THE ROUGH GUIDE TO
CAPE TOWN
THE WINELANDS &
THE GARDEN ROUTE

**ROUGH
GUIDES**

This sixth edition updated by
James Bainbridge and Barbara McCrea

Introduction to
Cape Town
the Winelands & the Garden Route

Cape Town is southern Africa's most beautiful, most romantic and most visited city. Its precolonial Khoikhoi inhabitants recognized its extraordinary physical setting when they referred to Table Mountain, the city's emblematic landmark, as Hoerikwaggo – the mountain in the sea. If the landscape doesn't take your breath away, its high-octane activities from paragliding to kitesurfing should do the trick, and that's before you've sampled the nightlife. Which isn't to say Cape Town is just about adrenaline. Away from the thrills and pumping party scene, you'll find a city boasting breathtaking beaches, rolling vineyards and fine museums – enough to keep you busy over an extended visit. Despite this, most visitors find the time to escape the city – to the Winelands, to sample South Africa's celebrated wines, and further east along the Garden Route, whose draws include unparalleled whale watching, crashing seascapes, dappled forests and lions, leopards and elephants in the best game reserve in the southern half of the country.

Cape Town has a rich urban texture too, etched in its diverse **architecture**. In the suburbs, shimmering white Cape Dutch homesteads, rooted in seventeenth-century northern European traditions, characterize the grand estates of the Constantia Winelands; in the city, Muslim slaves, freed in the nineteenth century, added their minarets to the centre's skyline; and the English, who invaded and later freed these slaves, introduced Georgian and Victorian buildings. In the tight terraces of the Bo-Kaap quarter and the tenements of District Six, the coloured descendants of slaves evolved a unique, evocatively Capetonian brand of jazz, which is well worth catching live. Indeed great sounds, along with high standards of accommodation, smart restaurants, laidback cafés and a vibrant gay scene, make visiting Cape Town a truly cosmopolitan experience.

ABOVE V&A WATERFRONT

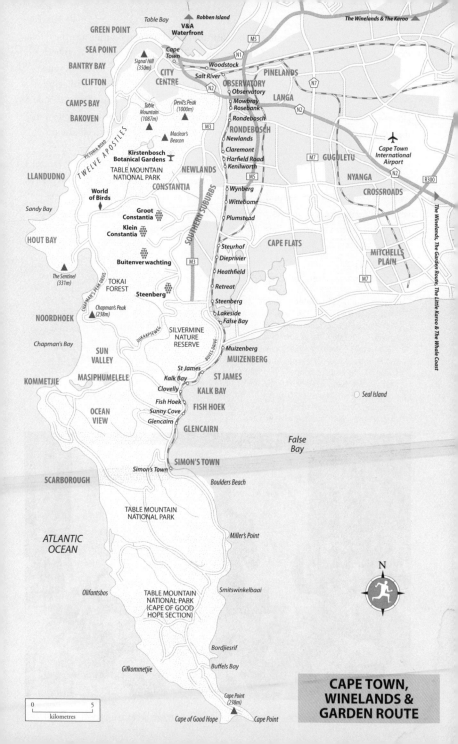

But despite a reputation for greater **liberalism** and racial tolerance during apartheid than the rest of the country, Cape Town has been the slowest South African city to embrace post-apartheid multiracialism. Ever since the mid-seventeenth century when Jan van Riebeeck, leader of the first white people to settle in South Africa, thought of digging a canal across the Cape Peninsula to cut it off from the rest of Africa, Cape Town has stood aloof from the rest of the country. For 350 years its white establishment endeavoured to maintain an illusion that the city was somehow really European, despite its location.

Under apartheid, black people were forcibly removed from the Western Cape, where coloured people were given preference in the job market. Consequently, black Africans make up less than forty percent of the Mother City, whereas they comprise over eighty percent nationwide; the Western Cape and neighbouring Northern Cape are the only provinces where coloured, rather than black, people form the majority. For most Capetonians, living in crowded **townships**, poverty and sky-high crime rates are part of everyday life.

CINE CITY

Following the success of *U-Carmen eKhayelitsha* at the Berlin Film Festival in 2005, Cape Town was not only lauded for showing its grittier face on film, but Hollywood directors began to realize the city's **chameleon-like** ability to recreate anything from French boulevards to hectic New York traffic. Cape Town was subsequently able to stand in for 35 diverse locations for the 2005 Nicolas Cage movie *Lord of War*, including Bolivia, Beirut, Berlin, the Caribbean, Sierra Leone, Indonesia, Odessa and New York City.

Nowadays, Capetonians are increasingly spotting major **Hollywood names** in bars along the Atlantic seaboard beaches, as *24*, starring Kiefer Sutherland, *Blood Diamond* with Leonardo DiCaprio and Jennifer Connelly, and Clint Eastwood-directed *Invictus*, starring Matt Damon and Morgan Freeman, have been shot in the city. Following the arrival of the world-class R350m Cape Town Film Studios in 2010, the city has hosted the filming of major Hollywood productions, including *Dredd* and *Mandela: Long Walk to Freedom*, while scenes from the fourth season of TV drama *Homeland* were shot in the Mother City in 2014.

ABOVE IDRIS ELBA IN *MANDELA: LONG WALK TO FREEDOM* **OPPOSITE** OSTRICHES NEAR OUDTSHOORN

What to see

Table Mountain, frequently mantled by its "tablecloth" clouds, is the solid core of Cape Town, dividing the city into distinct zones, with public gardens, wilderness, forests, hiking routes, vineyards and desirable residential areas. To its north lies the **city centre**, home to the city's most important museums and galleries, and with a buzzing street life – buskers, hawkers and market traders. In the adjacent **Bo-Kaap** Muslim quarter, colourful terraces and restaurants serving Cape Malay curries add a local flavour to the city's heart. A stone's throw from the centre, the **V&A Waterfront** is a popular spot for shopping, eating and drinking in a highly picturesque setting among the piers and quays of a working harbour. It's also the embarkation point for ferries to **Robben Island**, the site of Nelson Mandela's notorious incarceration. The rocky shore west of the Waterfront is occupied by the inner-city suburbs of **Green Point**, **De Waterkant** and **Sea Point**, their seafronts and back-streets crammed with excellent restaurants and accommodation to suit all budgets. Equally good for accommodation, but quieter, more leafy and upmarket, the **City Bowl suburbs** gaze down from the slopes of Table Mountain foothills and the neighbouring peaks across the central business district to the ships in Duncan Dock.

South from Sea Point, a coastal road traces the chilly **Atlantic seaboard** under the heights of the Twelve Apostles and past some of Cape Town's most expensive suburbs and spectacular beaches to Hout Bay. From here, the road merges with the precipitous **Chapman's Peak Drive**, ten dramatically snaking kilometres of early twentieth-century engineering carved into the western cliff of the Table Mountain massif, high above the crashing waves. To the east, across Table Mountain, the exceptionally beautiful **Kirstenbosch National Botanical Garden** creeps up the lower slopes, as do the **Constantia Winelands** a little further south, while the middle-class **Southern Suburbs** stretch towards **Muizenberg** and **False Bay**. The scenic Metrorail train line cuts through these suburbs and continues along the **False Bay seaboard**, passing through village-like **Kalk Bay**, with its intact harbour and working fishing community, and **Fish Hoek**, which has the best bathing beach along the eastern peninsula, before the final stop at the historic settlement of **Simon's Town**.

Most visitors see only the areas that were classified under apartheid as "white" and which remain relatively safe and salubrious. But the townships of the **Cape Flats** to the east of the city can be visited on guided tours, and if you really want to get under the skin of the African areas, you can enjoy the hospitality of several B&Bs in **Xhosa homes**.

An hour's drive east of central Cape Town, the beautiful **Winelands** are rich in elegant examples of Cape Dutch architecture, wonderful wines and excellent restaurants. Southeast of town you can take the picturesque coastal route, winding around massive sea cliffs, to reach Hermanus, the largest settlement on the **Whale Coast**, and a fabulous spot for shore-based whale watching.

After Cape Town, the best-known tourist feature of the Western Cape is the **Garden Route**, half a day's drive along the N2 from Cape Town or from Port Elizabeth in the Eastern Cape. This coastal strip can be driven in a day, but to cover it so quickly would mean missing its essence, which lies off the road in its seaside towns, lagoons, mountains and ancient forests on the stretch between **Mossel Bay** and **Storms River Mouth**. Highlights include the holiday town of Knysna and **Tsitsikamma**, at the easternmost section of the Garden Route National Park, where the dark Storms River opens spectacularly into the Indian Ocean. Public transport along the Garden Route is better than anywhere in the country, partly because the route is a single stretch of highway served by the Baz Bus, and tour operators have begun turning it into the country's most concentrated strip for **adventure sports** and **outdoor activities**. Parallel to the Garden Route, **Route 62** provides a thoroughly rewarding inland route to and from Cape Town, traversing some of the most dramatic mountain passes in the region and taking in a number of picturesque Little Karoo *dorps*.

But the ultimate destination at the eastern end of the region, to which both the Garden Route and Route 62 lead, is **Addo Elephant National Park**, where sightings of elephants are virtually guaranteed, and there's a chance of seeing lions, buffalo and rhinos, among other wildlife.

When to go

Cape Town has a **Mediterranean climate**, the warm, dry summers balanced by cool wet winters. Come prepared for hot days in winter and cold snaps in summer, and pack a jumper and jacket whatever time of year you come. The **southeaster or "Cape Doctor"**, the cool summer wind that blows in across False Bay, forms a major obsession for Capetonians. Its fickle moods can singlehandedly determine what kind of day you're going to have, and

OPPOSITE BO-KAAP; SALT RIVER MOUTH; GIRAFFE IN A PRIVATE RESERVE

ANIMAL ATTRACTIONS

In Cape Town you're never far from the Table Mountain National Park and although this is no longer lion country (the last one was shot in the 1720s), you can still see countless varieties of animals, birds and reptiles here and along the city's coastline.

Commonest of the peninsula's large mammals are **baboons**, which number around five hundred and are mostly seen in the Cape of Good Hope section of the park. Another common species are **dassies**, or rock hyraxes, the fluffy beasts that resemble large guinea pigs and routinely sun themselves around the Upper Cableway Station on Table Mountain. Of the scores of other mammals present, including **caracals**, **genets**, **polecats**, **Cape foxes** and some twenty species of **mice**, among the ones you'll most likely see are **Cape Mountain zebras**, **bontebok** (a large antelope) and **mongooses**.

Moving offshore, **African penguins** can be seen in high numbers at the colony in Boulders Beach and at Stony Point, Betty's Bay. The city's most famous and glorious marine mammals, however, are the hefty **southern right whales** that arrive in False Bay during their calving season (peak period September and October), while **dolphins** are commonly spotted off the coast. And if you're willing to go under, you'll discover that False Bay is one of the best places in the country to meet a **great white shark** face to face on a shark-cage diving excursion.

when it gusts at over 60kph you won't want to be outdoors, let alone on the beach. Equally, it brings welcome relief on humid summer days, and lays the famous cloudy tablecloth on top of Table Mountain. The **Garden Route** falls within overlapping weather systems and as a result has rain throughout the year, falling predominantly at night, to water the lush vegetation that gives the region its name. It famously has the world's mildest climate after Hawaii.

For sun and swimming, the best time to visit is from **October to mid-December** and **mid-January to Easter**, when it's light long into the evening and there's an average of ten hours of sunshine a day. Between mid-December and mid-January, the whole region becomes congested as the nation takes its annual seaside holiday. In Cape Town, this is serious party time, with plenty of **major festivals** and events, while Knysna is gridlocked with traffic. If this is when you plan to visit, arrange accommodation and transport well in advance, and expect to pay considerably more for your bed than during the rest of the year.

Despite its shorter daylight hours, the **autumn** period, from April to mid-May, has a lot going for it: the southeaster drops and air temperatures remain pleasantly warm and the light is sharp and bright. For similar reasons the **spring** month of September can be very agreeable, with the added attraction that following the winter rains, wildflowers bloom and the peninsula tends to be at its greenest. Although spells of heavy rain occur in **winter** (June to August), it tends to be relatively mild, with temperatures rarely falling below 6°C. Glorious sunny days with crisp blue skies are common, and you won't see bare wintry trees either: indigenous vegetation is evergreen and gardens flower year-round. It's also in June that the first migrating **whales** begin to appear along the southern Cape coast, usually staying till the end of November.

Author picks

Despite many years living in Cape Town our authors remain amazed by the Mother City. Whether it's climbing the paths that criss-cross Table Mountain, enjoying a sundowner at a Kirstenbosch summer concert, or escaping to the Winelands, the Cape Town area offers innumerable adventures. Here are some of the experiences that make this city so special:

Top wildlife experience The five-day Whale Trail in De Hoop Nature Reserve is stunningly beautiful throughout the year – and sublime in season when there are whales to see every day (p.188).

Scenic public transport ride The revolving cable car up Table Mountain may be a head turner, but a favourite local ride is a weekend train trip to False Bay for a seaside beer in Muizenberg, Kalk Bay or Simon's Town (p.100).

Local laughs Catching a comedian such as Nik Rabinowitz or Marc Lottering at the Baxter Theatre is an evening of Capetonian humour, attracting audiences from the nearby University of Cape Town and beyond (p.137).

Best café in town *Tamboers Winkel*, for its neighbourhood vibes, rustic feel and excellent coffee, breakfasts and lunches (p.125).

Easy mountain walk Don't like the look of those paths ploughing up Table Mountain? The Pipe Track contour path is relatively flat, with views of the Twelve Apostles, Camps Bay and Lion's Head (p.74).

Wine estate With so many Cape Dutch beauties, your favourite winery will likely change as often as the Cape Doctor blows; top choices range from Ataraxia (p.182), with its chapel tasting room near Hermanus, to Babylonstoren (p.175) near Franschhoek, a perennial favourite for its gardens and restaurants.

Go out on a limb The beautiful timber-and-steel "Boomslang" walkway sways gently in the wind as it meanders through the forest canopy at Kirstenbosch National Botanical Garden (p.83).

> Our author recommendations don't end here. We've flagged up our favourite places – a perfectly sited hotel, an atmospheric café, a special restaurant – throughout the Guide, highlighted with the ★ symbol.

ABOVE FROM TOP THE PIPE TRACK; BABYLONSTOREN FARM SHOP; DE HOOP NATURE RESERVE

18

things not to miss

It's not possible to see everything that Cape Town and the Garden Route have to offer in one trip – and we don't suggest you try. What follows is a selective and subjective taste of the highlights, including outstanding national parks, spectacular wildlife, thrilling adventure sports and beautiful architecture. All entries have a page reference to take you straight into the Guide, where you can find out more. Coloured numbers refer to chapters in the Guide section.

1 TABLE MOUNTAIN AERIAL CABLEWAY
Page 73
The revolving cable car is the most spectacular way to ascend Cape Town's famous peak.

2 OCEAN SAFARIS
Page 180
Take to the waves for incomparable encounters with South Africa's whale and dolphin species.

3 SUNDOWNERS
Page 94
Relax with a tipple in Camps Bay as the sun turns into a glowing orb and sinks into the ocean.

4 TOWNSHIP TOURS
Page 90
See the reality of daily life for most Capetonians in one of the city's sprawling townships.

9

10

11

15

16

17

18

Itineraries

With Cape Town's unbeatable mix of culture, culinary delights and natural splendour, you can easily have both urban experiences and outdoorsy fun. Mix days of mountain walks, museum visits and lounging on the beach with nights of fine dining and partying. Be sure not to miss the beautiful areas beyond the city limits, where activities from wine tasting on historic Cape Dutch estates to exploring the Garden Route's old-growth forests await.

A WEEKEND IN CAPE TOWN

DAY ONE

❶ **Table Mountain** Get going early to beat the queue for the cable car, and enjoy exhilarating views of Cape Town from this 1000m-plus plateau. **See p.73**

❷ **Castle of Good Hope** The city's oldest building, the seventeenth-century fort's courtyards and rooms were the centre of colonial administration. **See p.58**

❸ **City Centre** African craft and grand edifices on Long Street and Greenmarket Square, and Bree Street's hip boutiques and cafés. **See p.44**

❹ **V&A Waterfront** Boats glide along the waterways of this harbourside complex between the aquarium, markets, museums, cafés and bars. **See p.64**

❺ **Bo-Kaap** Smartie box houses and mosques climb the Cape Muslim quarter's cobbled streets. **See p.50**

❻ **Dinner** One of the centre's more authentic African restaurants, *Addis in Cape* serves Ethiopian cuisine on injera (sourdough flatbread). **See p.122**

DAY TWO

❶ **Kirstenbosch National Botanical Garden** On Table Mountain's eastern slopes, wander one of the world's greatest botanical gardens. **See p.83**

❷ **Constantia** The world's oldest winemaking region outside Europe, with magnificent Cape Dutch estates. **See p.86**

❸ **Chapman's Peak Drive** Follow the Atlantic coast to this dramatic toll road cut into the cliffs. **See p.96**

❹ **Clifton Fourth** Take a picnic blanket to this beach beneath Lion's Head to toast to the sun melting into the Atlantic. **See p.94**

❺ **Dinner** Sea Point's *La Boheme Wine Bar & Bistro* emphasizes Cape Town's Mediterranean climate and lifestyle with its French dishes, pavement seating and neighbouring espresso and tapas bar. **See p.128**

❻ **Drink** An alternative to Clifton, *Grand Café & Beach* offers chichi sundowners on the sand. **See p.133**

ABOVE STELLENBOSCH

CAPE CUISINE

With its Mediterranean climate, the Cape is a breadbasket, fruit bowl and wine barrel all rolled into one glorious package. Weave the following into our other Cape Town itineraries or cover them in four days minimum.

❶ **Bascule Bar** The *Cape Grace* hotel's marina-side whisky bar has one of the southern hemisphere's best selections of the amber nectar, and offers tastings with a whisky sommelier. **See p.133**

❷ **Cape Malay cooking safari** Learn how to make local curries and specialities from a coloured culinary guru in a Bo-Kaap kitchen. **See p.51**

❸ **La Parada** Tapas bars have taken off in recent years; sample the craze at this Bree Street hangout with communal tables, street seating and Andalusian attitude. **See p.132**

❹ **Truth Café** It's the world's best café according to one British newspaper. Coffee roasters and flat-white aficionados abound, but none can compete with *Truth*'s steampunk decor and staff uniforms. **See p.123**

❺ **Neighbourgoods Market** Recalling the days when farmers sold fresh fruit and veg to seafarers, food markets are hugely popular for supplies, snacks, a meal or a beer. Woodstock Old Biscuit Mill's Saturday market began this latter-day trend. **See p.144**

❻ **Test Kitchen** Book months ahead to experience the innovative cuisine at British chef Luke Dale-Roberts' much-lauded restaurant. **See p.127**

❼ **Wine Tours** On the great Cape Dutch estates around Stellenbosch and Franschhoek, quaff wine including the locally devised pinotage. **See p.163**

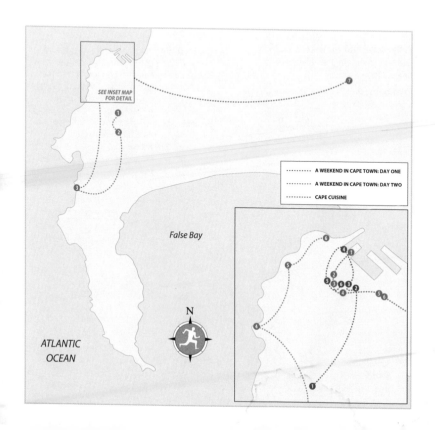

INTO THE CAPE WIDE OPEN

Travel from Cape Town to the nearby Winelands and beyond, where the mountainous landscape unfolds in a stream of postcard-perfect images. The following trip takes around ten days minimum.

❶ **Stellenbosch** The capital of the Winelands is an oak-shaded student town with Cape Dutch architecture, museums and pavement cafés. Cooling water gurgles along irrigation channels as tourists wander between wine tastings and African craft shops, making this little slice of Europe an inviting haven on hot summer days. See p.159

❷ **Franschhoek** Upmarket town among mountains and vineyards, with galleries, restaurants and a museum and monument honouring its French Huguenot heritage. Reached from Stellenbosch over the stunning Helshoogte Pass, "French corner" is a culinary capital with many of South Africa's oldest and most prestigious wine estates. See p.172

❸ **Whale Coast** Based in pretty, gastronomic Stanford, enjoy whale watching in Hermanus, shark-cage diving in Gansbaai and wine tasting in the Hemel-en-Aarde Valley. See p.176

❹ **Wilderness** Experience some wild African coastline in this aptly named Garden Route town with its long white beach. Explore the forest-covered mountains on horseback or fly into the blue on a tandem paragliding flight. See p.204

❺ **Knysna** Vibrant Garden Route tourist town offering activities from lagoon cruises to old-growth forest hikes. See p.209

❻ **Tsitsikamma** In the forested Garden Route National Park, cross Storms River Mouth on dramatic suspension bridges. Choose between basing yourself in Nature's Valley, with its lagoon-backed beach and tree-lined lanes, and the forest retreat of Storms River Village, which offers excellent accommodation and activities from zip-lining to tubing. See p.224

❼ **Addo Elephant National Park** The closest major park to Cape Town, with over six hundred elephants and private reserves nearby. See p.254

❽ **Prince Albert** Reached over mountain passes, this desert *dorpie* (town) offers an accessible taste of the Great Karoo. See p.244

❾ **Montagu** Returning to Cape Town along Route 62 through the Little Karoo, stop in this rustic farming town and climbing destination with its dramatic Cogmanskloof Pass. See p.234

❿ **Greyton** A final piece of rural bliss before descending Sir Lowry's Pass to Cape Town, this *dorpie* of picture-perfect cottages and former smallholdings has a few good restaurants and galleries, all occupying an idyllic position in the Riviersonderend Mountains. It's also the beginning of the Boesmanskloof Traverse trail, which crosses the mountains to pretty McGregor. See p.190

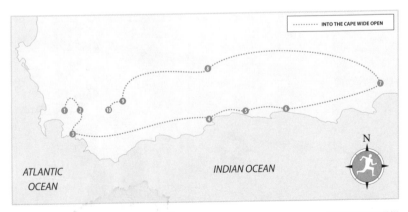

INTO THE CAPE WIDE OPEN

ATLANTIC OCEAN

INDIAN OCEAN

N

RIGHT KNYSNA LAGOON

ROUTE 62 THROUGH THE LITTLE KAROO

Basics

Getting there

Most overseas visitors to Cape Town travel there by air, either on a direct flight or via Johannesburg, which is connected to Cape Town by frequent domestic flights (see p.28). The few direct services from North America stop to refuel in West Africa, but there are nonstop flights from the UK, which allow you to travel from London in twelve hours. It can be cheaper, however, to fly via mainland Europe or the Middle East.

Airfares always depend on the **season**, with the highest prices and greatest demand in July, August, September, December and early January. Prices drop during April (except for around Easter), May and November, while the rest of the year is "shoulder season".

Flights from the UK and Ireland

From London there are nonstop flights to Cape Town with British Airways (Ⓦba.com), and more flights via **Johannesburg** (often a cheaper option). **Flying time** from the UK to Cape Town is around twelve hours and average high-season scheduled direct fares from London start around £1000. You can make major savings by flying via mainland Europe, the Middle East or Asia, and enduring at least one change of plane, often in Johannesburg.

There are no direct flights from **Ireland**, but a number of European and Middle Eastern carriers fly to Cape Town via their hub airports.

Flights from the US and Canada

There are no nonstop flights **from the US**, but there are direct **flights** from New York (JFK) and Washington (IAD) to Johannesburg stopping in West Africa to refuel, operated by South African Airways (SAA). These take between fifteen and seventeen hours. Most other flights stop off in Europe, the Middle East or Asia and involve a change of plane. For flights from New York to Cape

Town via Johannesburg, expect high-season return fares to start around $1200; you will save a lot if you fly via Europe, the Middle East or Asia.

From Canada, you'll have to change planes in the US, Europe or Asia on hauls that can last over thirty hours. High-season return fares from Toronto to Cape Town are similarly priced to those from the US east coast.

Flights from Australia and New Zealand

There are nonstop flights **from Sydney** (which take 14hr) and **Perth** (11hr) to **Johannesburg**, with onward connections to **Cape Town**; New Zealanders also tend to fly via Sydney. South African Airways (SAA) and Qantas (Ⓦqantas.com) are two of the airlines serving South Africa from Australia. Several Asian, Middle Eastern and European airlines fly to Cape Town via their hub cities, and tend to be less expensive, but their routings can often entail long stopovers.

Cape Town is not a cheap destination for travellers from Australia and New Zealand; high-season fares start around Aus$2000, low-season fares at Aus$1600, for an indirect return flight **from Sydney** to Cape Town with one change. A flight to Europe with a stopover in South Africa, or even a round-the-world ticket, may represent better value than a straightforward return. The most affordable return flights tend to travel via Dubai, Doha, Singapore and Kuala Lumpur, with the likes of Qatar Airways (Ⓦqatarairways.com) and Emirates (Ⓦemirates.com).

AGENTS AND OPERATORS

Abercrombie & Kent Australia ☎ 1300 851 800, Ⓦabercrombiekent.com.au; UK ☎ 01242 547 760, Ⓦabercrombiekent.co.uk; US ☎ 1800 554 7016, Ⓦabercrombiekent.com. Classy operator whose packages feature Cape Town and luxury rail travel with Rovos Rail.
Africa Travel UK ☎ 020 7843 3500, Ⓦafricatravel.com. Experienced Africa specialists, offering flights and packages including a thirteen-day Cape Town, Garden Route and Victoria Falls itinerary.
Cox & Kings UK ☎ 020 7873 5000, Ⓦcoxandkings.co.uk; US ☎ 323 271 4317, Ⓦcoxandkingsusa.com. Stylish operator with

---

A BETTER KIND OF TRAVEL

At Rough Guides we are passionately committed to travel. We believe it helps us understand the world we live in and the people we share it with – and of course tourism is vital to many developing economies. But the scale of modern tourism has also damaged some places irreparably, and climate change is accelerated by most forms of transport, especially flying. All Rough Guides' flights are carbon-offset, and every year we donate money to a variety of environmental charities.

classic luxury journeys, including an eleven-day itinerary geared towards families. Also deluxe safaris.

Exodus Travels UK ☎ 0203 553 0654, ⓦ exodus.co.uk; US ☎ 1 844 227 9087, ⓦ exodustravels.com. Small-group adventure tour operator with itineraries in and around Cape Town, overland trips taking in Kruger National Park and themed packages including activities such as cycling. Offices worldwide.

Expert Africa New Zealand ☎ 04 976 7585, UK ☎ 020 3405 6666, US ☎ 1 800 242 2434; ⓦ expertafrica.com. Mostly self-drive safari packages, including Addo and with the option of incorporating flights from the UK.

Explore Worldwide UK ☎ 01252 883 503, ⓦ explore.co.uk; US ☎ 1 800 715 1746, ⓦ exploreworldwide.com. Good range of small-group tours, expeditions and safaris, staying mostly in small hotels and taking in Cape Town and beyond.

Goway Travel US ☎ 1 888 414 0246, ⓦ goway.com. Wide range of packages from two days on the Blue Train to six weeks overland, including eleven days in Cape Town, the Winelands, the Garden Route and a private game reserve.

Joe Walsh Tours Ireland ☎ 01 241 0800, ⓦ joewalshtours.ie. Budget fares as well as hotels, golf packages and holidays from the Western Cape to Kruger. Also has offices in the UK.

Kuoni Travel UK ☎ 0800 422 0799, ⓦ kuoni.co.uk. Flexible package itineraries, including tailor-made tours, self-drive holidays and escorted small-group excursions, with a nine-night trip covering the classic sights around Cape Town. Good ideas for families too.

North South Travel UK ☎ 01245 608 291, ⓦ northsouthtravel .co.uk. Discounted fares worldwide. Profits are used to support projects in the developing world, especially the promotion of sustainable tourism.

Okavango Tours and Safaris UK ☎ 07721 387 738, ⓦ okavango .com. Top-notch outfit with on-the-ground knowledge of sub-Saharan Africa, offering fully flexible and individual tours across the country, including the Western Cape and family-focused packages.

On the Go Tours UK ☎ 020 7371 1113, US ☎ 1866 377 6147; ⓦ onthegotours.com. Group and tailor-made tours to South Africa including a two-week overland safari from Cape Town to Namibia. Offices worldwide.

Rainbow Tours UK ☎ 020 3131 2831, ⓦ rainbowtours.co.uk. Knowledgeable Africa specialists whose trips include a sixteen-day Cape Town, Garden Route and Kruger holiday.

STA Travel UK ☎ 0333 321 0099, US ☎ 1800 781 4040, Australia ☎ 134 782, New Zealand ☎ 0800 474 400, South Africa ☎ 0861 781 781; ⓦ statravel.co.uk. Worldwide specialists in independent travel; also student IDs, travel insurance, car rental and more. Discounts for students and youth travellers.

Trailfinders UK ☎ 020 736 81200, Ireland ☎ 01 677 7888; ⓦ trailfinders.com. A well informed and efficient agent for independent travellers, with numerous holiday packages on offer.

Tribes UK ☎ 01473 890 499, ⓦ www.tribes.co.uk; US ☎ 1800 608 4651. Unusual and off-the-beaten-track sustainable safaris and cultural tours, including Cape Town itineraries.

USIT Ireland ☎ 01 602 1906, ⓦ usit.ie. Ireland's main student and youth travel specialists offer Cape Town packages.

Wildlife Worldwide UK ☎ 01962 302 086, ⓦ wildlifeworldwide .com; US ☎ 1800 972 3982. Tailor-made trips for wildlife and wilderness enthusiasts, covering the Cape and the great reserves.

Entry requirements

Nationals of the US, Canada, Australia, New Zealand, Japan, Argentina and Brazil don't require a visa to enter South Africa. Most EU nationals don't need a visa, with the exception of passport holders from countries including the following, who will need to obtain one at a South Africa diplomatic mission in their home country: Bulgaria, Croatia, Estonia, Latvia, Lithuania, Romania, Slovak Republic and Slovenia.

As long as you carry a passport that is valid for at least thirty days from the date of exit from South Africa, and has at least two empty pages, you will be granted a temporary visitor's permit, which allows you to stay in South Africa for up to ninety days for most nationals, and thirty days for EU passport holders from Cyprus, Hungary and Poland. All visitors should have proof of a valid return ticket or another form of onward travel; immigration officers rarely ask to see it, but airlines will often check. Likewise, visitors should have a bank statement showing that they have sufficient funds to cover their stay, but officials seldom ask to see it.

Cross-border "visa runs" are not possible, but you can extend your visitor's visa for up to ninety days, or apply to stay for longer periods for purposes such as study. Applications should be made through VFS Global (☎ 012 425 3000, ⓦ vfsglobal.com/south africa), which will ask to see paperwork including proof of sufficient funds to cover your stay.

The easiest option is to use a consultant such as the immigration division of the International English School (☎ 021 852 8859, ⓦ english.za.net /immigration-services) in Somerset West, just outside Cape Town. Their services are recommended, and paying such a consultant's fees is far preferable to bureaucratic headaches.

See the box below for information on immigration requirements for children travelling to South Africa.

SOUTH AFRICAN DIPLOMATIC MISSIONS ABROAD

Australia Corner State Circle and Rhodes Place, Yarralumla, Canberra, ACT 2600 ☎ 02 6272 7300, ⓦ sahc.org.au.

CHILDREN TRAVELLING TO SOUTH AFRICA

It is important to be aware of paperwork requirements pertaining to kids aged under 18 years, which have caused families to miss flights since they were introduced in 2015.

Children travelling into or out of South Africa will be asked to show an unabridged (full) birth certificate in addition to their passport. Unlike abridged certificates, the unabridged version shows both parents' details.

Where only one parent is accompanying, parental or legal consent for the child to travel (eg an affidavit from the other parent or a court order) is required. There are other requirements for children travelling unaccompanied or with adults who are not their parents. The Department of Home Affairs has more details at Ⓦwww.dha.gov.za, while the British Foreign and Commonwealth Office (Ⓦwww.gov.uk/foreign-travel-advice/south-africa /entry-requirements) is a good starting point for clear guidance and helpful links.

Canada 15 Sussex Drive, Ottawa, ON K1M 1M8 ☎ 613 744 0330, Ⓦ southafrica-canada.ca. Consulate 110 Sheppard Ave East, Suite 600, Toronto, ON M2N 6Y8 ☎ 416 944 8825.
Netherlands 40 Wassenaarseweg 2596 CJ, The Hague ☎ 070 392 4501, Ⓦ zuidafrika.nl.
New Zealand Level 7, State Insurance Tower, 1 Willis St, Wellington ☎ 04 815 8484, Ⓦ sahc.org.au/consular_new-zealand.htm.
UK South Africa House, Trafalgar Square, London WC2N 5DP ☎ 020 7451 7299, Ⓦ southafricahouseuk.com.
US 3051 Massachusetts Ave NW, Washington, D.C. 20008 ☎ 202 232 4400, Ⓦ southafrica-newyork.net/homeaffairs/index .htm. Consulates 333 E 38th St, 9th floor, New York, NY 10016 ☎ 212 213 4880; 6300 Wilshire Blvd, Suite 600, Los Angeles, CA 90048 ☎ 323 651 0902; 200 South Michigan Ave, 6th floor, Chicago, IL 60604 ☎ 312 939 7929.

FOREIGN DIPLOMATIC MISSIONS IN CAPE TOWN

Most embassies are in Pretoria, but countries including the following also have a consulate in Cape Town.
Canada 19th Floor, South African Reserve Bank building, 60 St George's Mall. The consulate was temporarily closed at the time of writing; check the website for updates Ⓦ southafrica.gc.ca.
Netherlands 100 Strand St ☎ 021 421 5660, Ⓦ netherlandsworldwide.nl/countries/south-africa.
UK 15th floor, Norton Rose House, 8 Riebeek St ☎ 021 405 240, Ⓦ www.gov.uk/government/world/organisations/british -consulate-general-cape-town.
US 2 Reddam Ave, Westlake ☎ 021 702 7300, Ⓦ za.usembassy.gov.

Arrival

Cape Town International Airport, the city's international and domestic airport (CPT; Ⓦwww.airports.co.za), lies 22km east of the city centre. A bureau de change is open to coincide with international arrivals; there are also ATMs here and a tourist information desk. The

major car rental firms also have offices here. Pre-booking a vehicle is recommended, especially during the week when there is a big demand from domestic business travellers, and over the mid-December to mid-January and Easter peak seasons.

Metered 24-hour taxis operated by Touch Down Taxis (☎ 082 569 7555), the airport's officially authorised taxi service, rank in reasonable numbers outside both terminals and charge around R250 for the trip into the city.

The cheapest transport from the airport is the **MyCiTi bus** (every 30min; 5am–9.30pm; R88; ☎ 0800 65 64 63, Ⓦ myciti.org.za), a safe, clean and reliable option operated by the city. It goes to the Civic Centre on Hertzog Boulevard, near the central train and bus stations, and has connections further afield (see p.26). More expensive but considerably more convenient are the door-to-door **shuttle services** which offer transport around Cape Town, including airport transfers (see p.27).

Getting around

Cape Town's public transport system consists of a bus network that serves the city centre, the Northern Suburbs and the Atlantic seaboard, as well as a train line that runs through the Southern Suburbs and down the False Bay seaboard as far as Simon's Town.

For some attractions, you'll still need a **car** or else you'll have to rely on tours, **minibuses** and **metered taxis**. For getting further afield, there are several decent **intercity bus** lines as well as the **Baz Bus** backpacker service that serves some places the intercity buses don't reach.

GO TOPLESS

The open-top, hop-on, hop-off red **City Sightseeing Bus** (☎086 173 3287, ⓦcitysightseeing .co.za; one-day ticket R170, children R90) is an extremely convenient, informative and, on a fine day, fun way of getting to the major sights, especially with kids. Covering everywhere from **downtown** to the **Constantia wineries**, their routes and tours include the following (for which buses leave from their office by the Two Oceans Aquarium at the Waterfront):

Blue Mini Peninsula Tour (daily May to late Sept every 35min, late Sept to early May every 25min; 9am–3.25pm) stops on Long Street, *Mount Nelson Hotel*, Kirstenbosch, World of Birds, Imizamo Yethu township, Mariner's Wharf in Hout Bay, Camps Bay and Sea Point.

Red City Tour (daily May to late Sept every 20min, late Sept to early May every 15min; 8.40am–4.45pm) stops on Long Street before ascending Kloof Nek Road to the Table Mountain cable car station and crossing Kloof Nek to Camps Bay, Sea Point and Green Point.

City transport

Although Cape Town's city centre (aka the City Bowl or CBD) is compact enough to walk around, many of the major attractions are spread along the considerable length of the peninsula and require transport to reach. Between them, the **MyCiTi bus network**, introduced in 2011, and **Metrorail's** Southern Line down the peninsula cover Cape Town fairly comprehensively, as far south as Hout Bay on the Atlantic seaboard and Simon's Town on False Bay.

The **Golden Acre** shopping complex, at the junction of Strand and Adderley streets in the heart of Cape Town, can be a confusing muddle, but this, along with the central train station opposite and the nearby **Civic Centre**, is where all rail and most bus transport (both intercity and from elsewhere in the city) converges, along with most minibus taxis. Everything you need for your next move is within two or three blocks of here, including the main tourist office (see p.43).

Buses

The **MyCiTi bus** (☎0800 065 64 63, ⓦmyciti.org.za) is a safe and comprehensive commuter system that operates daily from roughly 5am to 10pm. With stations along dedicated trunk roads, MyCiTi is part of the municipality's initiative to improve public transport in the traffic-plagued city. Frequent buses service the **city centre**, **City Bowl suburbs**, **Atlantic seaboard** and **northern suburbs**, providing a reliable transport alternative to cars, although most middle-class Capetonians still rely on the latter. **Frequencies** vary between routes, but buses operate roughly every ten to twenty minutes during peak periods (6.45–8am & 4.15–5.30pm) and every twenty to thirty minutes during the off-peak period that falls between these times and over weekends. Importantly, MyCiTi is the safest public transport option in the evening and more routes are being added as the system evolves.

Cash is not accepted on buses and you'll need a **myconnect card**, which you load with credit to cover fares based on distance travelled. Fares include around R10 for routes within the city centre (with a variation of a few rand between peak and off-peak periods), around R20 from the centre to Hout Bay or Table View and R88 to the airport. Cards can be bought for R30 from MyCiTi stations and various retailers, or you can buy a single-trip card at some stations (R90 at the airport).

To use the card you tap your card against validators marked "in" when you board, and again on one marked "out" when you get off.

The MyCiTi **website** has user-friendly and up-to-date **information** on fares, routes and timetables.

Taxis

The term "**taxi**" refers, somewhat confusingly, to conventional metered cars, jam-packed minibuses and Rikkis.

Metered taxis

You will find regulated company-owned and independent **metered taxis** at the **taxi ranks** around town, including the Waterfront, the train station and Long Street. You can also hail one off the street, but to ensure you are using a regulated taxi, you'll need to phone to be picked up (see box, p.131). Taxis must have the driver's name and identification clearly on display and the meter clearly visible. **Fares** work out around R10 per kilometre, with minimum charges from R20, and rates go up after dark. Services are available around the clock.

Uber (ⓦuber.com/en-ZA/cities/cape-town) has become a popular and convenient option, although not without the controversy seen in other countries. Rates start around R7 per kilometre. Download the app to your smartphone.

For more taxi listings see the information in the Drinking chapter (see box, p.131).

Minibus taxis

Minibus taxis are cheap, frequent and race up and down the main routes at tearaway speeds. They can be hailed from the street – you'll recognize them from the whistling, hooting and booming music – or boarded at the central taxi rank, above the Cape Town train station. Once you've boarded, pay the assistant who sits near the driver and say where you want to get off. **Fares** are around R10 for trips around the centre. As well as dangerous driving, be prepared for **pickpockets** working the taxi ranks. Don't take minibus taxis after dark.

Rikkis and shuttle buses

The **Rikkis Taxis** fleet includes London-style black cabs, operating all hours and aimed principally at tourists; book through ☎086 174 5547 or ⊛rikkis .co.za. They offer airport shuttles, ride shares and a private door-to-door service.

In the same vein but a little cheaper, the **Backpacker Bus** (booking two days ahead recom-mended; ☎082 809 9185, ⊛backpackerbus.co.za) offers good-value transport between Cape Town, Stellenbosch and the airport. From Cape Town accommodation to Stellenbosch costs R300 (R550 return); R450 (R650 return) for two people, R550 (R750 return) for three and R650 (R850 return) for four. Their well-priced **airport shuttle** runs 24 hours a day as required to accommodate flight arrivals and departures (R220 one-way for the first person, two people R350, three people R400, four people R450).

Trains

Cape Town's suburban **train** service is run by **Metrorail** (☎021 449 6478, ⊛metrorail.co.za, ⊛cttrains.co.za). The only route likely to be useful to visitors is the relatively safe and reliable if slightly run-down **Southern Line**, which travels from Cape Town station through the Southern Suburbs and all the way down the False Bay seaboard to **Simon's Town**. Four other routes serve the Northern Suburbs, the Winelands and the Cape Flats; however, these journeys aren't recommended, as they run through less safe areas. Even on the Southern Line, never board an empty carriage, and only travel during daylight.

The Southern Line to the **False Bay seaboard** must be one of the world's greatest urban train journeys. It reaches the coast at Muizenberg and continues south to Simon's Town, sometimes so spectacularly close to the ocean that you can feel the spray and peer into rock pools. The stretch of the line to Fish Hoek is well served, with several trains an hour. Services to Simon's Town run roughly every twenty to sixty minutes.

There are often no signposts to the stations on the streets, so if you're staying in the Southern Suburbs, ask for directions at your accommodation. Tickets must be bought at the station before boarding – you'll be safer and more comfortable in the first-class MetroPlus carriages, which are reasonably priced (for example, Cape Town–Muizenberg is R13.50 one way). Week and month passes are available.

For more info on the Southern Line see details in Chapter 6 (see p.100).

Intercity buses

Baz Bus (☎086 122 9287, ⊛www.bazbus.com) operates an extremely useful hop-on, hop-off service five days a week between Cape Town and Port Elizabeth, via Mossel Bay, George, Knysna, Plettenberg Bay, Storms River and Jeffrey's Bay, with other stops possible along the N2. The service is aimed squarely at backpackers, with buses stopping off at hostels en route. The Cape Town–Port Elizabeth fare is R2300 one way, though there are also better-value seven-, fourteen- and 21-day passes costing R2600, R4100 and R5100. Bookings can be made through the website, by email, telephone or SMS (☎076 427 3003).

South Africa's three established **intercity bus** companies are Greyhound (☎083 915 9000, ⊛greyhound.co.za), Intercape (☎021 380 4400, ⊛intercape.co.za) and Translux (☎086 158 9282, ⊛translux.co.za); between them, they reach most towns in the country. Travel on these buses is generally safe, good value and comfortable; the vehicles are invariably equipped with air condi-tioning and toilets. Keep your valuables close on overnight journeys, when lone women should find a seat at the front near the driver.

Fares vary according to distances covered and the time of year, with peak fares corresponding approxi-mately to school holidays. As a rough indication you can expect to pay the following Greyhound fares for single journeys from Cape Town: Paarl (1hr) from R320; Mossel Bay (7hrs) from R430; and Port Elizabeth (12hr 30min) from R595.

Greyhound, Intercape and Translux intercity buses leave from around the interlinked complex in Cape Town's centre that includes the **train station** and Golden Acre shopping mall (see p.26), mostly from Old Marine Drive off Adderley Street on the northeast side of the station.

ENGLISH/AFRIKAANS STREET NAMES

Many towns along the Garden Route have **bilingual street names** with English and Afrikaans alternatives sometimes appearing along the same road. The Afrikaans name may bear little resemblance to the English one, although there is often some similarity, for instance if you spot a "Kerk" sign when looking for Church Street. In Cape Town you'll also find Afrikaans direction signs; for example signs for the airport may occasionally use the Afrikaans word "Lughawe".

We have included a list of Afrikaans terms you may encounter on signage in the "Language" section of the Guide (see p.276).

Translux and Greyhound also operate the no-frills budget bus lines **City to City** (**W** www.citytocity .co.za) and **Citiliner** (**W** citiliner.co.za) respectively, whose schedules and prices are listed on their websites. There is also a host of less reputable small private companies with ad hoc timetables; your best bet is to enquire at the long-distance bus terminus, on the corner of Adderley Street and Old Marine Drive, the day before you travel.

Domestic flights

Driving the Garden Route in one direction – say out from Cape Town – and flying back (or on to Johannesburg) from **George** or **Port Elizabeth** is a popular option. Expect to pay around R1000 for a budget flight from Cape Town to Port Elizabeth (1hr 15mins).

By far the biggest domestic airline is national carrier **South African Airways** (SAA; **☎** 086 160 6606, **W** flysaa.com), with its associates **SA Airlink** and **SA Express** (reservations through SAA) offering flights to George and Port Elizabeth among further-flung destinations. There are a number of smaller airlines that fly between Cape Town and Port Elizabeth, of which the most significant are **British Airways Comair** (**☎** 086 043 5922, **W** ba.com) and budget carrier **FlySafair** (**☎** 087 135 1351, **W** flysafair .co.za). Comair's budget subsidiary **kulula.com** (**☎** 086 158 5852, **W** kulula.com) links Johannesburg with Cape Town and Durban; budget carrier **Mango** (**☎** 086 100 1234, **W** flymango.com) connects Johannesburg with Cape Town, George and Port Elizabeth; and **Cemair** (**☎** 011 395 4473, **W** flycemair.co.za) flies from Cape Town and Johannesburg to Plettenberg Bay in the heart of the Garden Route.

Computicket Travel (**☎** 0861 915 4000, **W** computickettravel.com) is a useful booking engine for flights, buses and car rental.

Driving and cycling

Cape Town has good roads and several fast freeways that, outside peak hours (7–9am & 4–6pm), can whisk you across town in next to no time. The obvious landmarks of Table Mountain and its neighbouring peaks make orientation straightforward in the centre, while the two seaboards help in the south, and some wonderful journeys are possible. Notable drives include along the Atlantic seaboard to Hout Bay and **Chapman's Peak Drive**, a narrow, winding, cliff-edge road with the Atlantic breaking hundreds of metres below; and around the **Cape Point** section of the Table Mountain National Park, via the False Bay seaboard.

National roads (with an "N" prefix) and **provincial roads** (with an "R" prefix) in the rest of the Western Cape are of a generally high standard. The only time you're likely to encounter adverse conditions is during school holidays, particularly the Easter and December breaks, when the N1 and N2 become fairly congested, nerves fray, alcohol is copiously consumed and drivers' behaviour deteriorates accordingly.

Petrol stations are frequent on the major routes of the country, and usually open 24 hours a day. Off the major routes, though, stations are less frequent, so fill up whenever you get the chance. Stations are rarely self-service; instead, attendants fill up your car, check oil, water and tyre pressure if you ask them to, and often clean your windscreen even if you don't. A tip of R5–10 is normal.

Regulations

You drive on the **left-hand side**, with **speed limits** ranging from 40kph in wildlife parks and reserves and 60kph in built-up areas to 100kph on open roads and 120kph on highways and major arteries. In addition to roundabouts, which follow the British rule of giving way to the right, there are four-way stops, where the rule is that the person who got there first leaves first, and you are not expected to give way to the right. Note that traffic lights are often called **robots** in South Africa.

Foreign **driving licences** are valid in South Africa, provided they are printed in English. If you don't have such a licence, you'll need to get an International Driving Permit before arriving (available from national motoring organizations). When driving, make sure you have your driving licence and passport on you at all times.

Car and bike rental

Given Cape Town's scant public transport and car-centric culture, **renting** a vehicle is the most convenient way of exploring the Cape Peninsula, and needn't break the bank. There are dozens of competing car rental companies to choose from (see below). To get the best deal, either pick up a brochure at the Cape Town Tourism office or, a cheaper option, book beforehand with an international company, which might offer deals tied in with your airline or credit card, or a local player. Many backpacker hostels have cheaper deals with agencies too.

For **motorbike rental**, Cape Town Scooter Hire (9am–4pm; R250/day; ☎021 418 6885, Ⓦcapetownscooter.co.za), opposite the aquarium at the Waterfront, offers 125cc and 150cc scooters. For something more powerful, Cape Bike Travel, 125 Buitengracht (☎084 606 4449, Ⓦcapebiketravel.com), rents out BMWs and Harley-Davidsons along with protective gear (from R1300 for one day for a Harley, BMWs from R1600 for one day; BMW 1200GS R1800/day for seven days with unlimited mileage). Prices include comprehensive insurance and roadside assistance.

For **cyclists**, one of the most popular – and hair-raising – road routes is the serpentine **Chapman's Peak Drive**, which offers stupendous views of Hout Bay and the Atlantic. There are also dedicated mountain-biking routes in the peninsula's nature reserves; visit Ⓦmtbroutes.co.za for details. Mountain bikes are available from Downhill Adventures, Shop 1, Overbeek Building, corner of Kloof and Orange streets (☎021 422 0388, Ⓦdownhilladventures.co.za), from R400 a day. They also offer organized cycle outings that include trips to Cape Point, the Winelands and a Table Mountain descent.

CAR RENTAL AGENCIES

The big international names cover South Africa and local agencies such as Around About Cars offer good deals. They have offices at the airport and in the city.

TOP 5 SCENIC DRIVES

Atlantic seaboard Chapman's Peak Drive; see p.96.
City views Signal Hill Road; see p.74.
False Bay seaboard R44, Somerset West to Hermanus; see p.176.
Leafy affluence Rhodes Drive and Constantia Nek; see p.83.
Mountain pass Kloof Nek; see p.74.

Alamo Ⓦ alamo.com
Argus Car Hire Ⓦ arguscarhire.com
Around About Cars Ⓦ aroundaboutcars.com
Auto Europe Ⓦ autoeurope.com
Avis Ⓦ avis.co.za
Budget Ⓦ budget.co.za
Dollar Ⓦ dollar.com
Drive Africa Ⓦ driveafrica.co.za
Europcar Ⓦ europcar.co.za
First Ⓦ firstcarrental.co.za
Hertz Ⓦ hertz.co.za
Holiday Autos Ⓦ holidayautos.co.uk
SIXT Ⓦ sixt.global
Tempest Ⓦ tempestcarhire.co.za
Thrifty Ⓦ thrifty.co.za
Vineyard Car Hire Ⓦ vineyardcarhire.co.za

CAMPER VAN AND 4X4 RENTAL AGENCIES

Britz 4x4 Rentals Ⓦ britz.co.za
Cheap Motorhome Rental Ⓦ cheapmotorhomes.co.za
Drive South Africa Ⓦ drivesouthafrica.co.za
Kea Travel Ⓦ kea.co.za
Maui Ⓦ maui.co.za

Tours

Cape Town is awash with tour packages, from standard, through-the-window outings that take you from one sight to the other, to really excellent specialist packages. For some depth, opt for one of the cultural tours, which cover all aspects of Cape Town life, or feel the exhilaration of the peninsula's environment on foot or from a bike saddle. Operators generally pick you up from your accommodation and drop you back at the end of the day.

CULTURAL TOURS

A few excellent companies offer niche cultural tours; the most popular of these are township tours, the safest way to see the African and coloured areas that were created under apartheid.
Andulela ☎ 021 790 2592, Ⓦ andulela.com. Small selection of interactive adventures including a walking township tour, cookery- and gospel music-themed township tours and a Cape Malay cooking "safari" in the Bo-Kaap.
Bonani Our Pride ☎ 021 531 4291, Ⓦ bonanitours.co.za. Township tours to meet local people and understand the areas' tumultuous past and future aspirations. Also township evening tours, gospel tours to Xhosa churches on a Sunday morning, and Xhosa folklore tours.
Coffeebeans Routes ☎ 021 813 9829, Ⓦ coffeebeansroutes.com. Under the creative direction of Iain Harris, they are pioneers in cultural tourism in the townships, and the people to go to for hands-on, eye-opening experiences including the Jazz Safari, Township Futures tour and journeys themed around beer, fashion, art and more.

SAFE DRIVING TIPS

The main challenge you'll face on the roads is **other drivers**. South Africa has the world's seventh deadliest roads, placing it between Nigeria and Iraq on the list. Its abysmal accident statistics – resulting in 31.9 fatalities per 100,000 inhabitants, compared with 3.5 in the UK – are the result of reckless driving, drunken drivers (see p.37) and defective, overloaded vehicles. Keep your distance from cars in front, as domino-style pile-ups are common. Watch out also for **overtaking** traffic coming towards you. Overtakers often assume that you will head for the **hard shoulder** to avoid an accident (motorists commonly drive on the hard shoulder, but be careful as people frequently walk on it). If you do pull into the hard shoulder to let a car behind overtake, the other driver will usually thank you by flashing their hazard lights. It's wise to do so when it's safe, as aggressive and impatient South African drivers will soon start driving dangerously close to your back bumper to encourage you to give way. If oncoming cars **flash their headlights** at you, it probably means that there is a **speed trap** up ahead, or a hazard such as **baboons** in the road.

Driving in and around Cape Town presents a few peculiarities all of its own. Hurried **minibus taxis**, fiercely competing with rival cooperatives, will push in front of you without compunction and will routinely run through amber lights as they change to red – as will many Capetonians. Locals are often pushy behind the wheel, so drive defensively but stand your ground and remain calm in the face of uncourteous behaviour.

Take care approaching a **freeway** in Cape Town: the slip roads sometimes feed directly into the fast lane, and Capetonians routinely exceed the 100kph freeway and 120kph highway speed limits. Furthermore, there's often little warning of branches off to the suburbs, only the final destination of the freeway being signed. Your best bet is to plan your journey, and make sure you know exactly where you're going.

GENERAL TOURS

If you want a trip that covers more distance – the major peninsula sights and beyond – there are myriad operators. The most popular day-trips take in the Winelands or Cape Point. Knowledgeable independent guides often work with guesthouses and boutique hotels so ask your receptionist for suggestions.

Cape Convoy ☎ 076 146 8577, ⓦ capeconvoy.com. Tours with popular, passionate and fun Brit Rob Salmon to Cape Point (R999 including entrance fees), the Winelands, Cape Point and shark-cage diving.

Day Trippers ☎ 021 511 4766, ⓦ daytrippers.co.za. An excellent company if you want an active peninsula and Cape Point day tour that includes cycling and hiking (R850 including entrance fees and picnic lunch). They also go further afield to hike and cycle in the Winelands, Cederberg and Eastern Cape.

Discovery Tours ☎ 078 161 7818, ⓦ discoverytours.co.za. Specializing in private tours to the peninsula, the Winelands (two people R1400) and the West Coast.

WALKING TOURS

One of the best ways to orient yourself at the start of a visit is on a walking tour through central Cape Town. Tours with Cape Town on Foot and Footsteps to Freedom depart mid-morning at least three days a week, and last roughly three hours.

Cape Town Free Walking Tours ☎ 076 636 9007,
ⓦ nielsentours.co.za/capetown; free. Daily 90min tours, covering apartheid and liberation, more general history, the Bo-Kaap or the Waterfront. All four itineraries cost absolutely nada, though you might like to tip the guide; private tours can be arranged.

Cape Town on Foot ☎ 086 547 6833, ⓦ wanderlust.co.za; R250. Run by writer Ursula Stevens, these historical tours explore the city centre as well as the Bo-Kaap, and can be taken in English or German.

City Sightseeing ☎ 086 173 3287, ⓦ citysightseeing.co.za; free. The bus-tour operator offers daily 90min historical, Bo-Kaap, District Six and Waterfront walks. Tours are free but tips are appreciated.

Footsteps to Freedom ☎ 083 452 1112, ⓦ footstepsofreedom .co.za; one–four guests R1760. Historical and Mandela-themed tours taking in sights, buildings and local stories in the Company's Garden area. Book ahead.

Health

You can put aside most of the health fears that may be justified in some parts of Africa; run-down hospitals and bizarre tropical diseases aren't typical of Cape Town and the Garden Route, and malaria isn't an issue here at all. All tourist areas enjoy generally high standards of hygiene and safe drinking water. The only hazard you're likely to encounter, and the one the majority of visitors are most blasé about, is the sun.

Public **hospitals** are often well equipped and staffed, but are under huge pressure, undermining their attempts to maintain standards. Expect long waits and frequently indifferent treatment. **Private**

hospitals or clinics are a much better option for travellers and are well up to British and North American standards. You'll get to see a doctor quickly and costs are not excessive, unless you require an operation, in which case health insurance is a must.

Dental care in South Africa is also well up to British and North American standards, and is generally less expensive. You'll find dentists in Cape Town and most smaller towns.

Inoculations

No specific inoculations are compulsory if you arrive in South Africa from the West, although the CDC suggests several immunisations as routine for adults and children. In addition, it recommends inoculations against **typhoid** and **hepatitis A**, both of which can be caught from contaminated food or water – though this is extremely unlikely in the region covered by this guide. A **yellow fever** vaccination certificate is necessary if you've come from a country or region where the disease is endemic, such as Kenya, Tanzania or tropical South America.

If you need an armful of jabs, start organizing them **six weeks** before departure; some clinics will not administer inoculations less than a fortnight before departure. If you're going to another African country first and need the yellow fever jab, note that a yellow fever certificate only becomes valid ten days after you've had the shot.

MEDICAL RESOURCES FOR TRAVELLERS

Canadian Society for International Health ☎ 613 241 5785, ⓦ csih.org. Extensive list of travel health centres.
CDC ☎ 800 232 4636, ⓦ cdc.gov/travel. Official US government travel health site.
Hospital for Tropical Diseases Travel Clinic ⓦ www.thehtd .org. Health advice for travellers, with a link to the British government's online travel health advice, and a shop selling goods such as first-aid kits, mosquito nets and suncream.
International Society for Travel Medicine US ☎ 1 404 373 8282, ⓦ istm.org. Has a global directory of travel health clinics.
MASTA (Medical Advisory Service for Travellers Abroad) ⓦ masta-travel-health.com. The UK's largest network of private travel clinics.
The Travel Doctor ⓦ traveldoctor.co.nz. Travel clinics in New Zealand and an online shop.
Travel Doctor ☎ 0861 300 911, ⓦ traveldoctor.co.za. Travel clinics in Cape Town, Stellenbosch, George and beyond.
Travel Doctor ⓦ traveldoctor.com.au. Travel clinics in Australia.
Tropical Medical Bureau ☎ 086 0728 999, ⓦ tmb.ie. Offers extensive advice for travellers, with a number of clinics in Ireland.

STATE HOSPITALS AND CLINICS IN CAPE TOWN

Groote Schuur Hospital Main Rd, Observatory ☎ 021 404 9111. This large state hospital is just off the N2 and M3.
New Somerset Hospital Cnr Beach Road and Lower Portwood Road, Green Point ☎ 021 402 6911. A state hospital with emergency and outpatient departments, although it's generally overcrowded, understaffed and under-equipped.

PRIVATE HOSPITALS, DOCTORS AND CLINICS

The two largest **private hospital groups** are **Netcare** (emergency response ☎ 082 911, ⓦ www.netcare.co.za) and **Medi-Clinic** (emergency response operated by ER24 ☎ 084 124, ⓦ mediclinic.co.za) chains, with hospitals all over the Cape Peninsula; in addition to the hospitals listed here, which are open 24 hours for emergencies, Netcare runs over two dozen **Medicross Medical Centres** (ⓦ medicross.co.za) across the Western Cape, which are not open 24 hours, but do operate extended hours.
Cape Town Medi-Clinic 21 Hof St, Oranjezicht ☎ 021 464 5500; emergency ☎ 021 464 5555. Close to the city centre in the City Bowl.
Constantiaberg Medi-Clinic Burnham Road, Plumstead ☎ 021 799 2911; emergency ☎ 021 799 2196. In the southern suburbs, this is the closest private hospital to the False Bay seaboard.
Netcare Christiaan Barnard Memorial Hospital Cnr D.F. Malan and Rua Bartholomeu Dias Plain ☎ 021 441 0000. The most central of the Netcare private hospitals is convenient for the city centre, the V&A Waterfront, De Waterkant and the Atlantic seaboard.
UCT Private Academic Hospital Anzio Road, Observatory ☎ 021 442 1800. Netcare hospital adjacent to Groote Schuur Hospital in the Southern Suburbs.

Stomach upsets

Stomach upsets from food are rare. Salad and ice – the danger items in many other developing countries – are both perfectly safe. As with anywhere, though, don't keep food for too long, and be sure to wash fruit and vegetables as thoroughly as possible. Tap water is generally fine to drink, but bacteria levels rise as dam levels drop during the increasingly common droughts, when you may prefer to stick to bottled water.

If you do get a **stomach bug**, the best cure is lots of water and rest. Most pharmacies should have non-prescription anti-diarrhoea remedies and rehydration salts.

Avoid jumping for **antibiotics** at the first sign of illness. Instead keep them as a last resort – they don't work on viruses and they annihilate your gut flora (most of which you want to keep), making you more susceptible next time round. Taking probiotics helps to alleviate the latter side effect. Most tummy upsets will resolve themselves if you adopt a sensible fat-free diet for a couple of days, but if they do persist without improvement (or are accompanied by other unusual symptoms), see a doctor as soon as possible.

The sun

The **sun** is likely to be the worst hazard you'll encounter in South Africa, particularly, but not exclusively, if you're fair-skinned.

Short-term effects of **overexposure** to the sun include burning, nausea and headaches. This usually comes from overeager tanning, which can leave you looking like a lobster. The fairer your skin, the slower you should take tanning. Start with short periods of exposure and **high-protection sunscreen** (ideally SPF 30), gradually increasing your time in the sun and decreasing the factor of the sunscreen, if suitable. Many people with fair skin, especially those who freckle easily, should take extra care, starting with a very high factor screen (SPF 25–30) and continue using at least SPF 15 for the rest of their stay.

Extreme cases of overexposure to the sun, accompanied by dehydration, overexertion and intoxication, can lead to heat exhaustion or heatstroke.

Overexposure can also cause sunburn to the surface of the eye, inflammation of the cornea and can result in serious short- and long-term damage. Good **sunglasses** can reduce ultraviolet (UV) light exposure to the eye by fifty percent. A **broad-brimmed hat** is also recommended.

Protective measures are especially necessary for **children**, who should be kept well covered at the seaside. Don't be lulled into complacency on **cloudy days**, when UV levels can still be high. UV-protective clothing is available locally; if you don't have this gear, make sure children wear T-shirts at the beach, and use sunscreen of at least SPF 30 liberally and often.

Bites and stings

Bites and stings in South Africa are comparatively rare. **Snakes** are present, but hardly ever seen as they move out of the way quickly. The aggressive puff and berg adders are the most dangerous, because they often lie in paths and don't move when humans approach. The best advice if you get bitten is to note what the snake looked like and get yourself to a clinic or hospital. Most bites are not fatal and the worst thing you can do is to

panic: desperate measures with razor blades and tourniquets risk doing more harm than good. It's more helpful to immobilise the bitten limb with a splint and apply a bandage over the bite.

Tick-bite fever (rickettsia) is occasionally contracted from walking in the bush, where the greatest prevalence of ticks is found in long wet grass, especially during summer. The offending ticks can be minute and you may not spot them. Symptoms appear a week later – swollen glands and severe aching of the joints, backache and fever. The disease will run its course in three or four days, but it is worth visiting the doctor for antibiotics. Ticks you may find on yourself are not dangerous, just repulsive at first. It's extremely important to pull out the head as well as the body (it's not painful). A good way of removing small ones is to press down with tweezers, grab the head and gently pull upwards.

Scorpion stings and **spider bites** are painful but rarely fatal, contrary to popular belief. Scorpions and spiders abound, but they're hardly ever seen unless you turn over logs and stones. If you're collecting wood for a campfire, knock or shake it before picking it up. Another simple precaution when camping is to shake out your shoes and clothes in the morning before you get dressed. Seek medical attention for scorpion stings if your condition deteriorates.

Rabies is present throughout southern Africa with dogs posing the greatest risk, although the disease can be carried by other animals. If you are bitten, you should go immediately to a clinic or hospital. Rabies can be treated effectively with a course of injections (as long as these are administered within the time limits). If you'll be spending time in remote areas without medical facilities close at hand, you can get pre-trip jabs, which will buy you more time to reach the clinic or hospital if you are bitten.

Sexually transmitted diseases

HIV/AIDS and venereal diseases are widespread in southern Africa among both men and women, and the danger of catching the virus through sexual contact is very real. Avoid one-night stands with locals and follow the usual precautions regarding safe sex; international brand condoms are widely available from pharmacies and supermarkets. There's little risk from treatment in private medical facilities, but if you're travelling overland and you want to play it safe, take your own needle and transfusion kit.

The media

With two daily English-language newspapers, plus a few magazines devoted mainly to entertainment and tourism, Cape Town's media are unlikely to blow anyone away. Radio and TV are dominated by South Africa's national broadcasters, with a few local radio offerings that include a talk station, a pioneering black community station and several others that play sounds from classical to pop.

Newspapers and magazines

Cape Town has two fairly uninspiring English **newspapers**, owned by the same company: the **Cape Times** (Wiol.co.za/capetimes) broadsheet comes out on weekday mornings, while the tabloid-style **Cape Argus** (Wiol.co.za/capeargus) has daily editions. Both are dominated by local news, with a smattering of national and international coverage. In addition there's the national **Business Day** (Wbusinesslive.co.za), which is the best daily source of hard countrywide and international news.

Unquestionably the country's intellectual heavyweight ("heavy" being the operative word) is the **Mail & Guardian** (Wmg.co.za), which comes out on Friday; it benefits from its association with the London *Guardian* (from which it draws much of its international coverage). South Africa's **Sunday Times** (Wtimeslive.co.za) can claim the biggest circulation in the country – over three hundred thousand copies – thanks to its well-calculated mix of solid investigative reporting, gossip and material from the British press and foreign tabloids. The **Sowetan** (Wsowetanlive.co.za), targeted at a mainly black Johannesburg audience, is widely available across the country.

However, the liveliest of all South African news publications is the boundary-breaking, free online **Daily Maverick** (Wdailymaverick.co.za), which is brimful of news and analysis with a stable of some of South Africa's most challenging and provocative columnists.

For **events listings** in Cape Town, check out newspaper supplements as well as websites including **Cape Town Magazine** (Wcapetownmagazine.com) or **What's On in Cape Town** (Wwhatsonincapetown.com).

Both local papers and international publications such as *Time*, *Newsweek*, *The Economist* and the weekly overseas editions of the British *Daily Mail*, the *Telegraph* and the *Express* are available from corner stores, newsagents and book chains.

Television

The South Africa Broadcasting Corporation's three main TV channels churn out a mixed bag of domestic dramas, game shows, sport, soaps and documentaries, filled out with lashings of familiar imports. **SABC 1, 2 and 3** (Wsabc.co.za) share the unenviable task of trying to deliver an integrated service, while having to split their time between the eleven official languages. English is the best represented, with SABC 3 broadcasting almost exclusively in English, while SABC 2 and SABC 1 cover the remaining languages, with a fair amount of English creeping in even here. In the Afrikaans-dominated Western Cape, you will also come across much programming in that language.

A selection of movies, news, American programming and specialist channels are available to subscribers to the **M-Net** (Wm-net.dstv.com) satellite service, which is piped into many hotels. South Africa's first free-to-air independent commercial channel **e.tv** launched in 1998 with the promise of providing a showcase for local productions, although its output has consisted equally of imports.

There is no cable TV in South Africa, but **DSTV** (Wdstv.co.za) offers a **satellite television** subscription service with a selection of sports, movies, news (including BBC, CNN and Al Jazeera) and specialist channels, some of which are available in hotels. Sports fans should surf to **SuperSport** (Wsupersport.com) and everyone should catch an episode of KykNet's "Boer Soek 'n Vrou" (Farmer Seeks a Wife), an Afrikaans dating reality show for Boers from remote farms.

Radio

Given South Africa's low literacy rate and widespread poverty, it's no surprise that **radio** is a highly popular medium. The SABC operates a national radio station for each of the eleven official language groups, including the interesting English-language national service, **SAfm** (104–107FM, Wsafm.co.za). Heavily laden with phone-in shows interlaced with news bulletins, SAfm broadcasts current affairs programmes on weekdays from 6am to 9am ("AM Live"), midday to 1pm ("Midday Live") and 4pm to 6pm ("PM Live").

Cape Town stations include **Cape Talk** (567AM, Wcapetalk.co.za), which puts out wall-to-wall chatter consisting of news, reviews, discussions and phone-ins of varying interest, as well as wall-to-wall musical golden oldies during the daytime at weekends; and **Bush Radio** (89.5FM, Ⓦ bushradio .co.za), one of South Africa's first community stations, which actively involves members of Cape Town's black community, who were denied a voice under apartheid. Apart from hosting debates about significant issues and broadcasting informative social documentaries, Bush Radio also pumps out great local music. A number of other local stations are devoted to 24-hour music, the most successful being the entertaining **Heart Radio** (104.9FM, Ⓦ 1049.fm), which targets high-income black and coloured listeners in the Mother City with its mix of jazz fusion, funk, soul, r'n'b and often-engaging chat. Somewhat staid by comparison is **Fine Music Radio** (101.3FM, Ⓦ fmr.co.za), which politely delivers classical music and a smattering of respectable jazz.

Festivals

Many of the Western Cape's events take place outdoors in summer, and make full use of the city's wonderful setting. They include the Cape Town Minstrel Carnival, **a unique event rooted in the city's coloured community, while the** Kirstenbosch Summer Concerts, **on Sunday evenings from November to April, are a must. Winter tends to be quiet, but it does herald the arrival of calving whales, and in their wake the Hermanus Whale Festival, which packs out this Southern Cape town at the end of September. Winter is also trail-running season – for more information check** Ⓦ trailrunning.co.za.

Tickets for many of the events listed below are available from Computicket (☎ 0861 915 8000, Ⓦ computicket.co.za).

JANUARY

Cape Town Minstrel Carnival Jan 2. The city's longest-running and most raucous annual party, the carnival brings thousands of spectators to watch the parade through the city centre. It culminates on January 2 for the Tweede Nuwe Jaar or "Second New Year" celebrations – an extension of New Year's Day unique to the Western Cape. Central to the festivities are the brightly decked-out coloured minstrel troupes that vie in singing and dancing contests. Arrive early to get a spot with a good view.

Shakespeare in the Park Late Jan to late Feb; Ⓦ maynardville .co.za. A usually imaginative production of one of the Bard's plays is staged each year in the beautiful setting of the Maynardville Open-Air Theatre in Maynardville Park, Wynberg.

FEBRUARY

Cape Town Pride Pageant Ⓦ capetownpride.org. Series of gay-themed events over a week, kicking off with a pageant at which Mr and Miss Cape Town are crowned, and taking in a bunch of parties and a street parade.

MARCH

Cape Town Cycle Tour First half of the month;
Ⓦ capetowncycletour.org.za. The world's largest, and arguably most spectacular, individually timed bike race: some 40,000 participants on the 109km course – much of it along the ocean's edge – draw many thousands of spectators along the route. You can enter the Cape Argus (most locals still use its old name) online, and booking early is recommended, although sadly the event is often cancelled due to strong winds.

Cape Town Carnival Middle of the month; Ⓦ capetowncarnival .com. A Rio-style street extravaganza that kicked off in 2010, the carnival is centred on Green Point's Fan Walk with floats, parades and general euphoria intended to celebrate Cape Town's cultural diversity and richness. Festivities start at 3pm, and the parade takes place at 7pm.

Cape Town International Jazz Festival Last weekend of the month; Ⓦ capetownjazzfest.com. Initiated in 2000 as the Cape Town counterpart of the world-famous North Sea Jazz Festival (Rotterdam), Africa's largest jazz festival has come of age and acquired a local identity. Notable past performers have included Courtney Pine, Herbie Hancock, and African greats such as Jimmy Dludlu, Moses Molelekwa, Youssou N'Dour, Miriam Makeba and Hugh Masekela.

APRIL

Klein Karoo Nasionale Kunstefees First week of the month;
Ⓦ kknk.co.za. South Africa's largest Afrikaans arts and culture festival packs out the Karoo *dorp* of Oudtshoorn with festival goers, turning the otherwise dozy town into one big jumping, jiving party. If you don't understand Afrikaans, you'll find enough dance, music and other performance to keep you busy.

Fashion Week Cape Town First half of the month;
Ⓦ africanfashioninternational.com. Multiple catwalk shows over two days are aimed at showcasing new collections from leading South African designers, including the likes of Craig Port and Stefania Morland.

Two Oceans Marathon Easter Saturday; Ⓦ twooceansmarathon .org.za. Another of the Cape's big sports events, this is in fact an ultra-marathon (56km), with huge crowds lining the route to cheer on the participants. A less scenic half-marathon is held at the same time.

Pink Loerie Mardi Gras & Arts Festival End of the month;
Ⓦ pinkloerie.co.za. Gay pride celebration of parties, contests, cabaret, drag shows and performance over a long weekend in Knysna, South Africa's oyster capital.

MAY

Franschhoek Literary Festival Middle of the month; Ⓦ flf.co.za. Three-day celebration of books, writers and wine in the Winelands food capital, Franschhoek, featuring leading local and international writers, editors and cartoonists.

JUNE

Good Food & Wine Show Start of the month; W goodfoodand
wineshow.co.za. Celebrity chefs from around the world are just one of the
compelling attractions that make this Cape Town's foodie event of the year.
There are also hands-on workshops, kids' events, delicious nibbles and
wine as well as kitchen implements and books for sale.

**Encounters South African International Documentary
Festival** Middle of the month; W encounters.co.za. Fortnight-long
showcase of documentary film-making from South Africa and the world.

JULY

Franschhoek Bastille Festival Middle of the month;
W franschhoekbastille.co.za. Celebrating centuries-old French
Huguenot heritage in a splash of red, white and blue, this festival is
centred around a marquee where you can sample wine and food from
Franschhoek's acclaimed chefs and wine estates, while listening to live
music and watching the barrel-rolling competition.

Knysna Oyster Festival First half of the month; W oysterfestival
.co.za. Ten days of carousing and oyster eating on the Garden Route, kicked
off with the Knysna Cycle Tour and closed with the Knysna Forest Marathon.

AUGUST

Jive Cape Town Funny Festival Beginning of the month;
W baxter.co.za. Month-long comedy festival at the Baxter Theatre,
beginning in mid-July and attracting both local and international names.

SEPTEMBER

Hermanus Whale Festival End of the month; W whalefestival.co.za.
To coincide with peak whale-watching season, the Southern Cape town of
Hermanus stages a weekend festival of arts and the environment. Attractions
include marine displays, children's areas, a treasure hunt and live music.

OCTOBER

Rocking the Daisies Beginning of the month; W rockingthe
daisies.com. South Africa's premier rock and pop festival, featuring local
and international acts as well as much theatricality and debauchery. The
festival is held on Cloof Wine Estate near Darling. Most people make a
long weekend of it, camping for a few nights.

Cape Town International Kite Festival End of the month;
W capementalhealth.co.za/kite. This high-flying extravaganza attracts
over 15,000 visitors each year. Bring your own kite, watch flying displays,
join a kite-making workshop or buy one. All proceeds go towards Cape
Mental Health, providing services in resource-poor communities.

NOVEMBER

Kirstenbosch Summer Concerts Every Sun evening from end of
the month to early April; ☎ 021 799 8783, W sanbi.org. Among the
musical highlights of the Cape Town calendar are the popular concerts
held on the magnificent lawns of the botanical gardens at the foot of
Table Mountain. Performances begin at 5.30pm and cover a range of
genres, from local jazz to classical music. American rockers the Pixies
played their first African gig here in 2017. Come early to find a parking
place and picnic spot with a good view of the stage – and bring some
Cape fizz. Tickets available online or at the gate.

DECEMBER

Franschhoek Cap Classique and Champagne Festival
Beginning of the month; W www.franschhoekmcc.co.za.
Popular two-day bacchanalia of bubbly sampling – a vast selection of
local and French sparkling wine is on hand – and gourmandizing in the
Cape Winelands.

Mother City Queer Project Party Mid-month; W mcqp.co.za.
A hugely popular party attracting thousands of revellers, gay and
otherwise, to a vast venue. Outlandish get-ups, multiple dancefloors and
a mood of sustained delirium make this event a real draw.

Christmas Carols at Kirstenbosch Thurs–Sun before Christmas;
☎ 021 799 8783, W sanbi.org. The botanical gardens' annual carol
singing and nativity tableau is a Cape Town institution, drawing crowds of
families with their picnic baskets. The gates open at 6pm and the singing
kicks off at 7.45pm.

Spier Summer Festival Dec–March; W spier.co.za. A summer of
cultural happenings at Spier wine estate, near Stellenbosch, which are
increasingly taking on an African flavour. Featuring art installations, dance
and the lantern-lit performance of the Festival of White Lights.

Parks, reserves and wilderness areas

The region covered by this guide is bookended by two major national parks: at the western extreme is the Table Mountain National Park, a patchwork of wilderness that covers the full extent of the Cape Peninsula; and at the eastern end is Addo Elephant National Park, which, apart from hundreds of pachyderms, is home to lions, buffalos, leopards and rhinos – the only such major game reserve in the southern half of the country.

Between the two lie a series of provincial reserves, national parks and private operations, many of which are worth adding to a journey across the Southern Cape. In addition to the aforementioned, among the top wilderness areas in the country are **De Hoop Nature Reserve**, with its massive dunes and its claim to be one of the world's best places for land-based whale-watching; and the **Garden Route National Park**, especially the **Tsitsikamma section**, which draws many visitors to its ancient forests, rugged sea cliffs and dramatic Storms River Mouth.

All the national parks covered in this guide fall under the aegis of **South African National Parks** (SANParks, ☎ 012 428 9111, W sanparks.org). A few reserves mentioned, including De Hoop and Goukamma, are run by **CapeNature** (☎ 021 483 0190, W capenature.co.za).

TOP PARKS AND WILDLIFE AREAS

PARK	PRINCIPAL FOCUS	DESCRIPTION & HIGHLIGHTS	DETAILS
Addo Elephant National Park	Endangered species	The only Big Five national park in the southern half of the country, known for its six-hundred-strong elephant herd.	p.254
Agulhas National Park	Marine and coastal ecology	Rugged southernmost tip of Africa with rich plant biodiversity and significant archeological sites.	p.185
De Hoop Nature Reserve	Marine mammals and coastal fynbos	A combination of whales, massive dunes, *fynbos* and spectacular coastline.	p.188
Garden Route National Park	Marine, coastal, forestry and endangered species	Focused on three sections: • Wilderness and its lakes, rivers, lagoons, forest, *fynbos*, beaches and sea. • Knysna, a marine area that covers the lagoon and its dramatic headlands. The lagoon area protects the endangered Knysna sea horse. • Tsitsikamma, featuring cliffs, tidal pools, deep gorges and evergreen forests; offers snorkelling, scuba diving and forest trails.	Chapter 17
Goukamma Nature Reserve	Marine and coastal ecology	Comprises a river and estuary with some of the highest vegetated dunes in South Africa.	p.208
Robberg Nature Reserve	Rocky headland ecology	The promontory is a fine example of the interaction of plant and animal life on southern coastal headlands and a good place to spot seals. Good hiking trails, too.	p.219
Table Mountain National Park	The natural areas of the Cape Peninsula	Famed for the extraordinary diversity of flora and fauna living in the wild areas within and around Cape Town. The area spans Table Mountain, the Boulders Beach penguin colony and the Cape of Good Hope Nature Reserve.	p.110

Entry fees and accommodation

National parks charge a **daily conservation fee**, which is usually paid upfront when you enter. At most of the national parks covered by this guide, this entry fee comes to between R100 and R250 per day for foreign visitors (half-price for children), though citizens of the Southern African Development Community (SADC includes Angola, Botswana, DRC, Lesotho, Malawi, Mauritius, Mozambique, Namibia, Swaziland, Tanzania, Zambia and Zimbabwe) pay half the foreigner's rate. South African residents pay a quarter of the foreigner's rate.

In the case of the Cape of Good Hope Nature Reserve, part of the Table Mountain National Park, there is a daily conservation fee of R135 (children R70), which applies to all visitors. For Addo Elephant National Park it's R248 (children R124). Entry into CapeNature reserves generally costs around R40 (children R20) a day per person, irrespective of nationality.

Most national parks and some CapeNature reserves have **accommodation**, which generally has a pleasantly rustic atmosphere in keeping with the wilderness surrounds. Options include De Hoop Nature Reserve's luxurious De Hoop Collection cottages (⦿dehoopcollection.com) and comfortable, fully equipped en-suite cottages and chalets in the Garden Route and Addo Elephant national parks (respectively starting at R725 for a night in the

Garden Route for a couple and R870 a night for a couple in Addo). Some parks and reserves have family units sleeping several people, and most offer excellent **camping facilities**.

You can **book** accommodation in advance (to stay in high season, do so several months beforehand) through the SANParks or CapeNature website. Note that if you try booking for South African National Parks over the phone you could be in for a long wait; contacting them online is recommended.

Crime and personal safety

Despite horror stories of sky-high crime rates, most people visit South Africa without incident; be careful, but don't be paranoid. This is not to underestimate the issue – overcoming the ongoing crime epidemic is one of the country's most serious challenges. But some perspective is in order: crime is disproportionately concentrated in the townships rather than areas frequented by most visitors. Indeed, the greatest danger facing most visitors is navigating South Africa's roads, which claim well over ten thousand lives a year.

Protecting property and "security" are major national obsessions, and often a topic of conversation at dinner parties. A substantial percentage of middle-class homes subscribe to the services of armed private security firms. The other obvious manifestation of this obsession is the huge number of alarms, high walls and electronically controlled gates you'll see, not just in the suburbs, but even in less deprived areas of some townships. Fortunately, security at respectable tourist accommodation in the Western Cape is well managed and guests rarely feel unsafe or overwhelmed by burglar bars and trellis doors.

Guns are openly carried by police and women's handbags often sport a can of pepper spray past its expiry date. In some malls you'll spot firearms shops rubbing shoulders with places selling clothes or books, and you may see the odd notice asking you to deposit your weapon before entering the premises.

If you fall victim to a **mugging**, you should take very seriously the usual advice not to resist, and do as you're told. The chances of being mugged can be greatly minimized by using common sense and following a few simple rules (see box, p.38).

Drugs

Alcohol is unquestionably the most widely used and abused drug in South Africa, followed by dagga (pronounced like "dugger" with the "gg" guttural, as in the Scottish pronunciation of "loch") or cannabis in dried leaf form. Locally grown and produced, marijuana is fairly easily available and the quality is generally good – but this doesn't alter the fact that it is illegal.

Alcohol and drink-driving

Strangely, for a country that sometimes seems to be on one massive binge, South Africa has laws that prohibit drinking in public – not that anyone pays much attention to them. The **drink-drive laws** are routinely and brazenly flouted, making the country's roads a real danger that you should be concerned about. People routinely stock up their cars with booze for long journeys and levels of alcohol consumption go some way to explaining why, during the Christmas holidays, over a thousand people die in an annual period of road carnage. Attempts are being made to deal with the problem, including the widely publicized Arrive Alive campaign (Warrivealive.co.za), the confiscation of drunk drivers' vehicles and fining motorists travelling well over the speed limit. Don't risk drinking and driving, as nocturnal roadblocks are common in and around Cape Town.

Sexual harassment

South Africa's extremely high incidence of **rape** doesn't as a rule affect tourists. However, sexism is more common and attitudes are not as progressive as in Western countries, especially in black communities. Sometimes your eagerness to be friendly may be taken as a sexual overture – be sensitive to potential crossed wires and unintended signals.

Women should take care while travelling on their own, and should avoid hitchhiking or walking alone in deserted areas. This applies equally to Cape Town, the countryside or anywhere after dark. Minibus taxis should also be ruled out as a means of transport after dark; a taxi is the safest option, more so if you're travelling with others.

SAFETY TIPS

IN GENERAL

- Don't openly display expensive watches, jewellery, phones or cameras in cities.
- Use hotel safes.
- If you are accosted, remain calm and cooperative.

WHEN ON FOOT

- Grasp bags firmly under your arm.
- Don't carry excessive sums of money on you.
- Always know where your valuables are.
- Don't leave valuables exposed (on a seat or the ground) while having a meal or drink.
- Don't let strangers get too close to you – especially people in groups.
- Don't walk alone at night and always avoid isolated areas.

ON THE ROAD

- Lock all your car doors, especially in cities.
- Keep rear windows sufficiently rolled up to keep out opportunistic hands.
- Never leave anything worth stealing in view when your car is unattended.
- If you've concealed valuables in the boot, don't open it after parking.

ON THE BEACH

- Take only the bare essentials.
- Don't leave valuables, especially phones and cameras, unattended.
- Safeguard car keys by pinning them to your swimming gear, or putting them in a waterproof wallet or splash box and taking them into the water with you.

AT ATMS

Cash machines are favourite hunting grounds for sophisticated con men, who use cunning rather than force to steal money. Never underestimate their ability and don't get drawn into any interaction at an ATM, no matter how well spoken, friendly or distressed the other person appears. If they claim to have a problem with the machine, tell them to contact the bank. Don't let people crowd you or see your personal identification number (PIN) when you withdraw money; if in doubt, go to another machine. Finally, if your card gets swallowed, report it without delay.

WHEN PAYING WITH A CARD

- Never let your card out of your sight.
- At a restaurant, ask for a portable card reader to be brought to your table.
- At the till, keep an eye on your card.
- If the transaction fails, don't try a second time; pay with cash or another card.
- It's common for the amount being debited to not appear on the card-reader screen.

The police

Dismally paid, poorly trained, shot at (and frequently hit), underfunded, badly equipped, barely respected and demoralized, the **South African Police Service** (SAPS) keeps a low profile. If you ever get stopped, at a roadblock for example (one of the likeliest encounters), always be courteous. And if you're driving, note that under South African law you are required to carry your **driving licence** at all times. If you can't show your licence, a photocopy or another form of ID, you may be fined, although traffic police are often more lenient towards tourists. If you are fined and you suspect corruption, asking to be issued with a receipt will discourage foul play or at least give you a record of the incident.

If you are robbed, you will need to report the crime to the police, who should give you a case reference; keep all paperwork for insurance purposes. Don't expect too much crime-cracking enthusiasm, or to get your property back.

Travel essentials

Climate

As a winter rainfall area, Cape Town typically is at its coldest, wettest and stormiest from May to August. Having said that, it's not uncommon to have days or weeks of glorious sunshine at this time of year.

During the peak of the summer (November to February) you can expect long sunny days (and the blast of the seasonal southeasterly wind) with average temperatures peaking at 27°C in February. Droughts and bush fires are increasingly common during the summer.

In autumn and spring you can expect milder temperatures with occasional warm days without the summer wind and high UV index.

Costs

For budget and midrange travellers, the most expensive thing about visiting South Africa is getting there. Once you've arrived, you're likely to find it a relatively inexpensive and good-value destination. How affordable you find South Africa will depend partly on exchange rates at the time of your visit – since becoming fully convertible (after the advent of democracy in South Africa) the rand has seen some massive fluctuations against sterling, the dollar and the euro.

When it comes to **daily budgets**, your biggest expense is likely to be **accommodation**. If you're willing to stay in backpacker dorms and self-cater, you should be able to sleep and eat for under R500 (£31/US$39/€35) per person per day. Dorm beds cost around R140 to R390 in Cape Town, while backpacker doubles go for R350 to R1200. If you stay in B&Bs and guesthouses, eat out once a day, and have a snack or two you should expect to spend at least double that budget. Cape Town's

luxury hotels mostly charge between R5000 (£310/US$390/€350) and R10000 for a standard double; high-end guesthouses and boutique hotels are often a better deal, offering a special experience for under R3000. Luxury safari lodges around Addo and in the private game reserves are in roughly the same bracket as the top-end hotels, with packages available including **extras** such as safaris, car rental, horseriding and other outdoor activities. While most museums and art galleries impose an **entry fee**, it's usually quite low: only the most sophisticated attractions charge more than R50 (£3.10/US$3.90/€3.50).

Electricity

South Africa's **electricity** supply runs at 220/230V, 50Hz AC. Most sockets take unique plugs with three fat, round pins, although sockets taking European-style two-pin plugs are common. Most hotel rooms have sockets that will take 110V electric shavers, but for other appliances US visitors will need an adaptor to make their appliances compatible with South Africa's 220V system.

Emergencies

Police ☎10111; state ambulance ☎10177; cellphone emergency operator ☎112; ER24 private ambulance and paramedic assistance ☎084 124; Netcare ☎911 082 911.

Insurance

It's wise to take out an **insurance policy** to cover against theft, loss and illness or injury. A typical travel insurance policy usually provides cover for the loss of baggage, valuables and – up to a certain limit – cash and bank cards, as well as cancellation or curtailment of your journey. Most of them

AVERAGE MONTHLY TEMPERATURES AND RAINFALL

	Jan	Feb	Mar	Apr	May	Jun	Jul	Aug	Sep	Oct	Nov	Dec
CAPE TOWN												
max/min (°C)	26/16	27/16	25/14	23/12	20/9	18/8	18/7	18/8	19/9	21/11	24/13	25/15
max/min (°F)	79/60	80/60	78/58	73/53	69 48	65/46	65/45	65/46	67/48	70/51	74/56	77/59
Rainfall (mm/inches)	15/0.6	17/0.7	20/0.8	41/1.6	69/2.7	93/3.7	82/3.2	77/3.0	40/1.6	30/1.2	14/0.6	17/0.7
GARDEN ROUTE NATIONAL PARK (TSITSIKAMMA)												
max/min (°C)	23/17	22/17	21/16	20/14	19/12	18/10	17/10	17/10	17/11	19/13	20/14	22/16
max/min (°F)	73/63	72/63	70/61	68/57	66/54	64/50	63/50	63/50	63/52	66/55	68/57	72/61
Rainfall (mm/inches)	77/3.0	70/2.8	81/3.2	80/3.1	86/3.4	75/3.0	78/3.1	111/4.4	66/2.6	83/3.3	78/3.1	60/2.4

ROUGH GUIDES TRAVEL INSURANCE

Rough Guides has teamed up with WorldNomads.com to offer great travel insurance deals. Policies are available to residents of over 150 countries, with cover for a wide range of adventure sports, 24hr emergency assistance, high levels of medical and evacuation cover and a stream of travel safety information. Roughguides.com users can take advantage of their policies online 24/7, from anywhere in the world – even if you're already travelling. And since plans often change when you're on the road, you can extend your policy and even claim online. Roughguides.com users who buy travel insurance with WorldNomads.com can also leave a positive footprint and donate to a community development project. For more information, go to ⓦroughguides.com/travel-insurance.

exclude so-called **dangerous sports** unless an extra premium is paid: in South Africa this can mean scuba diving, white-water rafting, windsurfing, horseriding, bungee jumping and paragliding. In addition to these it's well worth checking whether you are covered by your policy if you're hiking, kayaking, pony trekking or game viewing on safari, all activities people commonly take part in when visiting South Africa.

Many policies can be chopped and changed to exclude coverage you don't need – for example, sickness and accident benefits can often be excluded or included at will. Do take **medical coverage**, as it will enable you to use South Africa's excellent-quality private healthcare with the prospect of a refund by your insurer, rather than relying on the less impressive state facilities. Ascertain whether benefits will be paid as treatment proceeds or only after you return home, if there is a 24-hour medical emergency number and if medical evacuation will be covered.

If you need to make a claim, you should keep receipts for medicines and medical treatment, and in the event you have anything stolen, you must obtain an official statement from the police.

When buying **baggage cover**, make sure that the per-article limit will cover your most valuable possession.

Internet

Accessing the **internet** is easy in and around Cape Town and the Garden Route: internet cafés are found even in small towns, and most backpacker hostels and hotels have internet facilities, albeit sometimes too slow for Skype calls. It's easiest to bring your own device, enabling you to use the paid or free wireless hotspots at airports, cafés, malls and accommodation. Bring your **smartphone** too, as South Africa is increasing its reliance on apps for ordering everything from taxis to takeaway food.

Mail

The deceptively familiar feel of South African post offices can lull you into expecting an efficient service. In fact, post within the country can be slow and unreliable, and certainly not safe for sending money or valuables. Expect domestic delivery times from one city to another of about a week – longer if a rural town is involved at either end.

International airmail deliveries are often quicker, thanks to the city's direct flights to London. A letter or package sent by surface mail can take up to six weeks to get from South Africa to London. Post is less reliable and trustworthy coming into the country, when items frequently disappear or take weeks to arrive.

Most towns of any size have a **post office**, generally open Monday to Friday 8.30am to 4.30pm and Saturday till noon (closing earlier in some places). A much better option, the ubiquitous private **PostNet** outlets (ⓦpostnet.co.za) offer many of the same postal services as the post office and more, including **courier services**. Courier companies like FedEx (☎0800 033 339, ⓦfedex .com/za) and DHL (☎086 034 5000, ⓦdhl.co.za), available only in the larger towns, are far more reliable than the mail.

Stamps are available at post offices and from newsagents such as the CNA chain. Postage is relatively inexpensive – it costs about R8 to send a postcard by airmail to anywhere in the world, while a small letter costs just over R9. You can open a **post box** at most post offices and PostNet branches.

Maps

You'll find up-to-date maps of Cape Town, its suburbs, the Winelands and the Garden Route in this guide, but if you're looking for more substantial maps, make sure they're up to date as many place and street names have been changed since the 1994 elections. **Bartholomew** produces an excellent map of South

Africa, including Lesotho and Swaziland, as part of its World Travel Map series. The best hiking and touring maps of the **Western Cape** are published by Cape Town's **Slingsby Maps** (Ⓦslingsbymaps.com) and available through **Map Studio** (Ⓦmapstudio.co.za) and bookshops. Maps cover the Cape Peninsula, Winelands, Garden Route and beyond.

South Africa's motoring organization, the **Automobile Association** (Ⓦaa.co.za), has free maps available to download from its website.

Money

South Africa's currency is the **rand** (R), often called the "buck", divided into 100 **cents**. Notes come in R10, R20, R50, R100 and R200 denominations and there are coins of 50 cents, and R1, 2, 5. The **exchange rate** often fluctuates wildly, generally in favour of visitors; in mid-2017, it averaged around R17 to the pound sterling (down from a pre-Brexit high of R24), R13 to the US dollar, R14 to the euro and R10 to the Australian dollar.

All but the tiniest settlement will have a **bank**, where you can withdraw and change money, or an ATM. **Banking hours** vary, but are at least from Monday to Friday 9am to 3.30pm, and Saturday 8.30am to 11am; banks in smaller towns usually close for lunch. In major cities, large hotels and banks operate **bureaux de change**. Outside banking hours, some hotel receptions will change money, although this entails a fairly hefty **commission**.

You can also change money at branches of American Express (Ⓦamericanexpressforex.co.za). In all cases, **keep exchange receipts**, which you'll need to show to convert your leftover rand at the end of your trip.

Cards and travellers' cheques

Credit and debit cards are the most convenient way to access your funds in South Africa. Most international cards can be used to withdraw money at **ATMs**, open 24 hours a day in the cities and elsewhere. South African banks usually charge a fee of around R30–45 for withdrawal. Plastic comes in very handy for paying for more mainstream and upmarket tourist facilities, including hotels, restaurants and tour operators, and a credit card with funds available to block as a security deposit is essential for renting a car. **Visa** and **MasterCard** are the cards most widely accepted.

American Express, Visa and Thomas Cook **travellers' cheques** are widely accepted. US dollar and sterling cheques are accepted, and better to carry than cheques in the weaker rand.

If you're heading into remote areas, you'll need to carry **cash** to tide you between ATMs, which are unreliable in rural regions. Stash it in a safe place, or even better in a few places on your person and baggage.

Opening hours and holidays

The **working day** starts and finishes early in South Africa: shops and businesses generally open on **weekdays** around 8.30am and close at 4.30pm. In small towns, many places close for an hour over **lunch**. Many **shops** and businesses close around noon on Saturdays, and most are closed on Sundays. However, in urban neighbourhoods, you'll find small shops and supermarkets where you can buy groceries and essentials after hours.

Some establishments have summer and winter opening times. In such situations, you can take **winter** to mean roughly April to September, while **summer** constitutes the rest of the year.

School holidays can disrupt your plans, especially if you want to camp, or stay in the national parks and the budget end of accommodation (self-catering, cheaper B&Bs, etc). All are likely to be booked solid during holiday periods, especially along the coast. If you travel to South Africa over a school holiday, book accommodation well in advance, particularly for the national parks.

The longest and busiest holiday period is **Christmas (summer)**, which for schools stretches from early December to mid-January. Flights and train berths can be hard to get from mid-December

> ## SOUTH AFRICAN PUBLIC HOLIDAYS
>
> Many tourist-related businesses and some shops remain open over public holidays, although often with shorter opening hours. Most of the country shuts down on Christmas Day and Good Friday. The main holidays are:
>
> **New Year's Day** (Jan 1)
> **Human Rights Day** (March 21)
> **Good Friday, Easter Monday** (variable)
> **Freedom Day** (April 27)
> **Workers' Day** (May 1)
> **Youth Day** (June 16)
> **National Women's Day** (Aug 9)
> **Heritage Day** (Sept 24)
> **Day of Reconciliation** (Dec 16)
> **Christmas Day** (Dec 25)
> **Day of Goodwill** (Dec 26)

to early January, when many businesses and offices close for their annual break. You should book your **flights** – long-haul and domestic – six months in advance for the Christmas period. The remaining school holidays roughly cover the following periods: **Easter**, late March to mid-April; **winter**, late June to mid-July; and **spring**, late September to early October. Exact **dates** for each year are listed at ⓦ gov.za/about-sa/school-calendar.

Phones

South Africa's **telephone** system, dominated by **Telkom** (ⓦ telkom.co.za), generally works well. Public phone booths are found in every city and town, and are either coin- or card-operated. While **international calls** can be made from virtually any phone, it helps to have a **phonecard** such as Telkom WorldCall. Prepaid WorldCall vouchers and recharge cards are available at Telkom offices, supermarkets, banks and more in denominations of R10 upwards.

Mobile phones (referred to locally as cell phones) are extremely widely used in South Africa, with more mobile than landline handsets in use. The competing networks – Vodacom, MTN, Cell C and Virgin Mobile – cover all the main areas and the national roads connecting them.

You can use 2G, 3G and 4G phones from outside South Africa, but you will need to arrange a **roaming agreement** with your provider at home. A far cheaper alternative is to buy a very inexpensive prepaid **local SIM card**. These can be bought for about R20 from the ubiquitous mobile phone shops and various other outlets, including supermarkets. You will need your ID and a proof of address, which

CALLING HOME FROM ABROAD

To make an international call, dial the international access code (in South Africa it's +00), then the destination's country code, before the rest of the number. In both cases, remember to omit the initial zero in the number of the place you're phoning.

Australia international access code + 61
New Zealand international access code + 64
UK international access code + 44
US and Canada international access code + 1
Ireland international access code + 353
South Africa international access code + 27

can be a hotel receipt or a signed letter from your accommodation or host. You can subsequently purchase data bundles as well as call credit.

It's also possible to **rent** a South African mobile phone through your car-rental provider.

PHONE RENTAL

B4i.travel ⓦ b4i.travel. Offers the same services, with collection points at Cape Town International Airport and the Waterfront.
Vodacom Rentals ⓦ vodacomrentals.co.za. SIM and phone rentals.

Taxes

Value-added tax (VAT) of fourteen percent is levied on most goods and services, though it's usually already included in the quoted price. Foreign visitors can claim back VAT on goods worth over R250 total. To do this, present an official tax receipt, which should carry your name and address in the case of purchases over R5000, along with a proof of payment for purchases over R10000, a non-South African passport and the purchased goods themselves, at the **airport** just before you fly out. You will also need to fill in a form, which can be obtained at international airports. At Cape Town International Airport, goods are inspected by customs officers in the arrivals terminal. For more information, visit ⓦ taxrefunds.co.za or call ☎ 011 979 0055.

Time

There is only one **time zone** throughout South Africa, two hours ahead of GMT year-round. If you're flying from anywhere in Europe, you shouldn't experience any jet lag.

Tipping

Ten to fifteen percent of the tab is the usual **tip** in restaurants, while taxi fares are generally rounded up. Don't feel obliged to tip if service has been shoddy, but keep in mind that many of the people who'll be serving you rely on tips to supplement a meagre wage on which they support huge extended families. **Porters** at hotels normally get about R10 per bag. At South African garages and petrol stations, someone will always be on hand to fill your vehicle, clean your windscreen and check your oil, water and tyre pressure, for which you should tip R5–10. Car guards meanwhile expect around R2–5. Many establishments, especially private game lodges, take (voluntary) communal tips when you check out – by far the fairest system, which ensures that all the low-profile staff behind the scenes get their share.

Tourist information

There are official **tourist information bureaus** in Cape Town and most towns have some sort of information office, but in smaller spots your accommodation will likely be a better source of local knowledge. If you're seeing South Africa on a budget, the useful notice boards, constant traveller traffic and largely helpful and friendly staff you'll encounter in **backpacker hostels** will greatly smooth your travels.

There are countless **guidebooks** on walks around Cape Town, hikes up Table Mountain, dive sites, fishing locations, surfing breaks, windsurfing spots and so on (see p.270). This guide includes bookshop recommendations (see p.142).

To find out **what's on**, check out websites such as *Cape Town Magazine* (Ⓦ capetownmagazine.com) and *What's On in Cape Town* (Ⓦ whatsonincapetown .com); the entertainment pages of the daily newspapers; and the *Mail & Guardian* (Ⓦ mg.co.za), which comes out every Friday and lists the coming week's offerings in a comprehensive pull-out supplement.

TOURIST INFORMATION BUREAUS

Cape Town Tourism Ⓦ capetown.travel ☎ 086 132 2223. Main office in the city centre at the Pinnacle, Burg & Castle streets, open Mon–Fri 8am–5.30pm, Sat & Sun 8.30am–1pm. Has a South African National Parks desk. Also at Cape Town International Airport and the Waterfront, while there is a non-accredited information desk at the lower Table Mountain Aerial Cableway station.

FOREIGN GOVERNMENT SITES

Australian Department of Foreign Affairs Ⓦ dfat.gov.au.
British Foreign & Commonwealth Office Ⓦ fco.gov.uk.
Canadian Global Affairs Ⓦ international.gc.ca.
Irish Department of Foreign Affairs Ⓦ foreignaffairs.gov.ie.
New Zealand Ministry of Foreign Affairs Ⓦ mfat.govt.nz.
US State Department Ⓦ state.gov.

Travellers with disabilities

Facilities for **disabled travellers** are not as sophisticated as those you might find in Europe and the US,

but they're sufficient to ensure you have a satisfactory visit. By accident, often, rather than design, you'll find pretty good accessibility to many buildings, as South Africans tend to build low (single-storey bungalows are the norm). As the **car is king**, you'll frequently find that you can drive to, and park right outside, your destination. Many attractions also offer boardwalks and Braille trails, including Kirstenbosch National Botanical Garden.

There are **organized tours** and holidays for people with disabilities, and **activity-based packages** are available. These offer the possibility for wheelchair-bound visitors to take part in safaris, sport and a range of adventure activities. Tours can either be taken as self-drive trips or as packages for groups.

If you want to be more independent on your travels, it's important to know where you can expect help and where you must be self-reliant, especially regarding transport and accommodation. Cape Town is a Westernised and relatively accessible destination, but other areas will offer fewer helpful facilities. If you do not use a wheelchair all the time but your walking capabilities are limited, remember that you are likely to need to cover greater distances while travelling (often over rough terrain and in hot temperatures) than you are used to. If you use a wheelchair, have it serviced before you go and take a repair kit with you.

USEFUL CONTACTS

Ⓦ **brandsouthafrica.com/tourism-south-africa/travel /advice/disabled** Useful overview and links.
Ⓦ **capetown.travel** Cape Town Tourism has a page on wheelchair-friendly activities.
Ⓦ **www.disabledtravel.co.za** Website of occupational therapist Karin Coetzee aimed at disabled travellers, with listings of accommodation, restaurants and attractions personally evaluated for accessibility as well as links to car rental, tours and orthopaedic equipment.
Ⓦ **epic-enabled.com** Accommodation, tours and safaris.
Ⓦ **flamingotours.co.za** Flamingo tours and Disabled Ventures specialize in tours for visitors with special needs.
Ⓦ **rollingsa.co.za** Accommodation, tours and safaris.
Ⓦ **sanparks.org/groups/disabilities/general.php** Lists what wheelchair- and mobility-impaired access and facilities are available at South African National Parks.

LONG STREET

The city centre

South Africa's oldest urban region pulses with the cultural fusion that has been Cape Town's hallmark since its founding in 1652. The city centre is spectacularly situated, dominated by Table Mountain to the south and the pounding Atlantic to the north. Strand Street marks the edge of the city's original beachfront (though you'd never guess it today), with the Lower City Centre to the northeast and Upper City Centre to the southwest. Another useful orientation axis is Adderley Street, which connects the main train station with St George's Cathedral, the landmark Anglican cathedral at the northeastern entrance to the Company's Garden. These venerated gardens are Cape Town's symbolic heart, surrounded by the Houses of Parliament, museums, historic buildings, archives and De Tuynhuys (the office of the president).

North of St George's is the closest South Africa gets to a European quarter – a tight network of streets with cafés, buskers, craft markets, street stalls and antique shops congregating around the pedestrianized **St George's Mall** and **Greenmarket Square**.

Parallel to St George's Mall, **Long Street**, the quintessential Cape Town thoroughfare, is lined with Victorian buildings containing pubs, bistros, nightclubs, backpacker lodges, bookshops and antique dealers. Climb to the colonial piles' wrought-iron balconies for glimpses of Table Mountain and the ocean. Two blocks further west is **Bree Street**, which has established itself as a quieter and more discerning alternative to Long Street, with an interesting choice of boutique stores and bars. The **Bo-Kaap**, or Muslim quarter, a few blocks further northwest across Buitengracht, is a piquant contrast with its colourful houses, minarets, spice shops and stalls selling curried snacks.

Southeast of Adderley Street lie three historically loaded sites. The **Castle of Good Hope** is the country's oldest building and an indelible symbol of Europe's colonization of South Africa (see p.58) – a process whose death knell was struck from nearby **City Hall**, the attractive Edwardian building from which Nelson Mandela made his first speech after being released. South of the castle lie the poignant remains of **District Six**, the coloured inner-city suburb that was razed in the name of apartheid.

GETTING AROUND   THE CITY CENTRE

BY BUS

MyCiTi ☎ 0800 65 64 63, ⊛ myciti.org.za. Useful and safe, the MyCiTi bus network has stations and stops on several routes around the City Bowl and beyond. Buses run through the city centre from Gardens and the neighbouring suburbs, on the south side of the City Bowl, to stops including Long St, the castle, the Civic Centre and Adderley (for the main train station), continuing to the Cape Town International Convention Centre and the Waterfront. The Civic Centre and Adderley are central transport hubs, where

you can get buses to all areas served by MyCiTi buses. A number of buses run through the city centre, bringing you within a short walk of most of the central attractions. Bus #106 to Camps Bay goes up Adderley St, Long St and Kloof Nek; the #101 to Gardens goes via Long St, while the #109 to Hout Bay crosses the centre at right angles to this, along Riebeek St and onto the Atlantic suburbs.

City Sightseeing ☎ 0861 733 287, ⊛ citysightseeing .co.za. Hop-on, hop-off sightseeing buses stop at the major attractions in the city centre.

Upper City Centre

Once *the* place to shop in Cape Town, **Adderley Street**, lined with handsome buildings spanning several centuries, is still worth a stroll today. Its attractive streetscape has been blemished by a series of large 1960s shopping centres, but just minutes away from these crowded malls, among the streets and alleys around Greenmarket Square, the area takes on a more human element and is full of historic texture.

Low-walled channels, ditches, bridges and sluices once ran through Cape Town, earning it the name **Little Amsterdam**. During the nineteenth century, the canals were buried underground, and, in 1850, Heerengracht (Gentlemen's Canal), formerly a waterway that ran from the Company's Garden down to the sea, was renamed Adderley Street (see box, p.48). There's little evidence of the canals today, except in name – the lower end of Adderley is still called Heerengracht and a parallel street to the west is called Buitengracht (Outer Canal). The destruction of old Cape Town continued well into the twentieth century, with the razing of many of the older buildings.

Trafalgar Place Flower Market

Trafalgar Pl • Mon–Sat 9am–4pm

Local coloured people, originally from Constantia and more recently from the Bo-Kaap, have run this **flower market** for well over a century. Look out for Cape classics such as proteas, petunias and daisies at the market, which spills onto Adderley Street.

1

THE LANGUAGE OF COLOUR

It's striking just how un-African Cape Town looks and sounds. Halfway between East and West, this city drew its population from Africa, Asia and Europe, and traces of all three continents are found in the genes, language, culture, religion and cuisine of Cape Town's coloured population.

Afrikaans (a close relative of Dutch) is the mother tongue of around forty percent of the city's residents, mostly coloured people and Afrikaners. However, about thirty percent of Capetonians are born English speakers, and English punches well above its weight as the local lingua franca, which, in this multilingual society, virtually everyone can speak and understand.

The term "coloured" is contentious, but in South Africa it doesn't have the same tainted connotations as in Britain and the US; it refers to South Africans of mixed race. Over forty percent of Capetonians are coloured people, with Asian, African and Khoikhoi ancestry – compared with around fifteen percent whites and the growing black African contingent of close to forty percent.

In the late **nineteenth century**, Afrikaans-speaking whites, fighting for an identity, sought to create a "racially pure" culture by driving a wedge between themselves and coloured Afrikaans speakers. They reinvented Afrikaans as a "white man's language", eradicating the supposed stigma of its coloured ties by substituting Dutch words for those with Asian or African roots. In 1925, the white dialect of Afrikaans became an official language alongside English, and the dialects spoken by coloured people were treated as inferior deviations from correct usage.

For Afrikaner nationalists this wasn't enough, and after the introduction of apartheid in 1948, they attempted to codify perceived racial differences. Under the **Population Registration Act**, all South Africans were classified as white, coloured or African. These classifications became fundamental to what kind of life you could expect. There are numerous cases of families in which one sibling was classified coloured with limited rights, and another white with the right to live in comfortable white areas, enjoy superior job opportunities and send their children to better schools and universities.

With the demise of **apartheid**, the make-up of residential areas is shifting – and so is the thinking on ethnic terminology. In Afrikaans, the term *kleurling* (coloured) is slowly being superseded by *bruinmense* (brown people). Far from rejecting the term "coloured" and its apartheid associations, most coloured people proudly embrace it, as a means of acknowledging their distinct culture, with its slave and Khoikhoi roots. Many middle class coloured people drop Afrikaans in favour of English, choosing a world language over one that was perceived under apartheid as the language of the white oppressor. However, the quavering coloured dialect of Afrikaans, which is distinct from the version spoken by Afrikaners, remains ubiquitous on the streets of Cape Town.

Standard and First National banks

15 & 82 Adderley St · First National Bank: Mon–Fri 9am–4pm, Sat 8.30am–noon · ⓦ standardbank.co.za, ⓦ fnb.co.za

Two grandiose bank buildings, one still a major working bank, stand on opposite sides of Adderley Street: the **Standard Bank** is fronted by Corinthian columns and covered with a tall dome; and the **First National Bank**, completed in 1913, is the last South African building designed by Sir Herbert Baker (see box, p.102). If you pop into the latter for a quick look, still in place inside the banking hall you'll find a solid-timber circular writing desk with the original inkwells, resembling an altar.

Groote Kerk

43 Adderley St · Mon–Fri 10am–2pm; services Sun 10am & 7pm · Free · ⓦ grootekerk.org.za (Afrikaans only)

The **Groote Kerk** (Great Church) was the first church erected in South Africa, shortly after the Dutch arrived in 1652, bringing their rigorous Protestant beliefs with them. The current church replaces an earlier structure, which had become too small for the swelling ranks of the Dutch Reformed congregation at the Cape. The building is essentially Classical, with Gothic and Egyptian elements, and was designed and built between 1836 and 1841 by Hermann Schutte, a German who became one of the Cape's leading early nineteenth-century architects. The beautiful freestanding clock tower is a remnant of the original church.

CITY CENTRE

SEE "V&A WATERFRONT & DE WATERKANT" MAP

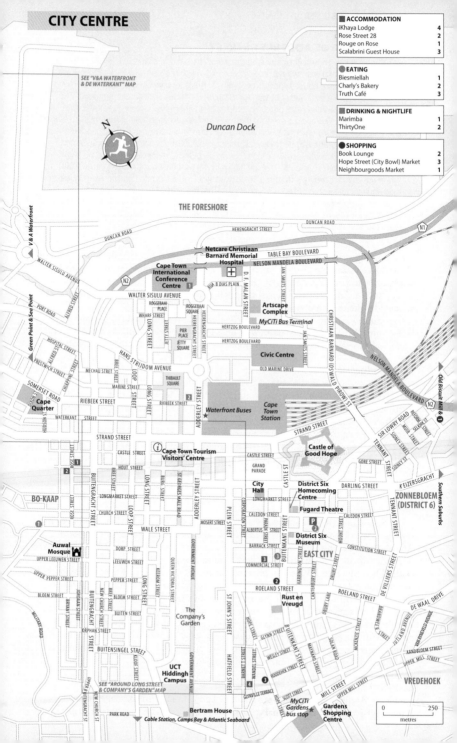

■ ACCOMMODATION	
iKhaya Lodge	4
Rose Street 28	2
Rouge on Rose	1
Scalabrini Guest House	3

● EATING	
Biesmiellah	1
Charly's Bakery	2
Truth Café	3

■ DRINKING & NIGHTLIFE	
Marimba	1
ThirtyOne	2

● SHOPPING	
Book Lounge	2
Hope Street (City Bowl) Market	3
Neighbourgoods Market	1

Duncan Dock

THE FORESHORE

Netcare Christiaan Barnard Memorial Hospital
Cape Town International Conference Centre
Artscape Complex
MyCiTi Bus Terminal
Civic Centre
Waterfront Buses
Cape Town Station
Castle of Good Hope
Cape Town Tourism Visitors' Centre
City Hall
Grand Parade
District Six Homecoming Centre
Fugard Theatre
District Six Museum
EAST CITY
ZONNEBLOEM (DISTRICT 6)
Cape Quarter
BO-KAAP
Auwal Mosque
The Company's Garden
Rust en Vreugd
UCT Hiddingh Campus
Bertram House
VREDEHOEK
MyCiTi Gardens bus stop
Gardens Shopping Centre

SEE "AROUND LONG STREET & COMPANY'S GARDEN" MAP

Cable Station, Camps Bay & Atlantic Seaboard

0   250
metres

1

THE NAMING OF ADDERLEY STREET

Although the Dutch used Robben Island (see p.68) as a political prison, in the 1800s the South African mainland only narrowly escaped becoming a second Australia, which at that time was a **penal colony** where British felons and enemies of the state could be dumped. In the 1840s, "respectable" Australians were lobbying for a ban on the transportation of criminals to the Antipodes, and the British authorities responded by trying to divert convicts to the Cape.

The British ship *Neptune* set sail from Bermuda for Cape Town in 1848, carrying 282 prisoners. There was outrage when news of its departure reached the Cape; five thousand citizens gathered on the Grand Parade to hear prominent liberals denounce the British government, an event depicted in *The Great Meeting of the People at the Commercial Exchange* by Johan Marthinus Carstens Schonegevel, which hangs in the Rust en Vreugd Museum (see p.58). When the ship docked in September 1849, governor Sir Harry Smith forbade any criminal from landing; meanwhile, back in London, politician **Charles Adderley** successfully addressed the House of Commons in support of the Cape colonists. In February 1850, the *Neptune* set off for Tasmania with its full complement of convicts, and grateful Capetonians renamed the city's main thoroughfare **Adderley Street**.

The soaring space created by the vast vaulted ceiling and the magnificent pulpit, a masterpiece by sculptor Anton Anreith and carpenter Jan Jacob Graaff, are worth stepping inside for. The **pulpit**, supported on a pair of sculpted lions with gaping jaws, was carved by Anreith after his first proposal, featuring Faith, Hope and Charity, was rejected by the church council for being "too popish".

The Groote Kerk still has a keen family congregation, with a thundering organ and pealing bells. Across Parliament Street, slaves were once traded on **Church Square**, as the Slavery Memorial remembers, its eleven black granite blocks engraved with the names of slaves.

Slave Lodge

Cnr Adderley and Wale sts • Mon–Sat 10am–5pm • R30 • ⓦ iziko.org.za/museums/slave-lodge

The **Slave Lodge**, which sits at the southern corner of Adderley Street, just as it veers northwest into Wale Street, was built in 1679 to house the human chattels of the Dutch East India Company (VOC) – the Cape's largest slaveholder.

For nearly two centuries – more than half the city's existence as an urban settlement – Cape Town's economic and social structures rested on slavery (see box opposite). By the 1770s, almost a thousand slaves were held at the lodge. Under VOC administration, the lodge also became the Cape Colony's main **brothel**, its doors thrown open for an hour each night. From 1810, following the British takeover, the lodge variously housed government offices, the **Supreme Court**, the country's first library and first post office, finally becoming a museum in 1966.

The Slave Lodge has redefined itself as a museum of slavery as well as human rights museum, with displays showing the family roots, ancestry and peopling of South Africa, and changing exhibitions which have covered the likes of Steve Biko and slavery in Brazil. Taking an audio headset allows you to follow the footsteps of German salt trader Otto Menzl as he is taken on a tour of the lodge in the 1700s, giving a good idea of the miserable conditions at the time. Of note is a scale model of the *Meermin*, one of several ships sent to Madagascar in the eighteenth century to bring men, women and children into slavery in the Cape. Another memorable stop is an alcove, lit by a column of light, where the names of slaves are marked on rings that resemble tree trunks, symbolic of the Slave Tree under which slaves were bought and sold. Though the actual **Slave Tree** is long gone, the spot is marked by a simple and inconspicuous plinth behind Slave Lodge, on the traffic island in Spin Street.

Long Street

Parallel to Adderley Street, buzzing one-way **Long Street** is one of Cape Town's most diverse thoroughfares, and is best known as the city's main nightlife strip.

When Muslims first settled here some three hundred years ago, Long Street marked Cape Town's boundary; by the 1960s, it had become a sleazy alley of drinking holes and brothels. The libation and raucousness are certainly still here, but with a whiff of gentrification and a wad of fast-food joints, and the street deserves exploration roughly from the Greenmarket Square area upwards.

Mosques still coexist alongside bars, while antique dealers, craft shops, bookshops and cafés occupy the attractive Victorian buildings with New Orleans-style wrought-iron balconies. The street is packed with backpacker hostels and a few hotels, though the proliferation of nightclubs means it can be noisy into the early hours. Until the area quietens down for the night, it's relatively safe to pub or club crawl on foot, with pickpockets being the main danger, and you'll always find taxis and street food.

Long Street Baths

Cnr Long and Orange sts • Daily 7am–7pm, women only Tues 10am–4pm • Pools R22, Turkish baths R60 per hour • ☎ 021 422 0100

The **Long Street Baths** is an unpretentious and relaxing historic Cape Town institution, established in 1908 in an Edwardian building at the top of Long Street. Though shabby, behind its Art Nouveau facade are a 25m heated pool and a children's pool, overlooked by murals of city life. Call ahead to use the Turkish baths, which have a sauna and steam room with massages available.

Palm Tree Mosque

185 Long St • Closed to the public

The diminutive **Palm Tree Mosque** was named after two palm trees that stood outside; the fronds of one still caress the building's upper storey. South Africa's second-oldest mosque, it is also the street's only surviving eighteenth-century building, erected in 1780 by Carel Lodewijk Schot as a private dwelling. The house was bought in 1807 by Frans van Bengal, a member of the local Muslim community, and a freed slave, Jan van Boughies, who became its imam and turned the upper storey into a mosque, the lower into his living quarters.

SLAVERY AT THE CAPE

Slavery was officially **abolished** at the Cape in 1834, but its legacy lives on in South Africa. The country's **coloured inhabitants**, who make up over forty percent of Cape Town's population, are largely descendants of slaves, political prisoners from the East Indies and indigenous Khoisan people. The darkest elements of apartheid recalled the days of slavery, as did labour practices such as the "dop system", in which workers on wine farms were partially paid in rations of cheap wine. Even today, domestic service, which is widespread throughout South Africa, can be traced back to colonialism and slavery.

By the end of the eighteenth century, the almost 26,000-strong **slave population** of the Cape exceeded that of the free burghers. Despite the profound impact this had on the development of social relations in South Africa, slavery remained one of the most neglected topics of the country's history, until the publication in the 1980s of a number of studies on slavery. There's still reluctance on the part of most coloured people to acknowledge their slave origins. Common coloured surnames such as January and September generally indicate these roots, as they refer to the month the slave was acquired.

Few if any slaves were captured at the Cape for export, making the colony unique in the African trade. Paradoxically, while people were being captured elsewhere on the continent for export to the Americas, the Cape administration, forbidden by the VOC (see p.261) from enslaving the local indigenous population, had to look further afield. Of the 63,000 slaves imported to the Cape, most came from East Africa, Madagascar, India and Indonesia, representing one of the broadest cultural mixes of any slave society. This diversity initially worked against the establishment of a unified group identity, but eventually a **Creolized culture** emerged which, among other things, played a major role in the development of the **Afrikaans** language.

1

Pan African Market

76 Long St • Summer Mon–Fri 8.30am–5.30pm, Sat 9am–3.30pm; winter Mon–Fri 9am–5pm, Sat 9am–3pm • ☎ 021 426 4478

Behind the yellow facade of the **Pan African Market**, one of Cape Town's most enjoyable places to buy African crafts, is a three-storey warren of passageways and rooms bursting at the hinges with traders selling art and artefacts from all over the continent. The colourful mishmash includes terrific masks from West Africa, baskets from Zimbabwe, brass leopards from Benin and contemporary South African art textiles, as well as CDs and musical instruments. This is also the place to get kitted out in African garb – in-house seamstresses are at the ready.

South African Missionary Meeting-House Museum

40 Long St • Mon–Fri 8.30am–4pm • Free • ☎ 021 423 6755

The **South African Missionary Meeting-House Museum** was the first missionary church in the country, where slaves were taught literacy and instructed in Christianity. This exceptional building, completed in 1804 by the South African Missionary Society, boasts one of the most beautiful frontages in Cape Town. Dominated by large windows, the facade is broken into three bays by four slender Corinthian pilasters surmounted by a gabled pediment. Inside, an impressive Neoclassical timber **pulpit** perches on a pair of columns, and frames an inlaid image of an angel in flight.

Heritage Square

From Long Street, head northwest down Shortmarket Street to **Heritage Square**, one of the largest restoration projects ever undertaken in Cape Town. Saved from becoming a car park, the block of Cape Dutch, Georgian and Victorian buildings houses a cluster of restaurants and wine bars set around a tranquil courtyard, where South Africa's oldest known (and still fruit-bearing) vine continues to flourish. The square is worth visiting for the architecture and a good glass of Cape wine under shady umbrellas. Adjoining it is the *Cape Heritage Hotel*, one of the city centre's most stylish historic hotels (see p.113).

Bo-Kaap

Minutes from Parliament, on the slopes of Signal Hill, is the **Bo-Kaap**, one of Cape Town's oldest and most fascinating residential areas. Its streets are characterized by brightly coloured nineteenth-century Cape Dutch and Georgian terrace houses – an image familiar from tour brochures – concealing a network of alleyways which are the arteries of its **Muslim community**. The Bo-Kaap harbours its own strong identity, made all the more unique by the destruction of District Six (see p.60), with which it had much in common.

Bo-Kaap residents descend from slaves, dissidents and Islamic leaders brought over by the Dutch in the sixteenth and seventeenth centuries. They were known collectively as "**Cape Malays**", a term still heard today, even though it's a misnomer: as well as the Dutch colonies in present-day Malaysia and Indonesia, many came from Africa, India, Madagascar and Sri Lanka.

SLAVERY AND SALVATION

The **South African Missionary Society** was founded in 1799 by the Reverend Vos, who was alarmed that many slaveholders neglected the religious education of their "property". The owners believed that once their slaves were baptized, their emancipation became obligatory – a misunderstanding of the law, which merely stated that Christian slaves couldn't be sold. Vos, himself a slaveholder, saw proselytization to those in bondage as a Christian duty, and even successfully campaigned to end the prohibition against selling Christian slaves, which he believed was "a great obstacle in this country to the progress of Christianity", because it encouraged owners to avoid baptizing their human possessions.

1

EXPLORING THE BO-KAAP

The easiest way to get to the Bo-Kaap is by foot along **Wale Street**, which trails up from the south end of Adderley Street and across Buitengracht, to become the neighbourhood's main drag. The architectural charm of the colourful, protected historic core climbing Signal Hill, roughly bordered by Dorp, Strand and Buitengracht streets, is one of Cape Town's great surprises.

While there is still a solid **Muslim community** in the Bo-Kaap, it has been joined by new residents who like the area's aesthetics and slight edginess, not to mention its central location and stunning Table Mountain views. As such, in recent years a smattering of design boutiques, coffee shops and B&Bs has sprung up here.

The best way to explore the Bo-Kaap is by joining one of the **walking tours** that take in the Bo-Kaap Museum and explore the district, with Cape Malay snacks or lunch along the way. A number of these combine walking with a **cooking tour**.

The Bo-Kaap Cooking Tour (meet at Bo-Kaap Museum; R500, including three-course lunch; ☎074 130 8124, ⓦbokaapcookingtour.co.za) offers a two-hour tour including a forty-minute walk and lunch in culinary guru Zainie's home. From Tuesday to Thursday, the same outfit offers a three-hour tour (R750) featuring an interactive cooking lesson, in which Zainie teaches you to mix masala and produce a Cape Malay meal. You need to book at least a day in advance, but for the delicious food, the forward planning is definitely worth it.

Cooking With Love (109 Wale St; ☎072 483 4040, ⓦfacebook.com/Faldela1), run by the charismatic Faldela Tolker, Lekka Kombuis (☎079 957 0226, ⓦlekkakombuis.co.za) and Andulela (☎021 790 2592, ⓦandulela.com) also offer **Cape Malay cooking "safaris"**.

Bo-Kaap Museum

71 Wale St • Mon–Sat 10am–5pm • R20 • ☎021 481 3938, ⓦiziko.org.za/museums/bo-kaap-museum

If you're exploring the Bo-Kaap without a guide, a good place to start is the **Bo-Kaap Museum**. Occupying one of the neighbourhood's oldest houses, the museum explains the local culture and illustrates the lifestyle of a nineteenth-century Muslim family. It also explores the local form of Islam, which has its own unique traditions and two dozen *kramats* (shrines) dotted about the peninsula.

Auwal Mosque

39 Dorp St • Closed to the public

The **Auwal Mosque** was South Africa's first official mosque, founded in 1797 by the highly influential Imam Abdullah ibn Qadi Abd al-Salam (commonly known as **Tuan Guru** or Master Teacher), a Moluccan prince and Muslim activist who was exiled to Robben Island in 1780 for opposing Dutch rule in the Indies. While on the island, he transcribed the Koran from memory and wrote several important Islamic commentaries, which provided a basis for the religion at the Cape for a century. On being released in 1792, he began offering religious instruction from his house in Dorp Street, before founding the Auwal nearby.

Although it is closed to the public, you may be able to access the Auwal on a Cape Malay cooking safari (see box above). It's one of ten mosques serving the Bo-Kaap's Muslim residents, their minarets punctuating the quarter's skyline.

Greenmarket Square

Cnr Shortmarket and Burg sts

Turning east from Long Street into Shortmarket or Longmarket street, you'll skim the edge of **Greenmarket Square**, its cobblestones fringed by grand Art Deco buildings and coffee shops. As its name implies, the square started as a vegetable market, and, after many ignominious years as a car park, it is now home to a flea market (see p.142) where you can buy crafts, jewellery and hippie clobber. This is one of the best places in Cape Town to buy from Congolese and Zimbabwean traders, who sell masks and malachite carvings that make great souvenirs.

Evangelical Lutheran Church Complex

Alexander Bar, Café & Theatre **1**

Waterfront Buses ★

Forecourt Market

Cape Town Station

1

STRAND STREET

Koopmans-De Wet House

STRAND STREET

Golden Acre Shopping Mall

Cape Town Tourism Visitors' Centre ⓘ

1

CASTLE STREET

South African Missionary Meeting-House Museum

Flower Market

TRAFALGAR PLACE

GRAND PARADE

HOUT STREET

2

Waterfront Buses ★

HERITAGE SQUARE

3

Cape Heritage Hotel

2 **1**

Standard Bank

3 3

SHORTMARKET STREET

4

DARLING STREET

Groote Kerk

CHURCH SQUARE

Pan African Market **3**

GREENMARKET SQUARE **4**

First National Bank

2

5

BREE STREET

LONGMARKET STREET

3 4

LONGMARKET STREET

5

Old Town House

7

CHURCH STREET

Groote Kerk

BUREAU STREET

SPIN STREET

6

10

LONG STREET

6

9 8

9

Slave Lodge

7

7

WALE STREET

8

Bo-Kaap

8

St George's Cathedral

3

9

■ ACCOMMODATION

Cape Heritage Hotel	**2**
Daddy Long Legs Art Hotel	**3**
Dutch Manor Antique Hotel	**4**
Grand Daddy Hotel	**1**
Long Street Backpackers	**5**
St Paul's Guesthouse	**6**

DORP STREET

National Library of South Africa

Houses of Parliament

● SHOPPING

Afraid of Mice	**5**
African Music Store	**9**
Caroline's Fine Wines	**1**
Clarke's Bookshop	**10**
Greenmarket Square	**4**
Mememe	**6**
Monkeybiz	**8**
Mungo & Jemima	**7**
Pan African Market	**3**
Streetwires	**2**

4

LEEUWEN STREET

LOOP STREET

KEEROM STREET

🕌 Palm Tree Mosque

De Tuynhuys

District Six Museum

PEPPER STREET

11

10
5

● EATING

95 Keerom	**13**
Addis in Cape	**9**
Africa Café	**2**
Bardelli's Restaurant	**15**
Café Mozart	**8**
Café Roux	**4**
Chef's Warehouse & Canteen	**1**
Eastern Food Bazaar	**6**
Headquarters	**3**
Jason Bakery	**12**
La Parada	**5**
Love Thy Neighbour	**7**
Mama Africa	**11**
Mink & Trout	**10**
Royale Eatery	**14**

BUITENGRACHT STREET

12

BLOEM STREET

BREE STREET

The Company's Garden

9

10
12
13

GREEN STREET

11 ★ Dinner at Mandela's pick-up point

13

14

BUITEN STREET

6

LOOP STREET

13

ORPHAN ST

17

14 16

South African National Gallery

South African Jewish Museum

ST JOHN'S STREET

■ DRINKING & NIGHTLIFE

Aces 'n' Spades	**2**	La Parada	**4**
Alexander Bar,		Long Street Café	**14**
Café & Theatre	**1**	Murano Bar	**18**
The Beerhouse	**9**	Orphanage	
Cafe Mojito	**15**	Cocktail	
Dubliner @		Emporium	**17**
Kennedy's	**11**	Publik Wine Bar	**6**
Era	**3**	The Slug & Lettuce	**12**
Fiction	**13**	TjingTjing	**5**
The Gin Bar	**7**	Twankey Bar	**8**
Jo'burg	**10**	The Waiting Room	**16**

KLOOF STREET

ORANGE STREET

GREY'S PASS

Long Street Baths

MUSEUM ROAD

10

South African Museum & Planetarium

PADDOCK AVENUE

Cape Town Holocaust Centre

Great Synagogue ✡

HATFIELD STREET

15

Bertram House

QUEEN VICTORIA STREET

GOVERNMENT AVENUE

PARLIAMENT STREET

ADDERLEY STREET

ST GEORGE'S MALL

CORPORATION

PLEIN STREET

CITY CENTRE: AROUND LONG ST & COMPANY'S GARDEN

0	50
	metres

Michaelis Collection

Old Town House, Greenmarket Square • Mon–Sat 10am–5pm • R20 • ☎ 021 481 3933, ⓦ iziko.org.za

At the southern corner of Greenmarket Square are the solid limewashed walls and small shuttered windows of the **Old Town House**, entered from Longmarket Street. Built in 1755, this beautiful example of Cape Rococo architecture, with a fine interior, has seen duty as a guardhouse, a police station and Cape Town's city hall. Today it houses the **Michaelis Collection** of minor but interesting seventeenth-century Dutch and Flemish paintings. At the time of writing it was closed for maintenance.

The seventeenth century was one of great prosperity for the Netherlands and has been referred to as the Dutch "Golden Age", during which the nation threw off the yoke of its Spanish colonizers and sailed forth to establish colonies of its own in the East Indies and, of course, at the Cape. The wealth that trade brought to the Netherlands stimulated the development of the arts, and the paintings of the era reflect the values and experience of Dutch Calvinists. A notable example is **Frans Hals**' *Portrait of a Woman*, hanging in the upstairs gallery. Executed in shades of brown, relieved only by the merest hint of red, it reflects the Calvinist aversion to ostentation. The sitter for the picture, completed in 1644, would have been a contemporary of the settlers who arrived at the Cape some eight years later (see p.260). Less dour and showing off the wealth of a middle-class family is the beautiful *Couple with Two Children in a Park*, painted by **Dirck van Santvoort** in the late 1630s. The artist displays a remarkable facility for portraying sensuous fabrics which glow with reflected light; you can almost feel the texture of the lace trimming.

Other paintings, most of them quite sombre, depict mythological scenes, church interiors, still lifes, landscapes and seascapes; the latter are very close to the seventeenth-century Dutch heart, often illustrating Dutch East India Company vessels or the drama of rough seas encountered by trade ships. A tiny **print room** on the ground floor has a small selection of works by Daumier, Gillray, and Cruikshank, and others.

Small visiting exhibitions also find space here, and there are regular evening chamber-music concerts and cultural lectures; the website lists forthcoming events.

St George's Mall

Coffee shops, snack bars, street traders and buskers make the pedestrianized thoroughfare of St George's Mall a pleasant route between the train station and the Company's Garden.

St George's Cathedral

5 Wale St • Mon–Fri 9am–4.30pm, Sat 9am–noon; services Mon–Fri 7.15am & 1.15pm, also Tues–Thurs 8am & 4pm, Wed 10am, Sat 8am, Sun 7am, 8am, 9.30am & 6pm • Free • ☎ 021 424 7360, ⓦ sgcathedral.co.za

St George's Cathedral, at the southern end of St George's Mall, is as interesting for its history as for its Herbert Baker (see box, p.102) Victorian-Gothic design. There are daily **services**, as well as the main Sunday Mass at 9.30am, and the cathedral hosts good classical, jazz and choral **concerts** (check website for details). The most famous former archbishop of Cape Town is undoubtedly Nobel Peace Prize-winner **Desmond Tutu**, who hammered on the cathedral's doors symbolically on September 7, 1986, when he was enthroned as South Africa's first black archbishop. Three years later, he heralded the last days of apartheid by leading thirty thousand people from St George's to the City Hall, where he coined his now famous slogan for the new order: "We are the rainbow people!", and told the crowd, "We are the new people of South Africa!" In 2014, at the cathedral, Archbishop Tutu launched a book on a topic close to his heart, *The Book of Forgiving*, with his daughter, Reverend Mpho Tutu.

Church Street

Church Street and its surrounding area abound with antique dealers selling bric-a-brac and Africana. In the pleasant pedestrianized section, between Long and Burg streets, art galleries mingle with the smell of coffee, and you can rest your legs sitting at an outdoor table at *Café Mozart* (see p.123).

1

Government Avenue and around

A stroll down the oak-lined, pedestrianized **Government Avenue** makes for one of the most serene walks in central Cape Town. The leafy boulevard runs past the rear of Parliament through the Company's Garden, and its benches host everyone from office workers to *bergies* (homeless inhabitants of Cape Town).

Houses of Parliament

Public entrance 120 Plein St • **Tours** hourly tours Mon–Fri 9am–4pm, 1hr • Free • Book ahead and bring ID • ☎ 021 403 2266, ⓦ www .parliament.gov.za • **Debating sessions** Tues, Wed & Thurs afternoons, also occasionally Fri mornings • Free • Book at least a day in advance on ☎ 021 403 8219 or ⓔ mtsheole@parliament.gov.za

South Africa's **Houses of Parliament**, east of the north end of Government Avenue, are a complex of interlinking buildings, with labyrinthine corridors connecting hundreds of offices, debating chambers and miscellaneous other rooms. Many are relics of the 1980s reformist phase of apartheid, when, in the interests of racial segregation, three distinct legislative complexes catered to people of different "race".

The original wing, completed in 1885, is an imposing Victorian Neoclassical building which first served as the legislative assembly of the Cape Colony. After the Boer republics and British colonies amalgamated in 1910, it became the parliament of the Union of South Africa. This is the old parliament, where over seven decades of repressive legislation, including apartheid laws, were passed. It's also where 1960s prime minister **Hendrik Verwoerd**, the arch-theorist of apartheid, was stabbed to death by unstable parliamentary messenger Dimitri Tsafendas. The assassin reputedly claimed that he was following the orders of a tapeworm in his stomach, although police may have concocted this story to detract attention from his crime's political motivation. Due to his mental state, Tsafendas escaped the gallows to outlive apartheid – albeit in an institution.

Verwoerd's portrait, depicting him as a man of vision and gravitas, used to hang over the main entrance to the dining room. In 1996 it was removed "for cleaning", along with paintings of generations of white parliamentarians, and never returned.

The new chamber was built in 1983 as part of the **Tricameral Parliament**, P.W. Botha's attempt to avert majority rule by trying to co-opt Indians and coloureds – but in their own separate debating chambers. The "tricameral" chamber, where the three non-African "races" on occasions met together, is now the **National Assembly**, where you can watch sessions of parliament. One-hour **tours** take in the old and new debating chambers, the library and museum. You can get free day-tickets to **debating sessions** in the chambers of the National Assembly or National Council of Provinces (see above).

National Library of South Africa

5 Queen Victoria St • Mon–Fri 8am–6pm • Free • ☎ 021 424 6320, ⓦ nlsa.ac.za

If you head south from the top of Government Avenue, you'll soon come across the **National Library of South Africa** on your right. The building houses one of the country's best collections of antiquarian historical and natural history books, covering southern Africa. It opened in 1822 as one of the world's first free libraries.

Company's Garden

19 Queen Victoria St • Daily: March–Nov 7am–9pm; Dec–Feb 7.30am–8.30pm • Free • ☎ 021 426 1357

The **Company's Garden**, which stretches from the National Library of South Africa down to the South African Museum, was the *raison d'être* for the Dutch settlement at the Cape. Established in 1652 to supply fresh greens to Dutch East India Company (VOC) ships travelling between the Netherlands and the East, the gardens were initially worked by imported slave labour. This proved too expensive, as the slaves had to be shipped in, fed and housed, so the Company opted for outsourcing: it phased out farming and granted the land to free burghers, from whom it bought fresh produce.

At the end of the seventeenth century, the gardens were turned over to botanical horticulture for Cape Town's growing colonial elite. Ponds, lawns, landscaping and a crisscross web of oak-shaded walkways were introduced. It was during a stroll in these gardens that **Cecil Rhodes** (a statue of whom you'll find here) first plotted the invasion of Matabeleland and Mashonaland (which together became Rhodesia and subsequently Zimbabwe). He also introduced an army of small, furry colonizers to the gardens – North American grey squirrels.

Today, the gardens are full of local plants, the result of long-standing European interest in **Cape botany**; experts have been sailing out since the seventeenth century to classify and name specimens. In recent years, the vegetable patches have been revived to evoke the agricultural diversity and splendour of the VOC era, when Government Avenue was lined with citrus trees to supply the scurvy-ridden sailors. The garden-cum-park is a pleasant place to meander, with a good outdoor café situated under massive trees.

De Tuynhuys

Government Ave • Not open to the public

Peer through an iron gate to see the grand facade and tended flowerbeds of **De Tuynhuys**, the office (but not residence) of the president. In 1992, President F.W. de Klerk announced outside this beautiful eighteenth-century building that South Africa had "closed the book on apartheid".

Under the governorship of **Lord Charles Somerset** (1814–26), an official process of Anglicization at the Cape included his private obsession with architecture, which saw the demolition of the two Dutch wings of **De Tuynhuys** in Government Avenue. Imposing contemporary English taste, Somerset reinvented the entire garden frontage with a Colonial Regency facade, characterized by a veranda sheltering under an elegantly curving canopy, supported on slender iron columns.

South African National Gallery

Access via Paddock Ave, Company's Garden • Daily 10am–5pm • R30 • ⓦ iziko.org.za/museums/south-african-national-gallery

The **South African National Gallery** is an essential port of call for anyone interested in the local art scene, with a small but excellent permanent collection of contemporary South African art. Displays change every three months, as the number of items far exceeds the capacity of the exhibition space. However, one of the pieces that regularly makes an appearance is **Jane Alexander**'s powerfully ghoulish plaster, bone and horn sculpture, *The Butcher Boys* (1985–86), created at the height of apartheid repression. It features three life-size figures with distorted faces that exude a chilling passivity, expressing the artist's interest in the way violence is conveyed through the human figure. Alexander's work is representative of "**resistance art**", which exploded in the 1980s, broadly as a response to the growing repression of apartheid.

Paul Stopforth's powerful graphite-and-wax triptych, *The Interrogators* (1979), featuring larger-than-life-size portraits of three notorious security policemen, is a work of monumental hyperrealism. Many other artists, unsurprisingly for a culturally diverse country, aren't easily categorized; while works have tended to borrow from Western traditions, their themes and execution are uniquely South African. The late **John Muafangelo** employed biblical imagery in works such as *The Pregnant Maria* (undated), producing highly stylized, almost naive black-and-white linocuts; while in *Challenges Facing the New South Africa* (1990), **Willie Bester** used paint and found objects to depict the melting pot of the Cape Town squatter camps.

Since the 1990s, and especially in the post-apartheid period, the gallery has engaged in a process of redefining what constitutes contemporary **indigenous art** and has embarked on an acquisitions policy that "acknowledges and celebrates the expressive cultures of the African continent, particularly its southern regions". Material that would previously have been treated as ethnographic, such as a major **bead collection** as well as carvings and **craft objects**, is now finding a place alongside oil paintings and sculptures.

The permanent collection also includes minor works by British artists, including George Romney, Thomas Gainsborough, Joshua Reynolds and some Pre-Raphaelites.

1

South African Jewish Museum

88 Hatfield St • Mon–Thurs & Sun 10am–5pm, Fri 10am–2pm • R60 • Bring ID • ☎ 021 465 1546, ⓦ sajewishmuseum.org.za

The **South African Jewish Museum** is partially housed in South Africa's first synagogue, built in 1863. One of Cape Town's most ambitious permanent exhibitions, it tells the story of the South African Jewish community from its beginnings, over 150 years ago, to the present. Starting in the Old Synagogue, visitors cross, via a gangplank, to the upper level of a two-storey building, symbolically re-enacting the arrival by boat of the first Jewish immigrants at Table Bay harbour in the 1840s. Multimedia interactive displays, models and artefacts explore Judaism in South Africa, drawing parallels between the religion and the ritual practices and beliefs of South Africa's other communities. The **basement** level houses a walk-through reconstruction of a Lithuanian *shtetl* or village (most South African Jews have their nineteenth-century roots in Lithuania). The museum complex also has a restaurant, shop and noteworthy collection of ivory, staghorn and wood Japanese Netsuke figures. During the time of the Samurai, the affluent Japanese merchant classes used these miniature carvings to hang containers from their kimonos.

Cape Town Holocaust Centre

88 Hatfield St • Mon–Thurs & Sun 10am–5pm, Fri 10am–2pm • Free • Bring ID • ☎ 021 462 5553, ⓦ ctholocaust.co.za

Opened in 1999, the **Cape Town Holocaust Centre**, Africa's first centre of its kind, features one of the city's most moving and brilliantly constructed displays. The **Holocaust Exhibition** resonates sharply in a country that endured half a century of systematic racial oppression – a connection that the exhibition makes explicitly.

Exhibits trace the history of anti-Semitism in Europe, culminating with the Nazis' Final Solution; they also look at South Africa's Greyshirts, who were motivated by Nazi propaganda during the 1930s and were later absorbed into the National Party. A twenty-minute video tells the story of the Holocaust survivors who settled in Cape Town.

Great Synagogue

88 Hatfield St • Mon–Thurs & Sun 10am–4pm • Free • Bring ID • ☎ 021 465 1405, ⓦ gardensshul.org

The **Great Synagogue** or Gardens Shul is one of Cape Town's outstanding religious buildings. Designed by the Scottish architects Parker & Forsyth and completed in 1905, it features an impressive dome and two soaring towers in the style of Central European Baroque churches. Guides can show you (for free) around the elegant neo-Egyptian interior with its carved teak pulpit, gold-leaf friezes and stained-glass windows.

South African Museum

25 Queen Victoria St; accessed from Museum Rd • Daily 10am–5pm • Adults R30, children 6–18 R15 • ⓦ iziko.org.za/museums/south-african-museum

The nation's premier museum of natural history and human sciences, the **South African Museum** is notable for its **ethnographic galleries**, which contain some good displays on the traditional arts and crafts of several African groups. There are also some exceptional examples of rock art (entire chunks of caves are in the display cases), as well as casts of the stone birds found at the archaeological site of Great Zimbabwe, in southeastern Zimbabwe.

Upstairs, the **natural history galleries** display mounted mammals, dioramas of prehistoric Karoo reptiles and Table Mountain flora and fauna. The highlight is the four-storey "whale well", a hanging collection of beautiful whale skeletons, including a 20.5m blue whale skeleton, accompanied by recordings of the eerie strains of their song.

Planetarium

25 Queen Victoria St; accessed from Museum Rd • Shows daily; closed first Mon of every month • R40 • ⓦ iziko.org.za/museums/planetarium

Housed in the South African Museum building is the **Planetarium**, in which you can see the constellations of the southern hemisphere, with an informed commentary. The

FROM TOP THE BO-KAAP; STREET VENDORS ON LONG STREET >

1

changing programme of daily shows covers topics such as San sky myths, with some geared towards children and others to teenagers and adults, and you can buy a monthly chart of the current night sky.

Shows generally take place hourly from noon to 3pm, and at 7pm and 8pm, but times change during school holidays. Check the website for schedules.

Bertram House

University of Cape Town, Hiddingh Campus, accessed from Orange St • Daily 10am–5pm • Donation • ⓦ iziko.org.za/museums/bertram-house

At the southernmost end of Government Avenue, you'll pass **Bertram House**, whose beautiful two-storey brick facade looks out across a fragrant herb garden. The museum is significant as Cape Town's only surviving brick, Georgian-style house, and displays typical furniture and objects of a well-to-do colonial British family in the first half of the nineteenth century.

The house was built in 1839 by John Barker, a Yorkshire attorney who came to the Cape in 1823 and named the building in memory of his late wife, Ann Bertram Findlay. The reception rooms are decorated in the Regency style, while the **porcelain** is predominantly nineteenth-century English, although there are also some very fine Chinese pieces.

Rust en Vreugd

78 Buitenkant St • Mon–Fri 10am–5pm • R20 • ⓦ iziko.org.za/museums/rust-en-vreugd

The most beautiful of Cape Town's house museums, **Rust en Vreugd** was built in 1778 for Willem Cornelis Boers, the colony's Fiscal (a powerful position akin to the police chief, public prosecutor and collector of taxes rolled into one), who was forced to resign in the 1780s following allegations of wheeler-dealing and extortion. Under the British occupation, it was the residence of Lord Charles Somerset during his governorship (1814–26).

The house was once surrounded by countryside, but now stands along a congested route that brushes past the edge of the central business district. Designed by architect Louis Michel Thibault and sculptor Anton Anreith, the two-storey facade features a pair of stacked balconies, the lower one forming a stunning portico fronted by four Corinthian columns carved from teak. The front door, framed by teak pilasters, is an impressive work of art, rated by architectural historian De Bosdari as "certainly the finest door at the Cape". Above the door, the fanlight is executed in elaborate Baroque style.

Inside, the William Fehr Collection of artworks on paper occupies two ground-floor rooms and includes illustrations by important documentarists such as **Thomas Baines**, who is represented by hand-coloured lithographs and a series of watercolours recording a nineteenth-century expedition up Table Mountain. The work of **Thomas Bowler**, another prolific recorder of Cape scenes, is also on display here, with his striking landscape painting of Cape Point from the sea in 1864, which shows dolphins frolicking in the foreground.

The **garden** is a reconstruction of the original eighteenth-century semiformal one, laid out with herbaceous hedges, bay trees, gravel walkways, and a spacious lawn with a quaint gazebo.

Castle of Good Hope

Castle St • Daily 9am–4pm; tours Mon–Sat 11am, noon & 3pm; cannon firing & key ceremony Mon–Fri 10am & noon, Sat 11am & noon • R30 including optional tour, kids R15 • ☎ 021 787 1249, ⓦ castleofgoodhope.co.za

Despite its unprepossessing pentagonal exterior, South Africa's oldest official building is one of the city's most worthwhile historical sights. Built in 1666, the **Castle of Good Hope** still serves as a (significantly downscaled) military barracks site, and is considered the best-preserved example of a Dutch East India Company (VOC) fort. For a hundred and fifty years, this was the symbolic heart of the Cape administration, and a sense of self-importance lingers in its grand rooms and courtyards.

Finished in 1679, complete with the essentials of a moat and torture chamber, the castle replaced Van Riebeeck's earlier mud-and-timber fort which stood on the site of the Grand Parade. The building was designed along seventeenth-century European principles of fortification, comprising strong bastions from which the outside walls could be protected by crossfire.

Moving boundaries

The original, seaward **entrance** had to be moved to its present, landward position because the spring tide sometimes came crashing in; a remarkable thought given how far aground the castle is now, thanks to land reclamation. The entrance gate displays the coat of arms of the United Netherlands and those of the six Dutch cities in which the VOC chambers were situated.

Still hanging from its original wooden beams in the tower above the entrance is the **bell**, cast in 1697 by Claude Fremy in Amsterdam; it was used variously as an alarm signal, which can be heard from 10km away, and as a summons to residents to receive pronouncements. On the left after you enter, you can see the castle's original gate in the **Castle Military Museum**, which exhibits South African military uniforms and delves into the Anglo-Boer War (often referred to as the South African War).

From castle to prison

The castle was the main **prison** for the Cape Colony, and prisoners held here included indigenous Khoi people and slaves accused of transgressions against their owners. As punishment could only be administered once a confession was made, detainees were routinely questioned and tortured. The guided **tour** takes you to the dark, inconspicuous room where these acts took place, with the original iron chains, that were used to bind the prisoner, still firmly attached to the wall; as well as to the adjacent solitary-confinement room – the much feared *Donker Gat* (Dark Hole). In other prison cells and dungeons, you can still see the touching centuries-old poetry and graffiti painstakingly carved into the walls by prisoners.

The **inner courtyard** is home to the platform where families of slaves would stand as they were bought and sold. As no law existed to keep families together, a mother would watch her children being sold off individually to different farms and vineyards in the Western Cape.

The William Fehr Collection

Across the grassy courtyard from the entrance, **De Kat Balcony** is named after the adjoining *kat* (defensive cross wall in Dutch). The ornate balcony leads to interconnected rooms that were once the heart of VOC government at the Cape and which now house the bulk of the **William Fehr Collection**, one of the country's most important exhibits of decorative arts. The contents, acquired from the 1920s onwards by businessman William Fehr, and sold and donated to the government, continue to be displayed informally, as he preferred. The galleries are filled with items that would have been found in middle-class Cape households from the seventeenth to nineteenth centuries, with some fine examples of elegantly simple Cape furniture from the eighteenth century.

Early colonial views of Table Bay appear in a number of paintings, including one by Aernout Smit showing the Castle in the seventeenth century, right on the shoreline. Among the antique **oriental ceramics** are a blue-and-white Japanese porcelain plate from around 1660, which displays the VOC monogram; and a beautiful polychrome plate from China, dating from around 1750 and depicting a fleet of Company ships in Table Bay – against the backdrop of a very oriental-looking Table Mountain.

Grand Parade to City Hall

The **Grand Parade**, just northwest of the Castle of Good Hope, is a large open area where the residents of District Six used to come to trade. On Wednesdays and Saturdays it still transforms itself into a **market** (9am–4pm), where there is an array of bargains on offer, from cheap clothes to spicy food.

1

The Grand Parade appeared on TV screens throughout the world on February 11, 1990, when over sixty thousand people gathered to hear **Nelson Mandela** make his first speech after being released from prison, from the balcony of the **City Hall**. It's also where an interfaith prayer was made upon his death, on December 6, 2013. The City Hall is a grand Edwardian building dating to 1905, dressed in Bath stone and looking impressive against the backdrop of Table Mountain.

District Six

South of the Castle of Good Hope, in the shadow of Devil's Peak, is a vacant lot shown on maps as the suburb of **Zonnebloem**. Before being demolished by the apartheid authorities, it was an inner-city neighbourhood known as **District Six**, an impoverished but lively community of fifty-five thousand predominantly coloured people. Once regarded as the soul of Cape Town, the district harboured a rich – and much mythologized – multicultural life in its narrow alleys and crowded tenements: along the cobbled streets, hawkers rubbed shoulders with prostitutes, gangsters, drunks and gamblers, while craftsmen plied their trade in small workshops. This was a fertile place of the South African imagination, inspiring novels, poems and jazz, often with more than a hint of nostalgia, anger and pain of displacement. A case in point are the musicals of **David Kramer**, which are often staged at the resident Fugard Theatre (see p.136).

In 1966, the **Group Areas Act** declared District Six a white area and the bulldozers moved in, taking fifteen years to drive District Six's presence from the skyline, leaving only the mosques and churches. The accompanying **forced removals** saw the coloured inhabitants moved to the Cape Flats. But, in the wake of the demolition gangs, international and domestic outcry was so great that the area was never developed, apart from a few residential projects on its fringes and the hefty **Cape Technikon** college. After years of negotiation, the original residents are moving back under a scheme to develop low-cost housing in the area.

District Six Museum

25A Buitenkant St • Mon–Sat 9am–4pm • Entry R30; tours R15 • ☎ 021 466 7200, ⓦ districtsix.co.za

Few places in Cape Town speak more eloquently of the effect of apartheid on the day-to-day lives of ordinary people than the compelling **District Six Museum**. On the northern boundary of District Six, the museum occupies the former **Central Methodist Mission Church**, which offered solidarity and ministry to the victims of forced removals right up to the 1980s, and became a venue for anti-apartheid gatherings. Today, it houses a series of fascinating displays including everyday household items and the tools of bygone local trades, such as hairdressing implements, as well as **documentary photographs**, evoking the lives of the individuals who once lived here. Occupying most of the floor is a huge map of District Six as it was, annotated by former residents, who describe their memories, reflections and incidents associated with places and buildings that no longer exist. There's also a collection of original street signs, secretly retrieved at the time of demolition by the man entrusted with dumping them into Table Bay.

You can tour the museum with an ex-resident for an extra R15, and **guided walks** around the area can be organised. The coffee shop offers a variety of snacks, including traditional, syrupy *koeksisters*. The nearby **District Six Homecoming Centre** (15 Buitenkant St), a cultural centre in the old Sacks Futeran textile warehouse, hosts changing exhibitions on local subjects, as well as performances by musicians and poets.

Strand Street

A major artery from the N2 freeway to the central business district, **Strand Street** neatly separates the Upper from the Lower city centre. Between the mid-eighteenth and mid-nineteenth centuries, this was one of the most fashionable streets in Cape Town,

1

due to its proximity to the shore – it used to run along the beachfront, but now lies about a kilometre south of it. Its former cachet is now only discernible from the handful of quietly elegant national monuments left standing amid the traffic.

Evangelical Lutheran Church

98 Strand St, at Buitengracht • Mon–Fri 10am–2pm • Free • ☎ 021 421 5854, ⓦ lutheranchurch.org.za

This **Lutheran church** is South Africa's oldest church in permanent service and forms part of the country's oldest city block. German woodcarver Anton Anreith converted it in around 1780 from a warehouse, where services had taken place in secret for several years.

The establishment of a Lutheran church in Cape Town struck a significant blow against the extreme **religious intolerance** that pervaded under VOC rule. Before 1779 (when permission was granted for Lutherans to establish their own congregation), Protestantism was the only form of worship allowed, and the Dutch Reformed Church held an absolute monopoly over saving people's souls. The Lutheran Church's congregation was dominated by Germans, who at the time constituted 28 percent of the colony's free burgher population.

The church's facade has Classical details such as a broken pediment perforated by the clock tower, as well as Gothic features including arched windows. Inside, the magnificent **pulpit**, supported on two life-size Herculean figures, is one of Anreith's masterpieces; the white swan perched on the canopy is a symbol of Lutheranism.

Koopmans-De Wet House

35 Strand St • Mon–Fri 10am–5pm • R20 • ☎ 021 481 3935, ⓦ iziko.org.za/museums/koopmans-de-wet-house

Sandwiched between two office blocks, the **Koopmans-De Wet House** is an outstanding eighteenth-century pedimented Neoclassical townhouse and museum, which exhibits a fine collection of antique furniture and rare porcelain.

The earliest sections of the house were built in 1701 by **Reyner Smedinga**, a well-to-do goldsmith who imported the building materials from Holland. After changing hands more than a dozen times over the following two centuries, the building eventually fell into the hands of **Marie Koopmans-De Wet** (1834–1906), a prominent figure on the Cape social and political circuit.

The house represents a fine synthesis of Dutch elements with the demands of local conditions: typically Dutch sash windows and large entrances combine with huge rooms, lofty ceilings and shuttered windows, all installed with high summer temperatures in mind. The **lantern** in the fanlight of the entrance was a common feature of Cape Town houses in the eighteenth and early nineteenth centuries, its purpose to shine light onto the street and hinder slaves from gathering to plot.

Bree Street

Humming with design shops, boutiques, restaurants, cafés and bars, **Bree Street** has become the favourite haunt of hipsters, fashionistas and well-heeled Capetonians. The conversion of old buildings into new spaces enhances the lovely architecture, adding charm to equal Long Street's Victorian edifices, and even the car-loving locals are enticed to wander the pavements. The upper end of Bree, roughly between Buitensingel Street and Heritage Square, is your best bet to get a feel for this vibrant strip.

Lower City Centre

In the mid-nineteenth century, the city's middle classes viewed the **Lower City Centre** and its low-life activities with a mixture of alarm and excitement – a tension that remains today. **Lower Long Street** splits this area just inland from the docklands. To the east is the **Foreshore**, an ugly post-World War II wasteland of grey corporate architecture, among which is the **Artscape Centre**, Cape Town's premier arts complex. The Foreshore is gradually being redeveloped, with a centrepiece in the successful **Cape Town International Convention Centre** (CTICC), linked by a canal and pedestrian routes with the Waterfront. **Cape Town Station**, at the junction of Adderley and Strand streets, is the city's commuting nexus; it has its own bustling life of hooting and hollering taxi drivers, buskers and stallholders hawking cheap Chinese goods.

The Foreshore

The Foreshore is an area of reclaimed land northeast of Strand Street, stretching to the docks and northwest of Lower Long Street. The area was developed in the late 1940s in the spirit of modernism that was sweeping the world, with its penchant for large, highly planned urban spaces. It was intended to turn Cape Town's harbour into a symbolic gateway to Africa; instead, all that emerged was a series of large concrete boxes surrounded by acres of windswept tarmac car parks.

In 2013, the construction of the FNB-branded **Portside Tower** gave Cape Town its tallest building (139m), in the heart of a small financial and legal district. It's also the city's greenest building: LED lighting and low-energy technology are used throughout, with ample bicycle racks and changing rooms, electric car chargers and parking for hybrid vehicles.

Another recent development is the fourteen-storey, R285 million office block, **Roggebaai Place**. However, the area's street life pales in comparison with other parts of the city centre, and most visitors will prefer to spend their time elsewhere. The main attraction here is watching a performance at the dynamic Artscape Complex, while you may spot the glassy blue facade of the Foreshore's latest construction triumph, the Netcare Christiaan Barnard Memorial Hospital, from the Nelson Mandela Boulevard flyover.

Artscape Complex

D.F. Malan St, just east of Heerengracht • Performance times vary; visit website for listings • ☎ 021 410 9800, ⓦ artscape.co.za

The **Artscape Complex**, Cape Town's monumental **performance venue**, includes a huge theatre, an opera house and the compact Arena Theatre, collectively offering the city's liveliest calendar of drama, opera, comedy, dance and musicals. The concrete 1970s complex is the home of Cape Town Opera, which features the best of South Africa's singers; Jazzart, the Western Cape's longest-established contemporary dance company, going since 1973; and the century-old Cape Town Philharmonic Orchestra.

Netcare Christiaan Barnard Memorial Hospital

Cnr D.F. Malan St & Rua Bartholomeu Dias Plain • ⓦ www.netcare.co.za

One of the latest additions to the Foreshore is the **Netcare Christiaan Barnard Memorial Hospital**, a 250-bed private hospital, which superseded the 35-year-old hospital of the same name on the corner of Bree and Longmarket streets. If you are in the area, pass through reception, where artworks and **AV installations** honour the life and work of Barnard, the pioneering surgeon who performed the world's first successful heart transplant at Cape Town's Groote Schuur Hospital in 1967.

Jetty Square

Between Jetty St & Pier Pl • ⓦ capetownpartnership.co.za

Cape Town Partnership, the organisation driving the regeneration of the central city, has placed sculptures and installations in the Foreshore's plazas, bringing beauty and humour to these urban spaces. A good example is Ralph Borland's eerie **shark sculptures** in the small **Jetty Square**, reminders that the land here was reclaimed from the sea. The skeletal structures have infrared sensors in their noses, which make them swivel in accordance with the movements of passing pedestrians.

THE V&A WATERFRONT

V&A Waterfront, Robben Island and De Waterkant

The Victoria & Alfred Waterfront, known locally as the Waterfront, is Cape Town's original Victorian harbour, incorporating nineteenth-century buildings, shopping malls, waterside piers and a functioning harbour that all share a magnificent Table Mountain backdrop. Redeveloped in the 1990s, it is the city's most popular tourist precinct for shopping, eating and drinking, and incorporates the Nelson Mandela Gateway – the embarkation point for unmissable trips to Robben Island. West of the Foreshore, with the Waterfront to its north, is De Waterkant, a once down-at-heel district that has gentrified at a cracking pace to become Cape Town's self-styled gay quarter and a significant draw for tourists, with plentiful accommodation, bars and shops.

The V&A Waterfront

Throughout the first half of the nineteenth century, arguments raged in Cape Town over the need for a proper dock. The Cape was often known as the **Cape of Storms** because of its vicious weather, which left Table Bay littered with wrecks. Many makeshift attempts were made to improve the situation, including the construction of a lighthouse in 1823, and work began on a jetty at the bottom of Bree Street in 1832. With the increase in sea traffic arriving at the Cape in the 1850s, and over thirty vessels wrecked during the winter storms of June 1858, clamour for a harbour grew. It reached its peak in 1860, when insurer Lloyd's of London refused the risk of covering ships dropping anchor in Table Bay.

The British colonial government dragged its heels due to the costs involved, but eventually conceded. At a huge ceremony in September 1860, the teenage Prince Alfred, Queen Victoria's second son, tipped the first batch of stones into Table Bay to begin the **breakwater**, the harbour's westernmost arm. Convicts were enlisted to complete the job, and in 1869, the dock was completed, and the sea was allowed to pour in.

Victoria Wharf
Breakwater Blvd • Daily 9am–9pm • Ⓦ waterfront.co.za

The shopping focus of the Waterfront is the **Victoria Wharf**, an enormous flashy mall on two levels, extending along Quays 5 and 6. The restaurants and cafés on the mall's southeast side, with their outdoor seating, have fabulous views of Table Mountain across the busy harbour.

Wandering south, you'll pass the **Amphitheatre**, where local musicians regularly perform. Look out, too, for **Nobel Square**, with its bronze statues of South Africa's four Nobel Peace Prize-winners: Archbishop Desmond Tutu (1984); Nelson Mandela and F.W. de Klerk (both 1993); and the least familiar, Chief Albert John Lutuli (1960), former president of the African National Congress (ANC) and the first African to receive the award.

Watershed
Dock Rd • Daily 10am–7pm • Ⓦ waterfront.co.za

Superseding the old Red and Blue Shed craft markets, the **Watershed** is a colourful converted warehouse that houses over 150 shops and stalls. It's a pleasant space to pick up **African craftwork** and souvenirs, covering the spectrum from township art, traditional handicrafts and batiks to jewellery, leatherwork and contemporary design. The open-plan complex also features the **Wellness at the Watershed** spa and, upstairs, a public hot-desk space, **Workshop 17**.

The Waterfront's two other major markets are food-focused: the daily **V&A Food Market** (see p.144), immediately northeast of Watershed, and Saturday **Oranjezicht City Farm Market** (see p.144).

EXPLORING THE V&A WATERFRONT

Join a tour to get your bearings and discover the long history underlying the buskers' lazy steel drums and wandering shoppers at the Waterfront, with numerous options available. Cruise vessels from speedboats to the Jack Sparrow-worthy *Jolly Roger Pirate Ship* also tie up at Quay 5, where touts tempt landlubbers onto the water. Visit Ⓦ waterfront.co.za for details.

Historical Walking Tour ☎ 021 416 6230. Departing from Chavonnes Battery Museum (see p.67), the 1hr 30min tour takes in sights such as Breakwater Prison (now a hotel), where you can see markings left by nineteenth-century convicts (daily 11am & 2pm; adults R150, under-16s R20).

Awol Tours (see p.68). Their 3hr City Cycle Tour (R600) begins at the Waterfront Information Centre, at 10am daily.

City Sightseeing (see p.68). Between late September and April, their 25min harbour cruise (R40) departs from the jetty behind the Two Oceans Aquarium every 20min.

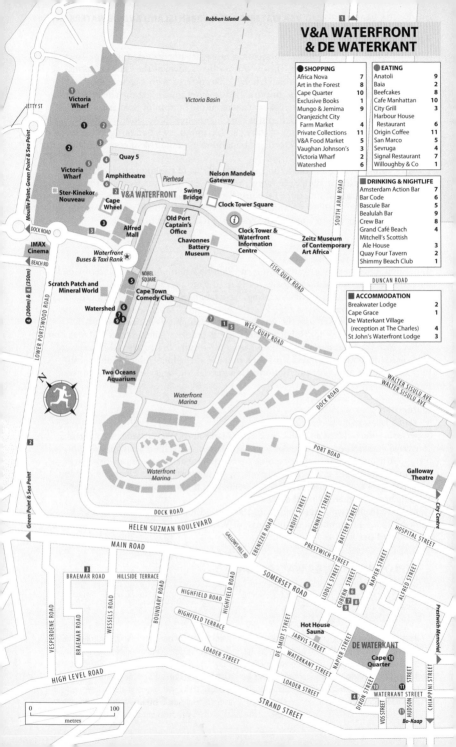

V&A WATERFRONT & DE WATERKANT

● SHOPPING	
Africa Nova	7
Art in the Forest	8
Cape Quarter	10
Exclusive Books	1
Mungo & Jemima	9
Oranjezicht City Farm Market	4
Private Collections	11
V&A Food Market	5
Vaughan Johnson's	3
Victoria Wharf	2
Watershed	6

● EATING	
Anatoli	9
Baia	2
Beefcakes	8
Cafe Manhattan	10
City Grill	3
Harbour House Restaurant	6
Origin Coffee	11
San Marco	5
Sevruga	4
Signal Restaurant	5
Willoughby & Co	1

■ DRINKING & NIGHTLIFE	
Amsterdam Action Bar	7
Bar Code	6
Bascule Bar	5
Bealulah Bar	9
Crew Bar	8
Grand Café Beach	4
Mitchell's Scottish Ale House	3
Quay Four Tavern	2
Shimmy Beach Club	1

■ ACCOMMODATION	
Breakwater Lodge	2
Cape Grace	1
De Waterkant Village (reception at The Charles)	4
St John's Waterfront Lodge	3

Robben Island

Victoria Basin

JETTY ST

Mouille Point, Green Point & Sea Point

Victoria Wharf

Quay 5

Victoria Wharf

Amphitheatre

Pierhead

Nelson Mandela Gateway

Ster-Kinekor Nouveau

Cape Wheel

V&A WATERFRONT

Swing Bridge

Clock Tower Square

DOCK ROAD

Alfred Mall

Old Port Captain's Office

Clock Tower & Waterfront Information Centre

Zeitz Museum of Contemporary Art Africa

BEACH RD

IMAX Cinema

(200m) & (350m)

Waterfront Buses & Taxi Rank

Chavonnes Battery Museum

SOUTH ARM ROAD

FISH QUAY ROAD

DUNCAN ROAD

Scratch Patch and Mineral World

NOBEL SQUARE

Cape Town Comedy Club

LOWER PORTSWOOD ROAD

Watershed

WEST QUAY ROAD

Two Oceans Aquarium

Waterfront Marina

DOCK ROAD

WALTER SISULU AVE
WALTER SISULU AVE

Green Point & Sea Point

Waterfront Marina

PORT ROAD

Galloway Theatre

City Centre

DOCK ROAD

HELEN SUZMAN BOULEVARD

MAIN ROAD

CARDIFF STREET

BENNETT STREET

BATTERY STREET

HOSPITAL STREET

GALLOWS HILL RD

EBENEZER ROAD

PRESTWICH STREET

NAPIER STREET

ALFRED STREET

Braemar Road

HILLSIDE TERRACE

SOMERSET ROAD

LIDDLE STREET

COBERN STREET

Prestwich Memorial

BRAEMAR ROAD

HIGHFIELD ROAD

HIGHFIELD ROAD

WESSELS ROAD

BOUNDARY ROAD

HIGHFIELD ROAD

VESPERDENE ROAD

HIGHFIELD TERRACE

DE SMIDT STREET

JARVIS STREET

Hot House Sauna

NAPIER STREET

DE WATERKANT

Cape Quarter

LOADER STREET

WATERKANT STREET

DIXON STREET

STREET

CHIAPPINI STREET

HIGH LEVEL ROAD

LOADER STREET

WATERKANT STREET

STRAND STREET

VOS STREET

HUDSON STREET

Bo-Kaap

0   100
metres

Two Oceans Aquarium

Dock Rd • Daily 9.30am–6pm, feeding times 11.30am, noon, 2pm, & 2.30pm • Adults R160, children 14–17 R115, 4–13 R75, under-4s free • ☎ 021 418 3823, ⊛ aquarium.co.za

At the Marina's North Wharf, the **Two Oceans Aquarium** showcases the Cape's unique marine environment, where the warm Indian Ocean mixes with the cold Atlantic. Its biggest and newest attraction, the **Ocean Exhibit**, houses rays, striped bonito, turtles, a giant guitarfish and more in 1.6 million litres of seawater, with a **jellyfish gallery** on the way in. Another major draw is the **Kelp Forest**, one of only a handful found in aquariums worldwide, with fish gliding through the kelp and abalone, sea urchins and rock lobsters clinging to the holdfasts. Scuba divers can explore the Kelp Forest and Ocean Exhibit. The **shark exhibit** is set to reopen in 2017, when the Kelp Forest will close for renovations until 2018.

The general route begins on the ground floor with the **Diversity Gallery**. Split over two floors, this gallery is home to tropical fish, honeycomb eels and a coral exhibit. It contains an astonishing variety of marine creatures, including giant spider crabs, octopuses and sea horses, the primitive eyeless and jawless hagfish and a display featuring floating gossamer jellyfish. Also on this level is the interactive **Touch Pool**, where visitors can get their hands wet while asking questions and inspecting animals such as anemones and crabs, and the **Microscope Exhibit**, where, with the assistance of highly knowledgeable staff, you can observe tiny animals that might otherwise go unnoticed.

The basement houses the **Children's Play Centre**, a good place to keep the little ones occupied, with free organized activities such as puppet shows, face painting and arts and crafts. The centre is combined with an area where the resident rockhopper penguins can sometimes be observed frolicking underwater during the day.

The top floor, accessed via a ramp, accommodates the **Penguin Exhibit**, featuring a small breeding colony of endangered African penguins (which you can see in their natural habitat at Boulders Beach; see p.108) and the rockhopper penguins.

Nelson Mandela Gateway

Clock Tower Precinct • Daily 7.30am–5.30pm • Free • ☎ 021 413 4200, ⊛ robben-island.org.za

The imposing **Clock Tower** by the Waterfront's swing bridge was built as the original Port Captain's office in 1882. Adjacent to this is the **Nelson Mandela Gateway**, the embarkation point for ferries to Robben Island (see p.68) and sometimes referred to as **Jetty 1**. Here, the Robben Island Museum has installed a number of exhibitions that are open to the public and free of charge. Displays cover the individual and collective struggles of those who went through this portal on their way to prison, including accounts by ex-political prisoners, ex-prison warders and the families of both.

Chavonnes Battery Museum

Clock Tower Precinct • Mon–Wed 9am–4pm, Thurs–Sun 9am–6pm; tour timings on demand • Adults R70, under-16s R30; guided tour & entrance adults R100, kids R50 • ☎ 021 416 6230, ⊛ chavonnesbattery.co.za

The Dutch East India Company built this **fortification**, named after an early-eighteenth century governor of the Cape, to protect Table Bay from their European rivals. Along with the Castle of Good Hope, it was part of a line of fortifications around the bay, built by the Dutch and later used by the British. Rediscovered in the 1990s during the development of the Clock Tower Precinct, the two levels of ruined walls, artefacts and informative displays provide much historical interest. The guided tour is well worth the extra R30.

Zeitz Museum of Contemporary Art Africa (Zeitz MOCAA)

Silo District • Under-18s free • ☎ 021 418 7855, ⊛ zeitzmocaa.museum

Occupying a historic grain silo, the ambitious **Zeitz MOCAA** is the world's leading museum dedicated to contemporary art from across Africa and its diaspora. Its foundation collection was amassed by the German sustainable business guru and philanthropist Jochen Zeitz, who turned around Puma's fortunes in the Nineties.

2

At the time of writing, excitement was mounting in advance of the nine-floor, eighty-gallery institution's opening; the fourteen inaugural exhibitions were set to include spotlights on young artists from Zimbabwe, Angola and Swaziland. Towering 57m above a plaza, the dynamic new addition to Cape Town's burgeoning cultural scene has regenerated this area of the Waterfront, with new hotels and businesses set to open.

INFORMATION & GETTING AROUND   THE V&A WATERFRONT

Information Waterfront Information Centre at Clock Tower Square (Mon–Fri 8am–5.30pm, Sat & Sun 8.30am–1pm; ☎086 132 2223, ⓦcapetown.travel).

By car If you have a car, you'll find yourself well catered for: there are several multistorey car parks along Dock Rd, which loops around the Waterfront.

By taxi There are a number of taxi ranks dotted about, such as the one next to the V&A Food Market.

By MyCiTi bus ☎0800 65 64 63, ⓦmyciti.org.za. This area is well served by public transport. Bus #104 between Sea Point and the Civic Centre has several stops at the

Waterfront, including the Two Oceans Aquarium. Service #T01 also runs to the Waterfront from the Civic Centre via Cape Town Stadium. To get to the airport, take a bus or taxi to the Civic Centre and pick up bus #A01 from there.

By sightseeing bus City Sightseeing buses link the Two Oceans Aquarium with a number of major sights in the city centre and on the peninsula (☎086 173 3287, ⓦcitysightseeing.co.za; see p.26).

By bicycle Awol Tours (☎021 418 3803, ⓦawoltours .co.za) rents out bikes from R200 per half-day. Call to arrange pick-up from the Waterfront Information Centre.

Robben Island

Flat and windswept **Robben Island**, only a few kilometres from the buzz of the Waterfront, is a symbol of the human spirit's triumph over adversity. Suffused by a meditative silence, this key site of South Africa's liberation struggle was intended to silence apartheid's domestic critics, but instead became an international focus for opposition to the regime. From the seventeenth until the late twentieth centuries, it variously served as a prison and leper colony, and as a World War II military base (see box, p.70).

Allow more than half a day for the trip, and book as far in advance as possible.

ESSENTIALS   ROBBEN ISLAND

Getting there The ferry from the Waterfront's Nelson Mandela Gateway (May–Aug daily 9am, 11am & 1pm; Sept–April daily 9am, 11am, 1pm & 3pm) takes 30min–1hr. Tours are sometimes cancelled due to bad weather or boat problems and refunds are issued, so check ahead.

Tours Visits are by guided tour only, led by former political prisoners who share their experiences. The 4hr tours are of varying quality. After arrival at Murray's Bay harbour, you go by bus around the island and on foot inside the prison.

Tickets Although a number of vendors sell tickets for

cruises that go close to Robben Island, the only ones that will get you onto it (adults R320, under-18s R180, for voyage, entry and tour) are from the Nelson Mandela Gateway (see p.67). Book in advance; the boats are often full, especially around December and January (☎021 413 4200, ⓦwww.robben-island.org.za). For online sales, the website links to ⓦwebtickets.co.za, which accepts credit and (most) debit cards; you must print out tickets. Although tickets are non-refundable, tours can be rescheduled at least 48hrs in advance.

The bus tour

The **bus tour** stops at several historical landmarks, including the **Moturu Kramat**, a shrine built in memory of Sayed Abdurahman Moturu. One of Cape Town's first imams, the Dutch exiled the Indonesian prince here, where he died in the mid-eighteenth century. The tour passes a leper graveyard and male leper church, built to a Sir Herbert Baker design in 1895. Both are reminders that leprosy sufferers were exiled here, until 1931, when they were relocated to Pretoria, and sadly leprosy is not yet beaten in South Africa.

Robert Sobukwe's house

Robert Sobukwe's house is perhaps the most affecting relic of incarceration on the island. It was here that Sobukwe, leader of the Pan Africanist Congress (a radical

CLOCKWISE FROM TOP NELSON MANDELA'S CELL, ROBBEN ISLAND (P.68); THE CLOCK TOWER (P.67); STREET PERFORMER AT THE WATERFRONT; DE WATERKANT (P.71) >

offshoot of the ANC; see p.265), was held in solitary confinement for nine years. He was initially sentenced to three years, but was regarded as so dangerous by the authorities that they passed a special law – the "Sobukwe Clause" – to keep him on Robben Island for a further six years. No political prisoners were allowed to speak to him, but he would sometimes gesture his solidarity with other sons of the African soil by letting sand trickle through his fingers as they walked past. After his release in 1969, Sobukwe was restricted to Kimberley under house arrest, until his death from cancer in 1978.

2

Lime quarry

Another stop is the **lime quarry** where Mandela and his fellow inmates spent hours of hard labour. The pale stone is extremely bright under the summer sun, which resulted in Mandela and others suffering eye disorders in later years. The quarry eventually became a place of furtive study for the prisoners, with the help of sympathetic warders.

"WE SERVE WITH PRIDE": THE HISTORY OF ROBBEN ISLAND

Nelson Mandela may have been the most famous Robben Island prisoner, but he wasn't the first. In the seventeenth century, the island became a place of banishment for those who offended the political order– initially the power belonged to the Dutch, then the British, and finally the apartheid-enforcing National Party. The island's first prisoner was the indigenous Khoikhoi leader **Autshumato**, who learnt English in the early seventeenth century and became an emissary of the British. After the Dutch settlement was established, he was jailed by Jan van Riebeeck in 1658. The rest of the seventeenth century saw a succession of East Indies political prisoners and Muslim holy men exiled here for opposing Dutch colonial rule.

During the nineteenth century, the **British** used Robben Island as a dumping ground for deserters, criminals and political prisoners, in much the same way as they used Australia. Captured **Xhosa leaders** who defied the British Empire during the Frontier Wars of the early to mid-nineteenth century were transported from the Eastern to the Western Cape to be imprisoned, and many ended up on Robben Island. In 1846 those imprisoned included a whole range of the **socially marginalized**: vagrants, prostitutes, and the mentally and chronically ill. All were subjected to a regime of brutality and maltreatment, even in the hospitals. In the 1890s, a leper colony numbering hundreds of sufferers existed here too; mentally ill patients were removed in 1921 and the leprosy sufferers in 1930. During World War II, the **Defence Force** took over the island to guard against a feared Axis invasion, which never came.

Robben Island's greatest era of notoriety began in 1961, when it was taken over by the **Prisons Department**, under the control of the National Party government. Prisoners arriving at the island prison were greeted by a slogan on the gate that read: "Welcome to Robben Island: We Serve with Pride." By 1963, when Nelson Mandela arrived, it had become a maximum-security prison. All the warders – but none of the prisoners – were white. Prisoners were only allowed to send and receive one letter every six months, and common-law criminals and political prisoners were housed together until 1971, when they were separated in an attempt to further isolate the political activists. Harsh conditions, including routine beatings and forced hard labour, were exacerbated by geographical location. There's nothing but sea between the island and the South Pole, so icy winds routinely blow in from across the Atlantic – and inmates were made to wear shorts and flimsy jerseys. Like every other prisoner, Mandela slept on a thin mat on the floor (until 1973, when he was given a bed because he was ill) and was kept in a solitary confinement cell, measuring two square metres, for sixteen hours a day.

Amazingly, the prisoners found ways of **protesting**, through hunger strikes, publicizing conditions (using visits from the International Committee of the Red Cross, for example) and, remarkably, by taking legal action against the prison authority to stop arbitrary punishments. They won improved conditions over the years, and the island also became a university behind bars, where people of different generations and political persuasions met; it was not unknown for prisoners to give academic help to their warders.

The last political prisoners were **released** from Robben Island in 1991 and the remaining common-law prisoners transferred to the mainland in 1996. The following year, the island opened as a **museum** and national monument, and was declared a **World Heritage Site** in 1999.

Wildlife spotting

The bus tour also takes in a stretch of coast dotted with shipwrecks and over 130 species of sea bird and waterfowl including the elegant **sacred ibis**. You may also spot some of the **antelope** population, including springbok, steenbok, eland and bontebok.

The Maximum Security Prison
The **Maximum Security Prison**, a forbidding complex of unadorned H-blocks on the island's eastern edge, is introduced with a tour through the famous **B-Section**. This small compound, full of tiny rooms, has become legendary in South African history; initially a place of defeat for the resistance movement, it came to incubate and concentrate the energies of liberation. Your ex-inmate guide will likely share their poignant memories of hunger strikes, solitary confinement and hardship alongside the great struggle heroes. **Mandela's cell** has been left exactly as it was, without embellishments or display, and the rest are locked and empty.

In the **A-Section**, the "Cell Stories" exhibition evokes the sparseness of prison life. The tiny isolation cells feature personal artefacts loaned by former prisoners (including a saxophone made of found objects), plus boards bearing quotations and photographs.

Towards the end of the 1980s, cameras were sneaked in here, and inmates took snapshots of each other, which have been mounted as the **Smuggled Camera Exhibition** in the **D-Section** communal cells. The prisoners' jovial demeanour shows they knew that the end was near.

Another interesting part of the prison visit is the **Living Legacy** tour in **F-Section**, in which ex-political prisoner guides describe their lives here and answer visitors' questions.

De Waterkant
An atmospheric central neighbourhood in easy striking distance of the city centre, the Waterfront and the Atlantic seaboard, **De Waterkant** is a decent place to base yourself. Its terraces, which date back to the mid-eighteenth century, line cobbled streets that climb the lower flanks of Signal Hill. The district plays up its assets for all they're worth, with many of its houses turned over to guesthouses and self-catering flats. Within easy wandering distance of everything are restaurants, clubs, art dealers and interior design boutiques, many clustered in and around the **Cape Quarter**, an upmarket shopping mall. With a clutch of **gay-friendly nightclubs and pubs** (see p.151) on both sides of main drag Somerset Rd, the area is unofficially known as the **Pink Village**.

Prestwich Memorial
St Andrew's Sq, cnr Buitengracht St and Somerset Rd • Mon–Fri 8am–6pm, Sat & Sun 8am–1pm • Free • ☎ 021 487 2755
The **Prestwich Memorial**, housed in an elegant modern structure with a facade of Robben Island slate, accommodates **2500 sets of human bones**, excavated in 2003, of forgotten and marginalized Capetonians. Many were slaves executed in the vicinity in the seventeenth and eighteenth centuries. The interesting interpretation boards provide accounts of burial practices, historic hospitals in the area and, across one wall, a reproduction of a beautiful panorama of Cape Town, painted by Robert Gordon in 1778.

Outside, the **Prestwich Memorial Garden** exhibits sculptures by homegrown artists, including two mosaic-adorned **Rock Girl benches** (ⓦwww.rockgirlsa.org), part of a city-wide scheme to create safe spaces for women and young people. The **Walk of Remembrance**, created for the 2010 World Cup and renamed from the Fan Walk after Mandela's death, passes by en route between the train station and Cape Town Stadium. The garden is also at one end of the art and architecture **City Walk** (ⓦcapetownbig7 .co.za) to/from the Company's Garden; this route can be explored at your own pace, with plenty of pointers on the website, or on a **free guided walking tour** (see p.30).

GETTING AROUND   **DE WATERKANT**

By car Street parking can be hard to come by; the easiest place to find a spot is the Cape Quarter mall, entered from Napier and Dixon streets.

DEVIL'S PEAK AND THE CITY BOWL SUBURBS

Table Mountain and the City Bowl

Table Mountain, the towering massif that announced Cape Town to seafarers for centuries, dominates the peninsula, and its flat top can be recognized from miles away. The 1086m-high rock formation, its dramatic cliffs and eroded gorges overlooking all walks of local life, is a Mother City icon and one of the world's great physical symbols. The mountain informs Cape lore, from the "tablecloth" – the cloud blanketing the plateau and cascading down the sides – to the tale of Van Hunks, who created that cloud with his pipe. Climbing the slopes of Table Mountain, Lion's Head and Signal Hill, the desirable residential suburbs of Vredehoek, Oranjezicht, Gardens and Tamboerskloof form the upper edge of the City Bowl. This natural amphitheatre is where many tourists stay, attracted by the harbour views, numerous restaurants, and easy access to the city centre, Waterfront and Table Mountain itself.

Table Mountain

The north face of **Table Mountain** overlooks the city centre, flanked by the distinct formations of **Lion's Head** and **Signal Hill** to the west and **Devil's Peak** to the east. A series of gable-like formations known as the **Twelve Apostles** makes up the mountain's drier west face and the southwest face towers over Hout Bay. The forested east, looming over the southern suburbs, gets the most rain.

The mountain is a wilderness where you'll find wildlife and 1400 species of flora, while indigenous mammals include baboons, **dassies** (see box below) and porcupines. No wonder then that Table Mountain was voted one of the world's New Seven Wonders of Nature in 2011, along with the Amazon and Vietnam's Ha Long Bay.

Getting up and down the mountain can be a doddle, via the highly popular **cable car**, though **walking** up will give you a greater sense of achievement; if you're up to the challenge, it's best to go on a **guided hike** (see p.78).

Table Mountain Aerial Cableway

Lower Cableway Station, Tafelberg Rd • Daily (every 10–15min): Jan & Dec 8am–8.30pm; Feb 8am–8pm; March 8am–7.30pm; April 8am–7pm; May–Aug 8.30am–6pm; Sept & Oct 8.30am–7pm; Nov 8.30am–8.30pm • Adults one-way R135, return R255; children 4–17 one-way R65, return R125; return tickets half price after 6pm Nov to mid-Dec & Jan–Feb • Last car up departs 1hr before last car down; operations can be disrupted by bad weather or maintenance work; for information on current schedules call ☎ 021 424 8181, or check Ⓦ tablemountain.net

3

The highly popular **cable car** offers dizzying views across town to Table Bay and the Atlantic. The state-of-the-art Swiss system completes a 360-degree rotation during the five-minute journey, giving passengers a full panorama. At the top, if you don't want to walk far, you can wander the concrete paths stopping at the viewpoints; grab a meal or beer in the **cafeteria** (open from 8am until 30mins before the last car down); and post jealousy-inducing photos in the free **Wi-Fi Lounge**. The upper-station area is of course one of the city's best spots to watch the sun go down.

Note that people start queuing early and finish late in summer, and weekends and public holidays tend to be very busy. If you're unlucky, you could stand in line for an hour or more, but you can shorten your queuing time by buying your ticket online. Additionally, buy an afternoon ticket, valid from 1pm, when the Cableway is quieter; or an online-only Early Access ticket (R375 return), available for travel from 7.30am, thirty minutes before the Cableway's normal opening time, from mid-December to mid-January.

Climbs and walks

Table Mountain, Lion's Head and Signal Hill (aka the Lion's Rump) all offer gorgeous hikes. There are hundreds of possible **walks and climbs** on its slopes, but unless you're going with a knowledgeable guide, it's recommended that you attempt one of the **routes** outlined below, which are the simplest. Every year the mountain takes its toll of

---

DASSIES

The outsized fluffy guinea pigs you'll encounter at the top of Table Mountain are **dassies** or rock hyraxes (*Procavia capensis*) which, despite their appearance, aren't rodents at all, but the closest living relatives of elephants. Pronounced like "dusty" without the "t", their name is the Afrikaans version of *dasje*, the nickname coined by the Dutch settlers, which means "little badger". Dassies have poor body temperature control and, like reptiles, rely on shelter against both hot sunlight and the cold. They wake up sluggish and seek out rocks where they can catch the sun in the early morning – one of the best times to look out for them. One adult stands sentry against predators and issues a low-pitched warning cry in response to a threat.

Dassies are very widely distributed, having thrived in South Africa with the elimination of predators, and can be found in suitably **rocky habitats** all over the country. They live in colonies consisting of a dominant male and eight or more related females and their offspring.

lives; it may look sunny and clear when you leave, but conditions at the top could be very different – the strong sun and Cape Town's infamous winds can be brutal, and mists that obscure the path can descend quickly. Plan well and keep safe (see box, p.75), and you will be rewarded with a worthwhile hike offering spectacular views.

Signal Hill and Lion's Head

From the roundabout at the top of **Kloof Nek** – the saddle between Table Mountain and Lion's Head, over which Kloof Nek Road runs to reach the Atlantic seaboard – the 3.5km Signal Hill Road runs the length of the **Signal Hill** ridge to a car park and lookout at the northern end, with good views over Table Bay and the city.

A cannon was formerly used for sending signals to ships at anchor in the bay, and the **Noon Gun**, still fired precisely at noon by the South African Navy, sends a thunderous rumble through the Bo-Kaap and city centre below. Hilltop cannons were fired from here to the Winelands to inform farmers that ships requiring their produce were docking; the Noon Gun was subsequently used for vessels to set their chronometers – and burghers to set their watches.

Halfway along Signal Hill Road, you'll see a sacred Islamic **kramat** (shrine), one of several dotted around the peninsula, which are said to protect the city (see box, p.76).

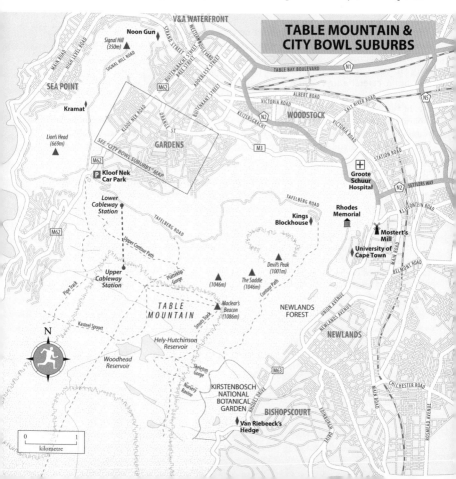

TABLE MOUNTAIN SAFETY

- Inform someone that you're going up the mountain; tell them your route, when you're leaving and when you expect to be back.
- Don't go up alone. As well as general mountain-safety issues (particularly for less experienced climbers), muggings are fairly common.
- Avoid quiet times of day (early or late), little-used paths and Devil's Peak.
- Leave early enough to give yourself time to complete your route during daylight.
- Don't try to descend via an unknown route. If you get lost in poor weather, seek shelter, keep warm and wait for help.
- Never make fires. No cooking is allowed, even on portable stoves – mountain fires are a serious hazard in Cape Town, especially during the dry, hot summer months.
- Never leave even the tiniest scrap of litter on the mountain.

WEAR:

- Good footwear. Walking boots or sturdy running shoes are recommended.
- A broad-rimmed hat.
- Long trousers to protect you from the sun and scratchy shrubs.

TAKE:

- A backpack.
- A water bottle; allow two litres per person.
- Enough food for the trip.
- A warm top.
- A windbreaker.
- Sunglasses.
- High-factor sunscreen.
- A map (available from Cape Union Mart at the Waterfront and in malls including the Gardens Centre and Cavendish Square, Claremont; and from ⓦ mapstudio.co.za).
- A fully charged mobile phone with Table Mountain Rescue number saved (☎ 021 937 0300).

3

You can also walk up **Lion's Head**, a hike that seems to bring out half the population of Cape Town every full moon. It's a local ritual, not just for the beautiful nocturnal views of the city below and the silvery procession of head torches snaking up the mountain, but for the camaraderie and the novelty of climbing the peak after dark.

One of the attractions of this two-kilometre ascent is that, as you spiral up around the mountain, there are constantly changing views of the city and the ocean. You can start the climb about 650m along Signal Hill Road from Kloof Nek, or at the *kramat*. The climb is relatively easy and manageable for all levels, as long as you leave enough time to descend, and it takes on average an hour and a half one-way. The hike is mostly on a track, followed by a path with minor rock scrambling and a ladder at one point, as well as chains to assist hikers up a short vertical ascent (a longer diversion bypasses the chains).

Be warned that Lion's Head gets extremely busy on and around full moon; the nights before and after are slightly quieter. Take a torch and watch your step at the top, where the ascent becomes steeper and rockier. Walk with others if possible, as muggings have occurred even on these busy nights.

Pipe Track

This easy and **scenic amble** follows the contour along the western side of Table Mountain, with Camps Bay stretching out below, the Twelve Apostles ahead and Lion's Head to one side. It's mostly flat, with only a little up and down and benches overlooking the view. You can walk for a few kilometres before retracing your steps, or make your way down the mountain to Camps Bay seafront for refreshments.

The **trailhead** is across Tafelberg Road from the Kloof Nek car park. It is popular with joggers and dog walkers, which makes it safe for an early-morning outing, especially at weekends.

Platteklip Gorge

The first recorded ascent to Table Mountain's summit was by Portuguese captain Antonio de Saldanha, in 1503. He chose **Platteklip Gorge**, the gap visible from the front table (the north side), the most accessible way up. The Platteklip route starts near the Lower Cableway Station and ends near the upper station (for a ride down).

From the lower station, walk east along Tafelberg Road until you see a high embankment built from stone and maintained with wire netting. Just beyond and to the left of a small dam is a sign pointing to Platteklip Gorge. A steep fifteen-minute climb brings you onto the **Upper Contour Path**. About 25m east along this, take the path indicated by a sign that says "Contour Path/Platteklip Gorge". The path zigzags from here onwards and is very easy to make out. The gorge is the biggest chasm on the whole mountain. It leads directly and safely to the top, but it's a very steep, three-hour slog, even if you're reasonably fit. Once on the top, turn right and ascend the last short section onto the **front table** for a breathtaking view of the city. A sign points to the Upper Cableway Station – a fifteen-minute walk along a concrete path thronging with visitors.

Maclear's Beacon

Maclear's Beacon is about 35 minutes from the top of the Platteklip Gorge (or about one hour from the Upper Cableway Station), on a path that leads eastward, with markers showing the way. The path crosses the front table with Maclear's Beacon, the highest point on the mountain (1086m), visible at all times. From the top, you'll get views of False Bay to the south and the Hottentots Holland Mountains to the east.

Skeleton Gorge

This eastern route (4–5hr) allows you to combine the Kirstenbosch gardens (see p.83) with an ascent of Table Mountain, returning down a different path. From the gardens' **restaurant** (just inside the upper entrance; turn right on the way in from Rhodes Drive) follow the **Skeleton Gorge** signs that lead onto the **Contour Path**. Here, a plaque indicates that this path forms part of the **Smuts Track**, the route to Maclear's Beacon favoured by Jan Smuts. The twentieth-century Boer leader, prime minister and international statesman was known for his love of Table Mountain.

The plaque marks the start of a broad-stepped climb up Skeleton Gorge, involving both wooden and stone steps, wooden ladders and loose boulders. Be prepared for steep **forested ravines** and the odd rock scramble – and under no circumstances stray off the path. It requires reasonable fitness, and can take about two hours to ascend.

The Skeleton Gorge descent can be unpleasant, especially in the wet season when it gets slippery; a recommended alternative is **Nursery Ravine**. From the top of Skeleton Gorge, a half-hour walk on the flat leads past the **Hely-Hutchinson Reservoir** to the head of Nursery Ravine. This descent returns you to the Contour Path, which leads back to Kirstenbosch.

SACRED CIRCLE

During the late seventeenth and early eighteenth centuries, the Dutch exiled a number of Muslim holy men and princes from the East Indies to the Cape, where some became revered as **auliyah**, or muslim saints. The **kramats**, of which there are around two dozen in Cape Town and the Winelands, are the *auliyah*'s burial sites, shrines and places of pilgrimage.

Signal Hill's *kramat* is a shrine to Mohamed Gasan Galbie Shah, a follower of Sheik Yusuf, an Indonesian Sufi scholar deported to the Cape in 1694 with a 49-strong retinue. According to tradition, Yusuf conducted Muslim prayer meetings in private homes and slave quarters, becoming South Africa's founder of Islam. His *kramat* at Macassar on the Cape Flats is said to be one of a sacred circle of six that protect Cape Town from natural disasters – as are the Signal Hill shrine and Robben Island's Moturu Kramat (see p.68). For more on the *kramats*, visit ⓦ capemazaarsociety.com.

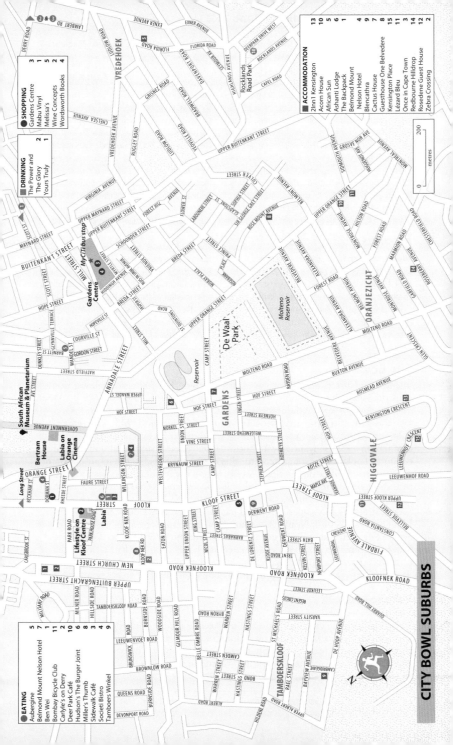

CITY BOWL SUBURBS

EATING

Aubergine	5
Belmond Mount Nelson Hotel	7
Ben Wei	1
Bombay Bicycle Club	11
Carlyle's on Derry	2
Deer Park Café	10
Hudson's The Burger Joint	6
Miller's Thumb	8
Sidewalk Café	3
Societi Bistro	4
Tamboers Winkel	9

SHOPPING

Gardens Centre	3
Mabu Vinyl	1
Melissa's	5
Wine Concepts	2
Wordsworth Books	4

DRINKING

The Power and The Glory	2
Yours Truly	1

ACCOMMODATION

2Inn1 Kensington	13
Acorn House	10
African Sun	5
Ashanti Lodge	6
The Backpack	1
Belmond Mount Nelson Hotel	4
Blencathra	9
Cactus House	7
Guesthouse One Belvedere	8
Kensington Place	15
Lézard Bleu	11
Once in Cape Town	3
Redbourne Hilldrop	14
Rosedene Guest House	12
Zebra Crossing	2

0   200
metres

You can also incorporate the plateau-top walk along the Smuts Track to **Maclear's Beacon**, which takes about two hours for a return trip from the top of Skeleton Gorge.

ARRIVAL AND DEPARTURE   TABLE MOUNTAIN

By car There's parking along Tafelberg Rd, but you may be in for a walk to the Lower Cableway Station in peak season – the stretch of parked cars can extend several hundred metres. If you find yourself in this situation after dark, walk back to your car with a friend, fellow motorist or car guard. **By MyCiTi bus** ☏ 0800 65 64 63, ⓦ myciti.org.za. Take bus #106 or #107 (running between the Civic Centre and Camps Bay via Adderley, Long and Kloof Sts and Kloof Nek Rd) and get off at Kloof Nek, which is at the junction of Tafelberg Rd. From here, catch the free #110 to the Lower Cableway Station or tackle the steep uphill 1km walk (the route is well signposted).

By City Sightseeing bus ☏ 086 173 3287, ⓦ citysightseeing.co.za. This open-topped bus stops at the Lower Cableway Station, between Buitengracht St and Camps Bay on its Red City Tour route. Cableway tickets can be bought from City Sightseeing offices and drivers.

By taxi You can travel by Uber or normal metered taxi to the Lower Cableway Station, where taxis wait to take you home at the end. Prices on the return journey will likely be higher than normal city fares, but it's a convenient option that eliminates parking hassles and waiting for buses.

ACTIVITIES

Adventure sports For an adrenaline thrill, you can abseil off Table Mountain (see p.147), paraglide from Lion's Head (see p.148) or mountain bike on Devil's Peak (see p.148). **Climbing** Experienced rock climbers will find enough satisfying routes to last a lifetime, on either granite or Table Mountain sandstone; the climbs are of varying degrees of difficulty, and some are thrillingly exposed (see p.148).

Hiking A recommended way to experience the mountain is on a guided half- or full-day hike (see p.147). Tailored to walkers' individual levels of fitness, the hikes offer a safe route into this wilderness in the heart of the city; there's also the 73km Hoerikwaggo Trail (ⓦ tmnp.co.za), a multiday hike up from the Lower Cableway Station and down the plateau and peninsula to Cape Point.

City Bowl

The residential areas of the **City Bowl** gently climbing Table Mountain's lower slopes are a district in which to consume, with good restaurants (see p.125), bars (see p.133) and cafés (see p.125) serving the affluent residents, tourists and city-centre workers.

A landmark of the district, as you arrive in the city along the M3, is the grand **Belmond Mount Nelson Hotel** (see p.116), which harks back to the heyday of British colonialism with its gigantic, white, pedimented gateway supported on Corinthian columns. Look out for it on the south side of Orange Street in the suburb of **Gardens**, which is named after the Company's Garden and the smallholdings that once climbed the mountain. Almost next door to the *Belmond Mount Nelson Hotel* is the **Labia**, an inexpensive art-house cinema (see p.138).

Kloof Street is a hip strip of shops and hangouts, especially around the Lifestyle on Kloof mall (see p.145). Nearby, look out for music shop Mabu Vinyl (see p.144), which featured in the Oscar-winning documentary, **Searching for Sugar Man**. Parallel with Kloof Street, busy Kloof Nek Road links central Cape Town to Kloof Nek and the cable car, and is the only central pass over the Table Mountain chain to the Atlantic seaboard. As you drive over the *nek* (neck), there are astounding vistas down to the ocean.

Molteno Reservoir

Molteno Rd • Daily 9am–5pm

The 800m asphalt path around the late nineteenth-century Molteno Reservoir, an Oranjezicht landmark, is popular with local runners, with **impressive views** of Table Mountain, Lion's Head and the city towers. You can walk up here through leafy **De Waal Park**, where free concerts are staged on summer Sundays.

GETTING AROUND   THE CITY BOWL

By MyCiTi bus Bus #103 runs between the Civic Centre and Oranjezicht via Buitenkant St and Gardens, and the #101 between the Civic Centre and Vredehoek via Long St, Orange St, Mill St and Gardens.

Southern Suburbs and Cape Flats

The suburbs of Woodstock and Observatory, slowly gentrifying but still rough around the edges, begin where the city centre ends. Beyond the latter, the formerly whites-only residential areas of the Southern Suburbs, Anglophone neighbourhoods with a British feel to their leafy avenues and prestigious schools, stretch down the eastern side of Table Mountain towards the False Bay coast. Greener and more forested than the Atlantic Coast, this side of the peninsula is home to the sublime Kirstenbosch National Botanical Garden. Further afield, in the Constantia winelands, lie South Africa's oldest wineries, and in the same vicinity is Tokai Forest, a relaxing refuge from the midsummer sun. Stretching east of the M5 highway are the Cape Flats; once the apartheid dumping ground for black and coloured people, these township-covered flatlands now offer rewarding experiences of everyday African life.

ARRIVAL AND DEPARTURE
SOUTHERN SUBURBS AND CAPE FLATS

By car The quickest way of reaching the Southern Suburbs from central Cape Town is the M3 highway; outside rush hour, it takes about 30min to drive the 20km to Tokai, where the highway ends. During the week, the traffic is appalling – avoid the M3 southbound between 3.30pm and 6pm, and use it only after 9am from the south to reach the centre.

By train Metrorail's Southern Line, from Cape Town Station to Fish Hoek and Simon's Town, runs through the Southern Suburbs, providing a handy and safe means of reaching many of these areas. However, there are no stops within walking distance of the Rhodes Memorial, Kirstenbosch, Constantia or Tokai, so you'll have to pick up a taxi or Uber from the closest train station. Metrorail's Central and Cape Flats lines serve the townships, but we recommend you avoid taking public transport to these areas and only visit on a guided tour (see p.90).

By minibus Shared minibus taxis run from Cape Town Station to Wynberg via Victoria/Main Rd (M4), passing through Woodstock, Observatory, the Baxter Theatre and close to the Irma Stern Museum. You can hail minibuses in both directions on this route. Minibus taxis also serve the Cape Flats and African townships, and most of the train stations (especially Cape Town, Mowbray, Claremont and Wynberg) have crowds of shared taxis outside waiting to rush people home from work. MyCiTi buses serve Mitchells Plain and Khayelitsha, although we don't recommend taking any public transport to the Cape Flats and African townships; the network is also set to expand to the Southern Suburbs.

By bus The hop-on, hop-off City Sightseeing bus' Blue Mini Peninsula Tour stops at Kirstenbosch and Constantia Nek; the latter links with the Purple Wine Tour, which visits three Constantia wine estates (☎ 086 173 3287, ⓦ citysightseeing.co.za).

Woodstock

4

One of Cape Town's oldest suburbs, and still a predominantly working-class coloured area, **Woodstock** is gradually gentrifying, having already become the city's premier **design district**. Newcomers snap up and renovate pretty old **Victorian houses**, while each block of Woodstock's stretches of Albert and Victoria/Main roads brings a new cluster of design and artisan coffee shops, **art galleries**, custom-made furniture stores and high-end shopping arcades. **Juma's Tours** (see p.90) offers walking tours of the area's street art and galleries.

Meanwhile, on the crumbling side streets, you will still pass old folk conversing on their *stoeps*, and keeping an eye on their grandchildren playing on the pavement – evoking an image of what nearby **District Six** (see p.60) must have been like before the forced removals to the Cape Flats.

Albert Road

Old Biscuit Mill Mon–Fri 10am–4pm, Sat 9am–2pm • ☎ 021 447 8194, ⓦ theoldbiscuitmill.co.za • **Woodstock Exchange** Mon–Fri 8am–5pm, Sat 8am–2pm • ☎ 021 486 5999, ⓦ woodstockexchange.co.za • **Woodstock Foundry** Mon–Fri 9am–4.30pm, Sat 9am–noon • ☎ 021 422 0466, ⓦ woodstockfoundry.co.za

A visit to these outer city fringes should take in three main hubs, all of which are situated along the Woodstock section of **Albert Road**; best known is the **Old Biscuit Mill**, at number 375, where you can eat yourself silly and wander around craft and design shops. The former biscuit factory houses two of the city's best contemporary restaurants, *Test Kitchen* (see p.127) and *Pot Luck Club* (see p.127), and the terrific organic and artisanal **Neighbourgoods** food market (see p.144).

The **Woodstock Exchange** (66 Albert Rd), 1km west of the Old Biscuit Mill, has become a byword for everything hip and creative in Cape Town's coolest neighbourhood with its vibrant community of boutiques, all housed in a **converted warehouse**. The appealing items on offer range from Grandt Mason Originals' handmade footwear to Honest's raw organic chocolate, while the complex's café, *Superette*, serves craft beers and locally roasted coffee.

Between the two, at 170 Albert Road, the **Woodstock Foundry** fills a renovated heritage building with a creative mix of shops, Tribe coffee roastery and studio space. Check their website and Facebook page for occasional Open Studio Nights.

Observatory

Abutting the southeastern end of Woodstock, "Obs" is generally regarded as Cape Town's **bohemian hub**, a reputation fuelled by its proximity to the University of Cape Town in Rondebosch and its large student population. Many of the houses here are student digs, but the narrow Victorian streets are also home to a fun-loving crowd of young professionals, artists and musicians. With their wrought-iron balconies, the attractively dilapidated and peeling buildings on **Lower Main Road**, and the streets off this atmospheric main drag, have some inviting neighbourhood cafés and bars, while the shops sell everything from wholefood and cheese to African fabrics and antiques.

Heart of Cape Town Museum

Old Building, Groote Schuur Hospital, Main Rd • Daily 9am–5pm; guided tours at 9am, 11am, 1pm & 3pm • R300 including tour • ☎ 021 404 1967, ⊛ heartofcapetown.co.za

Towering over "hospital bend" on the N2 as it curves around Devil's Peak, the hulking Groote Schuur Hospital witnessed history in 1967, when pioneering cardiac surgeon

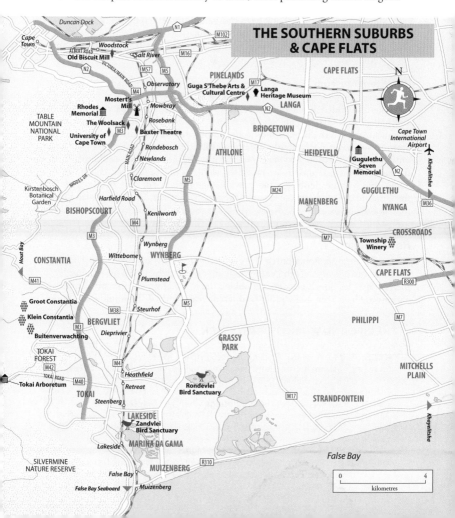

THE SOUTHERN SUBURBS & CAPE FLATS

Christiaan Barnard performed the world's first successful heart transplant here. Inside, the **Heart of Cape Town Museum** covers the groundbreaking procedure, including the ethical issues raised at the time, and features the restored theatres where the operation took place. You can visit the museum under your own steam, but taking the informative **two-hour guided tour** is recommended given the expensive entrance fee. The city's Netcare Christiaan Barnard Memorial Hospital (see p.63) provides more information on the Karoo-born Barnard's life and work.

Mowbray and Rosebank

South of Observatory is **Mowbray**, originally called Drie Koppen (Three Heads) after the heads of three slaves were impaled here in 1724, following their execution for insurrection. In the nineteenth century, Mowbray was the home of German linguist **Wilhelm Bleek**, who lived here with a group of San convicts given up by the colonial authorities so he could study their languages and attitudes. Bleek's pioneering work still forms the basis of much of what we know about traditional Khoisan life.

To Mowbray's south, **Rosebank** has a substantial student community, and university residences, blocks of flats and sports fields dominate the area. The main reason to pass through these largely residential areas is to visit one of Cape Town's cultural gems, the Irma Stern Museum.

Irma Stern Museum

Cecil Rd, Rosebank · Tues–Fri 10am–5pm, Sat 10am–2pm · R10 · ⓦ irmastern.co.za

Irma Stern is lauded as one of South Africa's greatest artists, for her vividly expressive and sensual portraits, still lifes and landscapes, which brought modern European ideas to South Africa in the twentieth century and now sell for millions of dollars. The **Irma Stern Museum** was the famously larger-than-life artist's home and studio for 38 years, until her death in 1966, and is definitely worth visiting to see her collection of African, Iberian, oriental and ancient artefacts. The whole house, in fact, reflects Stern's fascination with exoticism, from her own Gauguinesque paintings of African figures to the fantastic carved doors she brought back from Zanzibar. Even the garden brings a touch of the tropics to Cape Town, with its exuberant bamboo thickets and palm trees.

Rondebosch

South of Rosebank, **Rondebosch** is home to the **University of Cape Town** (UCT), whose handsome nineteenth-century buildings sit grandly on the mountainside, their creeper-festooned facades overlooking the M3 highway. University campuses nationwide have seen many protests in recent years, and UCT's found focus in the

---

THE LIFE AND WORK OF IRMA STERN

Born in South Africa's North West Province in 1894 to German-Jewish parents, **Irma Stern** studied at Germany's Weimar Academy. In reaction to the academy's conservatism, she adopted **expressionist distortion** in her paintings, and exhibited alongside the German Expressionists in Berlin. Returning to Cape Town in 1920, over the following decades she went on several expeditions to Zanzibar and the Congo, where she found the colourful and exotic inspiration for her intensely **sensuous paintings**, which shocked conservative South Africa.

Although Stern's work was appreciated in Europe, South African critics initially derided her style as simply a cover for technical incompetence; "ugliness as a cult", said one headline. South African art historians now regard her as the towering figure of her generation, and at Bonhams London in 2011, her *Arab Priest* (1945) fetched £3.1 million, the **highest auction price** ever achieved by a South African artwork. Stern's portraits range from the much-reproduced *The Eternal Child* (1916), a simple but vibrant depiction of a young girl, to her many later portrayals of African women.

2015 **#RhodesMustFall** movement, which toppled its prominent statue of Cecil Rhodes, the nineteenth-century British imperialist, diamond-mining magnate and founder of De Beers. The movement objected to the statue's colonial associations.

With one of Cape Town's premier arts complexes, the **Baxter Theatre** (see p.136), and many of the city's best schools nearby, this is the heartland of liberal, educated, English-speaking Cape Town.

The Woolsack

Woolsack Drive, UCT Middle Campus • Leave the M3 (Rhodes Dr) at exit 7, just after the Mostert's Mill windmill if you are coming from the city centre

Sir Herbert Baker designed **The Woolsack** as "cottage in the woods for poets and artists" for **Cecil John Rhodes**, prime minister of the Cape (1890–1896) and much-maligned colonial poster boy. Rhodes duly invited **Rudyard Kipling** to "hang up his hat there" whenever he visited the Cape. Taking his friend at his word, Kipling fled the English winter every year from 1900 to 1907, bringing his family to Cape Town and spending five to six months at the Woolsack, where he is said to have written his famous poem *If*. Restored in 2003, the house is now a student residence.

Rhodes Memorial

Rhodes Memorial St • Restaurant and tea garden daily 9am–5pm • ☎ 021 687 0000, Ⓦ rhodesmemorial.co.za • Leave the M3 (Rhodes Dr) at exit 8

On a site chosen by Herbert Baker and Rudyard Kipling, the **Rhodes Memorial**, a monument to Cecil Rhodes stands grandiosely against the slopes of Devil's Peak as herds of wildebeest and zebra nonchalantly graze nearby. Built in 1912 to resemble a Greek temple, the memorial celebrates Rhodes' energy with a sculpture of a wildly rearing horse. Carved in stone beneath the empire-builder's bust is a ponderous inscription by Kipling: "The immense and brooding spirit still shall order and control." Also on site is a relaxing **restaurant and tea garden** with terrific views of Cape Town.

Newlands and Claremont

If you continue south from Rondebosch along either the M3 or the more congested Main Road, you'll pass some of Cape Town's most prestigious suburbs. **Newlands** is home to the city's famous rugby and cricket stadiums, and its **Montebello Craft and Design Centre** (see p.141) is worth a stop.

Further south, the well-heeled suburb of **Claremont** is an alternative focus to the city centre for shopping at **Cavendish Square Mall** (see p.145). Its layout is a little bewildering for first-time visitors, but it is well equipped with high-quality shops, restaurants and a cinema, while vendors in the adjoining **street market** sell clothes, vegetables, herbs and more. You will find more street snacks across busy Main Road in the train station area.

Kirstenbosch National Botanical Garden

Rhodes Drive • Gardens April–Aug daily 8am–6pm, Sept–March daily 8am–7pm; open-air concerts Sun evenings, late Nov to early April; coffee shop daily 7am–7pm; tea room daily 8.30am–5pm; restaurant Sat–Thurs 9am–6pm, Fri 9am–11pm • Adults R60, children 6–17 R15, children under 6 free; adult concert tickets R125–190 • ☎ 021 799 8783, Ⓦ sanbi.org/gardens/kirstenbosch • The City Sightseeing Bus stops at the garden every 20min on its Blue Mini Peninsula Tour; Golden Arrow buses run six services every weekday from Mowbray train station to the garden (7am–4pm), with the 12.35pm service originating at the Golden Acre terminus in the city centre

The unmissable **Kirstenbosch National Botanical Garden** climbs the eastern slopes of Table Mountain, 13km from the city centre. Established in 1913, this is one of the Earth's great natural treasure troves; a status acknowledged in 2004 when the biodiverse Cape Floristic Region, which Kirstenbosch showcases, became South Africa's sixth UNESCO World Heritage Site – making Kirstenbosch the world's first botanical garden to achieve this. The listing recognizes the international significance of the *fynbos* (see box, p.110) vegetation and the Cape plant kingdom that predominate here, attracting botanists from all over the world.

Little signboards and paved paths guide you through the garden's highlights, with trees and plants identified to enhance the rambling. Allow a couple of hours to visit Kirstenbosch, a stunning picnic spot with ample shelter from Cape Town's battering summer winds.

An exciting feature is the **Tree Canopy Walkway** or "Boomslang", a steel-and-timber bridge that snakes its way up and through the trees of the **Arboretum**, with panoramic views of the garden and surrounding mountains. Five trails of varying difficulty explore the garden, including the **Braille Trail** starting at the **Fragrance Garden**; created for blind visitors, it has information signs in Braille and an abundance of aromatic and textured plants.

The garden has a pleasant **tea room** (see p.127), serving breakfast, lunch and picnics just inside Gate 2, as well as a *Vida e Caffè* **coffee shop** just outside Gate 1 and a *Moyo* **restaurant** between the two gates.

Walks

The garden trails off into the **wild vegetation** covering a huge expanse of the rugged eastern slopes and wooded ravines of Table Mountain – its setting is quite breathtaking. Two popular paths that climb the mountain from the **Contour Path** above Kirstenbosch are Skeleton Gorge and the Nursery Ravine (see p.76). While the garden is safe from crime, if you are hiking up Table Mountain, or onwards to **Constantia Nek** along the Contour Path, the usual safely precautions should be followed (see box, p.75). The northern route to Newlands Forest and the Rhodes Memorial is not recommended following a spate of muggings.

Concerts

If you're visiting Kirstenbosch National Botanical Garden in **summer**, one of its undoubted delights is to bring a picnic for a Sunday-evening **open-air concert**, where you can lie back on the lawn, sip Cape wine and savour the mountain air and sunset. Try to catch a local act such as Hugh Masekela, Jeremy Loops, Goldfish or Freshlyground, and arrive early to secure a good spot for your blanket.

Bishopscourt

Affluent **Bishopscourt** is south of Newlands, most easily reached from the M3 by turning off after the Kirstenbosch garden junction. As its name suggests, the suburb is home to the Anglican Archbishop of Cape Town, and it was in a mansion here that **Archbishop Desmond Tutu** lived even in the years when black people weren't supposed to live in white-only suburbs. Partly because of its prime siting – some plots have views of both the mountain-hugging Newlands Forest and False Bay – this area is one of the city's most *larney* ('posh' in South African slang). Diplomats and old money are secreted in huge properties behind high walls, which are about all you see as you pass through.

Wynberg

Three stops down the train line from Claremont is **Wynberg**, known for its Shakespearean **Maynardville Open-Air Theatre** (see p.137) in the park of the same name. On the park's western side is quaint **Wynberg Village**, where the thatched Cape Georgian cottages house art galleries and boutiques.

By contrast, Wynberg's Main Road offers a more African shopping experience: street vendors and fabric shops ply a lively trade as minibus taxis and pedestrians hustle along the thoroughfare.

4

CAPE DUTCH ARCHITECTURE

The **Cape Dutch** style, which developed in the Western Cape from the seventeenth to the early nineteenth century, is so distinctively rooted in Constantia and the Cape Winelands that it has become an integral element of the landscape. The dazzling limewashed walls glisten in the midst of glowing green vineyards, while the thatched roofs and elaborate curvilinear gables mirror the undulations of the surrounding mountains. Although there were important developments in the internal organization of Cape houses during this period, their most obvious element is the external **gable**. Central gables set into the long side of roofs were unusual in Europe, but became the quintessential feature of the Cape Dutch style.

In central Cape Town, the gable only survived until the 1830s, to be replaced by buildings with flush facades and flat roofs. **Arson** appears to be a major reason for this; fires, purportedly started by slaves, including the one that razed Stellenbosch in 1710, and Cape Town's **great fires** of 1736 and 1798, led officials to ban thatched roofs and protrusions on building exteriors. With the disappearance of pitched roofs, the urban gable withered away, surviving symbolically in some instances as minimal roof decoration; an example of this is the wavy parapet on the **Bo-Kaap Museum** (see p.51).

The threat of fire spreading from one building to another was a less serious consideration in the countryside. Consequently, Dutch East India Company building regulations carried little weight and the pitched roof survived, as did gables, becoming the hallmark of country manors. From functional origins, gables evolved into **symbols of wealth**, with landowners vying to erect the biggest, most elaborate and most fashionable examples. Some fine gables can be found on the historic estates of the Winelands, as well as at Tokai Manor (see p.88), Groot Constantia (see p.86), Klein Constantia (see p.86) and Buitenverwachting (see p.87).

Constantia and its winelands

There is no public transport to this area, although several tours run from central Cape Town daily; the City Sightseeing bus' Purple Wine Tour circles from Constantia Nek (a stop on its Blue Mini Peninsula Tour) to Groot Constantia, Eagles' Nest and Beau Constantia estates; driving, take exit 14 (Constantia Main Rd) from the M3

South of Kirstenbosch lie the elegant suburb of **Constantia** and the Cape's oldest **winelands**. Luxuriating on the lower slopes of Table Mountain and the Constantiaberg, with tantalizing views of False Bay, Constantia's nine wine estates are an easy drive from town, all within ten minutes of the M3.

The winelands began cultivated life in 1685 as the farm of **Simon van der Stel**, the governor charged with opening up the fledgling Dutch colony to the interior. Now Cape Town's oldest and most prestigious residential area, with a gentle ambience of landed wealth, Constantia is a green and pleasant shaded valley with **vineyards** carpeting its upper slopes. Famous past residents include Charles Spencer, Princess Diana's brother, and Mark Thatcher, the late British prime minister's son, who allegedly planned 2004's failed coup in Equatorial Guinea while living here.

Constantia grapes have been making wine since Van der Stel's first output in 1705. After his death in 1712, his estate was divided up and sold off as the modern **Groot Constantia**, **Klein Constantia** and **Buitenverwachting**. The major wine estates are open to the public and offer tastings; they're worth visiting for their history and architecture as well as viticulture, even if you're heading out of town to the Cape Winelands proper (see p.158).

Groot Constantia

Groot Constantia Rd · **Grounds** Daily 9am–6pm · Free · **Wine tasting** Daily 9am–5.30pm · R75 including five wines to taste and a souvenir glass · **Cellar tours** Daily on the hour 10am–4pm · R100; booking essential · **Visitors Route Experience** R95 · **Museum** Daily 10am–5pm · R30 · ☎ 021 794 5128, ⓦ grootconstantia.co.za

The largest Constantia estate and the one most geared to tourists is **Groot Constantia**, a terrific example of Cape Dutch grandeur reached along an oak-lined drive that passes through vineyards with the hazy blue Constantiaberg as its backdrop. The dozen high-end reds, whites and rosés produced here include local signature varietal Pinotage and Constantia's celebrated Vin de Constance (see p.87). The estate is restful and serene, and if you don't want to taste the wines, you can simply walk around the vineyards and enjoy the architecture. Groot Constantia's big pull is that it retains the rump of Van der Stel's original farm, as well as its original buildings, which powerfully evoke life on an estate in the early Cape.

The **manor house**, a quintessential eighteenth-century Cape Dutch homestead rebuilt from Van der Stel's original house, forms part of the **museum**. It is decorated in a style typical of eighteenth- and nineteenth-century Cape landowners, containing interesting Louis XVI Neoclassical furniture and Delft and Chinese ceramics.

If you walk straight through the house and across the yard, you'll come to the **Cloete Cellar** (actually a two-storey building above ground), fronted by a brilliant relief pediment. Attributed to the sculptor Anton Anreith, it depicts a riotous bacchanalia, featuring Ganymede, a young man so handsome that Zeus, in the form of an eagle, carried him off to be the cup-bearer of the gods. Also included in the museum are a coach house, wine cellar and **orientation centre**, the latter covering the estate's history including the role of slavery here.

The estate has two restaurants and a deli offering **picnics**. Its **Visitors Route Experience** offers access to the manor house, the Cloete Cellar, a wine tasting and two audio walking tours. Tickets are available at Groot Constantia or through Webtickets (ⓦ webtickets.co.za).

Klein Constantia

Klein Constantia Rd · Mon–Fri 10am–5pm, Sat 10am–4.30pm, Sun 10am–4pm · R50 · ☎ 021 794 5188, ⓦ kleinconstantia.com

Smaller in scale than Groot Constantia, **Klein Constantia** offers more casual wine tastings than at the bigger estate, and although the buildings are humbler, the setting is equally

MITCHELLS PLAIN

If you're driving east from the Muizenberg area to the Cape Winelands or the far end of False Bay, it's possible to take the coastal **Baden Powell Drive** (R310). This route avoids detouring all the way up the M3 or M5 to join the N2, but seek local advice before taking it: the road is unsafe later in the day and, over weekends and public holidays, it fills with beach traffic.

Along the way you will skirt the bottom of **Mitchells Plain**, a coloured area. More salubrious than the African townships, Mitchells Plain reflects how, under apartheid, lighter skin meant better conditions, even if you weren't quite white. Coloured people had their share of trauma during the **forced removals** from the city centre, when many were summarily forced to vacate family homes because the Group Areas Act had declared their suburb a white area. Many families were relocated to Mitchells Plain when **District Six** was razed (see p.60), and their communities never fully recovered. One of the symptoms of this dislocation and poverty is the violent gangs that have become an everyday part of Mitchells Plain youth culture.

beautiful. Klein Constantia has a friendly atmosphere and produces several fine wines, most famously its **Vin de Constance**. This is a recreation of a historic Constantia wine that was quaffed by eighteenth- and nineteenth-century luminaries including Frederick the Great and Bismarck; as well as Napoleon, who ordered it on St Helena; and the poet Baudelaire, who compared its sweet delights to his lover's lips. It's a delicious **dessert wine**, packaged in a replica of the original bottle, and makes an original souvenir.

Buitenverwachting
Klein Constantia Rd • **Tastings** Mon–Fri 9am–5pm, Sat 9am–3pm • R50 • ☎ 021 794 5190, ⓦ buitenverwachting.co.za

Buitenverwachting (roughly pronounced "bay-tin-fur-vuch-ting", with the "ch" as in the Scottish rendition of loch) is another great wine estate tucked away in the Constantia suburbs, where sheep and cattle graze in the fields as you approach the main buildings. Its name means 'beyond expectation' in Dutch.

The architecture and setting at the foot of the Constantiaberg are as lovely as any, while their wines have attracted accolades including a five-star rating in Platter's Wine Guide 2015. Overlooking the vineyards and backing onto the garden, the late-eighteenth-century **homestead** features an unusual gabled pediment broken with an urn motif. The original **wine cellar** and adjoining terrace are the venue for tastings and cheese and pâté platters, and the estate has a **restaurant** and a **coffee shop**.

Tokai
To drive to Tokai from central Cape Town, head south along the M3 and exit north (left) onto Ladies Mile Road. Continue for 500m before turning south (left) into Spaanschemat River Road (M42), signposted Tokai, which runs through the suburb. Alternatively, take the next exit and turn right onto Tokai Road (M40)

Effectively the southern extension of Constantia, forested **Tokai** is a popular area for leafy recreation away from the city centre. It offers relaxed and child-friendly places for eating and drinking, and shelter from the strong southeastern wind. You can easily combine Tokai with a trip to the seaside, as the suburb is fifteen minutes' drive from the False Bay seaboard.

Tokai Forest
Tokai Rd • Daily: April–Sept 8am–5pm, Oct–March 7am–6pm • Free, mountain bikers R80 • ☎ 021 712 7471, ⓦ tmnp.co.za

Most people come out to Tokai to picnic and mountain bike in the pine plantations of **Tokai Forest**, which was granted a reprieve from logging in early 2017. It is best to come in a group and stick together, as muggings have occurred. A challenging and exposed trail zigzags 6km up the Constantiaberg from the arboretum to the **Elephant's Eye Cave** (see p.104). Phone the arboretum for an update before coming; hikers had no access and mountain bikers had limited access at the time of writing, following summer

4

bush fires. Mountain bikers can ride up to the cave on Saturday and Sunday, with permits and car parking available in the picnic area and plans to extend the access to weekdays. Visit ⓦtokaimtb.co.za for more information.

You can get here from the M3 via Tokai Road, which runs west into the forest. About 500m west of Orpen/Steenberg Road (M42), you'll pass through pine forests equipped with **picnic tables**, though it's worth carrying on to the arboretum when it reopens. A little further along the road from the picnic sites, you can't fail to see the imposing and famously haunted **Tokai Manor House** (not open to the public). Designed by Louis Michel Thibault and built around 1795, this National Monument is an elegant gem of Cape Dutch architecture combined with the understated elegance of French Neoclassicism.

Tokai Arboretum

This **historic tree plantation** and National Monument is the work of Joseph Storr Lister, Conservator of Forests for the Cape Colony. In 1885, he experimented with planting 150 species of tree from temperate countries, including many oak and eucalyptus, as well as some beautiful California redwoods. Storr discovered that conifers were best suited to the Cape, hence the surrounding plantations consisting mainly of pines. Sadly, following devastating **bush fires**, the arboretum was closed at the time of writing; when it reopens, it is the best place in Tokai Forest to begin rambling and an ideal spot for **children**, with outdoor seating, plenty of shade and logs to scramble over.

4

The Cape Flats and the townships

The windswept **Cape Flats**, reaching well beyond the airport, is Cape Town's largest residential quarter, taking in the **coloured districts**, **African townships** and **informal settlements** (shantytown squatter camps). The Cape Flats are exactly that: flat, barren and populous, inhabited by black and coloured people in mostly separate areas and varying degrees of poverty. But they are certainly not without hope.

While countless projects are under way to foster entrepreneurship, alleviate social problems and attract tourists to the townships, everyday life in these grey and littered

---

THE HISTORY OF THE TOWNSHIPS

The African **townships** were historically set up as dormitories to provide labour for white Cape Town – not as places to build a life, which is why they had no facilities and no real communal hubs. The **men-only hostels**, another apartheid relic, are at the root of many of the area's social problems. During the 1950s, the government set out a blueprint to turn the tide of Africans flooding into Cape Town. No African was permitted to settle permanently in the Cape west of a line near the **Fish River**, the old frontier over 1000km east of Cape Town; women were entirely banned from seeking work in Cape Town and men prohibited from bringing their wives to join them. By 1970, there were ten men for every woman in Langa (see p.264). At the end of apartheid, hostels nationwide saw scenes of violence when black-on-black conflict began to erupt, as the **Bang-Bang Club** book and film recount.

The apartheid strategists ultimately failed to prevent the influx of job-seekers desperate to come to Cape Town. Where people couldn't find legal accommodation, they set up **squatter camps** of makeshift iron, cardboard and plastic sheeting. During the 1970s and 1980s, the government attempted to demolish these – but no sooner had the police left than the camps reappeared, and they remain a permanent feature of the Cape Flats.

One of the best known of all South Africa's squatter camps is **Crossroads**, located across the N2 highway from Cape Town International Airport. Its inhabitants suffered campaigns of harassment that included killings by apartheid collaborators and police, and continuous attempts to bulldoze it out of existence. Through sheer determination and desperation they hung on, eventually winning the right to stay, and now the shacks have been joined by tiny brick houses, with electricity supplies and running water improving the residents' quality of life.

TOWNSHIP HIGHLIGHTS

While we don't recommend independent trips to the townships, you can ask to visit these highlights on your guided tour.

Gugulethu Seven Memorial and Amy Bielh Memorial Gugulethu. Seven solid and powerful granite statue-like constructions honour the struggle and death of the Gugulethu Seven, an anti-apartheid group who were shot and killed by members of the South African police force in 1986. Nearby, a cross marks the site where Amy Biehl, a white American anti-apartheid activist, was murdered by local residents in 1993. A moving tribute to her courageous, all-too-short life (Steve Biko St; ⓦamybiehl.co.za).

★ **Guga S'Thebe Arts & Cultural Centre** Langa. With art studios, a shop, an outdoor amphitheatre and a theatre constructed from recycled materials, this dynamic community centre nurtures creativity from drumming, theatre and pottery to sand art, beadwork and mosaics. There's free wi-fi and *Kaffa Hoist Café* (see p.126) serves locally roasted Deluxe Coffeeworks coffee. The centre's location just off the N2 makes it easy to visit with your own wheels, although you will get more out of the experience on a guided tour; a car guard watches vehicles parked outside. Jazz in the Native Yards concerts (ⓦfacebook.com/nativeyards) take place here from time to time (cnr King Langalibalele/Washington Dr and Church St; daily 8.30am–6pm; free; ☎021 695 3493).

Ikhaya Le Langa Part of the Langa Quarter scheme to regenerate this neighbourhood, this social enterprise in an old primary school has attractions including a craft shop, café and "old skool toilets" with piped music. Facing it, ten homes with brightly painted facades have opened up their front rooms as art galleries. When we visited, the centre and home galleries were not running, but there were hopes of reopening so make enquiries if you visit the nearby Guga S'Thebe Arts & Cultural Centre (cnr Ndabeni and Rubuasna Sts; ⓦikhayalelanga.co.za).

★ **Langa Heritage Museum** Cape Town's only major township museum is dedicated to the "*dompas*" or pass system, which, during the apartheid years, required black citizens to carry a pass to enter "white-only" areas for work. The museum is located in the Old Pass Court, where people were tried for transgressing the pass laws. (King Langalibalele/Washington Dr; Mon–Fri 9am–4pm, Sat 9am–1pm, Sun by appointment; free; ☎084 949 2153 or ☎072 975 5442).

The Township Winery Philippi. This is Cape Town's first township- and black-owned winery, situated in an area where patches of farmland exist amid mass housing. The winery aims to increase community ownership by giving hundreds of individual homesteads Sauvignon Blanc vines to grow at their homes. Once harvested, they will go towards production of a wine called "Township Winery". Tastings by appointment (☎021 447 4476, ⓔinfo@townshipwinery.com, ⓦtownshipwinery.com).

neighbourhoods has considerable vibrancy, with children playing, hairdressers galore, people selling sheep's and goats' heads, and shisa nyama (township braais) smoking away on street corners. Some Africans who can afford to move out say they find the white-dominated suburbs sterile and unfriendly, and stay on in smart suburban houses. Nearby are former men-only hostels, where now as many as three families share one room, and shacks lining the N2.

Most tours visit **Langa**, the oldest (established 1927) and most central township, located across the M17 from the middle-class suburb of Pinelands; **Gugulethu** ('Gugs'), dating to the 1960s; or **Khayelitsha** (established 1983), one of South Africa's largest and fastest growing townships, with a population of around 2.5 million.

Visiting the Townships

The safest, easiest and most informative way to experience the townships is on a guided **tour**. These typically last half a day, cover one or two townships and include a visit to a local home for some food, as well as a crèche, church or community centre, and often a *sangoma* (traditional healer). Book ahead and check the price includes transport from your city-centre accommodation. It's possible, too, to gain a deeper understanding of the daily lives of the majority of South Africans by **staying overnight** in a township homestay or B&B (see box, p.115).

Visiting the townships under your own steam is not recommended: besides the threat of possible opportunistic crime, road signage is poor and opening and closing times erratic, so it's hard to find your way around.

TOURS

★**Andulela Tours** (see p.29). Recommended cultural tour company offering themed explorations, mostly of Langa; including the African Cooking Safari, gospel music tour and more general township tour.

Awol Tours ☎021 418 3803, ⌾awoltours.co.za. Walking tours of Gugulethu or the gardens of Seawinds (Muizenberg) and a cycling tour of Masiphumelele (Kommetjie).

★**Coffeebeans Routes** (see p.29). The cultural tour company offers day tours including Township Futures, which visits Khayelitsha CBD, the Langa Quarter and more, with a positive focus on township projects and potential; and night tours including the Jazz Safari.

Juma's Tours ☎073 400 4064, ⌾townshiparttours .co.za. Zimbabwean artist Juma Mkwela offers tours focused on the street art of Khayelitsha or Woodstock, with a Sunday itinerary incorporating lunch at a *shisa nyama*.

THE CAPE FLATS AND THE TOWNSHIPS

★**Maboneng Township Arts Experience** ☎021 824 1773, ⌾maboneng.com. The winner of an African Responsible Tourism Award 2017 (for engaging people and culture), Maboneng's Langa Home Gallery Tour of art galleries in township homes also includes the Guga S'Thebe Arts & Cultural Centre (see p.89) as well as street art and the Langa Heritage Museum (see p.89). One-hour, half- and full-day experiences are available, with African home cooking offered on longer itineraries.

Laura's Township Tours ☎082 979 5831, ⌾laurastownshiptours.co.za. Itineraries themed around cooking or gospel music, as well as a general tour, with Gugulethu local Laura Ndukwana.

Uthando ☎021 683 8523, ⌾uthandosa.org. Popular tours of Uthando's community projects, focused on work such as urban agriculture and animal welfare.

Vamos ☎072 499 7866, ⌾vamos.co.za. Walking and cycling tours and more.

4

Atlantic seaboard

Cape Town's chichi Atlantic suburbs cling in a dramatic ribbon to the lower slopes of Table Mountain, Lion's Head and Signal Hill. Although the open water on these northern and western flanks of the mountains can be chilly, the Atlantic seaboard offers mind-blowing views from some of the world's most scenic coastal roads, particularly beyond Sea Point. The coast itself consists of a series of bays and white-sand beaches edged with smoothly sculpted, bleached rocks; inland, the Twelve Apostles, a series of rocky buttresses, gaze down on the Camps Bays surf. The beaches are ideal for sunbathing, and it's from this side of the peninsula that you can watch the sun create fiery reflections on the sea and mountains as it sinks into the ocean. You'll find some of the city's most glamorous outdoor cafés and bars on this strip, where you can beautiful-people watch and enjoy the ocean views.

5

ARRIVAL AND DEPARTURE   **ATLANTIC SEABOARD**

BY BUS

MyCiTi ☎0800 65 64 63, ⊛myciti.org.za. From the city centre, buses #108 and #109 run down the Atlantic seaboard to Hout Bay, and the #106 and #107 cross Kloof Nek to Camps Bay. See individual listings for more details.

City Sightseeing ☎086 173 3287, ⊛citysightseeing .co.za. The clockwise Blue Mini Peninsula Tour runs from the Two Oceans Aquarium at the Waterfront via Long Street, the *Mount Nelson Hotel*, Kirstenbosch and Constantia

Nek to: World of Birds (1hr 5min), Imizamo Yethu (1hr 10min), Hout Bay Harbour (1hr 30min), Camps Bay (1hr 50min), Sea Point (2hr 7min) and Green Point (2hr 11min).

BY MINIBUS TAXI

Noordhoek, Kommetjie and Scarborough are not served by organized public transport; however, there are minibus taxis from Fish Hoek Train Station to Noordhoek and Kommetjie, at various times during the day, but most frequently during the morning and evening rush hours.

Green Point and Mouille Point

Green Point's proximity to the Waterfront – from which it's an easy ten-minute amble – and to the coast, as well as to the centre of Cape Town, has turned this once-sleazy district into a desirable location with good accommodation (see p.118) and cafés (see p.127). Adjoining Green Point is **Mouille** ("moo-lee") **Point**, known for its squat, rectangular, red-and-white-striped early nineteenth-century lighthouse. From here, you can walk or jog a few kilometres south along the safe and much-used coastal promenade to Sea Point and Bantry Bay.

Cape Town Stadium

Fritz Sonnenberg Rd • Tours Mon–Fri 10am, noon & 2pm • Adults R45, children under 12 R17 • ☎021 417 0120, ⊛capetown.gov.za

Hour-long tours explore the landmark Green Point **stadium built to host the 2010 World Cup** (see box below), mixing architectural information with a peek inside the football players' changing rooms. While here, take a tour or just wander across to **Green Point Park**, with its Biodiversity Showcase Garden, wetlands, maze and children's play park.

Sea Point

MyCiTi bus #104 (Sea Point to the Civic Centre via Beach Rd and the Waterfront); the City Sightseeing Bus also stops here

Nudging the western edge of Green Point, **Sea Point** is a **cosmopolitan area** known for its gay and Jewish communities, seafront apartment blocks and, for tourists, accommodation (see p.119) and restaurants (see p.128). The **Sea Point Promenade** is the best way to appreciate the rocky coastline and salty air, along with pram-pushing mothers, old ladies, power walkers and joggers. It's a symbol of the new nation, with locals of all colours enjoying the playgrounds, outdoor gym and public sculptures, in what was a white-only area. People picnic and play ball games on the **grassy parkland** beside the coastal walkway.

Driving through, take Beach Road rather than Main Road, which is busier and less scenic.

THE CAPE TOWN WORLD CUP STADIUM

Described by British architecture critic Jonathan Glancey as "a stunning white apparition … in a sublime setting", **Cape Town Stadium** was arguably the jewel in South Africa's 2010 World Cup crown. The towering, 68,000-seater stadium relies on natural light, and at night the open-meshed roof can light up to resemble an ethereal UFO. Controversy surrounded the high building costs, which were funded by taxpayers, and it was revealed that there had been **corruption** among the bidding construction companies in the tender process for the project.

While you may catch a **football match** in the stadium, it is seriously underutilized, and mostly fills during **concerts** by British and American pop and rock stars. Performances by the likes of U2, the Eagles and Kings of Leon still have serious novelty value here, following South Africa's pariah status under apartheid, when the country was roundly boycotted by international bands.

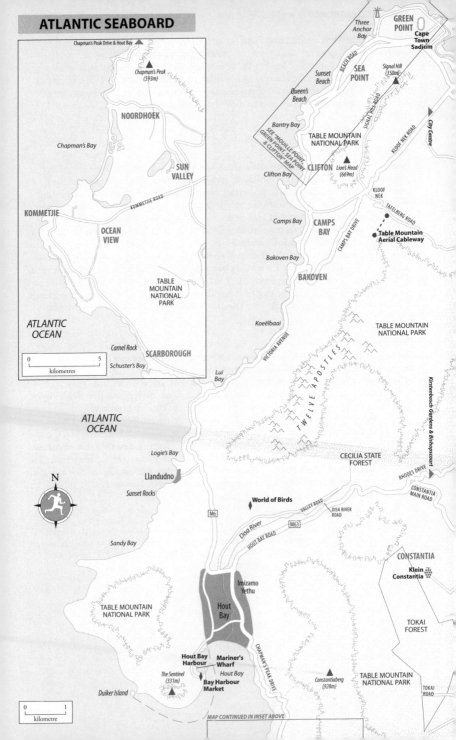

ATLANTIC SEABOARD

Chapman's Peak Drive & Hout Bay

▲ Chapman's Peak (593m)

NOORDHOEK

Chapman's Bay

SUN VALLEY

KOMMETJIE

OCEAN VIEW

KOMMETJIE ROAD

TABLE MOUNTAIN NATIONAL PARK

ATLANTIC OCEAN

Camel Rock

SCARBOROUGH

Schuster's Bay

0 — 5 kilometres

Three Anchor Bay

GREEN POINT

Cape Town Stadium

BEACH ROAD

SEA POINT

Signal Hill (350m)

Sunset Beach

Queen's Beach

SIGNAL HILL ROAD

KLOOF NEK ROAD

City Centre

Bantry Bay

TABLE MOUNTAIN NATIONAL PARK

SEE "MOUILLE POINT, GREEN POINT, SEA POINT & CLIFTON" MAP

CLIFTON

▲ Lion's Head (669m)

Clifton Bay

KLOOF NEK

TAFELBERG ROAD

Table Mountain Aerial Cableway

Camps Bay

CAMPS BAY

CAMPS BAY DRIVE

Bakoven Bay

BAKOVEN

Koeëlbaai

TABLE MOUNTAIN NATIONAL PARK

VICTORIA AVENUE

T W E L V E   A P O S T L E S

Lui Bay

ATLANTIC OCEAN

Kirstenbosch Gardens & Bishopscourt

CECILIA STATE FOREST

RHODES DRIVE

Logie's Bay

■ Llandudno

Sunset Rocks

World of Birds

M6

Disa River

VALLEY ROAD

DISA RIVER ROAD

M63

HOUT BAY ROAD

CONSTANTIA MAIN ROAD

Sandy Bay

CONSTANTIA

Klein Constantia

Imizamo Yethu

Hout Bay

TABLE MOUNTAIN NATIONAL PARK

TOKAI FOREST

CHAPMAN'S PEAK DRIVE

Hout Bay Harbour

Mariner's Wharf

Hout Bay

The Sentinel (331m) ▲

Bay Harbour Market

▲ Constantiaberg (928m)

TABLE MOUNTAIN NATIONAL PARK

TOKAI ROAD

Duiker Island

N

0 — 1 kilometre

MAP CONTINUED IN INSET ABOVE

5

Sea Point Pavilion Swimming Pool

Lower Beach Rd • Daily: May–Nov 9am–5pm; Dec–April 7am–7pm • Adults R22, children R11 • ☎ 021 434 3341

At the southwestern end of the Sea Point promenade is this set of four unheated filtered **saltwater pools**, beautifully located alongside the crashing surf. The largest of the four is Olympic-sized, making it a popular training tank for Cape Town's long-distance swimmers. There are also two children's splash pools and a fully equipped diving pool for the brave.

Clifton

MyCiTi bus #108 or #109 (Hout Bay to Adderley St via Victoria Rd, Sea Point and Green Point)

Rounding the coast from Bantry Bay to fashionable **Clifton**, you are now entering some of Africa's most expensive real estate, with house prices at the top end passing the R100 million mark. Beneath the fabulous seaside apartments, you can reach the four sandy, interlinked **beaches** via steep stairways. The sea here is good for surfing and safe for swimming, but bone-chillingly cold, though Clifton is notably sheltered from the southeasterly wind in summer. The northernmost and longest beach, Clifton First is frequented by muscular frisbee-players and laidback surfers, and is often the least crowded. Clifton Second is a **vibey hangout** for locals from teens upwards, while Third is the gay choice but open to all. If in doubt, head for Fourth, which is favoured by families with small kids by day, as it has the fewest steps; on still summer evenings, mellow groups of young people with candles hang out here from sunset onwards.

Camps Bay

The most direct MyCiTi buses from the city centre are #106 and #107 (from the Civic Centre via Adderley St, Long St, Kloof St and Kloof Nek Rd); #108 and #109 travel here along the Atlantic coast; and the City Sightseeing Bus stops here

The suburb of **Camps Bay** climbs the slopes of Table Mountain, scooped into a ridiculously scenic amphitheatre by Lion's Head and the Twelve Apostles. With views across the Atlantic in the other direction, this is one of the city's most affluent and downright gorgeous neighbourhoods. The coast-hugging main drag, **Victoria Road**, is packed with trendy restaurants, frequented by models on low-carb diets, while the wide sandy beach is enjoyed by families of all shapes and colours. Lined by a row of palms and some grassy verges with shade for picnics, the beach gets extremely busy around the Christmas and Easter breaks. However, it's exposed to the "southeaster" wind, and there's the usual Atlantic chill and the occasional dangerous backwash.

DUIKER ISLAND CRUISES

The best way to take in the Atlantic seaboard landscape is on one of the short cruises just out of Hout Bay, from the harbour to **Duiker Island**, sometimes called "seal island" because it's home to a massive **seal colony**. It makes for a great trip, and the seals are delightful clowns, even if their fishy smell will make you wish you'd packed your nose plugs.

South African, or Cape, fur seals are the largest of the fur seals, which accounts for their popularity among hunters, who began harvesting them in the seventeenth century. By 1893, when restrictions were introduced, the seal population was severely depleted. Controlled **hunting** in South Africa continued until 1990, when it was finally suspended, with the exception of two culls to protect gannet populations.

Of the operators running 45-minute tours to seal island, **Nauticat Charters** (8.45am, 9.45am, 11am, 12.45pm, 2.45pm & 3.45pm; R85; ☎ 021 790 7278, ⊛ nauticatcharters.co.za) and **Circe Launches** (8.45am, 9.30am, 10.15am & 11.10am; Adults R70, children under 14 R40; ☎ 021 790 1040, ⊛ circelaunches.co.za) have glass-bottomed boats which allow you to see the action underwater, as well as kelp forests when conditions are clear. The outings also provide **fabulous views** of the Sentinel, the distinctive formation on the promontory forming the bay's northwestern side, and Chapman's Peak.

Llandudno

MyCiTi buses #108 and #109 pass the entrance to Llandudno, from where it's a steep 20min walk down to the beach

There's little development between Camps Bay and the wonderful little cove of **Llandudno**, 20km from Cape Town along Victoria Road. A steep and narrow road winds down past smart homes to the shore, where the sandy beach is punctuated at either end by magnificent granite boulders and rock formations. A great spot for sunbathing and sunset watching alike.

Sandy Bay

A 20min walk from Llandudno

Isolated **Sandy Bay**, Cape Town's main nudist beach and a popular gay and lesbian hangout, can only be reached on foot from Llandudno. In the apartheid days, the police went to ingenious lengths to trap nudists, but nowadays the beach is relaxed, so feel free to come as undressed – or dressed – as feels comfortable. The path here leads from the Sunset Rocks car park, at the southern end of Llandudno, through *fynbos* vegetation and over rocks. There are no facilities whatsoever at Sandy Bay, so bring supplies.

Hout Bay

MyCiTi bus #108 or #109 (Civic Centre to Hout Bay via Camps Bay); the City Sightseeing Bus also stops here

Although no longer the quaint fishing village it once was, **Hout Bay** has a functioning fishing harbour and is the centre of the local crayfish industry. Some 20km from the centre (via Kloof Nek or the M3), it's a favourite **day-trip** for fish and chips at Mariner's Wharf (see p.128) or the lively **Bay Harbour Market** (see p.144), with a stunning bay overlooked by Chapman's Peak and the Sentinel.

The independently minded spot jokingly declared itself a republic in 1987, and began issuing **Hout Bay passports** and visas in defiance of President P.W. Botha's repressive government. Away from the harbour, the town is hanging onto a shred of its historic ambience, with a few art galleries on **Victoria Avenue**, but expanding townships and ugly modern developments are taking their toll.

Imizamo Yethu

Tours daily 10.30am, 1pm & 4pm • R75 • ☎ 083 719 4870, Ⓦ suedafrika.net/imizamoyethu • Tours start and end from the police station at the entrance to the township, where there are reserved parking places for visitors driving here; the City Sightseeing Bus also stops here

As you approach Hout Bay from Constantia Nek, you come to the township of **Imizamo Yethu**, a tightly packed shack-land settlement crawling up the hillside, more or less in the middle of Hout Bay. The **township** was first settled during the late 1980s, in the dying days of apartheid, by Xhosa job-seekers who had come from the Eastern Cape. Its population grew to tens of thousands before the terrible fire of March 2017, which destroyed over three thousand homes and displaced 15,000-plus people.

The awful tragedy followed positive developments such as the building of 450 brick houses with the help of Irish millionaire **Niall Mellon**. Mellon was so appalled by the conditions he saw in Imizamo Yethu during a visit in 2002 that he set up the Niall Mellon Township Trust (Ⓦ nmtownshiptrust.com) to provide subsidized housing in townships across South Africa – the trust is now one of the biggest housing charities in the country.

Enthusiastic guide **Afrika Moni**, who knows Imizamo Yethu and its history inside out, offers a two-hour **walking tour** of his home township. Along the way you stop to chat to proprietors of informal "spaza" shops, sip traditional beer at a *shebeen*, and pop into shacks and brick houses.

5

World of Birds

Valley Rd • Daily 9am–5pm; monkey jungle daily 11.30am–1pm & 2–3.30pm; feeding times: penguins 11.30am & 3.30pm, pelicans 12.30pm, cormorants 1.30pm, birds of prey 4.15pm • Adults R95, children R45 • ⓦ worldofbirds.org.za • The City Sightseeing Bus stops here

Hout Bay's biggest institutional attraction houses more than three thousand birds, in surprisingly pleasant and peaceful walk-through **aviaries**, as well as small mammals and reptiles. The setting, in lush gardens with a mountain backdrop, makes for a tranquil outing; you'll need about two hours to get the most out of your visit.

The four-hundred feathered species include **indigenous birds** such as cranes, vultures and pelicans, as well as a number of **exotics**. The large walk-in **monkey jungle** includes cute squirrel monkeys, which visitors are allowed to pet; there are also the popular meerkats.

Chapman's Peak Drive

Toll charge R42 • ☎ 021 791 8222, ⓦ chapmanspeakdrive.co.za

The thrilling **Chapman's Peak Drive**, which winds along a cliff-edge south of Hout Bay to Noordhoek, is one of the world's great ocean drives. There are a number of safe viewpoints along the route, some of which have picnic sites, so bring snacks and refreshments, and stop to enjoy the spectacular views. Affectionately known as "Chappies", the road is occasionally closed due to rockfalls, so phone or check online for the current situation before setting off.

Noordhoek

Alternatively minded **Noordhoek** is the heart of the "lentil curtain", as the peninsula's arty, surfy Atlantic seaboard is jokingly known (Cape Town's Afrikaner-dominated Northern Suburbs, meanwhile, are nicknamed the "boerewors curtain"). Noordhoek even has a **hemp house** available for the night, through Airbnb. The desirable settlement at the southern end of the descent from Chapman's Peak Drive, a 35km

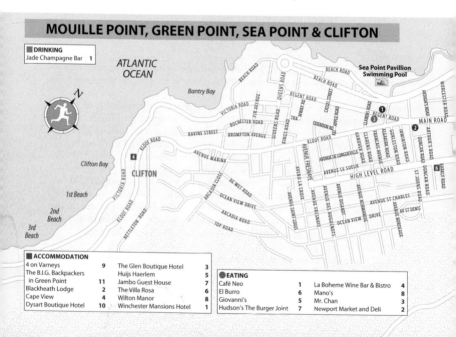

MOUILLE POINT, GREEN POINT, SEA POINT & CLIFTON

■ DRINKING
Jade Champagne Bar   1

ATLANTIC OCEAN

Bantry Bay

Sea Point Pavillion Swimming Pool

Clifton Bay

CLIFTON

1st Beach

2nd Beach

3rd Beach

■ ACCOMMODATION			
4 on Varneys	9	The Glen Boutique Hotel	3
The B.I.G. Backpackers in Green Point	11	Huijs Haerlem	5
		Jambo Guest House	7
Blackheath Lodge	2	The Villa Rosa	6
Cape View	4	Wilton Manor	8
Dysart Boutique Hotel	10	Winchester Mansions Hotel	1

● EATING			
Café Neo	1	La Boheme Wine Bar & Bistro	4
El Burro	6	Mano's	8
Giovanni's	5	Mr. Chan	3
Hudson's The Burger Joint	7	Newport Market and Deli	2

drive from the city centre, consists of smallholdings and riding stables in a gentle valley planted with oaks. When Chapman's Peak is closed, Noordhoek is accessible via the M3 south over Ou Kaapse Weg.

Long Beach

On the right, if you're heading from Chapman's Peak towards Noordhoek Farm Village (see below), is the turning for Avondrust Circle, which leads to **Long Beach**. Turn onto Beach Road and wind through a residential area until you reach a parking area, from where you can walk 8km across the white, kelp-strewn sands to Kommetjie. Each morning between 7.30am and 9am, **racehorses** are galloped along the sand, and you will invariably see riders (see p.148) sharing the wide beach with local dog walkers. The sea is cold, wild and spectacular to look at, framed by Chapman's Peak. Experienced **surfers** relish the area close to the rocks at the base of the peak.

Note that strong winds can sometimes turn the beach into a sandblaster. Signposted from Beach Road is *Monkey Valley Resort* (see p.120), which welcomes non-guests for reasonably priced meals with great views, and its groves of milkwood trees offer shelter from the wind.

Food markets take place at Noordhoek Farm Village on Wednesday and Cape Point Vineyards on Thursday (see p.98).

Noordhoek Farm Village

Village Lane • Opening hours vary for the different establishments, food market Weds 4–8pm • ⓦ noordhoekvillage.co.za

Close to the signposted entrance to Chapman's Peak Drive, **Noodhoek Farm Village** is a **rural mall** that is one of the Cape Peninsula's pleasantest shopping venues, and an excellent choice if you're on holiday with children. The village is laid out like a Cape Dutch farmstead; the manor houses a hotel and has outbuildings arranged around a yard. The complex is home to the excellent *Foodbarn* (see p.128) restaurant, deli and tapas bar, as well as a pub, café, sushi bar, children's playground, craft shops and more. The weekly outdoor **market** features food by the Village traders ranging from Italian to Mexican.

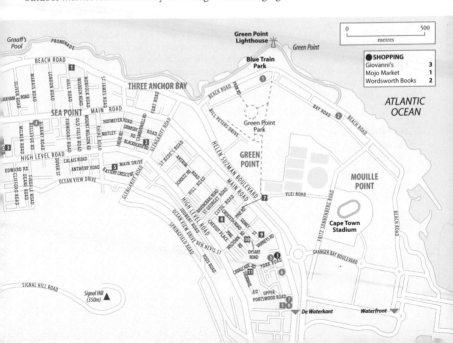

5

MASIPHUMELELE BICYLE TOUR

Tying in with a bike-based community scheme, Awol Tours (☎021 418 3803, ⓦawoltours.co.za) offers a **guided cycle tour** around Kommetjie's **Masiphumelele township**, learning about Xhosa customs en route, visiting a crèche and a *sangoma* (traditional healer) and stopping for lunch at a township café or home. The half-day tour costs R950 per person, R1850 including transfers. Prices are based on two people; single guests pay a supplement.

Cape Point Vineyards

Silvermine Rd · Tastings Mon–Weds & Fri–Sun 11am–6pm, Thurs 11am–2pm; picnics Mon–Weds & Fri–Sat noon–4pm; community market Thurs 4.30–8.30pm · Taster R10; platter R95–295; picnic basket for two R395 · ☎021 789 0900, ⓦcpv.co.za

Cape Point Vineyards, the main producer in the Cape Point wine region, is known for its mineral-characterised sauvignon blancs, made with the help of the cooling sea breezes. The vineyard offers a lavish picnic basket which you can eat on slopes close to the farm dam, with views over the distant beach and mountains. Order a day in advance.

Kommetjie

Kommetjie (pronounced "kom-ma-key"), the last major settlement as you follow the Atlantic coast south, and some 40km from central Cape Town, is a small, sleepy and attractive seaside town, dominated by Slangkop Lighthouse. It is built around a small rocky inlet, called **De Kom** (Afrikaans for basin), where you can walk around or take a dip in the water.

Kommetjie is another favourite **surfing** spot for the very experienced; if you want to learn, though, Muizenberg is the place (see p.100). Its stretch of the 8km **Long Beach**, which rolls all the way to Noordhoek, is a winner for a sunset stroll, with stunning views up the coast of Chapman's Peak and Hout Bay.

Imhoff Farm Village

Kommetjie Rd, opposite the Ocean View turn-off · Free · Opening hours vary for the different establishments · ☎021 783 4545, ⓦimhofffarm.co.za

With camels kneeling at the entrance, **Imhoff Farm Village** is a favourite place for kids (see p.154), with camel rides, farmyard delights and more. The complex also has several art galleries and craft shops, a cheesemaker, sushi bar, coffee shop and the **Blue Water Café** (see p.128), an excellent and well-priced restaurant in a Cape Dutch manor. Offering wood-fired pizza, a jungle gym and views onto the wetlands, it makes an inviting lunch stop on a peninsula tour.

Scarborough

The idyllic village of **Scarborough**, around 10km south of Kommetjie, is the most far-flung settlement along the peninsula, with cold, turquoise water and white sands. It's a lovely, easy drive to/from Simon's Town, winding over the spine of the peninsula, with a turning to **Cape Point** en route.

The False Bay seaboard to Cape Point

In summer, the waters of False Bay are several degrees warmer than those on the Atlantic seaboard, which is why Cape Town's oldest and most popular seaside towns line this flank of the peninsula. From Muizenberg down to Simon's Town via St James, Kalk Bay and Fish Hoek, this series of historic suburbs strung between mountain and beach are served by Metrorail stations. The train ride is reason enough to visit, and from Muizenberg most stations are situated close to the surf. Each suburb has its own character and places to eat, drink and sleep, while Simon's Town, one of South Africa's oldest settlements, makes either a pleasant day-trip or a relaxing base for visiting the penguins at Boulders Beach, just south of town, and Cape Point itself. This may be the peninsula's less moneyed coastline, but it is no less beautiful with Cape Point as its dramatic finale.

6

ARRIVAL AND DEPARTURE

By car Driving here from central Cape Town, the best route is along the M3 south to Muizenberg. Boyes Drive, a high-level alternative to coastal Main Rd, runs for about 7km between the suburbs of Lakeside at the southern end of the M3 and Kalk Bay, and offers spectacular views across to the Hottentots Holland Mountains on the east side of False Bay. The road is also one of several spots on the Cape Peninsula where, at the right time of year, you might spot whales (see box, p.103).

By train On Metrorail's safe and popular Southern Line from Cape Town to Simon's Town, there are roughly three trains an hour from Monday to Friday (5.10am–9.15pm;

FALSE BAY SEABOARD

1hr 15min; R16.50) and four as far as Fish Hoek (58min; R13.50). Trains travel via Muizenberg (48min; R13.50), St James (51min; R13.50) and Kalk Bay (55min; R13.50); on Saturday and Sunday, services are reduced to roughly one an hour from Cape Town to Simon's Town. Travel in MetroPlus (nominal first class) and stick to daylight hours, departing between about 7am and 6pm, for safety. The trains fill up heading into the city on weekday mornings before 9am, and leaving town on weekday afternoons after 4pm. Metrorail (☎ 021 449 6478, ⍟ metrorail.co.za, ⍟ cttrains.co.za) provides telephonic timetable information, and downloadable PDFs are available from their website.

Muizenberg

Once boasting South Africa's most fashionable beachfront, **Muizenberg** (pronounced "mew-zin-burg"), 27km from the city centre, is rising from the doldrums with the beautification of its seafront, where cafés, restaurants and bars overlook the sand. On its long, safe and fabulous **beach**, the brightly coloured Victorian **bathing chalets** are cheerful reminders of a more elegant heyday. During the 1920s, it was visited by the likes of crime novelist **Agatha Christie**, who learnt to surf – and wipe out – here. "One soon got the knack of coming in on the waves," she wrote. Today, the water is invariably bobbing with dozens of surfers; you can hire boards and organise lessons at the **surf shops** on Beach Road (see p.150).

The beach

Muizenberg Water Slides mid-Sept to April Mon–Fri 1.30–5.30pm, Sat & Sun 9.30am–5.30pm; night slide Fri 6–9pm • R45 per hr, R85 per day • ☎ 021 788 4759, ⍟ muizenbergslides.co.za

Muizenberg's gently shelving, sandy **beach** is the most popular stretch of sand along the peninsula for swimming, especially on Sundays in summer, though note that it can be windy.

At the eastern end of the esplanade, a **water park** with a trio of slides keeps kids well occupied. Muizenberg's shabby-chic hinterland is also worth a wander, frequented by the local artistic fraternity as well as a Congolese community.

Historical Mile

A short stretch of the shore, stretching south from **Muizenberg Station**, is known as the **Historical Mile**, dotted with notable buildings and easily explored on foot. The train station, a late Edwardian-style edifice completed in 1913, is now a National Monument, while the nearby **Posthuys** was once a lookout for ships entering the bay. A rugged whitewashed and thatched building dating from circa 1673, it is a fine example of the Cape vernacular style.

BEACH SAFETY TIPS

Don't take anything **valuable** to the beach, and don't leave anything unguarded while you're there, as opportunist **theft** is rife. Guards are present at the car park, so preferably leave valuables in your car boot – and place them there discreetly. False Bay is also home to **great white sharks**, and you will notice shark flags raised and a siren calling surfers and bathers out of the water when a shark is spotted.

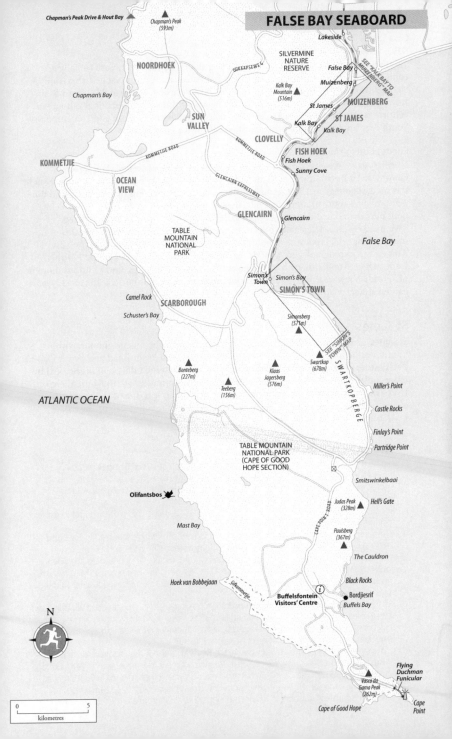

FALSE BAY SEABOARD

Chapman's Peak Drive & Hout Bay

Chapman's Peak
(593m)

Lakeside

SILVERMINE
NATURE
RESERVE

False Bay

Muizenberg

NOORDHOEK

SUUKAAPSEWEG

Kalk Bay
Mountain
(516m)

MUIZENBERG

St James

SUN
VALLEY

ST JAMES

Chapman's Bay

Kalk Bay

Kalk Bay

CLOVELLY

KOMMETJIE ROAD

FISH HOEK

KOMMETJIE

Fish Hoek

KOMMETJIE ROAD

Sunny Cove

OCEAN
VIEW

GLENCAIRN EXPRESSWAY

GLENCAIRN

Glencairn

False Bay

TABLE
MOUNTAIN
NATIONAL
PARK

Simon's
Town

Simon's Bay

SIMON'S TOWN

Camel Rock

SCARBOROUGH

Simonsberg
(571m)

Schuster's Bay

SWARTKOPBERGE

Swartkop
(678m)

Bonteberg
(227m)

Klaas
Jagersberg
(576m)

Miller's Point

ATLANTIC OCEAN

Teeberg
(156m)

Castle Rocks

Finlay's Point

Partridge Point

TABLE MOUNTAIN
NATIONAL
PARK
(CAPE OF GOOD
HOPE SECTION)

Smitswinkelbaai

Olifantsbos

Judas Peak
(328m)

Hell's Gate

CAPE POINT ROAD

Mast Bay

Paulsberg
(367m)

The Cauldron

Hoek van Bobbejaan

Gifkommetjie

Buffelsfontein
Visitors' Centre

Black Rocks

Bordjiesrif

Buffels Bay

Flying
Dutchman
Funicular

Vasco da
Gama Peak
(262m)

Cape
Point

N

Cape of Good Hope

0   5
kilometres

Casa Labia

192 Main Rd • Tues–Sun 10am–4pm • Free • ☎ 021 788 6068, ⓦ casalabia.co.za

The most idiosyncratic of the buildings along the Historical Mile, **Casa Labia** was completed in 1930 as the residence of the Italian consul, Count Natale Labia. Built in eighteenth-century Venetian style, it's a glorious piece of architectural bling on Main Road and worth popping into just for the palazzo's film-set interiors. It also houses a **cultural centre** that puts on concerts and talks, a **gallery** of modern and contemporary South African art, an opulently furnished **café** and a craft shop.

Rhodes Cottage Museum

246 Main Rd • Mon–Sat 10am–2pm • Admission by donation • ☎ 021 788 1816, ⓦ facebook.com/RhodesCottageMuseum

Controversial British mining magnate, politician and empire builder **Cecil Rhodes** bought this modest cottage in 1899, as a recuperative seaside retreat. His plan was to spend time here while his more monumental pile, **Rust en Vrede** (closed to the public), was being built next door. He died at the cottage in 1902, before the house was completed.

Manned by knowledgeable volunteers, the **Rhodes Cottage Museum** contains memorabilia which paints a (somewhat rosy) portrait of the infamous colonialist. Among the photographs are a model of the Big Hole in Kimberley in the Northern Cape, where Rhodes made his fortune at the diamond diggings, and a curious diorama of World's View in Zimbabwe's Matopos Hills, where he was buried. The lovely *fynbos* garden straggles up the mountainside.

St James

St James, 2km south of Muizenberg, is more upmarket than its neighbour, with its mountainside homes reached up long stairways between Main Road and Boyes Drive. The best reason to hop off the train here is for the **sheltered tidal pool**, overlooked by more multicoloured bathing chalets, and the twenty-minute walk to Muizenberg on the **paved coastal path**. Running along the rocky shore, it is one of the peninsula's easiest and most rewarding walks, with panoramas of the full sweep of False Bay. Look out for seals, and in season, whales.

THE CAPE DUTCH REVIVAL

During the 1890s, millionaire tycoons such as British expatriate **Cecil Rhodes** found themselves at the top of the South African pecking order. These men saw themselves as an Anglo-African aristocracy lording it over the country, much as the landed gentry did back in Britain. The **Randlords**, as Johannesburg's mining magnates were known, and characters like Rhodes in the Cape were among the biggest patrons of architecture, as they sought to express their new power and status.

Rhodes commissioned **Herbert Baker**, a young English architect schooled in the British Arts and Crafts Movement, to rebuild **Groote Schuur** following a fire in 1896. The grand mansion on Klipper Road in Rondebosch is now South Africa's official presidential residence. Looking for inspiration, Baker identified Cape Dutch architecture (see box, p.85) as a suitable model – it was old and it represented wealth, making it the closest local equivalent to the stately homes of England.

Baker used recognizable **Cape elements** such as gables, curving multi-paned windows and steeply pitched roofs. He also drew on English traditions, such as barley-sugar chimneys that hark back to Tudor architecture, while bird figures that Rhodes removed from Great Zimbabwe were used to suggest the gargoyles of Gothic architecture.

This style came to be known as **Cape Dutch Revival**, and was used again by the architect at **Rust en Vrede** (1902), Rhodes' seaside residence, adjacent to Muizenberg's Rhodes Cottage Museum (see above). The Cape Dutch Revival has become well established in South African architectural parlance: the twentieth century saw the appearance of Cape Dutch features, particularly **gables**, in suburban houses, no matter how inappropriate the scale or context.

WHALE SPOTTING ON THE FALSE BAY SEABOARD

The most common whales you'll see off the Cape are **southern rights**, and the warmer **False Bay** side of the peninsula has the best **whale-watching spots** in season (roughly June–Nov). There is some chance of spotting them on the **Atlantic seaboard**, too; whichever coastline you're visiting, you should have binoculars handy. The months when you are more or less guaranteed sightings are September and October.

Boyes Drive, which runs along the mountainside above Muizenberg, St James and Kalk Bay, provides an outstanding vantage point. To get here by car, take the M3 from the city centre to Muizenberg; at Lakeside, look for the sharp, signposted right turn into Boyes Drive. The road climbs from here, descending finally to join Main Road in Kalk Bay.

Alternatively, if you stick close to the shore along Main Road, the stretch between **Fish Hoek** and **Simon's Town** is recommended, with a nice spot above the rocks at the south end of Fish Hoek Beach, as you walk south towards Glencairn. As well as penguins, **Boulders Beach** (see p.108) has a whale signboard and smooth rocky outcrops above the sea to sit on and gaze across the water. Further south, you might also spot them in **Miller's Point**, Smitswinkelbaai and the Cape of Good Hope Nature Reserve.

Without a car, you can catch the train to Fish Hoek or Sunny Cove and whale-spot from the **Jager's Walk** beach path, which follows the coast between the two, just below the train line.

It's worth noting that there are more spectacular spotting opportunities further east, especially around **Hermanus** (see p.180) and **De Hoop** (see p.188).

Although False Bay is great for land-based whale watching, on a boat you get a different perspective: you're in the gargantuan marine mammals' own element and you may just get a closer look. There are also opportunities to spot other whales such as Bryde's, humpbacks and orcas, and other marine animals including dolphins and seals (both visible all year). Simon's Town Boat Company (☎083 257 7760, ⊚boatcompany.co.za), based at the Simon's Town pier, offers boat-based False Bay **whale-watching trips** (daily 10.30am & 2pm; adults R900, children under 12 R600). They also run cruises around Cape Point (adults R600, children under 12 R500) and to Seal Island (adults R450, children under 12 R350).

The beach

The compact St James **beach** draws considerable character from its much-photographed Victorian-style huts, whose bright, primary colours catch your eye as you pass by on the road or by rail. The beach tends to be overcrowded at weekends and during school holidays; far fewer visitors stroll south on the short footpath to the adjacent sandy stretch of **Danger Beach**, an excellent spot for sunbathing and building sand-castles. As the name suggests, its surf should be treated with respect, as there is a powerful undertow here.

Kalk Bay

One of Cape Town's smallest and most southerly suburbs, **Kalk Bay** centres around a lively working harbour with wooden fishing vessels, mountain views and a strip of shops brimming with collectables, antiques dealers and plenty of places to eat and drink. Uniquely, Kalk Bay managed to resist the Group Areas Act (see p.265), making it one of the few places on the peninsula with an intact coloured community. As well as coloured fishermen, the 275-year-old settlement is home to numerous artists and creative types, who thrive on Kalk Bay's village atmosphere and natural beauty.

The settlement is arranged around the small **harbour**, one of South Africa's oldest, where you can watch the boats come in. You can also buy **fresh fish**, which are flung onto the quayside and sold in a spirited fashion, though stocks are declining and fishing folk increasingly have to battle for permits. The harbour and seafront are busiest over weekends, when Capetonians descend to pick up something for the braai or to have lunch at the terrifically located **restaurants** (see p.129), some within spitting distance of the breakers.

Mellow Yellow Water Taxi runs an hourly service between Kalk Bay Harbour and Simon's Town (see p.110).

Silvermine Nature Reserve

Ou Kaapse Weg • Daily: May–Aug 8am–5pm; Sept–April 7am–6pm • R50 • ☎ 021 701 8692

Part of the Table Mountain National Park, the stunning **Silvermine Nature Reserve** rises behind Boyes Drive and stretches west across the peninsula's spine, almost to Chapman's Peak. The **walks** here in the Table Mountain chain of peaks provide fabulous views of False Bay, the mountains and montane *fynbos*, and you can **picnic** next to the idyllic Silvermine Dam.

It's possible to get into the eastern half of the reserve for free via paths that strike up from Boyes Drive, including a set of stairs in **Kalk Bay** that climbs from Boyes just as it turns to the harbour. The climb is worth it for the superb **views** of the ocean.

The **Silvermine Dam** area is the starting point for many of the reserve's best walks. To get here by car, take Ou Kaapse Weg (the M64 to Noordhoek), signposted at the southern end of the M3. The entrance is at the top of the tortuous **mountain pass** on the right-hand side. The road from the entrance gate leads through areas of *fynbos* to Silvermine Dam, where you can swim and picnic on the shore.

Alternatively, you can park at the entrance gate and do the easy and rewarding ninety-minute **River Walk** to the dam, which has no steep gradients, is well shaded and offers protection from the wind in summer. The other popular walk, which starts from the car park at the dam and offers sweeping views, is the two-and-a-half-hour climb up the Constantiaberg to **Elephant's Eye Cave**. Both walks are signposted.

Slingsby's excellent **Silvermine & Hout Bay map**, with hiking trails marked, is available at outdoor shops such as Cape Union Mart (ⓦcapeunionmart.co.za), which has branches at the Waterfront and the Gardens Centre, Cavendish Square, Constantia Village and Blue Route malls. Otherwise, the reserve's **brochure**, which is dispensed at the gate and can be downloaded from the SAN Parks website, features a sketchy map.

Fish Hoek

ⓦ fishhoek.com

Fish Hoek boasts one of the peninsula's finest family **beaches** along the False Bay coast. The best and safest swimming is at its southern end, where the surf is moderately warm, tame and much enjoyed by boogie boarders. Thanks to the beach, there's a fair

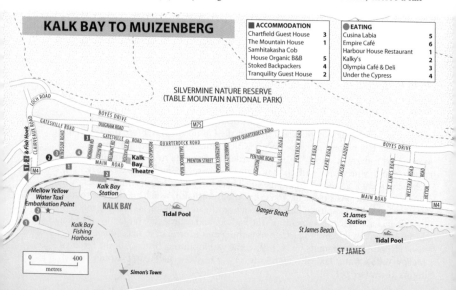

KALK BAY TO MUIZENBERG

■ ACCOMMODATION		● EATING	
Chartfield Guest House	3	Cusina Labia	5
The Mountain House	1	Empire Café	6
Samhitakasha Cob		Harbour House Restaurant	1
House Organic B&B	5	Kalky's	2
Stoked Backpackers	4	Olympia Café & Deli	3
Tranquility Guest House	2	Under the Cypress	4

amount of accommodation (see p.120), but this is otherwise one of the dreariest suburbs along the False Bay coast. An obscure by-law banning the sale of alcohol in supermarkets or bottle stores has cast Fish Hoek as the peninsula puritan, but liquor is now available in bars and restaurants.

Facilities include a playground, changing rooms, toilets, drinking water and the beachfront *Galley Restaurant*. From the restaurant, a picturesque pathway, **Jager's Walk**, provides a good vantage point for seeing whales. It skirts the rocky shoreline above the sea for 1km to Sunny Cove, from where it continues for 6km as an unpaved track to Simon's Town.

6

Simon's Town and around

Just 40km from Cape Town, roughly halfway down the peninsula to Cape Point, **Simon's Town** makes the perfect base for a mellow seaside break with good city access on Metrorail's Southern Line. Despite being the South African Navy's headquarters, having been a British Royal Navy base, Simon's Town isn't a hard-drinking port town. Rather, its well-preserved streetscape remains exceptionally pretty, bearing testament to its history as one of the country's oldest European settlements. The domineering **naval dockyard** mars the aesthetics, but this – and glimpses of naval squaddies square-bashing behind high walls or strolling to the station in their crisp white uniforms – adds to Simon's Town's distinct nautical flavour. A few kilometres to the south is the rock-strewn **Boulders Beach**, with its colony of nonchalant **African penguins** – reason enough to venture here.

Brief history

The Dutch East India Company founded Simon's Town in 1687 as their winter anchorage, and it became one of several places modestly named by **Governor Simon van der Stel** – after himself. Its most celebrated visitor was Lord Nelson, who convalesced here in 1776, as a midshipman en route home from the East Indies. Nineteen years later, the British sailed into Simon's Town and occupied it as a bridgehead for their first **invasion and occupation** of the Cape. They left after just seven years, but returned in 1806, and Simon's Town became a British base until 1957, when it was handed over to South Africa.

There are fleeting hints, such as the two **mosques** at the eastern end of Thomas Street, that the town's predominantly white appearance isn't the whole story. In fact, the first

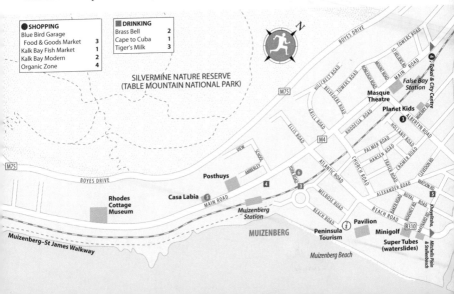

Muslims arrived from the East Indies in the early eighteenth century, imported as slaves to build the Dutch naval base. After the British banned the slave trade in 1807, ships were compelled to disgorge their human cargo at Simon's Town, where one district became known as Black Town.

In 1967, when Simon's Town was declared a White Group Area, there were 1200 well-established coloured families living here descended from these slaves. By the early 1970s, the majority had been forcibly removed under the Group Areas Act to the township of **Ocean View**, whose inspiring name belies its desolation.

Simon's Town Museum

Court Rd • Mon–Fri 10am–4pm, Sat 10am–1pm • R10 • ☎ 021 786 3046, ⓦ simonstown.com/museum/stm.htm

The town museum occupies the **Old Residency**, built in 1777 as the winter residence of the Governor of the Dutch East India Company, whose slave quarters (later a jail) can be seen in the basement. The museum's motley collection ranges from maritime exhibits and militaria to a whole room covering **Able Seaman Just Nuisance**, a much-celebrated **Great Dane**. He enjoyed drinking beer with the sailors he accompanied into Cape Town, and was adopted as a mascot by the Royal Navy in World War II, making Just Nuisance the only dog ever to have been enlisted in the Royal Navy.

The building also reputedly houses the **ghost** of Eleanor, the 14-year-old daughter of Cape governor Earl Macartney, who lived here in the closing years of the eighteenth century. Forbidden by her parents from playing on the sands with the children of coloured fishermen, Eleanor would escape to the beach through a secret tunnel she had discovered. The dankness of the tunnel supposedly gave her pneumonia, from which she tragically died.

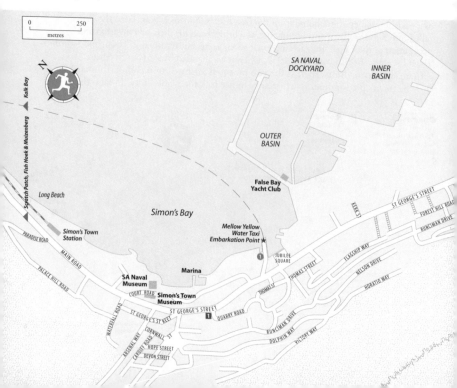

South African Naval Museum

West Dockyard, accessed from St George's St • Daily 9.30am–3.30pm • Free • ☎ 021 787 4686, ⓦ simonstown.com/navalmuseum/index.htm

The shipshape **South African Naval Museum's** lively displays include the inside of a submarine, a ship's bridge that simulates rocking, and numerous official portraits of South African naval commanders from 1922 to the present. Although much altered now, the museum occupies a mid-eighteenth-century Dutch East India Company **magazine and storehouse**, which was taken over by the Royal Navy when it installed its headquarters in Simon's Town in 1810. Ask about taking a guided tour of the **SAS Assegaai** submarine (ⓦnavy.mil.za/museum_submarine), which served thirty years in the South African Navy and closed for repairs in 2015.

6

Jubilee Square and the Marina

In the centre of Simon's Town, a little over 1km south of the station, lies **Jubilee Square**, a palm-shaded car park just off St George's Street. Flanked by some cafés and shops, the square has on its harbour-facing side a broad walkway with a statue of the ubiquitous **Just Nuisance** (see p.108) and stalls selling curios. In summer, a community food and craft **market** takes place here between 9.30am and 3pm on the second Saturday of the month.

A couple of sets of stairs lead down to the **Marina**, a modest development of shops and restaurants set right on the waterfront. This is a popular and scenic lunch stop, with the best **fish and chips** to be had at the *Salty Seadog* (see p.129).

Seaforth Beach

Seaforth Beach is the free version of the Boulders penguin reserve (see p.108), with many waddling visitors from the colony at neighbouring Boulders, especially in early morning and evening. The northern access point and car park for Boulders are also

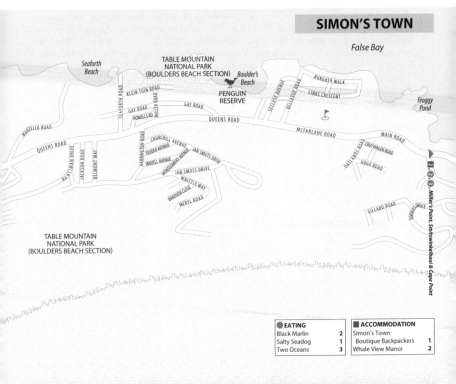

● EATING			■ ACCOMMODATION	
Black Marlin	2		Simon's Town	
Salty Seadog	1		Boutique Backpackers	1
Two Oceans	3		Whale View Manor	2

here. Seaforth is one of the best local beaches for **swimming**, with clear, deep waters lapping around rocks. It's calm, protected and safe, if not terribly pretty, being bounded on one side by the looming grey mass of the naval base. It does however have plenty of lawn shaded by palm trees, and a **restaurant** with outdoor seating and fresh fish on the menu.

Boulders Beach

Daily: Jan & Dec 7am–7.30pm; Feb, March, Oct & Nov 8am–6.30pm; April–Sept 8am–5pm • Adult R70, child R35 • ☎ 021 786 2329, ⓦ sanparks.org

6

Boulders Beach, Simon's Town most popular beach, takes its name from the huge rounded rocks that create a cluster of little coves with sandy beaches and clear, cold sea pools, which make for wonderful swimming. However, most people come to walk the boardwalks and see the colony of two thousand or more **African penguins** in the Boulders section of the Table Mountain National Park.

Also known as jackass penguins for their distinctive bray, African penguins usually live on islands off the Southern African coast, including Robben Island. The Boulders birds form one of only two mainland colonies, with the second 100km east in Betty's Bay. The reserve offers a rare opportunity to get a close look – and to hear that bray at its loudest, during the **breeding season** from March to May. Don't touch or feed the penguins, for they may look cute and cuddly but their beaks are razor sharp; if they feel threatened they have no qualms about nipping the odd finger or nose.

You can access Boulders from the signposted car park at Seaforth (see p.107), 2km east of Jubilee Square, or, further on, from the car park on the reserve's southern side, at the bottom of Bellevue Road.

Miller's Point

About 5km south of Simon's Town, this state-run **resort** and caravan park has a string of small sandy beaches and a tidal pool protected from the southeaster. Along Main Road, the *Black Marlin* **restaurant** (see p.129) attracts busloads of tourists, while the boulders around the point attract southern rock agama lizards, black zonure lizards and dassies.

Smitswinkelbaai

Heading south from Simon's Town, the last place you come to before the Cape of Good Hope Nature Reserve's gates is **Smitswinkelbaai** (pronounced "smits-vin-cull-buy"). This little cove has a small beach that is safe for swimming, but feels the full blast of the southeasterly wind. It's not accessible **by car**; to get here, you must park in the layby and walk down the steep path.

SHARK COUNTRY

False Bay is one of the best places in the country to encounter **great white sharks**. For one thing, the bay's sharks are on average about a third bigger than their counterparts in Gansbaai (near Hermanus), the main centre of the shark-cage diving industry.

Apex Shark Expeditions (Quayside Building, Main Rd; ☎ 021 786 5717, ⓦ apexpredators .com) is operated by naturalists Chris and Monique Fallows, who have worked with National Geographic and the BBC. They operate a range of marine trips in False Bay, among them shark-cage diving. Their emphasis is on observing shark behaviour – and that of other marine creatures you'll encounter on the trip out to Seal Island – rather than the adrenaline rush. Trips are in groups of a maximum twelve people, which means you have a personalized experience and everyone gets a good stint in the cage.

Trips leave from the pier in Simon's Town between February and September, and last three to four hours. Prices start at R2400 per person, and vary according to season (and the corresponding likelihood of encountering a shark).

6

By train If you're travelling by train to Simon's Town, you can arrange to be collected by HGTS Tours, who act as a taxi service and have an office on the station platform (☎021 786 5243, ⓦ hgtravel.co.za). A one-way trip to Boulders costs R30; an excursion to Cape Point, giving you 1hr 30min at the lighthouses and returning you to Simon's Town station at the end, is R500 excluding entry fees. Book ahead, especially for the latter tour.

Kalk Bay–Simon's Town water taxi Mellow Yellow

Water Taxi runs an hourly service between Kalk Bay Harbour and Simon's Town public jetty at the marina (daily 9am–4pm, on the hour from Simon's Town, half past the hour from Kalk Bay; R100 one-way, R150 return; ☎073 473 7684, ⓦ watertaxi.co.za). Although tickets can be bought on the boat, it's best to book ahead as the vessel takes a maximum of ten passengers and services are subject to the weather and whales crossing. The trip is highly recommended, and one of the few ways to get on the water in False Bay.

Cape of Good Hope Nature Reserve

Cape Point Rd • Daily: April–Sept 7am–5pm; Oct–March 6am–6pm • Adult R135, child R70 • ☎ 021 780 9010, ⓦ capepoint.co.za

Many people visit the **Cape of Good Hope Nature Reserve**, which is part of Table Mountain National Park, to see the southernmost tip of Africa and the place where the Indian and Atlantic oceans meet at **Cape Point**. In fact, this is the site of neither: the continent's real tip is at Cape Agulhas, some 300km southeast of here (see p.185). Cape Point is Africa's southwestern-most point, as well as being an awesomely **dramatic spot** and handily located compared with Cape Agulhas. You can also console yourself that the balmy **Agulhas Current**, which follows the Indian Ocean coast from Mozambique, meets the chilly **Benguela Current**, which heads up the Atlantic coast, on this stretch of coastline.

The 7750-hectare reserve sits atop massive sea cliffs with views, strong seas, and a wild wind which whips off caps and sunglasses as visitors gaze southwards from the old **lighthouse** buttress. European explorers called the headland the **Cape of Storms** for its treacherous weather; its ferocity also explains False Bay's name, given by mariners who confused it with Table Bay and realised they still had to round the stormy peninsula. The altogether sunnier title, Cape of Good Hope, came after **Vasco Da Gama** made it past in 1497, opening up a new trade route from Europe to India and the Far East.

FLORA, FAUNA AND FURRY FELONS

The majority of visitors to the **Cape of Good Hope Nature Reserve** make a beeline for Cape Point and take in the rest of the reserve through a vehicle window, but walking is the best way to appreciate indigenous **Cape flora**. At first glance the landscape appears rocky and bleak, with short, wind-cropped plants, but the vegetation is surprisingly rich. Amazingly, many bright blooms in Britain and the US, including varieties of geraniums, freesias, gladioli, daisies, lilies and irises, are hybrids grown from indigenous Cape plants.

Along with indigenous plants and flowers, there are animals living in the reserve's **fynbos** habitat, including over 250 species of bird. **Ostriches** stride through the low *fynbos*, and occasionally **African penguins** come ashore. A distinctive bird on the shores is the **black oystercatcher** which jabs limpets off the rocks with its red beak. You'll also see **Cape cormorants** in large flocks on the beach or rocks, often drying their outstretched wings. Running along the water's edge (where, as on any other beach walk in the Cape, you'll see piles of brown Ecklonia kelp) are **white-fronted plovers** and **sanderlings**, probing for food left by the receding waves.

As for mammals, **baboons** lope along the rocky shoreline, while **bontebok**, **eland** and **red hartebeest** graze along the heathery slopes, as do the smaller **grey rhebok** and **grysbok**. If you're very lucky, you may even see some of the extremely rare **Cape mountain zebras**.

Baboons may look amusing, but be warned: they can be a menace. Keep your car windows closed, as it's not uncommon for them to invade vehicles, and they're adept at swiping picnics. You should lock your car doors even if you only plan to get out for a few minutes to admire the view, as baboons have opened unlocked doors while the vehicle owner's back is turned. Do not ever unwrap food or eat or drink anything if baboons are in the vicinity. Feeding them is illegal and provocative, and can incur a R2500 fine. There are authorized **baboon chasers**, who ward off the animals, in several places across the reserve.

If you don't bring food, you can take in the view while you eat at *Two Oceans* (see p.129).

Flying Dutchman and the lighthouses

Flying Dutchman daily: April–Sept 9am–5pm; Oct–March 9am–5.30pm • Single: adult R50, child R20; return: adult R65, child R25 •
📞 021 780 9010, ⓦ capepoint.co.za

From the Cape Point car park, it's a short, steep walk – one crawling with tourists – up to the famous viewpoint, the original **lighthouse**. Leaving every three minutes, the **Flying Dutchman Funicular** runs to the top. It's named after the **ghostly galleon** that has haunted seafarers since 1641, when a Dutch ship sank off the Cape.

Built in 1860, the lighthouse was too often dangerously shrouded in cloud and failed to keep ships off the rocks, so in 1914 another was built lower down and closer to the Point. You can walk to this quieter **second lighthouse** from the base of the first, near the lower funicular station. It hasn't always been successful in averting disasters, but is still the most powerful light beaming onto the sea from South Africa.

Beaches

You'll find the **beaches** along signposted side roads branching out from the main Cape Point road through the reserve. The sea here is too dangerous for swimming, but there are safe tidal pools at the adjacent **Buffels Bay** and **Bordjiesrif**, midway along the east shore. Both have braai stands, but Buffels Bay is nicer, with grassy banks and sheltered spots to have a picnic (don't produce any food if there are baboons in the vicinity).

Walks

There are several marked **walks** in the Cape of Good Hope reserve. If you're planning a big hike it's best to set out early, as shade is rare and the wind can be strong, especially during summer, and it often increases in intensity as the day wears on. One of the most straightforward **hiking routes** is the signposted forty-minute walk from the car park at Cape Point to the more westerly **Cape of Good Hope**.

For exploring the shoreline, a clear path runs down the Atlantic side, which you can join at **Gifkommetjie**, signposted off Cape Point Road. From the car park, several sandy tracks drop quite steeply down the slope across rocks, and through bushes and milkwood trees to the shore, along which you can walk in either direction. Take plenty of **water** on any walk in the reserve, as there are no reliable fresh sources.

Navigators have been braving the rocks, winds and swells of Cape Point since the Portuguese first "rounded the Cape" in the fifteenth century. Several wrecks lie submerged off its coast, and at **Olifantsbos**, on the west side, you can walk to the *Lusitania*, a Portuguese ocean liner which hit the rocks in 1911; as well as the *Thomas T Tucker*, a US ship that sunk in 1942; and *Le Napoleon*, a French pirate ship that foundered in 1805 with the Royal Navy frigate *Narcissus* on its tail. Visit the **Shipwreck Trails** page of the Cape Point website for more details (ⓦ capepoint.co.za).

The multiday **Hoerikwaggo Trail** also leads to the reserve from Table Mountain (see p.78).

ARRIVAL AND INFORMATION   **CAPE OF GOOD HOPE NATURE RESERVE**

However you get to the reserve, go as early as you can in the day to avoid tour buses and the likelihood of the wind gusting more strongly as the day progresses.

By car Most visitors see the reserve as part of a circular driving trip, returning to town along the Atlantic seaboard and the scenic Chapman's Peak Drive (see p.96).
On a tour Numerous tours spend a day stopping off at Cape Point and other peninsula highlights. Day Trippers (📞 021 511 4766, ⓦ daytrippers.co.za) runs fun hiking and cycling tours for R850 (including entrance and picnic lunch); Baz Bus (see p.27) offers a similar tour for R750; and City

Sightseeing (📞 086 173 3287, ⓦ citysightseeing.co.za) visits on its daily Cape Point Explorer coach tour (R550).
Information The Buffelsfontein Visitor Centre (daily 9.30am–5.30pm; 📞 021 780 9204), 8km from the entrance gates and 6km from the Cape Point car park, boasts displays on the local fauna and flora as well as video screenings on the ecology of the area. Some tours stop here for lunch and guests cycle on to Cape Point.

CAPE HERITAGE HOTEL

Accommodation

Standards of accommodation are very high in Cape Town and cover an impressive range of options. In the city centre, you'll find outstanding boutique hotels, luxury guesthouses and welcoming hostels which often boast spectacular views of Table Mountain or the ocean. Move further along the Garden Route, and you'll discover country retreats in beautiful settings, ecolodges in old-growth forests and sumptuous beds in grand Victorian homes – at prices that would only get you a B&B in a Western country. Other than in the cheapest rooms, you'll always get a private bath or shower, and you'll often have use of a garden and pool, or even your own private patio. One unusual prospect – and one of the few ways to experience life as it is for the majority of South Africans – is to stay in an African township on the Cape Flats.

Although there's not much in the way of low-cost hotels, modest budgets are catered for by two main options. **Backpacker lodges** offer basic hostel accommodation in dorms, usually from around R200 per person, and private rooms. There's been a rise in **"boutique" backpackers**, which, as well as dorms, offer almost luxurious doubles, percale cotton sheets and feather duvets. Some backpacker places have family accommodation, some are quiet, but most, as is to be expected, are about socializing. They are independently run and listed in the free *Coast to Coast* guide, which covers the whole country and is widely available in tourist information offices and hostels countrywide.

Self-catering apartments are especially good if you are travelling as a family. You can expect kitchens to come with crockery and cutlery, and for linen and towels to be provided.

Nature lovers and hikers in search of isolated splendour can stay at the self-catering cottages and glamping sites dotted about **Table Mountain National Park** (book at the SAN Parks desk at Cape Town Tourism Office on Burg St, or on ⓣ021 487 6800, ⓦtmnp.co.za). For example, the four-bed *Orangekloof Tent* on the mountain costs R545 for two people; at the other end of the scale, the more luxurious, twelve-person *Olifantsbos Guest House*, right on the beach in the **Cape of Good Hope Nature Reserve** (see p.110), goes for R3620 for up to four people. Note that availability can be very limited over summer weekends.

Besides the many online booking services, the Cape Town Tourism website (ⓦcapetown.travel) can help you find accommodation for all budgets.

7

ESSENTIALS

Booking If you want to stay in a particular guesthouse in a central location, in high season, it's recommended that you book several months in advance.

Rates In this guide (including the "Beyond the city" chapters), accommodation prices are, unless stated otherwise, quoted as the lowest price for a double room with two people sharing in high season, though for backpacker hostels the rate for dorms is per person. Note, however, that on the ground many rates are quoted per person sharing rather than per room, with a single supplement applied to solo travellers – check on this when you book. Apart from at backpackers, an English breakfast is normally included – if not, it should be available to order. Wi-fi access is free unless noted in the review.

Seasons High season refers to the South African summer (Oct–March), when Cape Town is packed full to the brim – though note that prices rise again within this period, during Christmas and New Year and also over Easter. Autumn (April–May) and spring (Sept) are the shoulder seasons. There's a lull in the midwinter low season (June–Aug), during which time you can find good-value places to stay, often with hefty discounts.

THE CITY CENTRE

From **Long Street** and the surrounding area, you can walk to the museums, trawl Cape Town's best bars and clubs, eat at numerous restaurants and easily find transport to the Waterfront or out of the centre. There are backpacker lodges and hotels on Long Street itself, and you'll find several places to stay in quieter locations to the east, around the Company's Garden and the museums. Expect rooms fronting Long Street to be noisy.

★**Cape Heritage Hotel** 90 Bree St ⓣ021 424 4646, ⓦcapeheritage.co.za; map p.52. An exceptionally stylish, elegant and tastefully restored boutique hotel located in the redeveloped eighteenth-century complex at Heritage Square, where a walkway shaded by South Africa's oldest fruit-bearing grapevine links the hotel and central courtyard. The spacious rooms are decorated with contemporary handcrafted objects and original paintings. The service is charming and there's also a roof terrace and Jacuzzi. **R2850**

Daddy Long Legs Art Hotel 134 Long St ⓣ021 422 3074, ⓦdaddylonglegs.co.za; map p.52. Once part of the same chain as *Grand Daddy Hotel* (see p.114), and still affiliated with country cousin *Old Mac Daddy*, this playful boutique hotel's rooms were conceptualised by local artists, with themes from karaoke to the Karoo. One- and two-bedroom self-catering apartments are also available. Doubles and one-bedroom apartments **R1250**, two-bedroom apartments **R1450**

Dutch Manor Antique Hotel 158 Buitengracht, Bo-Kaap ⓣ021 422 4767, ⓦdutchmanor.co.za; map p.52. Travel back in time in this townhouse, which dates back to 1812 and is filled with period furniture, lavish tapestries and four-poster beds. Its pervasive sense of history is spoilt only by the proximity of busy Buitengracht, which the hotel's small balcony overlooks. The central location is certainly handy. **R2200**

Grand Daddy Hotel 38 Long St ☎021 424 7247, ⓦgranddaddy.co.za; map p.52. The *Grand Daddy* has a rooftop trailer park of seven retro-cool American Airstream caravans, decorated by local artists and linked by wooden walkways. Opt for one of these novel but small silver trailers or for one of the double rooms, which are also imaginative, colourful and funky. Doubles R2895, trailers R3695

iKhaya Lodge Dunkley Square, Wandel St ☎021 461 8880, ⓦwww.ikhayalodge.co.za; map p.47. This small hotel is on a pretty square, right by the Company's Garden and the museums, and close to a few good restaurants and bars in the regenerated East City area. There's a fun African decor, and accommodation ranges from rooms with balconies to single, doubles and triple loft apartments. Doubles R1225, loft apartments R1700

Long Street Backpackers 209 Long St ☎021 423 0615, ⓦlongstreetbackpackers.com; map p.52. Long Street may be famous for its backpacker hostels, but they mostly look tired compared with options in other areas – *Long Street Backpackers*, the strip's longest serving is one of the most dependable. It consists of a dozen small flats arranged around a leafy, mosaic-clad courtyard and bar. Dorms R190, doubles R350

Rose Street 28 28 Rose St, Bo-Kaap ☎021 424 3813, ⓦrosestreet28.co.za; map p.47. This good-value B&B consists of three townhouses on Rose street and Wale Street, simply but stylishly decorated with shared kitchen and courtyard and a friendly atmosphere. The main lodge occupies a grey-painted house in a row of colourful Bo-Kaap residences, with three dinky rooms inside. R890

Rouge on Rose 25 Rose St, at Hout St ☎021 426 0298, ⓦrougeonrose.co.za; map p.47. Nine modern, comfortable suites with bohemian studio chic reflecting the pastel Bo-Kaap facades outside. Beaded artworks liven up the muted urban decor and the suites are certainly spacious, with free-standing bath tubs, great views and self-catering facilities in some. R1800

St Paul's Guesthouse 182 Bree St, at Buiten St ☎021 423 4420, ⓦstpaul.org.za; map p.52. Established in 1933 by the neighbouring Anglican church, *St Paul's* is a welcome budget alternative to backpacker lodges for travellers who don't like reggae music. Appealingly simple and tranquil rooms have access to a vine-shaded courtyard, with breakfast included and secure parking available. R750

Scalabrini Guest House 47 Commercial St ☎021 465 6433, ⓦscalabrini.org.za; map p.47. This backpackers with a difference is attached to the Scalabrini Centre, which provides protection and support to vulnerable immigrants. Spacious, wooden-floored dorms and rooms, a kitchen, lounge and laundry service are on offer, and proceeds fund the centre's work – which guests can learn about in reception. It's an interesting area on the edge of the creative East City district, with numerous pubs and cafés nearby. Dorms R260, doubles R660

V&A WATERFRONT AND DE WATERKANT

In keeping with the gentrified ambience of the **V&A Waterfront** (usually referred to simply as the Waterfront), accommodation here tends to be expensive and you will find better value elsewhere. The waterside tourist precinct is a good choice nonetheless, offering shopping in a safe and self-contained area, pedestrianized walkways leading to restaurants and cafés, and a charming harbour atmosphere. Nearby, **De Waterkant** is an area of pretty, cobbled streets and terraced houses, with upmarket self-catering accommodation and good restaurants within easy reach of the city's best nightlife.

Breakwater Lodge Portswood Rd, Waterfront ☎021 406 1911, ⓦwww.breakwaterlodge.co.za; map p.66. One of the Waterfront's more affordable options occupies a historic nineteenth-century building – a prison to be exact. The modern hotel inside is linked to the University of Cape Town's Graduate School of Business, and offers a bar, restaurant, secure parking, and accommodation from studios to family rooms. R2150

★**Cape Grace** West Quay Rd ☎021 410 7100, ⓦcapegrace.com; map p.66. Among the Waterfront's many top-end hotels, the *Cape Grace* stands out for its sheer style, amenities and gracious customer service. *Bascule Bar* (see p.133) and *Signal Restaurant* (see p.124) are here, plus a range of luxurious rooms and suites, and sumptuous public areas overlooking the marina and Zeitz MOCAA. Staying here is memorable: the doormen greet you by name, champagne corks nudge the fruit juice in the lavish breakfast spread, and the introductory Cape wine tasting is on the house – as are the nightly port and sherry in the library, when the concierge team relieves parents of their little ones. R9948

De Waterkant Village 137 Waterkant St, De Waterkant ☎021 409 2500, ⓦdewaterkant.com; map p.66. These comfortable and contemporary self-catering properties include studios and one- to three-bedroom apartments and houses, dotted around De Waterkant's hilly streets. Guests can use the café, travel desk and services at affiliated guesthouse the *Charles*, thus enjoying a mix of hotel facilities and apartment privacy. Apartments (two person) R1400

St John's Waterfront Lodge 6 Braemar Rd, Green Point ☎021 439 1404, ⓦstjohns.co.za; map p.66. A 15min walk from the Waterfront, this solid, no-frills choice occupies a salmon-hued suburban house on a hillside street. Accommodation comes in dorms and private rooms, all with shared ablutions, and an en-suite flatlet, while the communal facilities include a swimming pool, an outdoor BBQ area, a sun deck and a travel centre. Dorms R140, doubles R530

AFRICAN TOWNSHIP HOMESTAYS

One of the best ways to get a taste of the African townships is to spend a night there, which is made possible by the growing number of township residents offering **B&B accommodation**. You'll have a chance to experience the warmth of **ubuntu** – traditional African hospitality – by staying with a family and sitting down to eat with them. They will often take you around their local area to **shebeens** (unlicensed bars), music venues, church, or just to meet the neighbours. **Prices** start around R400 for a double or twin room, which is considerably cheaper than the centre of Cape Town, and you'll get to experience something totally different.

Some B&Bs will send someone to meet you at the airport; if you're driving, they'll likely give you detailed directions or meet you at a convenient and obvious landmark. Many properties are listed on **Airbnb** and you can make bookings through Khayelitsha Travel (☎021 361 4505, ⓦ khayelitshatravel.com), while Maboneng Township Arts Experience (see p.90) and the Guga S'Thebe Arts & Cultural Centre (see p.89) can suggest options in Langa.

GUGULETHU

Liziwe's Guest House 121 NY 111 ☎021 794 1619, ⓦ mycapetownstay.com/Liziwe_s_Guest_House. Experience 'Gugs' while staying in one of Liziwe Ngcokoto's seven en-suite rooms, which have simple African decor and, in some, balconies with Table Mountain views. There are traditional African meals, township tours and visits to Gugulethu's memorials (see p.89) and Mzoli's *shisa nyama* (township braai). R700

KHAYELITSHA

Kopanong B&B C329 Velani Crescent ☎021 361 2084 or ☎082 476 1278, ⓦ kopanong-township .co.za. One of Khayelitsha's most dynamic B&B operations, run by the tireless Thope Lekau, who is on a mission to replace the busloads of tourists with guests who engage with township life. This Khayelitsha tourism guru and her daughter will treat you to a history of the city's largest township, introduce you to local music and dish up a hearty breakfast. Traditional dinners and tours are available with advance notice. R780

Majoro's B&B 69 Helena Crescent ☎021 794 1619, ⓦ mycapetownstay.com/MajorosBB. The charming Maria Maile hosts guests in her family home, which has a double and a twin sharing a bathroom and kitchen, in an upmarket part of the township. Meals include traditional dishes such as *mielie pap* (maize porridge), after which you can watch TV with the family or visit a local *shebeen*. The next day there's an English breakfast of sorts, which may include bacon and egg alongside fish cakes, sausages and home-made steamed bread. R900

Malebo's 18 Mississippi Way ☎021 361 2391, ⓦ airbnb.com/rooms/2156844. This B&B consists of five rooms, three en-suite, in the welcoming family home of chef Lydia Masoleng and husband Alfred. Her generous breakfast and traditional Xhosa meals are a treat, and activities include *shebeen* outings, township tours and Sunday church visits. R550

LANGA

Nomase's Guesthouse Cnr King Langalibalele/ Washington Dr and Sandile Ave ☎021 694 3904 or ☎083 482 8377, ⓦ tinyurl.com/y7729hun. Just a few hundred metres from Langa train station, the Langa Heritage Museum (see p.89) and Guga S'Thebe Arts & Cultural Centre (see p.89), the matriarchal Nomase offers clean, homely and secure rooms. The four en-suite bedrooms have plasma screen TV, one has a fridge and there's a kitchen with fridge and microwave. Breakfast is R30, dinner can be arranged and minibus taxis pass along the main drag outside. R450

CITY BOWL SUBURBS

The **City Bowl suburbs** are popular for accommodation, and the most northerly sections are just a 5–10min walk from the Company's Garden and the museums. A few backpacker lodges can be found on and around **Kloof Street**, the vibey continuation of Long Street, with some great cafés and restaurants. It's quieter and leafier than the city centre, especially the further up the mountainside you go, and you'll find gardens, good views and swimming pools at the more comfortable guesthouses. **New Church Street** is also quieter than Long Street, and well located for both the city and Table Mountain.

GARDENS

Ashanti Lodge 11 Hof St ☎021 423 8721, ⓦ ashanti .co.za; map p.77. This massive two-storey Victorian mansion has marbling and ethnic decor, soaring ceilings, a nicely kept front garden and a swimming pool with sun terrace. The private double and twin rooms, available

7

en-suite or with shared bathroom, and six- to eight-bed mixed and female-only dorms are simple, colourful affairs, while campers can pitch their tent outside. The bar is very lively, so if you are not a party animal, you might prefer their guesthouse, which offers en-suite double, twin and triple rooms, round the corner on Union St. *Ashanti* also has a backpackers in Green Point. Camping R140, dorms R250, doubles R780

★**Belmond Mount Nelson Hotel** 76 Orange St, rear entrance on Kloof St ☎021 483 1000, ⓦmountnelson .co.za; map p.77. Cape Town's *grande dame*: a fine and famous high-colonial Victorian hotel, built in 1899 (and extended in the late 1990s). Perfectly located, the building is set in extensive gardens, and the main entrance is via a majestic palm-lined driveway. Behind its jolly pink facade (originally painted to celebrate the end of WWI), the *Nellie* reflects its historical clout in room rates. Its location and grounds make its rooms, suites and garden cottages popular among movie-industry internationals, parliamentarians and anyone whose work trip is being sponsored; everyone else enjoys visiting for afternoon tea (see p.125). R9185

★**Once in Cape Town** 73 Kloof St ☎021 424 6169, ⓦstayatonce.com; map p.77. One of the most exciting new backpackers to open in recent years, hip *Once* offers four-bed mixed and female-only dorms, doubles and twins, all with en-suite bathroom, safes, universal chargers, reading lights and breakfast included. The adjoining café-bar, *Yours Truly* (see p.133), has a stunning terrace and there's always something going on, from free walking tours to market visits. Dorms R315, doubles R1135

TAMBOERSKLOOF

★**The Backpack** 74 New Church St ☎021 423 4530, ⓦbackpackers.co.za; map p.77. An excellent backpackers made up of four interconnected houses, where the interior has a spacious maze-like effect. It's on the cusp of the City Bowl suburbs and the city centre, and easily walkable to the likes of Kloof St and the Company's Garden. *The Backpack* has some of the best communal and outdoor spaces in town, given funky flourishes by beadwork, *schwe schwe* fabric and township art; including a pool terrace, lounge area, restaurant, bar, courtyard, travel desk and craft shop. Choose between three- to eight-bed mixed and female-only dorms, including an en-suite option, as well as private rooms and self-catering studios. Dorms R390, doubles R920

Blencathra 4 Cambridge Ave, at De Hoop ☎021 424 9571, ⓦblencathra.co.za; map p.77. A large, relaxed family house with stunning views on the slopes of Lion's Head, 2km from the city centre and 4km from the Atlantic. Rooms are peaceful and spacious; many are en suite, and options include a four-bed women-only dorm. The sunny garden has seating, a swimming pool and a cute chalet with basic self-catering facilities. Dorms R200, doubles R500

Zebra Crossing 82 New Church St ☎021 422 1265, ⓦzebra-crossing.co.za; map p.77. A no-frills backpacker lodge, with a leafy garden and limited off-street parking – perfect if you are looking for something affordable that's close to town. On the northern edge of the City Bowl suburbs, it's an easy walk to the Kloof Street restaurants and pubs, as well as those in the city centre, with amenities including a travel desk and a café-bar, pleasant courtyards and terraces under vines. Accommodation is in spacious dorms and private rooms including a family option, with the best offering views of the mountain. Dorms R190, doubles R690

ORANJEZICHT

2Inn1 Kensington 21 Kensington Crescent ☎021 423 1707, ⓦ2inn1.com; map p.77. Entering from a broad, quiet street into these two adjacent renovated houses, with bright, sleek furnishings and quiet music drifting over the lounge and dining area, gives the feel of walking into a soothing urban hideaway. The building backs onto a 10m swimming pool and deck area with sunbeds, complimentary sundowners and mountain views. The tasteful rooms mostly have private terraces and there are spa treatments available on site. R2700

★**Acorn House** 1 Montrose Ave ☎021 461 1782, ⓦacornhouse.co.za; map p.77. Set among a row of guesthouses high on the slopes of Table Mountain, this century-old residence has maintained its grandeur with a sweeping lawn, colonial furnishings and elegant lounge, and added comforts such as the pool and sun loungers. Each room is unique; those at the front of the house offer great city views, while the back shows off Table Mountain. Family rooms have their own lounge and courtyard. Excellent value for money, great service and small touches make a stay here personal and memorable. R1700

Lézard Bleu 30 Upper Orange St ☎021 461 4601, ⓦlezardbleu.co.za; map p.77. This guesthouse offers six en-suite rooms, furnished with maple beds and private patio or balcony in a spacious open-plan 1960s house. The cosy lounge is perfect for reading, and a wall of sliding doors opens onto an outside deck, plus each bedroom overlooks the garden and swimming pool. It also boasts one of the best accommodation spaces in central Cape Town – a treehouse room. R1800

Redbourne Hilldrop 12 Roseberry Ave ☎021 461 1394, ⓦredbourne.co.za; map p.77. This small and intimate B&B, with just a few rooms in a house dating to 1928, oozes hospitality and the quiet charm of being a guest in someone's home. Behind the modernised facade, the interior is all high ceilings, wooden floors and antique furniture. There's an outside plunge pool and a small breakfast room with a panoramic view of the city. R1750

TOP 5 SLEEPS

Backpackers *Once in Cape Town* (see p.116)
Seafront hotel *Winchester Mansions Hotel* (see p.119)
Coastal getaway *Tintswalo Atlantic* (see p.120)
Five star *Cape Grace* (see p.114)
Good-value guesthouse *Rosedene* (see p.118)

HIGGOVALE

Kensington Place 38 Kensington Crescent ☎ 021 424 4744, ⊛ kensingtonplace.co.za; map p.77. High on the side of Table Mountain, this stylish eight-room boutique has sweeping city views from its contemporary lounge, which is adorned with artworks and coffee-table books. There's a dazzling little pool and attentive staff. **R4200**

★ **Rosedene Guest House** 28 Upper Kloof St ☎ 021 424 3290, ⊛ rosedene.co.za; map p.77. Long-running *Rosedene* has struck a balance of relative affordability in this exclusive area, and of lofty views with restaurants nearby and the city centre below. Likewise, chatty staff run the reception, where tour guides ferry guests away, but the rooms up top feel far removed from the urban bustle. **R1850**

VREDEHOEK

African Sun 3 Florida Rd ☎ 021 461 1601, ⊛ airbnb .com/rooms/771176; map p.77. A small self-catering apartment, attached to a family house a little over 1km from the city centre. Furnished with pared-back ethnic decor, it's run by friendly couple Don and Patricia, a travel writer and poet respectively. Expect well-informed local knowledge, a good bottle of Cape red on arrival and a bush shower on the patio. **R507**

SOUTHERN SUBURBS

The southern suburbs – **Rosebank, Claremont, Newlands** and **Rondebosch**, on the mountain's forested side – are home to the Kirstenbosch gardens, Newlands cricket and rugby grounds and Cape Town's university. Bohemian **Observatory** is a few minutes' drive from the city centre and offers buzzing cafés, a couple of backpacker lodges and lively nightlife.

African Heart 27 Station Rd, Observatory ☎ 021 447 3125, ⊛ backpackersincapetown.co.za. This creatively decorated hostel is set in a Victorian house with wooden floors, comfy couches, bold murals and mosaics. There are several chill-out areas and an outdoor braai area, and main drag Lower Main Road is nearby. Great if you are connected with nearby Groote Schuur Hospital, the university or various humanitarian aid projects in the neighbourhood – or just want to stay in vibey Observatory. Dorms **R175**, doubles **R600**

Carmichael Guesthouse 11 Wolmunster Rd, Rosebank ☎ 021 689 8350, ⊛ carmichaelhouse.co.za. Round the corner from the Irma Stern Museum, a Swiss-French couple offers six spacious rooms in a grand yellow two-storey Victorian mansion, among stained-glass windows, pine floors and period fireplaces. There's a garden, a swimming pool and secure parking. **R1800**

Elephant's Eye Lodge 9 Sunwood Drive, Tokai ☎ 021 715 2432, ⊛ elephantseyelodge.co.za. This friendly four-star B&B has four rooms in a converted Cape Dutch farmhouse and two self-catering cottages. Set in large grounds with a pool, it's minutes from Tokai Forest, a golf course and Constantia's wine estates. It's a 40min drive or train (to Retreat station) from the centre. **R1200**

★ **Vineyard Hotel** Colinton Rd, off Protea Rd, Newlands ☎ 021 657 4500, ⊛ vineyard.co.za. One of the city's top stays, where the rooms are luxurious and better value than in the city centre. It's in a grand 120-year-old hotel, on the site of a cottage built in 1799 by Georgian diarist Lady Anne Barnard. The extensive gardens are like those of a peaceful country estate, offering guided walks and children's activities, all with views of Table Mountain's forested slopes. Has a spa and indoor and outdoor pools – a great choice for a pampered stay. **R4040**

ATLANTIC SEABOARD

There's a range of accommodation in **Sea Point**, which makes it a good alternative to the City Bowl if you want to be close to both the city centre and the ocean. **Green Point** is another appealing choice, as it's the closest suburb to the Waterfront, city centre and De Waterkant, though it's not directly on the water. The mountainside suburb of **Camps Bay** offers views over the Atlantic, with an upmarket Californian feel to its laidback restaurants and bars, and it's just a hop over Kloof Nek to the Table Mountain Aerial Cableway and city centre. Neighbouring **Clifton** has similar appeal. Further south and isolated around a bay is **Llandudno**, which, although it lacks shops or restaurants, boasts some similar vistas and a beautiful beach. **Hout Bay** is the main urban concentration along the lower half of the peninsula, with a harbour, waterfront development and bus lines to town. Below Chapman's Peak, **Noordhoek** and **Kommetjie** offer coastal seclusion with mountain views.

GREEN POINT

★ **The B.I.G. Backpackers in Green Point** 18 Thornhill Rd ☎ 021 434 0688, ⊛ bigbackpackers.com; map pp.96–97. A backpacker lodge with a light, clean, modern feel, catering to a quieter crowd looking for a short-term home away from home. It has three fully equipped self-catering kitchens, computer facilities, a library and two games rooms with big-screen TV, while outside are a sunny garden with braai facilities, a plunge pool and parking. The rooms and four-bed dorms are spacious, stylish and include breakfast and en-suite bathroom. Dorms R380, doubles R1200

Dysart Boutique Hotel 17 Dysart Rd ☎ 021 439 2832, ⓦ dysart.de; map pp.96–97. This luxury boutique hotel is styled in Afro chic, with artworks dotting the slick and polished interior. The dozen rooms and villas have flat-screen TV and minibar and most have a private balcony or patio. The real draw, however, is what lies outside: two infinity pools, and wooden decking with sunbeds, umbrellas and tables – perfect for relaxing with a cocktail. R2000

Jambo Guest House 1 Grove Rd ☎ 021 439 4219, ⓦ jambo.co.za; map pp.96–97. In a quiet cul-de-sac off Main Rd, this small, atmospheric establishment offers four luxury en-suite rooms, each decorated in a unique style, and one garden suite. The lush, leafy exterior and enclosed garden with a pond are delightfully soothing, and the service is excellent. R1900

Wilton Manor 15 Croxteth Rd ☎ 021 434 7869, ⓦ wiltonguesthouses.co.za; map pp.96–97. This beautifully renovated Victorian guesthouse is set on a quiet street, close to Cape Town Stadium and the Waterfront. Outside is a spacious and sunny deck with a homely atmosphere, breakfast tables and a plunge pool. R1800

SEA POINT AND THREE ANCHOR BAY

Blackheath Lodge 6 Blackheath Rd ☎ 021 439 2541, ⓦ blackheathlodge.co.za; map pp.96–97. Down a quiet backstreet, but close to the Sea Point action, this guesthouse gets everything right. The sixteen rooms in the Victorian home are large and airy (some with Lion's Head and sea views), and the king-size beds are the most comfortable you'll find in Cape Town. Breakfast is served in a courtyard-garden deck overlooking the pool and bar. R3200

Huijs Haerlem 25 Main Drive ☎ 021 434 6434, ⓦ huijshaerlem.co.za; map pp.96–97. This elegant and gay-friendly guesthouse is made up of two adjacent houses furnished with antiques and separated by a pool. Rooms have a sea view, a vista of Signal Hill or overlook the lovely garden. R2100

The Villa Rosa 277 High Level Rd ☎ 021 434 2768, ⓦ villa-rosa.com; map pp.96–97. A friendly guesthouse in a two-storey Victorian house on the lower slopes of Signal Hill, 500m from the beachfront promenade. Decorated with simplicity and style, all rooms have TV, phone and safe, but only some have sea views. R1300

★**Winchester Mansions Hotel** 221 Beach Rd ☎ 021 434 2351, ⓦ winchester.co.za; map pp.96–97. In a prime spot across the road from the seashore, this 1920s hotel has an atmosphere straight from the pages of Agatha Christie, though the rooms are fresh and contemporary. A cool Italianate courtyard restaurant is overlooked by balconies draped in luxuriant creepers. R2850

CAMPS BAY, CLIFTON AND BAKOVEN

★**Boutique@10** 10 Medburn Rd, Camps Bay ☎ 021 438 1234, ⓦ boutique10.co.za. A stay here is as if you're a welcome guest at a friend's lavishly appointed house, occupying one of only four suites, each supremely comfortable with unique decor. Restored with reclaimed timber from an old hotel, the light and airy open-plan lounge features French doors that open onto the outside decking area, which is complete with sunbeds, plunge pool and a stunning view of the Atlantic Ocean and Lion's Head. R3295

★**Camps Bay Retreat** 7 Chilworth Rd, Camps Bay ☎ 021 437 8300, ⓦ campsbayretreat.com. The secluded Earls Dyke Manor, set on a four-acre nature reserve beneath Lion's Head, is located a 5min walk away from the beach. Stay in the mansion which dates from 1929, with its plush colonial furnishings, lounge, reading room, fine-dining restaurant and bar, or cross the ravine on a rope bridge to the contemporary Deck House and Villa. The estate has a spa, three swimming pools (including one made to look like a natural mountain pool) and a tennis court. R5000

Cape View 232 Kloof Rd, Clifton ☎ 021 438 8748, ⓦ capeviewclifton.co.za; map pp.96–97. Sunk into the mountainside, this exclusive guesthouse has views down the coast of the Twelve Apostles from its pool terrace. All suites are sea facing and have a balcony overlooking the ocean. R6800

★**Ocean View House** 33 Victoria Rd, Bakoven ☎ 021 438 1982, ⓦ oceanview-house.com. A mountain stream runs through the grounds of this family-run boutique hotel, set among ancient milkwood trees and koi ponds in a gorgeous garden bordering a *fynbos* reserve. The dozen spacious rooms are comfortably and stylishly furnished and have either mountain or sea views. R2650

HOUT BAY, NOORDHOEK AND KOMMETJIE

Eco Wave Lodge 11 Gladioli Way, Kommetjie ☎ 073 927 5644, ⓦ ecowave.co.za. A short stroll from the beach, *Eco Wave* offers simple and stylish backpacker accommodation in a two-storey house with balconies overlooking the sea as well as a TV lounge and small garden. There is also a self-contained apartment with fully equipped kitchen, braai and garage. R600

Hout Bay Hideaway 37 Skaife St, Hout Bay ☎ 021 790 8040, ⓦ houtbay-hideaway.com. An outstanding guest-house bursting with luxurious touches and decorative verve, from the Persian rugs and Art Deco armchairs to the huge beds. Each of the four rooms has a mountain or sea view and decks where your private breakfast is served. At the back, there's a saltwater pool in a *fynbos* mountainside garden. R2100

7

7

Houtkapperspoort Hout Bay Main Rd, Constantia Nek; around 4km from Hout Bay and 17km from the city centre ☎021 794 5216, ⌨houtkapperspoortresort .co.za. These rustic one- to three-bedroom, stone-and-brick self-catering cottages sit right by the Table Mountain National Park, in the valley between Hout Bay and Constantia. You can take paths straight from the estate up the mountain slopes, play tennis or take a dip in the pool. R1470

Monkey Valley Resort Mountain Rd, Noordhoek ☎021 789 8000, ⌨monkeyvalleyresort.com. Spread over several acres of Chapman's Peak, some 40km south of the city centre, is this attractive group of mainly wooden-and-thatched rooms and cottages. Overlooking Noordhoek's Long Beach, the site is surrounded by indigenous vegetation and has a restaurant and both self-catering and B&B accommodation. Doubles R1480, cottages R2360

Sunbird Mountain Retreat & Lodge Boskykloof Rd, Hout Bay ☎021 790 7758, ⌨sunbirdlodge.co.za. Four pleasant, spacious, self-catering cabins and a guesthouse that includes a family unit, all nestled in a forest high up on the mountainside. Every room has a great view, and there's a secluded swimming pool. Cabins R800, doubles R1200

★**Tintswalo Atlantic** Chapman's Peak Drive, Hout Bay ☎021 201 0025, ⌨tintswalo.com/atlantic. Perched on the rocks below Chapman's Peak, with a view of the dramatic Sentinel Peak and the Atlantic Ocean, this stunning luxury lodge is the only hotel in Table Mountain National Park. The large bedrooms are lavishly furnished with tropical beach-house chic, each with ocean views and unique in style, and you might spot whales from the wooden deck as you wander to the pool, lounge, bar and restaurant. Dining here is a gastronomic pleasure, with multiple courses making for a lingering, atmospheric dinner as you gaze across the black water at the twinkling lights of Hout Bay. R10780

FALSE BAY SEABOARD

This is a great area if you want to enjoy the beach and some excellent restaurants. Once a favourite because of its stunning beach views, **Muizenberg**, 25km from the centre, is becoming popular again, especially amongst surfers. To its south is salubrious **St James**, but the real crown jewel is **Kalk Bay** with its harbour, antique shops and arty cafés. Accommodation is limited in Kalk Bay – look for an apartment with ⌨safarinow.com. **Fish Hoek**, further south, is recommended for its beach but not much else; a better option is pretty **Simon's Town**, 40km from the city centre. The historic seafaring town is now technically part of the Cape Town metropolis, but still regarded by many as a separate entity.

MUIZENBERG, KALK BAY AND FISH HOEK

★**Chartfield Guest House** 30 Gatesville Rd, Kalk Bay ☎021 788 3793, ⌨chartfield.co.za; map pp.104–105. This well-kept, rambling house sits halfway up the hill overlooking the harbour, with terrific sea views from some rooms and a hop and a skip down the cobbled road or steps to some of the peninsula's finest restaurants. R900

The Mountain House 7 Mountain Rd, Clovelly ☎083 455 5664, ⌨themountainhouse.co.za; map pp.104–105. Built in the garden of local architect Carin Hartford, this beautiful two-bedroom self-catering cottage has windows on all sides to capitalize on the incredible mountain setting, and the living space flows out to a timber deck. Between Fish Hoek and Kalk Bay. R1100

Samhitakasha Cob House Organic B&B 13 Watson Rd, Muizenberg ☎021 788 6613, ⌨cobhouse.co.za; map pp.104–105. One of Cape Town's greenest B&Bs, this mud-and-straw cob house is run by a friendly couple and set just 200m from the beach. It contains just one room, which works as a double or can sleep up to four, and the reasonable rate includes a room-service organic breakfast. Owner Simric Yarrow, a teacher, storyteller and musician, offers interesting local tours (⌨offbeatcapetown.yolasite .com). Double R750, family R950

Stoked Backpackers 175 Main Rd, Muizenberg ☎082 679 3651, ⌨stokedbackpackers.com; map pp.104–105. Vibey, well-run backpackers next to the station, over the railway line from Surfers Corner. There's a vegetarian café and the travel centre can organize activities in False Bay and beyond. There's a range of quality in the four- to twelve-bed dorms; the best en-suite rooms are on the upper levels with sunrise sea views. When there's no wind, the upstairs terrace overlooking the beach is stunning. Dorms R200, doubles R865

Tranquility Guest House 25 Peak Rd, Fish Hoek ☎021 782 2060, ⌨tranquil.co.za; map pp.104–105. This warm and welcoming place, walking distance to the beach, is situated on Fish Hoek mountainside and offers good ocean views. There are four flowery B&B en-suite rooms, and guests can soak in the outdoor Jacuzzi. R1800

SIMON'S TOWN

Simon's Town Boutique Backpackers 66 St George's St ☎021 786 1964, ⌨capepax.co.za; map pp.106–107. Conveniently located in the heart of Simon's Town, 1km south of the station, this boutique backpacker joint offers bunk-bed dorms and fairly spacious doubles, plus there's a large balcony with a view of the waterfront. You can rent bicycles here and ride to Cape Point, or arrange a kayak tour to paddle past the penguin colony. Dorms R220, doubles R660

Whale View Manor Main Rd ☎021 786 3291, ⌨whaleviewmanor.co.za; map pp.106–107. In the guesthouse area on the south side of town, this imposing white villa houses a four-star boutique hotel and spa. It's right next to the surf and the ten rooms come with a sea or mountain view, while the contemporary public spaces are sunny and relaxing. R1950

LUNCHTIME AT *KALKY'S*

Eating

Eating out is one of the highlights of visiting this world-class culinary capital, where the Mediterranean climate nurtures farms, vineyards and small producers galore. The city has a bottomless selection of relaxed and convivial restaurants and cafés serving imaginative food of a high standard. Prices are inexpensive compared with Western countries; for the cost of an unmemorable meal back home, you can experience innovative dishes cooked by outstanding chefs in an upmarket restaurant. One thing that unites South Africa is a love of meat, and Cape Town is an ideal place to try all kinds of interesting varieties, such as ostrich and springbok. As for seafood, fresh fish features on most restaurant menus, and in the many sushi and tapas bars. Cape Town itself is a good source of cold-water fish such as hake, often served as English-style fish 'n' chips, and snoek, a delicious but bony fish.

> ### ETHICAL EATING
>
> It's a sad fact, but fish stocks are declining worldwide. If you want to do your bit and be ecologically responsible, go for a tasty Cape fish like **yellowtail**, which is not endangered and has a low carbon footprint, coming straight from the seas around the city. Although they are on many menus, Cape salmon (Geelbek) and to a lesser degree kingklip are best avoided ethically. The **Southern African Sustainable Seafood Initiative (SASSI)** can inform you about the conservation status of different kinds of seafood and other issues related to fishing (W wwfsassi.co.za).

While meat is certainly popular, **vegetarians** need not despair, as there's always at least one concession to meatless food on menus. Even steakhouses will have a meat-free option, and generally offer reasonable salad bars. Menus often feature a low-carb, high-fat option for diners on the **Banting** diet, which is popular locally and sometimes called the Noakes diet, having been promoted by controversial media personality Professor Tim Noakes of the University of Cape Town.

Cape Malay cuisine (see box, p.124) must be sampled at least once. It's the exclusive focus of some restaurants in the city, though many of the dishes considered as Cape Malay have crept into the staple South African diet and can be found on menus nationwide.

The obvious accompaniment to your meals is locally produced **Cape wine**, costing R60 and up for a bottle of something quaffable, though **beer** is definitely the national drink, and there are some delicious craft beers to sample (see p.134). Note that some Muslim establishments serving Cape Malay cuisine don't allow alcohol at all.

Dining is generally rather **early**, with most people sitting down at 7pm or 8pm. Don't expect to walk into a restaurant at 10pm and get a full or decent meal. **Booking** is essential for the top restaurants. Most cafés and many restaurants offer free wi-fi of varying quality.

A great addition to eating out in Cape Town is the collection of **neighbourhood food markets**, located in different areas of the city, in interesting venues such as a converted warehouse, old fish factory and former aeroplane hangar. Whether you're after artisanal cheese, **organic produce**, scrumptious burgers, craft beer or a glass of bubbly, you'll be spoilt for choice. The markets are on specific days and times – a few of the best-known ones are a great attraction for breakfast on Saturday mornings (see box, p.144).

THE CITY CENTRE

95 Keerom 95 Keerom St ☎021 422 0765, W 95keerom.com; map p.52. Flash, fabulous and expensive, *95 Keerom* offers fresh and light Italian nouvelle cuisine, with dishes such as grilled beef, butternut ravioli or seared tuna (average mains R250). In 2013, the Italian chef Giorgio Nava won gold in the World Pasta Championship in Parma; sample his gnocchi, penne and linguine dishes in contemporary surrounds. Mon–Sat 6.30–10pm.

Addis in Cape 41 Church St ☎021 424 5722, W addisincape.co.za; map p.52. This friendly and authentic restaurant has a lovely laidback atmosphere, with traditional furnishings and coffee ceremonies available. You'll find delicious Ethiopian dishes on the menu, such as spicy red lentils (R137), served on tasty *injera* (sourdough flatbread) to soak up the flavours and eat with your fingers. Set menus cost R105–260. Mon–Sat noon–10.30pm.

Africa Café 108 Shortmarket St ☎021 422 0221, W africacafe.co.za; map p.52. This enduringly popular tourist restaurant is a good place to try African cuisine, with a fantastic selection of dishes from across the continent. Given that you're served a communal feast of sixteen dishes, and the evening includes a performance of African song and dance, the R250/head price tag is pretty reasonable. Booking essential. Mon–Sat 6–11pm.

Bardelli's Restaurant 18 Kloof St ☎021 423 1502; map p.52. A reliable, bustling Italian restaurant, this branch of Kenilworth's long-running favourite occupies a historic Cape Dutch building. The wood-fired pizzas such as the Pablo (bacon, feta, rosemary and fresh tomatoes; R95) are some of the best around. Daily 8am–10pm.

Biesmiellah Cnr Wale and Pentz Sts, Bo-Kaap ☎021 423 0850, W biesmiellah.co.za; map p.47. This is one of the oldest restaurants to sample traditional Cape Malay cuisine (see p.124), serving halal mains such as *bobotie* (beef mince topped with a milk egg glaze; R95) and tomato *bredie* (cubes of lamb cooked in sweet-sour tomato sauce; R99). For a bite on a Bo-Kaap walk, join local residents in the queue for takeaway samosas and delicious savoury wraps called *salomes*. No alcohol. Mon–Sat noon–10pm.

★**Café Mozart** 37 Church St ☎021 424 3774, ⓦthemozart.co.za; map p.52. Sit under trees on cute Church St, or in the quaint interior among printed wallpaper, porcelain and antiques, for hearty breakfasts, burgers (R90), sandwiches (R75) or a glass of Cape wine. Part of the city's theatrical Madame Zingara group, it feels like a cross between a twee English teahouse and a bohemian boudoir. Mon–Fri 8am–3.30pm, Sat 9am–3pm.

Charly's Bakery 38 Canterbury St, East City ☎021 461 5181, ⓦcharlysbakery.co.za; map p.47. For three decades, this fun-loving bakery in a psychedelically painted heritage building has produced Cape Town's most spectacular and decorative cakes. Try the red velvet cupcakes or wheat- and gluten-free lemon meringue cupcakes (R30). They also do breakfasts and light lunches (from R50), and this is a good refuelling spot if you're visiting Cape Town's best bookshop, the Book Lounge (see p.142). Tues–Fri 8am–5pm, Sat 8.30am–2pm.

★**Chef's Warehouse & Canteen** 92 Bree St, Heritage Square ☎021 422 0128, ⓦchefswarehouse.co.za; map p.52. Alongside a culinary wonderland selling everything from coffee machines to pink Himalayan salt, chef Liam Tomlin serves a foodie tapas feast (R650 for two) in a casual setting. Featuring a global mix of French and Asian flavours, the three-course small-plate banquet takes up to one hour. They don't take reservations, so arrive early or head downstairs to the dinky basement bar. There's a second branch at the Constantia winery Beau Constantia. Mon–Fri noon–2.30pm & 4.30–8pm, Sat noon–2.30pm.

Eastern Food Bazaar 96 Longmarket St ☎021 461 2458, ⓦeasternfoodbazaar.co.za; map p.52. Bustling canteen-style food court with a dozen stalls selling hearty and affordable dishes from India, China, the Bo-Kaap and beyond (mains R50). You buy a token before queuing at your chosen counter, and there are often long waits at lunchtime. No alcohol. Mon–Sat 11am–10pm.

Headquarters 100 Shortmarket St, Heritage Square ☎021 424 6373, ⓦhqrestaurant.co.za; map p.52. There is only one main dish on the menu at *Headquarters* – prime free-range Namibian sirloin steak and Café de Paris butter sauce with perfect matchstick chips and salad (R198). Snack boards and tapas are also offered (R100), and the drinks menu compensates for its short culinary counterpart. Check the website for regular specials and events, including two steaks for the price of one on Monday evenings. On Friday nights, they have a DJ with relaxing beats; things hot up around 10.30pm, when the tables are pushed back for dancing. Book ahead. Mon–Sat noon–midnight.

Jason Bakery 185 Bree St ☎021 424 5644, ⓦwww .jasonbakery.com; map p.52. With an unswerving local following, baker Jason Lilley is renowned for his pastries, pies and sourdough rye bread. Lunch favourites at the fashionable spot include pulled pork shoulder (R75) and curried Chalmar

beef burger (R90), while the menu also features numerous breakfasts, salads and sandwiches (chicken Caesar with bacon and parmesan R87). Look out, too, for *Bardough* by Jason at 33 Loop St. Mon–Fri 7am–3.30pm, Sat 8am–2pm.

La Parada 107 Bree St ☎021 426 0330; map p.52; 35 Victoria Rd, Camps Bay ☎021 286 2106; Constantia Main Rd, Constantia Nek ☎021 795 0620, ⓦlaparada .co.za. Cape Town has fallen heavily for tapas, and this open-fronted restaurant with street seating on Bree St serves some of the most authentic Spanish nibbles around (R55–89). There are mains also on offer (R300), along with cocktails. The food is served at long, wooden communal tables, and there's a lively atmosphere. Bree St daily 7am–2am; Camps Bay daily 8am–2am; Constantia Nek daily 8am–2am.

Love Thy Neighbour 110 Bree St ☎021 422 2770, ⓦfacebook.com/lovethyneighbourct; map p.52. Occupying the basement of a former church and spilling into a leafy courtyard, *Love Thy Neighbour* serves Mediterranean dishes such as meze (R50) and souvlaki, while the burgers (R75) are also popular. Tues–Sat 12.30–11.30pm.

Mama Africa 178 Long St ☎021 424 8634, ⓦmamaafricarestaurant.co.za; map p.52. With food from around the continent, the menu here includes *bobotie* and a wild-game mixed grill of springbok, kudu, ostrich and crocodile (mains R150). You can also sit beneath the Coke-bottle chandelier in the *Snake Bar* and listen to live marimba music from 8pm. Mon & Sat 6.30–11pm, Tues–Fri noon–3pm & 6.30–11pm.

Mink & Trout 127 Bree St ☎021 426 2534, ⓦfacebook .com/minkandtrout; map p.52. Taking over from the artisanal *Birds Café* – and offering some of the same dishes –this elegant wine bar and bistro serves mains such as Karoo lamb *bredie*, gnocchi and bouillabaisse (average R150), with a good selection of Cape wines and bubblies to accompany. Mon–Sat noon–3.30pm & 6.30–10.30pm.

★**Royale Eatery** 273 Long St ☎021 422 4536, ⓦroyaleeatery.com; map p.52. A hip hangout serving inexpensive gourmet burgers, with mouthwatering toppings such as mozzarella, jalapeños, salsa and guacamole. Choose from lamb, beef, pork and ostrich patties and eight vegetarian cheeseburgers. The Miss Piggy burger with bacon and guacamole (R92) is a favourite. It's usually packed, so book ahead, especially if you would like a balcony seat with Long St views. Mon–Sat noon–11.30pm.

★**Truth Café** 36 Buitenkant St, East City ☎021 200 0440, ⓦtruthcoffee.com; map p.47. *Truth* are artisan coffee roasters who supply some of the city's best restaurants and train baristas, so you'll get a great caffeine kick at this hip coffee shop with its creative industrial interior centred on a cast-iron vintage roaster drum. It's worth going for the "steampunk" decor alone, which moved the UK *Telegraph* to proclaim this the world's best café. They also do breakfast and lunch (mains R100). Mon–Fri 7am–6pm, Sat 8am–6pm, Sun 8am–2pm.

8

V&A WATERFRONT AND DE WATERKANT

The **Waterfront** offers a variety of food, from chain eateries and quick eats – perfect after a bout of shopping or before you take in a movie – to outdoor people-watching cafés and smart fish restaurants. You'll also find some of the best sushi in town here. **De Waterkant** has some nice places to eat; head for the Cape Quarter building with its array of restaurants and cafés.

THE WATERFRONT

Baia Upper Level, Victoria Wharf, Quay 6 ☎021 421 0935, ⓦbaiarestaurant.co.za; map p.66. Sit on the terrace and take in the views of Table Mountain while dining on masterfully cooked fresh fish and seafood; including line-fish papillote (baked in a parchment paper parcel with tomato, courgettes, fennel and thyme; R172) and a few kingklip dishes (R200). Booking recommended, especially for dinner. Daily noon–3pm & 7–11pm.

City Grill Shop 155, Victoria Wharf, Quay 5 ☎021 421 9820, ⓦcitygrill.co.za; map p.66. An excellent, if rather touristy and pricey steakhouse, celebrating the meaty heart of South African cuisine. From the appetizer plate of beef biltong and dry sausage (R99) to the ostrich kebab (R245), numerous dishes offer local flavours (helpfully accompanied by South African flags on the menu). You also can't go far wrong with a full-blooded rump steak (R160 for 250g). The wine list is encyclopaedic, and there are lovely water views from the umbrella-shaded outdoor tables. Daily 11am–1pm.

San Marco Lower Level, Victoria Wharf ☎021 418 5434, ⓦsanmarco.co.za; map p.66. This bar-restaurant with outdoor seating offers a breakfast menu, good sandwiches on Italian breads (R85), wraps and fresh salads. Mains range from grilled calamari (R129) to fillet steak (R175), and there are cocktails and Cap Classique bubbly while you wait. Daily 8am–11pm.

★Sevruga Quay 5 ☎021 421 5134, ⓦsevrugarestaurant .co.za; map p.66. With its crisp white tablecloths and walnut walls, *Sevruga* impresses everyone from local sushi lovers to the *New York Times*, which called it the "only reason to go to the V&A Waterfront". Book a shaded outdoor table for some people-watching while you enjoy your sushi platter (R200), dim sum or seafood main (R200). Daily noon–11pm.

Signal Restaurant Cape Grace, West Quay Rd ☎021 410 7100, ⓦcapegrace.com; map p.66. In a quietly elegant dining room with maritime scenes on the walls, the *Cape Grace* hotel's restaurant serves seven-course tasting menus (from R625, including wine from R945), featuring dishes such as goat's cheese mousse and beef fillet with truffled potato, and dinner mains such as *bobotie*-spiced springbok (R280). Lunch is a lighter affair, offering dishes including fish and chips (R95), and the Waterfront location makes *Signal* perfect for a cream tea (R75) or the full afternoon tea (R185), served in the adjoining library. Daily 6.30am–10.30pm.

Willoughby & Co Lower Level, Victoria Wharf ☎021 418 6115, ⓦwilloughbyandco.co.za; map p.66. Despite its lack of sea views, many locals rate this as the Waterfront's best fish restaurant. It serves fantastic sushi (platters R85 to R309) and seafood (mains around R200) and brings a lively atmosphere to its patch of mall. Daily noon–10.30pm.

DE WATERKANT

Anatoli 24 Napier St ☎021 419 2501, ⓦanatoli.co.za; map p.66. This Turkish restaurant, a little on the pricey side but bursting with personality, has transformed an early twentieth-century coach house into a culinary caravanserai. It's great for vegetarians: the excellent meze selection includes *dolmades* (vine leaves stuffed with rice, pine nuts, blackcurrants and spices), with at least twenty other meze to choose from (R26–53). For a meaty main, look no further than the kebabs (R149), and leave room for desserts (R42–53) such as baklava. Mon–Sat 6.30–10.30pm.

★Origin Coffee 28 Hudson St ☎021 421 1000, ⓦoriginroasting.co.za; map p.66. These coffee devotees serve single-origin, home-roasted beans from across Africa

---

CAPE CUISINE

Styles of cooking brought by Asian and Madagascan slaves have evolved into **Cape Malay** cuisine. Associated with Cape Town's Muslim community, who predominate in the brightly painted Bo-Kaap neighbourhood (see p.50), the food is characterized by mild, semisweet and aromatic curries with a strong Indonesian influence. Dishes include **bredie** (stew), among which **waterblommetjiebredie**, made using water hyacinths, is a highlight; **bobotie**, a spicy minced dish served under a savoury custard; and **sosaties**, a local version of kebab, made using minced meat. For dessert, dates stuffed with almonds make a light and delicious end to a meal, while **malva** sponge pudding is a rich combination of milk, sugar, cream and apricot jam.

"Cape Malay" is a misnomer given that less than 25 percent of slaves came from Malaysia and Indonesia, with over 75 percent originating from mainland Africa, Madagascar, Mauritius, **India** and Sri Lanka. However, while many Bo-Kaap locals prefer to be called "Cape Muslim", these wonderful dishes are still generally referred to as Cape Malay. You can try them in Cape Town restaurants or on a Cape Malay cooking "safari" (see box, p.51).

and beyond to Asia and Latin America, and their range of teas is equally appealing. You can complement your drink with something to eat, making the converted warehouse

CITY BOWL SUBURBS

GARDENS

Aubergine 39 Barnet St ☎021 465 0000, ⓦaubergine .co.za; map p.77. This is an unbeatable choice for an elegant five-star dinner, with a courtyard to sit in and enjoy German chef Harald Bresselschmidt's top-quality fusions of African, Asian and European flavours. There's a strong emphasis on fresh and local ingredients, and vegetarians will also find inspired dishes. The three-course lunch menu will set you back R445; the dinner equivalent is R580 (R790 with wine pairing). Mon, Tues & Sat 6–10pm, Wed–Fri noon–2pm & 6–10pm.

★**Belmond Mount Nelson Hotel** 76 Orange St ☎021 483 1000, ⓦmountnelson.co.za; map p.77. Colonial-style afternoon tea, with a smart-casual dress code, in Cape Town's gracious hospitality legend is a slow-paced culinary delight. The large tea tables are piled high with hot and cold pastries, classic savouries like smoked-salmon sandwiches and scrumptious cakes. You can skip dinner after this R325 feast. Book in advance online. Tea at 1.30pm & 3.30pm.

★**Ben Wei** Wembley Square, Solan St ☎021 461 2966, ⓦfacebook.com/BenWeiSushi; map p.77. This intimate sushi and Asian fusion restaurant offers some of Cape Town's freshest, most flavoursome and visually striking dishes. Its name means "original taste" in Mandarin and everything is certainly bursting with flavour, from the tom kha gai (Thai coconut milk and lemongrass broth; R50) and the tuna tataki (spiced and seared tuna; R58) to the crispy fried wonton (R38) and the "rainbow reloaded" (California roll with salmon, tuna and avocado, topped with seven-spice seasoning, mayo and teriyaki sauce; R109). Mains are available (around R75), but the best option is to share several bites. The most convenient parking is outside the Wembley Square complex's boom gates on Mckenzie Street. Mon–Sat 11.30am–9pm.

★**Bombay Bicycle Club** 158 Kloof St ☎021 423 6805, ⓦthebombay.co.za; map p.77. Don't expect Indian cuisine here, but do expect a great place for a fun evening out. There are things to play with in every area, whether you're sitting at a table with swings, or wearing silly hats. Food includes grills, pastas and decadent desserts (average mains R150). Booking essential, as it's often full. Mon–Sat 6–11pm (bar 4–11pm).

Carlyle's on Derry 17 Derry St ☎021 461 8787, ⓦcarlyles.co.za; map p.77. A friendly neighbourhood Italian restaurant where you'll need to book in advance for a table. They serve a great selection of thin-based, gourmet pizzas (R65–135) such as bacon, blue cheese, walnut and rocket, Thai chicken and coriander, and Parma ham and lemon-infused rocket. Meat dishes (R70–180), pasta

popular among savvy city workers for breakfast (R60) and lunch (R90). Mon–Fri 7am–5pm, Sat & Sun 9am–2pm.

(R80–120) and salads (R80–92) are also on the menu. Tues–Fri 5.30–10.30pm, Sat & Sun noon–10.30pm.

Hudson's The Burger Joint 69 Kloof St ☎021 426 5974; map p.77; cnr Main & Upper Portswood Rds, Green Point; map pp.96–97; 25 Protea Rd, Claremont; 77 Dorp St, Stellenbosch; ⓦtheburgerjoint .co.za. This Kloof St joint is a good choice for gourmet burgers (R44–97), with trendy young patrons, loud rock music, craft beer, home-made lemonade and Bar One milkshakes (R49). Besides the huge choice of burgers, there are decent salads, such as "The Good Girl" – roasted butternut with feta (R78). All branches daily noon–11pm.

★**Societi Bistro** 50 Orange St ☎021 424 2100, ⓦsocieti.co.za; map p.77. This popular bistro serves good Italian and South African food, in a lovely restored building and garden near the *Belmond Mount Nelson Hotel* (see p.116) and Labia cinema (see p.138), with a fireplace for winter evenings. The risotto is always a hit (R66–85), and the other mains include Karoo lamb shank (R206) and free-range ostrich burger (R94). There is generally a vegan dish on the menu, such as Thai curry, cauli-rice, autumn vegetables and pawpaw salsa (R129). Mon–Sat noon–10pm.

★**Tamboers Winkel** 3 De Lorentz St ☎021 424 0521, ⓦfacebook.com/Tamboerswinkel; map p.77. Like most residents of Gardens, this café seems to be suggesting it lives in posher Tamboerskloof, but we can forgive it for its excellent coffee and craft beer. The menu offers rustic tastes of the Cape *platteland* (farmland) with a creative twist, making this *winkel* (shop) a top choice for bloggers, media types, models and all discerning Capetonians. Mon & Wed–Sun 8am–10pm, Tues 8am–6pm.

TAMBOERSKLOOF

Miller's Thumb 10b Kloof Nek Rd ☎021 424 3838, ⓦmillersthumb.co.za; map p.77. Amidst ill-advised oranges and green walls, the *Thumb* serves consistently good seafood dishes, with a selection of line fish prepared in various ways from Cajun to Moroccan. If you're not into fish, you can try their juicy 300g rump steak (mains R125–185). Mon & Sat 6.30–10.30pm, Tues–Fri 12.30–2pm & 6.30–10.30pm.

VREDEHOEK

Deer Park Café 2 Deer Park Drive ☎021 462 6311, ⓦdeerparkcafe.co.za; map p.77. On the lower slopes of Table Mountain, and with an enclosed park and playground sloping below its outdoor tables, this is the best central

8

8

AFRICAN FOOD

Around the centre of Cape Town you will find a couple of restaurants offering African food, but these are geared towards tourists – most Xhosa locals would scoff at Long Street's prices. The best way to experience African food in the **townships** is by staying over in a B&B (see box, p.115), taking a tour that incorporates a township meal or a drink in a *shebeen* (see p.90), or by visiting one of the following.

Department of Coffee 158 Ntlazane St, Khayelitsha ☎078 086 0093, ⓦtwitter.com /Dpmofcoffee. At the first artisan coffee house in a township, you can get real coffee, hot chocolate, tea and muffins (all under R10 each), and sit at the outdoor tables under orange umbrellas. The convenient location outside Khayelitsha train station (iLitha Park side) makes this an option for groups to visit independently. Mon–Fri 6am–6pm, Sat 8am–3pm.

Dinner at Mandela's Departing from 259 Long St or accommodation ☎021 790 5817, ⓦdinnerat mandelas.co.za; map p.52. Priced at R395 including transfers (from your accommodation and back), this evening of African singing, dancing and food in Imizamo Yethu township near Hout Bay is a fun way to learn more about township culture. Reserve in advance. Mon &

Thurs 6.15–11pm.

★**Kaffa Hoist Café** Guga S'Thebe Arts & Cultural Centre, King Langalibalele/Washington Dr, Langa ☎071 120 6345, ⓔkaffa.hoist@gmail.com; map p.81. *Kaffa Hoist* is situated at the back of Langa's buzzy Guga S'Thebe Arts & Cultural Centre (see p.89), adjoining an amphitheatre made of shipping containers. Xhosa owner Chris serves locally roasted Deluxe Coffeeworks coffee (R19), muffins (R5), sweet or savoury pancakes (R30), toasted sandwiches (R30) and burgers (R50). The "Hoist" in the name refers to owner Chris's mission to uplift locals by keeping them out of the *shebeen*. With free wi-fi, the courtyard cafe is the perfect place for young township residents to study or send off their CV. May–Sept daily 8.30am–5.30pm; Oct–April daily 7am–7pm.

place to take children. Besides the children's menu, featuring dishes from fruit salad to spaghetti bolognaise, it's a great place for all the family – not only for the setting, but for the fresh, well-priced soups, salads, sandwiches and more (mains average R80). Daily 8am–8pm.

★**Sidewalk Café** 33 Derry St ☎021 461 2839, ⓦsidewalk.co.za; map p.77. This modern, funky café has

large windows and an enticing and imaginative menu (mains around R120). Whether you're after healthy and fresh or something more substantial, you're sure to find a breakfast, lunch or dinner to suit your mood. There's a good vegetarian selection, too – from quinoa salad to aubergine and spiced lentil moussaka. Mon–Sat 8am–10.30pm, Sun 9am–2pm.

SOUTHERN SUBURBS

Bistro Sixteen82 Steenberg Estate, Constantia ☎021 713 2211, ⓦsteenberghotel.com. On the historic and scenic Steenberg wine estate, this chic and contemporary bistro is popular for decadent weekend breakfasts – followed by a visit to the adjoining tasting room or a wander across the lawns dotted with sculptures by South African-Italian artist Edoardo Villa. Treats such as oysters, truffles and Eggs Benedict feature on the breakfast menu (mains R90), while lunch (mains R150) is served from noon and tapas (plate R65) from 5pm. Daily 9–11am, noon–3pm & 5–8pm.

Catharina's Steenberg Estate, Constantia ☎021 713 2222, ⓦsteenberghotel.com. Serving beautifully plated food on Steenberg estate, *Catharina's* is an elegant choice for a special occasion. Evenings here are cosy, and you can lounge in the comfy bar chairs while sipping bubbly made on the estate. During the day, the imposing windows make the most of the vineyard views. Seafood and venison regularly feature on the menu, while game and steaks appear alongside vegetarian options such as carrot, orange and cardamom risotto (mains R200). Daily 7–10am,

noon–3pm & 6.30–9.30pm.

Common Ground Café 23 Milner Rd, Rondebosch ☎021 686 0154. Attached to a church, this is an unlikely contender for the best coffee in town, but the baristas are true artists who make an excellent double-shot cup using locally roasted beans from Origin Coffee. They also offer reasonably priced breakfasts (around R50) and gourmet sandwiches, whole-wheat wraps, burgers, salads and quesadillas for lunch (average R60). Mon–Fri 7am–4pm, Sat 8am–2pm, Sun 8.30am–2pm.

The Dining Room 117 Sir Lowry Rd, Woodstock ☎021 461 0463, ⓦdining-room.co.za. From Karen Dudley, the culinary brains behind Woodstock's famous *The Kitchen* (see p.127), this restaurant focuses on fresh seasonal produce among the whimsical array of screens, mirrors and portraits in its stylish vintage interior. Expect unusual dishes such as Kentucky fried quail and glazed duck with olive relish. Lunch R100, three-course dinner R350. Mon, Weds & Fri 8.30am–4pm, Tues & Thurs 8.30am–4pm & 7–10pm.

Kirstenbosch Tea Room Restaurant Kirstenbosch National Botanical Garden, Rhodes Drive, Newlands ☎021 797 4883, ⦿ktr.co.za. The gorgeous setting in one of the world's greatest botanic gardens (see p.83) complements the pleasing, Cape country food. Recommended dishes include the pickled fish (R145) and home-made burgers (R128), and they serve some good vegetarian options and tea for two (R280). You can order a gourmet picnic (R210/person) and even rent a picnic blanket (R30). It's located just inside Gate 2. Daily 8.30am–5pm.

★**The Kitchen** 111 Sir Lowry Rd, Woodstock ☎021 462 2201, ⦿lovethekitchen.co.za. Famously visited by former US First Lady Michelle Obama, chef Karen Dudley's fun but food-obsessed deli-café uses the freshest ingredients to create inventive breakfasts and lunches. The "love sandwiches" on artisanal bread (R60) are especially popular, and there is an ever-changing range of salads (R70). This is one of the best lunch stops around, especially if you are vegetarian, but arrive early (or come for a quieter breakfast). The service is fast, efficient and the whole place buzzes; it's not a spot to linger. Mon–Fri 8am–3.30pm.

★**Pot Luck Club** Top Floor, Silo Building, Old Biscuit Mill, 375 Albert Rd, Woodstock ☎021 447 0804, ⦿thepotluckclub.co.za. Perched atop a converted silo, British chef Luke Dale-Roberts' second South African restaurant is all about inventive and tantalising tapas dishes (around R100 each). The menu is arranged according to sweet, sour, salty, bitter and *umami* (savoury or meaty) flavours; order several to share with friends. Sweet tapas, such as springbok rump with beetroot ketchup or Burrata cheese with grilled nectarines, are not to be confused with the "sweet ending" desserts, including braaied banana risotto. You'll need to book at least a few weeks in advance and will be allocated a seating time. Mon–Sat 12.30–2.30pm & 6–8.30pm, Sun 11am–12.30pm.

★**Test Kitchen** Old Biscuit Mill, 375 Albert Rd, Woodstock ☎021 447 2337, ⦿thetestkitchen.co.za. For a table at South Africa's top, award-winning fine-dining contemporary restaurant you'll need to book months in advance. Should you be lucky enough to get in, prepare to be overwhelmed by the sensual feast of tastes, smells and colours provided by the astonishing creative mastery and craft of chef Luke Dale-Roberts. The innovative dishes on the ever-changing menu are rich in unusual ingredients and combinations, from cauliflower and cheese with black-garlic salsa, to lamb minestrone with potato parmesan dumpling and lamb and tomato extraction. Menus range from R1200 to R2650; enjoy one in the industrial-style setting with its contemporary art and casual ambience. Tues–Sat 6.30–8.30pm.

8

ATLANTIC SEABOARD

GREEN POINT

El Burro 81 Main Rd ☎021 433 2364, ⦿elburro.co.za; map pp.96–97. This fun, casual spot offers Mexican food without too much cheese and grease (mains R130), plus a good view of Green Point Stadium from the balcony. There are a few options for vegetarians too. Mon–Sat noon–11.30pm.

Giovanni's 103 Main Rd ☎021 434 6893; map pp.96–97. With both indoor and pavement seating, this lively Italian deli and coffee shop is right across from the stadium and has its own screen for watching sports. It offers delicious coffee, excellent made-to-order sandwiches, salads and good prepackaged meals (R45–65). Daily 7.30am–8.30pm.

Mano's 39 Main Rd ☎021 434 1090, ⦿mano.co.za; map pp.96–97. Popular with Capetonian glitterati, chic *Mano's* serves seafood, grills and pasta from an unpretentious menu featuring Caesar salads, Prego rolls, lemon chicken and lamb chops (mains R100). After dinner, the party continues in champagne bar *Jade*, upstairs (see p.134). Mon–Sat noon–2am.

MOUILLE POINT

★**Café Neo** 129 Beach Rd ☎021 433 0849; map pp.96–97. *Neo* serves up deli-style food with a Greek influence, with mains going for around R80. There are tasty breakfast options, such as Greek yoghurt with nuts and honey, or milky porridge with berries, and at other times there are meze platters, salads and sandwiches. A big draw is the umbrella-shaded outdoor seating area that offers views of the stripy lighthouse. Vegetarians can do well here, too. Daily 7am–7pm.

★**Newport Market and Deli** Amalfi, 125 Beach Rd ☎021 439 1538, ⦿newportdeli.co.za; map pp.96–97. This two-floor deli, with views onto Table Bay, serves coffee, juices, gourmet sandwiches (R80), tasty salads such as watermelon and feta (R80), and hot dishes including macaroni cheese (R70) and burgers. The smoothies are packed with interesting blends such as pawpaw, mixed berries and mango (R38) – just right if you are walking or jogging along the Sea Point promenade. Daily 6.30am–6.30pm.

TOP 5 CAPE EATS

Sushi and people watching *Sevruga* (see p.124)

Experimental tapas *Pot Luck Club* (see above)

Coffee and breakfast *Origin Coffee* (see p.124)

Afternoon tea *Belmond Mount Nelson Hotel* (see p.125)

Vegetarian *The Kitchen* (see above)

SEA POINT

La Boheme Wine Bar & Bistro 341 Main Rd ☎021 434 6539, ⓦlabohemebistro.co.za; map pp.96–97. Come here for an enjoyable and good-value night out. The menu is full of interesting, well-presented rural French food and lovely wines by the glass; dishes, which are around the R100 mark, include the likes of confit rabbit and slow-braised pork belly. There's pavement seating for people-watching too. Next door is their sister espresso and tapas bar *La Bruixa* – great for a small bite to eat, and fantastic coffee. Mon–Sat noon–11pm.

Mr Chan 17 Regent Rd ☎021 439 2239, ⓦmrchan .co.za; map pp.96–97. This Cantonese restaurant has been keeping customers happy for years with excellent Hong Kong-style beef, seafood, roast duck and, for vegetarians, braised bean curd and mixed vegetables. Mains are around R90, with set dinner menus also available. Daily noon–2.30pm & 6–10.30pm.

CAMPS BAY

Café Caprice 37 Victoria Rd, Camps Bay ☎021 438 8315, ⓦcafecaprice.co.za. Across the road from Camps Bay Beach, this lively, albeit pretentious, Mediterranean-style restaurant's pavement tables are a time-honoured place to soak up the chichi suburb's street life, sunshine and sunsets. You can get nibbles like hummus and ciabatta (R45), more substantial meat, pasta or seafood dishes (R90), and myriad sexy cocktails (R85). Mon 12.30pm–midnight, Tues–Sun 9.30am–midnight.

Paranga Shop 1, The Promenade, Victoria Rd, Camps Bay ☎021 438 0404, ⓦparanga.co.za. Popular hangout at the beach, a place to see and be seen while you pick at salads, seafood, sushi or burgers (mains R130). There's a variety of champagnes and local MCC bubblies on offer (glass from R95), plus all sorts of wines, single malts and cocktails while you watch the sun sinking into the ocean. Daily 9am–midnight.

HOUT BAY

★**Kitima** 140 Main Rd, Hout Bay ☎021 790 8004, ⓦkitima.co.za. One of Cape Town's best Asian-fusion restaurants, with a definite Thai slant, is situated in a lovely Cape Dutch homestead, where the food couldn't be fresher. There's sushi and sashimi, dim sum and a plethora of seafood, meat stir-fries and curries, with dishes ranging from salmon *panang* (R175) to ostrich with lemongrass (R140). *Kitima* is best known for its sumptuous Sunday buffet (R250), for which you'll definitely need to book. Tues–Sat 5.30–10.30pm, Sun noon–3.30pm.

La Cuccina Victoria Mall, Victoria Rd, Hout Bay ☎021 790 8008, ⓦfacebook.com/lacuccina. This high-quality deli and café occupies a roomy and appealing space, and its delicious food compensates for the lack of sea views. Its mall location on the main road through town

makes it a great pit stop for wholesome breakfasts (R70), quiches, salads, lasagne and the like, with a pay-by-weight lunch buffet offered from noon to 3pm (R195 for 1kg). Daily 7.30am–5pm.

Wharfette Bistro Mariner's Wharf, Harbour Rd, Hout Bay ☎021 790 1100, ⓦmarinerswharf.com. A relaxed and popular seafood restaurant, decorated with nostalgic photographs and memorabilia from Cape Town's passenger-liner days. The views from the terrace seating overlooking the harbour outshine the food, but it's a fine spot to eat hake 'n' chips (R70) while sipping a cold beer. Daily 10am–8.30pm.

NOORDHOEK

Café Roux Noordhoek Farm Village ☎021 789 2538; 74 Shortmarket St ☎061 339 4438; map p.52; ⓦcaferoux.co.za. This chilled-out café in Noordhoek Farm Village offers wholesome and healthy food with a contemporary feel, as well as regular evenings of live music or comedy. They serve breakfasts (R70), lunch mains such as a Cape Malay roti wrap (R85) and other energizers for a day on the peninsula, with a menu and garden catering to children. Sit under umbrellas with a butternut and goat's cheese salad (R85), or have a cup of tea after driving Chapman's Peak, and gaze at the surrounding mountains. The kitchen closes at 3.30pm. Noordhoek Farm Village daily 8.30am–5pm; 74 Shortmarket St Tues–Fri noon–2am, Sat noon–midnight.

★**The Foodbarn** Noordhoek Farm Village ☎021 789 1390, ⓦthefoodbarn.co.za. Gourmet French food from acclaimed chef Franck Dangereux is served at reasonable prices here, compared to the top restaurants in the city centre. Starters such as fish tartare (R95) will get your taste buds humming, and the mains (R180) include fish and vegetarian choices as well as meats such as Karoo lamb rack and seared duck breast. Every dish has a suggested wine pairing, so you may need to organize a taxi to take you home after a lingering lunch. Booking is essential; check out the deli or tapas bar for something more casual. Mon & Sun noon–2.30pm, Tues–Sat noon–2.30pm & 7–9.30pm.

KOMMETJIE

★**Blue Water Café** Imhoff Farm, Kommetjie Rd, opposite the Ocean View turn-off ☎021 783 4545, ⓦimhofffarm.co.za. A great stop if you are on a Cape Point round route, *Blue Water* offers good seafood dishes (mussels R115), pastas (R100), wood-fired pizzas (R100) and local wines, as well as breakfast and tea. Set in a handsome Cape Dutch homestead, there are good views onto the wetlands and ocean beyond, and there's a fire to warm the place in winter. Service is attentive, and you can book outdoor tables next to the large lawn, where children can play – plus there's plenty at the farm to keep them occupied. Tues 9am–5pm, Wed–Sun 9am–9pm.

FALSE BAY SEABOARD

MUIZENBERG

Cusina Labia Casa Labia, 192 Main Rd ☎ 021 788 6062, ⓦ casalabia.co.za; map pp.104–105. At *Casa Labia* (see p.102), you can expect contemporary Italian food and English-style high teas in seafront *palazzo* surroundings, furnished with oil paintings, antiques and beautiful table linen. Lavish breakfasts are on the menu and classical pianist Jean-Paul Grimaldi-Lasserre adds to the pervading elegance on weekends between 1pm and 3pm. There's usually a good art exhibition on upstairs, and the small craft shop sells carefully chosen pieces. Courtyard dining comes with mountain views, and you can soak up the historical experience of being inside the grandest house along Muizenberg's historical mile. Tues–Sun 10am–4pm.

Empire Café 11 York Rd ☎ 021 788 1250, ⓦ empirecafe .co.za; map pp.104–105. Enjoy Woodstock-roasted Tribe coffee and munch on fresh pastries while sitting upstairs at this local hangout, gazing at passing trains and the blue ocean beyond, and waiting for the surf to come up. It's a popular breakfast spot and the ever-changing lunch menu features burgers, fish 'n' chips, pastas, salads, sticky pork ribs and chicken wraps, while drinks range from craft beer to gourmet milkshakes. Mon–Thurs & Sat 7am–4pm, Fri 7am–9pm, Sun 8am–4pm.

KALK BAY

Harbour House Restaurant Kalk Bay Harbour ☎ 021 788 4133; map pp.104–105; Quay 4, Ground Floor, V&A Waterfront ☎ 021 418 4744; map p.66; Hout Bay Rd, Constantia Nek ☎ 021 795 0688, ⓦ harbourhouse.co.za. This memorable Kalk Bay venue serves seafood and Mediterranean dishes (mains around R200), in a spectacular setting on the breakwater of Kalk Bay harbour. Book a table with bay views or enjoy sundowners on the deck, and in winter retire to the fireplace and comfortable sofas. Seafood options are the obvious choice – the Mozambique grilled prawns are worth a try, but the menu also features lamb, beef and salads. Portions are small, but rich and beautifully plated. Booking is essential. Kalk Bay Harbour daily noon–4pm & 6–10pm; V&A Waterfront & Constantia Nek daily noon–10pm.

Kalky's On the harbour ☎ 021 788 1726; map pp.104–105. For years, this no-frills seafood cabin has been serving the best traditional fish 'n' chips on the peninsula, as well as calamari, snoek, crayfish, prawns and good-value platters (R215). Fish is hauled off the boats and straight into the frying pan; wait a bit longer and you can have your catch grilled. You sit at benches to eat, and fish 'n' chips will set you back R55. Daily 10am–8pm.

★ **Olympia Café & Deli** 134 Main Rd ☎ 021 788 6396, ⓦ olympiacafe.co.za; map pp.104–105. Good enough to draw uptown Capetonians down to the False Bay seaboard,

Olympia is always buzzing, thanks to the harbour views, great coffee and their freshly baked goods. Gourmet lunch menus are chalked up on a board, with local fish and mussels often featured (mains around R100). They don't take bookings, so arrive early for dinner or join the queue. Their bakery is round the corner, where you can get bread, pastries, excellent takeaway coffee and sandwiches. Daily 7am–9pm, bakery 7am–7pm.

Under the Cypress 124 Main Rd, above Kalk Bay Books ☎ 021 788 2453, ⓦ underthecypress.co.za; map pp.104–105. Formerly the *Annex* restaurant, this historic building has tables under red umbrellas, on a terrace with superb views of the harbour and bay beyond. Accompany the views with local craft beers, ciders, wines and bar snacks such as fried calamari and squid heads (R65), or mains from Kalk Bay line fish (R145) to smoked and barbecued Greek lamb (R125). Mon–Sat 8am–9pm, Sun 8am–4pm.

FISH HOEK

C'est La Vie 2 Recreation Rd, Fish Hoek ☎ 083 676 7430. This unassuming and tiny French-style bakery is popular locally for its pavement breakfasts and sandwiches (R55), breadsticks, muffins, croissants, coffee and orange juice. Tues–Sun 7.30am–3pm.

SIMON'S TOWN AND THE DEEP SOUTH

Black Marlin Main Rd, south of Simon's Town ☎ 021 786 1621, ⓦ blackmarlin.co.za; map pp.106–107. Every kind of sea denizen, apart from the restaurant's namesake, is on the menu at this popular place on the road to Cape Point. While there's nothing wrong with the food, don't expect pyrotechnics, but the clifftop views from the outdoor tables certainly compensate – especially when there are whale sightings. Catch of the day costs R145, and the breakfasts are good value – scrambled eggs on toast go for R35. Daily 9am–10pm.

Salty Sea Dog 2 Wharf St, Waterfront, Simon's Town ☎ 021 786 1918, ⓦ saltyseadog.co.za; map pp.106–107. There's nothing fancy about this small restaurant on the wharf, but they do plain old fish 'n' chips (R70) extremely well, and they serve beer and wine. With indoor and alfresco seating, it makes a great lunch stop on an outing to Cape Point. Mon–Sat 8.30am–9pm, Sun 8.30am–4.30pm.

Two Oceans Cape Point ☎ 021 780 9200, ⓦ two -oceans.co.za; map pp.106–107. This touristic restaurant should more accurately be called "Two Ocean Currents", but no one seems upset on the alfresco deck that seems to float out a million miles above the ocean, taking in the whole of False Bay and its mountains. It's also a great place to see whales in season. As well as fish and seafood, they do sushi and some meaty options (mains from R145), plus gourmet breakfasts (R70) till 10.45am. Daily 9am–11am & noon–4.30pm.

8

HAPPY HOUR COCKTAILS ON LONG STREET

Drinking and nightlife

Cape Town has come a long way from the ribald port town nicknamed the Tavern of the Severn Seas, but it remains a hedonistic city – especially in summer, when the notoriously seasonal Capetonians emerge from hibernation. Travellers meanwhile drift into the famous "Cape coma", a blur of wild nights, lazy beach days and repeated extensions of their stay here. In the centre, Long and Bree Streets cater to most tastes and are relatively safe and busy, with taxis to take you home. In the summer, the Atlantic seaboard, notably chichi Camps Bay, is a great option for seafront sundowners and a glamorous crowd throughout the night. Clubs and venues play the same broad musical range as you'll find in a Western city, creating a varied nightlife encompassing sweaty electronic music dancefloors, grungy hangouts, hip wine bars and open-air artisanal beer gardens.

ESSENTIALS

Opening hours Most alcohol licences stipulate that the last round is served at 2am, although recently some have been granted until 4am. Clubs get going after 10pm and are pretty international in flavour, with DJs mixing house hits you're bound to recognize. Laws prohibit most bottle stores from selling liquor from 6pm on Saturday and all day Sunday.

Food Many watering holes are also restaurants, and may be better known as the latter; in a city where wine is produced, food and the grape definitely go together. Many bars and clubs offer food as well.

Safety It's really not a good idea to walk around late at night, with dangerous drunk drivers on the road and muggers on the street. Take along a friend or two if possible, and have a taxi number to get to the next bar or back to your hotel (see box below).

THE CITY CENTRE

Aces 'N' Spades 62 Hout St ☎076 070 4474, ⓦacesnspades.com; map p.52. This place is usually jam-packed from the bar (craft beers R35, wine R30), where chic meets grunge, to the heaving dancefloor where rock 'n' roll (or electronic on Wednesdays) sets the tempo for enthusiastic dancing. A safe bet for a great night out, with nightly DJs and live bands on Thursdays. Wed–Sat 6pm–2am.

Alexander Bar, Café & Theatre 76 Strand St ☎021 300 1088, ⓦalexanderbar.co.za; map p.52. Handsomely furnished in old-world decor, this is a good spot for a quiet conversation or a nightcap, and a much needed addition to Cape Town's social scene. Old rotary phones even allow you to call the cutie at the next table – or order a single malt (R40) from the bar. Upstairs is an intimate theatre space which hosts music, comedy and plays. Mon–Sat 11am–1am, Sun 3pm–midnight.

The Beerhouse 223 Long St ☎021 424 3370, ⓦbeerhouse.co.za; map p.52. With a beer menu comprising 25 on tap and 99 bottles, most of which are local craft brews, it's no wonder a whole day can go by at this industrial-styled "beer hall" without moving from the large balcony overlooking Long St. Beers cost R30–70, with tastings, food and regular events adding to the appeal. Daily 11am–2am.

Cafe Mojito 265 Long St ☎021 422 1095, ⓦfacebook .com/Cafe.Mojito.Cpt; map p.52. With a red star in its punchy signage, *Mojito* dishes up Cuban, Latin American and Caribbean cuisine and attitude. Pictures of Che Guevara and Ernest Hemingway overlook the tables spilling onto the pavement, where cocktails (from R45), happy hours (daily 4–7pm) and tapas keep the comrades happy. Daily 11am–2am.

Dubliner @ Kennedy's 251 Long St ☎021 424 1212, ⓦdubliner.co.za; map p.52. Crammed, wildly popular Irish pub with Guinness on tap (R30), a good selection of single malts, pub meals (burgers R80), and live music from 10pm every night. Other features include flat screens for sporting events and a nightclub upstairs. Daily 11am–4am.

★Era 71 Loop St ☎021 422 0202, ⓦeracapetown .com; map p.52. Rated one of the world's best clubs by *Mixmag*, *Era* promotes up-and-coming electronic DJs alongside seasoned artists. Local turntable stars such as Agugio and Killer Robot spin house flavours and devious techno cuts, with killer aesthetics and a café serving tapas. Cover charge R50–100, drinks R40. Men must be over 23, women over 21. Thurs–Sat 10pm–4am.

Fiction 226 Long St ☎021 422 0400, ⓦfacebook.com /Fictiondjbar; map p.52. Hosting standout electronic music nights since 2006, *Fiction* never fails to bring in

GETTING HOME SAFELY

Most Capetonians will tell you that walking around after dark, alone and inebriated, is to be avoided at all costs. Heed their words; and even if you are in a group, never carry your wallet or phone in your front or back pockets, as you will be quickly relieved of your possessions by light-fingered thieves. There are many independent and official cabs roaming the streets, but we recommend the following for a prompt, reliable and safe service.

Excite Taxis ☎021 448 4444, ⓦexcitetaxis.co.za. Fares are R9 a kilometre within their normal operating area (city centre to southern suburbs; open 24hr), but there may be an additional charge if your pick-up or drop-off point is further flung than this.

Intercab ☎021 447 7799. Available 24/7, this decade-old company charges R8.80 per kilometre.

Rikki's Taxis ☎0861 745 547, ⓦrikkis.co.za. Long-running Rikki's charges R10 per kilometre and offers cheaper ride shares and airport shuttles.

Sport Taxis ☎021 447 4444, ⓦsport24hrs.co.za. Rikki's affiliate charging the same rates. Tours and airport shuttles available.

Uber ⓦuber.com/en-ZA/cities/cape-town. A popular and convenient option, with rates from R7 per kilometre (and R0.70 per minute) with a R5 base fare and a minimum charge of R20. Download the app to your phone.

9

high-quality local and international DJs, attracting names from Skrillex to Johannesburg's Spoek Mathambo. Lose yourself on the energetic dancefloor, then head out to the balcony overlooking Long St to recover. Weekly nights range from Tuesday's Untamed Youth (indie) to It Came from the Jungle (drum and bass) on Thursday. Drinks R30; cover charge R50–70. Tues–Sat 10pm–4am.

The Gin Bar 64 Wale St ☎060 606 6014, ⏏www .theginbar.co.za; map p.52. This single-minded bar from the guys behind Honest Chocolate Café, with which it shares a courtyard, offers four artisan gin cocktails, called Head, Heart, Soul and Ambition. G&T fans can also design their own drink from a long list of gins and tonic waters (from R50). Mon–Sat 5pm–2am.

Jo'burg 218 Long St ☎021 422 0142; map p.52. A good, if crowded, place to hang out, grooving to a fresh soundtrack or playing pool with the thirsty crowd of backpackers, students and locals. Many people end up here at some point during a night out on Long St, especially on quiet Sunday nights. Cool off on the open-air patio outside. Drinks R30. Daily 5pm–4am.

★**La Parada** 107 Bree St ☎021 426 0330, ⏏laparada .co.za; map p.52. With its open frontage, vibrant atmosphere and Spanish tapas menu, *La Parada* is a highlight of the hip bars on Bree, and well-heeled Capetonians fill its long, sociable tables from lunch until late. House, classic and frozen cocktails go for R55–65, while a glass of wine will set you back R35. Downstairs in the basement, DJs spin in *Catacombs Bar* from 7pm to 2am Wednesday to Saturday. Daily 7am–2am.

Long Street Café 259 Long St ☎021 424 2464; map p.52. This local favourite near the top of Long St, identified by its neon sign and Art Deco windows, is popular for its great-value cocktails (R40) and bar food. It's easy to while away a few hours people-watching at the outside tables. Daily noon–1am.

Marimba CTICC, cnr Heerengracht St & Walter Sisulu Ave ☎021 418 3366, ⏏marimbasa.com; map p.47. This smooth restaurant and cigar bar at the Cape Town International Convention Centre offers what its name promises – live music from marimba maestro Bongani Sotshononda. Cocktails R40. Mon–Thurs 8am–midnight.

Murano Bar African Pride 15 on Orange Hotel, cnr Orange St and Grey's Pass ☎021 469 8000, ⏏marriott .com; map p.52. Like everything in this chic hotel, this

glittering bar is an extraordinary piece of design, draped with twenty thousand handmade Italian Murano glass links. Atop this art installation of a bar is an elevated pod, offering Table Mountain views and the feeling of floating in a chandelier. A glass of wine costs R40–60. Daily 24hr.

Orphanage Cocktail Emporium Cnr Bree and Orphan St ☎021 244 1995, ⏏theorphanage.co.za; map p.52. This concept cocktail bar's drinks are every bit as remarkable as its styling, which sends the roaring Twenties down the rabbit hole. Gargoyles watch over as the bar serves up artisan elixirs, twisted classics and tantalising intoxications on the drinks menu (from R70). The range of gourmet snacks adds to the decadent fun. Daily 4pm–late.

Publik Wine Bar 81 Church St ⏏publik.co.za; map p.52. This neighbourhood wine bar focuses on the more interesting and unusual products of the Cape's vineyards, which it also sells online. Settle in for a glass of "the best damned wines you've never heard of, yet" (R45–85); perhaps a red accompanied by some biltong from the adjoining artisan butcher, Frankie Fenner Meat Merchants. There's also a good charcoal restaurant, *Ash*, on site. Mon–Sat noon–11pm.

The Slug & Lettuce 224 Long St ☎021 424 7328, ⏏slugandlettuce.co.za; map p.52. This small South African chain (no relation to the UK chain of the same name) offers a jolly British experience, with a rocking horse, unicycle and bookshelves overlooking the barstools. It is not an English theme park however, and some reassuringly South African shooters, snacks and mains are on offer (drinks R35). There is another branch nearby at 64 Kloof St. Daily 11am–2am.

ThirtyOne 31st floor, ABSA Centre, 2 Riebeek St ☎021 421 0581, ⏏facebook.com/thirtyone.absacentre; map p.47. Take the lift to the thirty-first floor of the ABSA Centre, one of Cape Town's landmark towers, for a night of wraparound views. At its Friday and Saturday shindigs and special events, the recently renovated club makes the party people feel on top of the world. Cover charge R100, drinks R50. Men must be over 23, women over 21. Fri & Sat 10pm–3am.

★**TjingTjing** 165 Longmarket St ☎021 422 4374, ⏏tjingtjing.co.za; map p.52. This rooftop cocktail bar is a low-key favourite for young professionals with its indie and electronica soundtrack and tempting menu of classic and house cocktails (R58–95) – expect unusual ingredients like candyfloss-infused vodka, Jelly Babies and cinnamon. Tapas are also offered, while *Torii* serves Asian food downstairs, and free wine tastings take place from 5pm to 7pm on Wednesdays. Tues–Fri 4pm–2am, Sat 6.30pm–2am.

Twankey Bar Cnr Wale and Adderley Sts ☎021 819 2000, ⏏tajcapetown.co.za; map p.52. Run by the neighbouring *Taj Hotel*, *Twankey* is an elegant spot specializing in cocktails (R85) devised by award-winning local mixologist AJ Snetler. Every infusion, syrup and garnish is made from scratch, and unusual cocktail-making methods are employed from wood-chip smoking to teapot brewing. Champagne (R60), craft beers on tap (R40) and snacks are also served in the historic

---

TOP 5 MUSIC VENUES

Electronic dance *Era* (see p.131)
Alternative rock *Aces 'N' Spades* (see p.131)
Live bands *The Waiting Room* (see p.133)
Pop *Zhivago* (see p.133)
Smooth tunes *Shimmy Beach Club* (see p.133)

marbled interior. Mon–Sat 3–11pm.

★**The Waiting Room** 273 Long St ☎021 422 4536, ⓦfacebook.com/WaitingRoomCT; map p.52. With gourmet burger aromas drifting up from *Royale Eatery* (see p.123), this long-running club is a good bet for live music and a boogie. Bands play on Tuesdays, Wednesdays and Thursdays; hip hop DJs hit the decks on Fridays; and Saturdays are all about house and disco. Cover charge R50–70, drinks R25. Tues–Sat 7pm–2am.

V&A WATERFRONT

The Waterfront is good for a quiet drink, with *Mitchell's Scottish Ale House* (see p.134) and a couple of other pleasant bars close to each other. Nearby, the party gets going on Somerset Road and up in De Waterkant, and there are a couple of good spots in Green Point, near the Cape Town Stadium. Most places in De Waterkant are listed in the "LGBT Cape Town" chapter (see p.151).

★**Bascule Bar** Cape Grace, West Quay Rd ☎021 410 7100, ⓦbasculebar.com; map p.66. Lovers of the dram have been known to splurge thousands of rand on a bottle, or even just a glass, of single malt at the *Cape Grace* hotel's whisky bar, one of the best stocked south of the equator. The whisky-tasting experiences are recommended and, with its terrace alongside the yacht marina, the bar is equally good for a beer or cocktail (R65). Daily 10am–midnight.

★**Grand Café & Beach** Haul Rd, Granger Bay ☎021 425 0551, ⓦwww.grandafrica.com; map p.66. This chichi beach paradise hidden between the Waterfront and Cape Town Stadium has sun loungers on the sand and a bulging menu of exquisite cocktails (R80). Book ahead for a prime sundowner spot. Sept–June Mon–Sat noon–2am, Sun noon–5pm.

Quay Four Tavern Quay Four ☎021 419 2008, ⓦquay4 .co.za; map p.66. Going for two decades, the *Tavern* is an old favourite with tourists and locals alike. Watch the world go by with a pint of tap beer or a cocktail (R50) on the terrace overlooking the Waterfront, enjoy a hearty pub meal or catch the nightly free live music. Daily 7am–2am.

Shimmy Beach Club 12 South Arm Rd ☎021 200 7778, ⓦshimmybeachclub.com; map p.66. With a private beach, outdoor deck and an infinity plunge pool to boot, it's no wonder the luxurious *Shimmy Beach Club* is draped with beautiful people day and night. Completing the flashy setup are an upmarket restaurant, indoor dancefloor, cocktail menu (R80) and live local and international electronic-music acts every Sunday during summer. Cover charge R150–250. Daily 11am–2am.

CITY BOWL SUBURBS

Kloof St is a fun strip for drinking; it's slightly less wild than Long St and dotted with bars that slowly peter out, like the drinkers, as it ascends Table Mountain.

The Power and The Glory 13d Kloof Nek Rd ☎021 422 2108; map p.77. On any night of the week, this diminutive bar-restaurant is a magnet for hipsters sporting neatly trimmed beards and checked shirts, red lipstick and vintage dresses. The stylish bistro, kitted out with old-school metal chairs and botanical drawing prints, serves coffee during the day and morphs from 5pm into a cosy bar serving craft beers and local wine (R40). Mon–Sat 9am–1am.

★**Yours Truly** 73 Kloof St ☎021 426 2587, ⓦyourstrulycafe.co.za; map p.77. This popular branch of a local mini-chain of cafés and bars attracts hillside hipsters and backpackers from adjoining *Once in Cape Town* (see p.116) to its elongated terrace. Draught beer (R40) and iced coffee, pizzas and wraps are accompanied by city views and a dependably uplifting soundtrack. Daily 6am–11pm.

SOUTHERN SUBURBS

Foresters Arms 52 Newlands Ave, Newlands ☎021 689 5949, ⓦforries.co.za. Happy local drinkers from students to families gather to quaff beer at the popular and busy "Forries" in the heart of leafy Newlands. A big wood-panelled pub, it boasts a hedged-in courtyard with a playground and benches for a lazy afternoon pizza (R90) and pint (R30). Going since 1852, it was once a regular overnight stop for carriages bound from the city to Simon's

Town. Mon–Sat 11am–11pm, Sun 9am–10pm.

Zhivago 103 Main Rd, Claremont ☎083 784 1644, ⓦzhivago.co.za. On the site of the old *Tiger Tiger*, *Zhivago* is fast becoming a Southern Suburbs party staple with its happy crowd dancing to Nineties and Noughties house and commercial tunes. Get ready for drinks specials for under R20. Cover charge R40 after 10pm. Thurs & Sat 9pm–4am.

ATLANTIC SEABOARD

★**Café Caprice** 37 Victoria Rd, Camps Bay ☎021 438 8315, ⓦcafecaprice.co.za. This beach-facing hangout, popular with tanned and gorgeous local celebs and wannabes, is just right for cocktails (R85). Families are welcome during the day for breakfast and lunch (see p.128), but the pace increases at sunset and the

9

ALL ABOUT THE BEER

While the bulk of South African **beer** production is monopolized by the huge South African Breweries (SAB; tours Mon 11am and 3pm, Tues–Sat 10am and noon, with additional tours on weekdays; R80; ☎021 658 7440, ⓦnewlandsbrewery.co.za), one of the world's largest beer makers and the oldest brewery in Africa, the country's beer landscape has recently undergone a small transformation. Propelled by the global **microbrew** renaissance in the USA, Australia, New Zealand and the UK, microbreweries have popped up nationwide, making excellent versions of popular American and European beer styles like weiss, IPA, amber and pale ales. Look out for the Western Cape's **Jack Black**, Boston Breweries, Darling Brew, Mitchell's and Cape Brewing Company. An interesting trend to watch out for is the beer-wine hybrids and experimental beers aged in wine barrels, produced by Cape Town microbreweries such as Devil's Peak and **Triggerfish** who are taking cues from the local winemaking industry.

Many of the microbreweries offer tours and tastings, and you can dip into the world of South African craft beer and find out about the latest festivals at ⓦbrewmistress.co.za. Good places to sample **craft beer** in Cape Town include:

Banana Jam Cafe 157 2nd Avenue, Kenilworth ☎021 674 0186, ⓦbananajamcafe.co.za. Although not centrally located, this Caribbean-themed restaurant is the place to go for a relaxed introduction to the spectrum of South African beer. Staff can talk you through their impressive selection of local and imported beers (330ml from R22), including some thirty on tap, eighty bottled and regular specials – try the six-sample tasting plate. Caribbean food, rum cocktails (happy hour daily 5–6pm) and reggae music are further reasons to trek to the Southern Suburbs. It's next to Kenilworth train station, served by the Southern Line to/from Simon's Town. Tues–Sun 11am–10pm.

★**Devil's Peak Taproom** 95 Durham Ave, Salt River ☎021 200 5818, ⓦdevilspeakbrewing.co.za. Sample the Devil's Peak range in their eclectic bar-restaurant (beers R21–42), adjacent to the brewery where the magic happens. As well as an excellent regular menu, they also offer beer and food pairing (R110). Mon–Sat 11am–2am, Sun noon–6pm.

Mitchell's Scottish Ale House Cnr East Pier & Dock Rd, V&A Waterfront ☎021 419 5074, ⓦmitchells -ale-house.com; map p.66. This no-frills pub serves the half-dozen ales made by the country's oldest microbrewery, Mitchell's of Knysna (established 1983), including the 7 percent Old Wobbly lager. Mon–Sat 11am–2am, Sun 11am–midnight.

pavement tables are like gold dust. Mon 12.30pm–midnight, Tues–Sun 9.30am–midnight.

Dunes 1 Beach Rd, Hout Bay ☎021 790 1876, ⓦdunesrestaurant.co.za. Right on Hout Bay beach, this whitewashed restaurant is a popular hangout for families, especially on sunny weekend afternoons when kids enjoy the jungle gym. Savour the sea view with a cocktail (R50) or glass of Krone bubbly (R50), made in Tulbagh. Daily 9am–10pm.

Jade Champagne Bar 39 Main Rd above Mano's restaurant, Green Point ☎021 758 4008, ⓦjadelounge.co.za; map pp.96–97. Classy lounge-bar with DJs, plush sofas, chandeliers and a semi-enclosed balcony to relax on with a cocktail (from R80). Entry for over 23 years only; reservations recommended. The entrance is on Vesperdene Rd. Thurs & Sun 10pm–4am.

FALSE BAY SEABOARD

★**Brass Bell** Kalk Bay Station, Main Rd, Kalk Bay ☎021 788 5455, ⓦbrassbell.co.za; map pp.104–105. The *Brass Bell* has arguably the best location on the peninsula, with False Bay's waves breaking against the wall of its outdoor terrace. There are twin decks overlooking a beach and kids' tidal pool and its station-side position is handy for that train home. Drinks include a range of draught beers and wines by the glass (R40), and there's decent fish and chips if liquid nourishment is not enough. Daily 11.30am–10pm.

Cape to Cuba 165 Main Rd, Kalk Bay ☎021 788 1566, ⓦcapetocuba.com; map pp.104–105. Bringing Cuban panache to False Bay, this rambling bar-restaurant is

crammed with an impressive hotchpotch of chandeliers, devotional objects, vases and references to Guevara and Hemingway. With trains trundling along the shoreline outside, it's an atmospheric setting for cocktails (R45) and live music (Sat & Sun 4–7pm). Daily 9am–midnight.

Tiger's Milk Cnr Beach and Sidmouth Rds, Muizenberg ☎021 788 1860, ⓦtigersmilk.co.za; map pp.104–105. With a sweeping view of Muizenberg Beach, this coastal outpost of Cape Town hip (there's also a city-centre branch at 44 Long St) fills to the gills beneath its exposed beams and high ceiling. Burgers and pizzas are on offer (R100), but simply gazing at False Bay over your craft beer or vino is appealing enough. Drinks around R40. Daily 11am–2am.

The arts and film

You'll find a satisfying and easily accessible range of dramatic and musical
performances on offer in Cape Town, while the visual arts and design are
thriving across the city. Theatres normally have seats available and tickets are
a bargain compared to the prices you'd pay in London or New York. You are
likely to find something appealing at the two major arts venues, the Baxter
and Artscape, be it a play, a classical concert, some opera, contemporary
dance or a sample of the burgeoning comedy scene, while the Fugard
Theatre is also worth investigating. The city is known for its Cape jazz,
developed by local musicians including Dollar Brand (now known as
Abdullah Ibrahim), and you can catch jazz in venues and on tours. The best
jazz event of the year is the Cape Town International Jazz Festival in late
March or early April (see p.34).

ESSENTIALS

Listings Social media, websites of venues and ticket retailers, posters tied to street lights and the daily *Cape Times* and *Argus*, which carry listings and reviews, are good for discovering what's on. Listings magazine *021* (w021magazine.co.za), on sale at Vida e Caffè cafés and bookshops, has a comprehensive selection of cultural listings. *Cape Town Magazine* (w capetownmagazine.co.za)

is another good source of local knowledge.

Tickets Tickets for most of the venues and performances listed in this chapter are available from Computicket (t0861 915 8000, w computicket.com) or Webtickets (t086 111 0005, w webtickets.co.za). Most ticket prices are very reasonable at R100–200.

10

THEATRE AND MUSICALS

Cape Town's premier physical theatre company, **Magnet** (w magnettheatre.co.za), produces consistently excellent, politically conscious, non-didactic physical theatre. Some productions collaborate with contemporary dance and theatre company **Jazzart** (w jazzart.co.za), which attracts the finest black dancers in town, who have forged a fusion of Western and African dance in their work.

Alexander Bar, Café & Theatre 76 Strand St t021 300 1088, w alexanderbar.co.za; map p.52. An intimate 45-seat space which hosts music, comedy, play readings and theatre, many of which are written and performed by local playwrights, actors and artists, giving a real taste of the South African arts scene. From R40.

Artscape D.F. Malan St, Foreshore t021 410 9838, w artscape.co.za; map p.47. Cape Town's most central and largest arts venue, where major productions are staged. Catch contemporary dance, ballet, opera, orchestral music, comedy and musicals, with some adventurous new dramas appearing periodically. Don't be intimidated by the brutalist 1970s architecture; this is one of the city's liveliest venues.

Baxter Theatre Centre Main Rd, Rondebosch t021 685 7880, w baxter.co.za. This mammoth brick theatre complex is the cultural heart of Cape Town, and its doors remained open to everyone throughout apartheid. Mounting an eclectic programme of innovative plays,

comedy festivals, jazz and classical concerts and kids' theatre, it's the first place to check out what's on in Cape Town.

Fugard Theatre Caledon St, East City t021 461 4554, w thefugard.com. Named after South Africa's greatest living playwright (see box below), the Fugard runs a cross-section of interesting productions in the historic Sacks Futeran building, on the east side of central Cape Town in the old District Six. It's entered through the stylishly renovated Congregational Church Hall, which has a particularly nice ambience for a pre- or post-show drink.

Kalk Bay Theatre 52 Main Rd, Kalk Bay t021 788 7257, w kalkbaytheatre.co.za. Stages a lively programme including musicals, comedy, theatre and tribute bands in a converted church, and its restaurant offers dinner-and-a-show deals.

Masque Theatre 37 Main Rd, Muizenberg t021 788 1898, w masquetheatre.co.za. Small community theatre

CAPE TOWN'S FINEST

Athol Fugard is historically the best known of South African playwrights internationally, continuing to produce a steady trickle of innovative plays. Concerned with forging a new African or fusion theatre, Fugard's powerful and nuanced plays evolved from didactic protest theatre; his critically acclaimed, anti-apartheid work includes *Boesman and Lena* (1969) and *"Master Harold" and the Boys* (1982). Director Gavin Hood turned Fugard's novel **Tsotsi** (1980) into the Oscar-winning film of the same name (2005).

More visceral is the brilliant **Brett Bailey**, who creates electrifying, chaotic visual and physical theatre with his company **Third World Bunfight** (w thirdworldbunfight.co.za). The company does theatre productions, installations, house music shows and opera, mostly concerned with the post-colonial landscape of Africa. You're as likely to catch his works in Europe as you are in Cape Town. The city's most famous son is Cape Town-born Royal Shakespeare Company actor **Sir Antony Sher**, who regularly returns to the Mother City to appear in fabulous productions.

David Kramer and the late **Taliep Petersen** produced several hit **musicals**, including *District Six – The Musical* (1987). Kramer (w davidkramer.co.za) is well known for his show *Karoo Kitaar Blues* (2001), presenting the unique finger picking and guitar tunings of marginalized people in the South African hinterland; pick up the soundtrack or DVD from w takealot.com or the African Music Store (see p.144). His recent work includes an adaptation of Willy Russell's Liverpool-set hit *Blood Brothers*.

offering everything from brow-furrowing modern drama to sparky comedy. Conveniently located next to False Bay Station.

Maynardville Open-Air Theatre Piers/Wolfe St, Wynberg ☎ 021 410 9838, ⓦ maynardville.co.za. Every year from late January to late February, an imaginative production of a Shakespeare play is staged by the cream of Cape Town's actors and designers under the summer stars in Maynardville Park. Tickets R80–180. Take a picnic and something warm to put on as the evening wears on.

Moyo Cape Town's branches are at Kirstenbosch gardens & Bloubergstrand beach ☎ 021 762 9585, ⓦ moyo.co.za. These African-themed restaurants offer a theatrical albeit commercial experience, with hand-washing and face-painting ceremonies, colourful costumes, song and dance to accompany your meal. Check the website for details of upcoming acts.

Theatre On The Bay 1 Link St, Camps Bay ☎ 021 438 3301, ⓦ pietertoerien.co.za/venues. Known for adapting headline shows from overseas to the local stage using South African actors, Theatre On The Bay puts on Liberace-esque performances of drama, musicals, comedy, cabaret, music and dance. The bistro and bar make it a pleasant venue for an evening out.

UCT Drama Department Hiddingh Campus, 31–37 Orange St ☎ 021 650 7121, ⓦ drama.uct.ac.za. The University of Cape Town's drama faculty has a few performance spaces on its campus near the Company's Garden. The 75-seat Intimate Theatre (ⓦ facebook.com /TheIntimateTheatre), the 240-seat Little Theatre (ⓦ facebook.com/UCTLittleTheatre), and the smaller, more experimental Arena Theatre nurture the local student theatre scene, with productions by UCT groups and others. Check also "UCT Drama" on Facebook.

V&A Waterfront ⓦ waterfront.co.za/events /overview. There's always something going on at the Amphitheatre, from buskers to dance troupes – part of the Waterfront's lively programme of outdoor entertainment.

10

COMEDY

Comedy has a well-established following, particularly among coloured Capetonians, making the mix of Afrikaans slang and cultural references educating, if potentially bewildering, for outsiders. A great place to see a few is the Baxter Theatre (see p.136) from late July to late August, when **Jive Cape Town Funny Festival** hosts local and international comedians. The genre's star is **Trevor Noah**, the lovable coloured boy from Soweto who was "born a crime" under apartheid and, in 2015, succeeded Jon Stewart as host of American news satire programme *The Daily Show*. If you can get a seat at one of his sold-out home-coming shows, the 35-year-old remains one of South Africa's funniest stand-ups, whose leading themes are often political and centred around his mixed-race heritage.

Another renowned stage satirist is **Pieter-Dirk Uys**, whose character **Evita Bezuidenhout**, South Africa's answer to Dame Edna Everidge, has relentlessly roasted South African society since apartheid days. He often performs in Cape Town, though the best place to catch him is his venue in Darling, 85km north of the city (see below). New-generation comedians to look out for include **Marc Lottering**, a coloured Capetonian who derives his material from his own community; **Nik Rabinowitz**, an irreverent middle-class Jewish boy who uses his fluency in Xhosa to poke fun at cultural stereotypes; **Riaad Moosa**, a Muslim doctor-turned-comedian; and **Loyiso Gola**, anchor of the e.tv news satire show *Late Nite News with Loyiso Gola*.

In addition to the following, many of the venues listed under Theatre and Musicals host comedy.

★ **Cape Town Comedy Club** The Pumphouse, 6 Dock Rd, V&A Waterfront ☎ 021 418 8880, ⓦ capetowncomedy.com. The city's only major dedicated comedy venue, run by comedian Kurt Skoonraad, the former Jou Ma Se Comedy Club features up-and-coming South African comedians as well as established acts like Rob van Vuuren. If you like irreverent puppets, look out for Conrad Koch and Chester Missing. The stone-walled nineteenth-century building with a full restaurant menu available makes for a great evening out.

★ **Evita se Perron** Old Darling Station, 8 Arcadia St, Darling ☎ 022 492 2831, ⓦ evita.co.za. Just over an hour's drive north of Cape Town, the town of Darling is well worth visiting for its campily converted train station, which plays host to the satirical shows of Tannie Evita aka Pieter-Dirk Uys. It makes for a fantastic day out, and is a notable highlight of a stay in Cape Town. Since performances are dependent on Uys's schedule, check the website for dates.

ImproGuise ☎ 072 939 3351, ⓦ facebook.com /ImproGuise. Going for two decades, the city's oldest and best-loved improvisational comedy group regularly performs its *TheatreSports* show (akin to *Whose Line is it Anyway?*) at venues including the Waterfront's Galloway Theatre.

Obviouzly Armchair 135 Lower Main Rd, Observatory ☎ 021 460 0458, ⓦ facebook.com/pg/armchaircomedy. The backpackers and pub hosts the *Armchair Sundays* comedy night from 8pm on Sunday.

Premium Comedy Premium Sports Bar, Westridge, Mitchells Plain ☎ 072 399 3338, ⓦ facebook.com/pg /PremiumComedyAtPremiumSportsBar. It doesn't get much more authentically local than this comedy night at a sports bar in the coloured area of Mitchells Plain on the Cape Flats (see p.87). It takes place on Tuesday nights, once or twice a month.

CLASSICAL AND JAZZ MUSIC

Classical music is thriving, albeit for small and elite audiences, and one of the best things you could see on a visit to Cape Town is an opera. As in all areas of the arts, there is a quest for fusion, which has given rise to some fascinating performances, usually with a black cast boasting some of the most superb voices in the country: a great statement about opera crossing cultural barriers and centuries. **Cape Town Opera** (w capetownopera.co.za) and the century-old **Cape Town Philharmonic Orchestra** (w cpo.org.za) are both based at the Artscape (see p.136). The latter regularly performs **symphony concerts** at the City Hall, while UCT Symphony Orchestra, based at the university's South African College of Music (SACM; Woolsack Dr, UCT Lower Campus, Rondebosch ☎ 021 650 2626, w music.uct.ac.za), appears at the Baxter Theatre (see p.136). Free **lunchtime concerts**, showcasing the work of SACM students and staff, take place on Thursdays during term time in the Baxter's Concert Hall or nearby in the college's Chisholm Recital Room. The 40min concerts start at 1pm. You can also watch performers' classes in either venue on Wednesdays at 2pm, as well as examination recitals.

Recitals by visiting soloists and chamber ensembles are put on by an organization called **Cape Town Concert Series** (w ctconcerts.co.za), and there are excellent performances in churches by Cape Town's only baroque ensemble, Camerata Tinta Barocca. Check their Facebook page (w bit.ly/CamerataTintaBarocca) for upcoming concerts.

Jazz was the soundtrack to the struggle against apartheid, with dissenters listening all night in illegal clubs and stars like Miriam Makeba going into exile. Jazz-themed township **tours** run by the likes of Coffeebeans Routes (see p.29) tell this story and include performances in musicians' homes. Try to catch a concert by a local jazz legend such as Abdullah Ibrahim or Hugh Masekela. Popular jazz venues are **The Crypt Jazz Restaurant** (1 Wale St; ☎ 079 683 4658, w thecryptjazz.com), atmospherically located in the crypt beneath St George's Cathedral, and **The Piano Bar** (cnr Napier and Jarvis sts, De Waterkant ☎ 021 418 1096, w thepianobar.co.za).

On Sunday evenings from November to April, **Kirstenbosch Summer Concerts** (see p.84) are an unmissable experience, offering live music of all styles with a backdrop of Table Mountain. Bring a picnic and a bottle of Cape bubbly to enjoy during the show, and arrive a couple of hours early to get a spot of lawn with a good view.

CINEMA

With its low production costs compared with the likes of L.A. and London, Cape Town is booming as a filmmaking centre, having appeared in everything from *Homeland* season four (doubling for Islamabad) to the Ryan Reynolds movie *Safe House*. On the N2 to Somerset West and the Cape Winelands, you'll spot the pirate ship from the series *Black Sails* outside Cape Town Film Studios. Sadly, local feature films remain scarce, but some excellent documentaries are produced. There are several film festivals of note: **Cape Town International Animation Festival** (w ctiaf.com) screens animations from far and wide in March; each June, South Africa's leading film school shows short films by students at the **AFDA Experimental Film Festival** (w afda.co.za); the **Encounters South African International Documentary Festival** (w encounters.co.za) in June or July features riveting South African documentaries as well as award-winning international films; the **Tri Continental Film Festival** (w tcff.org.za) in October has a strong sociopolitical emphasis on the developing world; and you can catch screenings of around thirty new South African short films and documentaries at the **Cape Town & Winelands International Film Festival** (w films-for-africa.co.za) in November.

★**Labia** 68 Orange St, Gardens ☎ 021 424 5927, w thelabia.co.za. The retro Labia (Lah-bia) shows an intelligent mix of art-house films, mainstream features and cult classics, and is Cape Town's only independent cinema. Tickets cost R50. Check the website for excellent movie-and-a-meal deals at local restaurants.

Ster-Kinekor Nouveau Victoria Wharf, Waterfront ☎ 086 166 8473, w sterkinekor.co.za. One of two cinemas in the Victoria Wharf mall, this reliable art-house cinema shows films throughout the day (tickets R65–90).

OPEN AIR CINEMAS

Galileo Open Air Cinema ☎ 071 471 8728, w thegalileo.co.za. Catch an all-time classic under the stars at locations from the Castle of Good Hope to the Cape Winelands. Sunset over the Kirstenbosch gardens or Waterfront is a pretty spectacular backdrop. Tickets cost R80–160. Nov–April.

Pink Flamingo Grand Daddy Hotel, 38 Long St ☎ 021 424 7247, w granddaddy.co.za. The urban rooftop setting, complete with vintage Airstream trailers, makes this a memorable option for open-air cinema, with tickets from R125. Grab a drink from the adjoining *Sky Bar*. Mondays at sunset.

DESIGN ON THE EDGE OF AFRICA

Winning the **World Design Capital 2014** award (ⓦ www.wdccapetown2014.com) confirmed Cape Town's status at the forefront of South African contemporary design. The twelve-month stint and its legacy projects injected a new enthusiasm for design and its potential for social improvements, with highlights ranging from sustainable development projects to graphics.

To get a feel for Cape Town design, head to **Woodstock** (see p.80), with its design-orientated shopping complexes and art galleries, and stop for a coffee at the **Field Office** cafés (34 Salisbury Rd and Woodstock Exchange, 66 Albert Rd ⓦ fieldoffice.co.za) owned by local designers Pedersen + Lennard. Closer to the centre, check out **Southern Guild** (Shop 5B, Silo 5, V&A Waterfront ⓦ southernguild.co.za), which showcases high-end South African design in the Waterfront's new **Silo District**, also home to the Zeitz MOCAA (see p.67).

Another place to check out is the **East City**, the area southwest of the Castle of Good Hope, roughly bordered by Darling, Roeland, Buitenkant and Canterbury streets. Between 2009 and 2013, the area was promoted as **The Fringe** (ⓦ thefringe.org.za), a hub for creativity, entrepreneurship and innovation created by organizations including the Cape Town Partnership (ⓦ capetownpartnership.co.za). Based on an "urban science park" model, the area is home to a host of design studios and institutes working to put Cape Town on the global design map.

Shops and galleries in the East City and the city centre open late until 9pm on the first Thursday of the month, during **First Thursdays** (ⓦ first-thursdays.co.za/cape-town). Started in a bid to get people walking around at night, the free event has helped to rejuvenate areas such as Bree and Harrington streets. If you're in Cape Town in March, keep an eye out for the ever-growing **Design Indaba** (ⓦ designindaba.com), which hosts international and local speakers, music, film, exhibitions and more. Another design festival to look out for is **Open Design** (ⓦ opendesignct.com), held over twelve days in mid-August.

10

MODERN AND CONTEMPORARY ART GALLERIES

Most of South Africa's substantial collections of modern and contemporary art can be seen in private galleries and corporate environments. From serious commercial players dealing at the highest level, to small galleries showcasing urban pop art, Cape Town has a small but passionate community of curators, auction houses and art lovers. Both the local scene and art across the continent are attracting a greater share of the international limelight thanks to the opening of the Waterfront's major **Zeitz MOCAA** see p.67. The city's calendar of annual art events includes the **Cape Town Art Fair** (ⓦ capetownartfair.co.za) in February.

Erdmann Contemporary and The Photographers Gallery 84 Kloof St ☎ 021 422 2762, ⓦ erdmann contemporary.co.za. Committed to promoting contemporary South African photography and fine art, with past exhibitions showing the likes of Walter Battiss. Visits by appointment.

Everard Read 3 Portswood Rd, V&A Waterfront ⓦ everard-read-capetown.co.za. First opened as a bric-a-brac shop in Johannesburg in 1913, before opening in Cape Town in 1996, this is one of the country's oldest and most prestigious galleries. It contains the work of international and local artists in a range of media including sculpture, painting, lithography, multimedia, craft and photography. Mon–Fri 9am–6pm, Sat 9am–1pm.

Goodman Gallery 176 Sir Lowry Rd, Woodstock ⓦ goodman-gallery.com. Housed in an old textile factory, this industrial-chic gallery is at the forefront of contemporary art in South Africa. It houses an A-list of local artists, including William Kentridge, Willem Boshoff and photographer David Goldblatt, alongside emerging artists engaging with African issues. Tues–Fri 9.30am–5.30pm, Sat 9.30am–4pm.

Johans Borman Fine Art 16 Kildare Rd, Newlands ⓦ johansborman.co.za. A satisfying collection of works by South African old masters like Sydney Kumalo and Neville Lewis, as well as contemporary artists, housed in a smart suburban home. Mon–Fri 9.30am–5.30pm, Sat 10am–1pm.

The South African Print Gallery 109 Sir Lowry Rd, Woodstock ⓦ printgallery.co.za. This small gallery is the only one that focuses solely on South African printmaking, with a thousand-plus prints by artists including Alice Goldin, Joshua Miles and Anton Kannemeyer. Mon–Fri 9am–4.30pm, Sat 9am–1pm.

Stevenson 160 Sir Lowry Rd, Woodstock ⓦ stevenson .info. With a focus on conceptual art and photography, Stevenson hosts solo and group exhibitions, featuring the likes of internationally acclaimed photographers Pieter Hugo and Jo Ractliffe. Mon–Fri 9am–5pm, Sat 10am–1pm.

Whatiftheworld 1 Argyle St, Woodstock ⓦ whatiftheworld.com. This tiny gallery has been gaining a reputation as a platform for a new generation of emerging artists, hosting group and solo exhibitions and publishing catalogues and monographs. Watch out for Athi-Patra Ruga, Cameron Platter and Julia Rosa Clark to name a few. Tues–Fri 9.30am–5pm, Sat 9.30am–2pm.

TRADITIONAL AFRICAN BEADWORK

Shopping

The V&A Waterfront is the city's most popular shopping venue: it has a vast range of shops, the setting on the harbour is lovely and there's a huge choice of places to eat and drink. Nearby, the Cape Quarter complex, accessed off Somerset Road on the border of Green Point and De Waterkant, is smaller and more exclusive. The city centre itself offers much variety: Long Street is great for South African crafts, gifts, antiques and secondhand books, while Bree and Kloof offer unique designer goods. For something edgier, the increasingly gentrified city-fringe districts of Woodstock and the East City are destinations in their own right, with clusters of cutting-edge design shops, markets and some of the city's best restaurants and cafés. Cape Town's Green Map (ⓦgreenmap.org) is a great source of information about ethical shopping, organic markets, delis and health shops.

ESSENTIALS

Opening hours Shops have traditionally opened from Monday to Friday 8.30am–5pm and Saturday 8.30am–1pm, though lots of supermarkets, bookshops and other specialist outlets are now open beyond 5pm and also on Sunday. That said, don't expect much to be open on Sunday afternoons, except at the Waterfront or Cavendish Square (Claremont), and no alcohol is sold in shops on Sunday in South Africa. The Waterfront has the latest opening hours, with many shops staying open until 9pm.

FASHION, CRAFTS AND JEWELLERY

Designers abound in Cape Town, and with the added fillip of the city being crowned World Design Capital 2014, you'll find plenty of interesting clothes and handmade objects to fill your luggage. Cape Town is not known for its indigenous arts and crafts, and apart from some beadwork, wirework and township tableaus, many of the goods you'll buy here are from elsewhere in Africa, especially Zimbabwe and Zambia. There are several crafts outlets in the city centre and the V&A Waterfront; in the latter, the **Watershed** (see p.65) is a relaxing space with myriad retailers under one roof. You can pick up the same wares for less at the pavement **markets** scattered around town, but prepare to be overwhelmed by choice and varying quality. Don't expect exotic West African-style affairs: with the exceptions of Greenmarket Square and the Pan African Market, Cape Town's markets are more like European or North American flea markets. If you're after South African gold and diamonds, you'll find the **V&A Waterfront** is one of the best places to browse – but price tags are high.

11

FASHION

In addition to Long St and Woodstock's stores, the Watershed at the Waterfront has several designers in one spot. Hope Street Market (see box, p.144) also hosts a monthly fashion market, where you'll find everything from handmade jewellery to vintage clothing in addition to its usual food stalls.

Afraid of Mice 86 Long St ⓦafraidofmice.com; map p.52. Afraid of Mice offers hand-picked vintage women's wear, one-of-a-kind pieces and "the clothes you wish your mother had kept for you". Brands such as Chanel, Marc Jacobs, Ralph Lauren and Stella McCartney are displayed in a clean white environment. Mon–Fri 9.45am–5pm, Sat 10am–2pm.

Mememe Cnr Church & Long sts ⓦmememe.co.za; map p.52. A selection of somewhat edgy women's clothing and accessories characteristic of Capetonian style, such as sassy summer dresses, leather handbags and costume jewellery. Mon–Fri 9.30am–5.30pm, Sat 9am–3pm.

Mungo & Jemima 108 Long St; map p.52; also in the Watershed ⓦmungoandjemima.com; map p.66. Provides a platform for a variety of local designers, including the owners' labels Coppelia and Good, selling small-run women's clothing collections encompassing bikinis, soft cotton dresses and maxi-dresses in their elegant, white-painted boutique. 108 Long St Mon–Fri 10am–6pm, Sat 10am–5pm; Watershed daily 10am–6pm.

The Space Cavendish Square, Claremont ⓦthespace.co.za. A women's clothing store celebrating local designers from Adam & Eve dresses to Zamaan turbans. Find a designer one- or two-piece swimsuit, handmade sandals or casual-chic afternoon wear. Mon–Sat 9am–7pm, Sun 10am–5pm.

CRAFT SHOPS

★**Africa Nova** 72 Waterkant St, De Waterkant; map p.66; also in the Watershed ⓦafricanova.co.za; map p.66. A better-than-average selection of ethnic crafts and curios as well as contemporary African textiles and artwork, with an emphasis on the individual and handmade. In Cape Quarter mall, it is a dependable stop for quality souvenirs including Ardmore porcelain. Both stores: Mon–Fri 9am–5pm, Sat 10am–5pm, Sun 10am–2pm.

Ethno Bongo 35 Main Rd, Hout Bay ⓦandbanana.com. A charming shop selling quirky and well-priced crafts, jewellery and accessories made from reclaimed wood and recycled metal, as well as textile masks and bags – recommended for unique gifts and souvenirs. Mon–Fri 10am–5.30pm, Sat & Sun 10am–4pm.

Kalk Bay Modern 136 Main Rd, Kalk Bay ⓦkalkbaymodern.co.za; map pp.104–105. Contemporary photography, ceramics and jewellery as well as fine art and San textiles, with solo and group shows making this a cultural hub and a place to pick up something collectable. Daily 9.30am–5pm.

Monkeybiz 61 Wale St, Bo-Kaap ⓦmonkeybiz.co.za; map p.52. A nonprofit income-generating project that sells unique, handmade items by 450 bead artists, aiming to create sustainable employment, particularly for women. Mon–Fri 9am–5pm, Sat 9.30am–1pm.

★**Montebello Design Centre** 31 Newlands Ave, Newlands ⓦmontebello.co.za. A great selection of South African crafts – jewellery, beadwork, ceramics, sculptures and even musical instruments – are created here by small studios, many training people from townships to become artisans. Besides watching the craftsmen at work, you can eat at the restaurant under the oaks. Check the website for details of their occasional late-opening night markets. Mon–Fri 9am–5pm, Sat 9am–4pm, Sun 9am–3pm.

★**Streetwires** 77 Shortmarket St, Bo-Kaap ⓦstreetwires.co.za; map p.52. At this shop and working artists' studio you can try your hand at beading, purchase wire and bead craft artworks from lion heads to minibus taxis or even get something custom made. Mon–Fri 9am–5pm, Sat 9am–1pm.

MARKETS

★**Greenmarket Square** Burg St; map p.52. City-centre open-air market on a cobbled square where you can pick up loads of presents to take home, from all over the continent. To the sound of bongo drums, marketers tout items from beaded rhinos to batik. Mon–Sat 9am–4pm.

★**Pan African Market** 76 Long St; map p.52. A multicultural hothouse of township and contemporary art, artefacts, curios and crafts. There's also a café specializing in African cuisine, a bookshop, a Cameroonian hairbraider and a West African tailor. Mon–Fri 9am–5pm, Sat 9am–3pm.

Victoria Road Market Between Camps Bay and Llandudno. Carvings, beads, fabrics and baskets sold from a roadside market spectacularly sited on a clifftop overlooking the Atlantic. No set times, but usually daily 9am–4pm.

Watershed Dock Rd, V&A Waterfront ⓦwaterfront.co.za; map p.66. A creatively converted warehouse space with over 150 shops and stalls selling local art, craftwork, fashion, jewellery and more (see p.65). Daily 10am–7pm.

Wola Nani 9 Drake St, Observatory ⓦwolanani.co.za. A nonprofit organization established in 1994, Wola Nani supports crafters whose works include recycled papier-mâché bowls, jewellery, lampshades, tea light candle holders, beadwork and recycled-magazine mirrors. Mon–Fri 8.30am–4.30pm.

CERAMICS

Art In The Forest Off Constantia Nek Circle, Rhodes Drive, Constantia Nek; ⓖ also in the Watershed ⓦartintheforest.com; map p.66. Perched within a hillside forest with sweeping views, this is a thriving ceramic centre and gallery. The studio, run by ceramicist Anthony Shapiro, offers workshops and produces ceramics, while the gallery hosts exhibitions of leading South African ceramicists and showcases their Forestware range. Profits support their outreach programs for vulnerable children. Constantia Nek Mon–Fri 9am–4.30pm, Sat 10am–3pm; Watershed daily 10am–7pm.

Clementina Ceramics The Old Biscuit Mill, 375 Albert Rd, Woodstock ⓦclementina.co.za. Specializing in ceramics by Clementina van der Walt and other leading South African ceramicists, the shop also stocks unusual cards and other designer crafts. Clementina's tableware, vases and tiles, handcrafted in her Karoo studio, deliberately subvert the sterility of mass production. Mon–Fri 9am–5pm, Sat 9am–3pm.

FURNITURE

Private Collections 22 Hudson St, at Waterkant St ⓦprivatecollections.co.za; map p.66. Among the Cape Quarter mall's numerous upmarket arty shops, Private Collections is easy to miss yet possibly the most extraordinary offering. A massive warehouse on two levels, it's packed to the rafters with fantastic wooden architectural pieces, furniture and interior items from all over India, many of them antiques. Even if you're not planning on buying anything, just pop in and prepare to be awed. Mon–Fri 8am–5pm, Sat 9am–2pm.

BOOKS

South Africa has some very talented authors, and there are good, locally published novels as well as volumes on history, politics and natural history. Exclusive Books is the main chain you'll find in the airport and malls, while Upper Long St has several secondhand bookshops and a couple of notable independent bookshops.

★**Book Lounge** 71 Roeland St ⓦbooklounge.co.za; map p.47. The most congenial central bookshop, with comfy sofas and a downstairs café, stocks an excellent selection of local books and an imaginative list of imported titles, as well as hosting launches and stimulating events with local writers and intellectuals. Mon–Fri 8.30am–7.30pm, Sat 9am–5pm, Sun 10am–4pm.

Clarke's Bookshop 199 Long St ⓦclarkesbooks.co.za; map p.52. The best place in Cape Town for Africana has well-informed staff who can help you find what you want among the huge selection of local titles covering literature, history, politics, natural history, the arts and more. It also deals in out-of-print and collectors' editions of South African books. Mon–Fri 9am–5pm, Sat 9.30am–1pm.

Exclusive Books Victoria Wharf, V&A Waterfront ⓦexclus1ves.co.za; map p.66. Though small by British and American standards, Exclusive Books' well-stocked shelves include magazines and a wide choice of coffee-table books on Cape Town and South African topics. There are also branches in the Cavendish Square (Claremont) and Constantia Village malls, though their opening times may vary. Daily 9am–9pm.

Kirstenbosch Shop Gate 1 & Gate 2, Kirstenbosch National Botanical Gardens, Rhodes Dr, Newlands ⓦsanbi.org. A good selection of natural-history books, field guides and travel guides covering southern Africa, as well as a range of titles for kids. You don't need a Gardens ticket to browse. The shop inside Gate 2 is smaller than the one inside Gate 1. Gate 1 daily 9am–6pm; Gate 2 daily 9am–4.30pm.

Wordsworth Books Gardens Centre, off Mill St, Gardens; map p.77; 395 Main Rd, Sea Point; map pp.96–97 ⓦwordsworth.co.za. A good general bookshop, with a strong selection of literature and travel. Both stores Mon–Fri 9am–7pm, Sat 9am–5pm, Sun 9am–2pm.

CLOCKWISE FROM TOP LEFT OSTRICH EGGS FOR SALE; SHOPPING ON LONG STREET; BEACH TOWELS IN PORT ELIZABETH (P.248); TRIBAL MASK >

NEIGHBOURHOOD FOOD AND CRAFT MARKETS

Evening and weekend markets are weekly rituals for lovers of fresh air and food in Cape Town and the Winelands, with an ever-changing array of popular neighbourhood markets. Browse interesting craft and food stalls, grab breakfast, a gourmet burger or craft beer and often catch some live music. Most of the markets fill up as the day or evening wears on, so get there as early as possible. Also check out the excellent and family-friendly markets on Winelands estates such as Blaauwklippen, Lourensford and Vergenoegd Löw (see p.157).

Bay Harbour Market 31 Harbour Rd, Hout Bay ⓦbayharbour.co.za; map p.93. Hout Bay's lively weekend market fills a cavernous old fish factory with stalls selling African crafts and local designer clothes, alongside a host of artisan food traders – one even offering oysters and bubbly – and live acoustic acts. Fri 5–9pm, Sat & Sun 9.30am–4pm.

Blue Bird Garage Food & Goods Market 39 Albertyn Rd, Muizenberg ⓦbluebirdgarage.co.za; map pp.104–105. A lively Friday-night institution in the south, with stalls selling food, wine, craft beer, clothing and jewellery, often accompanied by live music, in a former aeroplane hangar next to the railway line. Fri 4–10pm.

Hope Street (City Bowl) Market 14 Hope St ⓦcitybowlmarket.co.za; map p.47. This indoor market's popularity has fluctuated over the years, but it remains a Thursday-evening staple, as much about meeting for a beer as grazing. Entering the market hall is a sensory experience, with jam-packed stalls laden with everything from curries to burgers and a live band creating a bubbly atmosphere. Take your pick from the mouthwatering options, then grab a spot at one of the communal tables. Thurs 4.30–8.30pm.

Mojo Market 30 Regent Rd, Sea Point ⓦfacebook .com/TheMojoMarket; map pp.96–97. Beneath Sea Point's colourful *Mojo Hotel*, the city's newest market has 45 craft, design and fashion stalls in addition to twenty food vendors, a fresh produce section, 24hr coffee shop, three bars and live entertainment. Daily 8am–11pm.

★**Neighbourgoods Market** Old Biscuit Mill, 373–375 Albert Rd ⓦneighbourgoodsmarket .co.za; map p.47. For over a decade, this Victorian warehouse has been one of the best places to experience the Cape's serious foodie credentials. Arrive when it opens to beat the devoted crowds, and wander around marvelling at the array of artisanal cheese, wood-fired bread, coffee, beer, fresh flowers, fruit and vegetables. Not cheap, but it sells the best produce of its kind in the Cape, as well as exceptional local designer crafts, homewares and clothing. Sat 9am–3pm.

★**Oranjezicht City Farm Market** Beach Rd, Granger Bay ⓦwaterfront.co.za/Shop/markets; map p.66. Despite its relocation from the mountainside farm to the Waterfront, locals pick up fabulously fresh organic produce at this market, stopping for a coffee and breakfast or lunch with a beer and sea views. Sat 9am–2pm, though produce sells out fast.

V&A Food Market Dock Rd, V&A Waterfront ⓦwaterfrontfoodmarket.com; map p.66. An enjoyable if commercialised lunch choice with forty stalls selling food from empanadas to ice cream in the historical Pumphouse. Daily 10am–6pm.

MUSIC

African Music Store 62 Lower Main Rd, Observatory ⓦfacebook.com/TheAfricanMusicStore;map p.52. Sadly relocated from its longstanding home on Long St, this small shop specializes in African music from around the continent. It also has a modest collection of instruments, such as shakers and thumb pianos. Mon–Sat 10.30am–5.30pm.

Mabu Vinyl 2 Rheede St, Gardens ⓦmabuvinyl.co.za; map p.77. The aficionado's choice for a great selection of both new and secondhand CDs, vinyl and even cassettes, of many genres. Since it featured in *Searching for Sugarman*, the Oscar-winning Rodriguez documentary, it has made a splash with tourists who drop by to see some musical history. Mon–Fri 9am–7pm, Sat 9am–6pm, Sun 11am–3pm.

Musica Cavendish Square, Claremont ⓦmusica.co.za. A generalist musical megastore for mainstream pop purchases, as well as African music, classical, jazz, rock, DVDs and video games. Mon–Sat 9am–7pm, Sun 9am–5pm.

FOOD AND PROVISIONS

Buying food from one of the weekly neighbourhood **markets** is always fun, while well-stocked delis provide more options. Of the major **supermarket** chains, Woolworths, which you'll find all over the city, is the most upmarket. It measures up to quality supermarkets in Western countries, with good food, bread and wine for picnics or packaged salads and microwaveable meals to eat at your lodgings. Otherwise look for a Pick n Pay or Spar. The larger branches of the better supermarkets have fishmonger counters, though by far the most atmospheric places to buy **seafood** are the Hout Bay and Kalk Bay harbours.

Cape Town also has a sprinkling of stores specializing in **health foods** and modest selections of organic fruit and vegetables, which you will also find at Woolworths. Supermarkets tend to have decent wine at competitive prices, but for more interesting labels, there are some first-rate specialist wine merchants. Otherwise, you can buy alcoholic beverages at **bottle stores** (the equivalent of the British off-licence), though most close at 6pm on Saturday and all Sunday, so plan ahead.

DELIS

Giovanni's 103 Main Rd, Green Point; map pp.96–97. Excellent breads and Italian foods to take away and – if temptation overcomes you – there's always the option of sitting down for a pavement coffee with a view of Cape Town Stadium. Daily 7.30am–8.30pm.

Melissa's 94 Kloof St, Gardens ⓦ melissas.co.za; p.77. Highly delectable imported and local specialities at this popular gourmet deli with the option of eating in. Three Southern Suburbs branches include Constantia Village Courtyard mall. Not cheap, but always worth it. Mon–Sat 7am–7pm, Sun 8am–6pm.

Organic Zone Lakeside Shopping Centre, Main Rd, Lakeside ⓦ organiczone.co.za; map pp.104–105. Always fresh and well-stocked organic fruit and vegetables, as well as grains, honey, breads and dairy products. Reasonably priced for the quality. Mon–Fri 9am–6pm, Sat 8am–5pm, Sun 9am–5pm.

FRESH FISH

Fish Market Mariner's Wharf, Hout Bay Harbour; map p.93. Fresh seafood from South Africa's original waterfront emporium, although it's slicker and less atmospheric than Kalk Bay Harbour. Daily 10am–8.30pm.

Kalk Bay Fish Market Kalk Bay Harbour, off Main Rd, Kalk Bay; map pp.104–105. Buy fresh fish directly from the fishermen and have it gutted and scaled on the spot.

Your best bet is during the morning, especially at weekends, though catches are dependent on several factors including the weather and rough seas, so you may not get any. Yellowtail fish are in good supply and excellent cooked on a braai. Daily 9am–5pm.

WINE

Caroline's Fine Wines 62 Strand St; map p.52; Forest Glade House, Tokai Rd, Tokai ⓦ carolineswine.com. Caroline Rillema has been in the wine business for decades and stocks the Cape's finest and most exclusive wines, with prices ranging from under R100 to over R1000. 62 Strand St Mon–Fri 9am–5.30pm, Sat 9am–1pm; Tokai Mon–Fri 9.30am–6pm, Sat 9.30am–1.30pm.

Vaughan Johnson's Dock Rd, V&A Waterfront ⓦ vaughanjohnson.co.za; map p.66. One of Cape Town's best-known wine shops, with a range of South African wines from far and wide, although it can be pricey. Mon–Fri 9am–6pm, Sat 9am–5pm, Sun 10am–5pm.

Wine Concepts Lifestyle on Kloof Centre, 50 Kloof St, Gardens; map p.77; Cardiff Castle, cnr Kildare Rd and Main St, Newlands; ⓦ wineconcepts.co.za. An excellent selection of South African and foreign wines from a knowledgeable and helpful outfit, with local estates often offering tastings. Lifestyle on Kloof Centre Mon–Fri 10am–7pm, Sat 9am–5pm; Newlands Mon–Fri 9am–7pm, Sat 9am–4pm.

MALLS AND SHOPPING CENTRES

South African shopping tends to follow the American model, with **malls** offering a sterile and safe indoor environment for browsing, banking and eating. The Waterfront, however, offers waterside cafés and fabulous views.

Blue Route Mall Tokai Rd, Tokai ⓦ blueroutemall .co.za. Major retailers and supermarkets are represented here, handy if you're staying in Constantia or along False Bay. Mon–Sat 9am–7pm, Sun 9am–5pm.

Cape Quarter 27 Somerset Rd, De Waterkant ⓦ capequarter.co.za; map p.66. This upmarket centre has a range of shops and boutiques selling everything from everyday essentials to quality souvenirs (see p.141). It's also a pleasant coffee stop. Mon–Fri 9am–6pm, Sat 9am–4pm, Sun 10am–2pm.

Cavendish Square Vineyard Rd, Claremont ⓦ cavendish.co.za. An upmarket multistorey complex, the major shopping focus for the Southern Suburbs. Mon–Sat 9am–7pm, Sun 10am–5pm.

Constantia Village Main Rd, Constantia ⓦ constantiavillage.co.za. Small, exclusive mall including two supermarkets, a post office and general, practical

shopping facilities. Next door is the similar Constantia Village Courtyard mall (ⓦ constantiavillagecourtyard.co.za). Mon–Fri 9am–6pm, Sat 9am–5pm, Sun 9am–2pm.

Gardens Centre off Mill St, Gardens ⓦ gardens shoppingcentre.co.za; map p.77. Close to the Company's Garden and city centre, this is a good-sized shopping mall with a broad selection of shops including two large supermarkets, a bookstore, pharmacy, opticians and local South African craft and fashion stores. Mon–Fri 9am–7pm, Sat 9am–5pm, Sun 9am–2pm.

Victoria Wharf Breakwater Boulevard, V&A Waterfront ⓦ waterfront.co.za; map p.66. It would be possible to visit Cape Town and never leave the Waterfront complex, which has a vast range of upmarket shops packed into the Victoria Wharf mall. You'll find the major South African chains, selling books, clothes, food and crafts, as well as two cinemas, one with art-house films. Daily 9am–9pm.

11

NEWLANDS CRICKET GROUND

Sports and outdoor activities

One of Cape Town's most remarkable features is its seamless fusion with Table Mountain National Park – a patchwork of mountains, forests and wild coastline – giving rise to myriad outdoor pursuits. In fact, there are few, if any, other cities in the world where so many activities are so easily available and affordable. For land lovers, there's the obvious draw of hiking up the imposing faces of Table Mountain, as well as mountain biking, rock climbing and horseriding. Surrounded by ocean beaches, the many surf schools and activity companies offer watersports from sea kayaking to kiteboarding, while daredevils can marvel at aerial views of the city by paragliding from Lion's Head. Alternatively, hit the spa, swing a golf iron or sink a few beers and watch high-calibre cricket, rugby or football – there's no denying it, South Africa is a sports-mad country.

PARTICIPATION SPORTS AND OUTDOOR ACTIVITIES

ABSEILING

Abseil Africa ☎ 021 424 4760, ⓦ abseilafrica.co.za. You can abseil off Table Mountain for R995, while a guided walk up Platteklip Gorge to the plateau goes for R495. Kloofing (canyoning) is also on offer.

BIRDWATCHING

Although Cape Town has fewer species of birds compared to the east of the country, its pelagic population raises the number over four hundred, including seven species of the endangered albatross. Good birdwatching spots include Lion's Head, Kirstenbosch Gardens, the Cape of Good Hope Nature Reserve, Kommetjie and Hout Bay.

Birding Africa ☎ 021 531 4592, ⓦ www.birdingafrica .com. Runs birdwatching tours throughout Africa and their website has a wealth of information on birding around Cape Town, with more at ⓦ capebirdingroute.org. Their fourteen-day Cape to Kruger itinerary costs from GBP3250 per person.

Cape Town Pelagics ☎ 021 531 4592, ⓦ www .capetownpelagics.com. Affiliated with Birding Africa, they run pelagic trips by boat if you're after the albatross and other rarities off the Cape coast. Day trips cost R2495 per person (including lunch).

World of Birds Valley Rd, Hout Bay ⓦ worldofbirds.org .za. The largest bird park in Africa with around three thousand birds and four hundred species. Entry R95. Daily 9am–5pm.

CYCLING

Cycling is very popular and a great way to take in the scenery, though you have to be vigilant about intolerant car drivers – cyclists are frequently knocked down.

Cape Town Cycle Tour ☎ 087 820 7223, ⓦ capetowncycletour.com. Spectacular annual 109km race around the peninsula, with up to forty thousand riders. Sadly the March event, formerly known as the Cape Argus, is often cancelled due to strong winds.

Moonlight Mass ⓦ moonlightmass.co.za. A nocturnal night bicycle ride once a month, starting at 9pm at the Green Point Circle. It began as a social experiment on Twitter to promote non-motorized transport, and has been gaining popularity since to become Africa's biggest social ride.

Pedal Power Association ⓦ pedalpower.org.za. Organizes and lists road and mountain biking events throughout the Cape.

GOLF

Cape Town has several well-maintained golf courses, all with dress codes and caddies. The courses are good value and the conditions are excellent.

Milnerton Golf Club Bridge Rd, Milnerton ☎ 021 552 1047, ⓦ milnertongolf.co.za. Tucked away on Woodbridge Island, between a lagoon and Table Bay, with classic views of Table Mountain. A challenging coastal links experience.

Non-members pay R650 to play eighteen holes.

Westlake Golf Club Westlake Ave ☎ 021 788 2020, ⓦ westlakegolfclub.co.za. Situated at the southern end of the Constantia valley where the M3 south ends, with a mountainous backdrop, Westlake is one of the nicest courses to play on, with visitors always welcome. Non-members pay R700 to play eighteen holes.

GYMS

Virgin Active ☎ 086 020 0911, ⓦ virginactive.co.za. These gyms are upmarket, well-appointed and dotted conveniently around the peninsula, all with large swimming pools and spotless changing rooms. There are branches in Wembley Square, Gardens and the Netcare Christiaan Barnard Memorial Hospital. Prices vary between gyms, but a month membership at the Netcare Christiaan Barnard Memorial Hospital branch costs R1200.

HEALTH SPAS

Most of Cape Town's luxury hotels have spas attached, which you can use as a day visitor.

Twelve Apostles Hotel and Spa Victoria Rd, Camps Bay ☎ 021 437 9060, ⓦ 12apostleshotel.com. One of Cape Town's most lavish spas, in the most beautiful setting imaginable with mountain and ocean views. There are hot and cold plunge pools as well as all the usual treatments. They also offer massages in the open air and an excellent high tea. A 90min treatment costs R1900. Daily 8am–8pm.

Vineyard Hotel Colinton Rd, Newlands ☎ 021 674 5005, ⓦ angsanaspa.com. A gorgeous garden setting with mountain backdrop and Zen-style decor makes this a truly serene spot. The treatment rooms are decorated in silks and everything at the spa, like the rest of the hotel, is elegant and pleasing. A 1hr massage costs R550. Daily 10am–8pm.

HIKING

The best places for easy walks are Kirstenbosch Gardens, Table Mountain's Pipe Track, the Sea Point Promenade and the beaches. A Table Mountain hike is to be taken seriously, so be prepared with a map and adverse weather gear. For safety advice see our information on Table Mountain (see box, p.75). Less experienced hikers can take a tour.

Guided by Mike ☎ 079 772 9808, ⓦ guidedbymike .co.za. Experienced and personable mountaineer Mike Wakeford leads hikes including Table Mountain, Silvermine Nature Reserve, the Cape Peninsula and beyond (half day R1500; full day R2200). Also offers rock climbing (see p.148).

Table Mountain Walks ☎ 021 715 6136, ⓦ tablemountainwalks.co.za. A registered Table Mountain guide, as well as offering other routes along the peninsula, Margaret Curran provides free pick-up from your accommodation, refreshments and lunch. Classic Table Mountain hike costs from R650/person.

12

HORSERIDING

Horse Trail Safaris Ottery ☎021 704 6908, ⓦ horsetrailsafaris.co.za. Rides lasting 1hr (R250) or 2hr 30min (R450), heading through the dunes to the coast and seeing endemic flora and fauna en route.

Sleepy Hollow Horse Riding Noordhoek ☎021 789 2341, ⓦ sleepyhollowhorseriding.co.za. Morning and afternoon rides on Noordhoek's spectacular Long Beach (2hr R530). Also bush trails and pony rides for children.

KAYAKING

Downhill Adventures ☎021 422 0388, ⓦ downhilladventures.co.za. One-hour, half-day and sunset paddles from Mouille Point, Simon's Town and Hermanus. From R650 per half day, with the option of incorporating a trip to Cape Point.

Kayak Cape Town ⓦ kayakcapetown.co.za. Two-hour trips from Simon's Town to the Boulders Beach penguin colony (R300).

Real Cape Adventures ⓦ seakayak.co.za. Half- and full-day sea-kayaking tours out of Hout Bay and Simon's Town, plus longer packages further afield. From R300.

KITEBOARDING

Kiteboarding has taken off in Cape Town and many companies offer lessons in Langebaan, a 90min drive north. This lagoon is one of the best spots, offering better conditions than the ocean around Cape Town, which has a bigger swell and is choppier. Closer to town, Blouberg and Big Bay, which host the Red Bull King of the Air competition every Feburary (ⓦ redbullkingoftheair.com), are well set up for beginners and the more advanced. For more tips see ⓦ kitespotters.co.za.

Cabrinha Kiteboarding Eden on the Bay Mall, Big Bay ☎021 554 1729, ⓦ cabrinha.co.za. Gear rental, repairs, lessons for kitesurfing (2hr introduction from R990, 4hr R1980, 12hr over three or four days R5346) as well as surfing (1hr R390) and stand-up paddleboarding (1hr R490, 2hr R980).

Cape Sports Center Langebaan ☎022 772 1114, ⓦ capesports.co.za. Offers kitesurfing, stand-up paddleboarding, kayaking and surfing, and has a range of accommodation. Lessons cost R400/hr or R3550 /10hr.

Surfstore Africa Muizenberg ☎021 788 5055, ⓦ surfstore.co.za. While not as good as options further afield, Surfstore Africa is accessible and great for beginners. Three-day lessons cost R4800; a tandem ride is R1600. They also offer stand-up paddleboarding and surfing.

MOUNTAIN BIKING

Day Trippers ☎021 511 4766, ⓦ daytrippers.co.za. Offers expert mountain-bike tours, including on Devil's Peak or to Cape Point. Downhill Adventures (see p.150) offers similar adventures, such as Devil's Peak or Tokai Forest.

PARAGLIDING

Cape Town has great air thermals for paragliding: the usual spot is from Lion's Head (or Signal Hill), drifting down to Camps Bay (or Sea Point).

Cape Town Tandem Paragliding ☎076 892 2283, ⓦ www.paraglide.co.za. Tandem flights R1150. Flights last 5–30min depending on wind conditions and pilots are certified by the South African Hang Gliding and Paragliding Association (SAHPA).

Wallend-Air School ☎021 762 2441, ⓦ wallendair .com. Peter Wallenda, one of SA's paragliding champs, offers tandem flights (from R1150), tours, introductory lessons and courses to get your paragliding licence.

ROCK CLIMBING

Table Mountain has fantastic rock-climbing routes for all abilities and there are some excellent guides. The cable car makes access to some pitches relatively easy.

City Rock 21 Anson Rd, Observatory ☎021 447 1326, ⓦ cityrock.co.za. For practice walls, you'll find serious climbers at this indoor climbing centre, which has good facilities including a bouldering area, a small wall for children and more challenging surfaces. Courses and yoga are also on offer. Day pass and gear rental cost R150.

Guided by Mike ☎079 772 9808, ⓦ guidedbymike .co.za. Offers climbs, hikes and kloofing (canyoning) throughout the Table Mountain Range, as well as further afield in the Western Cape (see p.147). Half day costs R1500.

High Adventure Africa ☎021 689 1234, ⓦ highadventure.co.za. Well known city rock-climber Ross Suter will take you to unusual and unique locations depending on your ability. Packages start at R550 per person, with a minimum of two climbers. Guided hikes are also offered (2–4hr costs R480 per person).

RUNNING

Two of the best places to jog are the Sea Point Promenade and Table Mountain's Pipe Track. Trail running (ⓦ trailrunning.co.za) is popular, with events on wine farms and elsewhere, especially during the winter. Local Parkruns (ⓦ parkrun.co.za) include Green Point Park, Rondebosch Common, Constantia, Fish Hoek and Root 44 Market.

Two Oceans Marathon ⓦ www.twooceansmarathon .org.za. Held every Easter Saturday, this one of the world's most exciting runs – athletes come from around the globe to run the arduous 56km ultra-marathon around the peninsula. The website also carries details of other events.

SAILING

Yachtmaster Sailing School ☎021 788 1009, ⓦ yachtmaster.co.za. Offers a range of courses from competent crew (five days R7150) to professional training.

Yacoob Yachts ⓦ yacoobyachts.co.za. Catamaran and

12

pirate boat cruises taking in Table and Bantry bays and Clifton beaches. Available twice daily, weather permitting, plus champagne sunset cruises (adult R260, child R130).

SANDBOARDING

Downhill Adventures 🕿 021 422 0388, ⓦ downhilladventures.com. The local pioneers of this sandy adventure sport. Boards, boots and bindings are provided, as well as expert instruction for beginners. Half day R950, full day R1100.

Sunscene Outdoor Adventures 🕿 021 783 0203, ⓦ sunscene.co.za. For extreme thrill junkies, Sunscene offers a full day of sandboarding (R1200) and combinations for paragliding (R2500), surfing (R1600) or sky diving (R3000).

SCUBA DIVING

While the Cape waters are cold, they're also good for seeing wrecks, reefs and magnificent kelp forests.

Scuba Shack Kommetjie 🕿 072 603 8630, ⓦ scubashack.co.za. Boat and shore dives, from R1900 for two boat dives including equipment, as well as dives in the Two Oceans Aquarium shark tank or kelp forest. You can also take the internationally recognized PADI Open Water Diver qualification. If you don't want to dive, you can snorkel with Cape fur seals off Kommetjie or Hout Bay.

SKYDIVING

The ultimate way to see Table Mountain and Robben Island is from a tandem jump from 3000m up.

Skydive Cape Town 🕿 082 800 6290, ⓦ skydivecape town.za.net. A 40min drive from Cape Town, this long-established business offers reliable, quality dives (R2300).

SURFING

Cape Town and its surrounding coastline are home to world-class waves including Dungeons off Hout Bay, one of the world's gnarliest (and most shark infested), while Jeffery's Bay is along the east coast. The Atlantic coast between Table Bay and Cape Point offers a host of beach and point breaks for all levels. Top surfing spots include Big Bay at Blouberg, Llandudno, and Long Beach near Noordhoek and Kommetjie. Muizenberg is the best place for beginners, with surf shops and schools along Beach Rd. Check out ⓦ wavescape.co.za for more information.

Gary's Surf School Muizenberg 🕿 021 788 9839, ⓦ garysurf.com. In the surf business since 1989, Gary's offers a 2hr lesson including gear for R450, which generally gets novices up and riding.

Surf Shack Muizenberg 🕿 021 788 9286, ⓦ surfshack .co.za. Various lesson packages available or just board and wetsuit rental R100 for 90min.

SWIMMING

Sea swimming is best in False Bay, as it is far warmer than the Atlantic side, especially at Muizenberg and Fish Hoek beaches, as well as St James Pool.

Long Street Baths Cnr Long and Orange sts 🕿 021 422 0100. Heated 25m indoor pool, with steam and sauna rooms to help you warm up on winter days (R22). Daily 7am–7pm.

Newlands Swimming Pool Cnr Main and Sans Souci rds 🕿 021 444 2828. An Olympic-sized pool with trees, lawns, mountain views and a paddling pool for children (R22). Daily 10am–5pm.

Sea Point Pavilion Swimming Pool Lower Beach Rd 🕿 021 434 3341. An Olympic-sized filtered saltwater pool, right on the edge of the ocean with lovely lawns to laze on, and watch the ships go by (R22). Daily: May–Nov 9am–5pm; Dec–April 7am–7pm.

YOGA AND PILATES

Cape Town is full of high-quality and excellent-value yoga and pilates studios. Visit ⓦ pilatesafrica.co.za for listings.

Wynberg Pilates Studio 18 Mortimer Rd, Wynberg 🕿 021 797 2351, ⓦ wynbergpilates.co.za. Experienced trainers for classes or individual tuition in a tranquil studio with a beautiful garden setting.

SPECTATOR SPORTS

CRICKET

Newlands Cricket Ground Campground Rd, Newlands 🕿 021 657 2003, ⓦ cricket.co.za. The city's cricketing heart, and one of the world's most beautiful grounds, Newlands nestles beneath the elegant profile of Devil's Peak. It plays host to provincial, test and one-day international matches.

FOOTBALL

Though football matches aren't as well attended as cricket or rugby, Cape Town football is burgeoning with talent and received a boost from the 2010 FIFA World Cup. The Cape Flats' streets have produced superb footballers such as Benni McCarthy (Porto, Ajax Amsterdam, Celta Vigo) and Quinton Fortune (Atlético Madrid, Manchester United). The city's most professional club is Ajax Cape Town (ⓦ ajaxct .com), while the most exciting games are those between a local outfit and one of the Soweto glamour teams, Orlando Pirates and Kaizer Chiefs. Matches take place at Cape Town Stadium (see p.92) in Green Point, which was built for the World Cup, and at Athlone Stadium, off Klipfontein Rd (M18) on the Cape Flats. For fixtures go to ⓦ psl.co.za.

RUGBY

The Western Cape is one of the world's rugby heartlands, and the game is followed religiously here.

Newlands Rugby Stadium Boundary Rd, Newlands 🕿 021 659 4600, ⓦ wprugby.com. Provincial, international and Super Rugby contests are fought on this hallowed turf.

12

THE CAPE TOWN GAY PRIDE FESTIVAL

LGBT Cape Town

South Africa has the continent's most developed and diverse LGBT scene –
and Cape Town is its capital, attracting LGBT travellers from across the
country and the globe. Cape Town is the only South African city with a
gay-friendly district, De Waterkant (aka the Pink Village), which is centrally
located with great cafés, nightlife and accommodation. Wandering around
the Pink Village, and to a lesser degree neighbouring Green Point and Sea
Point, you'll find a selection of places to drink and party. Happily, the country
has one of the world's first pro-homosexual constitutions: homosexuality is
legal between consenting adults of 16 or over, and same-sex marriage is
legal. Moffies (as local gays affectionately call themselves in Afrikaans slang)
can look forward to an enjoyable stay in the Mother City, but should be more
circumspect as they head out of town.

13

Outside the big cities, in Cape Town's suburbs and especially the townships, attitudes are largely conservative and homophobic. Open displays of affection by gays and lesbians are unlikely to go down well; white people may find it un-Christian, while black people may think it un-African. It's still especially hard for African and coloured gay men and women to come out, and homophobic attacks are a threat whatever your ethnicity, so be discreet and take care outside the city centre. If you are considering having a one-night stand, remember that South Africa has the world's largest population of people with HIV/AIDS.

As you'd expect in a city where the great outdoors figures so prominently, there are a number of beaches popular with the LGBT community, including **Clifton Third Beach** (see p.94) and the nudist **Sandy Bay** (see p.95). You can also get some fresh air with the **Cape Town Gay Hiking Club**, which has a Facebook page (bit.ly/CapeTownHiking).

RESOURCES AND CONTACTS

Health The Triangle Project (2nd floor, Leadership House, cnr Burg and Shortmarket Sts; phone line: daily 1–9pm; ☎ 021 712 6699, ⓦ triangle.org.za) is the longest established organization offering care and support for LGBT people including HIV testing, ARV advice and other medical services. They run a clinic most Tuesday evenings from 6pm. Johannesburg-based Health4Men (ⓦ health4men.co.za) is a health resource for gay men, providing advice on how to access screening and treatment for sexually transmitted infections including HIV.

Information The best resources for travel information and inspiration are ⓦ pinksa.co.za, ⓦ gaycapetown4u.com, ⓦ mapmyway.co.za/printed-maps, ⓦ www.mambaonline.com and ⓦ www.mambagirl.com.

Media Look out for monthly newspaper *The Pink Tongue* and other Lunch Box Media titles (ⓦ lunchboxmedia.co.za) in bars and restaurants in De Waterkant, and download the app or listen online to GaySA Radio (ⓦ gaysaradio.co.za).

Travel GAP Leisure (ⓦ gapleisure.com) is a travel agency specializing in gay holiday accommodation in both De Waterkant and countrywide. It's on the corner of Napier and Waterkant streets.

ACCOMMODATION

Most establishments have a relaxed attitude towards same-sex couples, especially in inner-city neighbourhoods such as De Waterkant, Green Point and Sea Point, and LGBT travellers should generally feel welcome. Listed below are half a dozen places to stay that are particularly accommodating.

4 on Varneys 4 Varneys Rd, Green Point ☎ 021 434 7167, ⓦ 4onvarneys.co.za; map pp.96–97. A little less extravagant than the other options, but still warm, welcoming and comfortable, this six-room Victorian townhouse boasts a gorgeous plunge pool and terrace, not to mention big, soft beds. Decorative flourishes such as crystal chandeliers and Afro-furnishings are complemented by excellent service from Thierry and Philip. R1200

Cactus House 4 Molteno Rd, Gardens ☎ 021 422 5966, ⓦ cactushouse.co.za; map p.77. Centrally located, this gay men guesthouse has five rooms in a beautifully renovated late nineteenth-century property with a pool, terrace and mountain views. R1200

★ **The Glen Boutique Hotel** 3 The Glen, Sea Point ☎ 021 439 0086, ⓦ glenhotel.co.za; map pp.96–97. This gay-friendly boutique hotel a few streets from Sea Point Promenade has two-dozen luxurious en-suite rooms and apartments, all with private terrace or garden. It has a spa, pool and restaurant and even organizes rental of cute convertible Mini Coopers and Renault Clios. R2160

LESBIAN PARTIES

For the newcomer, the gay scene in Cape Town is accessible: parties, clubs and bars geared towards men abound. But the **lesbian scene**, which is relatively tight knit and more elusive, has only recently found its feet. Following the global trend in the lesbian scene of using burlesque performance as a way of embracing female sexuality, a selection of new events has emerged.

The event company **MISS** (Make It Sexy Sisters; ☎ 083 760 8499, ⓦ missmakeitsexysisters .wordpress.com) is the best platform for lesbian DJs, performers and parties. Check their Facebook page (bit.ly/FacebookMISS) for details of upcoming events such as the monthly **Unofficial Pink Parties** (ⓦ facebook.com/pinkpartyza) and the **Rouge Revue Burlesque Company's** performances and classes (ⓦ therougerevue.co.za; ⓕ facebook.com /TheRougeRevue). Also check out **Beaulah Bar** (see p.153).

Guesthouse One Belvedere 1 Belvedere Ave, Oranjezicht ☎021 461 2442, ⚑onebelvedere.co.za; map p.77. A gay-friendly guesthouse in a lovely, two-storey colonial house dating to 1914 with views of Table Mountain. Rooms come with TV, DVDs, safe, and an entrance to the wraparound veranda, plus there's a pool, jacuzzi and steam room. R1700

13

EATING

★**Beefcakes** 40 Somerset Rd, De Waterkant ☎021 425 9019, ⚑beefcakes.co.za; map p.66. This is one seriously camp burger bar, with feather boas, balloons, flamingo wallpaper and seatbacks, where Capetonians of all persuasions don a sequinned cowboy hat, order a fabulous Martini (R60) and build their own juicy burger (R80). There is nightly live entertainment, from Drag Divas (Monday) to "Bitchy Bingo" (Tuesday), attracting a R80–250 cover charge. Mon–Sat 7–11.30pm.

Café Manhattan 74 Waterkant St, De Waterkant ☎021 421 6666, ⚑manhattan.co.za; map p.66. A stalwart of the gay scene since 1994, and recently taken over by the flamboyant and fantastic Madame Zingara group, this buzzing bar-restaurant's attractive oak-shaded terrace is ideal for people watching on the busy street. With an affordable and largely meat-orientated menu (R100), it's always bustling and lively, especially when the weather is good. Patrons of all genders and orientation will feel comfortable, though it is primarily a gay venue. Mon–Fri 4–11pm, Sat & Sun noon–11pm.

DRINKING AND NIGHTLIFE

Amsterdam Action Bar 10–14 Cobern St, off Somerset Rd, De Waterkant ⚑amsterdambar.co.za; map p.66. Old-school gay bar (men only) with a more mature crowd, keen on full leathers. There's no disco but they have a pool table, discreet booths and a small balcony overlooking the Pink Village. Next door, the affiliated *Backroom Bar* is renowned for its topless barmen and shower shows. Daily 4pm–2am.

Bar Code 18 Cobern St, De Waterkant ☎021 421 5305, ⚑leatherbar.co.za; map p.66. Men-only leather, rubber, uniform and jeans bar with dark rooms and an outdoor deck. There is a different theme every night, from underwear to fetish pig, so check the website beforehand. Cover charge R80. Weds–Sun 10pm–3am.

Beaulah Bar Cnr Somerset Rd & Cobern St, De Waterkant ☎021 418 5244, ⚑facebook.com/Beaulahbar; map p.66. Popular with lesbians and (to a lesser degree) gays for its fun nights such as Priests and Prostitutes, *Beaulah Bar* has all the frills with disco lights, a dancefloor, screens showing VH1 music videos and a DJ playing all the latest tracks. You will find a good mixture of couples and singles, with the crowd often migrating to *Crew Bar* next door for an after-party. Cover charge R30. Fri & Sat 9pm–4am.

Crew Bar 30 Napier St, De Waterkant ⚑facebook.com/CrewBarCapeTown; map p.66. This stylish bar's topless barmen and dancing table-top hunks fill the house every weekend with gays and their fun-loving straight friends, with pop music downstairs and harder beats upstairs. The nightspot to see and be seen in summer. Daily 7pm–4am.

FESTIVALS

Cape Town Pride Late Feb ⚑capetownpride.org. The annual Gay Pride Festival, running for a week starting late February, has a small Mardi Gras street parade in Green Point, plus pageants, pink parties and other fun events.

Miss Gay Western Cape Late Nov ⚑missgay.co.za. Drag beauty pageant with an after-party at a city gay club, raising funds to support health initiatives in Cape Town's LGBTQI community.

★**Mother City Queer Project Party** December ⚑mcqp.co.za. Cape Town's most famous festival, this hugely popular one-day shindig is one of the year's biggest parties and attended by all orientations. The city's answer to Sydney's Mardi Gras festival, people dress as outrageously as possible according to the official yearly theme (past themes have included "Space Cowboys").

Pink Loerie Mardi Gras & Arts Festival Late April ⚑pinkloerie.co.za. This festival in Knysna is a good excuse to load up your car with pink accessories and bumble on down to the Garden Route to spend a long weekend dancing in the streets.

SAUNA

Hot House 18 Jarvis St, De Waterkant ☎021 418 3888, ⚑hothouse.co.za; map p.66. A luxurious, men-only pleasure and relaxation complex, and the only one of its kind in Cape Town, with all manner of jacuzzis and steam rooms, as well as a sundeck boasting superb views. There's also a bar and an adult store. Entrance R90–180 depending on days and times. Mon–Wed noon–2am, Thurs noon–4am, Fri & Sat 24hrs, Sun noon–midnight.

Cape Town for kids

Cape Town and the Winelands are an excellent place to travel with children. You'll find a multitude of parks, gardens, activities and markets to enjoy with the whole family, not to mention child-friendly restaurants and a few rainy-day options. Highlights include walking Kirstenbosch's twisting Boomslang bridge and marvelling at the Two Oceans Aquarium's jaw-dropping array of sea monsters, while there are several play parks and wildlife centres. Cape Town's beaches offer a classic and easy summer-weekend family outing, and kids may enjoy riding the Metrorail train to False Bay, while older children can learn to surf, sand board, rock climb or horse ride (see p.146). Kids' menus are widespread and most restaurants are sympathetic to families, but don't expect facilities such as high chairs and changing rooms apart from in larger chains and malls.

ESSENTIALS

Car rental Companies will give you child seats if you ask for them in advance. However, they often forget to install the seat in your vehicle, so be prepared to wait while they find a seat and to install it yourself.

Entrance fees Activities are either free or around half the cost of an adult ticket. Children's prices in this chapter apply to under-12s, unless otherwise stated.

Resources A good website for finding out what's on is ⓦcapetownkids.co.za, while ⓦchildmag.co.za is a local parenting guide. For reputable babysitters or even nannies to accompany you on road trips, try Sitters4U (☎074 656 0469, ⓦsitters4u.co.za) or Super Sitters (☎021 551 7082, ⓦsupersitters.net).

14

MUSEUMS AND INDOOR FUN PARKS

Cape Town Science Centre 370B Main Rd, Observatory ☎021 300 3200, ⓦctsc.org.za. Kids will love the interactive displays on science, new technologies and inventions here, which appeal to their innate sense of curiosity with things to touch, push and create. Highlights include a gyroscope, the brain-teasing Puzzling Things exhibits and an inflatable planetarium. Entry R50. Mon–Sat 9am–4.30pm, Sun 10am–4.30pm.

Planet Kids 3 Wherry Rd, Muizenberg ☎021 788 3070, ⓦplanetkids.co.za. A great indoor play centre for kids up to 13, designed by an occupational therapist, which is loads of fun, as well as offering healthy snacks and a calmer environment than the usual plastic, sugar-crazed scene

(R35/hr, parents free entry). With assistants on hand, you can drop off your child for 1hr (R30–55), or have a cup of tea while you wait. All abilities welcome, with facilities for kids with special needs. Thurs–Sun 10am–5pm.

Rush 109 Main Rd, Claremont ☎021 683 3841, ⓦrushsa.co.za. To really burn off some energy, take the kids to this indoor trampoline park with around 2000 square metres of fun, including dodge-ball courts, a foam pit, hydraulic slam-dunk basketball hoops and of course wall-to-wall interconnected trampolines. Check the website for details of toddler-only time slots (R185 for adult and toddler; kids or adults R145/hr; prices include compulsory non-slip socks). Mon–Thurs 10am–9pm, Fri

BEACHES AND SWIMMING POOLS

Most of Cape Town's sandy **beaches** are pretty undeveloped, so it's best to take what you need in the way of food and drink, although you may come across vendors. Get to the beach as early as possible so you can leave by 11am before the sun gets too strong, and to avoid the wind, which often gusts up in the afternoon in summer.

On the False Bay seaboard, **Boulders Beach** (see p.108) is one of the few beaches to visit when the southeaster is blowing. It has safe, flat water, making it ideal for kids – and its resident penguin colony is an added attraction. **Fish Hoek** (see p.104) is another great peninsula beach, with gentle waves that are warm in summer, a long stretch of sand and a playground. The paved **Jager's Walk**, which runs along the rocky coast here, is suitable for pushchairs and offers beautiful views of the Hottentots Holland Mountains. **St James** (see p.102) boasts a safe tidal pool with a small sandy beach and photogenic bathing chalets, but gets overcrowded on the weekend. From here you can walk to **Muizenberg** and its water park (see p.100) along a pushchair-friendly coastal pathway, with more views of distant mountains across the water.

The **Atlantic seaboard** is too cold for serious swimming, but does have some lovely stretches of sand, boulders and rock pools – and astonishing scenery. The beaches here are excellent for picnics, and on calm summer evenings are an idyllic setting for sundowners and sunsets. In the summer they're less windy than the False Bay beaches, but the afternoons are often baking hot. The closest stretch of coast to the centre, ideal for prams – and rollerblading – is the paved **Sea Point Promenade**, stretching 3km from the lighthouse in Mouille Point to Sea Point Pavilion, with the draw of playgrounds and ice-cream sellers en route. The tidal pool and small rock pools of **Camps Bay** (see p.94) make this popular beach very child-friendly, and it's easily reachable from the centre by car or bus. Finally, the 8km stretch of white sand from **Noordhoek to Kommetjie** (see p.97) provides fine walking, kite-flying and horseriding opportunities, with stupendous views of Chapman's Peak. If you're heading for Kommetjie, consider a spot of camel riding at **Imhoff Farm Village** (see p.98).

As regards child-friendly swimming pools, **Newlands Pool** (see p.150) has a kids' paddling pool and large grounds, while the marvellous **Sea Point Pavilion Pool** (see p.94) has two splash pools for children and lawns to laze on, but is overcrowded on warm weekends, unless you go early or late in the day.

14

& Sat 9am–10pm, Sun 9am–8pm.

Scratch Patch and Mineral World Dido Valley Rd, off Main Rd, Simon's Town ☏021 786 2020; Dock Rd, V&A Waterfront ☏021 419 9429, ⊚scratchpatch.co.za. Over-3s can search for jewels, filling a bag (R17–95) with the colourful polished gemstones that cover the floor. At the Simon's Town venue you can also see Topstones (⊚topstones .co.za), one of the world's biggest gemstone tumbling plants, in operation (Mon–Fri only). Simon's Town daily 9am–4.45pm; V&A Waterfront daily 9am–6pm.

South African Museum and Planetarium See p.56. Great for rainy days, especially for 5- to 12-year-olds, who'll enjoy the four-storey "whale well" and African animal dioramas, as well as the dinosaur displays. The hands-on Discovery Room features live ants, pinned and preserved spiders and insects, and a crocodile display. The adjoining planetarium's changing programme of daily shows covers topics such as San sky myths, with some geared towards children. It was closed at the time of research; check ⊚iziko.org.za/museums/planetarium for schedules. Daily 10am–5pm.

★**Two Oceans Aquarium** See p.67. One of Cape Town's most rewarding museums, the aquarium has loads to interest a wide range of ages. Apart from the excitement of just looking at weird and wonderful sea creatures from sea horses to jellyfish, kids can actually handle species such as anemones and crabs in the touch pool. The Children's Play Centre usually has puppet shows, face painting and craft activities, as well as a window on the penguin pool. Daily 9.30am–6pm.

OUTDOOR PARKS AND PICNIC SPOTS

Blue Train Park Beach Rd, Mouille Point ☏084 314 9200, ⊚thebluetrainpark.com. Take a trip on Cape Town's favourite miniature train (R20) for a view of the sea, passing ships and Robben Island. There's also plenty to wear kids out afterwards in the park including a jungle gym, climbing rock, outdoor obstacles, basketball net, ice rink and toddler push-bike track. Tues–Sun 9.30am–6pm.

Bugz Playpark 56 Tarentaal St, Joostenbergvlakte, Kraaifontein ☏021 988 8836, ⊚bugzplaypark.co.za. This fun park offers all manner of activities, including a carousel, choo-choo trains, water slides, go-carts, toddler tractors, horseriding and zip-lining. Rides are open weekends only during term time. It's just off the N1, about 35km from the centre towards Paarl. From R45. Daily 9am–5pm.

★**Deer Park Café** See p.125. The most central outdoor family venue, adjoining a popular enclosed park (sadly no deer) with a good selection of jungle gyms, swings and so on, all overlooked by the towering massif of Table Mountain. There are outdoor tables with easy access to the park and a children's menu. Daily 8am–8pm.

Green Point Park Bill Peters Dr, Green Point ⊚gprra .co.za/green-point-urban-park. Offering vistas over the city and stadium, this grassy park has an educational Biodiversity Showcase Garden, tracks for jogging and cycling, a play park for small children and an outdoor gym for those a little older. Go for a picnic or join the 5km Saturday-morning Parkrun (⊚parkrun.co.za/greenpoint). Free entry. Daily 7am–7pm.

Imhoff Farm Village See p.98. Activities here include camel rides, horseriding on the beach, paintball, a farmyard petting zoo and reptile park. There's also a good café, restaurant and farmers' shop with fabulous cheeses. Daily 9am–5pm.

★**Kirstenbosch National Botanical Garden** See p.83. Top of the list for a family outing, with extensive lawns for running about, trees and rocks to climb, trickling streams for paddling and the beloved Boomslang treetop walkway. There's no litter, no dogs, it's extremely safe and you can push a pram all over the walkways; it's also great for picnics or to have tea outdoors at the café. For older kids there are short waymarked walks. Daily 8am–6pm.

Noordhoek Farm Village See p.97. A small, grassy green, surrounded by cafés, a deli, crafts stores and a gift shop, with gentle country charm. At the Weds food market (4–8pm) kids can tear around and enjoy the playground while their parents choose between stalls offering Mexican, Italian, craft beer and more. Daily 9am–5pm.

Oude Molen Eco Village Alexandra Rd, Pinelands ☏021 448 9442, ⊚oudemolenecovillage.co.za. A working model of a sustainable eco-village in a suburban area. You can sample home-grown organic produce and wood-fired bread at the *Millstone Farmstall and Café* before taking the kids to play in the garden tree house, swing and play area. Children are also encouraged to feed the horses and pigs nearby, while horseriding and nature walks can be organised. Tues–Sun 9am–5pm.

Silvermine Nature Reserve See p.104. A good place to see *fynbos* vegetation at close quarters while strolling around the lake and picnicking with small children; however, it is exposed, and not recommended in heavy winds or mist. For older children there are some mountain walks with relatively gentle gradients, which give spectacular views over both sides of the peninsula – try the hike to Elephant's Eye Cave on the Constantiaberg. Daily 8am–5pm.

Tokai Arboretum See p.88. When it reopens, the Tokai Forest arboretum will once again offer good walks and be a great place for young children to explore, with logs to jump off and a gentle walk to a stream; best of all it is sheltered from the wind. The roadside forest picnic area en route to the arboretum remains open. Free entrance. Daily dawn–dusk.

Western Province Live Steamers Bertie Genade St, off Frans Conradie Dr, Parow ☏021 788 2539, ⊚www .wpls.co.za. This model steam and electric train society, its tracks enjoying distant Table Mountain views, holds an open day once a month. Kids love trundling down the line and a snack bar sells refreshments. With families from the surrounding Afrikaans suburbs picnicking by the track, it's a local experience. Tickets cost just a few rand each, but get there early to beat the queues. First Sat of the month 1–4pm.

DAY-TRIPS FROM CAPE TOWN

With less of a premium on the price of real estate, and families trekking out from town for suburban space and an outdoors lifestyle, the Winelands offer at least as many child-friendly activities and venues as Cape Town.

14

★**Blaauwklippen Family Market** R44 between Stellenbosch and Somerset West ☎021 880 8653, ⓦblaauwklippen.com/family-market. The leafy environs, farm animals and rides make this food and craft market a hit among local families. Sun 10am–3pm.

Butterfly World Zoo R44, Klapmuts ☎021 875 5628, ⓦbutterflyworld.co.za. This sanctuary for butterflies, birds, exotic animals and reptiles is just off the N1 to Paarl. Wander the lush tropical gardens among fluttering wings, birdsong and trickling water – just take care not to step on the green iguana. Entry R45. Mon–Sat 9am–5pm.

Caveman Café 33 Canterbury Lane, Paradyskloof, Stellenbosch ☎021 880 0799, ⓦwww.specialized-stellenbosch.com. Attached to Specialized bike shop, this café has an enclosed play area with a sand pit and an impressive rubber bike track for kids to whizz around. On the menu are healthy, pedal-powering Banting, raw and chocaholic treats including organic muesli, quiche with salad (R50), beetroot juice, trail bars (R20) and locally roasted Deluxe Coffeeworks coffee. It's just off the R44 as you head south out of Stellenbosch towards Somerset West. Mon–Fri 7.30am–6pm, Sat 8am–3pm.

Giraffe House Old Paarl Rd, off R304, Muldersvlei ☎021 884 4506, ⓦgiraffehouse.co.za. This wildlife awareness centre is a fun place for kids to get some fresh air and learn about Africa's four-legged residents, through meeting animals including Gerry the hand-reared giraffe, antelopes, meerkats and zebras. Interactive creepy-crawly encounters take place at 11am, 1pm and 3pm on weekends. Entry R30. Daily 9am–5pm.

Kids Carnival Weltevreden Estate, off R304, Stellenbosch ☎021 889 6588, ⓦweltevredenestate .com. This Cape Dutch estate offers "a unique platform where a fusion exists between the wishes of the child and the cravings of the parent": in other words, kids can play on jungle gyms worthy of Willy Wonka's chocolate factory, bounce on the trampolines and build their own pizza while adults enjoy a drink and some food. Gourmet picnics are also available (R390 for two including a bottle of wine). Tues–Sun 9am–5pm.

★**Lourensford Market** Lourensford Wine Estate, Somerset West ☎072 284 1654, ⓦlfhm.co.za. In the idyllic surrounds of a historic wine estate, this food and craft market is great for families with its adjoining fairground and choo-choo rides. In summer, there's a Twilight Market every other Friday. Sun 10am–3pm; Twilight Market summer alternate Fri 4–9pm.

Radloff Park Hillcrest Rd, off Lourensford Rd, Somerset West. This public park tucked away in Somerset West is a lovely spot to experience some Winelands nature without having to pack the Kendal Mint Cake, with paths running along the Lourens River. Kids love riding bikes and paddling here, while the mountain views attract local dog walkers. It's close to the child-friendly Lourensford and Vergelegen Wine Estates. Free entry. Dawn–dusk.

★**Vergenoegd Löw Wine Estate** Baden Powell Dr, Faure, Stellenbosch ☎021 843 3248, ⓦvergenoegd .co.za. Not far off the N2 from Cape Town, this wine estate has popular daily parades of over a thousand Indian Runner ducks, which waddle past en route to pick pesky snails from the vines. Watching the spectacle is free, and duck tours are available (R10). The Cape Dutch estate also offers a garden restaurant, wine tastings, picnics, a kids' playroom with childminders and a bucolic Saturday food market (9am–3pm). Daily 8am–5pm; duck parade 9.45am, 12.30pm & 3.30pm.

VIEW ACROSS THE VINES, DELAIRE WINE ESTATE

The Winelands

An hour from Cape Town, the Winelands is all about indulgence – eating, drinking and relaxing. Each of the Western Cape's earliest European settlements, at Stellenbosch, Paarl, Franschhoek and Somerset West, has its own established wine route, packed with picture-perfect Dutch colonial heritage in the form of shimmering white, gabled homesteads, surrounded by vineyards and tall, slatey crags. To top it all off, the area has a disproportionate concentration of South Africa's stellar restaurants. Franschhoek, the smallest of the towns, is a centre of culinary excellence draped in heavily cultivated Provençal character. In a region of striking settings, it has the best – located at the head of a narrow valley. This is where you should go if you're principally after a great lunch and a beautiful drive out of Cape Town.

Stellenbosch, by contrast, has some attractive historical streetscapes, a couple of decent museums, cafés and shops and, as far as great restaurants go, it gives Franschhoek stiff competition. One of the region's scenic highlights is the drive along the **R310** across the heady **Helshoogte Pass** between Stellenbosch and the R45 Franschhoek–Paarl road. **Paarl**, also a pretty drive from Stellenbosch, is a workaday farming town set in a fertile valley overlooked by granite rock formations. Beyond, head to the sprawling town of **Somerset West** for its one simply outstanding drawing card: **Vergelegen**, one of the most stunning of all the Wineland estates.

GETTING AROUND   THE WINELANDS

By car All the wineries are an easy drive from Cape Town; if you're not staying overnight, you can easily visit four to six in a day.

By train Use the train line from Cape Town via Stellenbosch and Paarl with caution, as trains pass through rough areas

of the Cape Flats, and it is slow and unreliable.

On a tour Organized tours are operated from Stellenbosch (see p.163) and Cape Town, with many backpacker hostels and guesthouses running excursions. Stellenbosch's tourism office is also a good source of information.

INFORMATION

When to go Summer is the best time to visit, when opening hours are longer, the vines are in leaf and there's activity at the wineries. In winter the wine has been made and there are fewer cellar tours, though the landscape is still gorgeous, and many upmarket guesthouses charge half-price.

Wine tasting Wine tasting and buying are supposed to

be fun, so don't take them too seriously. If you aren't a wine buff, you'll often find staff at tasting rooms are happy to talk you through a wine. Most estates charge a fee for a wine-tasting session (anywhere up to R40) and some only have tastings at specific times. Note also that some wineries are closed on Sundays.

15

Stellenbosch

Dappled avenues of three-century-old oaks are the defining feature of **STELLENBOSCH**, 46km east of Cape Town – a fact reflected in its Afrikaans nickname Die Eikestad (the

---

TASTING THE FORBIDDEN FRUIT: SOUTH AFRICA'S WINES

Despite South Africa having the longest-established **New World** winemaking tradition (going back more than 350 years), its rapid growth in wine production is remarkable for having taken place in the decades since apartheid. Before that, South Africa's isolation had led to a stagnant and inbred industry that produced heavy Bordeaux-style wines. After the arrival of democracy in 1994, winemakers began producing fresher, fruitier wines. Many South African winemakers are finding their feet in wines that combine the best of Old and New World styles, and new wineries are opening up all the time, with more and more farms planting vines.

South Africa produces wines from a whole gamut of major cultivars. Of the **whites**, the top South African Sauvignon Blancs can stand up with the best the New World has to offer; among the **reds**, it's the blends, created from Cabernet Sauvignon, Merlot and Shiraz that really shine. Also look out for red wine made from Pinotage grapes – a somewhat controversial curiosity unique to South Africa – which its detractors feel should stay on the vine. **Port** is also made, and the best vintages come from the Little Karoo town of Calitzdorp along the R62 (see p.242). There are also a handful of excellent **sparkling wines**, including Champagne-style, fermented-in-the-bottle bubbly, known locally as **méthode cap classique** (MCC).

The most enjoyable way to sample wines is by visiting wineries. The oldest and most rewarding wine-producing regions to tour are the **Constantia** estates in Cape Town (see p.86) and the **Winelands**; other wine-producing areas covered by this guide include **Walker Bay** around Hermanus (see p.182) and the **Little Karoo** along the R62 (see p.230). If you're serious about your wine tasting, think about buying the authoritative and annually updated *John Platter's South African Wine Guide* (also available as an iPhone app), which rates wines from virtually every producer in the country. *Wine* magazine (Ⓦ winemag.co.za), published every month, has useful features on wineries, places to eat, wine reviews, information on latest bottlings, and a diary of events and wine festivals.

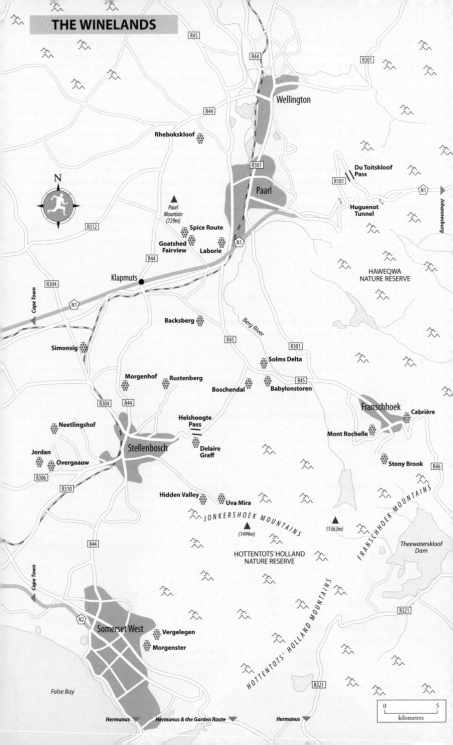

oak city). Stellenbosch's attractions lie principally in its setting and architecture, rooted in the seventeenth century, which make it a lovely place to simply wander around and one that's safe at night. Besides its historical and architectural sights, you'll find cafés and some good-quality galleries and arts and crafts shops down Church and Dorp streets.

Stellenbosch today is the heart of the Winelands, having more urban attractions than either Paarl or Franschhoek, while at the same time being at the hub of the largest and oldest of the Cape **wine routes**. The city is also home to Stellenbosch University, Afrikanerdom's most prestigious educational institution, which does something to enliven the atmosphere. But even the thousands of students and the heady promise of plentiful alcohol haven't changed the fact that at heart this is a conservative place, which was once the intellectual engine room of apartheid, and fostered the likes of Dr Hendrik Verwoerd, the prime minister who came up with the system (see p.264).

The tourist office is a good place to start your explorations. Heading east up this road, you'll soon reach a whitewashed block that was the **VOC Kruithuis**, the Dutch East India Company's powder magazine. From here, a right turn south down the side of the **Braak**, the large green occupying the centre of town, will take you past the **Rhenish Church** in Bloem Street, built in 1823 as a school for slaves and coloured people.

15

Village Museum
18 Ryneveld St • Mon–Sat 9am–5pm, Sun 10am–4pm • R25

Stellenbosch's highlight, the extremely enjoyable **Village Museum**, cuts a cross section through the town's architectural and social heritage by means of four fortuitously adjacent historical dwellings from different periods. They're beautifully conserved and furnished in period style, and you'll meet the odd worker dressed in period costume.

Earliest of the houses is the homely **Shreuderhuis**, a vernacular cottage built in 1709. With its small courtyard garden filled with aromatic herbs, pomegranate bushes and vine-draped pergolas, it bears more resemblance to the early Cape settlement's European aesthetics than to modern South Africa.

Across the garden is **Blettermanhuis**, which was built in 1789 for the last Dutch East India Company-appointed magistrate of Stellenbosch. It is an archetypal eighteenth-century Cape Dutch house, built on an H-plan with six gables. **Grosvenor House**, opposite, was altered to its current form in 1803, reflecting the growing influence of English taste after the 1795 British occupation of the Cape. The Neoclassical facade, with fluted pilasters supporting a pedimented entrance, borrows from the high fashion that was the style then at the heart of the growing empire. The more modest **O.M. Bergh House**, across the road, is a typical Victorian dwelling that was once similar to Blettermanhuis, but was "modernized" in the mid-nineteenth century on a rectangular plan, with a simplified facade without gables.

Dorp Street
Stellenbosch's best-preserved historic axis, **Dorp Street** lies south of the museum and is well worth a slow stroll just to soak up the ambience of buildings, gables, oaks and roadside irrigation furrows. Look out for **Krige's Cottages**, nos. 37–51 between Aan-de-Wagenweg and Krige streets, an unusual terrace of historic townhouses. The houses were built as Cape Dutch cottages in the first half of the nineteenth century; Victorian features were added later, resulting in an interesting hybrid, with gables housing Victorian attic windows and decorative Victorian verandas with filigree ironwork fronting the elegantly simple Cape Dutch facades.

ARRIVAL AND INFORMATION   STELLENBOSCH

By train Metrorail trains (☎ 0800 65 64 63, ⊛ metrorail .co.za) travel between Cape Town and Stellenbosch roughly every 90min during the day and take about 1hr, but use this line with caution.

By bus The Baz Bus runs daily from Cape Town to Somerset West, where it drops passengers off at the BP filling station next to the *Lord Charles Hotel*. Some hostels operate shuttle services from there, but you need to arrange this in advance.

STELLENBOSCH

Franschhoek

Jan S. Marais Park

UNIVERSITY

UNIVERSITY

Stellenbosch University Botanical Garden

MERRIMAN AVENUE

SOETEWEIDE ROAD

BANGHOEK ROAD

JOUBERT ROAD

SMUTS ROAD

DE VILLIERS ROAD

RYNEVELD STREET

BANGHOEK ROAD

BORCHERD ROAD

ANDRINGA STREET

BIRD STREET

MOLTENO ROAD

PAUL KRUGER ROAD

DENNESIG ROAD

HOFMAN ROAD

MERRIMAN AVENUE

DU TOIT ROAD

KOETSIEF

BERGZICHT ROAD

DU TOIT ROAD

ALEXANDER ROAD

MARKET

DENNESIG ROAD

ADAM TAS

MARAIS ROAD

VICTORIA STREET

HOFMEYR ROAD

DE WAAL ROAD

CLAASEN ROAD

BOSMAN ROAD

VICTORIA STREET

NEETHLING STREET

CROZIER ROAD

VICTORIA STREET

RYNEVELD STREET

PLEIN STREET

ANDRINGA STREET

City Hall

DROSTDY ROAD

Village Museum

CHURCH/KERK STREET

DORP STREET

BIRD STREET

The Braak

VOC Kruithuis

BLOEM

Rhenish Church

HERTE ROAD

KRIGE ROAD

HAMMAN ROAD

Oom Samie se Winkel

MARKET

PAPEGAAI ROAD

HEROLD ROAD

STRAND ROAD

WEIDENHOF STREET

Stellenbosch Station

CLUVER RD

VAN DER STEL RD

JONKERSHOEK RD

COETZENBURG ROAD

NOORDWAL-OOS ROAD

VAN RIEBEECK STREET

DIE LAAN

RATTRAY AVENUE

MINISERIE ROAD

VAN RIEBEECK STREET

THE AVENUE

SUIDWAL

Coetzenburg Stadium

Danie Craven Stadium

HELDERBERG ROAD

NOORDWAL-WES ROAD

LOUW ROAD

DORP STREET

BIRD STREET

PIET RETIEF STREET

MILL

SUIDWAL

AAN-DE-WAGENWEG

Eerste River

ADAM TAS

N

0   250   metres

ACCOMMODATION
10 Alexander	6
Banghoek Place	3
De Oude Meul	8
Glenconner	5
Knorhoek Country Guest House	2
Natte Vallej	1
Ryneveld Country Lodge	4
Stumble Inn	7

● EATING
Bird Cage	2
De Warenmarkt	1
Genki Sushi and Japanese Tapas Bar	3
Jordan Restaurant	5
Overture	7
Schoon de Companje	4
Terroir	6

DRINKING
Bohemia Bar	1
The Happy Oak Pub & Grill	2
Wijnhuis	3

1, 2 & Pearl

3

5

6, 7, Kleine Zalze Wine Esate & Somerset West

5, Oude Libertas Estate, Airport & Cape Town

Tourist information The busy tourist office about 1km from the station at 36 Market St (Mon–Fri 8am–5pm, Sat & Sun 9am–2pm; ☎021 883 3584, ⓦstellenbosch.travel), provides information on local attractions and a comprehensive accommodation booking service.

TOURS

WALKING TOURS

Walking tours leave the tourist office in the morning and afternoon, and are a great way to see Stellenbosch's architectural highlights and get a feel of the town (by appointment with Sandra ☎021 887 9150; R100 per person; minimum of six in a group).

WINE TOURS

If you want to get out of town and visit the vineyards, the tourism office represents a number of wine tour operators and can steer you towards the right one, depending on your time and budget. Expect to pay a minimum of R350 for a half-day tour and R550 for a full-day, inclusive of tasting fees. Recommended companies include:

Bikes n Wines ☎074 186 0418, ⓦbikesnwines.com. If you are feeling energetic, you can tour the vineyards by bicycle with Bikes n Wines, who do a half-day tour to Stellenbosch (R600) and to Franschhoek (R800).
Easy Rider Wine Tours ☎021 886 4651, ⓦwinetour .co.za. Based at *Stumble Inn* backpacker lodge (see below), Easy Rider Wine Tours offers packages to four wineries, with lunch at Franschhoek thrown in (R600).
The Vine Hopper ☎084 492 4992, ⓦvinehopper .co.za. A convenient hop-on, hop-off bus, which goes to a dozen wineries, including Van Ryn's Brandy Cellar. Call in advance for their days and routes, which will vary depending on the season and demand (day-ticket R300).

15

ACCOMMODATION

Accommodation can be difficult to find in Stellenbosch in the summer months, when you can expect to find many places full, so book well in advance at this time of year. The tourist office can be helpful in finding you a place.

10 Alexander 10 Alexander St ☎021 887 4414, ⓦ10alexander.co.za. This guesthouse is functional, quiet and pleasant, and very well run by the chatty owner. Rooms are small and spotless, plus there's a nice garden and pool. There are also facilities for self-catering for those trying to keep down costs. There is a two-night minimum stay. R1850
Banghoek Place 193 Banghoek Rd ☎021 887 0048, ⓦbanghoek.co.za. Slightly more upmarket sister hostel to *Stumble Inn* (see below), with mostly en-suite double, twin and triple rooms that offer terrific value, and three small dorms. There are discount packages available, which include two nights' accommodation plus a wine tour. Dorms R180, doubles R600
De Oude Meul 10A Mill St (off Dorp St) ☎021 887 7085, ⓦdeoudemeul.com. Located in the middle of town on a fairly busy street, above an antique shop, these pleasant rooms are good value. Ask for one at the back to ensure a quiet night's sleep. R1400
Glenconner Jonkershoek Rd, 4km from the centre ☎021 886 5120 or ☎082 354 3510, ⓦbit.ly/Glenconner. Both self-catering and B&B options are available at these farm cottages. The tranquil valley setting is spectacular – there are grazing horses in the fields below the cottages – and it's close to the walks in the Jonkershoek Nature Reserve. Breakfast can be taken under an old oak tree, and you may be tempted to buy photos from the photographer owner. R1200

Knorhoek Country Guest House Knorhoek Wine Estate, off the R44, 7km north of town ☎021 865 2114, ⓦknorhoek.co.za. With a bucolic setting in a snug valley, these old farm buildings have been turned into modern guest rooms and cottages. Each has a sunny patio, lawn and a feeling of calm luxury, plus guests can wander the gardens and vineyard. R1200
Natte Valleij On the R44, 12km north of town ☎021 875 5171, ⓦnattevalleij.co.za. Guests have a choice of a large cottage sleeping six, a smaller one-bedroom unit attached to an old wine cellar or an en-suite room with its own entrance. There's a swimming pool, and breakfast is served on the veranda. R900
Ryneveld Country Lodge 67 Ryneveld St ☎021 887 4469, ⓦryneveldlodge.co.za. Elegant late-nineteenth-century building, now a National Monument and furnished with Victorian antiques. The rooms are spotless, with the two best rooms upstairs leading onto a wooden deck. There are also two family cottages, which sleep up to four, and a pool. R1700
Stumble Inn 12 Market St ☎021 887 4049, ⓦstumbleinnbackpackers.co.za. The town's best and longest-standing hostel, spread across two houses that date from the turn of the last century and are run by friendly, switched-on staff. Just down the road from the tourist office, the hostel is also noted for its good-value tours. Dorms R150, doubles R410

EATING

A meal at a **vineyard** is one of the top eating experiences in South Africa (see box, p.164). You'll need to reserve a table weeks or months in advance, particularly in the summer. In **Stellenbosch** there are several fairly alluring café's and restaurants along Dorp and Church streets, with a nice crop in the leafy De Wet Square, a courtyard scattered with outdoor tables. On Saturday mornings it's worth visiting the fabulous and very popular farmers' market in the Oude Libertas Estate grounds, off the R310 just south of the centre (⦿ slowmarket.co.za; 9am–2pm). You'll find a range of locally produced and organic food to eat and take away, including breads, cheeses, meats, vegetables, fruit, beers and estate wines.

Bird Cage 5 Plein St ☎ 021 882 9790. Great daytime spot for coffee and cake, home-made biscuits and cupcakes, or alfresco light lunches of fresh salads and sandwiches. The home-made granola topped with fresh berries (R65) is delicious. Mon–Fri 9am–5pm, Sat 9am–1pm.

De Warenmarkt Cnr of Ryneveld & Plein sts ☎ 021 883 2274, ⦿ dewarenmarkt.com. A market-style venue, in a handsome listed building, where you can pitch up at any time of day and find something delicious and reasonably priced, from egg breakfasts (R45) and freshly squeezed juices to seafood platters and salads. The coffee is brilliant, there's a champagne and oyster bar and perhaps most interesting, if you are a carnivore, an excellent butchery where you can choose your hunk of meat and have it prepared on the spot. Mon–Sat 8am–10pm.

Genki Sushi and Japanese Tapas Bar, De Wet Centre, Cnr Bird & Church Sts ☎ 021 887 5699. Great setting in a leafy courtyard with characteristic whitewashed walls, come here for fresh Japanese dishes from sushi (R100) and noodles to tempura and skewers of meat. The wine comes from local estates. Mon–Sat 11.30am–3pm & 5.30–10pm.

★ **Schoon de Companie** Cnr Bird & Church sts ☎ 021 883 2187, ⦿ decompanje.co.za. A café combined with a deli, with various nooks to settle down in with some good coffee and croissants. The pavement seating is one of the big draws in summer, as are the ice creams and locally brewed Stellenbrau craft beer. For lunch try the quinoa tabbouleh salad (R75), and a variety of sandwiches. Mon 7am–1.30pm, Tues–Sun 7.30am–5pm.

DRINKING

In Stellenbosch there are some appealing pavement cafés, especially down Church Street, while in the evenings the student presence ensures a relaxed, and occasionally, raucous drinking culture.

Bohemia Bar 1 Victoria St ☎ 021 887 8375, ⦿ facebook .com/bohemiabar. There's a good chance of catching local live music, usually alternative punk rock, with Thursday as the most reliable night. During the day, there is a pleasant wrap-around veranda with tables looking onto the street. Food like pizzas and toasties is exceptionally cheap, or try an

egg and bacon breakfast (R30). Daily 11am–2am.

The Happy Oak Pub & Grill 62 Andringa St ☎ 021 882 9672. Central and cheap, a studenty vintage pub and grill where you can get a variety of beers and ciders, a bottle of decent local wine (R80) and meals like steak and egg (R70) or a plate of potato wedges to line the stomach while you sit

---

STELLENBOSCH'S BEST WINE ESTATE RESTAURANTS

Jordan Restaurant Jordan Wine Estate (see p.165), 11.5km west of Stellenbosch, off the R310 ☎ 021 881 3612, ⦿ jordanwines.com. One of the country's top chefs rules the roost here. Expect exquisite food, service and wines, which can be enjoyed on a deck overlooking a lake and distant mountains. The reasonably-priced set menu is based on seasonal ingredients (R350 for two courses, R425 for three) and you can even visit their cheese tasting room in between courses. Next to the restaurant is *Bakery at Jordan* (⦿ thebakery.co.za), which does interesting breakfasts, lighter meals and cheese and charcuterie platters (R200). Jordan Restaurant summer Mon–Wed & Sun noon–2pm, Thurs–Sat noon–2pm & 6.30–8.30pm; winter Tues & Wed noon–2pm, Thurs–Sat noon–2pm & 6.30–9pm; Bakery at Jordan daily 8am–4pm.

Overture Hidden Valley Wine Estate, Annandale Rd ☎ 021 880 2646, ⦿ www.dineatoverture.co.za. Top of the town in more ways than one, *Overture* looks down

magnificently from the hills into the Annandale Valley – and it consistently wins awards as one of the country's top ten restaurants. Based on classical French cuisine, with fresh ingredients and everything made from scratch, the dishes throw up interesting contemporary twists. Sample the works with the six-course tasting menu (R690). Book way in advance. Mon–Wed & Sun noon–2.30pm, Thurs–Sat noon–2.30pm & 7–11pm.

Terroir Kleine Zalze Wine Estate, Strand Rd (R44) ☎ 021 880 0717, ⦿ kleinezalze.co.za. Some 8km from Stellenbosch on a wine and golf estate, *Terroir* has a surprisingly relaxed dining room (for a nationally fêted restaurant) and tables outside under shady oaks. The fairly expensive French-inspired chalkboard menu is based as far as possible on local seasonal produce, including appealing desserts like marinated mango with coconut, vanilla brioche and banana (R110). Mon–Sat noon–2.30pm & 6.30–9pm, Sun noon–2.30pm.

at the outdoor beer-garden-style trestles and benches. Not much scope for vegetarians. Daily 11am–2am.

Wijnhuis Wine Bar & Grill Cnr Church & Andringa sts ☎ 021 887 5844. Dazzling array of local wines sold by the glass, and artisanal beers to sample (R50), in a clean-cut environment with rather stylish wooden tables and fittings. It's a good place too, for steaks, bruschetta, salads, pasta, fish, and game dishes. Daily 8am–11pm.

THE WINERIES

Stellenbosch was the first locality in the country to wake up to the marketing potential of a **wine route**. It launched its wine route in 1971, a tactic that has been hugely successful; today tens of thousands of visitors from all over the world are drawn here annually, making this the most toured area in the Winelands. Although the region accounts for only a fraction of South Africa's land under vine, its wine route is the most extensive in the country, with around three hundred establishments. Apart from the selection here (all of which produce creditable wines and are along a series of roads that radiate out from Stellenbosch) there are scores of other excellent places, which taken together would occupy months of exploration. If you're planning your own route, all the wineries are clearly signposted off the main arteries, or you can take a tour from Stellenbosch (see p.163). Several vineyards offer sit-down luxury meals (see box, p.164) or picnic baskets (reserve in advance), but many only lay on tastings. Opening hours may be shorter in the winter.

Delaire Graff Estate On the Helshoogte Pass, 6km east of Stellenbosch along the R310 to Franschhoek ☎ 021 885 8160, ⓦ delaire.co.za. The highly regarded *Delaire Graff* restaurant has possibly the best views in the Winelands, looking through pin oaks across the Groot Drakenstein and Simonsig mountains and down into the valley. Outstanding wines aren't hard to find here as most of their output delivers the goods: the majority are whites, but they also produce a great red blend. A tasting of three wines costs R50. Mon–Sat 10am–5pm, Sun 10am–4pm; restaurant Mon–Sat noon–2pm & 6.30–9pm, Sun noon–2pm. Winter hours are subject to change.

Jordan Wine Estate 11.5km west of Stellenbosch off the R310 ☎ 021 881 3441, ⓦ jordanwines.com. A pioneer among the new-wave Cape wineries, Jordan's high-tech cellar and modern tasting room is complemented by its friendly service. The drive there is half the fun, taking you into a *kloof* bounded by vineyards that get a whiff of the sea from both False Bay and Table Bay, which has clearly done something for its output – it has a list of outstanding wines as long as your arm and a highly rated restaurant (see box, p.164). Tasting R120 for six premier wines, redeemable against purchases. Daily 9am–4pm.

Morgenhof 4km north of Stellenbosch on the R44 ☎ 021 889 2007, ⓦ morgenhof.com. French-owned chateau-style complex on the slopes of the vine-covered Simonsberg, owned by Anne Cointreau-Huchon (granddaughter of the founder of Remy Martin cognac). Morgenhof has a light and airy tasting room with a bar, and delicious light lunches are served outside, which can be followed with ice cream enjoyed on the lawns. They produce the excellent Morgenhof Estate red blend and a couple of brilliant whites (including a Chenin Blanc, Chardonnay and Sauvignon Blanc) under the same label, while the Fantail range is their second, more affordable label. Tasting R35 for five wines. Mon–Fri 9am–5pm, Sat & Sun 9am–4pm; restaurant daily 9am–4pm.

Neethlingshof 6.5km west of Stellenbosch on

Polkadraai Rd (the R306) ☎ 021 883 8988, ⓦ neethlingshof.co.za. Centred around a beautifully restored Cape Dutch manor dating back to 1814, reached down a kilometre-long avenue of stone pines, Neethlingshof's first vines were planted in 1692. Their flagship wines include the Caracal, a Bordeaux-style red blend and the Pinotage Old Post. Tasting R40 for five wines. Mon–Fri 9am–4.30pm, Sat & Sun 10am–4pm; restaurant Mon, Tues & Sun 9am–5pm, Wed–Sat 9am–9pm.

Overgaauw 6.5km west of Stellenbosch, off the M12 ☎ 021 881 3815, ⓦ overgaauw.co.za. Notable for its elegant Victorian tasting room, this pioneering estate was the first winery in the country to produce Merlots, and it's still the only one to make a wine with Sylvaner, a well-priced, easy-drinking dry white. Tasting R30 for five wines, redeemable against purchase. Mon–Fri 9am–4pm, by appointment only.

Rustenberg Wines Off Lelie Rd, Ida's Valley ☎ 021 809 1200, ⓦ rustenberg.co.za. One of the closest estates to Stellenbosch, Rustenberg is also one of the most alluring, reached after a drive through orchards, sheep pastures and tree-lined avenues. An unassuming working farm, it has a romantic pastoral atmosphere, which contrasts with its architecturally stunning tasting room in the former stables; the first vines were planted in 1692, but the viniculture looks to the future. Their high-flyers include the Peter Barlow Cabernet Sauvignon, and Five Soldiers Chardonnay. Tasting R25 for six wines, redeemable against purchase. Mon–Fri 9am–4.30pm, Sat 10am–3.30pm, Sun 10am–3pm.

Simonsig Estate 9.5km north of Stellenbosch, off Kromme Rhee Rd, which runs between the R44 and the R304 ☎ 021 888 4900, ⓦ simonsig.co.za. This winery has a relaxed outdoor tasting area under vine-covered pergolas, offering majestic views back to Stellenbosch of hazy stone-blue mountains and vineyards. The first estate in the country to produce a bottle-fermented bubbly some three decades back, it also makes a vast range of first-class still wines. Tasting R75 for five bubblies and R50 for three

15

wines. Mon–Fri 8.30am–4.30pm, Sat 8.30am–3.30pm, Sun 11.30am–2.30pm.

★**Uva Mira** About 8km south of Stellenbosch, off Annandale Rd, which spurs off the R44 ☎ 021 880 1683, ⓦ uvamira.co.za. Enchanting boutique winery that punches well above its weight, but is worth visiting just for the winding drive halfway up the Helderberg. The highly

original tasting room, despite being fairly recently built, gives the appearance of a gently decaying historic structure, and there are unsurpassed views from the deck across mountainside vineyards to False Bay some 50km away. Their 2006 Chardonnay stands out as an international winner and their flagship Bordeaux-style red blend is also noteworthy. Tasting R50 for three wines. Daily 10am–6pm.

Somerset West

The only compelling reasons to trawl out to the unpromising town of **SOMERSET WEST**, 50km east of Cape Town along the N2, are to visit the wine estates of **Vergelegen**, and its immediate neighbour **Morgenster**. Both of these are officially part of the Helderberg wine route, but can easily be included as an extension to a visit to Stellenbosch, just 14km to the north.

Vergelegen

Lourensford Rd • Daily 9.30am–4pm • R20 • Wine tasting R50 for six wines • ☎ 021 847 2100, ⓦ vergelegen.co.za

An architectural treasure as well as an estate producing a stunning range of wines, **Vergelegen** was the only wine estate visited by Queen Elizabeth II during her 1995 state visit to South Africa – a good choice, as there's enough here to occupy even a monarch for an easy couple of hours.

The **interpretive centre**, just across the courtyard from the shop at the building's entrance, provides a useful history and background to the estate. Next door, the **wine-tasting centre** offers a professionally run sampling with a brief talk through each label. They produce a vast range of wines, almost every one of which is excellent.

The **homestead**, which was restored in 1917 to its current state by Lady Florence Phillips, wife of a Johannesburg mining magnate, can also be visited. Its pale facade, reached along an axis through an octagonal garden that is dotted with butterflies in summer, has a classical triangular gable and pilaster-decorated doorways. Extensive grounds planted with chestnuts and camphor trees, which feature ponds around every corner make this one of the most serene places in the Cape.

EATING
VERGELEGEN

Vergelegen Lourensford Road ☎ 021 847 2131, ⓦ vergelegen.co.za. Food options at Vergelegen are varied. One of the best ways to enjoy the surrounds is to order a gourmet picnic basket (R250/person; summer only, booking essential), which will be laid-out under the camphor trees, complete with checked tablecloth and wicker basket. *The*

Stables offers breakfast, lunch and coffee in a bistro environment, while *Camphors Restaurant* is one of the top Winelands eating experiences and in the top ten in South Africa – the seasonal menu might include steak tartare from their own Nguni cattle, local cheeses and vegetables grown on the estate (R395 for three courses). The Stables daily

---

THE HISTORY OF VERGELEGEN

Vergelegen represents a notorious episode of corruption and the arbitrary abuse of power at the Cape in the early years of Dutch East India Company rule. Built by Willem Adriaan van der Stel, who became governor in 1699 after the retirement of his father, Simon, the estate formed a grand Renaissance complex in the middle of the wild backwater that was the Cape at the beginning of the eighteenth century. Van der Stel acquired the land illegally and used Dutch East India Company slaves to build Vergelegen, as well as company resources to farm vast tracts of land in the surrounding areas. At the same time he abused his power as governor to corner most of the significant markets at the Cape. When this was brought to the notice of the bosses in the Netherlands, they sacked Van der Stel and ordered the destruction of Vergelegen to discourage future miscreant governors. It's believed that the destruction was never fully carried out and the current building is thought to stand on the foundations of the original.

THE HISTORY OF AFRIKAANS

Afrikaans is South Africa's third mother tongue, spoken by fifteen percent of the population and outstripped only by Zulu and Xhosa. English, by contrast, is the mother tongue of only nine percent of South Africans, and ranks fifth in the league of the eleven official languages.

Signs of the emergence of a new southern-African dialect appeared as early as 1685, when a VOC official from the Netherlands complained about a "distorted and incomprehensible" Dutch being spoken around modern-day Paarl. By absorbing English, French, German, Malay and indigenous words and expressions, the language continued to diverge from mainstream Dutch, and by the nineteenth century was widely used in the Cape by both white and coloured speakers, but was regarded by the elite as an inferior creole, unsuitable for literary or official communication.

Ironically, it was the British defeat of the Afrikaner republics in the second Anglo-Boer War at the start of the twentieth century that provided the catalyst for a mass white Afrikaans movement. The official British policy of anglicizing South Africa helped unite a demoralized white Afrikaner proletariat and elite against the common English enemy.

In 1905, **Gustav Preller**, a young journalist from a working-class Boer background, set about reinventing Afrikaans as a "white man's language". Substituting Dutch words for those with non-European origins, Preller began publishing the first of a series of populist magazines written in Afrikaans and glorifying Boer history and culture. In 1925 Afrikaans became recognized as an official language.

When the National Party took power in 1948, its apartheid policy went hand in hand with promoting the interests of white Afrikaners, which they did through a programme of **uplifting poor white people**. Despite there being more coloured than white Afrikaans speakers, the language became associated with the **apartheid** establishment. When the government tried to enforce Afrikaans as the sole medium of instruction in African schools, the policy led directly to the **Soweto uprising** in 1976, which marked the beginning of the end for Afrikaner hegemony in South Africa. The repression of the 1970s and 1980s and the forced removals of coloured and black people led many coloured Afrikaans-speakers to adopt English in preference to their tainted mother tongue.

There are few signs, though, that Afrikaans will die out. Under the new constitution, language rights are protected, which means that Afrikaans will continue to be almost as widely used as before, except now it is as much with coloured as white people that the future of the *taal* (language) rests.

15

9.30am–4pm; Camphors Restaurant Wed, Thurs & Sun noon–2.30pm, Fri & Sat noon–2.30pm & 6.30–9.30pm.

For Camphors Restaurant booking, as far in advance as possible, is essential.

Morgenster

Mon–Sat 10am–5pm, Sun 10am–4pm • Olive oil tastings R40; wine & chocolate tastings R65 • ⓦ morgenster.co.za

As well as its exquisite rustic setting, the tasting room at **Morgenster**, Vergelegen's immediate neighbour, has a veranda that looks onto a lovely lake with mountains in the distance. Its two stellar blended reds aside, the estate offers the unusual addition of olive tasting, with several types of olive and oil (including an award-winning cold-pressed extra virgin olive oil) and some delicious olive paste.

Paarl

Although **PAARL** is attractively ensconced in a fertile valley brimming with historical monuments, at heart it's a parochial *dorp*, lacking the sophistication of Stellenbosch or the striking setting and trendiness of Franschhoek. It is, however, a prosperous farming centre that earns its keep from the agricultural light industries – grain silos, canneries and flour mills – on the north side of town, and the cornucopia of grapes, guavas, olives, oranges and maize grown on the surrounding farms. Despite its small-town feel, Paarl has the largest municipality in the Winelands, with its most exclusive areas on the vined slopes of **Paarl Mountain** overlooking the town.

Brief history

In 1657, just five years after the establishment of the Dutch East India Company refreshment station on the Cape Peninsula, a party under Abraham Gabbema arrived in the Berg River Valley to look for trading opportunities with the Khoikhoi, and search for the legendary gold of Monomotapa. With treasure on the brain, they woke after a rainy night to see the glistening dome of granite dominating the valley, which they named **Peerlbergh** (pearl mountain), which in its modified form, Paarl, became the name of the town. Thirty years later, the commander of the Cape, Simon van der Stel, granted strips of the Khoikhoi lands on the slopes of Paarl Mountain to French Huguenot and Dutch settlers. By the time Paarl was officially granted town status in 1840, it was still an outpost at the edge of the Drakenstein Mountains, a flourishing wagon-making and last-stop provisioning centre. This status was enhanced when the first **rail line** in the Cape connected it to the peninsula in 1863. Following in the spirit of the first Dutch adventurers of 1657, thousands of treasure-seekers brought custom to Paarl as the gateway to the interior during the diamond rush of the 1870s and the gold fever of the 1880s.

The town holds deep historical significance for the two competing political forces that forged modern South Africa. **Afrikanerdom** regards Paarl as the hallowed ground on which their language movement was born in 1875 (see box, p.167), while for the **ANC** (and the international community), Paarl will be remembered as the place from which Nelson Mandela made the final steps of his long walk to freedom, when he walked out of **Groot Drakenstein Prison** (then called Victor Verster) in 1990.

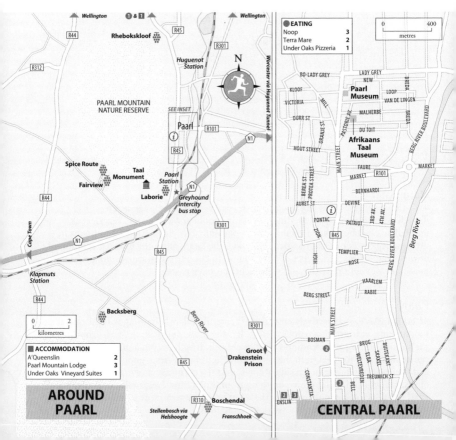

AROUND PAARL

CENTRAL PAARL

Paarl's best-preserved historical frontage is along oak-lined **Main Street**, which stretches for some 2km – not ideal for strolling, especially on a hot day.

Paarl Museum
303 Main St • Mon–Fri 9am–4pm, Sat 9am–1pm • R20

Housed in a handsome, thatched Cape Dutch building with one of the earliest surviving gables (dating back to 1787) in the "new style", characterized by triangular caps, the contents of the **Paarl Museum** don't quite match up to its exterior. Exhibits include some reasonably enlightening panels on the architecture of the town, and several eccentric glass display cases of Victorian bric-a-brac. Post-apartheid transformation has introduced some coverage of the indigenous Khoisan populations of the area and the changes that came with European colonization, including slavery.

Taal Monument
South along Main St past the head office of the KWV; follow signs to the right up the slope of the mountain • Daily 9am–5pm • Free

The only other sight of any interest in Paarl itself is the grandiose **Taal Monument**, the controversial memorial to the Afrikaans language, standing just outside the centre on the top of Paarl Mountain. The monument used to be as important a place of pilgrimage for Afrikaners as the Voortrekker Monument in Pretoria, although when it was erected in 1973 detractors joked that monuments were usually erected to the dead. From the coffee and curio shop you can admire a truly magnificent panorama across to the Cape Peninsula and False Bay in one direction and the Winelands ranges in the other.

Groot Drakenstein (Victor Verster) Prison
Roughly 9km south of the N1 as it cuts through Paarl, along the R301 (the southern extension of Jan van Riebeeck St)

The **Victor Verster Prison**, renamed **Groot Drakenstein** in 2000, was Nelson Mandela's last place of incarceration. It was through the gates at Victor Verster that Mandela walked to his freedom on February 11, 1990, and it was here that the first images of him in 27 years were bounced around the world (under the Prisons Act, not even old pictures of him could be published during his imprisonment). The working jail looks rather like a boys' school fronted by rugby pitches beneath hazy mountains, and there's something bizarre about seeing a prison sign nonchalantly slipped in among all the vineyard and wine-route pointers.

ARRIVAL AND INFORMATION	PAARL

By bus Daily Greyhound intercity buses from Cape Town (1hr) stop at the Monument Shell Garage, on the corner of Main Road and South Street, about 2km from the tourist office.

By train Metrorail and Spoornet services from Cape Town (18 daily; 1hr 15min) pull in at Huguenot Station in Lady Grey Street at the north end of town, near to the central shops.

Tourist information The tourist office, corner of Main and Plantasie streets (Mon–Fri 8am–5pm, Sat & Sun 10am–1pm; ☎ 021 872 4842, ⍵ paarlonline.com), has a good selection of maps, including the wine routes, and can help with booking accommodation.

ACCOMMODATION

A'Queenslin 2 Queen St ☎ 021 863 1160, ⍵ queenslin .co.za. Two en-suite rooms with their own entrances and garden spaces, and three doubles that share a bathroom, in a family home set in a quiet part of town, bounded on one side by vineyards and towered over by Paarl Rock. The rooms are large, each with a deck or patio and limited self-catering is possible – there's a fridge and microwave. **R900**

Paarl Mountain Lodge 21 Enslin St ☎ 021 869 8045, ⍵ paarlmountainlodge.co.za. Clean white rooms in a large home on a quiet street on the slopes of the Paarl mountain, 2km from the centre. There's a deck with mountain views

where you can drink your complimentary wine on arrival, and a swimming pool. Breakfasts are done buffet-style. **R900**

Under Oaks Vineyard Suites Off R45, 8km north of Paarl ☎ 021 869 8045, ⍵ underoaks.co.za. Good-value-for-money luxury rooms, with ultra-comfy beds and linen, in a purpose-built, modern guesthouse on a vineyard overlooking the wide, fertile valley towards Wellington. Breakfast is served in a historic wine-estate dining room overlooking pastures, while dinner is at their pizzeria. You can try their flagship Sauvignon Blanc or Cabernet Sauvignon at the adjoining boutique winery. **R1350**

15

EATING

A working town, Paarl has none of the Winelands foodie pretensions of Franschhoek or Stellenbosch, but you'll find a number of places along the main street for a decent coffee or a meal, as well as a couple of outstanding places in the surrounding vineyards.

Noop 127 Main St ☎021 863 3925, ⊛noop.co.za. This super-cool pavement wine bar and restaurant in an elegant period house has an extensive list of wines by the glass. *Noop* is well regarded for its steaks (R140) and seafood. Vegetarians can find at least one starter, salad or main. Risotto with truffle oil is a favourite (R120). Mon–Sat 11am–9.30pm.

★**Terra Mare** 90A Main St ☎021 863 4805. Italian- and Mediterranean-influenced dishes, such as three-mushroom risotto for starters (R95) and chalkboard specials like ostrich fillet (R170), which use local ingredients and are infused with considerable flair. The glass and steel restaurant has great sweeping views of the Paarl Mountain. Mon–Sat 11am–2pm & 6–10pm.

Under Oaks Pizzeria Paarl Main Rd, 8km from centre ☎021 869 8962. The best thing about eating a delicious wood-fired pizza (R80) here, and drinking wine from grapes grown on the farm, is the setting beneath majestic oaks. There is a relaxed vibe, with children running about on the lawns; it is very popular with local families. Tues–Sat 11.30am–8.30pm, Sun noon–3.30pm.

THE WINERIES

There are a couple of notable **wineries** in Paarl itself, but most are on farms in the surrounding countryside. Boschendal, one of the most popular of these, is officially on the Franschhoek wine route (see p.175), but is in easy striking distance of Paarl. Most of the wineries have a restaurant, which is generally of a high standard, and some have accommodation in beautiful rooms, which is often more appealing than staying in central Paarl.

Backsberg Estate 22km south of Paarl on Simondium Rd (WR1) ☎021 875 5141, ⊛backsberg.co.za; map p.160. Notable as the first carbon-neutral wine estate in South Africa, Backsberg produces some top-ranking red blends, especially the Cabernet and Merlot, and a delicious Chardonnay, in its Black Label ranges. Outdoor seating, with views of the rose garden and vineyard on the slopes of the Simonsberg, makes this busy estate a nice place to while away some time. There's also a restaurant and a maze to get lost in. Tasting R40 for five wines. Tasting Mon–Fri 8am–5pm, Sat 8.30am–4pm, Sun 9.30am–4.30pm; restaurant daily 11.30am–3pm.

The Goatshed Fairview Estate Suid Agter Paarl Rd, on the southern fringes of town ☎021 863 2450, ⊛fairview.co.za; map p.160. One of the most fun of all the Paarl estates (especially for families), with a resident population of goats who clamber up the spiral tower – you will see them also featured in the estate's emblem, at the entrance. A deli sells breads and preserves, and you can also sample and buy the goats', sheep's and cows' cheeses made on the estate. As far as wine-tasting goes (six wines and cheese selection R40), Fairview is an innovative, family-run place, but it can get a bit hectic when the tour buses roll in. The restaurant, no surprises here, offers a cheese platter with ten cheeses, bread and preserves (R115) and they are well known for their Sunday lunches. Tasting and restaurant daily 9am–5pm.

Laborie Taillefert St ☎021 807 3390, ⊛laboriewines .co.za; map p.160. One of the most impressive Paarl wineries, all the more remarkable for being right in town. The beautiful manor is fronted by a rose garden, acres of close-cropped lawns, historic buildings and oak trees – all towered over by the Taal Monument. There's a truly wonderful tasting room with a balcony that juts out over the vineyards trailing up Paarl Mountain, as well as a great restaurant with terrace seating offering good views of the town vineyards and mountains. Their flagship is the Jean Taillefert Shiraz, and their brandy is also worth a try. Tasting R25 for five wines. Mon–Sat 9am–5pm, Sun 11am–5pm.

HORSE AND QUAD-BIKE TRAILS

Hopping into the saddle and trotting off through the countryside offers a great alternative to seeing the Winelands from behind a restaurant table. At Rhebokskloof wine estate (see p.172), 11.5km northwest of Paarl, you can do both.

Wine Valley Horse Trails ☎083 226 8735, ⊛horsetrails-sa.co.za. This company, based at Rhebokskloof, offers 1–4hr equestrian trails for novices and experts through the surrounding countryside – a choice spot for some riding. Prices start from R450 for a 1hr trail. For experienced riders who want some speed, there is a 3hr beach trail at Grotto Bay, from R1500 per person. They also do quad-bike trips which start at R450 for 1hr.

Rhebokskloof Signposted off the R45, 11.5km northwest of Paarl ☎ 021 869 8386, ⓦrhebokskloof .co.za; map p.160. A highly photogenic wine estate, Rhebokskloof sits at the foot of sculptural granite *koppies* overlooking a lake with a shaded terrace for summer lunches and gourmet meals. Meat is the house speciality, with exciting combinations of flavours that are both Cape and international. It's also a good place for morning or afternoon teas, and they can prepare picnics on the lawns outside (R400 for two). Their Sunday lunch buffets (R225) are tremendously popular. In terms of wine, Shiraz is where they make their mark. Wine tasting R20 for five wines. Mon–Sun 9am–5pm.

Spice Route Suid Agter Paarl Rd ☎ 021 863 5222, ⓦspiceroute.co.za; map p.160. The Spice Route farm offers unusual tastings drawn from several artisanal producers who have grouped together in different buildings on the same premises. You can try beer at the *Cape Brewing Company*, handmade chocolate tasting at the *DV Artisan Chocolate* (R150), or local grappa at *La Grapperia Pizza and Tapas Bar*, the only place open in the evening after 5pm. Other residents include an art gallery, glass blowers and farm shop. Like nearby The Goatshed Fairview Estate, it is favoured by groups, so book in advance for tastings. Daily 9am–5pm.

Franschhoek

15

If indulgence is what the Winelands is really about, then **Franschhoek** is the place that does it best. Despite being a fairly small *dorp*, it has managed to establish itself as the culinary capital of the Western Cape, if not the whole country. Its late Victorian and more recent Frenchified rustic architecture, the terrific setting (it's hemmed in on three sides by mountains), and the vineyards down every other backstreet have created a place you can really lose yourself in, a romantic set piece that unashamedly draws its inspiration from Provence.

Brief history

Between 1688 and 1700 about two hundred French Huguenots, desperate to escape religious persecution in France, accepted a Dutch East India Company offer of passage to the Cape and the grant of lands. They made contact with the area's earliest settlers, groups of Khoikhoi herders. Conflict between the French newcomers and the Khoikhoi followed familiar lines, with the white settlers gradually dispossessing the herdsmen, forcing them either further into the hinterland or into servitude on their farms. The establishment of white hegemony was swift and by 1713 the area was known as *de france hoek*. Though French-speaking died out within a generation because of explicit Company policy, many of the estates hereabouts are still known by their original French names. **Franschhoek** itself, 33km from Stellenbosch and 29km from Paarl, occupies parts of the original farms of La Cotte and Cabrière and is relatively young, having been established around a church built in 1833.

Huguenot Museum and Huguenot Monument

Summer daily 9am–5pm , winter Mon–Sat 9am–5pm, Sun 2–5pm • R10

Driving through Franschhoek, you can't fail to miss the **Huguenot Memorial Museum**, thanks to its location next to the town's most obvious landmark, the **Huguenot Monument**. Set in a prime position at the head of Huguenot Road, where it forms a T-junction with Lambrecht Street, the monument consists of three skinny interlocking arches, symbolizing the Holy Trinity. The museum gives comprehensive coverage of Huguenot history and culture, and of their contribution to modern South Africa.

Museum van de Caab

Solms Delta Wine Estate • Mon–Thurs & Sun 9am–5pm, Fri & Sat 9am–6pm • Free • ⓦsolms-delta.co.za

Twelve kilometres north of Franschhoek along the R45, at the Solms Delta Wine Estate, the highly recommended **Museum van de Caab** gives a condensed and riveting slice through South African vernacular history as it happened on the farm and its surrounds. Housed alongside the atmospherically understated tasting room in the original 1740s gabled Cape Dutch cellar, the display begins with Stone Age artefacts found on the site and goes on to trace the arrival of the aboriginal Khoisan people, their colonization by Europeans, the introduction of slavery and how this eventually evolved into the apartheid system and its eventual demise.

ARRIVAL AND INFORMATION   FRANSCHHOEK

By car There's no scheduled public transport to Franschhoek or around the town itself, though everything is within walking distance. From Stellenbosch take the R310 heading north, then east out of town. The route winds through the beautiful Helshoogte Pass, with a bunch of first-class wineries lining the mountainside along the way. Roughly 16km from Stellenbosch the R310 hits a T-junction with the R45, where you should turn east (right) and take the road for 18km to Franschhoek.

Tourist office Just north of the junction with Kruger St the tourist office at 62 Huguenot Rd (Mon–Fri 8am–6pm, Sat 9am–6pm; winter Mon–Sat 9am–5pm, Sun 9am–4pm; ☏ 021 876 2861, ⓦ franschhoek.org.za) has some excellent maps of the village and its winelands.

ACTIVITIES

Equestrian wine tours Paradise Stables (Roberstsvlei Rd ☏ 021 876 2160 or ☏ 084 586 2160, ⓦ paradisestables .co.za) runs tours that visit Rickety Bridge and Mont Rochelle wineries: wine tasting is included in the price, though lunch is not (2hr 30min in the saddle, 30–45min stop at each winery; R850; Mon–Sat 8.45am and 1.15pm). Their Arabian horses, ridden with halters, are as good as gold, and beginners can be accommodated. The farm itself, where you start the ride, has a couple of reasonably priced cottages for rent (R500).

Hiking The best hike in the vicinity is the Cat se Pad (Cat's Path), which starts as you head out of town up the Franschhoek Pass. The walk leads into *fynbos* with proteas, and gives instant access to the mountains surrounding the valley, with good views. The first 2km section gets you to the top of the pass, and you can keep going for another 10km in the direction of Villiersdorp (though you don't actually reach it).

15

ACCOMMODATION

On the whole, **guesthouse accommodation** here is pricey, but the rooms are of high quality and frequently in unparalleled settings; budget accommodation is hard to find, but there are a couple of reasonably priced **self-catering cottages** and a backpackers. It can be hard to find a bed in Franschhoek during the summer, so book as far ahead as possible. Some of the **wine estates** outside town also offer luxury rooms.

★**Akademie Street Boutique Hotel** 5 Akademie St ☏ 082 517 0405, ⓦ aka.co.za. Luxury guesthouse offering total privacy in each of its tastefully decorated and spacious suites set in beautiful gardens, with a number of original and striking artworks. Facilities include DVDs, a fridge stocked with free drinks and a long, saltwater swimming pool. Gourmet breakfasts with regional specialities are served poolside by the charming hosts who'll happily recommend a restaurant for dinner and book a table for you. R5000

Avondrood Guest House 39 Huguenot St ☏ 021 876 2881, ⓦ avondrood.com. A guesthouse with six rooms in a beautifully restored home, which gets accolade after

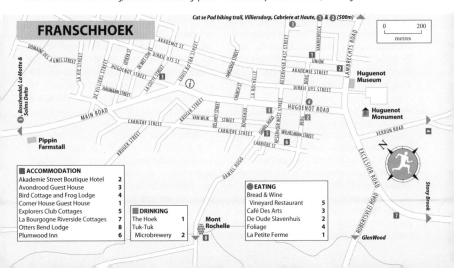

FRANSCHHOEK

Cat se Pad hiking trail, Villiersdorp, Cabriere at Haute, ① & ② (500m)

0   200
metres

Boschendal, La Motte & Solms Delta

Pippin Farmstall

■ ACCOMMODATION	
Akademie Street Boutique Hotel	2
Avondrood Guest House	3
Bird Cottage and Frog Lodge	4
Corner House Guest House	1
Explorers Club Cottages	5
La Bourgogne Riverside Cottages	7
Otters Bend Lodge	8
Plumwood Inn	6

■ DRINKING		
The Hoek	1	Mont
Tuk-Tuk		Rochelle
Microbrewery	2	

● EATING	
Bread & Wine	
Vineyard Restaurant	5
Café Des Arts	3
De Oude Slavenhuis	2
Foliage	4
La Petite Ferme	1

Huguenot Museum

Huguenot Monument

GlenWood

Stony Brook

15

accolade for the level of comfort and aesthetic experience offered. There are extensive lawns, a manicured garden and a pool. R2850

Bird Cottage and Frog Lodge Verdun Rd, 4.5km from town ☎021 876 2136, ✉grahamh@radionet.co.za. Two artistically furnished cottages that each sleep four, surrounded by beautiful indigenous gardens close to the mountains, with a dam to swim in. This is about as remote as you'll find this close to Franschhoek, and it's thoroughly laidback and exceptional value. R800

Corner House Guest House Cnr of Riebeeck & Union sts ☎021 876 4729, ⊛thecornerhouse.co.za. One of the few moderately priced popular guesthouses, Dutch-run Corner House offers six bright and spotless rooms, and a pretty garden with pool. It's a good base from which to explore the area. They're especially pet-friendly. R1400

★**Explorers Club Cottages** Cabrière St ☎021 876 4229, ⊛explorersclub.co.za. A collection of centrally located self-catering houses – all absolutely luxurious, modern and tasteful. Each house sleeps two to ten people. The Map Room is ideally suited to couples, with a living space upstairs and folding glass doors opening onto a terrace with vineyard and mountain views. Their portfolio now includes cottages on La Cotte wine farm, 7km from Franschhoek. Explorers Club can also arrange meals to be delivered to you, or the services of a private chef. R2850

La Bourgogne Riverside Cottages Excelsior Rd ☎021 876 3245, ⊛labourgogne.co.za. Six simply but very tastefully furnished converted labourers' cottages set in gardens along a river. They are self-catered but you can get breakfast and coffee from the deli/farmshop on the property. The working farm presses their own olive oil and produces wines, including the highly rated Progeny Sémillon (R250); wine tasting is offered for free when you stay here. R900

Otters Bend Lodge Dassenberg Rd ☎021 876 3200, ⊛ottersbendlodge.co.za. Rustic lodge with double and twin-bedded cabins, dorms, and camping on the lawn, 5min drive from town and surrounded by orchards and vineyards. There is an inviting communal area, complete with a roaring fire in winter, a well-equipped kitchen and an outside braai area. Camping R200, dorms R200, doubles R550

Plumwood Inn 11 Cabrière St ☎021 876 3883, ⊛plumwoodinn.com. Unfailingly excellent boutique guesthouse with smart, clean and modern furnishings. They've paid close attention to detail throughout – from the custom-made cotton tablecloths to the luxurious beds and bathrooms, and the impeccable service. R3000

EATING

Eating and drinking is what Franschhoek is all about, so plan on sampling at least one or two of its excellent **restaurants**, some of which rate among the country's best; it goes without saying that there is excellent wine at every turn. Franschhoek's cuisine tends to be French-inspired, but with an emphasis on local ingredients. Restaurants in town are concentrated along Huguenot Rd, but there are a number of excellent alternatives in the more rustic environment of the surrounding wine estates, several of which do picnics in their beautiful grounds. Booking is essential, particularly for the most flash of the restaurants, and winter opening hours may be reduced. Every Saturday (9am–3pm) there is a Farmers' Market in the churchyard on Main Rd. Come here for delicious goodies, and coffee, and to stock up on food for the weekend.

Bread & Wine Vineyard Restaurant Moreson Farm, Happy Valley Rd ☎021 876 3692, ⊛moreson.co.za. Signposted off the R45 and surrounded by lemon orchards and vineyards, this is a genial and child-friendly venue, consistently in the top twenty restaurants in the country. The two or three-course menus (R300) change with the seasons, and the chef Neil smokes the meat and fish himself, while his wife Tina bakes outstanding bread. Daily noon–3pm.

Café Des Arts 7 Reservoir St, next to the library ☎021 876 2952, ⊛cafedesarts.co.za. Service and food are consistently good here, with unfussy but flavoursome dishes. It's a relaxed spot – you can walk in barefoot. They are known for their fish, but it's also good for dinner, or coffee and breakfast, when favourites include the truffled scrambled eggs with wilted baby spinach (R95). Mon–Sat 8am–3pm & 6.30–10pm.

De Oude Slavenhuis Huguenot Museum, Huguenot St ☎021 876 2192. Reasonably priced and uncomplicated food served both indoors and outdoors under umbrellas, with plenty of play space on the lawns, for children. Dishes include smoked salmon and scrambled egg (R65), salads, tea and scones. Daily 8am–4pm.

★**Foliage** 11 Huguenot Rd ☎021 876 2328. Sophisticated comfort food, with a forest-to-plate philosophy showcasing the chef's skills in foraging, pickling and preserving, using free-range meat, wild vegetables and herbs. Try the pan-fried Angel fish, river greens and Cape Malay velouté (R150). In winter sit in the kitchen with an open fire, and in summer relax next to the street. Mon–Sat noon–3pm & 6–9pm.

La Petite Ferme Franschhoek Pass Rd ☎021 876 3016, ⊛lapetiteferme.co.za. With gorgeous views across a vineyard-covered valley, this restaurant is a Franschhoek institution, and if you start off here it will set the bar for your whole visit. You may be tempted to lie on the grass after lunch, and order bottle after bottle. Slow roasted lamb has been on the menu for thirty years and never fails to please (R190). Daily: summer noon–4pm & 7–9pm; winter noon–4pm.

DRINKING

The Hoek 36 Huguenot St ☎ 079 451 3019. For coffee fanatics, this is the only pure espresso bar in town and it's a double-shot unless you request otherwise. There's excellent ice cream too, and casual seating at wooden tables. Mon–Sat 7am–3pm, Sun 8am–3pm.

Tuk Tuk Microbrewery 14 Huguenot Rd ☎ 021 492 2207.

Delicious craft beers (which you can also buy to take home) with a European café feel, sitting out on the terrace on a balmy evening. Mexican bites like a plate of cheese quesadillas with chicken, tomato and cream sauce and guacamole go down well (R100) and a favourite dessert is cinnamon *churros* dipped in chocolate (R90). Daily 11am–10pm.

THE WINERIES

Franschhoek's **wineries** are small enough and sufficiently close together to make it a breeze to visit two or three in a morning. Heading north through town from the Huguenot Monument, you'll find most of the wineries signposted off Huguenot Rd and its extension, Main Rd; the rest are off Excelsior Rd and the Franschhoek Pass Rd.

★**Babylonstoren** Simondium Rd ☎ 021 863 3852, ⓦ babylonstoren.com. There are tourists aplenty here, but for good reason. Babylonstoren is a less traditional estate, beautifully set against the high Drakenstein mountains, with beautiful, extensive gardens, a shop (look for South African cookery books and upmarket crafts), ducks, chickens and olive trees as well as many acres under vine. They're the new kid on the block in terms of wine, but are already accruing a reputation for their red blend, Babel, and their Viognier. Of the two restaurants, the *Green House* is less formal while *Babel* is known for more traditional South African food, and inspired by the completely edible garden. Booking is required. Entry to the estate costs R20. Estate daily 9am–5pm (last entry 4pm; Green House daily 10am–4pm; Babel Mon & Tues 7–8.30pm, Wed–Sun noon–3.30pm & 7–8.30pm.

Boschendal Pniel Rd, just after the junction of the R45 and R310 to Stellenbosch ☎ 021 870 4274, ⓦ boschendalwines.com. One of the world's longest-established New World wineries, Boschendal draws busloads of tourists – around 200,000 visitors a year – with its impressive Cape Dutch buildings, tree-lined avenues, beautiful gardens, restaurants and cafés and, of course, its wines. Of their six labels the Pavilion range delivers high-class, well-priced plonk (Shiraz–Cabernet Sauvignon, Rosé and a white blend); but their top ranges consistently deliver with classy wines like the Cecil John Reserve Shiraz and Sauvignon Blanc, and their Reserve range Cabernet Sauvignon, Shiraz and Bordeaux-blend Grande Reserve. Tasting R50. Try their famous "pique nique" basket (R360 for two) on the extensive lawns. Book in advance on their website. There is also a vegetarian picnic, a low carb option, a kids option and more enticingly, full moon picnics in the summer. Daily 9am–4.30pm.

Cabrière at Haute Cabrière About 2km from town along the Franschhoek Pass Rd ☎ 021 876 8500, ⓦ cabriere.co.za. Atmospheric winery notable for its Pinot Noirs and colourful wine-maker Achim von Arnim, whose presence guarantees an eventful visit; try to catch him or, more commonly now, his son Takuan, when they

demonstrate *sabrage* – slicing off the upper neck of a bubbly bottle with a French cavalry sabre. Cabrière is noted for its top-notch Pierre Jourdan range of sparkling wines and it specializes in Pinot Noir and blends made with the cultivar. Tasting R30 for five wines and R60 for five bubblies. Mon–Fri 9am–5pm, Sat 10am–4pm, Sun 11am–4pm.

★**Mont Rochelle** Dassenberg Rd ☎ 021 876 2770, ⓦ montrochelle.co.za. Set against the Klein Dassenberg, Mont Rochelle has one of the most stunning settings in Franschhoek – one that was seized upon by Richard Branson and given a contemporary and vibrant make-over. Chardonnay is what they do best here, but don't overlook their also stellar Sauvignon Blanc and Syrah. It is best visited in the evening (bar and restaurant open until 10pm) to catch the sunset or moonrise. They also offer very comfortable accommodation and have two restaurants and picnics available (R360 for two). Tasting for five wines costs R45. Daily 10am–6pm.

★**Solms Delta** 13km north of Franschhoek along the R45 ☎ 021 874 3937, ⓦ solms-delta.co.za. Pleasantly bucolic Solms Delta produces unusual and consistently outstanding wines, which, on a summer's day, you can taste under ancient oaks at the edge of the vineyards with a picnic (R365 for two people). Half the profits from the wines produced go into a trust that benefits residents of the farm and the Franschhoek Valley. The Solms-Wijn de Caab range, with some new cultivars, includes the excellent Hiervandaan (an unusual blend dominated by Shiraz, and including Carignan, Mourvèdre and Viognier grapes) and the even more highly rated Amalie (vine-dried Grenache Blanc and Viognier). Tasting R25 for five wines. Daily 9am–5pm.

Stony Brook Vineyards About 4km from Franschhoek, off Excelsior Rd ☎ 021 876 2182, ⓦ stonybrook.co.za. Family-run boutique winery, with just 140,000 square metres under vine, that produces first-rate wines, including its acclaimed flagship Ghost Gum Cabernet Sauvignon, which takes its name from a magnificent old tree outside the rather informal tasting room. Tastings are convivial affairs conducted by the owners and are by appointment only (R35). Mon–Fri 10am–5pm, Sat 10am–1pm.

15

TRADITIONAL FISHERMAN'S HUTS, ARNISTON

The Whale Coast and Overberg Interior

From roughly July to November, southern right whales can be seen in the warm, sheltered bays of the Western Cape, and the southern Cape coast is prime territory for sightings. The Whale Coast, as the section from roughly Kleinmond to De Hoop has come to be known, is close enough for an easy outing from Cape Town, and yet, with the exception of popular Hermanus, is surprisingly undeveloped. The Overberg Interior – the stretch as far as Swellendam, along the N2 towards the Garden Route – is dominated by the towns of Greyton, a peaceful, oak-lined country town 35km off the main road, and Swellendam, a town brimming with historical guesthouses and decent restaurants, as well as the Bontebok National Park.

Hermanus

On the edge of rocky cliffs and backed by mountains, 112km east of Cape Town, **HERMANUS** sits at the northernmost end of **Walker Bay**, an inlet whose protective curve attracts calving whales as it slides south to Danger Point. The town trumpets itself as South Africa's whale capital – an official whale crier (purportedly the world's only one) struts around with a mobile phone and a dried kelp horn through which he yells sightings. Hype aside, the bay here does provide some of the world's finest shore-based whale-watching and, even if there are better spots nearby, the town is the most geared-up place for tourists. There is still the slightest trace of a once-quiet fishing village around the historic harbour, but for the most part the town has gorged itself on its whale-generated income, which has produced shopping malls, supermarkets and craft shops.

   Main Road, the continuation of the R43, meanders through Hermanus, briefly becoming Seventh Street. **Market Square**, just above the old harbour and to the south of Main Street, is the closest thing to a centre, and it's here you'll find the heaviest concentration of restaurants, craft shops and flea markets.

   Apart from whales, Hermanus is also known for its wines, grown in the nearby Hemel-en-Aarde Valley, which sits inland from the R43. The valley is home to some sensational places to eat and drink (see box, p.182).

Old Harbour Museum

The Old Harbour • Mon–Sat 9am–4.30pm, Sun noon–4pm • R25

Just below Market Square is the **Old Harbour Museum** where, among the uncompelling displays, you'll find lots of fishing tackle and some sharks' jaws. Outside, a few colourful boats, used by local fishermen from the mid-eighteenth to mid-nineteenth centuries, create a photogenic vignette in the tiny harbour.

16

The Cliff Path

An almost continuous 5km **cliff path** through *fynbos* hugs the coastline from the Old Harbour to Grotto Beach in the eastern suburbs. For one short stretch, the path heads

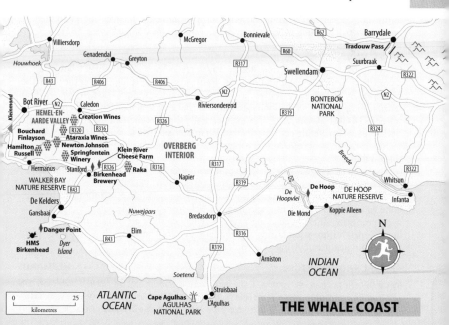

SWIMMING AND BEACHES

East of the Old Harbour, just below the *Marine Hotel*, a beautiful tidal pool offers the only **sea swimming** around the town centre's craggy coast; it's big enough to do laps. For **beaches**, you have to head out east across the Mossel River to the suburbs, where you'll find a decent choice, starting with secluded **Langbaai**, closest to town, a cove beneath cliffs at the bottom of Sixth Avenue that has a narrow strip of beach and is excellent for swimming. **Voëlklip**, at the bottom of Eighth Avenue, has grassed terraces, toilets, a nearby café for tea and is great for picnics if you prefer your sandwiches unseasoned with sand. Adjacent is **Kammabaai**, with the best surfing break around Hermanus, and 1km further east, **Grotto Beach** (which despite its name is not a rocky cove), marking the start of a twelve-kilometre curve of dazzlingly white sand that stretches all the way to De Kelders.

away from the coast and follows Main Road before returning to the shore. This path makes an excellent place to spot whales, and you can do as little of the walk as you like.

Fernkloof Nature Reserve
Theron St • Dawn–dusk • Free

On the east side of town, off Main Road, the **Fernkloof Nature Reserve** encompasses fifteen square kilometres of mountainous terrain and offers sweeping views of Walker Bay. This highly recommended wilderness area is more than just another nature reserve on the edge of town – it has some 40km of **waymarked footpaths**, including a 4.5km circular nature trail. Visiting is an excellent way to get close to the astonishing variety of delicate montane coastal *fynbos* (over a thousand species have been identified in the reserve), much of it flowering species that attract scores of birds, including brightly coloured sunbirds and sugarbirds endemic to the area.

New Harbour

A couple of kilometres west of town along Westcliff, the **New Harbour** is a working fishing harbour, dramatically surrounded by steep cliffs, projecting a gutsy counterpoint to the more manicured central area. Whales sometimes enter the harbour – and there's nowhere better to watch them than from the *Harbour Rock Seagrill* (see p.181).

Rotary Way

On the eastern edge of Hermanus, **Rotary Way** is a fantastic 10km drive that follows the mountain spine through beautiful montane *fynbos*, offering sweeping views of the town, the Hemel-en-Aarde Valley and Walker Bay from Kleinmond to Danger Point. To get here from town, turn right just after the sports ground, and take a track straddled by a pair of white gateposts labelled "Rotary Way". The road is tarred for part of the way, then becomes a dirt track, eventually petering out altogether, which means you have to return the same way.

Wine Village
Hemel-en-Aarde Village, at the junction of R43 and R320 • Mon–Fri 9am–6pm, Sat 9am–5pm, Sun 10am–3pm • ☎ 028 316 3988, ⓦ www.winevillage.co.za

Just on the outskirts of Hermanus is possibly the best wine shop in South Africa, the **Wine Village**, with a staggering selection of labels from all of the country's various wine-producing districts, covering a vast price range. There are usually at least six bottles open for free wine-tasting and the staff are very knowledgeable. This is the place to stock up just before flying out – or have some cases shipped.

ARRIVAL AND DEPARTURE   **HERMANUS**

By car There are two routes to Hermanus, 125km from Cape Town. It's more direct to take the N2 and head south onto the R43 at Bot River (1hr 30min drive), but the winding road that hugs the coast from Strand, leaving the N2 just before Sir Lowry's Pass, is the more scenic and one of the best coastal drives in South Africa (2hr).

By bus The Baz Bus (☎021 422 5202, ⊛www.bazbus .com) drops off at Bot River, 34km northwest of Hermanus on the R43, where you can arrange to be collected by your hostel. Two shuttles – Bernadus (☎028 316 1093 or ☎083 658 7848) and Splash (☎028 316 4004) – ply the route between Hermanus and Cape Town (1hr 30min). They are effectively a taxi service, operating on demand, so you need to book in advance, though it is conveniently door-to-door. The journey one-way costs from R400–800 per person to the airport or centre of Cape Town; the price depends on the number of people taking the shuttle.

INFORMATION

Tourist information The tourist office at the old station building in Mitchell Street (May–Aug Mon–Sat 9am–5pm & Sun 9am–2pm; Sept–April Mon–Sat 8am–6pm; ☎028 312 2629, ⊛hermanustourism.info) is a helpful place, with maps, useful brochures about the area and a free accommodation-finding service. They can take bookings for boat-based and aerial whale-watching, as well as shark-cage diving trips.

Whale festival During the last week in September, the town puts on a fun show of anything that's got a whale connection – check ⊛whalefestival.co.za for more details.

ACCOMMODATION

The most popular coastal destination outside Cape Town, Hermanus is awash with **accommodation**. If you want something more countrified, head to Stanford, 20mins drive around the the bay (though there are no beaches there). Alternatively, head further along the coast to Gansbaai (see p.184), home to ugly holiday houses, but with great whale-viewing in season.

Auberge Burgundy 16 Harbour Rd ☎028 313 1201, ⊛auberge.co.za. A Provençal-style country house in the town centre, close to the water, projecting a stylish Mediterranean feel. The rooms are light and airy with imported French fabrics, and a lavender garden. R1870

Eastbury Cottages 36 Luyt St ☎028 312 1258,

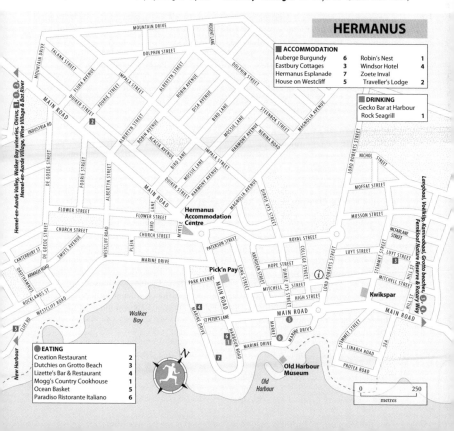

Ⓦeastburycottage.co.za. Four fully equipped self-catering cottages close to the *Marine Hotel*. Prices vary depending on whether you are a couple or a group, and breakfast is available for R100. R800

Hermanus Esplanade 63 Marine Drive ☎028 312 3610, ✉info@hermanusesplanade.com. Self-catering apartments of varying sizes, some are sea facing, while others face onto a courtyard. Go for the more expensive ones that feature views of the bay. R1000

House on Westcliff 96 Westcliff Rd ☎028 313 2388, Ⓦwestcliffhouse.co.za. This homely B&B is situated just out of the centre near the new harbour and boasts six bedrooms in a classic Cape-style house with a protected, tranquil garden and swimming pool. All rooms are en suite and have their own entrance off the garden, and there is also a three-bed family room, with a baby's cot available. R1000

Robin's Nest 10 Meadow Ave ☎028 316 1597, Ⓦrobinsnest-guesthouse.co.za. Three fully equipped, but

WHALE-WATCHING

The Southern Cape, including Cape Town, provides some of the easiest and best places in the world for **whale-watching**. You don't need to rent a boat or take a pricey tour to get out to sea; if you come at the right time of year, whales are often visible from the shore, although a good pair of binoculars will come in useful when they are far out.

All nine of the great whale species of the southern hemisphere pass by South Africa's shores, but the most commonly seen off Cape Town are **southern right whales** (their name derives from being the "right" one to kill because of their high oil and bone yields and the fact that they float when dead). Southern right whales are black and easily recognized from their pale, brownish **callosities**. These unappealing patches of raised, roughened skin on their snouts and heads have a distinct pattern on each animal, which helps scientists keep track of them.

Female whales come inshore to calve in sheltered bays, and stay to nurse their young for up to three months. **July to October** is the best time to see them, although they start appearing in June and some stay around until December. When the calves are big enough, the whales head off south again, to colder, stormy waters, where they feed on enormous quantities of plankton, making up for the nursing months when the females don't eat at all. Though you're most likely to see females and young, you may see **males** early in the season boisterously flopping about the females, though they neither help rear the calves nor form lasting bonds with females.

What gives away the presence of a whale is the blow or spout, a tall smoky plume which disperses after a few seconds and is actually the whale breathing out before it surfaces. If luck is on your side, you may see whales **breaching** – the movement when they thrust high out of the water and fall back with a great splash.

THE WHALE COAST'S HOTTEST WHALE SPOTS

In **Hermanus**, the best vantage points are the concrete cliff paths that ring the rocky shore from New Harbour to Grotto Beach. There are interpretation boards at three of the popular vantage points (Gearing's Point, Die Gang and Bientang's Cave) – these are the most congested venues during the whale season. There are equally good spots elsewhere along the Walker Bay coast; aficionados claim that **De Kelders** (see p.184), some 39km southeast of Hermanus, is even better, while **De Hoop Nature Reserve** (see p.188), east of Arniston, is reckoned by some to be the ultimate place along the entire southern-African coast for whale-watching.

Several **operators** offer boat trips from Hermanus, all essentially offering the same service. Try Hermanus Whale Cruises (☎028 313 2722, Ⓦwww.hermanus-whale-cruises.co.za), which is a coloured fishing village community project. A boat for 87 passengers goes out four times daily from the New Harbour, for the two-hour trip (June–late Nov; R800). Boats must give a 50m berth to whales, but if a whale approaches a boat, the boat may stop and watch it for up to twenty minutes.

Further around Walker Bay, close to Gansbaai, **Dyer Island Cruises** (Geelbek St, Kleinbaai; ☎028 384 0406, Ⓦwhalewatchsa.com) does whale cruises during whale season in the Dyer Island area, and on each trip there is a marine biologist on hand to answer questions. Whale-watching trips depart daily (2hr 30min; R1100) from Kleinbaai at various times depending on weather conditions. Book in advance.

Perhaps the ultimate way to see whales is from the air. David Austin, based in Hermanus (African Wings; ☎082 555 7605, Ⓦafricanwings.co.za), flies a maximum of three people in a small plane over the bay to see whales, dolphins, sharks and other sea life. Flights range from thirty minutes (R3850 for three people) to an hour (R7300 for three people), all of which guarantee whale-spotting in season, and offer the opportunity to observe mothers and baby whales interacting.

plain, self-catering studio flats above a garage in a garden, 4km west of the centre. Reached through the Hemel-en-Aarde shopping village, these purpose-built, two-storey flats sleep two guests and have good mountain views. R700
Windsor Hotel 49 Marine Drive ☏ 028 312 3727, ⓦ windsorhotel.co.za. This old, but popular, seafront hotel offers a full range of accommodation right on the cliff edge. It's ideally situated in the centre of Hermanus and guests can enjoy sea views from the dining room, lounges

and almost half of the bedrooms. R1500
Zoete Inval Traveller's Lodge 23 Main Rd ☏ 028 312 1242, ⓦ zoeteinval.co.za. A quiet and relaxing hostel, with a distinct lack of party vibe, comprising dorms, doubles and family suites, with extras like good coffee, a Jacuzzi and a fireplace. If you're travelling with a baby, there is a baby bed that can be moved into your room. They can also organize all tours and outings in the area. Dorms R225, doubles R600, family room sleeping four R1200

EATING

Seafood is the obvious thing to eat in Hermanus – and you'll find plenty of restaurants serving it – though the views are generally better than the food. There are a couple of excellent restaurants in the wine estate valley of Hemel-en-Aarde (see p.182), west of town, and further afield in Stanford. **Book well ahead** at weekends and in summer; without a booking, you can always get fish and chips at the harbour. Food features large at the **market** held every Saturday morning at the Hermanus Cricket Grounds (8am–noon; ⓦ hermanus.co.za/hermanus-market). Here you'll find a variety of organic foods, excellent cheeses from Bot River as well as fresh pasta, pesto, muffins, hummus and baked goods.

★**Creation Restaurant** Hemel-en-Aarde Valley ☏ 028 212 1107, ⓦ creationwines.com. A fabulous place with an elegant, yet informal, setting. Tables, both inside and out, look onto the *fynbos*-clad mountains. The antipasto dishes and canapés are sublime, and the food is created to complement the wines (food and wine pairing R335). Children are well catered for, with their own tasting menu of five pairings of food with five surprise drinks (R75). Booking essential. Daily 11am–4pm.
Dutchies on Grotto Beach 10th Avenue, Grotto Beach, Voëlklip ☏ 028 314 1392, ⓦ dutchies.co.za. The only place to eat right on the beach, and a good one at that. There isn't much of a Dutch character in the menu, but the management and service sparkle. Prices are reasonable – a "health breakfast" (hot drink, fresh orange juice, fruit salad, Greek yoghurt and muesli) will set you back just R70, while a Dutch cheese and ham ciabatta sandwich is R80. Book ahead, especially to get outdoor seating. Daily 9am–9pm.
★**Lizette's Bar & Restaurant** 20 8th St, Voëlklip ☏ 028 314 0308, ⓦ lizetteskitchen.com. Well-known chef Lizette Crabtree cooks up a storm in this spacious restored house, which has plenty of outdoor seating, a play area for kids and a cosy interior. With her experience of cooking in the East, you can expect Vietnamese street food (R100), curries, Moroccan dishes, and some South African

favourites with a twist. Takeaway available, too, but no deliveries. Daily 9am–10pm.
★**Mogg's Country Cookhouse** Hemel-en-Aarde Valley, 12km from Hermanus along the R320 to Caledon ☏ 076 314 0671, ⓦ moggscookhouse.com. A most unlikely location for one of Hermanus's most successful restaurants – a farm cottage – with superb views across the valley. *Mogg's* is an intimate place that's always full and unfailingly excellent, serving whatever takes the fancy of chefs Jenny Mogg and her daughter Julia. Mains, which might include pan-fried line fish on red pepper risotto with a mushroom sauce (R125), are followed by a selection of great desserts. Booking is essential and kids are welcome. Wed–Sun noon–2.30pm.
Ocean Basket Fashion Square, Village Square ☏ 028 312 1313. As part of a reasonably priced and consistently reliable seafood chain, this restaurant is popular thanks in no small part to its fabulous setting, serving up cheap fish and chips (R70) and a variety of salads and other fish dishes. Mon–Sat noon–9pm, Sun noon–8pm.
Paradiso Ristorante Italiano 83 Marine Drive ☏ 028 313 1153. Situated behind Village Square, near the water in a zone of tourist restaurants, this reliable Italian place does seafood dishes and chicken, alongside delicious pizza (R100) and pasta. Daily 11am–9.30pm.

DRINKING

Gecko Bar at Harbour Rock Seagrill New Harbour ☏ 028 312 2920. One of the best places in Hermanus for a sundowner (R60), this packed, noisy bar has excellent views and serves cocktails, pizzas, burgers and other pub

grub. It allows smoking in some parts of the bar. For a more upmarket bite head next door to the *Harbour Rock Seagrill*. Daily 12.30pm–midnight.

Stanford

East of Hermanus, the R43 takes a detour inland around the attractive Klein River Lagoon, past the village of **STANFORD**, 155km from Cape Town. This historic village,

WALKER BAY WINERIES

Some of South Africa's top **wines** come from the **Hemel-en-Aarde (heaven and earth) Valley** along the **R320** to Caledon, which branches off the main road to Cape Town, 2km west of Hermanus. Several small **wineries** are dotted along the same road and are worth popping into for their intimate tasting rooms and first-class wines, with views of the stark, scrubby mountains just inland. The whole route is 20km, and some wineries also offer meals, notably Creation and Newton Johnson.

Hamilton Russell Winery (off R320, Hemel-en-Aarde Road; Mon–Fri 9am–5pm, Sat 9am–1pm; ☎ 028 312 3595, ⓦ hamiltonrussellvineyards.com) is the longest established of the Walker Bay wineries and produces some of South Africa's priciest wines. They are especially known for their Pinot Noir and Chardonnay.

Adjacent to Hamilton Russell, towards Caledon, **Bouchard Finlayson** (Mon–Fri 9.30am–5pm, Sat 9.30am–12.30pm; ☎ 028 312 3515, ⓦ bouchardfinlayson.co.za) is another establishment with a formidable reputation, and a wider range of wines than its neighbour. Their flagship and award-winning wine, the Galpin Peak Pinot Noir, is grown on the slopes of Galpin peak. Their dry white blend, Blanc de Mer, alludes to the fact that these wines are hugely influenced by their proximity to the cool ocean. Two-thirds of the way down the route is **Newton Johnson** (Mon–Fri 9am–5pm, Sat & Sun 10am–1pm; ☎ 028 312 3862, ⓦ newtonjohnson.com); its estate restaurant is rated for lunch. Getting towards the top of the valley, **Ataraxia Wines** (Mon–Fri 9am–4pm, Sat 10am–5pm; ☎ 028 212 2007, ⓦ ataraxiawines.co.za) is contemporary and stylish; its wine-tasting lounge, which is built like a chapel to contemplate the heavenly wines, has gorgeous mountain views. At the end of the line, **Creation** (daily 10am–5pm; ☎ 028 212 1107, ⓦ creationwines.com) has fabulous wines and is known for its gourmet food and wine pairings (daily 11am–4pm), as well as chocolate- and tea-tasting. Book well in advance at weekends.

16

established in 1857, has become something of a refuge for arty types – something that can best be appreciated on the **arts and crafts route** that takes in over a dozen artists' studios. But apart from the town's excellent microbrewery and some wine estates, Stanford's principal attraction is its streetscape of simple **Victorian architecture** that includes limewashed houses and sandstone cottages – as well as an Anglican church – with thatched roofs that glow under the late afternoon sun.

The Klein River

The town's northern boundary is the attractive **Klein River**, which can be explored on a boat trip or by yourself in a kayak. For trips on the river, contact Ernie (☎ 083 310 0952) a two- to three-hour boat trip costs R150, while canoe and kayak rental is R100; book in advance, especially at the weekend. The price is for the entire day, if you choose. There's rich birdlife in and among the rustling reed beds lining the riverbanks where you stand a chance of spotting the flashy malachite kingfisher.

Walker Bay Estate and Birkenhead Brewery

Just across the R43 from Stanford along the R326 • Beer and wine tasting daily 11am–5pm, R30 for six wines, R60 for six beers; Lunch daily 11am–4pm • ☎ 028 341 0013, ⓦ walkerbayestate.com

Although **Birkenhead Brewery** bills itself as a "craft brewery estate", the gleaming stainless-steel pipes and equipment inside soon dispel any images of bloodshot hillbillies knocking up a bit of moonshine on the quiet. This is a slick operation and a great place to go for a pub lunch or to buy craft beers, which put those of SAB, South Africa's big brewing near-monopoly, in their place. They have also added winemaking to their talents, so you can try both wine and beer.

ARRIVAL AND INFORMATION   STANFORD

By car Stanford is 155km from Cape Town. Take the Hermanus off-ramp from the N2 (about 90km from Cape Town), and follow the R43 for another 65km through

Hermanus to Stanford.
Tourist office Located on Main Road (Mon–Fri 8.30am–4.30pm, Sat 9am–4pm, Sun 9am–1pm;

📞 028 341 0340, 🌐 stanfordtourism.co.za), the tourist office can help with booking accommodation, and can also provide a brochure for a walkabout you can do that takes in the various historical houses in the village. Their website has a list of cottages to rent, and many are bookable via the website. They can provide information on wineries to visit and other activities, as well as the arts and crafts route.

ACCOMMODATION

B's Cottage 17 Morton St 📞 028 341 0430 or 📞 083 293 5512, 🌐 www.stanford-accommodation.co.za. This centrally located, small, thatched house features open-plan self-catering and sleeps two upstairs, with a sleeper couch in the downstairs living room. There's also an English-style country garden, as well as another, similar adjoining cottage. It's popular so book well ahead. Weekend bookings are for two nights only. R750

Mosaic Farm 10km from the centre, exit from Queen Victoria St 📞 028 313 2814, 🌐 mosaicsouthafrica.com. Stone, canvas and thatch self-catering chalets on the river here, with 4km of lagoon frontage. Chalets can sleep a couple or a group. Cruises, nature walks, canoeing and 4WD excursions to the beach are available. At the luxury end, the full-board *Lagoon Lodge* on the same site (R6200) is a lagoon-side safari camp. The natural setting of the farm and access to a wild part of the lagoon and coast is fabulous. R900

★ **Stanford River Lodge** 4km from the centre, exit from Queen Victoria St 📞 028 341 0444, 🌐 stanfordriverlodge.co.za. Sunny, spacious and modern self-catering cottages with river and mountain views. It's a lovely, upmarket place with river swimming and canoeing in summer. Bring all you need by way of supplies, though it is possible to order a breakfast basket 24hr in advance. R900

EATING

In addition to the **restaurants** listed below, Stanford is also home to a number of lovely **coffee shops** located along the quiet main road. Like every small town in the Western Cape, Stanford has a Saturday morning **market** (9am–noon). Located on the veranda of the *Stanford Hotel*, in Queen Victoria Street, this is the place to buy ready-made meals, bread, pastries, quiches and ingredients for picnics and self-catering. On Wednesdays (9am–noon) there are organic vegetables and other goodies for sale outside *Graze Restaurant*, opposite the *Stanford Hotel*. Outside of town, the most outstanding food is to be found at Springfontein Winery (see box below), and should be top of the list for food and wine.

★ **Madres Kitchen** Robert Stanford Estate, 1km west of Stanford 📞 028 341 0647. The best place to have breakfast on the edge of town, and the lunches, with platters of home-made bread, pâtés and cheeses, plus herbs and vegetables from the garden, complemented with wines from their own estate, are also fabulous (R130).

It is great for children, with lawns, a jungle gym and ducks to feed, and they also do picnics. Thurs–Sun 8am–4pm.

★ **Mariana's Bistro and Home Deli** Du Toit St 📞 028 341 0272. The innovative and reasonably priced, award-winning country food served at this Victorian cottage is good enough to draw Cape Town gourmands out for the

---

STANFORD FOOD AND WINE

Two kilometres beyond Birkenhead Brewery, and 7km from Stanford on the R326, is the **Klein River Cheese Farm** (Mon–Sat 9am–4pm; 📞 028 341 0693, 🌐 kleinrivercheese.co.za), which offers tastings of its famous Gruyère, Leiden, Colby and Dando cheeses. Buy one of their picnic baskets at lunchtime and enjoy it sitting under the trees next to the river; book online in advance, it is deservedly popular.

As everywhere else in the Cape, more and more vineyards are opening, *fynbos* giving way to grapes, but possibly Stanford's best wine is sold from **Raka** (Mon–Fri 9am–5pm, Sat 10am–3pm; 📞 028 341 0676, 🌐 rakawine.co.za), 17km from town along the R326. Even if you don't get out there, be sure to try their wine, they sell countrywide and internationally, and it is served up throughout the region.

Springfontein Winery, on the Stanford Lagoon, 5km from Stanford on the Queen Victoria St Extension (Mon–Wed & Fri–Sun 11.30am–8.30pm, closed Wed during winter; 📞 028 341 0651, 🌐 www.springfontein.co.za) is a great destination for wine tasting and enjoying good food. *The Barn* tasting room (R25) doubles up as a German-style pub with excellent cheese, salad and sausages on offer. There is also a separate, outstanding restaurant open for lunch (Thurs–Sun from 12.30pm), and dinner (Wed–Sun from 6.30pm), which does sophisticated three-course or six-course lunches and dinners (R440–720), with Springfontein and other boutique wines, cooked by Michelin-starred chef Jurgen Schneider. Book in advance.

16

day, and is an absolute food highlight of the region. Food and wines are local, and many of the vegetables are picked from the owners' garden. The owners host in a warm and engaged way. Vegetarians can enjoy chèvre tart or home-made ricotta in local vine leaves (R90). You'll need to book a couple of months beforehand, though cancellations may be a possibility. Try for a table on the *stoep* for a long lazy lunch. No children under 10. Thurs–Sun noon–4pm.

Gansbaai

GANSBAAI, 175km from Cape Town, is a workaday place, economically dependent on its fishing industry and the seafood canning factory at the harbour. This gives the town a more gutsy feel than the surrounding holiday lands, but there's little reason to spend time here unless you want to engage in **great white shark safaris**, Gansbaai's other major industry. It is an appropriately competitive and cut-throat business with operators engaged in a blind feeding frenzy to attract punters. Boats set out from Gansbaai to **Dyer Island** (see box, p.186), east of Danger Point, where great white sharks come to feed on the resident colony of seals.

De Kelders

A suburb of Gansbaai, **De Kelders** is a treeless area of bland holiday homes and ostentatious seafront mansions on cliffs that look out across Walker Bay to Hermanus. Its rocky coast, though, provides outstanding whale-watching and there is access to a beautiful, long sandy beach at the Walker Bay Nature Reserve.

Walker Bay Nature Reserve and the Klipgat Strandloper Caves

Access is at the end of Cliff Rd • Daily 7am–7pm • R30

You can clamber over rocky sections and walk for miles along the beach at the **Walker Bay Nature Reserve**, known by everyone as "Die Plat". Swimming is very dangerous though, and it's best not to venture in more than knee-high. From the car park, a path leads down to the **Klipgat Strandloper Caves**, excavated in the early 1990s, when evidence was unearthed of modern human habitation from 80,000 years ago. The caves became unoccupied for a few thousand years, after which they were used again by Khoisan people 20,000 years ago. Shells, middens, tools and bones were uncovered; some of these are now displayed in the South African Museum in Cape Town (see p.56). From the caves, the waymarked **Duiwelsgats hiking trail** goes east for 7km as far as Gansbaai and is a good way to explore the coastline, which can also be accessed at a number of other points.

ARRIVAL AND INFORMATION

GANSBAAI

By car Gansbaai is 175km from Cape Town. Take the Hermanus off-ramp from the N2 (about 90km from Cape Town), and follow the R43 for another 85km through Hermanus, Stanford, De Kelders and Gansbaai.

By bus The shuttle Bernadus (☎ 028 316 1093 or ☎ 083 658 7848) does the trip 45km around the coast from Cape Town to Gansbaai for around R900 per person (2hr).

Tourist office Great White Junction, Kapokblom St (Mon–Fri 8.30am–5.30pm, Sat 9am–4pm, Sun 10am–2pm; ☎ 028 384 1439, ⓦ gansbaaiinfo.com).

GROOTBOS PRIVATE NATURE RESERVE

Set among the hills 6km before De Kelders, *Grootbos Private Nature Reserve* (☎ 028 384 8000, ⓦ grootbos.com) is an exceedingly tasteful, **luxurious ecolodge** that offers whale-watching safaris, horseriding and *fynbos* tours. Even if you can't stay – and it is undoubtedly the **top accommodation along the Whale Coast** – you can visit for the day and enjoy superb gourmet meals at reasonable rates, though you'll need to book ahead. Full board, including all activities, ranges from R4500–7400 per person per night. If it's outside of Christmas and Easter, they offer a last-minute special, which gives thirty percent off the normal rates, and can be booked 48 hours in advance via their website.

ACCOMMODATION

Cliff Lodge 6 Cliff St ☎ 028 384 0983, ⊛ clifflodge .co.za. A stylish seafront guesthouse, with friendly owners, perched on the cliffs of De Kelders, with breathtaking views from all four luxurious bedrooms and the spacious penthouse suite, plus a deck for whale-watching and a pool for your own splashing. R2900

★ **Crayfish Lodge** Killarney St ☎ 028 384 1898,

⊛ crayfishlodge.com. This is the top stay in town; a palatial guesthouse with sea views and an individual patio or courtyard for all five rooms. If you're treating yourself, go for the upstairs suites with Jacuzzis. A path leads down to a rocky beach with a channel for bathing or there's a heated swimming pool. Doubles R2800, suites R3800

EATING AND DRINKING

Blue Goose 12 Franken St ☎ 028 384 1106. Fresh, locally sourced seafood and meat, complemented with regional wines. Their spicy fish curry (R150) and tempura prawns are recommended, and there is always a pasta for vegetarians. Daily 7–10pm.

Boat House Restaurant and Pub Gansbaai Harbour. This is the place to come for over-the-counter traditional fresh fish and chips (R70) in big portions, or to enjoy a beer sitting on the veranda while watching the fishing boats come in. Daily 9am–5pm.

Coffee on the Rocks Cliff St ☎ 028 384 2017. A small bistro that does great coffee, cakes and light meals, with a

deck in an unsurpassed position for whale-watching; also a good choice for leisurely Sunday roasts (R130). Booking is essential. Wed–Sun 10am–5pm.

★ **Grootbos Nature Reserve** Off R43, 8km west of Gansbaai ☎ 028 384 8008. This delightful ecolodge is one of the culinary highlights of the area – offering fine-dining traditional cuisine with a modern twist. What's more, it's surprisingly reasonable for the quality of food you receive. They run a set menu only; a three-course lunch will set you back R300 while the dinner is R460. Definitely arrive early before dinner to enjoy a sundowner while taking in the view. Daily 1–3pm & 7–9pm.

16

Danger Point

Danger Point, the southernmost point of Walker Bay, is where British naval history was allegedly made. True to its name, the Point lured the ill-fated HMS *Birkenhead* onto its hidden rocks on February 26, 1852. As was the custom, the captain of the troopship gave the order "Every man for himself". Displaying true British pluck, the soldiers are said to have lined up in their ranks on deck where they stood stock-still, knowing that if one man broke ranks it would lead to a rush that might overwhelm the lifeboats carrying women and children to safety. The precedent of "women and children first", which became known as the **Birkenhead Drill**, was thus established, even though 445 lives were lost in the disaster.

Cape Agulhas and around

Along the east flank of the Danger Point promontory, the rocky and shallow coastline with heavy swells and strong currents makes this one of South Africa's most treacherous stretches of coast – it has claimed over 250 wrecks and around 2500 lives. Its rough terrain also accounts for the lack of a coastal road from Gansbaai and Danger Point to **Cape Agulhas**, the southernmost tip of Africa.

The plain around the southern tip of South Africa has been declared the **Agulhas National Park** to conserve its estimated two thousand species of indigenous plant, marine and intertidal life as well as a cultural heritage which includes shipwrecks and archeological sites – stone hearths, pottery and shell middens have been discovered here.

The actual tip of the continent is marked by a rock and plaque about 1km below the landmark of Agulhas Lighthouse, towards Suiderstrand. There is no fee to walk around the tip, which is part of the Agulhas National Park. Undramatic as it is, the famous spot is definitely worth seeing, where Africa simply tails off into a few rocks in the sea. Following the dirt road to **Suiderstrand** itself takes you to some beautiful undeveloped beaches, and the National Park beach cottages, but the road is very corrugated and rough. **L'AGULHAS**, referred to simply as Agulhas, is the rather windblown, treeless settlement associated with the southern tip. Consisting of a small collection of holiday houses and a few shops, it's a much quieter coastal destination than anywhere along the

DYER ISLAND AND SHARK ALLEY

How a black American came to be living on an island off South Africa in the early nineteenth century is something of a mystery. But, according to records, **Samson Dyer** arrived here in 1806 and made a living collecting guano on the island that subsequently took his name.

Dyer Island is home to substantial **African penguin and seal breeding colonies**, both of which are prized morsels among great white sharks. So shark-infested is the channel between the island and the mainland at some times of year that it is known as **Shark Alley**, and these waters are used extensively by operators of great-white viewing trips. If you go on a trip, you'll be safely contained within a sturdy boat or cage. This is a luxury that a group of West African castaways could not afford when, in 1996, they found themselves washed up here as the Taiwanese merchant vessel they were riding on sank en route to the Far East. One of them drowned, but the rest (amazingly) survived five days at sea, including a stint down Shark Alley, clinging to pieces of timber and barrels.

Garden Route. The centre of Agulhas is along Main Road, where you'll find a couple of restaurants, a small supermarket and a craft shop. There is a large tidal pool on the left, just before you reach the Lighthouse, which is perfect if you fancy a swim.

STRUISBAAI, 4km before you reach Agulhas, is worth considering staying in, rather than Agulhas itself, if you want access to sandy beaches, as the coastline around Agulhas is very rocky. It has the added attraction of a small harbour and a couple of restaurants.

Agulhas Lighthouse

Daily 9am–4.30pm • R40

The red-and-white **Agulhas Lighthouse**, commissioned in 1849, offers vertiginous views from its top, reached by a series of steep ladders, and is a landmark not to be missed. The appeal of lonely lighthouses on rugged coastal edges beaming out signals to ships at night is explored here through interesting exhibits about lighthouses around South Africa.

Struisbaai

East of Agulhas is **STRUISBAAI** (pronounced "strace-bye", often simply referred to as Strace), notable for its endless white-sand beach. The further away you walk from the uninspiring holiday homes and camping site, the better it gets, and you could literally walk the whole day on the beach around the bay. Swimming is fantastic too, and safe, with the typically dark turquoise-coloured water of these parts.

It is worth going to the small harbour at Struisbaai where there are frequently sightings of giant stingrays gracefully gliding through the water and wooden struts of the slipway. Totally safe, the resident giant ray, Parrie, even has his own Facebook page. From the jetty, there is a lovely wooden walkway to take you along the coast to some rocky beaches.

ARRIVAL AND INFORMATION

CAPE AGULHAS AND AROUND

By car Agulhas is 230km from Cape Town. Take the N2 to Caledon (115km), then the R316 to Bredasdorp; here, the westerly branch of the R319 will take you down to Agulhas (43km). The drive takes you through rolling farmlands where you are almost certain to see South Africa's national bird, the elegant and endangered blue crane, feeding in the fields. Both the small towns of Napier and Bredasdorp en route have appealing cafés and restaurants to tempt you to break the journey.

By taxi transfer Mrs Marie Johannes runs a daily door-to-door taxi company from Cape Town, which can drop you in Agulhas or Struis (☎ 082 691 9075, R350).

Tourist information At Agulhas Lighthouse (daily 9am–5pm; ☎ 028 435 7185, ⓦ discovercapeagulhas .co.za) is astoundingly good and they have a comprehensive map of the area with useful listings, as well as the comprehensive *Overberg Wine* (free), which covers estates in Elim, Greyton, Stanford, Napier and Hermanus. It is really worth leaving the beach and venturing out to explore wine farms in the region. If you want to taste and buy wines from the region, the infallibly excellent Wine Boutique (☎ 082 567 7858) on the Main Road, across the road from *Seagulls Pub and Restaurant*, stocks wines of the region and can certainly advise.

ACCOMMODATION

Cape Agulhas Backpackers Cnr of Duiker & Main roads, Struisbaai ☎082 372 3354, ⓦcapeagulhas backpackers.com. The only budget place around Agulhas has camping, dorms and doubles, all with good bedding, plus a pool and garden. It's run by a couple who are big on helping you enjoy the outdoors and will organize fishing, surfing lessons, kite-surfing or horseriding. Camping R100, dorms R160, doubles R450

Cape Agulhas National Park Rest Camp Suiderstrand 7km west of Agulhas ☎028 435 6078, ⓦsanparks.org. If you want a remote beach experience, and some hiking, opt for one of the sea view cottages in Suiderstrand. They are fully equipped for self-catering, and you need to collect the key from the National Park office near the Lighthouse before 6pm during the week, or 5pm at the weekend, and pay the R150 per person

conservation fee. Take everything with you, as you won't want to be bumping along this road to the shops. R1100

Langezandt Fishermans Village Murex St, Struisbaai ☎028 435 7547, ⓦlangezandt.co.za. Self-catering, exclusive beach villas on an estate, built to look like traditional white-washed, thatched local houses. They are geared to families, but there are some smaller units. The location is fabulous, right at the edge of town, with direct access to miles of sandy beach for walking or swimming. R1200

Southermost B&B Cnr of Van Breda & Lighthouse sts ☎028 435 6565, ⓦsouthermost.co.za. A well-loved and rather dilapidated historic beach cottage, run by the welcoming Meg, opposite the tidal pool with an indigenous garden sloping down to the water's edge. It is an easy walk from here to the centre to get an evening meal. It's closed in winter. R800

EATING

Agulhas Seafoods 118 Main Rd, Agulhas ☎028 435 7207. The fish and chips at *Agulhas Seafoods* is so succulent and delicious that Capetonians have been known to travel all the way out here to enjoy it (R65). As well as local fish, they also serve calamari and sushi, accompanied by a selection of wine and beers. Mon–Sat 10am–7pm, Sun 10am–3pm.

Pelicans Harbour Café Struisbaai Harbour ☎028 435 6526. Straightforward fish and chips place with wooden tables and benches. This could be a good place to try

legitimately farmed and harvested abalone (R190), a delicacy normally associated with poaching, otherwise go for the mussels or locally caught line fish. Daily 10am–9pm.

Twisted Fork Restaurant and Bar 184 Main Rd, Agulhas ☎028 435 6291. This is the place to go for a night out at the pub, and the food is not bad either. The Thai chicken and prawn curry is recommended (R120), and the catch of the day is served with excellent chips. Daily 11am–2am.

16

Arniston

After the deep blues of the Atlantic to the west, the azure of the Indian Ocean at **ARNISTON** is startling, made all the more dazzling by the white dunes. Situated 220km from Cape Town, this is one of the best places to stay in the Overberg – if you want nothing more than the sea. The colours may be tropical, but the wind can howl unpredictably here, as anywhere else along the Cape coast, and when it does, there's nothing much to do. The village is known to locals by its Afrikaans name, Waenhuiskrans ("wagon-house cliff"), after a cliff containing a huge cave 1500m south of town (see p.188), which trekboers reckoned was spacious enough for a wagon and span of oxen (the largest thing they could think of). The English name derives from a British ship, the *Arniston*, which hit the rocks here in 1815.

The shallow seas, so treacherous for vessels, provide Arniston with safe swimming waters. You can swim next to the slipway or at **Roman Beach**, the main swimming beach, just along the coast as you head south from the harbour.

ELIM MISSION STATION

ELIM, a Moravian mission station 40km northwest of Agulhas, founded in 1824, has streets lined with thatched, whitewashed houses and fig trees, though feels rather run-down and forsaken. You can wander about the central area, which is the most attractive part, and take in the architecture and history by visiting the church, the restored water mill where wheat is still ground, and the memorial commemorating the **emancipation of slaves** in 1834, the only such monument in South Africa. Its presence reflects the fact that numerous freed slaves found refuge in mission stations like Elim. The Mission is best visited on a day-drive if you are exploring the area or visiting several good wine farms in the area – all on unpaved roads.

Kassiesbaai

A principal attraction of Arniston is **Kassiesbaai**, a district of starkly beautiful, limewashed cottages, now declared a National Monument and home to fishing families who have for generations made their living here. But Kassiesbaai sits a little uneasily as a living community, as it's also a bit of a theme park for visitors stalking the streets with their cameras. Heading north through Kassiesbaai at low tide, you can walk 5km along an unspoilt beach unmarred by buildings until you reach an unassuming fence – resist the temptation to climb over this, as it marks the boundary of the local testing range for military material and missiles.

Arniston Caves

Heading south of the harbour for 1500m along spectacular cliffs, you'll reach the vast **cave** after which the town is named. The walk is worth doing simply for the *fynbos*-covered dunes you'll cross on the way. From the car park right by the cave, it's a short signposted walk down to the dunes and the cave, which can only be reached at low tide. The rocks can be slippery and have sharp sections, so be sure to wear shoes with tough soles and a good grip.

ARRIVAL AND INFORMATION
ARNISTON

By car From Cape Town (225km), take the N2 to Caledon (115km), then the R316 to Bredasdorp, continuing along the R316 afterwards for 25km to Arniston.

By taxi There is no public transport to Arniston, though you can try the daily door-to-door taxi service run by Mrs Johannes from Cape Town (☎ 082 691 9075, R400).

Tourist office There is no tourist office in Arniston, but the one in Agulhas covers the area (see p.186).

ACCOMMODATION

There is holiday accommodation in the new section of town, adjacent to the traditional fishing village quarter of Kassiesbaai. You won't find pumping nightlife or adrenaline-packed attractions here, only azure sea, and peace and quiet.

Arniston Lodge 23 Main Rd ☎ 028 445 9175, ⓦ arnistonlodge.co.za. In the residential area, this B&B offers four rooms in a two-storey thatched home with a pool. The upstairs rooms have views and better bathrooms than those downstairs. R1300

Arniston Seaside Cottages Huxham St, signposted as you arrive from Bredasdorp ☎ 028 445 9772, ⓦ arniston seasidecottages.co.za. A series of attractive and modern self-catering establishments built in the style of traditional fisherman's cottages with limewashed walls and thatched roofs. Clean and bright, they're in a good position just a few minutes' walk from the beach and come fully equipped. R760

★**Arniston Spa Hotel** Beach Rd ☎ 028 445 9000, ⓦ arnistonhotel.com. Dominating the seafront, this luxurious spa hotel boasts every comfort, including a spa with massage and beauty treatments. The best rooms have a fireplace, or a balcony with sea views. If it's way out of your budget, go during the week or in winter when prices drop. It is one of the best-set beach hotels in the country, and the only one in town. R2550

EATING AND DRINKING

Arniston Hotel Beach Rd. Pleasing fresh fish dinners (R140), with outdoor seating to take in the sea views. It also holds the town's only bistro bar, which serves burgers and the like and has sport on TV. Daily 10am–9.30pm.

Willeen's Meals Arts and Crafts House C26, Kassiesbaai ☎ 028 445 9995. An authentic fisherman's cottage where you'll be served traditional Cape Malay meals by family members. You can try *bobotie* (R60) or fried fish. They have a BYO booze policy, though soft drinks are available. You can also just have tea and something sweet in the garden that boasts sea views. Daily 9am–9pm.

De Hoop Nature Reserve

Daily 7am–6pm • R40

De Hoop is the wilderness highlight of the Western Cape and one of the best places in the world for land-based whale-watching. July to October is the best time for this, with the highest number of whales in August and September, but you stand a very good

chance of a sighting from June through to November. There's no need to take a boat or use binoculars – in season you'll see whales blowing, breaching – leaping clear of the water – or perhaps slapping a giant tail. Although the reserve could technically be done as a day-trip from Agulhas, Arniston or Swellendam, you'll find it far more rewarding to come here for a night or more. The Whale Trail hike is one of South Africa's best walks and is among the finest wildlife experiences in the world (see box, p.191).

The breathtaking coastline is edged by bleached sand dunes standing 90m high in places, and rocky formations that at one point open to the sea in a massive craggy arch. The flora and fauna are impressive, too, encompassing 86 species of mammal, 260 different birds and 1500 varieties of plants. Inland, rare **Cape mountain zebra**, **bontebok** and other **antelope** congregate on a plain near the reserve accommodation.

ARRIVAL AND DEPARTURE   DE HOOP NATURE RESERVE

By car De Hoop is signposted off the N2, 13km west of Swellendam, the quickest route from Cape Town. Alternatively, if you are in the Overberg, take the signposted dirt road that spurs off the R319 as it heads out of Bredasdorp, 50km to its west.

ACCOMMODATION AND EATING

There are a couple of places to stay outside of the park, but accommodation within the National Park is only available through the De Hoop Collection (w dehoopcollection.co.za), and varies from **camping** to luxurious **cottages**. The accommodation and **restaurant** are some 20min drive on roughish dirt roads, from the sea.

There are **no food supplies** at De Hoop, except for a small shop selling basics, so be sure to stock up with everything you need before you arrive, in Swellendam or Bredasdorp.

★**De Hoop Cottages** De Hoop Nature Reserve ✆ 021 422 4522, w dehoopcollection.co.za. You'll find an array of accommodation here, none of them especially cheap, but all appealing and comfortable. At the top end, you can enjoy a bed and breakfast stay, with dinner included, in the converted manor house, eating at the restaurant next door. Camping is the cheapest way to visit the reserve, and there are also a number of appealing self-catering properties of varying sizes from basic rondavels with outdoor showers and views to a fully equipped cottage. Camping R375, rondavels R1050, cottage R1600, manor house R3000
Fig Tree On the reserve, close to reception ✆ 028 542 1254. De Hoop's only restaurant uses local ingredients complementing the Elim wines, with good-value set-menu dinners, often including fish (R275), plus a children's menu.

Reservations are required. Picnic baskets can be ordered (R275 for two) and there is a lovely spot outside that's perfect for sundowners after a good day at the beach. Daily 8–11am, noon–3pm & 7–9pm.
Verfheuwel Farm Potberg Road, in the direction of Malgas ✆ 028 542 1038 or ✆ 082 767 0148, w verfheuwelguestfarm.co.za. This cottage accommodation, attached to the main farmhouse, is run by hospitable Afrikaner farming folk who can bring dinner to your cottage if you ask in advance. It sleeps a couple, with beds in the living area for children. The garden is beautiful and has a swimming pool. If *Verfheuwel* is full, owner Matti can direct you to other friends and relatives in the area who have farm accommodation. R850

The Overberg Interior

Just off the N2, **Caledon** merits a quick visit for its refreshing hot springs, while a few towns are worth visiting for a night or two. Closer to Cape Town, **Greyton** makes a perfect weekend break, with enough good food, walks and lounging in garden cafés to occupy you for a couple of nights. Nearby, South Africa's oldest mission station, **Genadendal**, 6km west of Greyton, is also worth a look around. **Swellendam**, further along the N2, is often treated as the first night stop along the Garden Route, but makes a good base for visiting **De Hoop Nature Reserve** (see p.188), or to see some antelope and ostriches in the **Bontebok National Park**, a few kilometres away.

Greyton

GREYTON, a tranquil village 46km north of Caledon, is a favourite weekend destination for Capetonians. Based around a core of Georgian and Victorian buildings, shaded by

ON THE WHALE TRAIL

Only moderately difficult, the five-day, four-night, self-guided **Whale Trail** (☎021 483 0190, ⓦcapenature.co.za) is one of South Africa's most desirable hikes and follows a spectacularly beautiful 55km route from the Potberg Mountains along the deserted coast to Koppie Alleen. To walk in whale season, however, you'll need to book a year in advance and take any date offered. Bookings are for a minimum of six and maximum of twelve people (with no children under 8), and you pay for six even if there are just two of you. Prices are about R2100 per person and include porterage of your supplies, clothes and bedding to each night's accommodation – comfortable cottages, each in splendid isolation. For the duration of the trail you see only your own group, and no other people or signs of habitation at all.

grand old oaks and tucked away at the edge of the Riviersonderend (meaning "river with no end") Mountains, it is a great place to unwind, stroll and potter about the handful of galleries, antique shops and cafés, with good accommodation and excellent food on offer. It also boasts some lovely walks, most notably the superb **Boesmanskloof Traverse** trail, which crosses the mountains to a point 14km from McGregor, as well as several shorter walks in the reserve at the northern end of town, where you can find King Proteas and a rich diversity of Cape flowers and plants.

ARRIVAL AND INFORMATION GREYTON

By car Greyton is 145km from Cape Town. The best route is to take the signposted, sealed road R406 from the N2, just west of Caledon and 105km from Cape Town. Follow the R406 for 30km – ignore any other signs to Greyton on the N2 as they are for unsealed, difficult roads. Allow 2–2hr 30min for the journey.

Tourist office 29 Main St, along the main road as you come into town (Mon–Fri 8am–5pm, Sat & Sun 10am–1pm; ☎028 254 9414, ⓦgreytontourism.com).

ACCOMMODATION

Definitely stay somewhere with a fireplace if you're here in winter, as it can be cold in this mountainous terrain, and conversely look for a pool or shady gardens in summer. Greyton is awash with self-catering cottages, of which the tourism office has lists and pictures.

Anna's Cottages 1 Market St ☎084 764 6012, ⓦgreyton-accommodation.com. A treehouse with an oak tree growing though it, complete with bath, and three lovely self-catering garden cottages, all attractively and eclectically furnished. Mark Cottage is a large space with two double bed alcoves, indoor and outdoor cooking facilities, fairy lights and fireplaces. There is a requirement of a minimum stay of two nights. Cottage R800, treehouse R1400

High Hopes 89 Main Rd ☎028 254 9898, ⓦwww .highhopes.co.za. One of the best B&Bs in town, in a beautiful country-style retreat centre, set in large gardens with a swimming pool. Besides four rooms, there's a self-contained unit with a kitchen, which can be taken on a B&B or self-catering basis. They have a variety of therapies, including massage, on offer. There are substantial midweek discounts. R1800

EATING

The town has a short, unmissable Saturday **market** at the corner of Main Road and Cross Market Street, opposite the church (10am–noon), to which locals bring their produce: organic vegetables, fabulous and well-priced cheeses, decadent cakes, breads, biscuits and preserves.

CALEDON SPA

The thermal springs at **Caledon Spa** (Tues–Sun 10am–7pm; R150; ☎028 214 5100, ⓦtsogosun .com/caledon_spa) make a fun day-trip out of Cape Town (111km away), or a restorative stop off the N2. The natural, hot, brown water that flows through the spa offers a wonderfully relaxing and rejuvenating experience, with a number of pools to loll in, including a number of waterfall pools that offer lovely views over the surrounding farmlands. A sauna and steam room are included in the price, but you'll need to bring your own towels. It can be a bit crowded over weekends, when it gets a bit grubby, but at other times you will often have the pools to yourself.

Abbey Rose Main Rd ☎ 028 254 9470. A nice garden and streetside setting, with the delightful rose garden that the name suggests, and hearty but uncomplicated food; try the oxtail stew (R150) and the malva pudding (R40). Wed 6–10pm, Thurs–Sat 11.30am–3pm & 6–10pm, Sun 11.30am–3pm.

Oak and Vigne Café DS Botha St ☎ 028 254 9037. An extremely popular restaurant situated in an old cottage with an oak-shaded terrace. Fresh bread and croissants are baked daily, plus cooked breakfasts (R50) and good cocktails, such as the Greyton Mule (vodka, ginger beer and lime; R40), though service can be slow. Daily 8am–5pm.

★**Peccadillo's** 23 Main Rd ☎ 028 254 9066. With the reputation for the best fine dining in town, *Peccadillo's* serves up food with a strong Mediterranean influence; try the local trout dishes, pork belly or wood-fired pizza (R100). A good place to try boutique wines. Book ahead. Mon & Thurs–Sun noon–3pm & 6–10pm.

Genadendal

GENADENDAL, 6km from Greyton, was founded in 1737 by Moravians. The village's focus is around **Church Square**, dominated by a very Germanic church building constructed in 1891. The old bell outside dates back to the eighteenth century, when it became the centre of a row between the local farmers and the mission station. The argument broke out when missionary Georg Schmidt annoyed the local white farmers by forming a small Christian congregation with impoverished Khoi and giving refuge to maltreated labourers from local farms. The farmers were enraged that while they, white Christians, were illiterate, Schmidt was teaching native people, whom they considered uncivilized, to read and write. The Dutch Reformed Church, under the control of the Dutch East India Company, waded in when Schmidt began baptizing converts, and prohibited the mission from ringing the bell, which called the faithful to prayer.

In 1838 Genadendal established the first teacher training college in the country, which the government closed in 1926, on the grounds that coloured people didn't need tertiary education and should be employed as workers on local farms – a policy that effectively ground the community into poverty. In 1995, in recognition of the mission's role in offering education, Nelson Mandela renamed his official residence in Cape Town "Genadendal".

Today, the population of this principally coloured town numbers around four thousand people, adhering to a variety of Christian sects – no longer just Moravianism. The **Mission Museum** adjacent to Church Square (Mon–Thurs 9am–1pm & 2–5pm, Fri 9am–3.30pm, Sat 9am–noon; free) is moderately interesting, as is a wander through the town, down to the rural graveyard, which is spiked with old tombstones.

Swellendam and around

SWELLENDAM is an attractive historic town at the foot of the Langeberg, 97km east of Caledon. With one of South Africa's best country museums, it's a congenial stop along the N2 between Cape Town and the Garden Route. With its good accommodation and its position – poised between the coastal De Hoop Nature Reserve and the Langeberg – it's a suitable base for spending a day or two exploring this part of the Overberg, with the **Bontebok National Park**, the stomping ground of an attractive type of antelope, to the south.

South Africa's third-oldest white settlement, Swellendam was established in 1745 by **Baron Gustav van Imhoff**, a visiting Dutch East India Company bigwig. He was deeply concerned about the "moral degeneration" of burghers who were trekking further from Cape Town and out of Company control. Of no less concern to the baron was the loss of revenue from these "vagabonds", who were neglecting to pay the company for the right to hold land and were fiddling their annual tax returns. Following a brief hiccup in 1795, when burghers declared a "free republic" (quickly extinguished when Britain occupied the Cape), the town grew into a prosperous rural centre known for its wagon-making, and for being the last "civilized" port of call for trekboers heading out into the interior. The income generated from this helped build Swellendam's gracious homes, many of which were destroyed in the fire of 1865.

The town is built along a very long main road with no traffic lights; it's most attractive at either end, with a mundane shopping area in the middle. The eastern end

HORSERIDING

Good horseriding is possible in the mountains and forests at the eastern edge of town in the Marloth Nature Reserve. **Two Feathers Horse Trails** (☎082 494 8279, ⊛ swellendambackpackers .co.za) offers short trips for all levels (R400), and two hours for experienced riders only (R600).

is dominated by the museum complex and tourist information, and is nearest to the mountain reserve for hiking or horseriding.

Oefeningshuis

36 Voortrek St

The only building in the centre to survive the town's 1865 fire is the Cape Dutch-style **Oefeningshuis**, which now houses the tourist office. Built in 1838, it was first used as a place for religious activity, then as a school for freed slaves, and has surreal-looking clocks with frozen hands carved into either gable end.

Dutch Reformed Church

11 Voortrek St

The unmissable **Dutch Reformed Church**, dating from 1910, incorporates Gothic windows, a Baroque spire, Renaissance portico elements and Cape Dutch gables into a wedding cake of a building that agreeably holds its own, against the odds, and certainly still draws a good crowd on Sundays.

Drostdy Museum

18 Swellengrebel St • Mon–Fri 9am–4.45pm, Sat & Sun 10am–2.45pm • R25

On the east side of town, a short way from the centre, is the excellent **Drostdy Museum**. It's a collection of historic buildings arranged around large grounds, with a lovely nineteenth-century Cape garden. The centrepiece is the *drostdy* itself, built in 1747 as the seat of the *landdrost*, a magistrate-cum-commissioner sent out by the Dutch East India Company to control the outer reaches of its territory. The building conforms to the beautiful limewashed, thatched and shuttered Cape Dutch style of the eighteenth century, but the furnishings are of nineteenth-century vintage. From the rear garden of the *drostdy* you can stroll along a path and across Drostdy Street to **Mayville**, a middle-class Victorian homestead from the mid-nineteenth century with an old rose garden.

16

ARRIVAL AND INFORMATION

SWELLENDAM AND AROUND

By car Swellendam is 220km from Cape Town, on the N2, about 3hr drive, and 533km from Port Elizabeth, another 7hr drive up the Garden Route.

By bus Coaches, including the Baz Bus, run between Cape Town and Port Elizabeth via Swellendam, dropping off at

the *Swellengrebel Hotel*, in the centre of town.

Tourist office 22 Swellengrebel St, in one of the Drostdy Museum buildings (Mon–Fri 9am–5pm, Sat & Sun 9am–2pm; ☎028 514 2770, ⊛ capetraderoute.co.za).

ACCOMMODATION

Anyone who enjoys the atmosphere of historic houses will be spoilt for choice in Swellendam, where places to stay in Cape Dutch and Georgian houses are ten a penny, and rates tend to be pretty reasonable.

★**Augusta de Mist** 3 Human St ☎028 514 2425, ⊛ augustademist.com. A two-hundred-year-old home-stead with beautifully renovated cottages and garden suites. Most of the accommodation comes with fireplaces and all have percale linen, and are altogether luxurious and stylish. A rambling terraced garden and a pool complete the picture. There is a great restaurant on site, but you need to book their dinner in advance. R2000

★**Cypress Cottage** 3 Voortrek St ☎028 514 3296, ⊛ cypress-cottage.co.za. The seven charming rooms here are great value, decorated with antiques in the back garden of a grand house. The house is one of the oldest in town and the friendly owner is a brilliant gardener. R900

Eenuurkop Huisie 8km from town on the Ashton Rd ☎028 514 1447, ⊛ eenuurkop.co.za. Two self-catering cottages, one with three bedrooms, the other with one, in a stunning setting with great views and access to mountain walks, with a dam on the farm to swim in. **R800**

Hermitage Huisies 3km from town on R60 to Ashton ☎028 514 2308 or ☎082 380 2080, ⓦwildebraam .co.za. These four restored labourers' self-catering cottages are on a berry farm, with a duck pond and grazing sheep and horses. They sleep two to five people, and are ideal for families. There's also a swimming pool with mountain views. On the farm next door, Wildebraam, there is berry picking in November and December, jams to taste and a liquor-tasting cellar all year round. **R800**

Swellendam Backpackers 5 Lichtenstein St ☎028 5142648 or ☎0824948279, ⓦswellendambackpackers .co.za. Swellendam's only hostel is well situated near the

Marloth Nature Reserve, and close to the Drostdy Museum, with a large campsite, and decent twins and doubles. No dorms, so if you are on your own, you can have the pleasure of a room to yourself. Friendly staff can arrange activities including horseriding and hiking permits for Marloth. Children are welcome and anyone wanting to get out into nature. Camping **R130**, doubles **R550**

Swellendam Country Lodge 237 Voortrek St ☎028 514 3629, ⓦswellendamlodge.com. Six garden rooms with separate entrances, reed ceilings and elegant, uncluttered decor in muted hues. There's a veranda, which is perfect for summer days, as well as a swimming pool and well-kept garden. **R1300**

EATING

De Companjie 5 Voortrek St ☎083 399 0299. Set in a most pleasing historic building that also functions as a lovely guesthouse. It offers good teatime eats and hearty dinners. They are best known for steaks (R160) and venison dishes. Mon, Tues, Thurs & Sun 4–10pm.

La Belle Alliance 1 Swellengrebel St ☎028 514 2924. Conveniently located just off the N2, near the Drostdy Museum, with a very restful garden setting and outdoor seating next to the river. It is ideal if you are simply passing through Swellendam and want uncomplicated, but tasty food, such as a Ploughman's Platter (R85), or fish with a salad (R110). Daily 8am–5pm.

La Sosta 145 Voortrek St ☎028 514 1470. One of the top restaurants in the Western Cape, this rather elegant establishment needs advance booking. They serve contemporary Italian food and there are three set menus:

one catering for fish eaters (R450), the second for carnivores and the third, appropriately named Garden, for vegetarians (R350). Tues–Sat 6.30–10pm.

The Old Gaol Coffee Shop Church Square, 8A Voortrek St ☎028 514 3847. A good place where you can get milk tart in a copper pan and *roosterkoek*, traditional bread made on an open fire, with nice fillings (R70). A great choice for kids, with an outdoor play area, though it is favoured by tour buses. Mon, Tues, Sat & Sun 8.30am–5pm, Wed–Fri 7.30am–10pm.

Woodpecker Deli 270 Voortrek St ☎028 514 2924. Casual and reasonably priced restaurant serving pizza, pasta, soups and burgers. A good choice if you are in town for one night and just want something simple. Mon–Sat 11.30am–9pm, Sun 11.30am–5pm.

Bontebok National Park

6km south of Swellendam • Daily: May–Sept 7am–7pm; Oct–June 7am–6pm • R100 • ☎028 514 2735

Set along the Breede River, **Bontebok National Park** is a compact, 28-square-kilometre reserve at the foot of the Langeberg range that makes a relaxing overnight stop between Cape Town and the Garden Route. The park was established in 1931 to save the Cape's dwindling population of bontebok, an attractive antelope with distinctive brown and white markings. By 1930, hunting had reduced the number of bontebok in the Cape to a mere thirty. Their survival has been secured and there are now three hundred of them in the park, as well as populations in other reserves in the province. There are no big cats in the park, but **mammals** you might encounter include rare Cape mountain zebra, red hartebeest and grey rhebok, and there are more than 120 **bird species**. It's also a rich environment for **fynbos**, with nearly five hundred species here, including erica, gladioli and proteas. Apart from wildlife viewing, you can swim in the Breede River, hike a couple of short nature trails and fish.

ACCOMMODATION   BONTEBOK NATIONAL PARK

★**Bontebok National Park** ☎028 514 2735, ⓦsanparks.org. Self-catering accommodation is available in ten, fully equipped chalets; the best have river views. There is also a campsite with very clean washing facilities

– the sites without their own electricity supply are cheaper. Stock up on supplies in Swellendam beforehand. Camping **R245**, chalet **R1100**

PLETTENBERG BAY

The Garden Route

The Garden Route, a slender stretch of coastal plain on the N2 between Mossel Bay and Storms River Mouth, has a legendary status as South Africa's paradise – reflected in local names such as Garden of Eden and Wilderness. This soft, green, forested swath, that stretches nearly 200km, is cut by rivers that tumble down from the mountains to the north, to its southern rocky shores and sandy beaches. The Khoikhoi herders who lived off its natural bounty considered the area a paradise too, calling it Outeniqua ("the man laden with honey"). Their Eden was quickly destroyed in the eighteenth century with the arrival of Dutch woodcutters, who had exhausted the forests around Cape Town and set about doing the same in Outeniqua, killing or dispersing the Khoikhoi and San in the process.

17

Birds and animals suffered too from the encroachment of Europeans. In the 1850s, the Swedish naturalist Johan Victorin shot and feasted on the species he had come to study, some of which, including the endangered narina trogon, he noted were both "beautiful and good to eat".

Despite the dense appearance of the area, what you see today are only the remnants of one of Africa's great **forests**; most of the indigenous hardwoods have been replaced by exotic pine plantations, and the only milk and honey you'll find now is in the many shops servicing the Garden Route coastal resorts. **Conservation** has halted the wholesale destruction of the indigenous woodlands, but a huge growth in tourism and the influx of urbanites seeking a quiet life in the relatively crime-free Garden Route towns threaten to rob the area of its remaining tranquillity.

The Garden Route coast is dominated by three inlets – Mossel Bay, the Knysna lagoon and Plettenberg Bay – each with its own town. Oldest of these and closest to Cape Town is **Mossel Bay**, an industrial centre of limited charm, which marks the official start of the Garden Route. **Knysna**, though younger, exudes a well-rooted urban character and is the nicest of the coastal towns, with one major drawback – unlike **Plettenberg Bay**, its eastern neighbour, it has no beach of its own. A major draw, though, is the **Knysna forest** covering some of the hilly country around Knysna.

Between the coastal towns are some ugly modern holiday developments, but also some wonderful empty beaches and tiny coves, such as **Victoria Bay** and **Nature's Valley**. Best of all is the **Tsitsikamma National Park**, which has it all – indigenous forest, dramatic coastline, the pumping **Storms River Mouth** and South Africa's most popular hike, the **Otter Trail**.

There are no serious Big Five game reserves in the Western Cape and certainly none that can offer anything like you'll get on a safari in the Kruger or a stay in one of the reserves near Port Elizabeth. Of the **game experiences** offered along the Garden Route, **Botlierskop**, inland from Mossel Bay and within half a day's drive from Cape Town, consistently gets rated as one of the best.

Most visitors take the Garden Route as a journey between Cape Town and **Port Elizabeth** (see p.248), dallying for little more than a day or two for shopping, sightseeing or a taste of one of the many outdoor activities on offer. The rapid passage cut by the excellent N2 makes it all too easy to have a fast scenic drive – and end up disappointed because you don't see that much from the road. To make the journey worthwhile, you'll need to slow down, take some detours off the highway and explore a little. Each town offers a plethora of adventure-based activities, including whale- and dolphin-spotting from land or boat and the more sedate pleasures of first-class restaurants, ultra-luxurious guesthouses and forest and beach walks.

GETTING AROUND   THE GARDEN ROUTE

The Garden Route is probably the best-served stretch of South Africa for **transport**. If time is tight, you may want to go by **plane** to George at the west end of the Garden Route, which is served by scheduled flights from Cape Town and Port Elizabeth, or a flight from either Johannesburg or Cape Town directly to Plettenberg Bay's tiny airport on Cemair (see p.28). Visiting Port Elizabeth from Cape Town, consider taking the magnificent interior **Route 62** to avoid having to drive the N2 in both directions.

By Baz Bus The most user-friendly among the public transport options is the Baz Bus (see p.27) service between Cape Town and Port Elizabeth (☎ 0861 229 287, ⓦ www .bazbus.com), which picks up passengers daily except Wednesday and Sunday in Cape Town (7.15–8.30am) and Port Elizabeth (6.45–7.30am). It provides a door-to-door service within the central districts of all the towns along the way, and has the advantage over the large intercity lines that it will happily carry outdoor gear, such as surfboards or mountain bikes. Although the buses take standby passengers if there's space available, you should book ahead to secure a seat.

By intercity bus Intercape, Greyhound and Translux intercity buses (see p.27) from Cape Town and Port Elizabeth are more direct than the Baz Bus, stopping only at Mossel Bay, George, Wilderness, Sedgefield, Knysna and Storms River (the village, but not the Mouth and National Park, which is some distance away). These buses often don't go into town, letting passengers off at petrol stations on the highway instead.

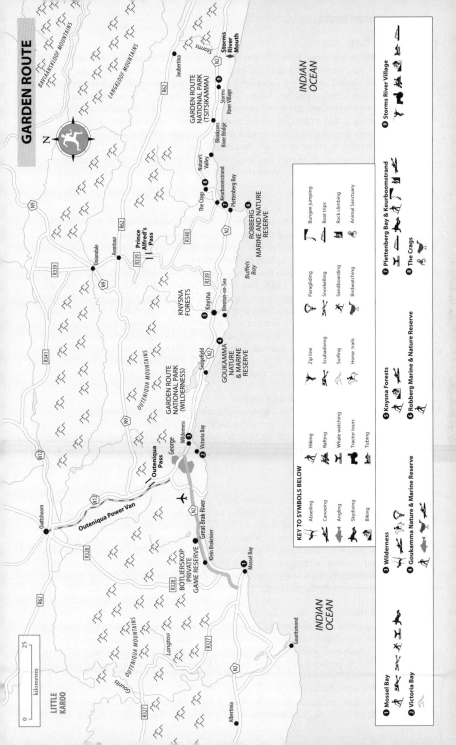

17 ## Mossel Bay

MOSSEL BAY, a mid-sized town 397km east of Cape Town, gets a bad press from most South Africans, mainly because of the huge industrial facade it presents to the N2. Don't panic – the historic centre is a thoroughly pleasant contrast, set on a hill overlooking the small working harbour and bay. Mossel Bay also has one of the best **swimming** beaches along the southern Cape coast and an interesting museum. Like other Garden Route destinations it is also a springboard for numerous adventure activities (see p.199). The town takes on a strong Afrikaans flavour over Christmas, when Karoo farmers and their families descend in droves to occupy its caravan parks and chalets.

If the urban nature of Mossel Bay holds no appeal, you are best heading off inland in the direction of Oudtshoorn, along the R328 Robinson Pass Road, where there are some great places to stay.

Brief history

Mossel Bay bears poignant historical significance as the place where indigenous Khoi cattle herders first encountered the Europeans in a bloody spat that symbolically set the tone for five hundred years of race relations on the subcontinent. A group of Portuguese mariners under Captain **Bartholomeu Dias** set sail from Portugal in August 1487 in search of a sea route to the riches of India, and months later rounded the Cape of Good Hope. In February 1488, they became the first Europeans to make landfall along the South African coast, when they pulled in for water to the safety of an inlet they called Aguado de So Bras ("watering place of St Blaize"), now Mossel Bay. The Khoikhoi were organized into distinct groups, each under its own chief and each with territorial rights over pastures and water sources. The Portuguese, who were flouting local customs, saw it as "bad manners" when the Khoikhoi tried to drive them off the spring. In a mutual babble of incomprehension the Khoi began stoning the Portuguese, who retaliated with crossbow fire that left one of the herders dead.

Bartholomeu Dias Museum Complex

Mon–Fri 9am–4.45pm, Sat & Sun 9am–3.45pm • R20; entry onto Dias caravel additional R20 • ⓦ diasmuseum.co.za

Mossel Bay's main urban attraction is the **Bartholomeu Dias Museum Complex**. Housed in a collection of historic buildings, which are well integrated into the small town centre, the museums are all near the tourist office and within a couple of minutes' walk of each other.

The Maritime Museum

The highlight of the Bartholomeu Dias Museum Complex is the **Maritime Museum**, a spiral gallery with displays on the history of European, principally Portuguese, seafaring, arranged around a full-size replica of Dias' original caravel. The ship was built in Portugal and sailed from Lisbon to Mossel Bay in 1987 to celebrate the five hundredth anniversary of Dias' historic journey. You can't fail to be awed by the idea of the original mariners setting out on the high seas into terra incognita on such a small vessel – particularly as the crew were accommodated above deck with only a sailcloth for protection against the elements.

Post Office Tree

Sixteenth-century mariners used to leave messages for passing ships in an old boot under a milkwood tree somewhere around the designated **Post Office Tree**, just outside the Maritime Museum; the plaque claims that "this may well" be the same tree. You can post mail here in a large, boot-shaped letterbox and have it stamped with a special postmark.

Shell Museum and Aquarium

Of the remaining exhibitions, the **Shell Museum and Aquarium**, next to the Post Office Tree, is the only one worth taking the time to visit. This is your chance to see some of the beautiful shells found off the South African coast, as well as shells from around the world. Exhibits include a history of the use of shells by humans and a fascinating display of living shellfish including cowries with their inhabitants still at home.

Santos Beach
A short walk north down the hill from the Maritime Museum gets you to **Santos Beach**, the main town strand, and purportedly the only north-facing beach in South Africa – which gives it exceptionally long sunny afternoons. Adjacent to the small town harbour, the beach provides some of the finest swimming along the Garden Route, with uncharacteristically gentle surf, small waves and a depth perfect for practising your crawl.

The Point
East of the harbour, the coast bulges south towards the **Point**. Here there are several places to eat and a popular restaurant bar (see p.200) with a deck at the ocean's edge, from which you may see dolphins cruising past along a surreal five-hundred-metre rocky channel known as the aquarium, which is used as a natural **tidal pool**.

St Blaize Lighthouse and Cape St Blaize Cave
A couple of hundred metres to the south of the harbour, atop some cliffs, the **St Blaize Lighthouse**, built in 1864, is still in use as a beacon to ships. Below it, the **Cape St Blaize Cave** is both a marvellous lookout point and a significant archeological site. A boardwalk leads through the cave past three information panels describing the history of the interpretation of the cave as well as the modern understanding of it. In 1801 Sir John Barrow insisted that **shells** found at the site had been brought by seagulls, while others argued that they were relics of human habitation. It turned out that Barrow's opponents were right, but it wasn't till 1888 that excavations uncovered **stone tools** and showed that people had been using the cave for something close on 100,000 years. The path leading up to the cave continues onto the Cape St Blaize trail (see p.200).

ARRIVAL AND DEPARTURE
MOSSEL BAY

By Baz Bus Only the daily Baz Bus comes right into town, dropping passengers off at *Mossel Bay Backpackers* and *Park House Lodge*.

By intercity bus Greyhound, Intercape, SA Roadlink and Translux buses stop at Shell Voorbaai Service Station on the N2, 7km from the centre, at the junction of the national highway and the road into town. Voorbaai Truckport offers a centralized bus booking service ☎ 044 695 1172.

Destinations Cape Town (3 daily; 6hr); George (1–2 daily; 45min); Knysna (1–2 daily; 2hr); Oudtshoorn (1–2 daily; 1hr 15min); Plettenberg Bay (1–2 daily; 2hr 30min); Port Elizabeth (1–2 daily; 6hr 30min).

By taxi The town itself is small enough to negotiate on foot, but should you need transport, call 24/7 Taxi on ☎ 082 932 5809.

INFORMATION

Tourist information Bang in the town centre, the tourist information office on the corner of Church and Market sts (Mon–Fri 8am–6pm, Sat & Sun 9am–4pm; ☎ 044 691 2202, ⍾ visitmosselbay.co.za) has brochures about Mossel Bay and the rest of the Garden Route, and a map of the town. Their website has comprehensive listings of Mossel Bay's main attractions, businesses, accommodation and restaurants.

ACTIVITIES

Mossel Bay is a springboard for popular **activities**, including skydiving, sandboarding and deep-sea fishing, all of which can be booked through the Garden Route Adventure Centre at *Mossel Bay Backpackers* (☎ 044 691 3182, ⍾ gardenrouteadventures.co.za). It is worth noting that although fishing is available at Mossel Bay, you should question operators about what catch they target. Some operators are known to recreationally catch threatened or endangered species that are on the Red or Orange list of WWF SASSI (World Wildlife Fund, Sustainable Seafood Initiative; ⍾ wwfsassi.co.za).

17

DIVING AND SNORKELLING

These aren't tropical seas, so don't expect clear warm waters, but with visibility usually between 4m and 10m you stand a good chance of seeing octopus, squid, sea stars, soft corals, pyjama sharks and butterfly fish. There are several rewarding diving and snorkelling spots around Mossel Bay.

Electro Dive ☎ 082 561 1259, ⊛ electrodive.co.za. This outfit rents out gear and provides shore- and boat-based dives to local reefs and wrecks (R240/400 including kit), certification courses (R5000) and guided snorkelling trips (R300).

HIKING

On the mainland you can check out the coast on the St Blaize hiking trail, an easy 15km walk (roughly 4hr each way; a map is available from the tourist office) along the southern shore of Mossel Bay. The route starts from the Cape St Blaize Cave, just below the lighthouse at the Point, and heads west as far as Dana Bay, taking in magnificent coastal views of cliffs, rocks, bays and coves.

SANDBOARDING

Billeon Surf Meeting Point Engen One-Stop Garage ☎ 082 97 11 405, ⊛ dragondune.com. Mossel Bay is one of the best places in the country for sandboarding: the dunes are big and the operation well run. Billeon Surf runs trips to the so-called "Dragon Dune", which they claim, at 320m, is the longest runnable stretch of sand in the country. The activity is suitable for all levels, from beginner to extreme. It is extremely popular so book in advance (R400/person for a 2hr trip). From their meeting point, you are taken by 4x4 to the dunes, and a shuttle service is offered from the hostels.

SKYDIVING

Skydive Mossel Bay Mossel Bay Airfield ☎ 044 695 1771, ⊛ skydivemosselbay.com. For the ultimate adrenaline junkies, the Garden Route has some of the country's best sky diving. Skydive Mossel Bay offers tandem sky-dives (3000m for R3000) and skydiving courses.

WHALE-WATCHING AND SEAL ISLAND CRUISES

The Romonza ☎ 044 690 3101, ⊛ mosselbay.co.za. Cruises around Seal Island (hourly 10am–3pm, adults R160), about 10km northwest of Santos Beach, to see the African penguin and seal colonies, can be taken on the *Romonza*, a medium-sized yacht that launches from the yacht marina in the harbour. The *Romonza* is also the only registered vessel allowed to run boat-based whale-watching cruises (adults R700; 2–3hr) in Mossel Bay. As elsewhere along this coast, the whale season is variable with southern rights appearing from June till late October. If you're extremely lucky, you may also see a humpback whale.

ACCOMMODATION

Edward Charles Manor Hotel 1 Sixth Ave ☎ 044 691 2152, ⊛ edwardcharles.co.za. An upmarket two-storey guesthouse in a central location overlooking Santos Beach. There are fifteen en-suite rooms, a swimming pool and a courtesy shuttle to take you to town if you don't have your own car. **R1150**

Mossel Bay Backpackers 1 Marsh St ☎ 044 691 3182, ⊛ mosselbaybackpackers.co.za. Well-run lodge with squeaky clean rooms, only 300m from the sea, accommodating 65 people. They also do adventure activity bookings, and there's a swimming pool, garden and football table. Dorms **R150**, doubles **R550**

Park House Lodge 121 High St ☎ 044 691 1937, ⊛ parkhouse.co.za. Top-notch budget accommodation in twenty rooms distributed across three buildings, one of which is a beautiful nineteenth-century sandstone manor house. There is a communal kitchen and place to braai. Some rooms have private entrances leading onto the garden and doubles with a shared bathroom are very affordable – en-suite rooms cost a bit more (R780). Dorms **R170**, doubles **R600**

Protea Hotel Mossel Bay Bartholomeu Dias Museum Complex, Market St ☎ 044 691 3738, ⊛ proteahotels .com/mosselbay. Opposite the tourist office, in an old Cape Dutch manor house, this quaint place in the town centre overlooks Santos Bay and the harbour. Breakfast is served at *Café Gannet*, Mossel Bay's nicest restaurant (see below). **R2016**

EATING AND DRINKING

You don't come to Mossel Bay for the food, but there are a number of reasonable places to eat, some of them with superb sea views. The small Point Village shopping development at the north end has a couple of inexpensive to mid-priced family restaurants, opening daily from the morning until 11pm-ish.

Café Gannet Market St ☎ 044 691 1885, ⊛ oldposttree .co.za. Close to the Bartholomeu Dias Museum Complex, Mossel Bay's smartest restaurant serves local fish, sushi and delicacies like wild Mossel Bay oysters (R25 per oyster) at moderate prices. The stylish garden has glimpses across the harbour, and is a good spot for sundowners. Daily 7.30am–10pm.

Delfino's Espresso Bar and Pizzeria Point Village

☎ 044 690 5247. A good place to get pasta (R70), pizza and steak, as well as decent coffee all at reasonable prices. There are great views of the sea. Daily 7am–11pm.

★**Kaai 4** Mossel Bay Harbour ☎ 044 691 0056, ⓦ kaai4.co.za. Relaxed, rustic, open-air beach restaurant, with sprawling picnic tables in a stunning location on the beach, where you can watch your seafood braai on an open fire (R90). Although the menu is small, the servings are large and good value for money. Daily 10am–10pm (closed when raining).

King Fisher Point Village ☎ 044 690 6390, ⓦ thekingfisher.co.za. A relaxed joint that, as its name suggests, specializes in seafood, from humble fish and chips (R60) to local line-fish. It also has a kids' menu. Its elevated position above *Delfino's* means it has excellent views. Daily 11.30am–11pm.

Mossel Bay to Oudtshoorn

Heading inland towards Oudtshoorn (see p.238) from Mossel Bay on the R328 takes you over the forested coastal mountains of **Robinson Pass** into the desiccated Little Karoo. The draw of this road is some great scenery and accommodation, and an alternative, prettier route to Oudtshoorn than travelling via George. Day-visitors are welcome at **Botlierskop Private Game Reserve** (see below), with activities including game drives (R450; 3hr) and horserides (R310; 1hr) that can be booked in advance.

ACCOMMODATION   MOSSEL BAY TO OUDTSHOORN

Botlierskop Private Game Reserve 22km from Mossel Bay ☎ 044 696 6055, ⓦ botlierskop.co.za. While there is nothing wild about it, the tented accommodation here works hard to provide a safari atmosphere, with decks and outdoor seating to admire the lovely views. You will usually (although not always) see lions in their huge enclosure, and there's a good chance of spotting rhinos, elephants, giraffes and antelope too. Their packages are professionally put together and include a number of activities for both day- and overnight-visitors. Cost per person for half-board, including a game drive R3100

Eight Bells Mountain Inn 35km from Mossel Bay ☎ 044 631 0000, ⓦ eightbells.co.za. A firm favourite with well-heeled families wanting a fully catered hotel-style holiday, with all sorts of activities laid on for children, including horseriding, swimming, tennis and walking. There are even special meal times for younger kids. The atmosphere is friendly and it's superbly run. Out of school holidays it remains a restful stop-off with lovely gardens and extensive grounds, close to the top of the mountainous pass. R1500

★**Outeniqua Moon Percheron Stud and Guest Farm** 23km from Mossel Bay, just below the Robinson Pass ☎ 044 631 0093 or ☎ 082 564 9782, ⓦ outeniquamoon.co.za. Comfortable and classy self-catering or B&B accommodation in four, colonial farm-style cottages on a working farm with beautiful views of the Outeniqua mountains. The huge, serene draft horses are given a sanctuary on the farm and you can spend time with them, petting foals or taking a carriage ride. You can swim laps in the 25m ozone pool or explore the large forest on the farm. If you choose not to self-cater, prepare to be spoilt with home-made bread and other farm delights. Prices are reasonable, and drop further outside of school holidays. Two-bed self-catering cottage R1500, half-board cottage R1980

George

There's little reason at all to visit **GEORGE**, a large inland town 66km northeast of Mossel Bay, unless you need what a big centre offers – airport, car rental, hospital and shops. Sadly, all that's left of the forests and quaint character that moved Anthony Trollope, during a visit in 1877, to describe it as the "prettiest village on the face of the earth" are some historic buildings.

If you're pushed for time, however, George is conveniently right in the middle of the Garden Route, halfway between Cape Town and Port Elizabeth, and there are regular flights here from both Cape Town and Johannesburg. By road, the town is a 5km detour northwest off the N2 and 9km from the nearest stretch of ocean at Victoria Bay.

Dutch Reformed Church
Davidson St

The most notable of George's historic buildings is the beautiful **Dutch Reformed Church**, at the top end of Meade Street. Completed in the early 1840s, the church is

17

PRESIDENT BOTHA AND APARTHEID'S LAST STAND

Pieter Willem Botha believed that by setting up a powerful "Imperial Presidency" in South Africa he could withstand the inevitable tide of democracy. A National Party hack from the age of 20, Botha worked his way up through the ranks, getting elected as an MP in 1948 when the first apartheid government took power. He was promoted through various cabinet posts until he became **Minister of Defence**, a position he used to launch a palace coup in 1978 against his colleague, Prime Minister John Vorster. Botha immediately set about modernizing apartheid, modifying his own role from that of a British-style prime minister, answerable to parliament, to one of an executive president taking vital decisions in the secrecy of a President's Council heavily weighted with army top brass.

Informed by the army that the battle to preserve the apartheid status quo was unwinnable purely by force, Botha embarked on his **Total Strategy**, which involved reforms to peripheral aspects of apartheid and the fostering of a black middle class as a buffer against the ANC, while pumping vast sums of money into building an enormous military machine that crossed South Africa's borders to bully or crush neighbouring countries harbouring groups opposed to apartheid. South African refugees in Botswana and Zimbabwe were bombed, Angola was invaded, and arms were run to anti-government rebels in Mozambique, reducing it to ruins – a policy that has returned to haunt South Africa with those same weapons now returning across the border and finding their way into the hands of criminals. Inside South Africa, security forces enjoyed a free hand to murder, maim and torture **opponents of apartheid**.

Botha blustered and wagged his finger at the opposition through the late 1980s, while his bloated military sucked the state coffers dry as it prosecuted its dirty wars. Even National Party stalwarts realized that his policies were leading to ruin, and in 1989, when he suffered a stroke, the party was quick to replace him with **F.W. de Klerk**, who immediately proceeded to announce reforms.

Botha lived out his unrepentant retirement near George, declining ever to apologize for any of the brutal actions taken under his presidency to bolster apartheid. Curiously, when he died in 2006, he was given an uncritical, high-profile state funeral, broadcast on national television and attended by members of the government, including then-president, Thabo Mbeki.

---

definitely worth a stop if you happen to be passing through, with its elegantly simple classical facade, Greek-cross plan with an impressive, centrally placed pulpit and wonderful domed ceiling, panelled with glowing yellowwood.

St Mark's Cathedral
Cathedral St • ⓦ stmarkscathedral.co.za

St Mark's Cathedral, consecrated in 1850, is worth seeing, but unlike the Dutch Reformed Church, which is open to the public, it can only be visited by appointment. Ask at the tourist office for bookings (see below). It also holds regular worship services.

ARRIVAL AND INFORMATION   GEORGE

By plane Kulula and SAA fly between Johannesburg and the small George airport, 10km west of town on the N2 (6 daily; 1hr 50min). SAA also flies here from Cape Town (2 daily; 50min). Most tourists flying in rent a car from one of the companies at the airport and set off down the Garden Route.

By Baz Bus The Baz Bus drops off at *Outeniqua Backpackers* on Merriman St on its daily run between Cape Town and Port Elizabeth.

By intercity buses Intercape, Translux and Greyhound intercity buses pull in at George station, adjacent to the railway museum, and at the Sasol garage station on the N2 east of town.

Destinations Cape Town (2 daily; 7hr); Joburg (daily; 16hr); Knysna (2 daily; 1hr 30min); Mossel Bay (6–7 daily; 45min); Oudtshoorn (daily; 1hr 10min); Plettenberg Bay (2 daily; 2hr); Port Elizabeth (2 daily; 5hr 30min).

Tourist information The George tourist office at 124 York St (Mon–Fri 7.45am–4.30pm, Sat 9am–1pm; ☏ 044 801 9295, ⓦ georgetourism.org.za) can provide town maps and help with accommodation bookings.

THE OUTENIQUA POWER VAN

Sadly South Africa's main-line railways are slowly dying. The Garden Route's train line once penetrated some of the region's most visually stunning back country making the Cape Town-to-Port Elizabeth run one of the great railway journeys of the world. That ended when some of the tracks were washed away and never replaced.

Fortunately, you can still get a taster of the line on the **Outeniqua Power Van**, a single cab diesel-powered train that trails into the Outeniqua Mountains just outside George. The train stops at a scenic site for a picnic before returning to the town. En route you pass through forest, negotiate passes and tunnels, and can see waterfalls and *fynbos*.

BOOKING

The train departs from the Outeniqua Transport Museum, 2 Mission Rd, George (Mon–Sat on demand, booking essential ☎ 082 490 5627; R140; 2.5hr). Bring your own picnic, sunglasses, a hat and a warm jacket.

ACCOMMODATION

10 Caledon Street 10 Caledon St ☎ 044 873 4983. The pick of the mid-priced B&Bs, this spotless guesthouse is on a quiet street, within an easy walk to the city centre. There's a garden and the rooms feature balconies with mountain views. The owners are superb hosts and provide an excellent breakfast. **R1200**

Die Waenhuis 11 Caledon St ☎ 044 874 0034, ⓦ diewaenhuis.co.za. Mid-nineteenth-century home that has retained its period character. There are eleven spacious en-suite rooms, a beautiful garden, and it's run by gracious hosts. English breakfasts are served in a sunlit dining room, which is warmed in the winter by a Dover stove. **R1300**

Mount View Resort & Lifestyle Village York St ☎ 044 874 5205, ⓦ mountviewsa.co.za. Modern complex that lacks some character, but offers great value in its one-,

two- and three-bedroom en-suite chalets and rondavels. The gardens are well-kept and pleasant. The complex also has a gym as well as an indoor and outdoor swimming pool. Rondavels **R580**, chalets **R750**

Oakhurst Hotel Cnr Meade & Cathedral sts ☎ 044 874 7130, ⓦ oakhursthotel.co.za. Charming, centrally located manor house with a country feel. There are green lawns, a peaceful garden with pool, a lovely dining area and views of the Outeniqua Mountains. **R1000**

Outeniqua Backpackers 115 Merriman St ☎ 082 316 7720, ⓦ outeniqualodge.co.za. Friendly hostel in a bright and airy suburban house with comfortable dorms and doubles, some with mountain views. There's a swimming pool, and they provide free airport pick-ups. The Baz Bus also pulls in here. Dorms **R140**, doubles **R500**

EATING AND DRINKING

Fat Fish 124 York St ☎ 044 884 1012. A good choice for a well-priced meal, from meze for one (R85) to rump steaks at varying sizes (R145), in a popular, central and well-run venue. Daily 11.30am–10pm.

La Capannina 122 York St ☎ 044 874 5313. Italian restaurant that in addition to excellent pizzas and pasta, has other tricks up its sleeve such as beef fillet on a bed of polenta and some distinctly un-Italian dishes such as ostrich jambalaya with a hint of curry (R160).

Mon–Sat noon–10pm.

The Old Town House Cnr York and Market sts ☎ 044 874 3663. There's a lovely ambience in this original townhouse, where the food is well-cooked with attention to detail in an intimate setting. Despite the place's carnivorous inclination – they specialize in venison and beef – vegetarians are catered for and their baked pasta is delicious (R65). Mon–Fri noon–3pm & 6–10pm, Sat 6–10pm.

Victoria Bay

Some 9km south of George and 3km off the N2 lies the minuscule hamlet of **VICTORIA BAY**, on the edge of a small sandy beach wedged into a cove between cliffs, with a grassy sunbathing area, safe swimming and a tidal pool. During the December holidays it packs out with day-trippers, and rates as one of the top **surfing** spots along the Garden Route. Because of the cliffs, there's only a single row of buildings along the beachfront, with some of the most dreamily positioned guesthouses along the coast (and therefore some of the priciest for what you get).

17

ARRIVAL AND DEPARTURE   VICTORIA BAY

By car Arriving by car, you'll encounter a metal barrier as you drop down the hill to the bay, and you'll have to try and park in a car park that's frequently full (especially in summer). If you're staying at one of the B&Bs, leave your car at the barrier and collect the key from your lodgings to gain access to the private beach road.

By Baz Bus The daily bus, which provides the only transport to Victoria Bay, drops off at the *Vic Bay Surfari*.

ACCOMMODATION

Land's End Self-Catering The Point, Beach Rd ☎ 044 889 0123, ⓦ vicbay.com. Spectacularly sited right on the shoreline, this place offers a variety of rooms, the price depending on views and facilities. You can bring your own food to cook, or go down to the beachside restaurant. R1600

Sea Breeze Holiday Resort Along the main road into the settlement ☎ 044 889 0098, ⓦ seabreezecabanas .co.za. A variety of budget self-catering units, including two-storey holiday huts and wooden chalets, sleeping two, four or eight people. The huts have no sea views, but it's an easy walk to the beach. R900

VicBay Surfari Lodge Victoria Bay Rd ☎ 044 889 0113, ⓦ vicbaysurfari.co.za. Predominantly a surfers' lodge with home comforts including a DSTV, a self-catering kitchen and BBQ areas. The lodge offers surfboard and wetsuit hire as well as lessons on request for all levels at the local easy, right-hand point break. There's also a trampoline, pool table, table tennis and volleyball. They run shuttles to the beach and George, if you don't have a car. Dorms R200, doubles R650, family room R900

EATING

There are no food shops and just one restaurant at Victoria Bay itself. It's best to bring your own supplies, or drive back to a shopping mall in George. There is a marvellous service, however, offered by Mr Delivery in George (☎ 044 873 6677) which will collect pre-ordered takeaways from George, as well as groceries bought online at Pick n Pay, and even DVDs.

Vikki's @ The Beach ☎ 044 899 0212. Right on the seafront, with tables and umbrellas out in the sun, Victoria Bay's only restaurant serves rather dull, but reasonably priced food including burgers and chips, egg breakfasts, pizzas and fish and chips (R70), in a setting which may make up for the food. It often closes when the weather is poor or when there are no customers. Daily 9am–5pm.

Wilderness

East of Victoria Bay, across the Kaaimans River, the beach at **WILDERNESS** is so close to the N2 that you can pull over for a quick dip with barely an interruption to your journey, though African wilderness is the last thing you'll find here. Wilderness village earned its name, so the story goes, after a young man called Van den Berg bought the property in 1830 for £183 as a blind lot at a Cape Town auction. When he got engaged, his fiancée insisted that their first year of marriage should be spent out of town in the wilderness, so he romantically (or perhaps opportunistically) named his property Wilderness and built a hut on it.

If the hut still exists, you'll struggle to find it among the sprawl of retirement homes, holiday houses and thousands of beds for rent in the vicinity. The beach, which is renowned for its long stretch of sand, is backed by tall dunes, rudely blighted by holiday houses. Once in the water, stay close to the shoreline: this part of the coast is notorious for its unpredictable currents.

ARRIVAL AND INFORMATION   WILDERNESS

By Baz Bus The Baz Bus drops off at *Fairy Knowe Backpackers*, a 20min walk into Wilderness.

Tourist office The tourist office is in Milkwood Village Mall, Beacon Rd, off the N2 opposite the Caltex garage (Mon–Fri 7.45am–4.30pm, Sat 9am–1pm; ☎ 044 877 0045, ⓦ george.org.za).

Services Wilderness's tiny village centre, on the north side of the N2, has a petrol station and a few shops.

ACTIVITIES

Abseiling, kloofing and canoeing Eden Adventures at *Fairy Knowe Hotel* (☎ 044 877 0179 or ☎ 083 628 8547, ⓦ eden.co.za) offers daily kloofing adventures (8am–1pm, R550) and abseiling trips (1.30–4.30pm, R550); a full day taking in both activities costs R1000, which includes lunch. Explore the river yourself by renting a two-seater canoe from them, starting at Fairy Knowe (R300 for 5hr).

Horseriding Black Horse Trails 19km into the mountains, up the Hoekwil Rd ☎ 082 494 5642, ⓦ blackhorsetrails.co.za. Mountain and forest horseriding tours using bitless bridles (R500 for 3hr ride to rock pools, R350 for shorter plantation ride). Probably the best trail riding along the Garden Route.

Paragliding Cloudbase Paragliding Adventures ☎ 082 777 8474, ⓦ cloudbase-paragliding.co.za. To see it all from the air, sign up for a tandem paragliding jump that starts from R750 for a minimum of 15min. You'll only be taken up when the weather offers absolutely safe conditions. They also offer paragliding courses.

ACCOMMODATION

Beach House Backpackers Western Rd ☎ 044 877 0549, ⓦ wildernessbeachhouse.com. Set on the hill, with ocean views from the hammocks on the terrace and bar, *Beach House Backpackers* has very basic dorm rooms and doubles. There is a bar and a communal kitchen. Internet can be sketchy but it is free for 20mins. Surf lessons and board rental are available. Dorms R170, doubles R550

Fairy Knowe Backpackers 6km from the village, follow signs from the N2 east of Wilderness ☎ 044 877 1285, ⓦ wildernessbackpackers.com. Built in 1897, this is the oldest home in the area. It's set in the quiet woodlands near the Touw River, though nowhere near the sea, and features a wraparound balcony. Note that during peak season it gets busy and can be very noisy near the bar. The Baz Bus drops off here. Dorms R160, doubles R600

Island Lake Holiday Resort Lakes Rd, 2km from the Hoekwil/Island Lake turn-off on the N2 ☎ 044 877 1194, ⓦ islandlake.co.za. Camping and self-catering rondavels that sleep four on one of the quietest and

prettiest spots on the lakes. The rondavels are basic one-room affairs with kitchenettes equipped with hotplates, microwaves and utensils, but you share communal washing and toilet facilities. Camping R300, rondavel R750

Mes-Amis Homestead Buxton Close, signposted off the N2 on the coastal side of the road, directly opposite the national park turn-off ☎ 044 877 1928, ⓦ mesamis .co.za. Nine double rooms, each of which has its own terrace, offering some of the best views in Wilderness, with a private path down to the beach. Rooms are elegantly furnished with crisp white bedding and curtains and there are luxurious touches such as bathrobes and espresso machines in each room. R1700

Wilderness Bush Camp Heights Rd (follow Waterside Rd west for 1600m up the hill) ☎ 044 877 1168, ⓦ boskamp.co.za. Six self-catering timber units with loft bedrooms, thatched roofs and ocean views. The camp, set on a hillside amid *fynbos* wilderness, is part of a conservation estate that you're free to roam around. R850

EATING

The Girls George Rd ☎ 044 877 1648, ⓦ thegirls.co.za. Deservedly one of the most popular restaurants in the village, *The Girls* fuses classic French dishes, such as steak tartare, with North African and Middle Eastern influences. The prawns are fantastic, they do a mean steak (R165) and vegetarians get a decent look in. Tues–Sun 5.30–11pm.

Salinas Beach Restaurant Cnr N2 and Zundorf Lane ☎ 044 877 0001. An easy stop-off on the N2 with a great view over the beach from the tables under umbrellas on the terrace. They're known for fresh fish brought in from Mossel Bay or Knysna (R165), good cocktails and excellent cheese cake. Daily 11am–10pm.

Serendipity Freesia Ave ☎ 044 877 0433, ⓦ serendipitywilderness.com. Located on the banks of the Touw River Lagoon, this fine-dining restaurant is one of the country's top places to eat. Come here for a fabulous dinner,

with Asian, Mediterranean and strong South African influences, cooked by a husband-and-wife team. Vegetarians may be seriously tempted by twice-baked goat's cheese soufflé or aubergine and pumpkin roulade. A seasonal, ever-changing five-course set menu is on offer (R550) and you need to book well ahead. Mon–Sat 7–10pm.

Zucchini Timberlake Organic Village ☎ 044 882 1240, ⓦ zucchini.co.za. This restaurant offers more sustainable food choices, including organic vegetables from their own garden and sourcing meat that is either free-range or organic. Their meals are simple and tasty with large portions – dishes include gourmet burgers like the "Dronk Bok" which is topped with brandy-soaked pears (R90), and gluten-free chocolate tart (R50). Drinks include thirteen types of locally brewed craft beer and sulphur-free wine. Phone before you go as opening times change according to seasons. Daily 9am–10pm.

Garden Route National Park: Wilderness Section

Reception open 7am–5.30pm • R120 • ☎ 044 877 1197

Stretching east from Wilderness village is the **Wilderness Section of the Garden Route National Park**, a rather inappropriate name, as it never feels very far from the N2. It's the **forests** you should come for, and the 16km of inland waterways; the variety of habitats here includes coastal and montane *fynbos* and wetlands, attracting 250 species of **bird** – as well as many holiday-makers.

17

ARRIVAL AND DEPARTURE   WILDERNESS SECTION

By car Driving along the N2, follow the road signs to Wilderness National Park to get to *Ebb and Flow* restcamps. There is also a western access to the park, reached by passing through the town of Wilderness, across the rail road bridge and a right turn for reception.

ACTIVITIES

Canoeing You can navigate the Touw River from the restcamp down to the beach in a canoe, which can be rented from Eden Adventures (see p.204).
Hiking There are five waymarked trails in the Wilderness Section ranging from 2km to 5km. A map of the trails, which also shows the location of three bird hides, is available at reception or you can download it from the SANParks website (ⓦsanparks.org).

ACCOMMODATION

There are two **restcamps**, *Ebb and Flow North*, and *Ebb and Flow South*, both on the west side of the park, which can be booked through SANparks (ⓦsanparks.org/parks/garden_route/camps/wilderness).

Ebb and Flow North Right on the river, this restcamp is cheap, old-fashioned and away from the hustle. It offers camping, fully equipped two-person rondavels with their own showers, and rondavels with communal washing and toilet facilities. Camping R200, rondavel R457
Ebb and Flow South This site has camping and modern accommodation in spacious log cottages on stilts and brick bungalows for up to four people (with private kitchen and bathroom). There are also en-suite two-sleeper forest huts with communal kitchens. Camping R200, forest huts R735, family cottages R1420

Sedgefield

The drive between Wilderness and Sedgefield gives glimpses on your left of dark-coloured lakes which eventually surge out to sea, 21km later, through a wide lagoon at **SEDGEFIELD**. A pleasantly old-fashioned holiday village – one of the last of its kind along the Garden Route – Sedgefield is a few kilometres off the road, with miles of beautiful beaches. In fact so proud is Sedgefield of its lack of pizzazz that the village has had itself registered as a "slow town", affiliated to the Cittaslow towns of Italy with its emblem a tortoise.

The entertainment highlight of Sedgefield's week is the **Wild Oats Community Farmers' Market** (ⓦwildoatsmarket.co.za; summer Sat 7.30–11.30am, winter from 8–11.30am), along the N2 on the west side of town, just before Swartvlei Lake, where you can pick up groceries and tasty nosh, such as preserves, cheeses, pickles and cured meats as well as delectable takeaway finger foods.

Sedgefield can be used as a base from which to explore Goukamma Nature and Marine Reserve and the western extent of Groenvlei, a freshwater lake that falls within the reserve's boundaries.

ARRIVAL AND DEPARTURE   SEDGEFIELD

By intercity bus Greyhound, Intercape and Translux buses stop in the middle of the village at the Sedgefield Garage, Main Rd, a service road running parallel to the N2, which passes through the town's shopping area.

Destinations Cape Town (2 daily; 8hr); Knysna (2 daily; 35min); Mossel Bay (2 daily; 1hr 15min); Plettenberg Bay (2 daily; 1hr 10min); Port Elizabeth (2 daily; 5hr 25min).

ACCOMMODATION

Afrovibe Adventure Lodge and Backpackers 2 Claude Urban Drive, Myoli Beach ☎044 343 3217, ⓦafrovibe .co.za. An unattractive, rectangular building, built questionably close to the beach on the ecologically sensitive dunes, but offering a stunning location and beach experience. It's on the Baz bus route too. Take advantage of their wide range of adventure activities. Dorms R185, doubles R630

★**Teniqua Treetops** 23km northeast of Sedgefield ☎044 356 2868, ⓦteniquatreetops.co.za. This is a genuinely unique and romantic forest retreat between Sedgefield and Knysna, a patch including 4km of woodland walks and a river with pools for swimming. Luxury tents are raised on timber decks, where, if you feel so inclined, you can leave the flaps open and wake up to

17

dappled light filtering through the leaves; one unit is wheelchair-accessible. It is a fascinating example of sustainable living in practice: not a single tree was felled to build *Teniqua*; recycled materials were used where possible; water is gravity fed; showers are solar-heated; and toilets use a dry composting system that preserves precious water. R1800

Goukamma Nature Reserve

Daily 7.30am–4pm • R40, free entry for overnight visitors • ☎ 044 383 0042

An unassuming sanctuary of around 220 square kilometres, **Goukamma** stretches from near Sedgefield east to Buffalo Bay (also known as Buffels Bay). The nature reserve takes in Groenvlei Lake and approximately 18km of beach frontage, some of the highest vegetated dunes in South Africa and walking country covered with coastal *fynbos* and dense thickets of milkwood, yellowwood and candlewood trees.

The area has long been popular with anglers, while away from the water, you stand a small chance of spotting one of the area's **mammals**, including bushbuck, grysbok, vervet monkeys, mongoose, caracals and otters. Because of the diversity of coastal and wetland habitats, more than 220 different kinds of **bird** have been recorded here, including fish eagles, Knysna louries, kingfishers and very rare African black oystercatchers. Offshore, southern right whales often make an appearance during their August-to-December breeding season, and bottlenose and common dolphins can show up at any time of year.

ARRIVAL AND DEPARTURE   GOUKAMMA NATURE RESERVE

By car Two roads off the N2 provide access to the reserve. The entrance and office are on the Buffalo Bay side accessed via the Buffalo Bay road, halfway along which is the reserve office. There are no public roads within the reserve. At the westernmost side, a dirt road that runs down to Platbank Beach takes you past the tiny settlement of Lake Pleasant on the south bank of Groenvlei, which consists of little more than a hotel and holiday resort.

ACTIVITIES

Apart from angling and birdwatching, the Goukamma offers a number of **self-guided activities**, including safe swimming in Groenvlei.

Hiking There are several day-long hiking trails that enable you to explore different habitats. A beach walk, which takes around 4hr one-way, traverses the 14km of crumbling cliffs and sands between the Platbank car park on the western side of the reserve and the Rowwehoek one on the eastern side. Alternatively, you can go from one end of the reserve to the other via a slightly longer inland trek across the dunes. There's also a shorter circular walk from the reserve office through a milkwood forest.

Canoeing You can canoe on the Goukamma River on the eastern side of the reserve; a limited number of canoes can be rented from the office during the week or at the gate over the weekend. Single or double canoes R100 a day.

ACCOMMODATION

There are two fully equipped bush camps on the Groenvlei side of the reserve and three thatched rondavels on the east side. Book through CapeNature (🖥 capenature.co.za). Over weekends, expect to pay roughly 25 percent more than the quoted prices.

Fish Eagle Lodge This loft, located on the top floor of *Otters Rest Lodge*, sleeps two people in single beds. There are wonderful sea and river views, an open-plan kitchen, dining room and lounge leading onto a deck and private braai facilities. R1025

Mvubu Thatched timber and reed bush camp on stilts, located at the edge of Groenvlei in a stand of milkwood trees. There are two en-suite bedrooms, sleeping four, both of which have doors opening onto a deck that overlooks the lake. R1600

Otters Rest Lodge Ground-floor lodge, with views of the ocean and river, sleeping four in two rooms with two single beds in each and a shared bathroom. Facilities include an open-plan kitchen, dining room and lounge with indoor fireplace, and large deck area with braai facilities. R1550

Stumpnose, Blacktail and Kabeljou Chalets Three basic double units on the Buffalo Bay side of the reserve, that overlook the river and estuary. Each unit sleeps four people and has rooms with two single beds, as well as one shared bathroom. There's a fully equipped kitchen with solar electricity and braai facilities (wood for sale at the gate). R1350

Knysna and around

South Africa's 1990s tourist boom rudely shook **KNYSNA** (pronounced "Nize-na") from its gentle backwoods drowse, which for decades had made it the hippie and craftwork capital of the country. The town, 491km and six hours' drive from Cape Town and 102km east of Mossel Bay, now stands at the hub of the Garden Route. Its lack of ocean beaches is compensated for by its hilly setting around the **Knysna lagoon**, its handsome **forests**, good opportunities for **adventure sports**, a pleasant **waterfront development** – and some hot marketing. If you want somewhere quiet or rural, Knysna is not for you: it is busy yet sophisticated with good restaurants and ever-burgeoning housing developments.

Knysna's distinctive atmosphere derives from its small historic core of Georgian and Victorian buildings, which gives it a character absent from most of the Garden Route holiday towns. Coffee shops, craft galleries, street traders and a modest nightlife add to the attractions. That the town has outgrown itself is evident from the cars and tour buses that, especially in December and January, clog Main Street, the constricted artery that merges with the N2 as it enters the town.

Knysna wraps around the lagoon, with its oldest part – the town centre – on the northern side. The lagoon's narrow mouth is guarded by a pair of steep rocky promontories called **The Heads**, the western side being a private nature reserve and the eastern one an exclusive residential area (confusingly, it's also called The Heads), along dramatic cliffs above the Indian Ocean.

Main Street, which used to be the hub of Knysna, lost some of its status as the heart of the town with the development of the waterfront area. But it has begun fighting back, with extensive redevelopment that has brought with it trendy coffee bars, restaurants and shops.

At the time of writing, devastating fires had swept through the town and surrounding forests, destroying houses and hotels in its wake – check with the tourist office (see p.211) for updates on the rebuilding process.

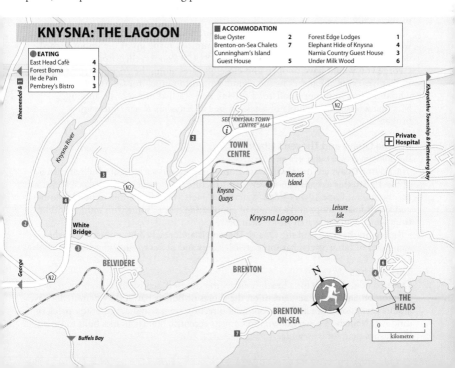

KNYSNA: THE LAGOON

ACCOMMODATION

Blue Oyster	2	Forest Edge Lodges	1
Brenton-on-Sea Chalets	7	Elephant Hide of Knysna	4
Cunningham's Island		Narnia Country Guest House	3
Guest House	5	Under Milk Wood	6

EATING

East Head Cafè	4
Forest Boma	2
Ile de Pain	1
Pembrey's Bistro	3

17

TOWNSHIP TOURS AND HOMESTAYS

Get a taste of Knysna's townships by joining one of the warts-and-all tours operated by **Eco Afrika** (tours daily 10am; R400; booking essential; ☎082 558 9104, ⊕eco-afrika-tours.co.za). Tours go to five areas, where you'll be given some historical background and get a chance to walk around and chat to people. You can also include lunch with a township family as part of the package (R60), but you need to book that in advance.

Eco Afrika also arrange **homestays** in one of the shanty towns within the townships, where you stay with a family in a corrugated iron shack (R300 per person). The tour operator will drop you off and pick you up the next morning.

Brief history

At the beginning of the nineteenth century, the only white settlements outside Cape Town were a handful of villages that would have considered themselves lucky to have even one horse. Knysna, an undeveloped backwater hidden in the forest, was no exception. The name comes from a Khoi word meaning "hard to reach", and this remained its defining character well into the twentieth century. One important figure was not deterred by the distance – **George Rex**, a colonial administrator who placed himself beyond the pale of decent colonial society by taking a coloured mistress. Shunned by his peers in Britain, he headed for Knysna at the beginning of the nineteenth century in the hope of making a killing shipping out hardwood from the lagoon.

By the time of Rex's death in 1839, Knysna had become a major **timber centre**, attracting white labourers who felled trees with primitive tools for miserly payments, and looked set eventually to destroy the forest. In 1872, **Prince Alfred**, on his visit to the Cape, made his small royal contribution to this destruction when he took a special detour here to hunt elephants. The forest only narrowly escaped devastation by far-sighted and effective conservation policies introduced in the 1880s.

By the start of the twentieth century, Knysna was still remote, and its forests were inhabited by isolated and inbred communities made up of the impoverished descendants of the woodcutters. As late as 1914, if you travelled from Knysna to George you would have to open and close 58 gates along the 75-kilometre track. Fifteen years on, the passes in the region proved too much for **George Bernard Shaw**, who did some impromptu off-road driving and crashed into a bush, forcing Mrs Shaw to spend a couple of weeks in bed at Knysna's *Royal Hotel* with a broken leg.

Knysna Quays and Thesen's Island
About 500m south of Knysna Tourism, at the end of Grey St

The **Knysna Quays** are the town's waterfront complex and yacht basin. Built at the end of the 1990s, this elegant two-storey steel structure with timber boardwalks resembles a tiny version of Cape Town's V&A Waterfront. Here you'll find a mix of hotels, clothes and knick-knack shops and a couple of good eating places, some with outdoor decks, from which you can watch yachts drift past.

Riding on the success of the Quays, **Thesen's Island**, reached by a causeway at the south end of Long Street, has some stylish shops and places to eat.

The beaches

Don't come to Knysna for a beach holiday: the closest beach is 20km from town at **Brenton-on-Sea**. A tiny settlement on the shores of Buffels Bay, it does admittedly have a quite exceptional beach. In the opposite direction from Knysna, the closest patch of sand is at **Noetzie**, a town known more for its eccentric holiday homes built to look like castles than for its seaside.

17

ARRIVAL AND DEPARTURE

KNYSNA AND AROUND

By Baz Bus The Baz Bus drops off at *Knysna Backpackers*.

By intercity bus Knysna is connected to Cape Town, Port Elizabeth and all major towns on the Garden Route by daily services on Greyhound, Intercape and Translux buses. Intercape and Translux buses drop passengers off at the old train station in Remembrance Avenue opposite

Knysna waterfront; Greyhound stops at the Toyota garage, 9 Main Rd.

Destinations Cape Town (2 daily; 8hr); Mossel Bay (2 daily; 1hr 45min); Plettenberg Bay (2 daily; 30min); Port Elizabeth (2 daily; 4hr 30min); Sedgefield (2 daily; 30min); Storms River Bridge (2 daily; 1hr 30min); Joburg (daily; 17hr 30min).

GETTING AROUND

By car Renting a car is the best way to explore Knysna and the surrounding forest – there are a number of rental agencies in town including Avis (7 Main Rd; ☎044 382 2222, ⓦavis.co.za), Europcar (1 Waterfront Drive, Caltex

Quay service station; ☎044 382 2733, ⓦeuropcar.co.za) and Tortoise Car Hire (23 Uil St, Sedgefield; ☎044 343 2991, ⓦtortoisecarhire.co.za).

INFORMATION AND ACTIVITIES

Tourist office Knysna Tourism, 40 Main St (Mon–Fri 8am–5pm, Sat 8.30am–1pm; ☎044 382 5510, ⓦvisitknysna.co.za), provides maps and runs a desk for booking activities around Knysna – including cruises to and abseiling down The Heads and bungee jumping from the Bloukrans River Bridge, as well as activities in Plett (see

p.221). They can also help with booking accommodation.

Mountain biking Knysna Cycle Works, 20 Waterfront Drive (☎044 382 5151, ⓦknysnacycles.com), offers bikes for rent (from R200/day) and has maps and information about trails in the Harkerville Forest, which is a brilliant area to explore.

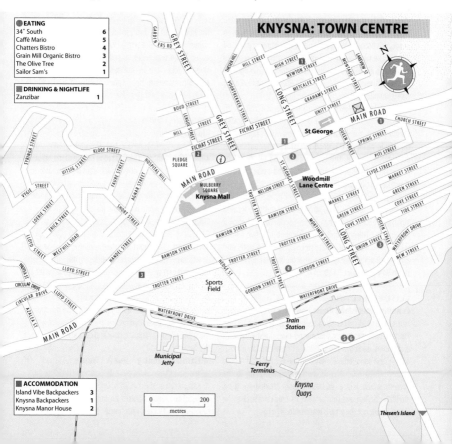

KNYSNA: TOWN CENTRE

● EATING	
34° South	6
Caffè Mario	5
Chatters Bistro	4
Grain Mill Organic Bistro	3
The Olive Tree	2
Sailor Sam's	1

■ DRINKING & NIGHTLIFE	
Zanzibar	1

■ ACCOMMODATION	
Island Vibe Backpackers	3
Knysna Backpackers	1
Knysna Manor House	2

17

KNYSNA CRUISES

One of the most pleasant diversions around Knysna is a **cruise** across the lagoon to the Heads. Knysna Featherbed Company (☎ 044 382 1693, ⓦ knysnafeatherbed.com) runs a number of trips of varying length, the shortest of which is Knysna Quays to the Heads (1hr 15mins; R150) and there is also an appealing daily sunset cruise on the lagoon (R160). The only way to reach the private **Featherbed Nature Reserve** on the western side of the lagoon is on a four-hour Featherbed Nature Tour (R635), which includes the boat there, a 4WD shuttle to the top of the western Head and a buffet meal. There's a slightly shorter version (3hr 45min) which excludes the meal. **Bookings** are essential, and can be made at the kiosk on the north side of Knysna Quays; **departures** are from the Waterfront Jetty and municipal jetty on Remembrance Avenue, 400m west of the quays and station.

ACCOMMODATION

The best places to stay in **Knysna** are well away from the N2 main road, with views of the lagoon and The Heads. Out of town there are some excellent establishments as well as reasonably priced self-catering cottages right in the forest. For somewhere quieter **on the lagoon**, make for the western edge at Brenton-on-Sea. At the time of writing, devastating fires had destroyed houses and hotels in the town, and the surrounding forest – check websites of accommodation establishments before you travel.

TOWN CENTRE AND KNYSNA QUAYS

Island Vibe Backpackers 67 Main Rd ☎ 044 382 1728, ⓦ islandvibe.co.za; map p.211. Part of the popular *Island Vibe Backpackers* group that are situated along the Garden Route, this branch has a good location, swimming pool and a deck. The facilities are not plush but it is a good cheap option and excellent place to meet buddies to join up with for adventure activities. It is on the Baz Bus route. Dorms R140, doubles R550

Knysna Manor House 19 Fichat St ☎ 044 382 5440, ⓦ knysnamanor.co.za; map p.211. A centrally located hundred-year-old house with yellowwood floors and colonial furnishings. It is good value for money although a little dated in style. The twin, double and family rooms come with the use of a swimming pool and garden. R1100

Knysna Backpackers 42 Queen St ☎ 044 382 2554, ⓦ knysnabackpackers.co.za; map p.211. Spotless, well-organized hostel in a large, rambling and centrally located Victorian house that has been declared a National Monument. This tranquil establishment has five rooms rented as doubles (but able to sleep up to four people) and a dorm that sleeps eight. It's also on the Baz Bus route. Dorm R140, doubles R480

LEISURE ISLE AND THE HEADS

Cunningham's Island Guest House 3 Kingsway, Leisure Isle ☎ 044 384 1319, ⓦ islandhouse.co.za; map p.209. Purpose-built two-storey, timber-and-glass guesthouse with eight suites, decked out in dazzling white relieved by a touch of blue and some ethnic colour (stripy cushions and African baskets). Each room has its own entrance leading to the garden, which has a swimming pool shaded by giant strelitzias. Stylish and comfortable, its only drawback is the lack of views, but the price is reasonable. R1010

Under Milk Wood George Rex Drive, The Heads ☎ 044 384 0745, ⓦ milkwood.co.za; map p.209. Luxury self-catering accommodation on the lagoon at the foot of The Heads with its own private beach, where it is safe for swimming. There are terrific views of the mountains and water. Three two-bedroom self-catering units, with their own sundecks, are surrounded by milkwood trees; rates vary depending on the position, and there are hefty off-season discounts. R1500

WEST OF TOWN

Blue Oyster Cnr Rio & Stent sts ☎ 044 382 2265, ⓦ blueoyster.co.za; map p.209. Hospitable three-storey, vaguely Greek-themed B&B set high on one of the hills that rise up behind Knysna, offering fabulous panoramas across the lagoon to The Heads. The four comfortable double rooms, of which the ones on the top floor have the best views, are done out in white and blue. R1400

Elephant Hide of Knysna Cherry Lane ☎ 044 382 0426, ⓦ elephanthide.co.za; map p.209. Overlooking the lagoon, 3km from the town centre, this peaceful guesthouse has seven rooms, each lavishly styled with warm and earthy textures and tones. The lagoon suites are a honeymooner's dream, each with a spa bath set with floor-to-ceiling windows overlooking the lagoon, as well as a private balcony and a king-sized bed. The guesthouse has a spacious communal lounge and a fireplace for winter; there's a dreamy swimming pool and deck area to laze on in the summer. R2300

★ Narnia Country Guest House Signed off Welbedacht Lane, 3km west of Knysna ☎ 044 382 1334, ⓦ narnia.co.za; map p.209. On a hillside with far-off views of the lagoon, this is an immensely fun stone and rough-hewn timber farmhouse in a glorious garden.

Decorated in a rustic-chic style, there are three comfortable cottages, lovely views, a swimming pool and small lake on the property. You can self-cater, or chose the more expensive B&B option. **R2000**

fittings. The cottages are private and romantic. Forest walks and cycling trails start from the cottages, from where you can walk to rock pools and waterfalls. A minimum stay of two nights is required. **R1025**

FOREST ENVIRONS

★**Forest Edge Lodges** Rheenendal turn-off, 16km west of Knysna on the N2 ☎082 456 1338, ⌨forestedge .co.za; map p.209. Ideal if you want to be close to the forest itself, these traditional two-bedroom woodcutters' cottages have verandas built in the vernacular tin-roofed style, and have been upgraded for extra comfort with good linen and

BELVIDERE AND BRENTON-ON-SEA

Brenton-on-Sea Chalets C.R. Swart Drive, Brenton beachfront ☎044 381 0081, ⌨brentononsea.net; map p.209. Right at the long sandy Brenton beach, a 20min drive from Knysna, these three-bedroom, self-catering chalets sleep six people, and are well equipped and comfortably furnished. **R1180**

EATING

As far as food goes, you'll find a lot of good **restaurants** catering to a wide range of palates and one or two excellent coffee shops. With so many forests, waterways and beaches, you may be tempted to have a **picnic**, and there's no shortage of tempting deli food in town. In summer and holiday periods, you'll need to make a restaurant reservation.

34° South Knysna Quays ☎044 382 7331, ⌨34-south .com; map p.211. A good deli, café, restaurant, bar and sushi joint with imported groceries, home-made food and an extensive menu that includes seafood in all its guises – from *peri-peri* calamari heads to a red Thai curry mussel pot (R145) and a variety of sushi. From here you can watch the drawbridge open to let yachts sail through. Daily 8.30am–10pm.

Caffè Mario Knysna Quays ☎044 382 7250; map p.211. An intimate Italian waterside restaurant with outdoor seating. The food is consistently good value, there's *paninoteca* and *tramezzini* on its snack menu as well as great pizza (R90) and pasta. Daily 8am–10pm.

Chatters Bistro Corner of Gray and Gordon sts ☎044 382 0203, ⌨chattersbistro.co.za; map p.211. With an enclosed garden, a roaring fire in winter and eighty wines on the drinks list, this is the place to go in Knysna for superb thin and crispy pizzas (with wheat and gluten-free bases available) and pastas (R80). Tues–Sun noon–9.30pm.

East Head Café 25 George Rex Drive ☎44 384 0933, ⌨eastheadcafe.co.za; map p.209. Very popular café with an outdoor area, panoramic views of the Knysna Heads and a kids' playground. Try their simple, delicious seafood dishes (R95), classic wraps and salads or a spirited milkshake as a cocktail. Note they don't take bookings and parking can be tricky. Daily 8am–3.30pm.

Forest Boma Phantom Forest Eco-Reserve, Phantom Pass Rd ☎044 386 0046; map p.209. Eating is secondary to the setting here, in a forest with views of the whole estuary, which places this spot among the most beautiful in South Africa. The six-course pan-African set menu (R490) ranges from game meats to tempting desserts, and changes on a daily basis. Booking essential. Daily 6.30–10pm.

★**Grain Mill Organic Bisto** 3 Union Street, Waterfront Drive ☎083 635 7634, map p.211. Fabulous restaurant, with sustainably grown food, freshly milled flour used for baked goods, as well as good coffee, teas, smoothies and

juices. The blackboard menu gives vegetarians a large choice of dishes like creamy vegan pumpkin soup (R60), and for meat eaters all the chicken, beef and fish on offer is ethically reared. There is no corkage fee if you want to bring your own bottle. The ambience is cosy, and seating is at wooden tables, some on the patio. There is a small farm stall/deli too. Mon–Sat 8.30am–3pm.

★**Ile de Pain** 10 The Boat Shed, Thesen's Island ☎044 302 5705, ⌨iledepain.co.za; map p.209. A trendy restaurant in an artisan bakery with stone floors and an open bakery that does salads, baguettes and pastas. Try the crusty wood-fired bread with butter and preserves for breakfast or enjoy one of the delicious pastries with coffee (R80). Tues–Sat 8am–3pm.

The Olive Tree 12 Wood Mill Lane Centre, Main Rd ☎044 382 5867; map p.211. This local favourite offers bistro dining, with fresh ingredients and Mediterranean-influenced and beautifully plated dishes. Vegetarians have a couple of options, including vegetarian pasta (R100). Mon–Sat 6–10pm.

Pembrey's Bistro Brenton Rd, Belvidere ☎044 386 0005, ⌨pembreys.co.za; map p.209. Highly rated restaurant that fuses country cooking with haute cuisine, run by the chef/owners. They use herbs and vegetables from the garden, and their desserts are full of tantalising fruity flavours such as sorbets and churned ice cream with lemon balm, elderflower and liquorice (R60). There is a Mediterranean-inspired salad buffet, and good meat dishes. The owners also have a great interest in wines so expect a most tempting wine list. Tues–Sat 6.30–10pm.

★**Sailor Sam's** Main Rd, opposite the post office ☎044 382 6774; map p.211. A warm-hearted, old-fashioned chippy that offers incredible value, brilliant fish and chips and the cheapest oysters in town (R16 per oyster). Don't tell a soul, but the delicious shellfish aren't local; they're shipped in from South Africa's west coast. Mon–Sat 11am–8pm.

17

DRINKING AND NIGHTLIFE

Knysna has perked up over the past decade, but it still isn't somewhere you come if your main aim is to party. Having said that, there are one or two clubs in town that burn the midnight oil and where you may catch some live music or DJs.

Zanzibar Corner of St George's and Main sts ☎ 044 382 0386; map p.211. Knysna's longest-established nightclub occupies the premises of the Old Barnyard Theatre and blends everything from pop to commercial house and beyond. It has occasional live acts – mostly bands, and best to check out their happenings on Facebook. Expect to pay around R60 for a spirit and mixer drink. Daily 7pm–2am.

DIRECTORY

Emergencies General emergency number from landline ☎ 107, from mobile phone ☎ 112; Police ☎ 044 302 6600; National Sea Rescue ☎ 082 990 5956.

Hospital Life Knysna Private Hospital, Hunters Drive (☎ 044 384 1083), is a well-run hospital and has a casualty department.

The Knysna forests

The best reason to come to Knysna is for its **forests**, shreds of a once magnificent woodland that was home to **Khoi** clans and harboured a thrilling variety of wildlife, including elephant herds. The forests attracted European explorers and naturalists, and in their wake woodcutters, gold-diggers and businessmen like George Rex, all bent on making their fortunes here.

The French explorer François Le Vaillant was one of the first Europeans to **shoot and kill** an elephant. The explorer found the animal's feet so "delicious" that he wagered that "never can our modern epicures have such a dainty at their tables". Two hundred years later, all that's left of the Khoi people are some names of local places. The legendary Knysna elephants have hardly fared better and are teetering on the edge of certain extinction.

Goudveld State Forest

Just over 30km northwest of Knysna • Daily sunrise–sunset • R100

The beautiful **Goudveld State Forest** is a mixture of plantation and indigenous woodland. It takes its name from the gold boom (*goudveld* is Afrikaans for goldfields) that brought hundreds of prospectors to the mining town of **Millwood** in the 1880s. The six hundred small-time diggers who were here by 1886, scouring out the hillsides and panning Jubilee Creek for alluvial gold, were rapidly followed by larger syndicates, and a flourishing little town quickly sprang up, with six hotels, three newspapers and a music hall.

GOUDVELD HIKES

A number of clearly **waymarked hikes** traverse the Goudveld. The most rewarding (and easy going) is along **Jubilee Creek**, which traces the progress of a burbling brook for 3.5km through giant woodland to a gorgeous, deep rock pool. It's also an excellent place to encounter **Knysna turacos** (formally known as Knysna louries); keep an eye focused on the branches above for the crimson flash of their flight feathers as they forage for berries, and listen out for their harsh call above the gentler chorus provided by the wide variety of other birdlife here. You can pick up a **map** directing you to the creek from the entrance gate to the reserve; the waymarked trail is linear, so you return via the same route. There's a pleasant **picnic site** along the banks of the stream at the start of the walk.

A more strenuous option is the circular **Woodcutter Walk**, though you can choose either the 3km or the 9km version. Starting at **Krisjan se Nek**, another picnic site not far past the Goudveld entrance gate, it meanders downhill through dense forest, passing through stands of tree ferns, and returns uphill to the starting point. The picnic site is also where the 19km **Homtini Cycle Route** starts, taking you through forest and *fynbos* and offering wonderful mountain views. Be warned though; you really have to work hard at this, with one particular section climbing over 300m in just 3km. The tourist office in town has maps of the area.

However, the singing and dancing was shortlived and bust followed boom in 1890 after most of the mining companies went to the wall. The ever-hopeful diggers took off for the newly discovered Johannesburg goldfields, and Millwood was left a deserted **ghost town**. Over the years, its buildings were demolished or relocated, leaving an old store known as Materolli as the only original building standing.

Today, the old town is completely overgrown, apart from signs indicating where the old streets stood. In **Jubilee Creek**, which provides a lovely shady walk along a burbling stream, the holes scraped or blasted out of the hillside are still clearly visible. Some of the old mine works have been restored, as have the original **reduction works** around the cocopan track, used to carry the ore from the mine to the works, which is still there after a century.

The forest itself is still lovely, featuring tall, indigenous trees, a delightful valley with a stream, and plenty of swimming holes and picnic sites.

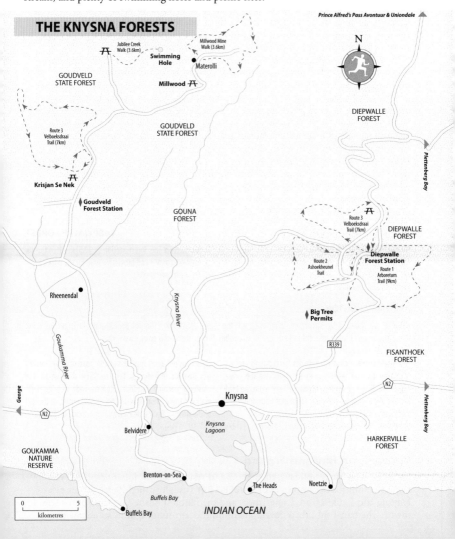

THE KNYSNA FORESTS

17

By car To get here from Knysna, follow the N2 west toward George, turning right onto the Rheenendal road just after the Knysna River, and continue for about 25km, following the Bibby's Koep signposts until the Goudveld sign.

Diepwalle Forest

Just over 20km northeast of Knysna • Daily 7.30am–4pm • R100 • ☎ 044 382 9762, ⊕ sanparks.org/parks/garden_route/camps/knysna_lakes

The **Diepwalle Forest** is the last haunt of Knysna's almost extinct elephant population, although the only elephants you can expect to see here are on the painted markers indicating the three main hikes through these woodlands. However, if you're quiet and alert, you do stand a chance of seeing vervet monkeys, bushbuck and blue duiker.

Diepwalle ("deep walls") is one of the highlights of the Knysna area and is renowned for its impressive density of huge trees, especially **yellowwoods**. Once the budget timber of South Africa, yellowwood was considered an inferior local substitute in place of imported pine, and found its way into thousands of often quite modest nineteenth-century houses in the Western and Eastern Cape. Today, its deep golden grain is so sought after that it commands premium prices at the annual auctions.

The three main hiking routes cover between 7km and 9km of terrain, and pass through flat to gently undulating country covered by indigenous forest and montane *fynbos*. If you're moderately fit, the hikes should take between two hours and two and a half hours. The 9km **Arboretum trail**, flagged by black elephant markers, starts a short way back along the road you drove in on, and descends to a stream edged with tree ferns. Across the stream you'll come to the much-photographed **Big Tree**, a six-hundred-year-old Goliath yellowwood. The easy 9km **Ashoekheuwel trail**, marked by white elephants, crosses the Gouna River, where there's a large pool allegedly used by real pachyderms. Most difficult of the three hikes is the rewarding 7km **Velboeksdraai trail**, marked by red elephants, which passes along the foothills of the Outeniquas. Take care here to stick to the elephant markers, as they overlap with a series of painted footprints marking the Outeniqua trail, for which you need to have arranged a permit.

By car To get here from Knysna, follow the N2 east towards Plettenberg Bay, after 7km turning left onto the R339, which you should take for about 16km in the direction of Avontuur and Uniondale.

Information The forest station is 10.5km after the tar gives way to gravel and provides a map for the park's trails, all of which begin here.

ACCOMMODATION

There are two National Parks accommodation options in the Forest, both booked through the SANparks Knysna Lakes office (Long St, Thesen's Island, adjacent to Jetty; ☎ 044 302 5606). Driving directions given on booking.

★ **Forest timber camping decks** Ten camping sites set within the forest make this an exceptional SANParks site – you can really get in touch with nature here amid the busy Garden Route. Braai facilities, communal bathrooms and electricity available. R210

Tree Top Forest Chalet This two-bedroomed timber chalet tucked away in forest at the head of a wide valley has luxuries including a Jacuzzi, DSTV, dishwasher and washing machine. Outdoors there's a wide viewing deck, walking trails, mountain-biking opportunities and great birdwatching. Book at least a month in advance. R1500

Plettenberg Bay and around

Over the Christmas holidays, forty thousand residents from Johannesburg's wealthy northern suburbs decamp to **PLETTENBERG BAY** (usually called Plett), 33km east of Knysna and 520km from Cape Town, and the flashiest of the Garden Route's seaside towns. The banal suburban development on the surrounding hills somehow doesn't

THE KNYSNA ELEPHANTS

Traffic signs warning motorists about elephants along the N2 between Knysna and Plettenberg Bay are rather optimistic: there are only a few indigenous pachyderms left and, with such an immense forest, sightings are rare. But such is the mystique attached to the **Knysna elephants** that locals tend to be a little cagey about just how few there are. By 1860, the thousands that had formerly wandered the once vast forests were down to five hundred, and by 1920 (twelve years after they were protected by law), there were only twenty animals left; the current estimate is three. Loss of habitat and consequent malnutrition, rather than full-scale hunting, seems to have been the principal cause of their decline. The only elephants you're guaranteed to see near Knysna are at the **Elephant Sanctuary** (see p.219), near Plettenberg Bay.

seem so bad because the bay views really are stupendous with lovely swimming and walking beaches. The deep-blue **Tsitsikamma Mountains** drop sharply to the inlet and its large estuary, providing a constant vista to the town and its suburbs. The bay generously curves over several kilometres of white sands separated from the mountains by forest, which makes this a green and temperate location with rainfall throughout the year.

Nevertheless Plett remains an expensive place to stay, with no cheap chalets or camping. For these you'll have to go to nearby **Keurboomstrand**, on the east of the bay. Further east lie **The Crags** (both of them more or less suburbs of Plett) with their trio of wildlife parks: Monkeyland, Birds of Eden and the Elephant Sanctuary are all worth a visit, especially if you're travelling with kids.

Plett's town **centre**, at the top of the hill, consists of a conglomeration of supermarkets, swimwear shops, estate agents and restaurants aimed largely at the holiday trade. Visitors principally come for Plett's **beaches** – and there's a fair choice. Southern right whales appear every winter, while dolphins can be seen throughout the year, hunting or riding the surf, often in substantial numbers. Swimming is safe, and though the waters are never tropically warm they reach a comfortable temperature between November and April. One of the best things to do is to take a marine tour, or go canoeing (see p.221).

Southeast of the town centre on a rocky promontory is **Beacon Island**, dominated by a 1970s hotel, an eyesore blighting a fabulous location. Development has been halted however, on the magnificent **Robberg Peninsula**, the great tongue of headland that contains the western edge of the bay, which offers the Garden Route's best short **hikes**, with spectacular scenery. Robberg also makes a good place to spend a night or two, if you are driving along the coast.

The beaches

Beacon Island Beach, or **Main Beach**, right at the central shore of the bay, is where the fishing boats and seacats anchor a little out to sea. The small waves here make for calm swimming, and this is an ideal family spot. To the east is **Lookout Beach**, which is also one of the nicest stretches of sand for bathers, or sun lizards. Lookout Beach has the added attraction of a marvellously located restaurant (see p.224), from which you can often catch sight of **dolphins** cruising into the bay. From here you can walk several kilometres down the beach towards Keurboomstrand and the **Keurbooms Lagoon**.

Keurboomstrand

Some 14km east of Plettenberg Bay by road, across the Keurbooms River, is the uncluttered resort of **KEURBOOMSTRAND** (Keurbooms for short), little more than a suburb of Plett, sharing the same bay and with equally good beaches, but less safe for swimming. The safest place to take the waves is at **Arch Rock**, in front of the caravan park, though **Picnic Rock Beach** is also pretty good. A calm and attractive

17 place, Keurbooms has few facilities, and if you're intending to stay here you should stock up in Plett beforehand. One of Keurbooms' highlights is **canoeing** up the river (see p.221).

Robberg Marine and Nature Reserve

Robberg Rd • Daily 8am–5pm • R40 • ☎ 021 483 0190, ⓦ capenature.co.za/reserves/robberg-nature-reserve

One of the Garden Route's most magnificent walks is the four-hour, 9km circular route around the spectacular rocky peninsula of **Robberg**, 8km southeast of Plett's town centre. Here you can completely escape Plett's development and experience the coast in its wildest state, with its enormous horizons and lovely vegetation. Much of the walk

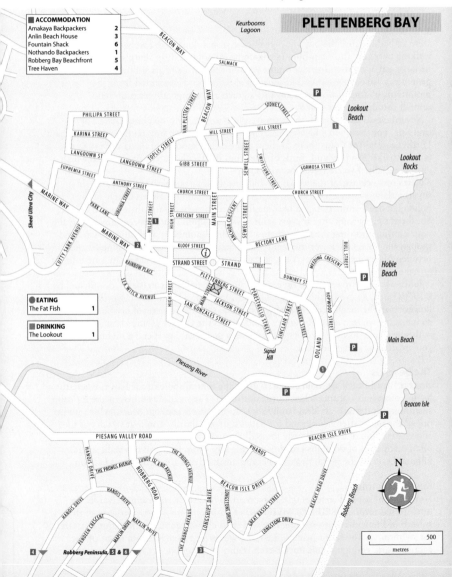

PLETTENBERG BAY

ACCOMMODATION	
Amakaya Backpackers	2
Anlin Beach House	3
Fountain Shack	6
Nothando Backpackers	1
Robberg Bay Beachfront	5
Tree Haven	4

EATING	
The Fat Fish	1

DRINKING	
The Lookout	1

0 — 500
metres

takes you along high cliffs, from where you can often look down to see seals surfacing near the rocks, dolphins arching through the water and, in winter, whales further out in the bay. If you don't have time for the full circular walk, there is a shorter two-hour hike, as well as a thirty-minute ramble; a map is provided at the entrance gate. There is one rustic hut, *Fountain Shack*, to stay overnight (see p.221).

The Crags

From Keurbooms, look out for the BP petrol station, then take the Monkeyland/Kurland turn-off and follow the Elephant Sanctuary/Monkeyland signs for 2km

The Crags, 2km east of Keurboomstrand, comprises a collection of smallholdings along the N2, a bottle store and a few other shops on the forest edge. The real reason most visitors pull in here though, is to visit the **Elephant Sanctuary**, **Monkeyland** and **Birds of Eden**.

Elephant Sanctuary

Daily 8am–5pm • Trunk-in-Hand Programme daily from 8am R580; elephant ride R580; elephant brush-down experience 7.30am & 3.15pm R705 • ☏ 044 534 8145, ⓦ elephantsanctuary.co.za

The **Elephant Sanctuary** offers a chance of close encounters with its half-dozen pachyderms, all of whom were saved from culling in Botswana and Kruger National Park. On the popular one-hour Trunk-in-Hand programme you get to walk with an elephant, holding the tip of its trunk in your hand and also to feed and interact with it. The programme includes an informative talk about elephant behaviour, and helping brush down the elephants is among the other packages on offer.

Monkeyland, Birds of Eden and Jukani

Daily 8am–5pm • R230, combined ticket for two sanctuaries R360, combined ticket for all three sanctuaries R450 • ⓦ monkeyland.co.za

Together these three rescue sanctuaries provide an impressive display of animals and birds, in well-kept, natural environments. Tickets can be booked online for the sanctuaries. If you wish to see all three places, the latest you may arrive is 2pm, although the ticket which allows visits to all three sanctuaries does not have to be used on the same day. At each sanctuary there is a café for light meals or a drink.

Monkeyland

Monkeyland, 400m beyond the Elephant Sanctuary, brings together primates from several continents, all of them orphaned or saved from a life as pets. None of the animals has been taken from the wild – and most wouldn't have the skills to survive there. The monkeys are free to move around the reserve, looking for food and interacting with each other and their environment in as natural a way as possible. For your own safety and that of the monkeys, you are not allowed to wander around alone. **Guides** take visitors on walking "safaris", during which you come across water holes, experience a living indigenous forest and enjoy chance encounters with creatures such as ringtail lemurs from Madagascar and squirrel monkeys from South America.

Birds of Eden

Birds of Eden is a huge bird sanctuary with birds from all over the world. The sanctuary took four years to create, as great effort was taken to place netting over a substantial tract of virgin forest with as little impact as possible. The result is claimed to be the largest free-flight aviary in the world. As with Monkeyland, most of the birds were already living in cages and are now free to move and fly around within the confines of the large enclosure (so large in fact that you can easily spend an hour slowly meandering along its winding, wheelchair-friendly, wooden walkway).

17

WHALING AND GNASHING OF TEETH

For conservationists, the monumental 1970s eyesore of the *Beacon Island Hotel* may not be such a bad thing, since previously the island was the site of a whale-processing factory established in 1806 – one of some half-dozen such plants erected along the Western Cape coast that year. Whaling continued at Plettenberg Bay until 1916. Southern right whales were the favoured species, yielding more oil and **whalebone** – an essential component of Victorian corsets – than any other. In the nineteenth century, a southern right would net around three times as much as a humpback caught along the Western Cape coast, leading to a rapid decline in the southern right population by the middle of the nineteenth century.

The years between the establishment and the closing of the Plettenberg Bay factory saw worldwide whaling transformed by the inventions of the Industrial Revolution. In 1852, the explosive harpoon was introduced, followed by the use of steam-powered ships five years later, making them swifter and safer for the crew. In 1863, Norwegian captain Sven Foyn built the first modern whale-catching vessel, which he followed up in 1868 with the **cannon-mounted harpoon**. In 1913 Plettenberg Bay was the site of one of seventeen shore-based and some dozen floating factories between West Africa and Mozambique, which that year between them took about ten thousand whales.

Inevitably, a rapid decline in humpback populations began; by 1918, all but four of the shore-based factories had closed due to lack of prey. The remaining whalers now turned their attention to fin and blue whales. When the South African fin whale population became depleted by the mid-1960s to twenty percent of its former size, they turned to sei and sperm whales. When these populations declined, the frustrated whalers started hunting minke whales, which at 9m in length are too small to be a viable catch. By the 1970s, the South African whaling industry was in its death throes and was finally put out of its misery in 1979, when the government banned all activity surrounding whaling.

Jukani

Jukani signposted off the N2 at the Crags, 7km west of Monkeyland, is the place to go to see big cats. There are a couple of large enclosures, with African cats, as well as jaguars, tigers and cougars. Other predators include hyenas, wild dogs, jackals and even some snakes. The animals have all been born in captivity or rescued, there is no breeding programme and lions are not used to supply the notorious canned lion hunting trade.

ARRIVAL AND INFORMATION   PLETTENBERG BAY AND AROUND

By Baz Bus The Baz Bus drops passengers off at accommodation in town.

By intercity bus Intercape, Greyhound and Translux intercity buses stop at the Shell Ultra City petrol station, just off the N2 in Marine Way, 2km from the town centre. As there's no transport around town, if you don't have your own car, you'll need to arrange for your guesthouse to collect you. Destinations Cape Town (2 daily; 9hr); George (2 daily;

2hr); Joburg (2 daily; 18hr); Knysna (2 daily; 1hr 30min); Mossel Bay (2 daily; 2hr 20min); Port Elizabeth (2 daily; 3hr 30min).

Tourist information The tourist office, Shop 35, Melville Corner, Main St (Mon–Fri 9am–5pm, Sat 9am–1pm; ☎044 533 4065, ⓦplett-tourism.co.za), has maps of the town, can help with booking accommodation, and has a good website with information on local facilities.

ACTIVITIES

BOAT TRIPS

Keurbooms River Ferries Signposted on the east side of the Keurbooms River Bridge ☎083 254 3551, ⓦferry.co.za. This company runs daily guided upriver boat trips (11am, 2pm, sunset; R180) with knowledgeable guides skilled at spotting rare birds – the indigenous forest comes right down to the edge. Booking required. Cape Nature entrance fee is R40 per person.

BUNGEE JUMPING

Bloukrans Bungy ☎042 281 1458, ⓦfaceadrenalin .com. The world's highest commercial bungee jump takes place off the 216m Bloukrans River Bridge and costs R9500 (excluding pictures or video) for the seven-second descent. Book 48hr in advance.

CANOEING

CapeNature On the east side of the Keurbooms River

Bridge along the N2, on the road marked Keurbooms River Ferry. Go to the kiosk to reserve a fairly basic craft, out of season you can easily get one (R135/day for a two-person canoe).

HIKING
The Robberg Marine and Nature Reserve offers one of the garden route's best hikes (see p.219).

ROCK CLIMBING
GoVertical Mountaineering Adventures ☎ 082 731 4696, Ⓦ govertical.co.za. An outfit which teaches the basics of rock climbing and takes experienced climbers out: kloofing or canyoning is the most adventurous way of exploring the deep river gorges between Knysna and Plett. Prices depend on the size of the group, and are given when you enquire. Their reach is country-wide for guided adventure expeditions.

SKYDIVING
Skydive Plettenberg Bay ☎ 082 905 7440, Ⓦ skydiveplett.com. If you fancy a bit of an adrenaline rush, you can go tandem skydiving (no experience required) with these guys, who charge R2300 for a 10,000ft jump, with the option of paying extra for a DVD or video of the event.

TOWNSHIP TOURS
Ocean Blue Central Beach ☎ 044 533 5083, Ⓦ oceanadventures.co.za. Ocean Blue arranges relaxed tours into Plett's township with a member of the community. Outings cost R250 per person and all the takings go into a development trust, which among other things, pays teachers' salaries and funds a crèche.

WHALE- AND DOLPHIN-WATCHING
Dolphin Adventures Central Beach ☎ 083 590 3405, Ⓦ dolphinadventures.co.za. Sea kayaking is one of the best ways to watch whales, and this outfit offers unforgettable trips with experienced and knowledgeable guides in two-person kayaks (2hr–2hr 30min, R300;) or just rentals (2hr R150).
Ocean Blue Central Beach ☎ 044 533 4897 or ☎ 083 701 3583, Ⓦ oceanadventures.co.za. Sea-kayaking (R300) and boat-based whale-watching, from July to September (R750), are among the offerings of this licensed outfit, which also runs township tours (see above).
Ocean Safaris Shop 3, Hopwood St ☎ 044 533 4963, Ⓦ oceansafaris.co.za. Tailor-made cruises from a licensed whale-watching company. Whale-watching by boat (R750) virtually guarantees sightings between July and September. Out of whale season it's still worth going out to see dolphins and seals (R450).

ACCOMMODATION

PLETTENBERG BAY
Amakaya Backpackers 15 Park Lane ☎ 044 533 4010, Ⓦ amakaya.co.za; map p.218. Located close to town and the beach, this place is well-set-up for backpackers with communal lounge areas, and outside fire pit and hammocks to while away your time. They also boast an upstairs veranda with bar and swimming pool with views of the lagoon and mountains. Note that the minimum stay over the weekend is two nights. Dorms R170, doubles R480
Anlin Beach House 33 Roche Bonne Ave ☎ 044 533 3694, Ⓦ anlinbeachhouse.co.za; map p.218. Stylish and comfortably kitted-out self-catering garden studios, a sea-facing double room and a larger family unit with three bedrooms and a kitchen, in a garden setting on the side of Plett nearest to Robberg Nature Reserve. Breakfast is an extra R85. Garden studio & sea-facing double R1800
Fountain Shack Robberg Nature Reserve ☎ 021 483 0190, Ⓦ capenature.co.za/reserves/robberg-nature-reserve; map p.218. A renovated fisherman's style bungalow sleeping eight, magically isolated with no electricity and beautifully set next the ocean. There is no vehicle access – you need to walk 2hr to reach it – though linen, cooking facilities and cutlery are provided, so you just need to bring in your food. It is the only place to stay in the nature reserve. R1400
Nothando Backpackers 5 Wilder St ☎ 044 533 0220, Ⓦ nothando.com; map p.218. Top-notch

child-friendly hostel. A 5min walk from Plett's shops, this suburban home has seven doubles, three dorms and a four-bedded family room. Breakfast and dinner are available for an extra R50/80. Dorms R180, doubles R550, family room R990
★ **Robberg Bay Beachfront** 2 Robberg Rd ☎ 082 809 3931, Ⓦ robbergbay.com; map p.218. Poised above Robberg Beach, with the full sweep of the bay in front of you, this stupendously located and immaculate guesthouse overflows with easy luxury and relaxation. All seven units have unobstructed sea views and there is a path from the house straight onto the beach 700m away. Without doubt, a top Garden Route stay. R2800
Tree Haven 45 Hanois Crescent ☎ 044 533 1989, Ⓦ treehavenholidays.co.za; map p.218. Tranquil and comfortable self-catering suite, part of the fascinating home of architect and artist couple, Carol and Feo Sachs. The house is surrounded by trees and garden, and the lack of sea view means they are sheltered from the wind. You can easily drive a few minutes to the beach or to Robberg and the airport. R900

KEURBOOMSTRAND AND EAST OF PLETT
Alkantmooi Keurboom Rd, Keurbooms River ☎ 044 535 9245, Ⓦ alkantmooi.co.za; pp.222–223. Four modern one- or two-bedroom self-catering units, all

17

varying in style, with lagoon rather than sea views, fully equipped kitchens and braai or outdoor patio facilities. Good value for money. R1400

Arch Rock Chalets & Caravan Park Arch Rock ☎044 535 9409, ⓦarchrock.co.za; map below. Seventeen self-catering chalets, some with one and the others with two bedrooms, in the best position at Keurbooms, right at the beach. It has one of the best locations of anywhere in the country, if you want a beach stay. Apart from the forest chalets and log cabins, which are set back among trees (R800), the rest have sea views. Chalet R1200

Bitou River Lodge Bitou Valley Rd (the R340), about 4km from the N2 ☎044 535 9577, ⓦbitou.co.za; map below. Great value in a lovely spot on the banks of the Bitou River, this intimate establishment has five

comfortable but unfussy bedrooms that overlook a pretty garden with a lily pond. Rate includes use of canoes on the river. R1700

Dune Park Keurboomstrand Rd, leading off the N2 and running along the shore to Keurbooms ☎044 535 9606, ⓦdunepark.co.za; map below. Luxury hotel whose airy bedrooms with crisp white linen are simple and stylish. Two-bedroom self-catering cottages built on top of high dunes provide great views within spitting distance of the sea. Doubles R990, cottages R1500

★Emily Moon River Lodge Rietvlei Rd, off the N2 (turn off at Penny Pinchers) ☎044 533 2982, ⓦemilymoon.co.za; map below. That the owner of this highly imaginative and luxurious lodge, perched on a ridge looking across the Bitou Wetlands, is a dealer in ethnic art is plain to see. The place is not only littered with

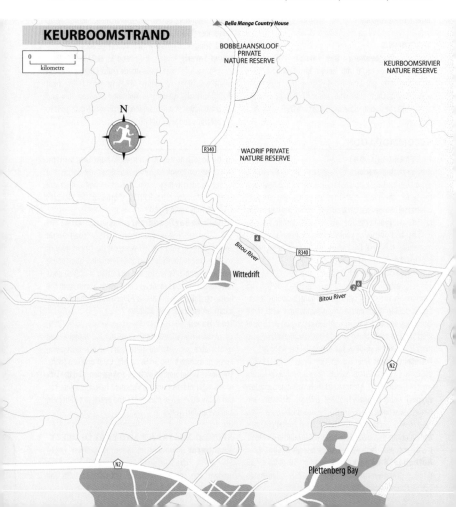

Batonga sculptures and Swazi crafts, it has in places been constructed out of artworks, such as the intricate Rajasthani arched screen that is the entrance to the magnificently sited restaurant. Each of its chalets jetties out of the hillside to offer views from a private deck (and bathroom) of the oxbowing Bitou, along which small game can occasionally be seen. There is a family suite that sleeps four in which kids are accommodated at a discounted rate. R3440

★ **Hog Hollow Country Lodge** Askop Rd, 18km east of Plettenberg Bay (turn south off the N2 at the signpost) ☎ 044 534 8879, ⓦ hog-hollow.com; map below. A touch of luxury on a private reserve where each of the chalets, done out in earthy colours and spiced up with African artefacts, has a bath or shower and its own wooden deck with vistas across the forest and Tsitsikamma Mountains; superb food is served as well. From here you could hike for a couple of hours through forest to Keurbooms beach, or drive there in 15min. R3680

Moonshine on Whiskey Creek 14km east of Plettenberg Bay along the N2, signposted north of the N2 ☎ 044 534 8515 or ☎ 072 200 6656, ⓦ whiskeycreek.co.za; map below. Fully equipped bungalows, three wooden cabins and one creatively renovated labourer's cottage (R950), nestled in indigenous forest, with a children's play area. One of the best reasons to come here is the access to a secluded natural mountain pool and waterfall at the bottom of the nearby gorge. There is a little office with views for guests to use the internet. R1440

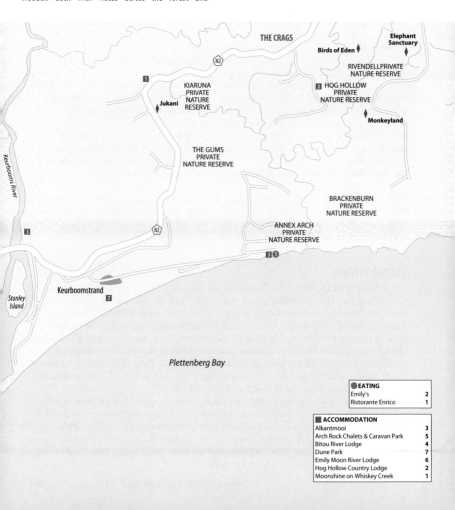

● EATING	
Emily's	2
Ristorante Enrico	1

■ ACCOMMODATION	
Alkantmooi	3
Arch Rock Chalets & Caravan Park	5
Bitou River Lodge	4
Dune Park	7
Emily Moon River Lodge	6
Hog Hollow Country Lodge	2
Moonshine on Whiskey Creek	1

17

WHALE- AND DOLPHIN-WATCHING VIEWPOINTS

Elevated ocean panoramas give Plettenberg Bay outstanding vantages for watching **southern right whales** during their breeding season between June and October. An especially good vantage point is the area between the wreck of the *Athene* at the southern end of Lookout Beach and the Keurbooms River. The Robberg Peninsula is also excellent, looming protectively over this whale nursery and giving a grandstand view of the bay. Other good town viewpoints are from Beachy Head Road at Robberg Beach; Signal Hill in San Gonzales Street past the post office and police station; the *Beacon Island Hotel* on Beacon Island; and the deck of the *Lookout* restaurant on Lookout Beach. Outside Plett, the Kranshoek viewpoint and hiking trail offers wonderful whale-watching points along the route. To get there, head for Knysna, taking the Harkerville turn-off, and continue for 7km. It's also possible to view the occasional pair (mother and calf) at Nature's Valley, 29km east of Plett on the R102, and from Storms River Mouth.

EATING

Restaurants come and go in Plett but one or two long-standing establishments remain afloat. Locally caught fresh **fish** is the thing to look out for. And because the town is built on hills, you should generally expect **terrific views**.

★**Emily's** Rietvlei Rd, off the N2 (turn off at Penny Pinchers) ☎044 533 2982; map pp.222–223. Fine dining restaurant attached to *Emily Moon's Lodge* that many regard as the best in the area, offering stunning views of the Bitou Wetland and classic, sustainable French cuisine with an edge. Vegetarians should try her superb lentil dal (R90) or goat's cheese and beetroot salad (R75). Booking essential, it opens two months in advance, especially for a table on the deck. Mon 6.30–10pm, Tues–Sun noon–3pm & 6.30–10pm.

The Fat Fish Milkwood Centre, Central Beach ☎044 533 4740; map p.218. Cheerful restaurant with reasonably priced seafood including tapas-sized portions of oysters, tempura prawns or salmon, and with various meze platters to share (R85), as well as steaks and heavier dishes, doused with good wines. Daily 11.30–4pm & 5.30–10pm.

Ristorante Enrico Main Beach, Keurboomstrand ☎044 535 9818; map pp.222–223. Casual holiday-feeling restaurant right on the beach with mid-priced Italian standards – thin-based pizzas, pasta and veal (R130) where you can eat outside and enjoy the sea breeze. Tues–Sun noon–9pm.

DRINKING

The Lookout Lookout Beach ☎044 533 1379, ⓦlookout.co.za; map p.218. There are marvellous bay views at this bar-restaurant, with umbrellas and outdoor tables, which focuses on seafood, but with appealing vegetarian options. It's undoubtedly the best place in town for cocktails (R60). Daily 9am–10pm.

Tsitsikamma

The **Tsitsikamma section** of the Garden Route National Park, roughly midway between Plettenberg Bay and Port Elizabeth, is the highlight of any Garden Route trip. Starting from just beyond Keurboomstrand in the west, the section extends for 68km into the Eastern Cape along a narrow belt of coast, with dramatic foamy surges of rocky coast, deep river gorges and ancient hardwood forests clinging to the edge of tangled, green cliffs. Don't pass up its main attraction, the **Storms River Mouth**, the most dramatic estuary on this exhilarating piece of coast. Established in 1964, Tsitsikamma is also South Africa's oldest marine reserve, stretching 5.5km out to sea, with an **underwater trail** open to snorkellers and licensed scuba divers.

Tsitsikamma has two sections: **Nature's Valley** in the west and **Storms River Mouth** in the east. Each section can only be reached down a winding tarred road from the N2 (apart from hiking, there's no way of getting from one to the other). Nature's Valley incorporates the most low-key settlement on the Garden Route, with a fabulous sandy beach stretching for 3km. South Africa's ultimate hike, the five-day **Otter Trail** (see box above), connects the two sections of the park.

OPPOSITE STORMS RIVER MOUTH BRIDGE, TSITSIKAMMA NATIONAL PARK >

17

GARDEN ROUTE LONG-DISTANCE WALKING TRAILS

Dolphin Trail This is the Garden Route's luxury, portered trail with stays in comfortable accommodation, and the only one suitable if you are on holiday on your own without gear. The rest are geared towards locals who are fit hikers in a group, with all the gear.

The terrain through the Tsitsikamma National Park is breathtaking, covering the rugged coastal edge and the natural forest. The price includes a guide, a boat trip up the Storms River Gorge and a 4WD drive through the Storms River Pass. *Start: Storms River Mouth; end: Sandrif River Mouth; distance: 20km; duration: three and a half days* (☎042 280 3588, ✆dolphintrail .co.za) *cost: R5990 per person sharing, including food, accommodation and permits.*

Otter Trail The Otter Trail is South Africa's flagship hike; it is simply magnificent hiking a pristine stretch of coastline and forest where there is no habitation or vehicle access. It is geared to locals, in a group. If you're desperate to walk the Otter Trail and have been told that the trip is full, don't despair – keep checking the website for cancellations. You need to be fit for the steep sections and be an experienced hiker – you carry everything from hut to hut and need to be able to manage river crossings. *Start: Storms River Mouth; end: Nature's Valley; distance: 42km; duration: five days; booking through South African National Parks, at least twelve months in advance* (☎012 428 911, ✆sanparks.org). The maximum number of people on the trail is twelve: Starts at R1150 per person.

Tsitsikamma Trail Not to be confused with the Otter Trail, this is an inland hike through indigenous forest, long stretches of open *fynbos* and the Tsitsikamma mountain range. Five overnight huts accommodate 24 people and it is a strenuous hike. They have now introduced porterage, which makes everything a lot easier. *Start: Nature's Valley; end: Storms River Bridge; distance: 60km; duration: six days, though shorter versions through: MTO Ecotourism* (☎042 281 1712, ✆mtoecotourism.co.za); *cost: R200 per person per night.*

Harkerville Coastal Trail Closer to the roads, this circular trail doesn't feel as remote as the Otter Trail but is a good second-best, taking in magnificent rocky coastline, indigenous forest and *fynbos*. Lots of rock scrambling and some traversing of exposed, narrow ledges above the sea is required, so don't attempt this without experience of scrambling on exposed rock, or a good degree of fitness. Because of its short duration, it is often a good choice if you don't have much time. *Start and end: Harkerville Forestry Station, 12km west of Plettenberg Bay, signposted off the N2; distance: 26.5km; duration: two days; cost: R260 per person. Bookings contact* ☎044 302 5600 *and* ✉reservations@sanparks.org.

The nearest settlement to Storms River Mouth, some 14km to its north at the top of a steep winding road, is the confusingly named **Storms River Village**, which is outside the national park and some distance from any part of the river, though appealingly set in forest. Storms River Village makes a convenient base for adventure activities in the vicinity and day-trips down to Storms River Mouth.

Nature's Valley

Nature's Valley, at the western end of the Tsitsikamma Section of the Garden Route National Park, 29km east of Plettenberg Bay and two and a half hours' drive from Port Elizabeth (204km), extends into the hilly interior. It incorporates a settlement of wooden houses set on the beautiful Groot River Lagoon, with 20km of beach and miles of forest to explore. The strict legislation here (highly unusual in South Africa) means there are no crass holiday houses, hotels or tour buses and only one small restaurant and village shop.

There are plenty of good **walks** at Nature's Valley, many starting from the national park campsite, 1km north of the village, where you can pick up maps and information. One of the loveliest places to head for is **Salt River Mouth**, 3km west of Nature's Valley, where you can swim and picnic – though you'll need to ford the river at low tide. This walk starts and ends at the café at Nature's Valley. Also recommended is the circular 6km **Kalanderkloof trail**, which starts at the national park campsite, ascends to a lookout point, and descends via a narrow river gorge graced with a profusion of huge Outeniqua yellowwood trees and Cape wild bananas.

ARRIVAL AND INFORMATION

By car There is no public transport to Nature's Valley and the only way of getting there is by car, taking the beautiful Groot River Pass road that winds down through riverine forest from the N2, 2km east of The Crags. Nature's Valley is at the bottom of the pass, 11km after the turn-off. The road continues from Nature's Valley and rejoins the N2 after 9km, just west of the Bloukrans River Bridge. The detour is

NATURE'S VALLEY 17

worth it – the last relic of the Garden Route as it was before the N2 sped through it – with a chance of encountering baboons and vervet monkeys along the way.

Tourist information The *Nature's Valley Trading Store* (see below) is effectively the village centre and acts as an informal information bureau. If you're self-catering, stock up on supplies before you get to Nature's Valley.

ACCOMMODATION

Accommodation in Nature's Valley itself is pretty limited, which contributes to its low-key charm, but there are options on the road leading off the N2 into the village, just before the switchbacks begin.

Four Fields Farm Nature's Valley Rd, 3km from the N2 along the R102 and 8km from Nature's Valley ☎044 534 8708, ⍈fourfields.iowners.net. A welcoming and charmingly unpretentious former dairy farm, less than 10min drive from the sea. The self-catering farmhouse has four bedrooms simply furnished with beautiful old pieces and with French doors leading to their own private decks, which in turn open onto a much-loved garden surrounded by fields. There is also a flat that sleeps four (R1200) and another which sleeps a couple (R660). R2400

Lily Pond Lodge 102 Nature's Valley Rd, 3km from the N2 along the R102 and 6km from Nature's Valley ☎044 534 8767, ⍈lilypond.co.za. Probably the most memorable accommodation in Nature's Valley, this lodge distinguishes itself through its commitment to luxury. The four en-suite rooms have patio doors opening onto private terraces, plus sound systems and TVs, while the spacious luxury suites also have their own lounge, under-floor heating and king-sized beds. The honeymoon suite that has its own private garden; there is also a large, shared garden on-site. R1980

★**Nature's Valley Restcamp** 1km to the north of the village. Campsites tucked into indigenous forest, and basic two-person forest huts with communal ablution facilities. Bookings through South African National Parks (☎044 531 6700, ⍈sanparks.org/parks/garden_route/camps/natures _valley) or if you're already in Nature's Valley, the camp supervisor ☎044 531 6700. Camping R205, hut R510

Rocky Road Backpackers 1.5km from the N2 along

the R102, 12 km from Nature's Valley ☎072 270 2114, ⍈rockyroadbackpackers.com. A tranquil backpacker retreat set on a large forested property. While the setting and landscaped gardens are the big draw, it also has an outdoor pizza oven, forest bathroom and a highly sociable Friday braai night. There is a range of sleeping options, the most appealing being the luxury tents with soft bedding and electric blankets. It's on the Baz Bus route. Camping R100, luxury tent R220, dorms R190, doubles R500

Tranquility Lodge 130 St Michael's Ave (next to the shop) ☎044 531 6663, ⍈tranquilitylodge.co.za. If Nature's Valley has a centre, then this comfortable lodge, next to the village's only shop, is bang in the middle of it. A two-storey brick and timber building set in a garden that feels as if it's part of the encroaching forest, it is just 50m from the beach. Breakfast is served on an upstairs deck among the treetops. All rooms are en-suite and there's also a larger honeymoon suite (R1800) with double shower, fireplace and private deck. R1500

★**Wild Spirit Lodge and Backpackers** Nature's Valley Rd, 8km from Nature's Valley ☎044 534 8888, ⍈wildspiritlodge.co.za. One of the best Garden Route lodges, which has an alternative focus, with accommodation in bunk-free dorms in three, two-storey garden cottages and safari tents. You can explore forests, or hang out in the tree house. There is a kitchen for self-catering, a yoga and meditation room, book exchange, live music and drumming nights and a big outdoor braai. It's on the Baz Bus route. Camping R90, bunk-free dorms R150, doubles R450

EATING AND DRINKING

Nature's Valley Trading Store Corner of Forest & St Michael's ☎044 531 6835. The only place in the village that does food and booze is a pretty informal and convivial

spot for seafood, steaks, burgers (R70) and toasted sandwiches, and provides the only nightlife – a large-screen TV. Daily 9am–8.30pm.

Storms River Mouth

55km east of Plettenberg Bay • Daily 7am–7pm • Day-visitor R90; overnight, on top of accommodation R200 • ☎042 281 1607

In contrast to the languid lagoon and soft sands of Nature's Valley, **Storms River Mouth**, 55km from Plettenberg Bay, presents the Garden Route's elemental face with the Storms River surging through a gorge to battle the surf. Don't confuse this with **Storms River Village** just off the N2, which is nowhere near the sea, but right in the forest.

17

Walking is the main activity at the Mouth, and at the visitors' office at the restcamp you can get **maps** of short, waymarked coastal trails that leave from here. These include walks up the forested cliffs, where you can see 800-year-old yellowwood trees with views onto a stretch of ocean. Most rewarding is the 3km **hike** west from the restcamp along the start of the Otter Trail to a fantastic **waterfall** pool at the base of 50m-high falls. Less demanding is the 1km **boardwalk stroll** from the restaurant to the suspension bridge to see the river mouth. On your way to the bridge, don't miss the dank *strandloper* (beachcomber) **cave**. Hunter-gatherers frequented this area between five thousand and two thousand years ago, living off seafood in wave-cut caves near the river mouth. A modest display shows an excavated midden, with layers of little bones and shells. The area's most popular walks, however, are the Dolphin and Otter trails (see box, p.226). **Swimming** at the Mouth is restricted to a safe little sandy bay below the restaurant, with a changing hut, though it can be cold in summer if there are easterly winds and cold upwellings of deep water from the continental shelf.

ARRIVAL AND DEPARTURE   STORMS RIVER MOUTH

By car Storms River Mouth is 18km south of Storms River Bridge: you'll need your own wheels to get around here as there's no public transport to the Mouth. Most people stop at the bridge, on the N2, to gaze into the deep river gorge

and fill up at the beautifully located petrol station.
By shuttle *Tsitsikamma Backpackers* (see p.229) can arrange a shuttle service for their guests from Storms River Village to the Mouth (R100/person; minimum three passengers).

ACCOMMODATION

Storms River Mouth Restcamp 18km south of Storms River Bridge ☎ 042 281 1607, ⚝ sanparks.org/parks /garden_route/camps/storms_river. Sited on tended lawns, *Storms River Mouth Restcamp* is poised between a craggy shoreline of black rocks pounded by foamy white surf and steeply raking forested cliffs, and is the ultimate location along the southern Cape coast. It has a variety of

accommodation options, not especially nice and rather modest and worn, but all with sea views and the ever-present sound of the surging surf. Advance booking through South African National Parks is essential and you may have to take whatever is available, as its location makes it understandably popular. Two units have disabled access. Camping R390, forest hut R755, chalet or oceanette R1385

EATING

Tsitsikamma Restaurant Storms River Mouth Restcamp. The only place to eat at the restcamp has such startling views that it can be forgiven its rather mediocre fare of English breakfasts, toasted sandwiches,

burgers, pastas and steak, and often indifferent service. They do a reasonable range of seafood dishes (R120) and you can get a drink out on the wooden deck. Daily 8.30am–10pm.

Storms River Village

About a kilometre south of the national road, **STORMS RIVER VILLAGE** is a tranquil place crisscrossed by a handful of dirt roads and with a few dozen houses, enjoying mountain vistas, with easy access to hike in the state-run forest, which is literally on the doorstep. The main attraction of the village is as a centre for adventure activities, of which the canopy tour zip-line is a highlight.

ARRIVAL AND DEPARTURE   STORMS RIVER VILLAGE

By Baz Bus The only transport into Storms River Village proper, the Baz Bus pulls in at the backpacker hostels daily on its way between Cape Town and Port Elizabeth.
By intercity bus Greyhound, Translux and Intercape intercity buses pull in on their daily hauls along the N2 between Cape Town and Port Elizabeth at the filling station at the Storms River Bridge, some 5km from the village.
Destinations Cape Town (2 daily; 10hr 25min); Knysna

(2 daily; 1hr 20min); Mossel Bay (2 daily; 3hr); Plettenberg Bay (2 daily; 50min); Port Elizabeth (2 daily; 2hr 30min); Sedgefield (2 daily; 1hr 40min).

By shuttle bus Some of the backpacker hostels, among them *Tsitsikamma Backpackers*, offer a free shuttle service to and from the bridge from 8am till 5pm, as well as a paid shuttle to Storms River Mouth, the Bloukrans Bungee site, Nature's Valley and Plettenberg Bay.

17

ACTIVITIES

BOAT TRIPS AND TUBING

SANParks ☎ 042 281 1607. Trips run for up to twelve people (R180 for 30min trip and conservation gate entry fee) about 1km up Storms River. Booking is at the *Storms River Mouth restcamp*, at the Untouched Adventures office, close to the boathouse, below the restcamp's restaurant.

Tube 'n Axe Backpackers ☎ 042 281 1757, ⓦ tubenaxe.co.za. Trips operate down the Storms River gorge, where you ride the river and its rapids buoyed up by a small inflatable (R595 half-day, R995 full day).

TOURS

Woodcutters' Journey ☎ 042 281 1836, ⓦ stormsriver .com. A relaxed jaunt organized by Storms River Adventures (trips R300–R400), headquartered next to the post office. It takes you through the forest to the river along the old Storms River Pass in a specially designed trailer, drawn by a tractor.

ZIP LINE

Storms River Adventures ☎ 042 281 1836, ⓦ stormsriver.com. The Canopy Tour (R750) gives a bird's-eye view of the forest as you travel 30m above ground along a series of interconnected cables attached to the tallest trees. The system has been constructed in such a way that not a single nail has been hammered into any tree.

Tsitsikamma Falls Adventures ☎ 042 280 3770, ⓦ tsitsikammaadventure.co.za. A faster, higher alternative, geared more to adrenaline junkies, is the zip-line tour across the Kruis River at Tsitsikamma Falls Adventures (R380), which at times is 50m above the ground and crisscrosses an awesome ravine, zipping over three waterfalls, with the longest slide measuring 211m.

ACCOMMODATION

The Armagh Fynbos Ave ☎ 042 281 1512, ⓦ thearmagh.com. A hospitable and very comfortable guesthouse with excellent bathrooms and bed linen, in a beautiful garden that drifts off into the *fynbos*. The rooms include two budget rooms, four standard ones, a garden cottage and an ultra luxurious and very private honeymoon room, all of which open onto the garden. There's a nice swimming pool and a decent restaurant. R1200

★**At the Woods Guest House** 49 Formosa St, along the main drag into town ☎ 042 281 1446, ⓦ atthewoods.co.za. Friendly, modern guesthouse that's the nicest place in town, with traditional reed ceilings and large, comfortable rooms with king-sized beds and French doors that open onto garden verandas, or, upstairs, onto private decks with mountain views. and there's a communal lounge with a fireplace where you can use the internet. They also have a very nice café for meals. R1190

Tsitsikamma Backpackers 54 Formosa St ☎ 042 281 1868, ⓦ tsitsikammabackpackers.co.za. Well-run hostel, whose accommodation options include luxury tents set in a beautiful garden that claims environmentally friendly and fair-trade credentials. You can self-cater or order a reasonably priced breakfast or dinner and there's a bar. They offer a shuttle service to local attractions and pick up guests for free from the Storms River Bridge. Dorms R180, luxury tent R500, doubles R600

Tsitsikamma Village Inn Darnell St, along the road into the village and left at the T-junction ☎ 042 281 1711, ⓦ tsitsikammahotel.co.za. An old-fashioned and consistently well-run hotel in the village amid the trees and with a well-tended garden. It has 49 rooms in eleven cottage units, which does draw tours, and has the advantage of a pub, micro-brewery and restaurant on the premises. R1400

Tube 'n Axe Backpackers Cnr Darnell and Saffron sts ☎ 042 281 1757, ⓦ tubenaxe.co.za. A wacky place that works hard to compete by offering drumming nights, a pool table and bonfires. On the Baz Bus route, and they can collect or drop off at the Storms River Bridge bus stop for mainline coaches, as well as offer shuttles around the area. They also give discounted rates for the adventure activities too. Camping R105, dorms R175, doubles R480

EATING AND DRINKING

De Oude Martha Tsitsikamma Village Inn, Darnell St. Acceptable, if unexceptional, hotel restaurant that serves up unpretentious breakfasts, lunches and dinners (mains average R160). Their cosy pub has a welcoming fireplace, and the micro-brewery is good. Daily 7am–9pm.

Rafters The Armagh, Fynbos Ave. The dinner menu has an emphasis on the local: South African cuisine using garden greens in their salads, fish from Plettenberg Bay and meat sourced nearby. Cape Muslim sweet and mild curries feature big on the menu (R130). Daily 8am–9pm.

Tsitrus Café At the Woods Guest House, 49 Formosa Street. The best choice for a light lunch, this place uses fresh ingredients and serves up a small menu of soups and salads (R75) as well as pizza and cheesecake. Daily 8am–8pm.

Route 62 and the Little Karoo

One of the most rewarding journeys in the Western Cape – an inland counterpart to the Garden Route (see p.195) – is the mountain route from Cape Town to Port Elizabeth, which is largely along the R62 and thus is often referred to as Route 62. Nowhere near as well known as the coastal journey, this trip takes you through some of the most dramatic passes and *poorts* (valley routes) in the country and crosses a frontier of *dorps* (villages) and drylands. This "back garden" is in many respects more rewarding than the actual Garden Route, being far less developed, with spectacular landscapes and quieter roads. It also has some of the nicest small towns in South Africa to visit, with characterful guesthouses and restaurants, bearing only a patina of tourism.

With no scheduled public transport, apart from intercity buses between Oudtshoorn and Cape Town, this is a journey best done by car – minibus taxis are available in some destinations but run on demand and cannot be organized much in advance. Though it's easily possible to drive to Oudtshoorn from Cape Town in a day, it's worth breaking up your journey to explore the pretty towns of **McGregor**, **Montagu** and **Barrydale**. Continuing east from Barrydale, the R62 landscape becomes more sparse as you get into the **Little Karoo** (or Klein Karoo), a vast, khaki-coloured hinterland (the name is a Khoi word meaning "hard and dry") with low, wiry scrub and dotted with flat-topped hills. One unsung surprise along the way is **Calitzdorp**, a rustic little *dorp*, five hours' solid driving from Cape Town, down whose backstreets a few unassuming wine farms produce some of South Africa's best port, with some first-rate guest houses. Staying here may be a lot more satisfying then Oudtshoorn itself, which is a lot busier.

18

By contrast, the well-trumpeted attractions of **Oudtshoorn**, half an hour further on, are the ostrich farms and the massive **Cango Caves**, one of the country's biggest tourist draws. Less than 70km from the coast, with good transport connections, Oudtshoorn marks the convergence of the mountain and coastal roads and is usually treated as a leisurely day-trip away from the Garden Route. From Oudtshoorn, over the most dramatic of all passes in the Cape – the unpaved **Swartberg Pass**, 27km of spectacular switchbacks and zigzags through the Swartberg Mountains – is **Prince Albert**, a favourite Karoo village whose spartan beauty and remarkable light make it popular with artists.

Worcester

WORCESTER, the large functional hub of the region, is on the N1 just 110km from Cape Town, and worth a stop if you are interested in Cape flora. Worcester is an agricultural centre at the heart of a wine-making region, consisting mostly of co-operatives producing bulk plonk, and for most travellers it marks the place to buy petrol and deviate from the N1 onto the scenic R62. However, it's worth considering stopping for a break and a cup of tea at the peaceful botanic gardens. An interesting piece of local knowledge is that J.M. Coetzee, South Africa's most internationally acclaimed writer, grew up here, though nothing yet in the town makes mention of its famous son.

Karoo Desert Botanic Gardens

108 Roux Rd · Gardens: daily 7am–7pm; restaurant: Mon–Sat 8.30am–9pm, Sun 8.30am–4pm · R25 · ☎ 023 347 0785, ⓦ sanbi.org

As you enter Worcester from Cape Town, signs point to the **Karoo Botanic Gardens**, a sister reserve to Kirstenbosch in Cape Town, known for its show of indigenous spring flowers and succulents. The pleasant **restaurant** here, which serves light meals, looks out over the gardens and the distant mountains. The best time to visit the gardens is from late July to early September when all the flowers people travel to see in Namaqualand bloom here in a profusion of purples, oranges and yellows. Three hiking trails meander through large wild areas, full of desert plants and prickly blooms, and in the winter, snow caps the dramatic backdrop of the Hex River mountain range.

McGregor

McGREGOR is an attractive small village, with whitewashed cottages that sparkle in the summer daylight amid the low scrub, vines and olive trees. Its quiet, relaxed atmosphere has attracted a small population of spiritual seekers and artists, and residents are urged to build in harmony with existing style and thus maintain the town's character. It makes a great weekend break from Cape Town, with a couple of first-rate restaurants, plenty of well-priced accommodation and a beautiful retreat centre with reasonably priced massages and other body-work. Spending a day wine tasting around McGregor and its environs is another drawing card, as long as it's not a Sunday when almost everything is closed.

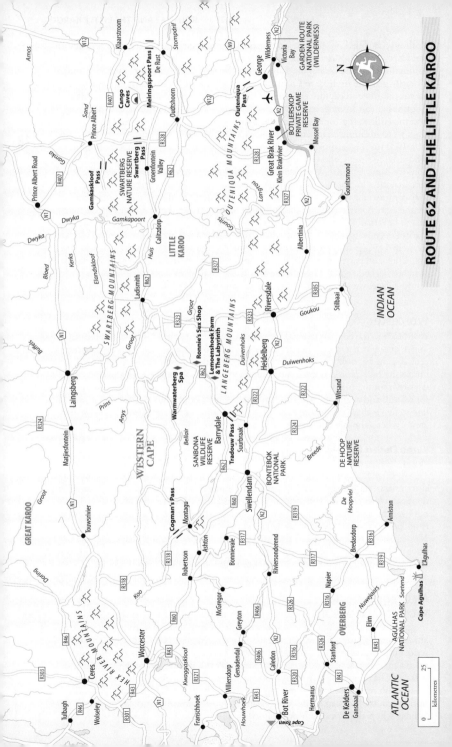

ROUTE 62 AND THE LITTLE KAROO

McGregor gained modest prosperity in the nineteenth century by becoming a centre of the whipstock industry, supplying wagoners and transport riders with long bamboo sticks for goading oxen. There aren't too many ox-drawn wagons today, and tourism, though developing, is still quite limited. One reason people come here is to walk the **Boesmanskloof Traverse** (see p.191), which starts 14km from McGregor and crosses to Greyton on the other side of the mountain. From McGregor you can walk a section of the trail, hiking to the main waterfall and back to the trailhead, which is a three- to four-hour round hike of exceeding beauty through the river gorge, or *kloof* in Afrikaans.

18

ARRIVAL AND INFORMATION — MCGREGOR

By car McGregor, 180km from Cape Town and 15min to the south of Robertson, is at the end of a minor road signposted off the R60. Don't be tempted by an approach from the south which may look like a handy back route – you'd need a 4WD for this. Allow 2hr 30min for the drive from Cape Town along the N1, turning onto the R62 at Worcester for Robertson.

Tourist office Voortrekker St (Mon–Sat 9am–1pm & 2–4.30pm, Sun 9am–1pm; ☎023 625 1954, ⓦtourismmcgregor.co.za). The office can book accommodation and issue permits for walking the whole Boesmanskloof Traverse or simply for the waterfall section (R40). They will also direct you to artists' studios in town, and to complementary health practitioners offering massage and yoga, and give you the times of the daily meditation sessions at the *Temenos Country Retreat*.

ACCOMMODATION

Green Gables Country Inn 7 Smith St ☎023 625 1626, ⓦgreengablesmcgregor.co.za. Country accommodation at the edge of the village, with a swimming pool, an English-style pub and a restaurant open three nights a week. The decor is cosy, if slightly cluttered, and the service is warm and personal; rates are very reasonable for what you get. **R900**

McGregor Backpackers Bree St ☎083 206 8007, ⓦmcgregorbackpackers.co.za. Comfortable, homely accommodation in a variety of room types catering for couples or groups. There's only room for twenty-five guests so the place is quiet enough. **R500**

The Old Village Lodge Voortrekker St ☎023 625 1692, ⓦoldvillagelodge.co.za. Upmarket B&B in a Victorian cottage on the main road, with a pretty garden, swimming pool and rooms furnished in an elegant and comfortable country style. **R1300**

Rhebokskraal Farm Cottages 2km south of town ☎082 896 0429, ⓦrhebokskraalolives.co.za. Secluded cottages, each on a different part of this beautiful fruit, olive and grape farm, which is within easy reach of the restaurants in town. **R700**

★**Tanagra Guest Wine Farm** 4.5km northeast of McGregor, towards Robertson ☎023 625 1780, ⓦtanagra-wines.co.za. Idyllic wine farm with stylish, light and airy cottages, all with private verandas and mountain views. One cottage is totally off-the-grid, with a private plunge pool, hammocks and a fireplace. There are walking trails on the farm itself or on the adjoining Vrolijkheid Nature Reserve. It is fully equipped for self-catering. **R900**

★**Temenos Country Retreat** Cnr of Bree and Voortrekker sts ☎023 625 1871, ⓦtemenos.org.za. Retreat centre with cottages dotted about beautiful gardens and walkways, a swimming pool, library and meditation spaces. Breakfast is included and it's safe and peaceful – an ideal place for solo women travellers. **R815**

Whipstock Farm 7km southwest of McGregor, towards Boesmanskloof ☎073 042 3919, ⓦwhipstock.co.za. Farm accommodation in a Victorian house with five cottages, each with whitewashed walls, wooden beams, fridges and tea-making facilities. Meals are served communally in a large dining room with a fireplace. It's ideal for families who want a nature-based holiday; self-catering rates are also available. **R560**

EATING AND DRINKING

Bemind Garagiste Wines 45 Voortrekker St ☎083 380 1648. A chance to try McGregor wines in a very relaxed atmosphere where you can chat to the winemaker Ilsa, who produces small quantities of Sauvignon Blanc, MCC Brut, Shiraz and Cinsault. The price of a bottle is reasonable (R90–R170). Wed–Fri 10am–5pm & Sat 10am–2pm.

Flora's Eating House & Gallery 54 Voortrekker St ☎082 070 9004. Great for fresh and interesting breakfasts and lunches. You can sit on the front or back porch to savour

home-made food, such as a Turkish-style breakfast, spicy lentil soup, free-range chicken dishes, vegan salads (R75) or bockwurst with mash. Delicious cakes, often gluten free. Booking essential. Mon 6–9pm, Thurs–Sun 9am–3pm.

Green Gables Country Inn 7 Smith St ☎023 625 1626, ⓦgreengablesmcgregor.co.za. Alfresco dinners on the terrace overlooking vineyards and the village, with a cosy dining room warmed with a fireplace in winter, plus a "village pub". There are generally three well-cooked dishes on offer, such as chicken curry, fish and chips, and lamb shank (R115). The simplicity of the dishes belies their quality. Booking in advance. Wed & Fri–Sun 6–10pm.

★**Karoux Restaurant** 42 Voortrekker St ☎023 625 1421. Award-winning gourmet food you wouldn't expect to find in a sleepy village, such as pan-roasted duck breast with cauliflower puree, wilted baby spinach, confit lamb croquettes and free-range chicken liver parfait with truffled blueberry vinaigrette (R140). Booking essential. Wed–Sat 7–10pm & Sun noon–3pm.

Tebaldi's at Temenos Cnr of Bree and Voortrekker sts ☎023 625 1871, ⓦtemenos.org.za. Fading a little alongside the upstart gourmet newcomers, but still reliable. Breakfasts and salad lunches served in a tranquil garden setting, or on the street-facing *stoep*. Tues & Sun 9.30am–3.30pm, Wed–Sat 9.30am–3.30pm & 7–9.30pm.

Montagu

Some 190km from Cape Town, and 47km from McGregor, is **MONTAGU**, the centre of a major peach- and apricot-growing region whose soaring mountains with twisted red and ochre strata dominate the town with its pleasing Victorian architecture.

The town was named in 1851 after **John Montagu**, the visionary British Secretary of the Cape, who realized that the colony would never develop without decent communications and was responsible for commissioning the first mountain passes connecting remote areas to Cape Town. Montagu is best known for its **hot springs**, but serious **rock climbers** come for its cliff faces, which are regarded as among the country's most challenging. You can also explore the mountains on a couple of trails or, easiest of all, on a tractor ride onto one of the peaks. Montagu is also conveniently positioned for excursions along both the Robertson and Little Karoo **wine routes**.

Highly photogenic, Montagu is ideal for exploring on foot. As you wander around you can take in the interesting buildings or simply enjoy the setting, with the Langeberg Mountains, valleys and farms.

Montagu Museum

41 Long St • Mon–Fri 9am–4.30pm, Sat & Sun 10.30am–noon • R10

The best thing about the **Montagu Museum**, housed in a pleasant old church, is its herbal project, which traces traditional Khoisan knowledge about the medicinal properties of local plants. Note the peach pips embedded in the floor, to give texture, and the peach kernels used to create the driveway, both of which are typical in these fruit-growing parts.

Montagu Springs Resort

3km northwest of Montagu on the R318 • Daily 8am–11pm • R100 • ⓦmontagusprings.co.za

Montagu's best known attraction, the **Montagu Springs Resort** is home to several chlorinated open-air pools of different temperatures and a couple of Jacuzzis, spectacularly situated at the foot of the cliffs – an effect slightly spoilt by the neon lights of a hotel complex and fast-food restaurant. It's a nice place to take kids, but the weekends become a mass of splashing bodies: if you want a quiet time, go first thing in the morning or last thing at night. The temperatures in winter are not hot enough to be entirely comfortable, when you're better off heading to the springs at **Caledon** (see p.191) or **Warmwaterberg** (see box, p.238), which are much hotter, and in many respects preferable.

ARRIVAL AND INFORMATION
MONTAGU

By car Montagu is 190km from Cape Town; take the N1 as far as Worcester and then head southeast on the R60. The journey from Worcester (roughly 60km) takes you through Robertson and Ashton.

By minibus Danie (☎072 750 3125) runs a very reasonably priced on-demand shuttle service (R170)

between Montagu and Cape Town, but you will need to be flexible about time of departure and arrival, as well as the number of stops.

Tourist office 24 Bath St (Mon–Fri 8am–6pm, Sat 9am–5pm, Sun 9.30am–2pm; ☎023 614 2471, ⓦmontagu-ashton.info).

ACCOMMODATION

★ **Aasvoelkrans** 1 Van Riebeeck St ☏ 023 614 1228, ⓦ aasvoelkrans.co.za. Set in a pretty part of town, these four exceptionally imaginative garden rooms are housed in a guesthouse situated on a farm with competition Arab horses grazing in the fields. There is also a two-bedroomed self-catering cottage suitable for a family or larger group. Cottage R900, doubles R1000

De Bos Guest Farm 8 Brown St ☏ 023 614 2532, ⓦ debos.co.za. Camping (in lovely shady sites), dorms and basic doubles on a farm at the western edge of town, close to the spectacular, twisted mountain slopes. The farm often accommodates rock climbers who bring their own kit to tackle climbs in the area, but you don't have to be a rock climber to enjoy staying here – there are also hikes on the doorstep. Camping R80, dorms R130, doubles R900

Montagu Rose Guest House 19 Kohler St ☏ 023 614 2681, ⓦ montagurose.co.za. All of the rooms in this well-run, modern guesthouse, decorated with plenty of paintings and knicknacks, have baths and mountain views; one is wheelchair-friendly, and there is a family room for four. R800

Montagu Springs Signposted off the R62, west of town ☏ 023 614 1050, ⓦ montagusprings.co.za. Large resort with fully equipped self-catering chalets, some more luxurious than others, sleeping four. It is especially suitable for families as children will love the pools and playing areas. Prices go down by roughly a third during the week. R1300

Squirrel's Corner Cnr of Bloem and Jouberts sts ☏ 023 614 1081, ⓦ squirrelscorner.co.za. A reasonably priced B&B situated two blocks from the main road, with four comfortable, spotless en-suite rooms in the main house, as well as an African-themed garden suite. You will be greeted with a glass of Montagu muscadel on arrival. R970

EATING AND DRINKING

The farm stalls as you drive through Montagu on the R62 are worth stopping at for nibbles and local produce, and there are several appealing **cafés** to choose from on Long Street. In summer, bags of peaches and apricots are often sold from backyards or along the roadside, for next to nothing. On Saturday mornings, don't miss the local **farmers' market** at the church, where you can get olives and olive oil, bread, cheese, almonds and dried fruit from the surrounding farms – all of which are exceptionally well priced. All **restaurants** need to be booked ahead for dinner.

Die Stal 8km out of town on the R318 ☏ 082 324 4318. A thoroughly pleasant venue on a farm, serving breakfast, lunches and tea. A good destination if you want to see something of the surrounding orchards and farmlands. A hearty favourite is the lamb rump (R130), while vegetarians can opt for the ploughman's platter (R85). Tues–Sun 9am–5pm.

Ma Cuisine Mimosa Lodge, 19 Church St ☏ 023 614 235. Reserve a candle-lit table for a memorable dinner along the R62, in a posh guesthouse. Expect to dine on South African dishes with a French influence, such as Karoo lamb with muscadel and thyme jus. Vegetarians are also catered for, with good and fresh ingredients. There's a four-course set menu for R500, which costs R670 with wine. Daily 6–9pm.

Mystic Tin 38 Bath St ☏ 082 572 0738, ⓦ themystictin.co.za. Tablecloths, candlelight and a winter fireplace create a cosy atmosphere to enjoy South African specialities done with flair. The ostrich fillet is worth a try (R110) and there are a couple of appealing vegetarian options, all accompanied by hand-crafted beers brewed in their Karoo microbrewery. Mon–Sat 5–9.30pm.

Simply Delicious Restaurant Four Oaks, 46 Long St ☏ 023 614 3483, ⓦ four-oaks.co.za. A good choice for a light lunch or dinner, set in a handsome 1860 thatched house with a shady courtyard. Dishes include steak with seasonal vegetables (R125) and various wraps and salads. Summer daily 12.30–2.30pm & 7–9pm; winter Mon–Sat 12.30–2.30pm & 6.30–9pm.

Barrydale

BARRYDALE, 240km from Cape Town, is perfect for a couple of days of doing very little other than experiencing small-town life in the Little Karoo, visiting the hot springs at **Warmwaterberg** (see box, p.238), picnicking along the Tradouw Pass and wine tasting. The village has a couple of excellent restaurants, some good, reasonably priced accommodation and a number of craft outlets. And the drive here, a 60km journey from Montagu, offers spectacular mountain scenery – as does the route from Swellendam via the Tradouw Pass. There's a distinct rural feel about the place: a large vineyard is just off the main road, farm animals are kept on large plots of land behind dry-stone walling, and you'll find fig, peach and quince trees thriving in the dryness.

Its arid beauty has attracted its fair share of artists, and every December, on the weekend closest to the December 16 public holiday, the Handspring Puppet Company,

18

famous for *War Horse*, have an open-air show at the local school with a street parade of puppets, as part of their annual community project in Barrydale.

ARRIVAL AND INFORMATION BARRYDALE

By car Allow 3–3hr 30min for the journey from Cape Town, either taking the N1 and R62, via Montagu, or the N2, and cutting inland on the R324 just east of Swellendam for the lovely drive through Suurbraak and the Tradouw Pass. Both routes are equally recommended for the scenery and ease of travel.

Tourist office There's a tiny visitor information centre

(Mon–Fri 9am–5pm, Sat & Sun 9am–2pm; ☏028 572 1572, ✉barrydale@swellendamtourism.co.za) on the R62, in the strip of shops and restaurants, closest to *Diesel and Cream Diner*. They can also help with finding accommodation.

Services There's a supermarket on the main drag, van Riebeeck Street, which houses an ATM and post office.

ACCOMMODATION

Inkaroo Cottage 2 Bain St, close to Clarke of the Karoo ☏028 572 1344. Beautifully restored and furnished in a contemporary style, this typical Karoo farmhouse cottage sleeps up to six people on a self-catering basis. It has dry stone walling and seating at the back of the house under vines, and a full kitchen and living room, with sunset views onto the mountains. R800

★**Tradouw Guest House** 46 van Riebeeck St ☏028 572 1434, �🌐tradouwguesthouse.co.za. One of

the best places to stay along the R62 is Leon and Denis' friendly *Tradouw Guest House*. The simple rooms have thick white cotton sheets and blankets, and feature sash windows – four of these rooms open out onto the courtyard, while two open onto the large garden. In the winter there's a roaring fire in the lounge, while in the summer guests can enjoy breakfast in the vine-shaded courtyard. The rates are reasonable, with breakfast an extra R100 per person. R700

EATING

There's a number of places to eat strung along the R62 – many of which are only open during the day and cater to the passing traffic. However, you will always find at least one restaurant open in the evening – it's best to book in advance.

Clarke of the Karoo Mud Gallery, on R62 ☏028 572 1017, �🌐clarkeofthekaroo.co.za. A great option for hearty country food, with a starter provided on the house. Their Karoo lamb burgers or curry and *roti* are recommended, and this is the most restful place to stop for a meal, if you are swinging through Barrydale, with pleasant dry-stone walled courtyard seating. They also serve dinner on Wednesday nights (R130 for two courses). Mon, Tues & Thurs–Sun 8am–4pm, Wed 8am–8pm.

Diesel and Creme Vintage Diner on R62 ☏028 572 1008. The most popular stop along the R62, this place is always packed. The interior is a retro style, having been

done up with junk to create the romance of Route 66 road trips. Their milkshakes are the thing to go for, and burgers the order of the day (R70). Daily 8am–5pm.

★**Mez Karoo Kitchen** van Riebeeck St ☏082 077 5980. Outstanding and reasonably priced Mediterranean food and wine, served at the chef's spacious home, including light tapas meals and their Greek lamb speciality (R140). The bright pink rose-water ice cream served with pistachios and fresh mint, or the honey and rose ice cream are memorable. Sitting in the garden on a summer's evening is a delight. Book ahead and check the hours, which can vary a bit. Tues, Thurs–Sat 6–10pm, Sun 11am–2pm; closed in winter.

SANBONA WILDLIFE RESERVE

The striking semi-desert landscape of the massive **Sanbona Wildlife Reserve** (☏021 010 0028, 🌐sanbona.com) is a luxurious option for time-strapped visitors set on seeing some big game, who can't make it to Kruger National Park. Twenty kilometres west of Barrydale, the reserve offers three ultra luxurious all-inclusive lodges, as well as a walking and camping option. Of the lodges, *Dwyka Tented Lodge* is closer to where most of the wildlife is to be found and has the more spectacular setting, though to get closer to nature opt for the *Explorer Camp* – a walking and mobile camping option (R4612 per person). The prices include all your meals and accommodation, plus two game drives a day, but, owing to the vegetation and climate, there are far fewer animals able to be supported here compared with Kruger National Park. Having said that, it is the only place in the Western Cape with free-roaming lions and cheetahs and there's a herd of elephants.

FROM TOP FEATHER PALACE, OUDTSHOORN (P.238); THE CANGO CAVES (P.241); THE SWARTBERG PASS >

WARMWATERBERG SPA

Thirty kilometres east of Barrydale (just beyond *Ronnie's Sex Shop*, a pub and well-known landmark in the middle of nowhere), is **Warmwaterberg Spa** (☎028 572 1609, ⓦwarmwaterbergspa.co.za), a Karoo farm blessed with natural hot water siphoned into two outdoor, unchlorinated hot pools and surrounded by lush green lawns and lofty palms. Primarily aimed at South Africans, it gets rather crowded and noisy during school holidays and over weekends, but is old-fashioned and lovely. The best time of day to enjoy the baths is after dark, when the steam rises into the cold, starry Karoo sky. The farm is attractively set, with mountain vistas to gaze at from the baths and fantastic birdlife drawn by this oasis in the deserty landscape.

Accommodation is basic, reasonably priced and all self-catering – in wooden cabins or rooms in the main farmhouse, each of which has an indoor spa bath (R750). There are also some campsites (R380 for two), a bar, and a restaurant serving dinners and breakfasts. Rates are lowered on weekdays and during the school term on all accommodation. If you are driving past, and want to have a swim, day-visitors pay R50 at the reception.

DRINKING

Barrydale Cellar 1 van Riebeeck St ☎028 572 1012. This is the place to enjoy handcrafted brandy, beer and ale tastings (two tastings for free, thereafter R30 per person). They have a lovely setting open to the river, and do a single offering at lunchtime, with delectable pizzas. Mon–Fri 9am–5pm, Sat 9am–3pm.

SHOPPING

Barrydale has a couple of wine outlets that are worth a visit for tasting and buying, and there are a couple of browsable craft shops along the R62.

Magpie Studio 27 van Riebeeck St ☎028 572 1997, ⓦmagpieartcollective.com. This craft shop makes colourful light fittings and chandeliers from recycled materials; their most famous customer is Michelle Obama. Tues–Fri 10am–5pm, Sun 9am–1pm.

Oudtshoorn

From Barrydale, vineyards and orchards give way to arid mountains and rocky, treeless plains vegetated with low, wiry scrub, making for a dramatic journey onwards, and another spectacular, twisting pass. **OUDTSHOORN**, 420km from Cape Town and 180km from Barrydale, has been called the "ostrich capital of the world" – the town's surrounds are indeed crammed with ostrich farms, several of which you can visit, and the local souvenir shops keep busy dreaming up 1001 tacky ways to recycle ostrich parts as comestibles and souvenirs. But Oudtshoorn has two other big draws: it's the best base for visiting the nearby **Cango Caves** (see p.241), and the town is known for its winter sunshine, at a time when it can be raining on the Garden Route. It's boiling hot in summer, though, so make sure you have access to a pool, and in winter the nights can be freezing.

Oudtshoorn's town centre has little more than a couple of museums, which are worth visiting; the town's main interest lies in its Victorian and Edwardian sandstone buildings, some of which are unusually grand and elegant for a Karoo *dorp*.

Brief history

Oudtshoorn started out as a small village named in honour of Geesje Ernestina Johanna van Oudtshoorn, wife of the first civil commissioner for George. By the 1860s, **ostriches**, which live in the wild in Africa, were being raised under the ideal conditions of the Oudtshoorn Valley, where the warm climate and loamy soils enabled lucerne, the favourite diet of the flightless birds, to be grown. The quirky Victorian fashion for large feathers had turned the ostriches into a source of serious wealth, and by the 1880s hundreds of thousands of kilogrammes of feathers were being exported, and birds were changing hands for up to £1000 a pair – an unimaginable sum in those days. On the back of this boom, sharp businessmen made their fortunes, ignorant farmers were ripped off, and labourers drew the shortest straw of all. The latter were mostly coloured descendants of the Outeniqua and Attaqua Khoikhoi and trekboers, who received derisory wages supplemented by rations of food, wine, spirits and tobacco – a practice that still continues on some farms. In the early twentieth century, the most successful farmers and traders built themselves "feather palaces", the ostentatious sandstone Edwardian buildings that have become the defining feature of Oudtshoorn.

18

C.P. Nel Museum

Cnr of Baron van Reede and Voortrekker sts • Mon–Sat 8am–5pm, Sat 9am–1pm • R25

The **C.P. Nel Museum** is a good place to start exploring Oudtshoorn. A handsome sandstone building, it was built in 1906 as a boys' school, but now houses an eccentric collection of items relating to ostriches. It's worth a visit mainly for the story it tells of the town's feather boom and decline, and the contrast between ostrich design items of the past – including gorgeous feather trimmings – compared to what you'll see in the tacky ostrich shops today.

18

Le Roux Town House

Cnr of Loop and High sts • Mon–Fri 9am–5pm • R25

Le Roux Town House is a perfectly preserved family townhouse, and the only way to get a glimpse inside one of the much-vaunted "feather palaces". The family's gracious, opulent style was enjoyed and appreciated by royalty and politicians alike during their visits here. The beautifully preserved furnishings were all imported from Europe between 1900 and 1920, and there is plenty to stroll around and admire, from the Art Nouveau glass panels inside to the corrugated iron verandas encircling the house.

Buffelsdrift Game Lodge

7km from Oudtshoorn • Elephant interactions 8am–4pm • Free; elephant interactions R280 • ☎ 044 272 0106, ⓦ buffelsdrift.com

The **Buffelsdrift Game Lodge**, just out of town on the Cango Caves road, offers an exciting opportunity to get close to **elephants**. Book ahead for a really worthwhile experience where you get to stroke elephants under the guidance of their handlers, and watch them at training and play. From the lodge's **restaurant** (see p.241) on the large dam, you are likely to see hippos, and may be lucky enough to see other animals coming to drink. There is safari-style accommodation too (see p.241).

Cango Wildlife Ranch

Just outside town on the Cango Rd • Daily 8.30am–5pm • R210 • ☎ 044 272 5593, ⓦ cango.co.za

The other wildlife activity around Oudtshoorn is **Cango Wildlife Ranch**. Guided tours lead you past white tigers and cheetahs, crocodiles and other creatures from other parts of Africa. The ranch offers a spectacle rather than authentic wildness, but it caters well for children who can frolic in water fountains or on climbing frames while you eat lunch.

ARRIVAL AND DEPARTURE   OUDTSHOORN

By car Allow 6hr from Cape Town for the 420km journey along the R62. Alternatively, take the N2 to George along the Garden Route and cut inland to Oudtshoorn on the N12.
By bus Intercity buses pull in at Queens Mall, off Voortrekker St, across the river from the main road, Baron van Reede St. Intercape (ⓦ intercape.co.za) has a daily service from Cape Town at 4.30pm, which takes 9hr, arriving at 1.30am. Their service to Cape Town leaves at 10.30pm and arrives at 6.30am. Greyhound does not

travel via Oudtshoorn.
By minibus There are two local transport companies which offer door-to-door services, on demand, from Oudtshoorn to Cape Town along the R62 (R300). The journey takes most of the day as about fifteen people need to be collected, and then dropped at their destinations. Try Hilton de Villiers at Divvies Transport (☎ 082 841 0107 or ☎ 078 209 3866) or Gysman Transport (☎ 044 272 0516 or ☎ 083 946 8862).

INFORMATION AND ACTIVITIES

Tourist office The office at 80 Voortrekker Rd, in front of the library (Mon–Fri 8.30am–5pm, Sat 9.30am–12.30pm; ☎ 044 279 2532, ⓦ oudtshoorn.com), is a good source of information about the caves and ostrich farms. They can

also help find you local accommodation.
Activities Backpacker's Paradise (see p.241) rents out bikes and arranges spectacular adventurous cycling trips down the Swartberg Pass, with motor vehicle back-up.

OSTRICH TOURS

Many people come to Oudtshoorn to see, or even ride, **ostriches**. You don't actually have to visit one of the ostrich farms to view Africa's biggest bird, as you're bound to see flocks of them as you drive past farms in the vicinity or past truckloads of them on their way to the slaughterhouse (feathers being no longer fashionable, these days ostriches are raised for their low-cholesterol flesh). A number of show farms offer **tours**, which include the chance to sit on an ostrich (if you are under 70kg). Best of the bunch is **Cango Ostrich Farm** on the main road between Oudtshoorn and the Cango Caves, in the Schoemanshoek Valley, which runs tours every twenty minutes, where you can sit on a bird, stand on their unbreakable eggs and look at ostrich chicks (45min; R100; ☎ 044 272 4623, ⓦ cangoostrich.co.za).

ACCOMMODATION

Oudtshoorn has a number of large **hotels** catering mainly to tour buses, plus plenty of good-quality **B&Bs** and **guesthouses**, a centrally located **campsite** with chalets, and one of the country's best-run **backpacker lodges**. Some of the nicest places to stay are in the attractive countryside en route to the Cango Caves. Rates fall dramatically during the winter months following the week-long **Klein Karoo Nasionale Kunstefees** (KKNK; ⓦ absakknk.co.za), a major arts festival, mostly in Afrikaans, and street party in the April Easter holidays when people from all over the country take every bed in town.

Backpacker's Paradise 148 Baron van Reede St ☎ 044 272 3436, ⓦ backpackersparadise.net. A well-run two-storey hostel along the main drag, which makes an effort to go the extra few centimetres with three-quarter beds, en-suite doubles and family rooms as well as dorms. There are nightly ostrich, and veg-friendly, braais, too, and a daily shuttle from the Baz Bus drop-off in George to the hostel. The on-site adventure centre organizes cycle trips in the Swartberg Pass and there's a daily shuttle to the caves, ostrich farm and wildlife ranch, as well as horseriding. Camping R100, dorms R160, doubles R520

Buffelsdrift Game Lodge 7km from town on the road to the caves ☎ 044 272 0106, ⓦ buffelsdrift.com. The town's top stay, in luxurious en-suite safari tents overlooking a large dam with hippo in it. Breakfast, served in the grand thatched dining area, is included, and game drives or horseback rides to view rhino, buffalo, elephant, giraffe and various antelope can be included in a package, or paid for separately. R2500

★ **De Oue Werf** Signposted off the R328 to Cango Caves, 12km north of Oudtshoorn ☎ 044 272 8712, ⓦ ouewerf.co.za. Luxurious and well-priced garden rooms on a working farm, run by the very welcoming sixth generation of the family. Green lawns run down to a dam,

which has a swinging slide and raft to play on, and lots of birdlife. A great option if you're visiting the caves and want to stay in the country. R1300

Gum Tree Lodge 139 Church St ☎ 044 279 2528, ⓦ gumtreelodge.co.za. Five rooms in a peaceful B&B, as well as a two-roomed self-catering cottage sleeping four, conveniently located a few minutes' walk from the centre, fronting onto a river with good birdlife. There's a pool and deck, a well-stocked pub, and rooms have modern bathrooms, a/c and TV. Doubles R1150, cottage R1800

Kleinplaas Holiday Resort 171 Baron van Reede St ☎ 044 272 5811, ⓦ kleinplaas.co.za. Well-run, shady sites for camping and fully equipped self-catering brick chalets, conveniently close to town, with a swimming pool and launderette. The owners know the town well and will show you the ropes, and can provide breakfast for a little extra. Camping R320, chalet R1300

Lodge 96 96 Langenhoven Rd ☎ 044 272 2996, ⓦ lodge96.co.za. Simple, neat house with clean rooms and pine furniture, one dorm and one family room, with a garden for a few tents, a pool, laundry service and good kitchen for self-catering. Ideal if you are on a budget and don't want a noisy hostel scene, and they can organise activities in the area. Camping R100, dorm R160, doubles R550

EATING

Oudtshoorn has a choice of several places to eat, mostly strung out along Baron van Reede Street and catering to the tourist trade, with the obligatory ostrich on the menu.

Bello Cibo 145 Baron van Reede St ☎ 044 272 3245. Relaxed and reasonably priced Italian place with indoor and outdoor seating, making it a good choice for children. Besides pizza and pasta, there are some creative ostrich (R90) offerings. Booking advisable. Mon–Sat 5–10pm.

Buffelsdrift Game Lodge 7km out of town towards Cango Caves ☎ 044 272 0106. Have a great breakfast or lunch on a wooden deck overlooking the waterhole, and do a spot of animal viewing at the same time. The lodge is open to non-guests for meals, and you could combine it with an elephant encounter or other wildlife activity.

Breakfast buffets with some local specialities such as *roesterkoek* – delicious sandwiches roasted on the coals (R90). Daily 10am–10pm.

Café Brule Queens Hotel, 5 Baron van Reede St ☎ 044 279 2412, ⓦ queenshotel.co.za. The nicest café in town, set in the restored *Queens Hotel* which has a rather grand, colonial ambience. The menu includes generous cooked breakfasts and ostrich burgers (R70) for lunch; it's also a great spot to sip a cappuccino overlooking the main street. They make their own pastries and breads too, and their deli counter is good for picnic supplies. Daily 7am–5pm.

Cango Caves

29km from Oudtshoorn • Daily 9am–4pm • R100 • ☎ 044 272 7410, ⓦ cango-caves.co.za

The **Cango Caves** number among South Africa's ten most popular attractions, drawing a quarter of a million visitors each year to gasp at their fantastic cavernous spaces, dripping rocks and rising columns of calcite. In the two centuries since they became known to the public, the caves have been seriously battered by human intervention, but they still represent a stunning landscape growing inside the Swartberg foothills. Don't go expecting a serene and contemplative experience, though: the only way of getting inside the caves is on a **guided tour** accompanied by a commentary.

San hunter-gatherers sheltered in the entrance caves for millennia before white settlers arrived, but it's unlikely that they ever made it to the lightless underground chambers. **Jacobus van Zyl**, a Karoo farmer, was probably the first person to penetrate beneath the surface, when he slid down on a rope into the darkness in July 1780, armed with a lamp. Over the next couple of centuries the caves were visited and pillaged by growing numbers of callers, some of whom were photographed cheerfully carting off wagonloads of limestone columns.

In the 1960s and 1970s the caves were made accessible to mass visitation when a tourist complex was built, the rock-strewn floor was evened out with concrete, ladders and walkways were installed, and the caverns were subsequently turned into a kitsch extravaganza with coloured lights, piped music and an indecipherable commentary. Even **apartheid** put its hefty boot in: under the premiership of Dr Hendrik Verwoerd, the arch-ideologue of racial segregation, a separate "non-whites" entrance was hacked through one wall, resulting in a disastrous through-draft that began dehydrating the caves. Fortunately, the worst excesses have now ended; concerts are no longer allowed inside the chambers, and the coloured lights have been removed.

ARRIVAL AND INFORMATION   **CANGO CAVES**

By car The drive here from Oudtshoorn involves heading north along Baron van Reede Street, and continuing 32km along a signposted scenic, quiet road (R328) to the caves. From the caves you can continue by car on the R328 to Prince Albert via the majestic Swartberg Pass (see p.244).

Information The visitors' complex includes an interpretive centre with quite interesting displays about the geology, people and wildlife connected with the caves, the decent *Cango Caves* restaurant, and a well-stocked souvenir shop. Below the complex you'll find shady picnic sites at the edge of a river that cuts its way into the mountains and along which there are hiking trails.

Calitzdorp

The small Karoo village of **CALITZDORP** hangs in a torpor of midday stillness, with its attractive, unpretentious Victorian streets and handful of wineries. It is another spot favoured by artists – dry, beautiful and undeveloped. Be sure not to miss exploring Queen Street, home to a handful of appealing guesthouses, quirky cafés and galleries, all of which are en-route to the three key wineries, a few hundred metres from the centre, and clearly signposted off the R62 (look for the Bo-Plaas sign). Don't leave without buying some port and olives – South Africa's finest ports are produced here, and there are groves of olive trees. Calitzdorp is at the turn-off to the beautiful Groenfontein (green fountain) Valley (see p.243). Since it is only 50km from Oudtshoorn, consider staying here instead, it is cheaper, smaller and with far more appeal.

CAVE TOURS

Two **tours** leave every hour, and you may only enter the caves on a tour. Tours must be booked in advance, by phone, otherwise you may not get on one. The one-hour Standard Tour (on the hour; R100) gets you through the first six chambers, but far more interesting is the ninety-minute Adventure Tour (on the half-hour; R150) which takes you into the deepest sections open to the public, where the openings become smaller and smaller. Squeezing through tight openings with names like **Lumbago Walk, Devil's Chimney** and **The Letterbox** is not recommended if you are claustrophobic, and you should wear oldish clothes and shoes with a grip to negotiate the slippery floors.

STARGAZING

The Karoo sky is heaven for astronomers due to the lack of pollution and few lights, and you get some of the southern hemisphere's sharpest views of the firmament from here. One of the most exciting things you can do in Prince Albert, if not in South Africa, is to watch the **night skies** with resident astronomer Hans Daehne (new moon only; R350 for a lecture and viewing; ☏072 732 2950, ⊛astrotours.co.za). Be sure to book far in advance.

ARRIVAL AND INFORMATION CALITZDORP 18

By car Calitzdorp is 370km from Cape Town, 50km east of Oudtshoorn on the R62. If you're driving from the capital, allow for a 5hr drive with a lunch stop; this would be a good halfway, overnight stop along the R62 if you are travelling between Cape Town and Port Elizabeth, and makes a good base, rather than staying in Oudtshoorn, to explore the area.

Tourist office At the Shell garage on Voortrekker St (Mon–Fri 8.30am–5pm, Sat 8am–1pm; ☏044 213 3775, ⊛calitzdorp.org.za).

ACCOMMODATION

Calitzdorp Country House Besemkop, Calitz Street ☏044 213 3760, ⊛cch.co.za. A luxurious and friendly guesthouse, with five rooms, a swimming pool and dam. Each unit has its own patio looking onto vines and the Swartberg beyond, and is furnished with antiques. Best of all, perhaps, though is the food, with dinners (R300) that can be booked in advance. R1800

PortWine Guest House Cnr of Queen and Station sts ☏044 213 3131, ⊛portwine.net. The smartest and most comfortable guesthouse in town, in a renovated early nineteenth-century homestead with local paintings on the walls, and a veranda overlooking the Boplaas wine estate. There is a pool and rose garden at the back too. R900

Welgevonden Guesthouse St Helena Rd ☏044 213 3642, ⊛welgevondenguesthouse.co.za. A comfortable country-style guesthouse, on a smallholding adjacent to Boplaas wine estate, 300m from the main road. The four en-suite bedrooms, set in an 1880 outbuilding, are furnished with brass or wooden bedsteads, patchwork quilts and wooden family heirloom furniture. R700

The Groenfontein Valley

The narrow dirt road through the highly scenic **Groenfontein Valley** twists through the Swartberg foothills, past whitewashed Karoo cottages and farms and across brooks, eventually joining the R328 to Oudtshoorn. Winding through these backroads is also an option to reach the Cango Caves (see p.241) and Prince Albert (see p.244), one of the best drives you'll ever do in South Africa. Many of the roads are unsealed but are perfectly navigable in an ordinary car if taken slowly.

ARRIVAL AND DEPARTURE THE GROENFONTEIN VALLEY

By car A circuitous minor route to the valley diverts just east of Calitzdorp from the R62, signposted *Groenfontein Retreat*.

ACCOMMODATION

Kruis Rivier Guest Farm 17km off the R62 (signposted turn-off 14km east of Calitzdorp) ☏044 213 3788, ⊛kruisrivier.co.za. Homely, simply furnished cottages right underneath the mountains, with lovely streams and waterfalls, which make an excellent base for hiking. The owners, who have a policy of keeping prices absolutely affordable, will also do breakfast on request and can provide braai packs, home-made bread and wood. R500

Red Stone Hills 6km off the R62 (signposted turn-off 14km east of Calitzdorp) ☏044 213 3783, ⊛redstone .co.za. Four lovely period-furnished Victorian cottages on a working farm in a landscape full of red rock formations. The owners can provide dinner on request as well as breakfast. Besides walking and cycling trails, there is birdwatching and the four horses on the farm can be ridden. R480

★**The Retreat at Groenfontein** 20km northeast of Calitzdorp and 59km northwest of Oudtshoorn ☏044 213 3880, ⊛groenfontein.com. No mobile phone reception or wi-fi. This isolated Victorian colonial farmstead borders the 2300-square-kilometre Swartberg Nature Reserve, an outstandingly beautiful area of gorges, rivers and dirt tracks. Accommodation is in comfortable en-suite rooms, each with its own fireplace, and rates include full board with vegetarians well catered for, and hospitable and helpful owners who turn every evening into a fine dinner party. R2000

18

Prince Albert

Isolation has left intact the traditional rural architecture of **PRINCE ALBERT**, an attractive little town 70km north of Oudtshoorn. Reached across the loops and razorbacks of the Swartberg Pass, this is one of the most dramatic drives and entries to a town imaginable. Although firmly in the thirstlands of the South African interior, on the cusp between the Little and Great Karoo, Prince Albert is all the more striking for its perennial spring, whose water trickles down furrows along its streets – a gift that propagates fruit trees and gardens. It is undoubtedly one of the best small towns outside Cape Town to spend a couple of days, with its great guesthouses, restaurants and craft shopping, plus the spectacular landscapes.

Many come to Prince Albert for the drives themselves, through its two southerly gateways – the aforementioned **Swartberg Pass** on the R328 and **Meiringspoort** on the N12. Once in town, though, it is small enough to explore on foot and you'll find everything you want on the main road.

The essence of the town is in the fleeting impressions that give the flavour of a Karoo *dorp* like nowhere else: the silver steeple of the Dutch Reformed church puncturing a deep-blue sky with a mountainous backdrop, and residents sauntering along or progressing slowly down the main street on squeaky bikes.

ARRIVAL AND DEPARTURE   PRINCE ALBERT

By car From Cape Town allow 5–6hr for the 420km trip. The fastest and least scenic route is along the N1, past Laingsburg, and involves no mountain passes; turn off onto the Prince Albert Road. The most scenic route is along the R62 to Calitzdorp or Oudtshoorn, and along the R328 over Swartberg. The pass is unpaved, with switchbacks, but fine in an ordinary car if you go slowly. If you want a gentler experience, approach the town via Meiringspoort from De Rust, a paved road which goes along a river and valleys with spectacular rock formations and little picnic spots. If you get a puncture or have car trouble Benny can help (24hr ☎073 455 1174). Petrol is available at the Agri Co-op, 99 Church Street, but note that it is closed on Saturdays from 11am and is closed on Sundays.

By train There is a one train per day, three times per week, between Cape Town and Johannesburg (Wed, Fri & Sun;

Shosholoza Meyl; ☎086 000 8888) which stops at Prince Albert Road station, 45km from the hamlet. Be warned that the trains are often late, and Prince Albert Road station has absolutely no facilities. From Cape Town the journey is some 7hr 30min. From Johannesburg it is an overnight trip, of approximately 19hr. Arrange to be collected by your guesthouse, or book a taxi in advance through Billy van Rooyen (☎072 337 3149; R450 for two people).

By bus Greyhound (☎083 915 9000, ⓦgreyhound.co.za) stops daily at the *North and South Hotel* in Prince Albert Road station, on the N1, on its Cape Town-to-Johannesburg run, but you will need to arrange to be picked up (see "By train", above) for the 45km journey to Prince Albert. Allow 7–8hr by bus from Cape Town, and another 14hr for the 1073km to Johannesburg.

INFORMATION AND ACTIVITIES

Banks and exchange There is limited use of credit cards in town, and no foreign exchange, but there is an ABSA ATM in Church Street.

Cinema and theatre The town's newly restored and handsome Art Deco cinema and theatre – totally unique in the Karoo – The Showroom 41 Church Street (☎023 541 1563, ⓦshowroomtheatre.co.za) is definitely worth a visit. Their site gives the dates of shows, music and movies, there is usually something on over the weekend and Wednesdays nights, and you can purchase tickets online.

Hiking permits *Lazy Lizard* (daily 7.30am–5pm; ☎023 541 1379), in Church Street, sells Cape Nature hiking

permits for exploring the Swartberg. You'll find good wi-fi here, if it is poor elsewhere.

Tourist office Church St (Mon–Fri 9am–5pm, Sat 9am–noon; ☎023 541 1366, ⓦprincealbert.org.za). Has maps with accommodation, restaurants and craft shops, and can point you to other activities in the area, such as olive oil tasting or visiting the largest fig farm in South Africa, Weltevrede – itself a fantastic 30min drive away, in the foothills of the Swartberg (ⓦfigfarm .co.za). The town's website has the dates of the Olive Festival in April, as well as details of photography courses and other activities.

ACCOMMODATION

Dennehof Guest House Off Christina de Wit St, on the outskirts of town ☎023 541 1227, ⓦdennehof.co.za.

Stay in one of seven rooms in this homestead that is a National Monument. Hiking trips are offered by the guesthouse, as well as mountain biking trips where you're driven up the Swartberg and descend the terrifying 18km on your own two wheels (R400). Renting a bike for a day around town is another, more sedate option (R200). R1300

Karoo Lodge 66 Church St ☎ 023 541 1467 or ☎ 082 692 7736, ⓦ karoolodge.com. You'll find reasonably priced, spacious accommodation at this B&B, which is run by a hospitable couple. Each of the suites, complete with pure cotton sheets and goose down duvets, leads onto the pool and the garden, which is filled with crimson bougainvillea. R1030

Karoo Views Margrieta Prinsloo Rd ☎ 023 541 1929, ⓦ karooview.co.za. Upmarket, comfortable self-catering in four modern Karoo-style cottages on the edge of town with views of the Swartberg and surrounding countryside, but close enough to walk into town. They do a light breakfast, and can provide firewood for braais. R1090

Mai's Guest House 81 Church St ☎ 023 541 1188, ⓦ maisbandb.co.za. You can expect a comfortable stay in this restored nineteenth-century house. The rooms have a/c, and the house has a pool and lots of cats. A fabulous breakfast is served under the vines, dished up by the full-of-beans Irish owner. R1000

★**Onse Rus** 47 Church St ☎ 023 541 1380, ⓦ onserus .co.za. Cool, thatched B&B rooms attached to a restored Cape Dutch house, with welcoming and knowledgeable owners who serve you tea and cake on arrival, and provide delicious home-made muesli and local yoghurt breakfasts, as well as the usual eggs in a gracious dining room. There is a pool, large garden full of birds and flowers and nice outdoor areas to relax in. R1040

EATING

★**Gallery Café** Church St ☎ 023 541 1197. Imaginative dishes by passionate chef Brent, who creates a relaxed ambience above Prince Albert Gallery, with balcony seating. Vegetarians and vegans are catered for, there are delightful starters, meat dishes including game (R160) and home-made ice creams. Daily 6–9.30pm.

Lazy Lizard 9 Church St ☎ 023 541 1379. This is the best place in Prince Albert to come for lunch or a coffee. You can sit on the veranda here and get a good salad, quiche (R60) or sandwich, while using the internet. Daily 7.30am–5pm.

★**Simply Saffron** 10 Church St ☎ 023 541 1040 or ☎ 082 873 9985. Aim to be in Prince Albert at the weekend simply to eat here. Meals are served by the owners, in their own dining room, using their kitchen garden or local ingredients where possible, with the flair and imagination you would expect from a top city restaurant. The three-course set menus offer a choice of two dishes, with plenty of options for vegetarians (R190) but you need to bring your own wine. Their talents extend beyond the kitchen, as it is also a healing centre with reflexology and other treatments on offer. Restaurant booking is essential as there is only one sitting, and a few tables. Fri & Sat 6–9pm.

SHOPPING

Prince Albert is known for its **mohair products**: magnificent blankets, rugs and mats, socks, scarves and other garments. Prince Albert Gallery (see p.246) is a good place to start looking for artworks and crafts, though there are a number of smaller shops on Church Street. Like most small towns, there is a modest Saturday morning **market** for locals, next to the Fransie Pienaar Museum (9am–11am) with home-made baked goods, fruit and vegetables, Karoo lamb, biltong, teas and

GO TO HELL

Prince Albert is one of the best places to begin a trip into **Die Hel** (also known as Hell, The Hell or Gamkaskloof), a valley that's part of the Swartberg Nature Reserve, and not on the way to anywhere. Although it doesn't look far on the map, you'll need to allow two-and-a-half hours in either direction to make the spectacular but tortuous drive into it along a dirt road. A 4WD isn't needed, but you should definitely not attempt the drive in the killing heat of December or January without air conditioning. The valley itself is 20km long and fertile, a deep cleft between the towering Swartberg Mountains, with the Gamka River running through it.

The attraction of the place is the silence, isolation and birdlife. Only opened up to road transport in 1962, the valley still has no electricity supply, petrol, ATMs, mobile phone reception or shops.

There's **accommodation** at *Fontein Guest Farm* (☎ 023 541 1107, ⓦ gamkaskloof.co.za), which is run by one of the original farming families. There are four different houses (R350 per person) and sites for camping (R200 per site). Meals and picnic baskets can be made on request, there's dinner if you book beforehand, and the farm's restaurant is always open for breakfast (7–10am). Another option for accommodation is the *Nature Conservation* (☎ 021 483 0190, ⓦ capenature.co.za/reserves), which has well-kept camping sites (from R150) and restored historical cottages (R640 per cottage).

18

coffee. Prince Albert is also well-known for its figs and olives – you'll find the dried varieties everywhere, and boxes of fresh figs in summer after Christmas, especially in February. The olive oil is outstanding.

18

Gay's Guernsey Dairy Christina de Wit St ☎023 541 1274, ⓦgaysguernseydairy.com. Award-winning home-made cheeses which you can taste before buying, as well as yoghurts and cream. If you're travelling with children, take them to watch the milking at sunrise, and walk around the farm. Mon–Fri 7–9am, 10am–noon & 4–6pm, Sat & Sun 7–10am & 4.30–6pm.

Karoo Looms 55 Church St ☎023 541 1363, ⓦkarooweavery.co.za. The best place in Prince Albert for mohair carpets and rugs with bright, funky designs. Also look out for cotton bath mats off the looms. Mon–Fri 9am–5pm, Sat 9am–1pm.

Prince Albert Gallery 57 Church St ☎023 541 1057, ⓦprincealbertgallery.co.za. The town's beauty has attracted a number of artists to live here and the excellent and not-to-be-missed, Prince Albert Gallery, set in an airy Victorian building, sells their work. Come here to buy paintings, sculpture, affordable beadwork, jewellery, ceramics and etchings by local artists, or to visit one of their occasional special exhibitions. Mon–Fri 9am–5pm, Sat 9am–1pm, Sun 10am–1pm.

The Watershed 19 Church Street ☎082 938 2531, ⓦwatershedprincealbert.co.za. The town's top gallery, set in a restored Victorian house, has photographic prints for sale by Berlin-born Schadeberg, famous for his iconic anti-apartheid images in the 1950s and 1960s of musicians, beautiful women, activists, including the mighty Nelson M, and magazine covers. There is also retro furniture, fabulous cushions and other unique interior design pieces you might like to acquire with a deep purse. Pieces are chosen from artists using the textures and colours of the Karoo. Their website has a catalogue and they do ship goods. Daily 10am–4pm.

CITY HALL, PORT ELIZABETH

Port Elizabeth, Addo and the private reserves

Port Elizabeth, the Eastern Cape's commercial and industrial centre, is for many visitors a practical place to start or end a trip along the Garden Route. The port's industrial feel is mitigated by a small historical centre with a selection of excellent restaurants and drinking spots. Nearby there are outstanding beaches around Nelson Mandela Bay as well as some beautiful coastal walks a few kilometres from town. Around an hour's drive inland from Port Elizabeth is its biggest draw, Addo Elephant Park, the closest Big Five reserve to Cape Town. Here you have virtually guaranteed sightings of elephants and a good chance of seeing other big animals.

Port Elizabeth

As a city, **PORT ELIZABETH** (always referred to as **PE**) is pretty functional and easy enough to navigate – it's a great deal smaller and more manageable than Cape Town or Johannesburg. The city does have an industrial feel, however it still has plenty to offer: excellent and safe beaches, sunset cruises on the bay, a small but interesting historical centre and rich past – both in colonial and anti-apartheid terms – and beautiful **coastal walks and beaches**, a few kilometres from town. A couple of classically pretty rows of Victorian terraces still remain in **Central**, the area on the hill above the bay, with a recommended walk around the Donkin Reserve and an interesting choice of places to eat in restored old houses. For accommodation however, visitors are better off staying near the beach in **Humewood** or **Summerstrand**.

Port Elizabeth's **city centre** is marred by a network of freeways that cuts a swath across the south of town, blocking off the city from the harbour. In the midst of this stands the slender tower of the Campanile, commemorating the landing of the 1820 British settlers. These British settlers left their mark on the architecture of the town centre, and today a number of English-speaking South Africans in the Eastern Cape can trace their roots back to these settlers. The city's white population, however, retreated to the suburbs some time ago, leaving the centre to African traders and township shoppers. The **suburbs** offer little to draw you away from the beachfront, unless you need something practical, in which case you should make a beeline for **Newton Park**, 5km west of the centre and home to the shopping malls of **Greenacres** and **The Bridge**.

Central

Central, the area on the slopes above the actual town centre, has seen pleasing regeneration in the last couple of years with a number of creative offices choosing to locate here, and some grand old hotels set to be restored – there's also a number of good places to eat in Richmond Hill. Running parallel to the freeway as it sweeps into town is Port Elizabeth's main street, **Govan Mbeki Avenue**. This street was renamed in honour of the veteran activist (father of Thabo Mbeki, South Africa's former president), who died in 2001; during the last century the Eastern Cape has been the heartland of the African National Congress, trade union movements and political resistance. The symbolic heart of town is the **City Hall**, standing in **Market Square**, a large empty space surrounded by some striking mid-Victorian buildings.

Just north of Market Square is the lofty Campanile monument. A block east from the Campanile is the former Sanlam Building where famous activist Steve Biko was severely tortured, and then died while being transported from here to Pretoria. Rather derelict and dismal now, it can't be visited, though there are plans to restore it as a political monument.

The dejection of the quarter, under the grimy shadow of a flyover, is lessened by taking a walk from the Campanile up to the Donkin Lighthouse and Pyramid. From the Campanile, the walk up to the lighthouse is rich in anti-apartheid history, with information plaques relating to Nelson Mandela, and some funky sculptures, such as the line of life-size laser-cut steel figures of voters giving triumphal fist pumps in 1994. Reaching the lighthouse, there's a pleasant green space and you can enjoy views of the harbour, beaches and bay.

Donkin Street

Heading west up hilly **Donkin Street**, you'll come upon a curious stone pyramid commemorating **Elizabeth Donkin**, after whom PE was named. Elizabeth was the young wife of the Cape's acting governor in 1820, Sir Rufane Donkin; she died of fever in India in 1818. The nineteen **Donkin Houses**, built in the mid-nineteenth century and declared National Monuments in 1967, reflect the desire of the English settlers to create a home from home in this strange, desiccated land.

Nelson Mandela Metropolitan Art Museum
1 Park Drive • Mon & Wed–Fri 9am–5pm, Tues 2–5pm • Free

The **Nelson Mandela Metropolitan Art Museum**, situated in two buildings framing
the entrance to St George's Park, sounds grander than it is, but has a collection of
contemporary local work, visiting exhibitions and a small shop selling postcards and
local arts and crafts. Their Eastern Cape art section is the thing to aim for, though they
do have some minor European and oriental artworks. Sadly there are no funds to keep
it open at weekends.

South End Museum
Cnr of Humewood Rd and Walmer Boulevard • Mon–Fri 9am–4pm, Sat & Sun 10am–3pm • Free

Based in the old Seamen's Institute, the **South End Museum** recalls the bygone days of
the South End, a once vibrant multicultural neighbourhood whose growth had much
to do with PE's then booming harbour. As a result of the Group Areas Act it was razed
street by street in the 1960s, save for a handful of churches and mosques. Today, the
area is full of pricey townhouses.

19

The beachfront and around
PE's **beaches** are its main attraction. The **beachfront strip**, divided from the harbour
by a large wall, starts at wide **King's Beach**, somewhat marred by a jumble of coal heaps
and oil tanks behind it. To the southeast lies **Humewood Beach**, across the road from
which is a complex housing the **Bayworld Museum and Snake Park** (daily 9am–4.30pm,
snake show daily at noon, seal and penguin talks daily 11am & 3pm; R40; ⓦwww
.bayworld.co.za), a research and education centre where you can visit the snake park,
and see seals and penguins in the Oceanarium. Brookes on the Bay and **Dolphin's Leap**
nearby are complexes of restaurants, pubs and clubs with great views.

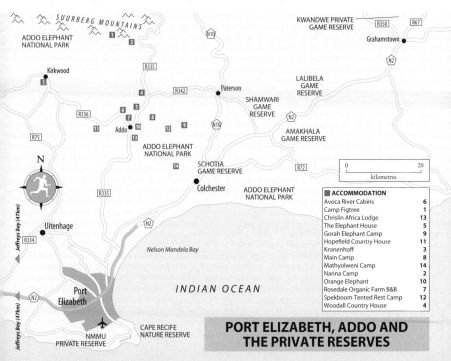

PORT ELIZABETH, ADDO AND
THE PRIVATE RESERVES

ACCOMMODATION	
Avoca River Cabins	6
Camp Figtree	1
Chrislin Africa Lodge	13
The Elephant House	5
Gorah Elephant Camp	9
Hopefield Country House	11
Kronenhoff	3
Main Camp	8
Mathyolweni Camp	14
Narina Camp	2
Orange Elephant	10
Rosedale Organic Farm B&B	7
Spekboom Tented Rest Camp	12
Woodall Country House	4

Beyond, to the south, **Hobie Beach** and **Summerstrand** are great for walking and sunbathing. Summerstrand's mammoth **Boardwalk Casino Complex** (⊗suninternational .com/boardwalk) houses a casino, places to eat and shop, and a cinema, plus adventure golf and ten-pin bowling, among other things.

Sardinia Bay and Schoenmakerskop

Marine Drive continues 15km down the coast from Summerstrand to the village of **Schoenmakerskop** ("Schoenies" to the locals), along an impressive coastline that alternates between rocky shores and sandy beaches, with the odd café to stop off at. From here you can walk the 8km **Sacramento Trail**, a shoreline path that leads to the huge-duned **Sardinia Bay**, the wildest and most dramatic stretch of coast in the area and the best part of Port Elizabeth, if you want nature, rather than city. It is also only fifteen to twenty minutes drive from the airport. To get to Sardinia Bay by road, turn right at the Schoenmakerskop intersection and follow the road until Sardinia Bay is signposted on the left.

19

ARRIVAL AND DEPARTURE — PORT ELIZABETH

BY PLANE

Port Elizabeth's airport is conveniently situated on the edge of Walmer suburb, 4km south of the city centre, and is served by Safair (⊕087 135 1351, ⊗safair.co.za), Kulula (⊕0861 585 852, ⊗kulula.com), SAA (⊕041 507 1111, ⊗flysaa.com) and Mango (⊕086 100 1234, ⊗flymango .com). Taxis wait outside the airport and the major car rental companies are here too.

Destinations Cape Town (3 daily; 1hr 15min); Durban (3 daily; 1hr 15min); Johannesburg (6–7 daily; 1hr 35min).

BY TRAIN

The train station (⊕041 507 2662) is centrally located on the Strand. The Shosholoza Meyl (⊗www.shosholozameyl .co.za) connects Johannesburg to PE (Wed, Fri & Sun; 20hr 35min). You will need to arrange to be met by your hotel or a

taxi (see p.252) beforehand, as this downtown area is prone to crime.

BY BUS

Intercity buses Greyhound, Intercape and Translux buses stop at Greenacres shopping mall in Newton Park suburb, 3km from the centre. It's best to arrange to be met here by your accommodation, though there are waiting taxis during business hours (see p.252). Leaving PE, buses stop at every major town along the Garden Route to Cape Town, and also head east to Mthatha and Durban.

Destinations: Cape Town (6–7 daily; 12hr); Durban (daily; 12hr 30min); Johannesburg (daily; 14hr 30min); Knysna (daily; 5hr); Mthatha (daily; 8hr 50min).

Baz Bus The Baz Bus will drop you off at the backpacker lodge that you are staying at.

INFORMATION

Nelson Mandela Bay Tourism (⊗nmbt.co.za) has several offices including: Port Elizabeth Airport, Arrivals Hall (Mon–Fri 7am–7pm, Sat 7am–6pm, Sun 8am–6pm; ⊕041 581 0456); Shop 48 at the Boardwalk, Marine Drive,

Summerstrand (Mon–Fri 8am–7pm, Sat & Sun 10am–7pm; ⊕041 583 2030); and Donkin Reserve Lighthouse Building, Belmont Terrace, Central (Mon–Fri 8.30am–4pm; ⊕041 582 2575).

TOURS AND ACTIVITIES

Horseriding Heavenly Stables (431 Sardinia Bay Rd, ⊕081 890 7080, ⊗heavenlystables.co.za; R450) offers

riding with lovely horses, for both beginners and experienced riders. The rides go through coast dune forest

---

THE ART IN MANDELA'S STEPS

Art Route 67 (⊗nmbt.co.za/listing/route_67.html) is a walk that incorporates **67 works of art** by artists from the Eastern Cape, which commemorate Mandela's 67 years of fighting for democracy. The art ranges from small tile mosaics and vinyl street stickers to metal installations and towering sculptures. Well-worth exploring, the walking route of 1km or so starts at the 52m-high Campanile Bell Tower (Strand St, Central; Tues–Sun 9am–12.30pm & 1–2pm), which offers views of the harbour and surrounds from the top; from here, the route continues to Vuyisile Mini Square, a place which saw many meetings of resistance during the 1980s, and up the staircase at St Mary's Terrace, to meander through the Donkin Reserve, before reaching a triumphal end on top of Donkin Hill.

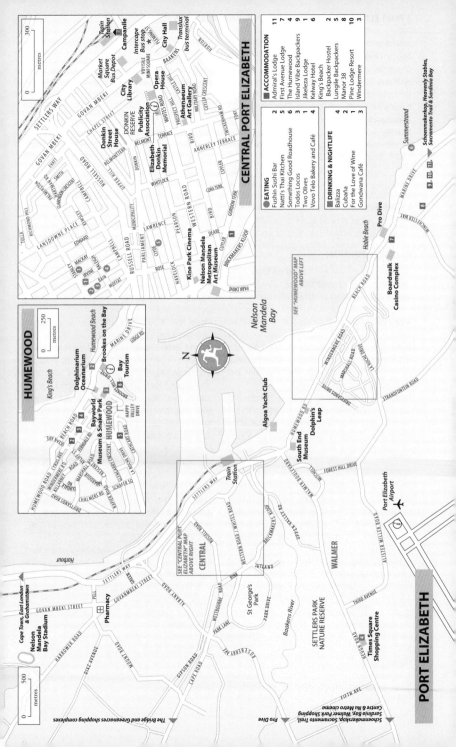

CENTRAL PORT ELIZABETH

HUMEWOOD

PORT ELIZABETH

and end up on the beach at Sardinia Bay.

Sea cruises Raggy Charters (☏073 152 2277, �🌐raggycharters.co.za; R1400) runs cruises from PE Harbour at the Algoa Yacht Club, with opportunities to see the massive penguin colony at St Croix Island, dolphins and humpback and southern right whales (July–Nov).

Watersports Although the ocean around PE is not tropically clear and warm, the diving is good, especially for soft corals, and there is the chance of diving with ragged tooth sharks. Pro Dive (189 Main Rd, Walmer ☏041 581 1144, �🌐prodive.co.za) offer diving,

snorkelling, kiteboarding, stand-up paddling, kayaking and dive courses.

Tours It's possible to explore Central on foot – the tourist office (see p.250) can provide a map which highlights the area's various historical buildings and landmarks. The best way to see the city, however, is on one of the excellent bus tours, which shed light on the culture and history of a city shaped by layers of political history. Calabash Tours (☏041 585 6162, �🌐calabashtours.co.za) is one of the best and operates "Real City Tours" by day (R550) and *shebeen* tours by night, as well as trips to Addo.

GETTING AROUND

By taxi PE's minibus taxis run regularly from town to the beachfront, but are the least recommended way to travel, in terms of safety. There are some metered taxis about, but

it's better to arrange transport beforehand; try King Cab (☏041 368 5559), or Uber.

ACCOMMODATION

The obvious place to stay in PE is the **beachfront**, with a wide choice of hotels, self-catering suites and B&Bs. During the December and January peak holiday period the beachfront becomes the focus for most of the city's action, while February, March and April are much quieter and offer perfect beach weather.

Admiral's Lodge 47 Admiralty Way, Summerstrand ☏041 583 1894, �🌐admiralslodge.co.za. Spacious and stylish rooms at a good B&B situated at the far end of Summerstrand, roughly 7km from the centre; airport transfers are available (R120). There's a braai area, communal lounge and pool. R1090

First Avenue Lodge 3 First Ave, Summerstrand ☏041 583 5173, �🌐firstavenuelodge.co.za. Sixteen en-suite rooms close to the beach with their own entrances, offered on a B&B or self-catering basis, in a popular and pleasant establishment with a lawn pool and chilling-out area. R1200

The Humewood 33 Beach Rd, Humewood ☏041 585 8961, �🌐humewoodhotel.co.za. A large, old-fashioned hotel with more than a nostalgic hint of 1950s family seaside holidays. The rooms are large and feature wicker furniture and older-style floral prints. Service is excellent and includes laundry facilities. There's a good bar and sun deck. R1120

★**Island Vibe Backpackers** 4 Jenvey Rd, Summerstrand ☏041 583 1256, ⓦislandvibe.co.za. Ideal for backpackers who want more creature comforts without sacrificing social atmosphere. An appealing location near the beach and nightlife spots, offering four-bed dorms with wooden bunks, as well as doubles, plus a swimming pool, Jacuzzi, pool table and soccer table. Dorms R180, doubles R650

Jikeleza Lodge 44 Cuyler St, Central ☏041 586 3721, ⓦhighwinds.co.za. Friendly backpacker place, with dorms, doubles and a family room. Its adventure centre, High Winds, can help you sort out tour and travel bookings; they do tours around Addo, as well as recommended

combo tours to Addo and Schotia for the evening or overnight. Dorms R140, doubles R360

Kelway Hotel Brookes Hill Drive, Humewood ☏041 584 0638, ⓦthekelway.co.za. Stylish hotel kitted out with timber panelling, seagrass chairs and handcrafted wooden tables. The pool area, swathed in green and with a natural rock wall, wooden decking and sunbeds overlooking the sea, is lovely. Standard, luxury and family rooms are available, and breakfast is included. R1180

King's Beach Backpacker Hostel 41 Windermere Rd, Humewood ☏041 585 8113. Spotless, slightly out-dated, well-established hostel, a block away from the beach, with camping facilities, dorms and double rooms, plus an outside bar and braai area. Although principally for self-catering, it lays on tea, coffee, and bread with various jams in the morning. The travel desk can book a range of trips including township and game park tours. Camping R100, dorms R150, doubles R400

Lungile Backpackers 12 La Roche Drive, Summerstrand ☏041 582 2042, ⓦlungilebackpackers.co.za. Large and popular beachfront hostel with a sociable party vibe, situated in the heart of PE's nightlife strip. It has a large lawn to relax on, twin rooms by the swimming pool and dorms inside the main house. Camping R100, dorms R160, doubles R500

Manor 38 38 Brighton Drive, Summerstrand ☏083 270 7771, ⓦmanorcollection.co.za. Modern, sparklingly clean boutique hotel in an excellent location close to Summerstrand and the Boardwalk. There's a lovely pool area with sunbeds, and two communal lounge areas. R1600

Pine Lodge Resort Off Marine Drive, Humewood ☏041 583 4004, ⓦpinelodge.co.za. The *Pine Lodge Resort* is located right on the beach near the wonderful historic

lighthouse and next to the Cape Recife Nature Reserve, where owls, mongooses and antelope make appearances. Accommodation is in excellent-value self-catering log cabins, some of which sleep up to eight people. There's a popular bar and restaurant, and the lodge also houses a swimming pool, spa for beauty treatments and a games room. R1075
Windermere 35 Humewood Rd, Humewood ☎041 582 2245, ⌨thewindermere.co.za. Nine large rooms

that have been given an almost Zen-like feel through the subtle use of off-white to oatmeal tones which contrast with dark, chocolatey hues and timber and granite surfaces. Full hotel facilities are available including a plunge pool, bar, laundry and secure parking. It's worth noting that the rooms with sea views don't have a higher price tag, so ask for one of those. R1990

EATING

The best area to trawl – both during the day and night – for an alfresco meal, rejuvenating coffee or tasty sandwich is Richmond Hill in Central. Here Art Deco and Victorian buildings give a historical feel, offsetting the overall functional feel of PE, and there's a lot of places for tapas and wine. Another obvious choice in a seaside town for having a meal or drink is along the beachfront.

Fushin Sushi Bar Stanley on Bain, Richmond Hill ☎041 811 7874. This is the place to head for the best sushi in town (R60–160). Rather than sitting at a counter, here you can order from a menu and enjoy pavement seating. They also serve salads and Eastern-influenced tapas-style small dishes. Mon–Sat 10am–10pm, Sun 11am–9pm.
Natti's Thai Kitchen 5 Park Lane, Central ☎041 373 2763. Reliable restaurant, which has been going for years, serving reasonably priced, authentic Thai cuisine (average mains R90) in a relaxed atmosphere, with a BYO alcohol policy. Mon–Sat 6.30–10pm.
★Something Good Roadhouse Marine Drive ☎041 583 6986. Stripped-down roadhouse/surfer bar on the beachfront, where you can get breakfast (until 11am; R70), pizzas, burgers, gourmet foot-long sandwiches and other classic roadhouse meals. Sit out on the deck, which is humming with people and has a beautiful view of the sea. Mon–Sun 7am–11pm.
Todos Locos 32 Bain St, Richmond Hill ☎041 582 2914.

Excellent Spanish restaurant with a Spanish owner, Ana who often welcomes guests to the light and spacious interior, and cooks up a storm. There are blackboard specials, tapas and old favourites like seafood paella (R80), sangria and Spanish omelette. Tues–Sat noon–3pm & 6–10pm.
★Two Olives 3 Stanley Street, Central ☎041 585 0371. Among the popular Richmond Hill strip of restaurants, *Two Olives* with its Mediterranean bias offers a great evening out – delicious, generously sized and varied tapas (R60) served with Cape wines on a first floor wrap-around balcony, with plenty of options for vegetarians and seafood lovers. Steaks and pizzas are also recommended. Mon–Sat 11.30am–10.30pm, Sun noon–10pm.
Vovo Telo Bakery and Café 16 Raleigh St, Richmond Hill ☎041 585 5606. This is a great place for breakfast and lunch, with Italian and French breads and pastries (R40), real coffee and veranda seating. Mon–Sat 7.30am–3pm.

DRINKING AND NIGHTLIFE

Balizza Times Square Shopping Centre, cnr Heugh Rd & 5th Ave, Walmer. This sprawling nightclub complex houses two bars, three lounges and two dancefloors. The DJs mix recent house anthems and old school tunes, and there's a range of cocktails and shooters to enjoy (cocktails from R56). Mon–Sun 11am–2am.
Cubaña 49 Beach Rd, Humewood ☎041 582 5282. A café during the day, at night this morphs into a cigar lounge and offers a large cocktail menu (drinks from R60) as well as reasonably priced Mexican-inspired food and burgers. The outside deck has a sea view, and on weekends there's Cuban music and DJs. Smart-casual dress code in the evenings (no trainers or shorts). Mon–Wed & Sun 8am–midnight, Thurs 8am–2am, Fri & Sat 8am–4am.

For the Love of Wine 1st Floor, 20 Stanley St, Richmond Hill ☎072 566 2692. This smart, compact bar is situated on the first floor with a wraparound balcony that overlooks Stanley Street. Despite being PE's only wine bar for the discerning, it is not overpriced and the selection is broad, either to drink there (from R45) or take home from their shop stocking interesting boutique wines. Tues–Sat 12–10pm.
Gondwana Café 2 Dolphin's Leap, Main Rd, Humewood ☎041 585 0990. This place is relaxed, with live music on Sunday nights, and DJs on other nights, though it's best to check out beforehand what is going on (beer from R26). Daily 4pm–4am.

DIRECTORY

Banks and exchange American Express Foreign Exchange, Boardwalk Casino Complex (☎041 583 2025;

Mon–Fri 9am–8pm, Sat & Sun 10am–4pm). There are ATMs at every shopping mall.

19

Cinema Nu Metro Cinema, Walmer Park Shopping Centre, Main Rd between 14th and 16th Sts, Walmer and at the Boardwalk Complex on the beachfront.
Hospitals St George's (private), 40 Park Drive, Settlers Park (☎ 041 392 6111).

Pharmacy Mount Road Pharmacy, 559 Govan Mbeki Avenue (daily 8.15am–11pm; ☎ 041 484 3838).
Post office 259 Govan Mbeki Avenue (Mon–Fri 8am–5pm & Sat 8.30am–1pm; ☎ 041 508 4039).

Addo Elephant National Park

73km northeast of Port Elizabeth • Daily 7am–7pm • R248 • ⓦ www.addoelephantpark.com

Home to the Big Five, but best known for its hundreds of pachyderms, **Addo Elephant National Park** is close enough to Port Elizabeth to be visited on a day-trip, though a couple of nights spent here are undoubtedly more rewarding.

You can drive around Addo yourself, but if you want to be taken around in an open-topped Land Rover and given a luxury safari experience, then stay in one of the nearby **private reserves** (see p.257). Another highly enjoyable way to roam the park is on a horseriding tour (see box, p.256).

One big attraction of Addo is that the Eastern Cape is **malaria-free** (unlike Kruger Park). And if you've driven out this way along the Garden Route and don't fancy heading back exactly the way you came, you've the option of returning to Cape Town via the inland **Route 62** (see p.230), branching off the N2 not far west of Port Elizabeth.

Wildlife-watching

The Addo bush is thick, dry and prickly, making it difficult sometimes to spot any of the six hundred or so elephants, four hundred Cape buffaloes and other animals; when you do, though, it's often thrillingly close up. A good strategy is to ask where the elephants are and the other four of the Big Five have last been seen (enquire with staff at the park reception), or to head for the waterhole in front of the restaurant to scan the bush for large grey backs quietly moving about. The best way to see wildlife, though, is to go on a **guided game drive** in an open vehicle with a knowledgeable national parks driver.

ARRIVAL AND DEPARTURE · ADDO ELEPHANT NATIONAL PARK

By car Addo's southern gate is accessed off the N2 at the village of Colchester, 43km northeast of Port Elizabeth; the gate is about 5km from *Mathyolweni Camp*. To get to *Main Camp*, north of *Mathyolweni*, take a slow, scenic drive through the park from the southern gate, which will take at least 1hr, or use the R335 that runs outside the western flank – take the N2 from Port Elizabeth east towards Grahamstown for 5km, branching off at the Addo/Motherwell/Markman signpost onto the R335 through Addo village. The R335 is also the way to reach the majority of accommodation outside the park. The Zuurberg section is reached by taking a turn-off marked "Zuurberg" 1km before you reach *Main Camp*, and travelling for 21km along a good gravel road; this is the way to *Narina Bush Camp* and the Zuurberg horse trails. The network of roads within the section of the park between *Main Camp* and *Mathyolweni* is untarred, but in good condition.

> ### CALL OF THE WILD
>
> Addo calls itself the "Big Seven" reserve due to the fact that the Alexandra State Forest/Woody Cape section of the park (the part of the coast which is protected and just south of the elephant park) has **whales** and **great white sharks**, pushing up the significant animal denizens to seven. **Elephants** remain Addo's most obvious drawing card, but there are also a few lions (don't count on seeing them), as well as the presence of the rest of the Big Five – **buffalo**, **hippos** and **leopards** – all of which make Addo a game reserve to be reckoned with. **Spotted hyenas** were introduced some years ago, as part of a programme to re-establish predators in the local ecosystem. Other species to look out for include **cheetah**, endangered and hard to spot **black rhino**, as well as **eland**, **kudu**, **warthog**, **ostrich** and **red hartebeest**.

CLOCKWISE FROM TOP LEFT THE RANGE OF WILDLIFE TO BE FOUND AT THE SHAMWARI PRIVATE RESERVE (P.258) >

HORSERIDES

A number of escorted **horserides** are on offer in Addo, at ridiculously low prices. Experienced riders (able to sit a gallop) can head into the Nyathi area, home to the Big Five (rides take place at 8.30am and 2pm; R510). In the beautiful Zuurberg section, 21km beyond *Main Camp*, there are one-hour rides for novices (three daily; R220), and longer excursions for more experienced riders (three or five hours starting at 9am; R330) – don't expect to see much wildlife here, though the mountain and steep river valley scenery is really beautiful (you'll need a head for heights on the longer trails). There is also a ride that overnights at *Narina Bush Camp* (R600). Advance booking, by phone only, for all trips is required (☎042 233 8657).

INFORMATION AND TOURS

Eating The restaurant at *Main Camp* is open for three meals a day (daily 7:30am–10pm), while the shop is well stocked with food and drink.

Guided tours Tours can be booked in advance at *Main Camp* or on the park's website. Two-hour guided game drives leave throughout the day and cost R370 per person for day-drives, R470 per person for sunset trips (including snacks and drinks), and R370 per person for night drives. The vehicles used are higher off the ground than a normal sedan to improve viewing opportunities. In PE, Calabash Tours (see p.252) runs day-trips here, as do most of the backpacker hostels.

Hop-on guide You can hire the exclusive services of a hop-on guide (R210) who joins you in your own car for 2hr and will direct you to where to find the animals.

Maps Park maps indicate the location of picnic and braai sites, and are available at *Main Camp* reception.

ACCOMMODATION

INSIDE THE PARK

Bear in mind that reservations, through SANParks (☎012 428 9111, ⓦaddoelephantpark.com), are essential in high season; although you can reserve directly with Addo if it's less than 72hrs in advance (☎042 233 8600). There are few villages in the area, so stock up on self-catering supplies in PE or Colchester. You are likely to have to take whatever kind of accommodation is available, as it's a popular destination.

Main Camp ☎012 428 9111, ⓦaddoelephantpark .com. *Main Camp* is the oldest and largest of the National Parks camps. In addition to camping facilities, there are forest cabins that sleep two people and share cooking facilities in communal kitchens, and more luxurious two-person chalets with their own kitchenettes. Some units sleep up to four people (minimum charge is for two occupants). The cheapest accommodation available is in well-designed, spacious safari tents, perfect during the summer months, with decks right next to the perimeter fence. Camping R330, safari tent R830, forest cabin R1010, chalet R1160

Mathyolweni Camp ☎012 428 9111, ⓦaddo elephantpark.com. National Parks accommodation in a dozen fully equipped self-catering chalets. These chalets sleep two people, and have showers and nice viewing decks. The chalets are set in a secluded valley surrounded by thicket that supports a wealth of birdlife. R1300

Narina Camp ☎012 428 9111, ⓦaddoelephantpark .com. A small, very attractive National Parks bush camp in the mountainous Zuurberg section, comprising four safari tents that sleep four people and share washing and cooking facilities. There is no restaurant here, so bring your own provisions. R1410

★**Spekboom Tented Rest Camp** ☎012 428 9111, ⓦaddoelephantpark.com. The most rustic of the National Parks accommodation, consisting of five fixed tents on decks with twin beds. Each tent is equipped with camp chairs, a table and solar light, with communal showers and toilets within short walking distance. There is no electricity, so you'll need to bring a torch; barbecue facilities and a communal gas fridge and stove plates are available. R1010

OUTSIDE THE PARK

Outside the park, but within easy striking distance, you'll find an abundance of private B&Bs and guesthouses, especially among the citrus groves of the Sundays River Valley. Many offer day and night drives in the game reserve.

Avoca River Cabins 13km northwest of Addo village on the R336 ☎082 677 9920, ⓦavocarivercabins.co.za. Reasonably priced B&B and self-catering accommodation on a farm in the Sundays River Valley. The range of self-catering spans from budget cabins (four- and five-sleeper) to more comfortable thatched huts, some of which are situated on the banks of the river. There is a swimming pool, some pleasant walks to be had on the citrus farm, plus a treetop course for kids, and canoes are available to rent. Four-sleeper cabin R700

★**Camp Figtree** 30 km northwest of Addo village on the R335 ☎082 611 3603, ⓦcampfigtree.co.za. Luxury mountain lodge, built on the Zuurberg slopes with glorious views, and built to satisfy every dream of romantic Africa. The rates include excellent food, and the packages they offer include a 3hr game drive into the park. It scores high on hilly scenery and total relaxation, though it is not near enough to nip in and out of the main part of the park, and the drive there is 15km on gravel road. R3692

Chrislin Africa Lodge 12km south of Addo main gate, off the R336 ☎042 233 0022 or ☎082 783 3553, ⊕chrislin.co.za. This quirky B&B offers accommodation in thatched huts that have been built using traditional Xhosa construction techniques. There's also a lovely *lapa* (courtyard) and pool, and they serve up hearty country breakfasts, as well as dinners (available on request). R1440

★**The Elephant House** 5km north of Addo village on the R335 ☎042 233 2462 or ☎083 799 5671, ⊕elephanthouse.co.za. Just minutes from Addo is one of the Eastern Cape's top places to stay, a stunning thatch-roofed lodge filled with Persian rugs and antique furniture that perfectly balances luxury with a supremely relaxed atmosphere. The eight bedrooms and six garden cottages (ideal for families and half the price of a room) open onto a lawn courtyard. Candlelit dinners are available, as are game drives (R1000/person) into Addo and the surrounding reserves. Doubles R3700, cottages R1450

Gorah Elephant Camp 9km west along the Addo Heights Rd leading from the N10 to Addo village ☎044 501 1111, ⊕gorah.hunterhotels.com. Ultra-luxurious outfit based around a Victorian homestead, with a landscaped pool and decked out with the appropriate paraphernalia including mounted antelope skulls above the fireplace. Meals are included in the price, as are game drives. R17543

Hopefield Country House 20km southwest of Addo main gate ☎042 234 0333, ⊕hopefield.co.za. An atmospheric 1930s farmhouse set in beautiful English-style gardens on a citrus farm. The nine bedrooms are imaginatively furnished with period pieces in a style the owners (a pair of classical musicians who occasionally give impromptu concerts for guests) describe as "farmhouse eclectic". R1300

Kronenhoff On the R336 as you enter Kirkwood ☎042 230 1448, ⊕kronenhoff.co.za. Situated in a small farming town, this is a hospitable, high-ceilinged Cape Dutch-style home, with five spacious suites, polished wooden floors, large leather sofas and a sociable pub. In summer the scent of orange blossom carries from the surrounding citrus groves. R1300

Orange Elephant On the R335, 8km from the National Park gate ☎042 233 0023, ⊕addobackpackers.com. Budget accommodation at a comfortable hostel, whose management will help you organize outings into the surrounding game reserves – an Addo full-day tour including a braai in the park, with an excellent guide, costs R1200. The lively bar is well known for its large portions of pub grub. Dorms R130, doubles R400

★**Rosedale Organic Farm B&B** On the R335, 1km north of Addo village ☎042 233 0404, ⊕rosedalebnb .co.za. Very reasonably priced accommodation in eight cottages on a certified organic farm that exports citrus fruits to the EU. Hosts Keith and Nondumiso Finnemore are seriously committed to sustainable farming and tourism – water for the cottages is solar-heated, and you can enjoy organic oranges and juice at breakfast. Keith offers a free 1hr walking tour of the farm to guests, on which you can get all those nagging questions about the state of the world's food industry answered. There is also a kitchen available for guests to self-cater and children are welcome. R950

Woodall Country House About 7km west of Addo main gate ☎042 233 0128, ⊕woodall-addo.co.za. Excellent luxury guesthouse on a working citrus farm with eleven self-contained suites and rooms. There's a swimming pool, gymnasium, spa and sauna (massages are available, and there's a resident beautician). A lovely sundowner deck overlooks a small lake full of swans and other waterfowl. Renowned for its outstanding country cuisine, its restaurant offers three- to six-course dinners. R3250

19

The Eastern Cape's private game reserves

Although self-driving through Addo can be extremely rewarding, nothing beats getting into the wild in an open vehicle with a trained guide – something the private reserves excel at. If you want the works – game drives, outstanding food, uncompromising luxury and excellent accommodation, you'll find it at top-ranking **Shamwari** between PE and Grahamstown, or at **Kwandwe Game Reserve**, another outstanding safari destination in the Eastern Cape, just north of Grahamstown.

If you aren't a jetsetter, a good option is one of the full-day safaris offered by **Amakhala** or **Schotia**. Accommodation rates are listed as the cheapest for two people in high season, although specials and season a variations may be available.

THE PRIVATE RESERVES

Amakhala Game Reserve 67km north of Port Elizabeth on the N2 ☎041 581 0993, ⊕amakhala.co.za. A fantastic, family-friendly reserve stocked with the Big Five as well as cheetah, giraffe, zebra, wildebeest and antelope. The Bushman's River meanders through the reserve allowing for riverboat sundowner cruises and canoeing for overnighting guests. Safaris for day-visitors must be booked in advance and include a 3hr game drive and a three-course lunch (R980). All accommodation comprises fabulous views, with three different tented camps to choose from. R5960

★**Kwandwe Private Game Reserve** On the R67, 34km north of Grahamstown and 160km from Port Elizabeth

19

☎ 046 603 3400, ⊛ kwandwe.com. This is the Eastern Cape's top wildlife destination, with 30km of Fish River frontage and the Big Five in attendance. Apart from twice-a-day game drives, *Kwandwe's* safari activities include guided river walks, canoeing on the Great Fish, rhino tracking and fascinating cultural tours with a resident historian. Children are well catered for with family game drives, bush walks, fishing and frog safaris. There are four lodges, ranging from a quintessential luxury thatched lodge to a stunning boutique-hotel-in-the-bush ingeniously designed with glass walls for panoramic views of the terrain. R1580

Lalibela Game Reserve 90km northeast of Port Elizabeth on the N2 to Grahamstown ☎ 041 581 8170, ⊛ lalibela.co.za. An excellent luxury choice, *Lalibela Game Reserve* is home to the Big Five and diverse flora and fauna. Safaris are included in the accommodation rate, along with all meals and drinks – you can dine on terrific Eastern Cape food and contemporary cuisine. There are three fabulous lodges with private viewing decks and swimming pools to choose from, and they also offer an African drumming and dancing session. R10000

Schotia Game Reserve On the eastern flank of Addo ☎ 042 235 1436, ⊛ schotiasafaris.co.za. *Schotia* is the smallest and the busiest of the private reserves, on account of the excellent value it offers. Although not (quite) a Big

Five reserve, it's really only missing elephants. Day-visitors can arrange to be collected from Port Elizabeth or anywhere in the Addo vicinity; full-day safaris 9am–9.30pm (R2500/person) involve a game drive through Addo and an evening game drive with lunch and dinner thrown in. They will collect you from PE or Addo. If you're pushed for time or money you can opt for the afternoon game drive at 2.30pm (R1500/person). An overnight stay here is the cheapest among the private reserves; packages always include a room rate plus game drives, and there's also a tented camp for the "Out of Africa" romance. R6000

Shamwari Game Reserve 65km north of Port Elizabeth on the N2 ☎ 041 509 3000, ⊛ shamwari.com. The largest and best known of the private reserves, *Shamwari* has cultivated a jetsetter fan base, hosting such celebrities as Tiger Woods and John Travolta, and consistently winning world travel accolades. The accolades are justified in the reserve's diverse landscapes, requisite animals and high standards of wildlife-viewing. A variety of accommodation in luxurious lodges dotted across different parts of the property is available, furnished with every conceivable comfort. One of the best options is the "explorers camp", which offers luxury combined with a chance to get in touch with nature. R10800

NELSON MANDELA

Contexts

History

Cape Town's history is complex and what follows is only a brief account of major events in the city's past. For more detailed coverage on both Cape Town's and South Africa's history in general, see the list in "Books".

Hunters and herders

Rock art provides evidence of human culture in the Western Cape dating back nearly 30,000 years. The artists were **nomadic** hunter-gatherers, known most commonly as **San**, a relatively modern term from the Nama language with roots in the concept of "inhabiting or dwelling", to reflect the fact that these were South Africa's aboriginals. At one time, they probably spread throughout sub-Saharan Africa, after pretty well perfecting their hunting and gathering, leaving them considerable time for artistic and religious pursuits. People lived in small, loosely connected bands comprising family units and were free to leave and join up with other groups.

About two thousand years ago, this changed when some groups in territory north of modern South Africa laid their hands on fat-tailed sheep and cattle from northern Africa, thus transforming themselves into **herding communities**, known as **Khoikhoi** or simply Khoi. The introduction of livestock had a revolutionary effect on social organization and introduced the idea of ownership and accumulation. Social divisions developed, as did political units, which, centred around a chief, became larger.

The Cape goes Dutch

Portuguese mariners, under the command of **Bartolomeu Dias**, first rounded the Cape in the 1480s, and named it Cabo da Boa Esperança, the **Cape of Good Hope**. Marking their progress, they left an unpleasant set of calling cards all along the coast – slaves they had captured in West Africa and had cast ashore to trumpet the power and glory of Portugal with the aim of intimidating the locals. Little wonder then, that the first encounter of the Portuguese with the indigenous Khoikhoi along the Garden Route coast was not a happy one. It began with a group of Khoikhoi stoning the Portuguese for taking water from a spring without asking permission, and ended with a Khoikhoi man lying dead with a crossbow bolt through his chest.

It was another 170 years before any European settlement was established in South Africa. In 1652, *De Goede Hoop* and two other vessels of the **Dutch East India Company** (Verenigde Oostindische Compagnie or **VOC**), which was engaged in trade between the Netherlands and the East Indies, pulled into Table Bay. Their mission was to set up a refreshment station to feed sailors on Company ships trading between Europe and the East. There were no plans at this time to set up a colony; in fact, the Cape post was given to the station commander **Jan van Riebeeck** because he had been caught with his hand in the till. Van Riebeeck dreamed up a number of schemes to keep "darkest Africa" at bay, including the very Dutch solution of building a canal that would cut the Cape Peninsula adrift. In the end he had to satisfy himself with

30,000 years ago	2000 years ago	1652 AD
Hunter-gatherers occupy Cape Peninsula	Khoikhoi herders with fat-tailed sheep migrate from the north	Dutch East India Company establishes supply station for trade ships sailing to Indies

planting a **bitter almond hedge** (still growing in Cape Town's Kirstenbosch Gardens) to keep the natives at arm's length.

Despite Van Riebeeck's view that the indigenous Khoikhoi were "a savage set, living without conscience", the Dutch were dependent on them to provide livestock, which were traded for trinkets. As the settlement developed, Van Riebeeck needed more **labour** to keep it going, and bemoaned the fact that he was unsuccessful in persuading the Khoikhoi to discard the freedom of their herding life to work for him. Much to his annoyance, the bosses in Amsterdam had forbidden Van Riebeeck from enslaving the locals, and refused his request for slaves from elsewhere in the Company's empire.

Creeping colonization

Everyone at the Cape at this time was under stringent contract to the VOC, which effectively had total control over all persons' activities and movements – a form of indentureship. But a number of Dutch men were released from their contracts in 1657 to farm as **free burghers** on land granted by the Company; they were now at liberty to pursue their own economic activities, although the VOC still controlled the market and set prices for produce. The resultant annexation of the lands around the mud fort, which preceded the construction of the more solid Castle of Good Hope, ultimately led to the inexorable process of **colonization**.

The only snag was that the land granted didn't belong to the Company in the first place, and the move sparked the first of a series of **Khoikhoi–Dutch wars**. Although the first campaign ended in stalemate, the Khoikhoi were ultimately no match for the Dutch, who had the tactical mobility of horses and the superior killing power of firearms. Campaigns continued through the 1660s and 1670s and proved profitable for Dutch raiders, who on one outing in 1674 rounded up eight hundred Khoikhoi cattle and four thousand sheep.

Meanwhile, in 1658, Van Riebeeck had managed to steal a shipload of **slaves** from West Africa, which whetted his insatiable appetite for this form of labour. The VOC itself became the biggest slaveholder at the Cape and continued importing slaves, mostly from the East Indies, at such a pace that, by 1710, there were more slaves than burghers in the colony. With the help of this ready workforce, the embryonic Cape colony expanded outwards and trampled the peninsula's Khoikhoi, who by 1713 had lost everything. Most of their livestock (nearly fifty thousand animals) and the majority of their land west of the Hottentots Holland Mountains had been gobbled up by the VOC. Dispossession, and diseases like smallpox, previously unknown in South Africa, decimated their numbers and shattered their social system. By the middle of the eighteenth century, those who remained had been reduced to a condition of miserable servitude to the colonists.

Kaapstad

During the early eighteenth century, **slavery** became the economic backbone of the colony, which was now a rude colonial village of low, whitewashed, flat-roofed houses. Passing through in 1710, Jan van Riebeeck's granddaughter, Johanna, commented contemptuously that the settlement was "a miserable place. There is nothing pretty along the shoreline, the Castle is peculiar, the houses resemble prisons", and "one sees here peculiar people who live in strange ways".

1657	**1713**	**1795**	**1834**
Company releases indentured labourers to farm as free burghers	Khoikhoi dispossessed of all livestock by Company and are reduced to servitude	Company goes bust and English becomes official language when British take Cape	Emancipation of slaves leads many Dutch to leave Cape and establish two Boer republics

Dutch global influence began to wane in the 1700s, but at the same time the Cape settlement began to develop an independent identity and a little prosperity, based on its pivotal position on the European–Far East trade route. People began referring to it as "**Kaapstad**" (Cape Town) rather than "the Cape settlement", and by 1750 it had a thousand buildings, with over three thousand diverse inhabitants. Some of these were indigenous Khoikhoi people, but the largest number were VOC employees, dominated by an elite of high-ranking Dutch-born officials. The lower rungs were filled by the poor from all over Europe, including Scandinavia, Germany, France, England, Scotland and Russia, while slaves came from East Africa, Madagascar, India and Indonesia. There was also a transient population from passing ships, which by the second half of the century were largely manned by Indian, Javanese and Chinese crews. If nothing else, the constant **maritime traffic** injected some life into this intellectual desert, which couldn't boast a single printing press, let alone a newspaper. Entertainment consisted mainly of carousing, whoring and gambling.

Britain takes the Cape

By the 1790s, the VOC was more or less bankrupt, and its control over the restive Cape burghers had become tenuous. As Dutch maritime influence declined, Britain and France were tussling for domination of the Indian Ocean. The outbreak of the French Revolution in 1789 and the establishment of a Francophile republic in the Netherlands a few years later made the **British** distinctly jittery about their strategic access to Cape Town. In August 1795, Rear Admiral George Keith Elphinstone was sent in haste with four British sloops of war to secure Cape Town; by mid-September the ragtag Dutch garrison had capitulated.

The British occupation heralded a period of **free trade** in which exports from the Cape multiplied, as tariffs were slashed, with the result that Cape wines, the largest Cape export, comprised ten percent of British wine consumption by 1822. The tightly controlled and highly restrictive Dutch regime was replaced with a more tolerant government, which brought immediate **freedom of religion**, the abolition of the slave trade in 1808, and the **emancipation** of slaves in 1834.

Although British-born residents were a minority during the first half of the nineteenth century, their influence was huge, and Cape Town began to take on a British character through a process of cultural, economic and political dominance. **English** became the language of status and officialdom, and by 1860 there were eight newspapers, six of them in English. A vibrant press fed a culture of **liberalism** which led Capetonians to thwart British attempts to transport convicts to the Cape (see box, p.48) – the first time since the American Revolution that an outpost of empire had successfully defied Whitehall. This gave the colonists the confidence to demand **self-government** and, in 1854, males, regardless of race, who owned property worth £25 or more won the right to vote for a lower house of parliament, which was based in Cape Town. A significant development of the second half of the nineteenth century was the rapid growth of **communications**, both within Cape Town and into the interior, which reinforced the city's status as the principal centre of a Cape Colony that by now extended 1000km to the east. The road from Cape Town to Camps Bay across Kloof Nek was started in 1848 and a telegraph line between Cape Town and Simon's Town was laid in 1860, but most

1864	1901	1899–1902	1910
Completion of Cape Town–Wynberg rail line facilitates development of outlying suburbs	First segregated black location, Ndabeni, established after bubonic plague outbreak	Britain defeats Afrikaner republics in Anglo-Boer War	Parliament comes to Cape Town when Afrikaner republics and British colonies (Cape and Natal) federate

significant of all was the introduction of steam. The first **rail line** from central Cape
Town to Wynberg was completed in 1864, which opened up the southern peninsula to
the growth of **middle-class suburbia**.

From backwater to breakwater

The development of an urban infrastructure wasn't enough to lift Cape Town from its
backwater provinciality. That required the discovery, in 1867, of the world's largest
deposit of **diamonds** around modern-day Kimberley. Coinciding with this, the city's
breakwater was started, and the **harbour** was completed just in time to accommodate
the massive influx of fortune-hunters and immigrants who flooded into Cape Town
en route to the diggings. More significant still was the **discovery of gold** around
Johannesburg in the Boer-controlled South African Republic in the 1880s, which gave
Cape Town a new significance as the gateway to the world's richest mineral deposits.

From the 1870s, growing middle-class self-confidence was reflected in the erection of
grand **Victorian frontages** on the city centre's shops, banks and offices. Echoing Victorian
London, this prosperous public facade hid a growing world of poverty, inhabited by
immigrants, Africans and people of mixed race (see box, p.46) who made up a cheap
labour force. The degradation and vice that thrived in Cape Town's growing slums were
disquieting to the Anglocentric middle class, which would have preferred Cape Town to be
like a respectably homogenous Home Counties town, rather than a cultural melting pot.

As the twentieth century dawned, the authorities attempted to achieve a closer
approximation to the white middle-class ideal by introducing laws to stem
immigration, other than from Western Europe, while other statutes sought to protect
"European traders" against competition from other ethnic groups. Racial segregation
wasn't far behind, and an outbreak of bubonic plague in 1901 gave the town council an
excuse to establish **Ndabeni**, Cape Town's first black ghetto, near present-day Pinelands.

Industrialization and segregation

Apart from contributing to Cape Town's development as a trading port, the discovery of
gold had more significant consequences for the city. By the end of the nineteenth century,
a number of influential capitalists, among them **Cecil John Rhodes** (prime minister of the
Cape from 1890 to 1897), were convinced that it would be a good idea to annex the two
Boer republics to the north to create a unified South Africa under British influence. In
1899, Britain marched on the Boer republics, in what was rashly described by Lord
Kitchener as a "teatime war", but became known internationally as the **Anglo-Boer War**,
Britain's most expensive campaign since the Napoleonic Wars. Today, it's often referred to
locally as the South African War, in recognition of the fact that South Africans of all
colours took part. After three bloody years, the war ended with the Boers' surrender. What
followed was nearly a decade of discussions, at the end of which the two Boer republics
(the South African Republic and the Orange Free State) and two British colonies (the
Cape and Natal) were federated in 1910 to become the **Union of South Africa**, in which
Cape Town gained a pivotal position as the **legislative capital** of the country.

African and coloured people, excluded from the cosy deal between Boers and Brits,
had to find expression in the workplace. They flexed their collective muscle on the docks

1920s	1948	1952
Influx of Africans leads to building of segregated township Langa, surrounded by barbed-wire fence	National Party, with its former-Nazi members, wins election and goes full throttle on segregation	Nelson Mandela leads defiance campaign against apartheid legislation

in 1919, when they formed the mighty **Industrial and Commercial Union**, which boasted 200,000 members in its heyday. Cape Town began the process of becoming a modern industrial city and, with the building of the South African National Gallery, promoted itself as the urbane cultural capital of the country. Accelerated **industrialization** brought an influx of Africans from the rural areas, and soon Ndabeni was overflowing. Alarmed that Africans were living close to the city centre in District Six and were also spilling out into the Cape Flats, the authorities passed the **Urban Areas Act**, which compelled Africans to live in what were named "locations" and empowered the city council to expel jobless Africans – measures that preceded apartheid by 25 years. In 1927, the new location of **Langa** (which ironically means "sun" in Xhosa) was opened next to the sewage works. Laid out along military lines, with barrack-style dormitories for the residents, it was surrounded by a security fence.

WWII accelerated this trend, bringing hardship to those at the bottom of the heap, and leading to an increased influx of Africans and poor white Afrikaners to the cities. This changed the demographics of the city of Cape Town, which lost its British colonial flavour and, for the first time in 150 years, had more coloured and black than white residents. New townships were built to accommodate the burgeoning African population.

Cape Town became a mixed bag of ad hoc official **segregation** in some areas of life, while in others, such as on buses and trains, there was none.

Apartheid and defiance

In postwar South Africa, ideological tensions grew between those pushing for universal civil rights and those whites who feared black advancement. In 1948, the **National Party** came to power, promising its fearful white supporters that it would reverse the flow of Africans to the cities. In Cape Town, the government introduced a policy that favoured coloured people

WORLD WAR II

During the 1930s, Cape Town saw the growth of several fascist movements, the largest of which was the **Greyshirts**, whose favourite meeting place was the Koffiehuis (coffee house) next to the Groote Kerk in Adderley Street. Its members included Hendrik Verwoerd (aka "the architect of apartheid"), a Dutch-born intellectual who became a fanatical Afrikaner Nationalist and South African prime minister from 1958 to 1966. When **World War II** broke out, there was a heated debate in parliament, which narrowly voted for South Africa to side with Britain against Germany. Local hero Jan Smuts (1870-1950), the great 20th-century statesman, philosopher and commander in the South African War and both world wars, was instrumental in persuading his fellow Afrikaners to side with the old British enemy. Smuts' many achievements include drafting the opening of the United Nations foundation charter, and you can walk the Smuts Track on Table Mountain (see p.76).

Members of all South African communities volunteered for service in WWII, and the **ANC** (**African National Congress**, founded in 1912) argued that their support should be linked to full citizenship for blacks. Afrikaners remained deeply divided, and **Nazi sympathizers**, among them John Vorster (Verwoerd's successor as prime minister), were jailed for actively attempting to sabotage the war effort. *Die Burger*, Cape Town's Afrikaans-language newspaper, backed Germany throughout the war.

1960	1964	1966
The PAC leads march from Langa against enforced carrying of passes by Africans	Mandela, Sobukwe and ANC leadership imprisoned on Robben Island	Coloureds and Africans evicted from "white areas" and relocated to Cape Flats townships

for certain unskilled and semi-skilled jobs, admitting only black African men who were already employed and forbidding the construction of family accommodation for Africans – hence the townships turned into predominantly male preserves.

During the 1950s, the National Party began putting in place a barrage of laws that would eventually constitute the structure of apartheid. Early **onslaughts on civil rights** included the Coloured Voters Act, which stripped coloured people of the right to vote; the Bantu Authorities Act, which set up puppet authorities to govern Africans in rural reserves; the Population Registration Act, which classified every South African at birth as "white, Bantu or coloured"; the Group Areas Act, which divided South Africa into ethnically distinct areas; and the Suppression of Communism Act, which made anti-apartheid opposition (communist or not) a criminal offence. Africans, now regarded as foreigners in their own country, had at all times to carry **passes** – one of the most reviled symbols of apartheid.

The ANC responded in 1952 with the **Defiance Campaign**, whose aim was to grant full civil rights to black people. A radical young firebrand called **Nelson Mandela** was appointed "volunteer-in-chief" of the campaign, which had a crucial influence on his politics. Up to that point, he had rejected political association with non-Africans, but the campaign's interracial solidarity brought him round to the conciliatory inclusive approach for which he became famous. The government swooped on the homes of the ANC leadership, which resulted in the detention and then banning of over a hundred ANC organizers. Unbowed, the ANC pressed ahead with the **Congress of the People**, held near Johannesburg in 1955. At a mass meeting of nearly three thousand delegates, four organizations – representing Africans, coloureds, whites and Indians – formed a strategic partnership.

From within the organization, a group of Africanists criticized cooperation with white activists, leading to the formation in 1958 of the breakaway **Pan Africanist Congress** (**PAC**), under the leadership of the charismatic **Robert Mangaliso Sobukwe**. Langa township became a stronghold of the PAC, which organized peaceful **anti-pass demonstrations** in Johannesburg and Cape Town on March 21, 1960. Over a period of days, work strikes spread to all Cape Town's locations, and a temporary nationwide suspension of the pass laws was achieved – the calm before the storm. As the protests gathered strength, the government declared a **State of Emergency**. They sent the army in to crush the strike, restored the pass laws and banned the ANC and PAC. Nelson Mandela continued to operate in secret for a year until he was finally captured in 1962, tried and later imprisoned – together with most of the ANC leadership – on **Robben Island**.

Soweto and the Total Strategy

With resistance stifled, the state grew more powerful, and for the majority of white South Africans, business people and foreign investors, life seemed perfect. The panic caused by the 1960 uprising soon became a dim memory, and confidence returned. For black South Africans, poverty deepened – a state of affairs enforced by apartheid legislation.

In 1966, the notorious **Group Areas Act** was used to uproot whole coloured communities from areas including District Six, and to move them to the soulless **Cape Flats**, where, in the wake of social disintegration, gangsterism took root (see box, p.87). It remains one of Cape Town's most pressing problems. Compounding the injury, the National Party stripped away coloured representation on the Cape Town city council in 1972.

1976	1981	1983
Police open fire on black school pupils opposing government; 128 Capetonians are killed	Botha moves Mandela to mainland prison, but also sends massed troops into townships to suppress rolling protest	15,000 delegates form ANC proxy the United Democratic Front, leading to escalation of violence

The **Soweto Revolt** of June 16, 1976, signalled the start of a new wave of anti-apartheid protest, when black youths took to the streets against the imposition of Afrikaans as a medium of instruction in their schools. The protests spread to Cape Town where, as in Joburg, the government responded ruthlessly by sending in armed police, who killed 128 and injured 400 Capetonians.

As protest spread to all sections of the community, the government was forced to rely increasingly on armed police to impose order. Even this strategy was unable to stop the mushrooming of new liberation organizations, many of which were part of the broadly based **Black Consciousness movement**. As the unrest rumbled on into 1977, the government responded by banning all the new black organizations and detaining their leadership.

From the mid-1960s to the mid-1970s, Prime Minister **John Vorster** had relied on the police to maintain the apartheid status quo, but it became obvious that this wasn't working. In 1978, he was deposed in a palace coup by his minister of defence, **P.W. Botha**, who conceived a complex military-style approach that he called the **Total Strategy**. The strategy was a two-handed one: the reform of peripheral aspects of apartheid, alongside the deployment of the armed forces in unprecedented acts of repression. In 1981, as resistance grew, Botha began contemplating change and moved Nelson Mandela and other ANC leaders from Robben Island to Pollsmoor Prison in mainland Cape Town. This was a symbolic gesture, as Pollsmoor had lower security, less harsh conditions and it was easier to access for (potential) negotiations. At the same time, however, he poured ever-increasing numbers of troops into the townships.

In 1983, Botha concocted what he believed was a master plan for a so-called **New Constitution**, in which coloured and Indian people would be granted the vote – in racially segregated chambers with no executive power. The only constructive outcome of this project was the extension of the Houses of Parliament to their current size.

Apartheid suffers a blow

As President Botha was punting his ramshackle scheme in 1983, fifteen thousand anti-apartheid delegates met at Mitchells Plain, on the Cape Flats, to form the **United Democratic Front (UDF)**, the largest opposition gathering in South Africa since the Congress of the People, in 1955. The UDF became a proxy for the banned ANC, and two years of strikes, boycotts and protest followed. As the government resorted to increasingly extreme measures, internal resistance grew and the international community turned up the heat on the apartheid regime. The Commonwealth passed a resolution condemning apartheid, the US and Australia severed air links, Congress passed disinvestment legislation and finally, in 1985, the Chase Manhattan Bank called in its massive loan to South Africa.

Botha declared his umpteenth **State of Emergency** and unleashed a last-ditch storm of tyranny. There were bannings, mass arrests, detentions, treason trials and torture, as well as assassinations of UDF leaders by sinister hit squads. At the beginning of 1989, **Mandela** wrote to Botha from prison describing his fear of a polarized South Africa and calling for negotiations. An intransigent character, Botha found himself paralyzed by his inability to reconcile the need for radical change with his fear of a right-wing backlash. When he suffered a stroke later that year, his party colleagues moved swiftly to oust him and replaced him with **F.W. de Klerk**.

1989	1990	1994	2006
Botha has stroke and is replaced by F.W. de Klerk, who lifts ANC ban and releases Mandela	Mandela walks free and addresses a crowd of over 60,000 from City Hall	ANC wins election and Mandela becomes president, but Western Cape returns National Party provincial government	Centrist Democratic Alliance takes control of Western Cape and Cape Town

Faced with the worst crisis in South Africa's history, President de Klerk realized that repression had failed. Even South Africa's friends were losing patience, and, in September 1989, US President George Bush Sr told de Klerk that if Mandela wasn't released within six months, he would extend US sanctions. Five months later, de Klerk lifted the ban on the ANC, PAC, the Communist Party and 33 other organizations, and released Mandela.

On February 11, 1990, Cape Town's history took a neat twist when, just hours after being released from prison, **Nelson Mandela** made his first public speech from the balcony of City Hall to a jubilant crowd, of over sixty thousand, spilling across the Grand Parade – the site of the very first Dutch fort.

A tale of two cities

Four years of negotiations followed, which eventually led to South Africa's current constitution. During the first-ever **democratic elections** in 1994, Mandela voted in national elections for the first time in his life – and became South Africa's president. One of the anomalies of the 1994 election was that while most of South Africa delivered an **ANC landslide**, the Western Cape, purportedly the most liberal region, chose the **National Party**, who had implemented apartheid, as its provincial government. Politics in South Africa were not divided along a fault line that separated whites from the rest of the population, as many had assumed; the majority of coloured people voted for the party that had once stripped them of the vote, regarding it with less suspicion than the ANC. Apart from between 2002 and 2006, when Capetonians elected an ANC mayor and administration, the Western Cape and its capital have bucked South Africa's trend of ANC dominance, by repeatedly electing the National Party and, after its dissolution, the **Democratic Alliance** (**DA**).

During the ANC's first term in national government under Mandela (1994–1999), affirmative action policies and a racial shift in the economy led to the rise of a **black middle class**, but even so this represented a tiny fraction of the African and coloured population, and many felt that transformation hadn't gone far enough. Indeed, after twenty-five years of non-racial democracy, Cape Town is still a very divided city.

On the one hand, the Mother City has been titivating itself for tourists and investors, helped by the establishment of the Cape Town Partnership in 1999, which has overseen the regeneration of the city centre. The post-apartheid period led to a wave of economic confidence expressed by investors in a number of monumental developments. Among these was the megalomaniacal **Century City** (1997) in the northern suburbs, a garish retail, residential and office complex that adopted faux Tuscan architecture and Venice-inspired canals. More tasteful was the expansion of the **V&A Waterfront** to include the **Nelson Mandela Gateway** (2001), from where the ferry to Robben Island departs. In preparation for South Africa's hosting of the 2010 FIFA World Cup, the iconic **Cape Town Stadium** (2009) went up on Green Point Common, and Cape Town International Airport got a brand-new **Central Terminal Building** (2009), which at last provided a facility that could cope with the city's expanding air traffic. To cap it all, the state-of-the-art **Cape Town Film Studio** (2010) was completed and went on to attract a string of major international productions, such as the 2012 hit *Chronicle*, *Safe House* starring Denzel Washington, futuristic 3D drama *Dredd*, *The Giver* with Meryl Streep and TV pirate drama *Black Sails*.

On the other hand, as the biggest city within a thousand kilometres, Cape Town continues to attract a steady **influx** of people seeking a better life, mostly from the rural

2010	2013	2014
City stages glittering FIFA World Cup extravaganza in new Cape Town Stadium	South Africa – and the world – mourns the death of Nelson Mandela	Cape Town is World Design Capital, chosen for its potential to alleviate social problems with design solutions

Eastern Cape, but also from all over Africa, making it one of the subcontinent's fastest-growing cities, with shacks proliferating wherever possible in the townships. Around a quarter of households occupy so-called "**informal dwellings**", ie shacks. The ANC launched the **N2 Gateway Project** in 2005 to replace some of the shacks lining the N2 with brick buildings. Nonetheless, **housing** remains one of the biggest problems facing the metropolis (and all South Africa), and it's a growing one: between 1998 and 2014 Cape Town's housing **backlog** grew from 150,000 to 375,000. At present rates of construction it would take decades to meet the shortfall – and that's without accounting for population growth.

With current birth rates and the influx of fifteen thousand families from the rural areas into the city each year, planners project that by 2030 the city's **population** will grow from its present 3.75 million to between five and six million inhabitants, having already increased by around 500 percent since 1950. The housing shortage means that hundreds of thousands of Capetonians have limited **access to services**, such as running water, waterborne-sewerage and electricity. It's also symptomatic of the city's slew of other problems: poverty, unemployment, rampant crime and high infection rates for HIV and TB.

In response to the tardy pace of South Africa's transformation since the end of apartheid, **street protests** became increasingly common and lack of housing provision remains one of the major complaints. While millions of South Africans are reduced to living in shacks, over R200m of taxpayers' money has been lavished on upgrading President Jacob Zuma's private residence at **Nkandla** in KwaZulu-Natal. This and the **death of Nelson Mandela** in late 2013 signalled a crisis for the ideals of the Freedom Charter, which had inspired the ANC for over half a century. It underlined the intractability of economic apartheid and the creeping entrenchment of corruption. With the ascendancy of the Guptas, a powerful trio of Indian brothers with a high level of influence over Zuma, the new buzzword is "state capture".

The ANC lost some support in the **2014 general election**, thanks to the Nkandla scandal and a record of poor delivery but still managed to win with a 62 percent majority. The local elections of 2016 were a different story however, with the ANC losing Johannesburg, Pretoria and Port Elizabeth to the DA. The following year, Zuma fired the well-respected finance minister, Pravhin Gordhan, prompting discontent in the ANC ranks and nationwide demonstrations as two credit rating agencies downgraded South Africa to 'junk' status. In August 2017, Zuma narrowly survived a no-confidence vote in parliament – the eighth such vote against him. The DA remains unlikely to win the 2019 election, however, as its image of being a white party persists – despite having a black leader, Mmusi Maimane.

In the **Western Cape**, the DA continues to dominate, reiterating the province's distinct demographic and political character. The DA's success may in part be due to its better-than-average record of delivery – a survey published in 2014 showed that seven of South Africa's ten best-performing municipalities were in the Western Cape. This included Cape Town, which was the only large city on the list.

However, this rapidly growing metropolis has a host of pressing problems, from burgeoning joblessness to chronic rush-hour traffic. The expansion of industry is a common route for urbanizing societies to rapidly create **employment**; the first signs of this are noticeable in Cape Town, such as the Chevron oil refinery processing 110,000 barrels a day. And yet, industrialization comes at an ecological cost, and Cape Town's **environment** is one of its greatest assets – through tourism, it is a tangible source of income and employment. Tourism creates over fifty thousand jobs, and contributes over R15 billion annually. But on its own, it's not enough. The city's planners and politicians face some tough choices.

2015	2016	2017
Aiming to "decolonize" education, #RhodesMustFall movement topples University of Cape Town's prominent statue of colonial poster boy Cecil Rhodes	DA retains Cape Town in local elections, helmed in the Western Cape by former party leader Helen Zille	There's severe drought, as dam levels drop to critical levels, and Cape Town draws up plans for the apocalyptic "day zero" – when the dams run dry

Books

For a country with a relatively small reading public, South Africa generates a huge number of books, particularly novels and politics and history titles.

FICTION

Tatamkhulu Afrika *The Innocents*. Set in the struggle years, this novel examines the moral and ethical issues of the time, from a Muslim perspective.

Mark Behr *The Smell of Apples*. Powerful first novel set in the 1970s recounts the gradual falling of the scales from the eyes of an eleven-year-old Afrikaner boy, whose father is a major-general in the apartheid army.

André Brink *A Chain of Voices*. Superbly evocative tale of nineteenth-century Cape life, exploring the impact of slavery on one farming family, right up to its dramatic and murderous end.

★**J.M. Coetzee** *Disgrace*. A subtle, strange novel set in a Cape Town university and on a remote Eastern Cape farm, where the lives of a literature professor and his farmer daughter are violently transformed. Bleak but totally engrossing, this novel won the Booker Prize in 1999.

Achmat Dangor *The Z Town Trilogy*. A well respected South African Indian novelist once shortlisted for the Booker Prize, Dangor sets this novel during one of apartheid South Africa's many states of emergency, which is burrowing in intricate ways into the psyches of his characters. The book portrays a brittle family, a dysfunctional society, and how we address – or fail to address – the past's deepest wounds.

Damon Galgut *In a Strange Room*. Galgut has scooped several literary awards: *In a Strange Room* was shortlisted for the 2010 Man Booker Prize for Fiction. Unusually for Galgut, this novel is set outside South Africa and describes the global travels and relationships of a protagonist named, like the author, Damon. Quirky, beautifully written and highly readable.

Lily Herne *Deadlands*. South Africa's street-smart answer to *Twilight* follows the adventures and romance of seventeen-year-old Lele as she navigates the shattered, zombie-infested suburbs of a postapocalyptic Cape Town.

Rayda Jacobs *The Slave Book*. A carefully researched historical novel dealing with love and survival in a slave household in 1830s Cape Town, on the eve of the abolition of slavery.

Ashraf Jamal *Love Themes for the Wilderness*. The inhabitants of a bohemian subculture are lovingly observed in this funny and free-spirited novel set in mid-1990s Observatory.

Pamela Jooste *Dance with a Poor Man's Daughter*. The fragile world of a young coloured girl during the early apartheid years is sensitively imagined in this hugely successful first novel, which won the 1998 Commonwealth Writers' Prize.

J.M. COETZEE

To read a **J.M. Coetzee** novel is to walk an emotional tightrope from exhilaration to sadness, with a sense throughout of being guided by a strong creative intellect and an exceptionally shrewd observer of human experience.

Coetzee's taut, measured style strikes some readers as cold and bloodless; he is relentlessly unsentimental, and plots tend to end on an unsettling note. But despite his reputation as a "difficult" writer, Coetzee never fails to involve us absolutely in the fates of his characters; in the words of Nadine Gordimer, Coetzee "goes to the nerve-centre of being".

Born in Cape Town in 1940 and trained as a linguist and computer scientist in South Africa and the US, Coetzee began to write fiction in the early 1970s. *Dusklands* and *In the Heart of the Country*, his first two novels, were dense and often overwrought dissections of settler psychology, but his prose reached a soaring maturity with *Waiting for the Barbarians* (1980), in which an imaginary desert landscape is the setting for a chilling exploration of the dynamics of imperial power.

In 1983, *Life and Times of Michael K*, following the wanderings of a refugee across a future South Africa ravaged by civil war, won the Booker Prize. The novel ends with a passage of extraordinary beauty, and stands as a postmodern masterpiece reflecting, like much of his work, the bleakness of apartheid. After *Michael K* came the novels *Foe*, *Age of Iron* and *The Master of Petersburg* and a moving childhood memoir, *Boyhood*, which was later followed by *Youth*.

When Coetzee won an unprecedented second Booker Prize for *Disgrace* in 1999, he became famous beyond literary circles for the first time. This has meant exasperation for soundbite-hungry media hounds, since Coetzee abhors publicity – he chose not to attend the Booker Prize award ceremony and is notoriously cagey in social interactions. In 2002, Coetzee emigrated to Australia, where he lives in Adelaide. In 2006, he became an Australian citizen.

Alex La Guma *A Walk in the Night and Other Stories*. One of the best proletarian writers South Africa has produced, La Guma, before his long exile in the UK and Cuba, focused on the conditions of life in Cape Town, particularly the inner-city areas like District Six. His social realism is gritty yet poignant, and it gives us many indelible portraits of Cape Town in the mid-twentieth century.

Anne Landsman *The Devil's Chimney*. A stylish and entertaining piece of magic realism about the Southern Cape town of Oudtshoorn, in the days of the ostrich-feather boom.

Sindiwe Magona *Mother to Mother*. Magona adopts the narrative role of the neighbour of the killer of Amy Biehl, an American student murdered in a Cape Town township in 1993. The novel is a trenchant and lyrical meditation on the traumas of the past.

Songeziwe Mahlangu *Penumbra*. Semi-autobiographical debut novel that etches a unique vision of Cape Town through the eyes of a young man employed by a large insurance company. Torn by turns between mindless web-surfing, drug-induced mania and charismatic Christianity, Manga charts his course through the southern suburbs of the Mother City.

★**Dalene Matthee** *Circles in a Forest*. A descendant of Sir Walter Scott, Matthee powerfully evokes the bygone world of woodcutters dodging wild elephants in the forests of the Garden Route. Look out for *Fiela's Child*, too.

Brent Meersman *Reports Before Daybreak*. This moving novel and its sequel, *Five Lives at Noon*, follow an interconnected group of disparate characters through apartheid-era Cape Town.

Deon Meyer *Thirteen Hours*. This riveting read from South Africa's hottest crime writer will appeal to backpackers especially – one thread follows Detective Benny Griessel's quest to find and save the life of an American overlander on the run from Cape Town gangsters after her travelling companion's murder.

Barbara Mutch *The Girl from Simon's Bay*. This follow-up to the UK-based South African writer's excellent debut, the Karoo-set *Housemaid's Daughter*, is a romantic tale set a century ago in nautical Simon's Town.

Mike Nicol *Payback*. This hard-boiled thriller, one of several by established novelist Nicol (who has been compared to Elmore Leonard and Cormac McCarthy), follows a pair of gun-runners drawn back from retirement into Cape Town's dark underworld.

Margie Orford *Water Music*. One of the Clare Hart novels by internationally acclaimed crime writer Orford, this riveting read, set in picturesque Hout Bay, delves into the dark depths of child abuse.

Richard Rive *Buckingham Palace, District Six*. The unique urban culture of District Six is movingly remembered in this short novel about the life of a now-desolate street and its inhabitants.

Linda Rode (ed) *Crossing Over*. Collection of 26 stories by emerging South African writers on the experiences of adolescence and early adulthood in a period of political transition.

Patricia Schonstein *Skyline*. Set in a crumbling apartment block in central Cape Town, Schonstein's novel examines a young girl's coming of age, her encounters with migrants from elsewhere in Africa, and the rising xenophobia in South Africa.

Jann Turner *Heartland*. A white farmer's daughter and a black labourer's son are childhood companions on a Boland fruit farm; a betrayal occurs, and years later the boy returns from political exile, ready to stake his claim to the land. An ambitious and popular novel.

Zoe Wicomb *You Can't Get Lost in Cape Town*. The author of a book of primarily short stories, Wicombe is remarkable for her sense of realism and the subtle way in which she produces her work. Social concern is transparent, humour is demonstrable, and yet none of it consents to the heavy-handed treatment anti-apartheid protest literature usually follows.

GUIDES AND REFERENCE BOOKS

G.M. Branch *Two Oceans*. Don't be put off by the coffee-table format; this is a comprehensive guide to southern Africa's marine life.

★**Richard Cowling and Dave Richardson** *Fynbos: South Africa's Unique Floral Kingdom*. Lavishly illustrated hardback which offers a fascinating layman's portrait of the *fynbos* ecosystem.

Mike Lundy *Best Walks in the Cape Peninsula*. An invaluable, not-too-bulky book for casual walkers, which contains plenty of possibilities for an afternoon's stroll.

L. McMahon and M. Fraser *A Fynbos Year*. Exquisitely illustrated and well-written book about the Western Cape's unique floral kingdom.

★**Philip van Zyl** (ed) *John Platter South African Wine Guide*. One of the best-selling titles in South Africa – an annually updated pocket book that rates virtually every wine produced in the country. No aspiring connoisseur of Cape wines should venture forth without it.

HISTORY, POLITICS AND SOCIETY

★**Vivian Bickford-Smith, Elizabeth van Heyningen and Nigel Worden** *Cape Town: The Making of a City* and *Cape Town in the Twentieth Century*. The first book is richly illustrated and exhaustively researched, and recounts the growth of Cape Town, from early Khoisan societies to the end of the nineteenth century. The second volume is a thorough and elegant account of modern Cape Town, which interweaves rich local history with international events.

Andrew Brown *Street Blues*. Advocate, police-reserve sergeant and award-winning novelist, Brown paints a gritty, and sometimes witty, picture of life on the beat, tackling the mean streets of Cape Town.

Richard Calland *Anatomy of South Africa: Who Holds the Power*. An incisive dissection of politics and power in South Africa today, from one of the most respected commentators in the country.

John Carlin *Playing the Enemy: Nelson Mandela and the Game that made a Nation*. Gripping account of Nelson Mandela's use of the 1995 Rugby World Cup to unite a fractious nation, in danger of collapsing into civil war. It was also published as *Invictus*, the title of the Clint Eastwood film, which starred Matt Damon and Morgan Freeman.

Andrew Feinstein *After the Party: Corruption, the ANC and South Africa's Uncertain Future*. A personal account of where South Africa's government has lost its way, by a former ANC member of parliament. Feinstein resigned in 2001 in protest at the government's cover-up of graft and corruption in negotiating the country's cripplingly expensive arms deal.

Hermann Giliomee and Bernard Mbenga *New History of South Africa*. A comprehensive, reliable and entertaining account of South Africa's history, published in 2010.

★ **Peter Harris** *In a Different Time: The Inside Story of the Delmas Four*. This brilliantly told, true historical drama is about four young South Africans sent on a mission by the ANC-in-exile, which ultimately led them to Death Row. As their defence lawyer, Harris had unique and sympathetic insight into their personalities and motivations.

★ **Antjie Krog** *Country of My Skull*. An unflinching and harrowing account of the Truth and Reconciliation Commission's investigations. Krog, a respected radio journalist and poet, covered the entire process, and skilfully merges private reaction with national catharsis.

Hein Marais *South Africa Pushed to the Limit: The Political Economy of Change*. An assessment of why the privileged classes remain just that – a handful of conglomerates dominate the South African economy – and how this relates to Jacob Zuma's rise to power.

Alan Mountain *An Unsung Heritage: Perspectives on Slavery*. An account of the nature of slavery in the Cape, and the contribution imported slaves made to the fabric of the area today. Best of all is the guide to slave heritage sites in

the Cape Peninsula, Winelands and West Coast and along the Garden Route, with attractive photos and illustrations.

★ **Pieter-Louis Myburgh** *The Republic of Gupta: A Story of State Capture*. Investigative journalist exposes the dodgy deals that have gone on behind the scenes during President Zuma's reign, covering the Indian Gupta family's influence on the governing party. A page-turning journey to the rotten core of contemporary South Africa.

Mike Nicol *Sea-Mountain, Fire City: Living in Cape Town*. One of the few non-fiction books covering the experience of living in Cape Town at the beginning of the new millennium. Nicol hinges his documentary narrative on moving back to the Cape after a year in Berlin, and maps many of those fissures, not to say abysses, that make Cape Town the divided city that it is.

★ **Nigel Penn** *Rogues, Rebels and Runaways*. A University of Cape Town history professor's hugely entertaining collection of essays on deviant types in the eighteenth-century Cape. Tragi-comic and written in a wry, engaging style.

Robert C-H Shell *Children of Bondage*. Definitive social history of Cape slavery in the eighteenth century – a compelling academic text that is accessible to the lay reader.

Allister Sparks *The Mind of South Africa* and *Beyond the Miracle: Inside the New South Africa*. In the first book, Sparks, an authoritative journalist and historian, traces the rise and fall of the apartheid state in a lively, economical and serious work. *Beyond the Miracle: Inside the New South Africa* examines the prospects for South Africa, looking beyond the initial buoyancy of democracy to emerging patterns in its government.

Stephen Taylor *The Caliban Shore: The Fate of the Grosvenor Castaways*. A gripping account of the wreck of the *Grosvenor* in the eighteenth century, along the Eastern Cape's aptly named Wild Coast. Meticulously researched history, it has the depth and pace of a well-crafted novel.

★ **Desmond Tutu** *No Future Without Forgiveness*. This is Tutu's gracious and honest assessment of the Truth and Reconciliation Commission that he guided. It's an important testimony, from one of the country's most influential thinkers and leaders.

Frank Welsh *A History of South Africa*. Solid scholarship and a strong sense of overall narrative mark this publication as a much-needed addition to South African historiography.

BIOGRAPHY AND AUTOBIOGRAPHY

★ **J.M. Coetzee** *Boyhood: Scenes from Provincial Life*. A moving fictionalized childhood memoir of the Southern Suburbs and Worcester by South Africa's greatest novelist.

★ **Sindiwe Magona** *To My Children's Children*. A fascinating autobiography – initially started so that her family would never forget their roots – which traces Magona's life from the rural Transkei to the hard townships of Cape Town.

Nelson Mandela *Long Walk to Freedom*. Superb best-selling autobiography of the former president and national

icon, which is wonderfully evocative of his early years and intensely moving about his long years in prison.

★ **Benjamin Pogrund** *How Can Man Die Better? The Life of Robert Sobukwe*. The story of one of the most important anti-apartheid liberation heroes, the late leader of the Pan Africanist Congress and a contemporary of Nelson Mandela. Sobukwe was so feared by the white government that they passed a special law – The Sobukwe Clause – to keep him in solitary confinement on Robben Island after he'd served his sentence.

★**Anthony Sampson** *Mandela, The Authorised Biography*. Released to coincide with Mandela's retirement from the presidency in 1999, Sampson's authoritative volume competes with *A Long Walk to Freedom* in both interest and sheer poundage. Firmly grounded in exhaustive research and interviews, it offers a broader perspective and sharper analysis than the autobiography.

Stephen Taylor *Defiance: The Extraordinary Life of Lady Anne Barnard*. Biography of the Georgian-era socialite who spent five years in Cape high society beginning in 1797.

THE ARTS

Marion Arnold *Women and Art in South Africa*. Comprehensive, pioneering study of women artists from the early twentieth century to the present.

Thorsten Deckler, Anne Graupner, Henning Rasmuss *Contemporary South African Architecture in a Landscape of Transition*. Lavishly illustrated coverage of fifty outstanding architectural projects that have been completed since 1994.

Stephen Francis and Rico Schacherl *Madam and Eve*. Various annual volumes of telling and witty cartoons that convey the daily struggle between an African domestic worker and her white madam in the northern suburbs of Johannesburg. These cartoons say more about post-apartheid society than countless academic tomes.

Steve Gordon *Beyond the Blues: Township Jazz in the Sixties and Seventies*. Portraits, in words and pictures, of the country's jazz greats, such as Kippie Moeketsi, Basil Coetzee and Abdullah Ibrahim (Dollar Brand).

★**Andy Mason** *What's So Funny? Under the Skin of South African Cartooning*. Insightful, fascinating and thoroughly collectable wade through the history of South African visual satire from the colonial period to the present.

Ralf-Peter Seippel *South African Photography: 1950–2010*. South Africa's history has provided a rich vein of material for photographers, and this volume covers the work of some of the country's most celebrated lensmen.

Sue Williamson *South African Art Now*. A survey of South African art from the "Resistance Art" of the 1960s to the present, covering movements, genres and leading artists such as Marlene Dumas and William Kentridge, by one of the country's most influential commentators and an accomplished artist in her own right.

★**Zapiro** Umpteen annual cartoon collections by South Africa's leading political cartoonist. Jonathan Shapiro, aka Zapiro, consistently reveals what needs to be exposed in satirical, hard-hitting and shocking cartoons depicting for example President Zuma raping Lady Justice or the South African nation (ⓦ zapiro.com).

POETRY

Ingrid de Kok *Transfer* and *Seasonal Fires*. Technically adroit and always moving work by an internationally acclaimed South African feminist poet.

★**Finuala Dowling** *Notes from the Dementia Ward*. At once cynical, humorous and sad, Dowling's award-winning collection explores the death of her brother and mental decline of her mother against the clearly delineated backdrop of Cape Town.

★**Denis Hirson** (ed) *The Lava of This Land: South African Poetry 1960–1996*. Comprehensive anthology of South African poetry that includes work from the oral period, as well as translations from Afrikaans and other languages.

Ingrid Jonker *Selected Poems*. One of the few Afrikaans-language poets whose work has been translated into a standard of English that does justice to their work. The poems display a remarkable rawness in depicting the outrage of 1960s apartheid, as well as a grief-stricken lyricism. The poet, who drowned herself off Sea Point in 1965, is often compared to Sylvia Plath.

★**Stephen Watson** *The Other City* and *The Light Echo*. No one better evokes Cape Town's changeable beauty, though Watson (who died of cancer in 2011) also writes about matters of the heart and great universal themes.

TRAVEL WRITING

Richard Dobson *Karoo Moons: A Photographic Journey*. If you need encouragement to explore the desert interior of South Africa, these enticing images should do the trick.

Justin Fox and Alison Westwood *Secret Cape Town*. Two local travel writers discover the obscure sights that tell the city's hidden stories.

Sihle Khumalo *Dark Continent, My Black Arse*. Insightful and witty account by a black South African who quit his well-paid job to realize a dream of travelling from the Cape to Cairo by public transport.

★**Ben Maclennan** *The Wind Makes Dust: Four Centuries of Travel in Southern Africa*. A remarkable anthology of fascinating travel pieces, meticulously unearthed and researched.

Julia Martin *A Millimetre of Dust: Visiting Ancestral Sites*. Sensitively crafted narrative that begins on the Cape Peninsula and takes the author, her husband and two children on a journey to important archeological sites in the Northern Cape, raising ethical, ecological and philosophical questions along the way.

Paul Theroux *Dark Star Safari: Overland from Cairo to Cape Town*. Theroux's powerful account of his overland trip from Cairo to Cape Town, with a couple of chapters on South Africa, including an account of meeting writer Nadine Gordimer.

Music

Cape Town's most proclaimed musical treasure is Cape jazz, the greatest exponent of which is Abdullah Ibrahim, a supremely gifted pianist and composer, born in the Cape Flats, who for decades has produced a hypnotic fusion of African, American and Cape Muslim idioms. Other Cape Town jazz legends include saxophonists McCoy Mrubata and the late Winston "Mankunu" Ngozi, Basil Coetzee and Robbie Jansen, plus guitarist Errol Dyers, pianist Hotep Galeta and bassist Spencer Mbadu. Three young stars stand out as heirs to the Cape jazz tradition: the astronomically cool guitarist Jimmy Dludlu; subtle, mellow pianist Paul Hanmer; and pianist Kyle Shepherd, who was taught by Robbie Jansen – catch them live if you can.

Among African township youth, two of the biggest sounds are **kwaito** and local **hip-hop**. In an accurate reflection of the depressed and nihilistic mood of township youth culture, *kwaito*'s vibe tends to be downbeat, and the music frequently carries a strong association with gangsterism and explicit sexuality. Although the supporters of local hip-hop eagerly proclaim that it is now replacing *kwaito*, the reality is more nuanced, and the difference between the two isn't always clear-cut.

DJ-mixed South African **house** manages to cross racial and cultural boundaries, attracting practitioners and fans from all sectors of the country, though it is dominated by black DJs such as **DJ Fresh**, **Glen Lewis**, **DJ Mbuso**, **Thibo Tazz**, **DJ Fosta** and **Oskido**. Meanwhile, South African **rap** has enjoyed sustained popularity since the early 1990s, remaining mostly ghettoized within the coloured community of the Western Cape apart from the likes of Soweto wunderkind Spoek Mathambo. Heavily influenced by African-American rappers, performers often exude a sense of being "Americans trapped in Africa", but many mix in Cape slang and mine local life for material. Pioneers of the

ENTER DIE ANTWOORD

Die Antwoord (meaning "the answer") – an unknown crew from Cape Town's northern suburbs **rapping** in Cape Flats slang – was an overnight sensation that stormed the internet in 2010. This was the true grit from the streets of the Mother City: a lowlife rap genre known as **zef** (from an Afrikaans word that denotes trashy style). That, at least, was the story.

Their **success** was real enough: in February 2010, traffic to their website (ⓦdieantwoord .com), which was streaming their debut album *o*, was so heavy (fifteen million hits) that it crashed, and they had to move to a US server. Their signature foul-mouthed lyrics aside, there's nothing rough and ready about their output – look at the tight machine-gun vocal style (likened by *Rolling Stone* to "Eminem's *Lose Yourself* on mescaline"), the slick art-direction, the careful choreography and the cool Keith Haring-esque graphics on their *Enter the Ninja* video.

Far from being the band that came from nowhere, Die Antwoord, made up of frontman Ninja, helium-voiced ¥o-landi Vi$$er and producer God (formerly known as DJ Hi-Tek), is the latest surreal vehicle for **Watkin Tudor Jones** (**Ninja**), whose previous excursions included hip-hop outfits Max Normal and the Constructus Corporation. Jones's history of taking on personas has led detractors to express disappointment that Die Antwoord "aren't real" (whatever that means in show business), while fans declare him a creative genius. Does it matter? The fact is, Die Antwoord have gone global by co-opting and developing an unmistakably Cape Town sound that really cooks. Rumours of their demise abounded in 2017, but everything about these masterful image manipulators, who can be seen on the big screen in Neill Blomkamp's *Chappie*, should be taken with a pinch of *sout*.

style were the heavily politicized **Prophets of Da City**, who included rapper Shaheen Ariefdien. Others who subsequently emerged include the group **Brasse vannie Kaap** (who rapped in Afrikaans) and DJ **Ready D.** Less easy to confine under the rubric of rap is **E.J. von Lyrik** (of hip-hop crew **Godessa**), who jams rap, reggae and funk influences into her sound. By far the most successful are **Die Antwoord**, who have stormed the world with their foulmouthed style known as **zef**, which is a mixture of English, Afrikaans and Cape Flats slang (see box, p.273). Back home, their one-time collaborator **Isaac Mutant**, with genuine roots in the Cape Flats, projects a menace-to-society image.

English-speaking South Africans have successfully replicated virtually every popular Western musical style going. Some have found fame in the outside world, but there are still many gifted performers who remain in the Mother City, including **Goldfish**, the **Parlotones**, string-maestro **Steve Newman** and **Tananas**, a string trio Newman plays with for a couple of months each year. A new Cape Town talent worth catching is folk singer **Jeremy Loops**, who hit the number-one spot on the South Africa iTunes store in 2014 with his skilful artistry on loop pedal, guitar, harmonica and beatbox.

Afrikaans music is a world unto itself, but from the late 1920s until the 1960s, American country was its greatest outside influence. Following the end of apartheid, a concern about the future of the Afrikaans language and culture spurred a revival of interest in Afrikaans music. There is undoubtedly more stylistic variety now than ever before: witness the house/disco of **Juanita**, the heavy rock of **Karen Zoid** and **Jackhammer**, the Neil Diamond-esque songs of **Steve Hofmeyer** (one of the bestselling Afrikaans music artists), as well as the punk-rock and indie riffs of **Fokofpolisiekar** and their spin-offs such as Die Heuwels Fantasties, aKING and the Van Coke Cartel. One of the most amusing Afrikaans bodies of musical work is the studied banality of rapper **Jack Parow**, who has collaborated with Die Antwoord. The Fokofpolisiekar documentary *Forgive Them for They Know Not What They Do* gives a sense of the challenges faced by rock bands in the still-conservative Afrikaans cultural universe.

Arguably the place where many contemporary South African artists sit most comfortably is the catch-all category known as **Afropop**. Characterized by a knack for combining various local African styles with Western popular influences, and the eschewing of computer-generated backing in favour of actual instruments, Afropop has the ability to attract a multiracial audience. Cape Town's most successful proponents of the style are **Freshlyground**, who, because of their broad appeal and engaging sound, were chosen to accompany Shakira in jamming to a billion viewers at the opening and closing ceremonies of the 2010 FIFA World Cup. The group are still going strong, with plenty of live performances – their bedrock – and album *The Legend* released in 2013. Spoek Mathambo offers an edgier take on the fusion of African and Western sounds in his "township tech", which merges lo-fi guitars, hip-hop beats and electronic noodling, along with sophisticated wordplay in English and several African languages. Check out the dark, gritty and gothic video for his cover of Joy Division's 'She's Lost Control'.

ESSENTIAL CAPE TOWN SOUNDS

★**Abdullah Ibrahim** *African Marketplace* (Discovery/ WEA). Ibrahim's best album – a wistful, nostalgic, otherworldly journey.

Basil Coetzee *Monwabisi* (Mountain). Smoky, energetic jazz record from one of the greatest Cape saxophonists.

Dantai *Operation Lahlela* (Nebula BOS). R&B-flavoured *kwaito* from one of Cape Town's up-and-coming dance acts.

Die Antwoord *O* (Rhythm Records). The signature album of the *zef* rave rap style that brought the trio to the world's attention and features their addictive and weird anthem track, *Enter the Ninja*.

Fokofpolisiekar *Swanesang* (Rhythm Records/The Orchard). One of South Africa's most successful live bands has helped redefine Afrikaner identity for the postapartheid generation with its punk-rock-influenced sound, while repeatedly outraging the establishment, starting with their name, which translates as "fuck off police car".

Freshlyground *Ma'Cheri* (Freeground Records/Sony BMG). Album of the Year at the 2008 SA Music Awards, *Ma'Cheri* sees the most enduring of South Africa's Afropopsters do what they're known for: crossing national and stylistic boundaries to deliver catchy hooks and accessible melodies.

★**Goldfish** *Perceptions of Pacha* (Pacha Recordings/ Finetunes). This Cape Town-based duo weave acoustic sounds into their predominantly electronica-based grooves to crank out one addictively upbeat Ibiza-style track after the other.

★**Jeremy Loops** *Trading Change* (Sheer Sound). Debut folk-pop album, which shot to number one on the South Africa iTunes store in 2014, beating Toni Braxton and Shakira. Tracks such as "Down South" are Cape anthems.

Jimmy Dludlu *Essence of Rhythm* (Universal). The essence of smooth jazz, and one of South Africa's most popular representatives of the commercially successful jazz style.

Paul Hanmer *Trains To Taung* (Sheer Sound). This album is constructed around Hanmer's dreamy, piano-based compositions. Now considered a classic, and one of the first expositions of the new jazz of the post-apartheid era.

Prophets of Da City *Ghetto Code* (Universal). Cape Town rap supremos' finest release, full of tough but articulate rhymes and some seriously heavy samples, all in true Cape Flats style.

Ringo *Sondelani* (CCP). A superb modern reworking of traditional Xhosa sounds by this bald Capetonian heart-throb, including the hit track "Sondela", which has become one of South Africa's most well-liked love songs.

Robbie Jansen *Nomad Jez* (EMI). Great, locally flavoured, album from veteran saxophonist Jansen, playing with other luminaries of the local jazz scene including Hilton Schilder and Errol Dyers.

Rodriguez *Cold Fact* (Light In The Attic/Naxos). The Dylanesque bard of Detroit had never visited Cape Town when he cut this cult classic, but unbeknown to him, he was bigger than Elvis in 1970s South Africa. Rodriguez eventually played sold-out shows across Southern Africa, as the Oscar-winning documentary *Searching for Sugar Man* relates, and his psychedelic '70s rock numbers remain local anthems.

Springbok Nude Girls *Afterlife Satisfaction* (Sony Music). The band, who performed as the opening act for U2 during their 2011 tour of South Africa, deliver a powerful, if not particularly original, belting rock set in this album.

Winston "Mankunu" Ngozi *Crossroads* (Nkomo/Sheer). Sinuous, upbeat township jazz from the veteran Cape Town saxman.

ESSENTIAL SOUTH AFRICAN SOUNDS

Bayete *Umkhaya-Lo* (Polygram). A seminal fusion of South African sounds with laidback soul and funk, blended by lead singer Jabu Khanyile's unique mixing talent and spiced with his beautifully soothing vocals.

Ladysmith Black Mambazo *Heavenly* (Gallo/Spectrum). An inspired and commercially successful foray into Afropop, featuring solo versions of various pop classics as well as vocal collaborations with Dolly Parton and Lou Rawls. There are also 'best of' compilations available and Paul Simon's *Graceland* features their dulcet voices.

Gloria Bosman *Tranquillity* and *Very Best Of* (Sheer/Limelight). A young and compelling jazz vocalist, Bosman juggles African and American styles with ease. Paul Hanmer arranges and tickles the ivories. The latter album is a retrospective of her best recordings up to 2009.

Lucky Dube *Prisoner* (Gallo). Originally a township jive singer, the late Dube made a switch to reggae that was both artistically and commercially inspired. *Prisoner* was South Africa's second-bestselling album ever, full of stirring Peter Tosh-style roots tunes.

Brenda Fassie *The Queen of Pop* and *Memeza* (CCP). The former is a posthumous survey that covers the greatest hits of South Africa's very own Madonna; the latter, featuring the massive hit "Vuli Ndlela", was Brenda's most commercially successful effort.

★**Hugh Masekela** *Hope* (Nashville Catalog/eOne). Jazz trumpeter and political exile under apartheid, Masekela treated Washington D.C.'s Blues Alley to this hot set in 1993, even including a Fela Kuti cover.

Mfaz'Omnyama *Ngisebenzile Mama* (Gallo). The title means "I have been working, Mum", and is amply justified by this superb set, which features some of the best maskanda (Zulu folk) ever recorded. There are also greatest hits compilations on the market.

★**Miriam Makeba** *Her Essential Recordings* (Manteca). A kind of Xhosa Billie Holiday who went into exile under apartheid, the jazz chanteuse's trademark hit 'Pata Pata' and 'Click Song', sung in the clicking Xhosa language, feature here.

Moses Taiwa Molelekwa *Genes and Spirits* (Melt2000). Fascinating jazz/drum'n'bass fusion by a talented young pianist, who died tragically in 2001.

★**Spoek Mathambo** *Father Creeper* (Sub Pop). It's not always an easy listen, but Mathambo's 2012 album, showcasing his boundary-blasting "township tech" in all its language- and genre-switching glory, captures the pulse of township streets.

Pops Mohamed *How Far Have We Come?* (Melt2000). An exciting celebration of traditional African instruments: *mbiras*, *koras*, mouthbows and various percussion instruments are supplemented by bass and brass in this ethereal but funky album.

Sibongile Khumalo *Ancient Evenings* (Sony Music). Though a classically trained opera singer, Khumalo takes on both jazz and a variety of traditional melodies on this wonderful album, demonstrating why she is one of South Africa's best-loved singers.

★**Various artists** *Amandla!* (ATO). The soundtrack to Lee Hirsch's excellent 2002 documentary about music's role in the fight against apartheid features the likes of Hugh Masekela, Miriam Makeba and Abdullah Ibrahim.

Vusi Mahlasela *Silang Mabele* (BMG). Lush harmonies and lilting melodies abound in this album by South Africa's sweet-voiced township balladeer.

Language

In Cape Town and along the Garden Route, you'll rarely, if ever, need to use any other language than English. Around thirty percent of whites are mother-tongue English speakers, and South African English has its own distinct character, as different from the Queen's English as Australian. Its most notable characteristic is its unique words and usages, some of which are drawn from Afrikaans and the indigenous African languages. The hefty *Oxford Dictionary of South African English* makes for an interesting browse.

Afrikaans, although a language you seldom need to speak, nevertheless remains very much in evidence in South Africa, and you will certainly encounter it on official forms and countless signs, particularly on the road (see p.279). A common one to look out for, when you are driving to Cape Town, is *Kaapstad*, the Afrikaans name for the city. If you talk to a Jo'burger about the relatively sleepy Mother City, they might jokingly refer to it as *slaapstad*.

The other main language spoken in Cape Town is **Xhosa**, the predominant mother tongue of the city's African residents and easily distinguished by the clicks that form part of the words. It is also Nelson Mandela's mother tongue, which he shares with over eight million other South Africans, predominantly in the Eastern Cape.

The glossary below is far from comprehensive, but it does include some of the more common words that are unique to South African English. Words whose spelling makes it hard to guess how to render them have their approximate pronunciation given in italics. Where **gh** occurs in the pronunciation, it denotes the **ch** sound in the Scottish word lo**ch**. Sometimes we've used the letter "r" in the pronunciation, even though the word in question doesn't contain this letter; for example, we've given the pronunciation of "Egoli" as "*air-gaw-lee*". In these instances the syllable containing the "r" is meant to represent a familiar word or sound from English; the "r" itself shouldn't be pronounced.

GLOSSARY

African In the context of South Africa, an indigenous South African

Afrikaner Literally "African": a white person who speaks Afrikaans

Aloe Family of spiky indigenous succulents, often with dramatic orange flowers

Apartheid (apart-hate) Term used from the 1940s for the National Party's official policy of "racial separation"

Arvie Afternoon

Baai Afrikaans word meaning "bay"; also a common suffix in place names, eg Stilbaai

Bakkie (bucky) Light truck or van

Bantu (bun-too) Unscientific apartheid term for indigenous black people; in linguistics, a group of indigenous southern-African languages

Bantustan Term used under apartheid for the territories such as Transkei, reserved for Africans

Bergie A vagrant living on the slopes of Table Mountain; a homeless person on the streets of Cape Town

Big Five A term derived from hunting that refers to the trophy animals hunters most want to bag: lion, leopard, buffalo, elephant and rhino; often now used generically to indicate top big game country (as opposed to game reserves that only have antelope and other small mammals)

Black Imprecise term that sometimes refers collectively to Africans, Indians and coloureds, but more usually is used to mean Africans

Boer (boor) Literally "farmer", but also refers to early Dutch colonists at the Cape and Afrikaners

Boland (boor-lunt) Southern part of the Western Cape

Bottle store Off-licence or liquor store

Boy Offensive term used to refer to an adult African man who is a servant

Bundu (approximately boon-doo, but with the vowels shortened) Wilderness or backcountry

Burgher Literally a citizen, but more specifically a member of the Dutch community at the Cape in the seventeenth and eighteenth centuries; free burghers were VOC employees released from contract to farm independently on the Cape Peninsula and surrounding areas

Bush See **bundu**

Bushman South Africa's earliest, but now almost extinct, inhabitants who lived by hunting and gathering

Cape Doctor The southeaster that brings cool winds during the summer months

Cape Dutch Nineteenth-century, whitewashed, gabled style of architecture

Cape Dutch Revival Twentieth-century style based on Cape Dutch architecture (see box, p.102)

CBD The Central Business District of central Cape Town

Coloured South African people of mixed race, descended from diverse ancestors including slaves and Islamic dissidents brought to Cape Town by the Dutch East India Company (see box, p.46).

Dagga (dugh-a) Marijuana

Dagha (dah-ga) Mud used in indigenous construction

Dassie (dussy) Hyrax

Disa (die-za) One of twenty species of beautiful indigenous orchid, most famous of which is the red disa or "Pride of Table Mountain"

Dominee (dour-min-ee) Reverend (abbreviated to Ds)

Dorp Country town or village (derived from Afrikaans)

Drostdy (dross-tea) Historically, the building of the landdrost or magistrate

Fundi Expert

Fynbos (fayn-boss) Term for vast range of fine-leafed species that predominate in the southern part of the Western Cape (see box, p.110)

Girl Offensive term used to refer to an African woman who is a servant

Gogga (gho-gha) Creepy-crawly or insect

Griqua Person of mixed white, Bushman and Hottentot descent

Group Areas Act Now-defunct law passed in 1950 that provided for the establishment of separate areas for each "racial group"

Homeland See **bantustan**

Hottentot Now-unfashionable term for indigenous Khoisan herders encountered by the first settlers at the Cape

Indaba Zulu term meaning a group discussion and now used in South African English for any meeting or conference

Is it? Really?

Jislaaik! (yis-like) Exclamation equivalent to "Geez!" or "Crikey!"

Jol Party, celebration

Just now In a while

Kaffir Highly objectionable term of abuse for Africans

Karoo Arid plateau that occupies a large proportion of the South African interior

Khoikhoi (ghoy-ghoy) Self-styled name of South Africa's original herding inhabitants

Khoisan A conflation of the terms "Khoikhoi" and "San" used to collectively refer to South Africa's aboriginal inhabitants; the two were socially, but not ethnically, distinct, the Khoikhoi having been herders and the San hunter-gatherers

Kloof (klo-ef) Ravine or gorge

Knobkerrie Wooden club

Koppie Hillock

Kramat (crum-mutt) Shrine of a Muslim holy man

Krans (crunce) Sheer cliff face; plural kranse

Lapa Courtyard of group of Ndebele houses; also used to describe an enclosed area at safari camps, where braais (see p.278) are held

Lekker Nice

Lobola (la-ball-a) Bride price, paid by an African man to his wife's parents

Location Old-fashioned term for segregated African area on the outskirts of a town or farm

Madiba Mandela's clan name, used affectionately

Malay Misnomer for Cape Muslims of Asian descent

Mbira (m-beer-a) African thumb piano, often made with a gourd

MK Umkhonto we Sizwe (Spear of the Nation), the armed wing of the ANC, now incorporated into the national army

Mlungu (m-loon-goo) African term for a white person, equivalent to honkie

Moffie (mawf-ee) Gay person

Mother City Nickname for Cape Town

Muti (moo-tee) See **umuthi**

Nkosi Sikelel' iAfrika "God Bless Africa", anthem of the ANC and now of South Africa

Pass Document that Africans used to have to carry at all times, which essentially rendered them aliens in their own country

Pastorie (puss-tour-ee) Parsonage

Platteland (plutta-lunt) Country districts

Poort Narrow pass through mountains along a river course

Protea National flower of South Africa

Raadsaal (the "d" is pronounced "t") Council or parliament building

Robot Traffic light

Rondavel (ron-daa-vil, with the stress on the middle syllable) Circular building based on traditional African huts

San A more common term for Bushmen (see above)

Sangoma (sun-gom-a) Traditional spirit medium and healer

Shebeen (sha-bean) Unlicensed township tavern

Southeaster Prevailing wind in the Western Cape

Spaza shops Small stall or kiosk

Stoep Veranda

Strandloper Literally "beach walkers"; Bushman or San social group who lived along the shores of the Western Cape and whose hunting and gathering consisted largely of shellfish and other seafood

Tackies Sneakers or plimsolls

Township Area set aside under apartheid for Africans

Transkei (trans-kye) Now-defunct homeland for Xhosa speakers

Trekboer (trek-boor) Nomadic Afrikaner farmers, usually in the eighteenth and nineteenth century

Umuthi (oo-moo-tee) Traditional herbal medicine

Vlei (flay) Swamp

VOC Verenigde Oostindische Compagnie, the Dutch East India Company

Voortrekkers (the first syllable rhymes with "boor") Dutch burghers who migrated inland in their ox wagons in the nineteenth century to escape British colonialism

FOOD AND DRINKS TERMS

Amarula Liqueur that is made from the berries of the marula tree

Begrafnisrys (ba-ghruff-niss-race) Literally "funeral rice"; traditional Cape Muslim dish of yellow rice cooked with raisins

Biltong Sun-dried salted strips of meat, that are chewed as a snack

Blatjang (blutt-young) Cape Muslim chutney that has become a standard condiment on South African dinner tables

Bobotie (ba-boor-tea) Traditional Cape curried mince topped with a savoury custard and often cooked with apricots and almonds

Boerekos (boor-a-coss) Farm food, usually consisting of loads of meat and vegetables cooked using butter and sugar

Boerewors (boor-a-vorce) Spicy lengths of sausage that are de rigueur at braais

Bokkoms Dried fish, much like salt fish

Braai (bry) Barbecue

Braaivleis (bry-flace) Barbecued meat

Bredie Cape vegetable and meat stew

Cane or **cane spirit** A potent vodka-like spirit distilled from sugar cane and generally mixed with a soft drink such as Coke

Cap Classique Sparkling wine fermented in the bottle in exactly the same way as Champagne; also called Méthode Cap Classic

Cape gooseberry Fruit of the physalis; a sweet yellow berry

Cape salmon or **geelbek** (ghear-l-beck) Delicious firm-fleshed sea fish (unrelated to northern-hemisphere salmon)

Cape Velvet A sweet liqueur-and-cream dessert beverage that resembles Irish Cream liqueur

Denningvleis (den-ning-flace) Spicy traditional Cape lamb stew

Frikkadel Fried onion and meatballs

Geelbek See **Cape salmon**

Haneepoort (harner-poort) Delicious sweet dessert grape

Kabeljou (cobble-yo) Common South African marine fish, also called kob

Kerrievis (kerry-fiss) See **pickled fish**

Kingklip Highly prized deepwater fish caught along the Atlantic and Indian ocean coasts

Kob See **kabeljou**

Koeksister (cook-sister) Deep-fried plaited doughnut, dripping with syrup

Maas or **amasi** or **amaas** Traditional African beverage consisting of naturally soured milk. It is available in a packaged dairy product in supermarkets

Maaskaas Cottage cheese made from **maas**

Mageu or **mahewu** or **maheu** (ma-gh-weh) Traditional African beer made from maize meal and water, now packaged and commercially available

Malva Very rich and very sweet traditional baked Cape dessert

Mampoer (mum-poor) Moonshine; home-distilled spirit made from soft fruit, commonly peaches

Mealie See **mielie**

Melktert (melk-tairt) Traditional Cape custard pie

Mielie Maize

Mielie pap (mealy pup) Maize porridge, varying from a thin mixture to a stiff one that can resemble polenta

Mqomboti (m-qom-booty) Traditional African beer made from fermented sorghum

Musselcracker Large-headed fish with powerful jaws and firm, white flesh

Naartjie (nar-chee) Tangerine or mandarin

Pap (pup) Porridge

Peri-peri Delicious hottish spice of Portuguese origin commonly used with grilled chicken

Perlemoen (pear-la-moon) Abalone

Pickled fish Traditional Cape dish of fish preserved with onions, vinegar and curry. It is available tinned in supermarkets

Pinotage A uniquely South African cultivar hybridized from Pinot Noir and Hermitage grapes and from which a wine of the same name is made

Potjiekos or **potjie** (poy-key-kos) Food cooked slowly over embers in a three-legged cast-iron pot

Putu (poo-too) Traditional African **mielie pap** (see p.278) prepared until it forms dry crumbs

Rooibos (roy-boss) **tea** Indigenous herbal tea, made from the leaves of a particular *fynbos* plant
Rooti Chapati
Salmon trout Freshwater fish that is often smoked to create a cheaper and pretty good imitation of smoked salmon
Salomie Roti
Sambals (sam-bills) Accompaniments, such as chopped bananas, green peppers, desiccated coconut and chutney, served with Cape curries
Samp Traditional African dish of broken maize kernels, frequently cooked with beans
Skokiaan (skok-ee-yan) Potent home-brew

Smoorsnoek (smore-snook) Smoked **snoek**
Snoek (snook) Large fish that features in many traditional Cape recipes
Sosatie (so-sah-ti) Spicy skewered mince
Spanspek (spon-speck) A sweet melon
Steenbras (ste-en-bruss) A delicious white-fleshed fish
Van der Hum South African **naartjie**-flavoured liqueur
Vetkoek (fet-cook) Deep-fried doughnut-like cake
Waterblommetjiebredie (vata-blom-a-key-bree-dee) Cape meat stew made with waterlily rhizomes
Witblits (vit-blitz) Moonshine
Yellowtail Delicious darkish-fleshed marine fish

AFRIKAANS STREET SIGNS

Derde	Third	**Perron**	Station platform
Doeane	Customs	**Polisie**	Police
Drankwinkel	Liquor shop	**Poskantoor**	Post office
Eerste	First	**Regs**	Right
Geen ingang	No entry	**Ry**	Go
Gevaar	Danger	**Sentrum**	Centre
Goof	Main	**Singel**	Crescent
Hoog	High	**Stad**	City
Ingang	Entrance	**Stad sentrum**	City centre
Inligting	Information	**Stadig**	Slow
Kantoor	Office	**Stasie**	Station
Kerk	Church	**Strand**	Beach
Kort	Short	**Swembad**	Swimming pool
Links	Left	**Verbode**	Prohibited
Lughawe	Airport	**Verkeer**	Traffic
Mans	Men	**Versigtig**	Carefully
Mark	Market	**Vierde**	Fourth
Ompad	Detour	**Vrouens**	Women
Pad	Road	**Vyfde**	Fifth
Padwerke voor	Roadworks ahead		

Small print and index

Rough Guide credits

Editor: Olivia Rawes
Layout: Jessica Subramanian
Cartography: Ashutosh Bharti, Richard Marchi
Picture editor: Aude Vauconsant
Proofreader: Stewart Wild
Managing editor: Keith Drew
Assistant editor: Shasya Goel

Production: Jimmy Lao
Cover photo research: Marta Bescos Sanchez
Editorial assistant: Aimee White
Senior DTP coordinator: Dan May
Programme manager: Gareth Lowe
Publishing director: Georgina Dee

Publishing information

This 6th edition published January 2018 by
Rough Guides Ltd,
80 Strand, London WC2R 0RL
11, Community Centre, Panchsheel Park,
New Delhi 110017, India
Distributed by Penguin Random House
Penguin Books Ltd, 80 Strand, London WC2R 0RL
Penguin Group (USA), 345 Hudson Street, NY 10014, USA
Penguin Group (Australia), 250 Camberwell Road,
Camberwell, Victoria 3124, Australia
Penguin Group (NZ), 67 Apollo Drive, Mairangi Bay,
Auckland 1310, New Zealand
Penguin Group (South Africa), Block D, Rosebank Office
Park, 181 Jan Smuts Avenue, Parktown North, Gauteng,
South Africa 2193
Rough Guides is represented in Canada by DK Canada, 320
Front Street West, Suite 1400, Toronto, Ontario M5V 3B6
Printed in Singapore
© Rough Guides, 2018
Maps © Rough Guides

A catalogue record for this book is available from the
British Library
ISBN: 978-0-24130-620-8
The publishers and authors have done their best to
ensure the accuracy and currency of all the information in
**The Rough Guide to Cape Town, the Winelands & the
Garden Route**, however, they can accept no responsibility
for any loss, injury, or inconvenience sustained by any
traveller as a result of information or advice contained in
the guide.
1 3 5 7 9 8 6 4 2

MIX
Paper from
responsible sources
FSC™ C018179

Help us update

We've gone to a lot of effort to ensure that the sixth edition
of **The Rough Guide to Cape Town, the Winelands &
the Garden Route** is accurate and up-to-date. However,
things change – places get "discovered", opening hours are
notoriously fickle, restaurants and rooms raise prices or lower
standards. If you feel we've got it wrong or left something
out, we'd like to know, and if you can remember the address,
the price, the hours, the phone number, so much the better.

Please send your comments with the subject line
"**Rough Guide to Cape Town, the Winelands & the
Garden Route Update**" to mail@uk.roughguides.com.
We'll credit all contributions and send a copy of the next
edition (or any other Rough Guide if you prefer) for the
very best emails.

Acknowledgements

James Bainbridge: Thanks to Olivia and Keith at Rough
Guides for your excellent brief-writing and question-
answering skills. Also to everyone on the home front for
cups of tea and patience as the deadlines, deadlines within
deadlines and extensions loomed – especially my in-laws
for the many hours of babysitting.

Barbara McCrea: Thank you to my fine editor for holding
it all together, to my family and friends for support, and to
the good people who provided accommodation, meals or
information along the way.

Readers' updates

Thanks to all the readers who have taken the time to write in with comments and suggestions (and apologies if we've
inadvertently omitted or misspelt anyone's name):

Angelika Bucher; Christina de Boni; Cilla Langdon-Down; Adrian Tahourdin; Tina Thomas; Sue Wall.

ABOUT THE AUTHORS

James Bainbridge grew up in Shropshire, UK and lived on a few continents before his wife-to-be persuaded him to swap London for her home patch of Cape Town. Seven years later, they're based among the good schools and high fences of the city's leafy Southern Suburbs, and, when he's not dropping the kids at crèche, James covers Africa and beyond for numerous publications.

Barbara McCrea was born in Zimbabwe, and taught African literature at the University of Natal. She lived in London for fifteen years authoring Rough Guides to Zimbabwe and Botswana, South Africa, Cape Town and the Garden Route, before returning to live in South Africa after the release of Nelson Mandela. She lives close to the beach in Cape Town, where she swims, rides and climbs mountains.

Photo credits

Index

Maps are marked in grey

Map index

Listings key

- ▪ Accommodation
- ● Eating
- ▪ Drinking/nightlife
- ● Shopping

City plan

The **city plan** on the pages that follow is divided as shown:

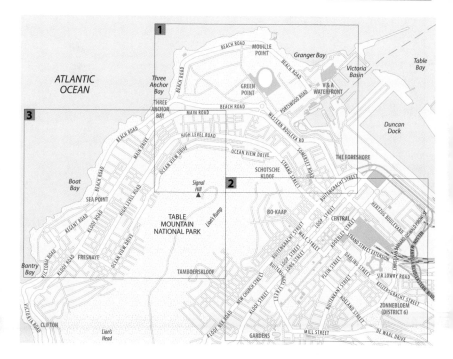

Map symbols

Province boundary	✈ Airport	♦ Place of interest	🐦 Bird sanctuary
Chapter division boundary	★ Bus/taxi	ⵛ Garden	Shipwreck
Motorway	P Parking	Vineyard	禾 Picnic site
Major road	✉ Post office	Golf course	Swimming area
Minor road	(i) Information office	🏛 Monument	Building
Path	+ Hospital	Ship wreck	Market
Railway	+ Pharmacy	Lighthouse	Church
Ferry route	Mosque	Windmill	Stadium
River	✡ Synagogue	▲ Mountain peak	Park
Funicular	⊠ Entrance gate	Cave	Beach
Cable car	Mountain range		

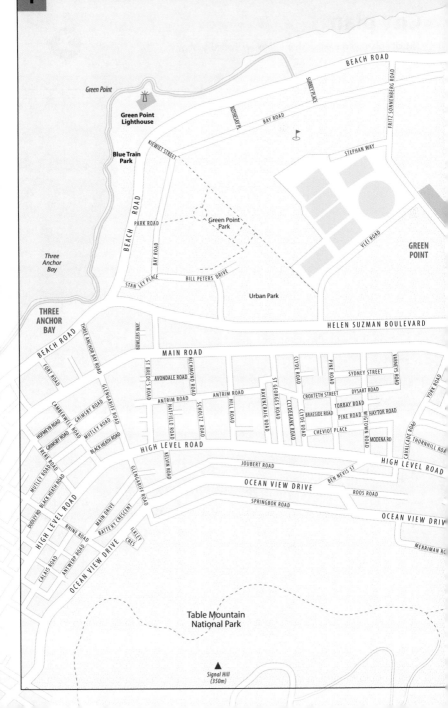

Green Point

Green Point Lighthouse

Blue Train Park

Three Anchor Bay

THREE ANCHOR BAY

BEACH ROAD

SUBBEY PLACE

ROTHESAY PL.

BAY ROAD

FRITZ SONNENBERG ROAD

KIEWIET STREET

STEPHAN WAY

BEACH ROAD

PARK ROAD

BAY ROAD

Green Point Park

VLEI ROAD

GREEN POINT

STAN LEY PLACE

BILL PETERS DRIVE

Urban Park

HELEN SUZMAN BOULEVARD

BOWLERS WAY

MAIN ROAD

BEACH ROAD

THREE ANCHOR BAY ROAD

FORT ROAD

GLENGARIFF ROAD

GRIMSBY ROAD

ST BREDE'S ROAD

AVONDALE ROAD

RICHMOND ROAD

CLYDE ROAD

PINE ROAD

SYDNEY STREET

VARNEY'S ROAD

YORK ROAD

CAMBERWELL ROAD

HOFMEYR ROAD

GRIMSBY ROAD

MUTLEY ROAD

ANTRIM ROAD

HATFIELD ROAD

ANTRIM ROAD

SCHOLTZ ROAD

HILL ROAD

RAVENCRAIG ROAD

ST GEORGES ROAD

CLYDEBANK ROAD

CLYDE ROAD

CROXTETH STREET

DYSART ROAD

BRAESIDE ROAD

PINE ROAD

TORBAY ROAD

HAYTOR ROAD

WIGTOWN ROAD

CHEVIOT PLACE

MODENA RD

CAVALCADE ROAD

THORNHILL ROAD

BLACK HEATH ROAD

TRERE ROAD

MUTLEY ROAD

BLACK HEATH ROAD

HIGH LEVEL ROAD

KELVIN ROAD

JOUBERT ROAD

GLENGARIFF ROAD

OCEAN VIEW DRIVE

BEN NEVIS ST

HIGH LEVEL ROAD

ROOS ROAD

DUDLEY RD

CALAIS ROAD

ANTWERP ROAD

RHINE ROAD

MAIN DRIVE

BATTERY CRESCENT

ILKLEY CRES

HIGH LEVEL ROAD

OCEAN VIEW DRIVE

SPRINGBOK ROAD

OCEAN VIEW DRIVE

MERRIMAN RD

Table Mountain National Park

Signal Hill (350m)

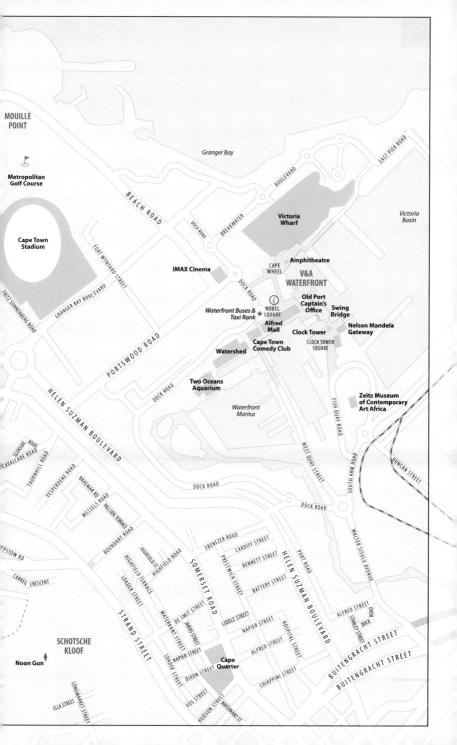

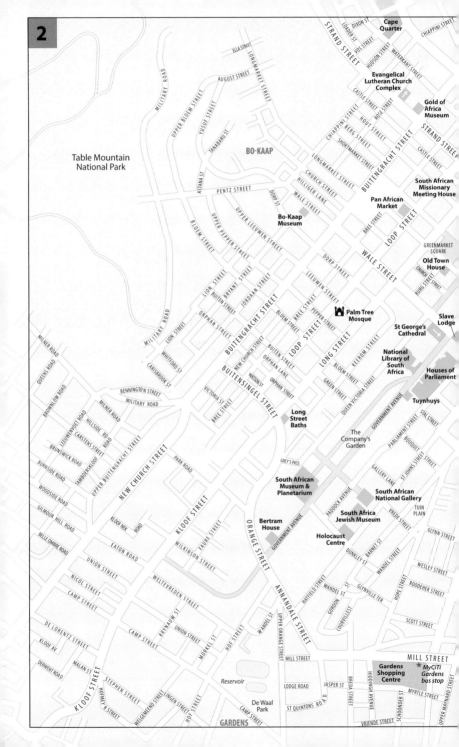

2

DIXON ST
LOADER ST
VOS STREET
STRAND STREET
HUDSON STREET
WATERKANT STREET
CHIAPPINI STREET
Cape Quarter

ELLA STREET
LONGMARKET STREET
AUGUST STREET
MILITARY ROAD
UPPER BLOEM STREET
YUSUF STREET
CASTLE STREET
ROSE STREET
Evangelical Lutheran Church Complex

STRAND STREET
Gold of Africa Museum

Table Mountain National Park

TAMBARU ST
BO-KAAP
CHIAPPINI STREET
BERG STREET
HOUT STREET
SHORTMARKET STREET
LONGMARKET STREET
BUITENGRACHT STREET
CASTLE STREET

ASTANA ST
PENTZ STREET
CHURCH STREET
HILLIGER LANE
DORP ST
WALE STREET
South African Missionary Meeting House

BLOEM STREET
UPPER PEPPER STREET
UPPER LEEUWEN STREET
Bo-Kaap Museum
BREE STREET
Pan African Market
LOOP STREET

DORP STREET
WALE STREET
GREENMARKET SQUARE

LION STREET
BRYANT STREET
JORDAAN STREET
LEEUWEN STREET
Old Town House
CHURCH STREET
BURG STREET

MILITARY ROAD
LION STREET
BUITEN STREET
ORPHAN STREET
BUITENGRACHT STREET
BLOEM STREET
BREE STREET
PEPPER STREET
🕌 **Palm Tree Mosque**
St George's Cathedral
Slave Lodge

WHITFORD ST
CARISBROOK ST
NEW CHURCH STREET
BUITEN STREET
ORPHAN LANE
LOOP STREET
LONG STREET
BLOEM STREET
KEEROM STREET
National Library of South Africa
Houses of Parliament

BENNINGTON STREET
MILITARY ROAD
WATSON ST
ORPHAN STREET
BUITENSINGEL STREET
GREEN STREET
QUEEN VICTORIA STREET
Tuynhuys

MILNER ROAD
QUEENS ROAD
BROWNLOW ROAD
VICTORIA ST
BREE STREET
GOVERNMENT AVENUE
STAL STREET

MILNER ROAD
HILLSIDE RD
LEEUWENVOET ROAD
CARSTENS ROAD
Long Street Baths
PARLIAMENT STREET
BOUQUET STREET
ST JOHNS STREET

BRUNSWICK ROAD
BURNSIDE ROAD
TAMBOERSKLOOF ROAD
UPPER BUITENGRACHT STREET
PARK ROAD
The Company's Garden
GREY'S PASS
GALLERY LANE

WOODSIDE ROAD
GILMOUR HILL ROAD
BELLE OMBRE ROAD
NEW CHURCH STREET
KLOOF STREET
KLOOF NEK ROAD
South African Museum & Planetarium
South African National Gallery
PADDOCK AVENUE
VREDE STREET
TUIN PLAIN
GLYNN STREET

UNION STREET
NICOL STREET
CAMP STREET
EATON ROAD
WILKINSON STREET
FAURE STREET
Bertram House
ORANGE STREET
GOVERNMENT AVENUE
South Africa Jewish Museum
Holocaust Centre
DUNKLEY ST
BARNET ST
WANDEL STREET
WESLEY STREET
ROODEHEK STREET

DE LORENTZ STREET
KLOOF AV
MALAN ST
KLOOF STREET
WELTEVREDEN STREET
KRYNAUW ST
UNION STREET
MORKEL ST
HOF STREET
WANDEL ST
HATFIELD STREET
GLYNVILLE TER
GORDON
COURTVILLE ST
HOPE STREET
SCOTT STREET

DERWENT ROAD
STEPHEN STREET
HOYMEY R STREET
WELGEMEEND STREET
LINGEN STREET
HOF STREET
WANDEL ST
UPPER ORANGE STREET
ANNANDALE STREET
UPPER ORANGE STREET
MILL STREET
BREDA STREET
HIDDINGH AVENUE
MILL STREET
Gardens Shopping Centre
★ *MyCiTi* **Gardens bus stop**

KLOOF STREET
Reservoir
LODGE ROAD
JASPER ST
ST QUINTONS RD
SCHOONDER ST
MYRTLE STREET
UPPER MAYNARD ST

De Waal Park
CAMP STREET
VRIENDE STREET
GARDENS

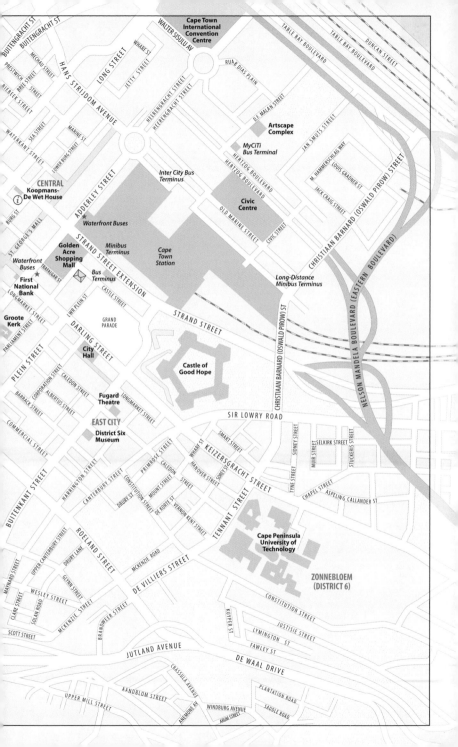

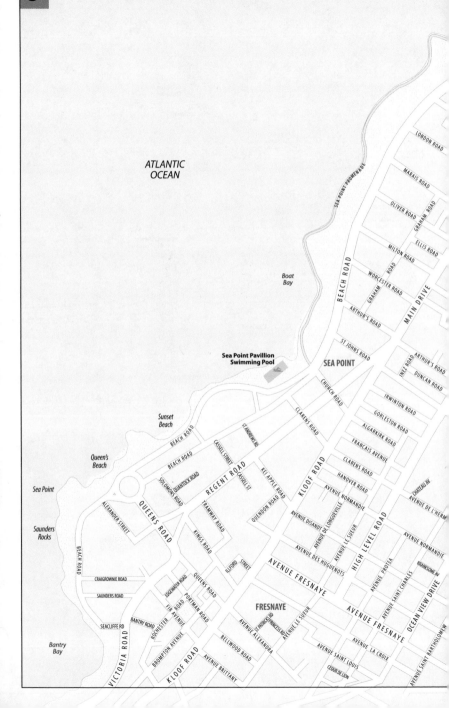

ATLANTIC
OCEAN

Boat
Bay

BEACH ROAD

SEA POINT PROMENADE

LONDON ROAD

MARAIS ROAD

OLIVER ROAD

GRAHAM ROAD

ELLIS ROAD

MILTON ROAD

WORCESTER ROAD

GRAHAM ROAD

MAIN DRIVE

ARTHUR'S ROAD

ST JOHNS ROAD

SEA POINT

ARTHUR'S ROAD

INEZ ROAD

DUNCAN ROAD

Sea Point Pavillion
Swimming Pool

CHURCH ROAD

IRWINTON ROAD

CLARENS ROAD

GORLESTON ROAD

ALGARKIRK ROAD

Sunset
Beach

BEACH ROAD

ST ANDREWS RD

FRANCAIS AVENUE

CLARENS ROAD

Queen's
Beach

BEACH ROAD

CASSELL STREET

KEI APPLE ROAD

KLOOF ROAD

HANOVER ROAD

AVENUE NORMANDIE

CASSELL ST

REGENT ROAD

CHATEAU AV

AVENUE DE L'HERM

Sea Point

SOLOMONS ROAD

QUANTOCK ROAD

TRAMWAY ROAD

QUENDON ROAD

AVENUE DISANOT

AVENUE DE LONGUEVILLE

AVENUE NORMANDIE

ALEXANDER STREET

QUEEN'S ROAD

AVENUE LE SUEUR

HIGH LEVEL ROAD

Saunders
Rocks

KINGS ROAD

AVENUE DES HUGUENOTS

AVENUE PROTEA

BEACH ROAD

ILFORD STREET

AVENUE FRESNAYE

BRANKSOME AV

CRAIGROWNIE ROAD

EDGEWATER ROAD

QUEENS ROAD

AVENUE SAINT CHARLES

OCEAN VIEW DRIVE

SAUNDERS ROAD

FIR AVENUE

PORTMAN ROAD

AVENUE FRESNAYE

SEACLIFFE RD

ROCHESTER

BANTRY ROAD

FRESNAYE

AVENUE SAINT BARTHOLOMEW

VICTORIA ROAD

BROMPTON AVENUE

KLOOF ROAD

BELLWOOD ROAD

AVENUE ALEXANDRA

ST PRINCESS RD

PRINCESS RD

AVENUE LE SUEUR

AVENUE LA CROIX

AVENUE SAINT LOUIS

Bantry
Bay

AVENUE BRITTANY

CEDUR DE LION

Saunders
Rocks

Sea Point